Exploring Social Psychology

SEVENTH EDITION

❖

David G. Myers

Hope College

EXPLORING SOCIAL PSYCHOLOGY, SEVENTH EDITION

Published by McGraw-Hill Education, 2 Penn Plaza, New York, NY 10121. Copyright © 2015 by McGraw-Hill Education. All rights reserved. Printed in the United States of America. Previous editions © 2012, 2009, and 2007. No part of this publication may be reproduced or distributed in any form or by any means, or stored in a database or retrieval system, without the prior written consent of McGraw-Hill Education, including, but not limited to, in any network or other electronic storage or transmission, or broadcast for distance learning.

Some ancillaries, including electronic and print components, may not be available to customers outside the United States.

This book is printed on acid-free paper.

1 2 3 4 5 6 7 8 9 0 DOC/DOC 1 0 9 8 7 6 5 4

ISBN 978-0-07-782545-4
MHID 0-07-782545-4

Senior Vice President, Products & Markets: *Kurt L. Strand*
Vice President, General Manager, Products & Markets: *Michael Ryan*
Vice President, Content Production & Technology Services: *Kimberly Meriwether David*
Brand Manager: *Nancy Welcher*
Executive Director of Development: *Lisa Pinto*
Associate Marketing Manager: *Alexandra Schultz*
Director, Content Production: *Terri Schiesl*
Senior Content Project Manager: *Melissa M. Leick*
Buyer: *Sandy Ludovissy*
Cover Designer: *Studio Montage, St. Louis, MO.*
Cover Image: © Heath Korvola/UpperCut Images/Getty Images
Media Project Manager: *Jenny Bartell*
Compositor: *MPS Limited*
Typeface: 10/12 Palatino LT Std
Printer: *R. R. Donnelley*

All credits appearing on page or at the end of the book are considered to be an extension of the copyright page.

Library of Congress Cataloging-in-Publication Data
Myers, David G.
    Exploring social psychology/David G. Myers, Hope College.—Seventh edition.
        pages cm
    ISBN 978-0-07-782545-4 (alk. paper)
1. Social psychology. I. Title.
    HM1033.M94 2015
    302—dc23

                                                        2013043099

The Internet addresses listed in the text were accurate at the time of publication. The inclusion of a website does not indicate an endorsement by the authors or McGraw-Hill Education, and McGraw-Hill Education does not guarantee the accuracy of the information presented at these sites.

www.mhhe.com

About the Author

❖

Since receiving his Ph.D. from the University of Iowa, David Myers has spent his career at Michigan's Hope College, where he is professor of psychology and has taught dozens of social psychology sections. Hope College students have invited him to be their commencement speaker and have voted him "outstanding professor."

With support from National Science Foundation grants, Myers's scientific articles have appeared in some three dozen scientific books and periodicals, including *Science,* the *American Scientist, Psychological Science,* and the *American Psychologist.*

He also communicates psychological science to the general public. His writings have appeared in four dozen magazines, from *Today's Education* to *Scientific American.* His 17 books include *The Pursuit of Happiness* and *Intuition: Its Powers and Perils.*

Myers's research and writings have been recognized by the Gordon Allport Prize, by an "honored scientist" award from the Federation of Associations in the Brain and Behavioral Sciences, and by the Award for Distinguished Service on Behalf of Personality-Social Psychology.

He has chaired his city's Human Relations Commission, helped found a thriving assistance center for families in poverty, and spoken to hundreds of college and community groups. In recognition of his efforts to transform the way America provides assistive listening for people with hearing loss (see hearingloop.org), he received the 2011 American Academy of Audiology Presidential Award.

Myers bikes to work year-round and plays pickup basketball. David and Carol Myers are parents of two sons and a daughter, and have one granddaughter.

Brief Contents

Contents

— ❖ —

Preface

———— ❖ ————

This is a book I secretly wanted to write. I have long believed that what is wrong with all psychology textbooks (including those I have written) is their overlong chapters. Few can read a 40-page chapter in a single sitting without their eyes glazing and their mind wandering. So why not organize the discipline into digestible chunks—say forty 15-page chapters rather than fifteen 40-page chapters—that a student could read in a sitting, with a sense of completion?

Thus, when McGraw-Hill psychology editor Chris Rogers first suggested that I abbreviate and restructure my 15-chapter, 600-page *Social Psychology* into a series of crisply written 10-page modules, I said "Eureka!" At last a publisher willing to break convention by packaging the material in a form ideally suited to students' attention spans. By presenting concepts and findings in smaller bites, we also hoped not to overload students' capacities to absorb new information. And, by keeping *Exploring Social Psychology* slim, we sought to enable instructors to supplement it with other reading.

As the playful module titles suggest, I have also broken with convention by introducing social psychology in an essay format. Each is written in the spirit of Thoreau's admonition: "Anything living is easily and naturally expressed in popular language." My aim in the parent *Social Psychology,* and even more so here, is to write in a voice that is both solidly scientific and warmly human, factually rigorous and intellectually provocative. I hope to reveal social psychology as an investigative reporter might, by providing a current summary of important social phenomena, by showing how social psychologists uncover and explain such phenomena, and by reflecting on their human significance.

In selecting material, I have represented social psychology's scope, highlighting its scientific study of how we think about, influence, and relate to one another. I also emphasize material that casts social psychology in the intellectual tradition of the liberal arts. By the teaching of great literature, philosophy, and science, liberal education seeks to expand our thinking and awareness and to liberate us from the confines of the present. Social psychology can contribute to these goals. Many undergraduate social psychology students are not psychology majors; most will enter other professions. By focusing on humanly significant issues such as belief and illusion, independence and interdependence, love and hate, one can present social psychology in ways that inform and stimulate all students.

This new seventh edition features updated coverage throughout:

- New and updated material on growing individualism within cultures examines changes in American, Chinese, and Indian cultures.
- Enhanced material on predicting one's own behavior.
- Revised discussions of aggression with new information on the effect of video games and poor diet on aggression.
- Expanded coverage of psychology and climate change, with discussions of the psychological effects of and public opinion about climate change.

In addition, the seventh edition features technology components designed to assist both professor and student. Icons throughout the text guide the student to the Online Learning Center (www.mhhe.com/myersesp7e) to gather more information on each module by viewing excerpts from the Social Connection video modules, participating in interactive exercises, and taking module quizzes to test their knowledge. The Social Connection video modules, produced by Frank Vattano at Colorado State University, enrich classic experiments by re-creating or providing footage from classic experiments, seasoned with interviews of leading social psychologists.

A comprehensive teaching package is also available on the Online Learning Center. The acclaimed *Instructor's Resource Manual* has been revised by Diane Willard to reflect changes in the seventh edition text. The OLC also includes a Test Bank, which has been revised by Alisha Janowsky to include a higher concentration of conceptual questions, and a set of PowerPoint slides (by Diane Willard) for classroom use. All instructors' resources are password-protected.

ACKNOWLEDGMENTS

I remain indebted to the community of scholars who have guided and critiqued the evolution of this material through ten editions of *Social Psychology*. These caring colleagues, acknowledged individually therein, have enabled a better book than I, alone, could have created.

I am grateful not only to Chris Rogers, for venturing this book, but also to editor Philip Zimbardo for his encouragement. As my friendship with Phil has grown, I have come to admire his gifts as one of psychology's premier communicators.

Others on the McGraw-Hill team also played vital roles. Psychology editor Nancy Welcher commissioned this new edition and editorial coordinator Adina Lonn, developmental editor Janice Wiggins-Clarke, and managing editor Penina Braffman Greenfield supported us throughout the revision process.

A special "thank you" goes to Jean Twenge, San Diego State University, for her contribution to Modules 3 (Self-Concept: Who Am I?), 4 (Self-Serving Bias), and 24 (The Nature and Nurture of Aggression). Drawing on her extensive knowledge of and research on the self and cultural changes, Professor Twenge updated and revised this material for *Social Psychology,* 11th edition.

Here at Hope College, Kathryn Brownson helped digest the *Social Psychology,* 11th edition material into these modules and prepare them for production. As in all of my published social psychology books with McGraw-Hill, I again pay tribute to two significant people. Were it not for the invitation of McGraw-Hill's Nelson Black, it surely never would have occurred to me to try my hand at text writing. Poet Jack Ridl, my Hope College colleague and writing coach, helped shape the voice you will hear in these pages.

To all in this supporting cast, I am indebted. Working with all these people has made my work a stimulating, gratifying experience.

David G. Myers
davidmyers.org

PART ONE

Introducing Social Psychology

"We cannot live for ourselves alone," remarked the novelist Herman Melville, "for our lives are connected by a thousand invisible threads." Social psychologists study those connections by scientifically exploring how we *think about, influence,* and *relate* to one another.

Video
1.1

In the first two modules I explain how we do that exploring, how we play the social psychology game. As it happens, the ways that social psychologists form and test ideas can be carried into life itself, enabling us to think smarter as we analyze everyday social thinking, social influences, and social relations.

If intuition and common sense were utterly trustworthy, we would be less in need of scientific inquiry and critical thinking. But the truth, as Module 2 relates, is that whether we are reflecting on research results or everyday events, we readily succumb to a powerful hindsight bias, also called the *I-knew-it-all-along phenomenon.*

MODULE

1

❖

Doing Social Psychology

There once was a man whose second wife was a vain and selfish woman. This woman's two daughters were similarly vain and selfish. The man's own daughter, however, was meek and unselfish. This sweet, kind daughter, whom we all know as Cinderella, learned early on that she should do as she was told, accept ill treatment and insults, and avoid doing anything to upstage her stepsisters and their mother.

But then, thanks to her fairy godmother, Cinderella was able to escape her situation for an evening and attend a grand ball, where she attracted the attention of a handsome prince. When the love-struck prince later encountered Cinderella back in her degrading home, he failed to recognize her.

Implausible? The folktale demands that we accept the power of the situation. In the presence of her oppressive stepmother, Cinderella was meek and unattractive. At the ball, Cinderella felt more beautiful—and walked and talked and smiled as if she were. In one situation, she cowered. In the other, she charmed.

The French philosopher-novelist Jean-Paul Sartre (1946) would have had no problem accepting the Cinderella premise. We humans are "first of all beings in a situation," he wrote. "We cannot be distinguished from our situations, for they form us and decide our possibilities" (pp. 59–60, paraphrased).

We are all amateur social psychologists. People-watching is a universal hobby. As we observe people, we form ideas about how human beings think about, influence, and relate to one another. Professional social psychologists do the same, only more systematically (by forming theories) and painstakingly (often with experiments that create miniature social dramas that pin down cause and effect).

3

FORMING AND TESTING THEORIES

We social psychologists have a difficult time thinking of anything more fascinating than human existence. As we wrestle with human nature to pin down its secrets, we organize our ideas and findings into theories. A **theory** is *an integrated set of principles that explain and predict* observed events. Theories are a scientific shorthand.

In everyday conversation, "theory" often means "less than fact"—a middle rung on a confidence ladder from guess to theory to fact. Thus, people may dismiss Charles Darwin's theory of evolution as "just a theory." Indeed, notes Alan Leshner (2005), chief officer of the American Association for the Advancement of Science, "Evolution *is* only a theory, but so is gravity." People often respond that gravity is a fact—but the *fact* is that your keys fall to the ground when dropped. Gravity is the *theoretical explanation* that accounts for such observed facts.

To a scientist, facts and theories are apples and oranges. Facts are agreed-upon statements about what we observe. Theories are *ideas* that summarize and explain facts. "Science is built up with facts, as a house is with stones," wrote the French scientist Jules Henri Poincaré, "but a collection of facts is no more a science than a heap of stones is a house."

Theories not only summarize but also imply testable predictions, called **hypotheses**. Hypotheses serve several purposes. First, they allow us to *test* a theory by suggesting how we might try to falsify it. Second, predictions give *direction* to research and sometimes send investigators looking for things they might never have thought of. Third, the predictive feature of good theories can also make them *practical*. A complete theory of aggression, for example, would predict when to expect aggression and how to control it. As the pioneering social psychologist Kurt Lewin declared, "There is nothing so practical as a good theory."

Consider how this works. Say we observe that people who loot, taunt, or attack often do so in groups or crowds. We might therefore theorize that being part of a crowd, or group, makes individuals feel anonymous and lowers their inhibitions. How could we test this theory? Perhaps (I'm playing with this theory) we could devise a laboratory experiment that simulates aspects of execution by electric chair. What if we asked individuals in groups to administer punishing shocks to a hapless victim without knowing which member of the group was actually shocking the victim? Would these individuals administer stronger shocks than individuals acting alone, as our theory predicts?

We might also manipulate anonymity: Would people deliver stronger shocks if they were wearing masks? If the results confirm our hypothesis, they might suggest some practical applications. Perhaps police brutality could be reduced by having officers wear large name tags and drive cars identified with large numbers, or by videotaping their arrests—all of which have, in fact, become common practice in many cities.

But how do we conclude that one theory is better than another? A good theory

- effectively *summarizes many observations*, and
- *makes clear predictions* that we can use to
  - confirm or modify the theory,
  - generate new exploration, and
  - suggest practical applications.

When we discard theories, usually it is not because they have been proved false. Rather, like old cars, they are replaced by newer, better models.

CORRELATIONAL RESEARCH: DETECTING NATURAL ASSOCIATIONS

Let's now go backstage and see how social psychology is done. This glimpse behind the scenes should be just enough for you to appreciate findings discussed later. Understanding the logic of research can also help us think critically about everyday social events.

Activity
1.1

Social psychological research varies by location. It can take place as *laboratory research* (a controlled situation) or as **field research** (everyday situations). And it varies by method—whether **correlational** (asking whether two or more factors are naturally associated) or **experimental** (manipulating some factor to see its effect on another). If you want to be a critical reader of psychological research reported in the media, it will pay you to understand the difference between correlational and experimental research.

Let's first consider the advantages of correlational research (often involving important variables in natural settings) and its major disadvantage (ambiguous interpretation of cause and effect). Today's psychologists relate personal and social factors to human health. In search of possible links between socioeconomic status and health, Douglas Carroll, George Davey Smith, and Paul Bennett (1994) ventured into Glasgow, Scotland's old graveyards. As a measure of health, they noted from grave markers the life spans of 843 individuals. As an indication of status, they measured the height of the grave pillars, reasoning that height reflected cost and therefore affluence. As Figure 1-1 shows, taller grave markers were related to longer lives, for both men and women.

Carroll and colleagues report that other researchers, using contemporary data, have confirmed the status–longevity correlation. Scottish postal-code regions having the least overcrowding and unemployment also have the greatest longevity. In the United States, income correlates

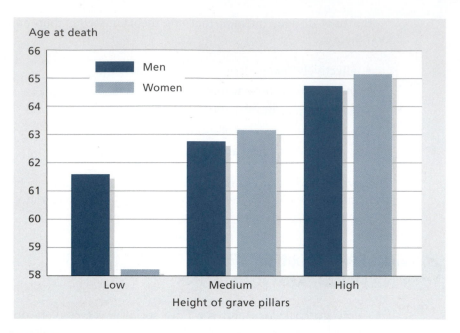

FIGURE 1-1
Correlating status and longevity. Tall grave pillars commemorated people who also tended to live longer.

with longevity (poor and lower-status people are more at risk for premature death). In today's Britain, occupational status correlates with longevity. One study followed 17,350 British civil service workers over 10 years. Compared with top-grade administrators, those at the professional-executive grade were 1.6 times more likely to have died. Clerical workers were 2.2 times and laborers 2.7 times more likely to have died (Adler & others, 1993, 1994). Across times and places, the status-health correlation seems reliable.

Correlation and Causation

The status–longevity question illustrates the most irresistible thinking error made by both amateur and professional social psychologists: When two factors such as status and health go together, it is tempting to conclude that one is causing the other. Status, we might presume, somehow protects a person from health risks. But might it be the other way around? Could it be that health promotes vigor and success? Perhaps people who live longer simply have more time to accumulate wealth (enabling them to have more expensive grave markers)? Or might a third variable, such as diet, be involved (did wealthy and working-class people tend to eat differently)? Correlations indicate a relationship, but that relationship is not necessarily one of cause and effect. Correlational research allows us to *predict*, but it cannot tell us whether changing one variable (such as social status) will *cause* changes in another (such as health).

The correlation–causation confusion is behind much muddled thinking in popular psychology. Consider another very real correlation— between self-esteem and academic achievement. Children with high self-esteem tend also to have high academic achievement. (As with any correlation, we can also state this the other way around: High achievers tend to have high self-esteem.) Why do you suppose that is true?

Some people believe a "healthy self-concept" contributes to achievement. Thus, boosting a child's self-image may also boost school achievement. Believing so, 30 U.S. states have enacted more than 170 self-esteem-promoting statutes.

But other people, including psychologists William Damon (1995), Robyn Dawes (1994), Mark Leary (1999), Martin Seligman (1994, 2002), and Roy Baumeister with John Tierney (2011), doubt that self-esteem is really "the armor that protects kids" from underachievement (or drug abuse and delinquency). Perhaps it is the other way around: Perhaps problems and failures cause low self-esteem. Perhaps self-esteem often reflects the reality of how things are going for us. Perhaps self-esteem grows from hard-won achievements. Do well and you will feel good about yourself; goof off and fail and you will feel like a dolt. A study of 635 Norwegian schoolchildren showed that a (legitimately earned) string of gold stars by one's name on the spelling chart and accompanying praise from the admiring teacher can boost a child's self-esteem (Skaalvik & Hagtvet, 1990). Or perhaps, as in a study of nearly 6,000 German seventh-graders, the traffic between self-esteem and academic achievements runs both ways (Trautwein & Lüdtke, 2006).

It is also possible that self-esteem and achievement correlate because both are linked to underlying intelligence and family social status. That possibility was raised in two studies—one a nationwide sample of 1,600 young American men and the other of 715 Minnesota youngsters (Bachman & O'Malley, 1977; Maruyama & others, 1981). When the researchers mathematically removed the predictive power of intelligence and family status, the relationship between self-esteem and achievement evaporated.

The great strength of correlational research is that it tends to occur in real-world settings where we can examine factors such as race, gender, and social status (factors that we cannot manipulate in the laboratory). Its great disadvantage lies in the ambiguity of the results. This point is so important that even if it fails to impress people the first 25 times they hear it, it is worth repeating a twenty-sixth time: *Knowing that two variables change together (correlate) enables us to predict one when we know the other, but correlation does not specify cause and effect.*

EXPERIMENTAL RESEARCH: SEARCHING FOR CAUSE AND EFFECT

The difficulty of discerning cause and effect among naturally correlated events prompts most social psychologists to create laboratory simulations of everyday processes whenever this is feasible and ethical. These simulations are akin to aeronautical wind tunnels. Aeronautical engineers do not begin by observing how flying objects perform in various natural environments. The variations in both atmospheric conditions and flying objects are too complex. Instead, they construct a simulated reality in which they can manipulate wind conditions and wing structures.

Control: Manipulating Variables

Like aeronautical engineers, social psychologists experiment by constructing social situations that simulate important features of our daily lives. By varying just one or two factors at a time—called **independent variables**—the experimenter pinpoints their influence. As the wind tunnel helps the aeronautical engineer discover principles of aerodynamics, so the experiment enables the social psychologist to discover principles of social thinking, social influence, and social relations.

To illustrate the laboratory experiment, consider an experiment that offers a cause–effect explanation of the correlation between television viewing and children's behavior.

The more violent television children watch, the more aggressive they tend to be. Are children learning and reenacting what they see on the screen? As I hope you now recognize, this is a correlational finding.

Social psychologists have therefore brought television viewing into the laboratory, where they control the amount of violence the children see. By exposing children to violent and nonviolent programs, researchers can observe how the amount of violence affects behavior. Chris Boyatzis and colleagues (1995) showed some elementary schoolchildren, but not others, an episode of the most popular—and violent—children's television program of the 1990s, *Power Rangers*. Immediately after viewing the episode, the viewers committed seven times as many aggressive acts per 2-minute interval as the nonviewers. The observed aggressive acts we call the **dependent variable.** Such experiments indicate that television can be one cause of children's aggressive behavior.

So far we have seen that the logic of experimentation is simple: By creating and controlling a miniature reality, we can vary one factor and then another and discover how those factors, separately or in combination, affect people. Now let's go a little deeper and see how an experiment is done.

Every social psychological experiment has two essential ingredients. We have just considered one—*control.* We manipulate one or more independent variables while trying to hold everything else constant. The other ingredient is *random assignment.*

Random Assignment: The Great Equalizer

We were reluctant, on the basis of a correlation, to assume that violence viewing *caused* aggressiveness. A survey researcher might measure and statistically extract other possibly pertinent factors and see if the correlations survive. But one can never control for all the factors that might distinguish viewers of violence from nonviewers. Maybe viewers of violence differ in education, culture, intelligence—or in dozens of ways the researcher has not considered.

In one fell swoop, **random assignment** eliminates all such extraneous factors. With random assignment, each person has an equal chance of viewing the violence or the nonviolence. Thus, the people in both groups would, in every conceivable way—family status, intelligence, education, initial aggressiveness, hair color—average about the same. Highly intelligent people, for example, are equally likely to appear in both groups. Because random assignment creates equivalent groups, any later aggression difference between the two groups will almost surely have something to do with the only way they differ—whether or not they viewed violence (Figure 1-2).

The Ethics of Experimentation

Our television example illustrates why some conceivable experiments raise ethical issues. Social psychologists would not, over long periods, expose one group of children to brutal violence. Rather, they briefly alter people's social experience and note the effects. Sometimes the experimental treatment is a harmless, perhaps even enjoyable, experience to which people

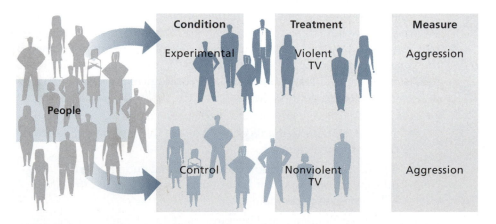

FIGURE 1-2
Random assignment. Experiments randomly assign people either to a condition that receives the experimental treatment or to a control condition that does not. This gives the researcher confidence that any later difference is somehow caused by the treatment.

give their knowing consent. Occasionally, however, researchers find themselves operating in a gray area between the harmless and the risky.

Social psychologists often venture into that ethical gray area when they design experiments that engage intense thoughts and emotions. Experiments need not have what Elliot Aronson, Marilynn Brewer, and Merrill Carlsmith (1985) called **mundane realism.** That is, laboratory behavior need not be like everyday behavior, which is typically mundane, or unimportant. But the experiment *should* have **experimental realism**—it should engage the participants. Experimenters do not want their people consciously play-acting or ho-humming it; they want to engage real psychological processes. An example of such engagement would be delivering electric shocks as part of an experiment on aggression. Forcing people to choose whether to give intense or mild electric shock to someone else can be a realistic measure of aggression. It functionally simulates real aggression.

Achieving experimental realism sometimes requires deceiving people with a plausible cover story. If the person in the next room actually is not receiving the shocks, the experimenter does not want the participants to know that. That would destroy the experimental realism. Thus, approximately one-third of social psychological studies (though a decreasing number) have used deception (Korn & Nicks, 1993; Vitelli, 1988).

Researchers often walk a tightrope in designing experiments that will be involving yet ethical. To believe that you are hurting someone, or to be subjected to strong social pressure, may be temporarily uncomfortable. Such experiments raise the age-old question of whether ends justify means. The social psychologists' deceptions are usually brief and mild compared with many misrepresentations in real life and in some of television's reality shows. (One network reality TV series deceived women into competing for the hand of a handsome supposed millionaire, who turned out to be an ordinary laborer.)

University ethics committees review social psychological research to ensure that it will treat people humanely and that the scientific merit justifies any temporary deception or distress. Ethical principles developed by the American Psychological Association (2010), the Canadian Psychological Association (2000), and the British Psychological Society (2009) mandate investigators to do the following:

- Tell potential participants enough about the experiment to enable their **informed consent.**
- Be truthful. Use deception only if essential and justified by a significant purpose and not "about aspects that would affect their willingness to participate."
- Protect participants (and bystanders, if any) from harm and significant discomfort.
- Treat information about the individual participants confidentially.

- Debrief participants. Fully explain the experiment afterward, including any deception. The only exception to this rule is when the feedback would be distressing, such as by making participants realize they have been stupid or cruel.

The experimenter should be sufficiently informative *and* considerate that people leave feeling at least as good about themselves as when they came in. Better yet, the participants should be compensated by having learned something (Sharpe & Faye, 2009). When treated respectfully, few participants mind being deceived (Epley & Huff, 1998; Kimmel, 1998). Indeed, say social psychology's advocates, professors provoke far greater anxiety and distress by giving and returning course exams than researchers provoke in their experiments.

GENERALIZING FROM LABORATORY TO LIFE

As the research on children, television, and violence illustrates, social psychology mixes everyday experience and laboratory analysis. Throughout this book, we do the same by drawing our data mostly from the laboratory and our illustrations mostly from life. Social psychology displays a healthy interplay between laboratory research and everyday life. Hunches gained from everyday experience often inspire laboratory research, which deepens our understanding of our experience.

This interplay appears in the children's television experiment. What people saw in everyday life suggested correlational research, which led to experimental research. Network and government policymakers, those with the power to make changes, are now aware of the results. The consistency of findings on television's effects—in the lab and in the field—is true of research in many other areas, including studies of helping, leadership style, depression, and self-efficacy. The effects one finds in the lab have been mirrored by effects in the field. "The psychology laboratory has generally produced psychological truths rather than trivialities," note Craig Anderson and colleagues (1999).

We need to be cautious, however, in generalizing from laboratory to life. Although the laboratory uncovers basic dynamics of human existence, it is still a simplified, controlled reality. It tells us what effect to expect of variable X, all other things being equal—which in real life they never are. Moreover, as you will see, the participants in many experiments are college students. Although that may help you identify with them, college students are hardly a random sample of all humanity (Henry, 2008a, 2008b). And most participants are from WEIRD (*W*estern, *E*ducated, *I*ndustrialized, *R*ich, and *D*emocratic) cultures that represent but 12 percent of humanity (Henrich & others, 2010). Would we get similar results with people of different ages, educational levels, and cultures? That is always an open question.

Nevertheless, we can distinguish between the *content* of people's thinking and acting (for example, their attitudes) and the *process* by which they think and act (for example, *how* attitudes affect actions and vice versa). The content varies more from culture to culture than does the process. People from various cultures may hold different opinions yet form them in similar ways. For example, college students in Puerto Rico have reported greater loneliness than do collegians on the U.S. mainland. Yet in the two cultures the ingredients of loneliness have been much the same—shyness, uncertain purpose in life, and low self-esteem (Jones & others, 1985).

Although our behaviors may differ, we are influenced by the same social forces. Beneath our surface diversity, we are more alike than different.

CONCEPTS TO REMEMBER

theory   An integrated set of principles that explain and predict observed events.

hypothesis   A testable proposition that describes a relationship that may exist between events.

field research   Research done in natural, real-life settings outside the laboratory.

correlational research   The study of the naturally occurring relationships among variables.

experimental research   Studies that seek clues to cause–effect relationships by manipulating one or more factors (independent variables) while controlling others (holding them constant).

independent variable   The experimental factor that a researcher manipulates.

dependent variable   The variable being measured, so called because it may depend on

manipulations of the independent variable.

random assignment   The process of assigning participants to the conditions of an experiment such that all persons have the same chance of being in a given condition. (Note the distinction between random *assignment* in experiments and random *sampling* in surveys. Random assignment helps us infer cause and effect. Random sampling helps us generalize to a population.)

mundane realism   Degree to which an experiment is superficially similar to everyday situations.

experimental realism   Degree to which an experiment absorbs and involves its participants.

informed consent   An ethical principle requiring that research participants be told enough to enable them to choose whether they wish to participate.

2

❖

Did You Know It All Along?

Anything seems commonplace, once explained.

Dr. Watson to Sherlock Holmes

Social psychology is everybody's business. For centuries, philosophers, novelists, and poets have observed and commented on social behavior. Every day, people observe, interpret, and influence others' actions. Thus it should not surprise us that many of this book's conclusions will already have occurred to people. So, does social psychology simply formalize what most folks already know?

Writer Cullen Murphy (1990) took that view: "Day after day social scientists go out into the world. Day after day they discover that people's behavior is pretty much what you'd expect." Nearly a half-century earlier, historian Arthur Schlesinger Jr. (1949), reacted with similar scorn to social scientists' studies of American World War II soldiers. Sociologist Paul Lazarsfeld (1949) reviewed those studies and offered a sample with interpretive comments, a few of which I paraphrase:

1. Better-educated soldiers suffered more adjustment problems than did less-educated soldiers. (Intellectuals were less prepared for battle stresses than were street-smart people.)

2. Southern soldiers coped better with the hot South Sea Island climate than did Northern soldiers. (Southerners are more accustomed to hot weather.)

3. White privates were more eager for promotion than were Black privates. (Years of oppression take a toll on achievement motivation.)

4. Southern Blacks preferred Southern to Northern White officers. (Southern officers were more experienced and skilled in interacting with Blacks.)

As you read those findings, did you agree that they were basically common sense? If so, you may be surprised to learn that Lazarsfeld went on to say, *"Every one of these statements is the direct opposite of what was actually found."* In reality, the studies found that less-educated soldiers adapted more poorly. Southerners were not more likely than Northerners to adjust to a tropical climate. Blacks were more eager than Whites for promotion, and so forth. "If we had mentioned the actual results of the investigation first [as Schlesinger experienced], the reader would have labeled these 'obvious' also."

One problem with common sense is that we invoke it after we know the facts. Events are far more "obvious" and predictable in hindsight than beforehand. Experiments reveal that when people learn the outcome of an experiment, that outcome suddenly seems unsurprising—much less surprising than it is to people who are simply told about the experimental procedure and the possible outcomes (Slovic & Fischhoff, 1977).

Activity
2.1

Likewise, in everyday life we often do not expect something to happen until it does. *Then* we suddenly see clearly the forces that brought the event about and feel unsurprised. Moreover, we may also misremember our earlier view (Blank & others, 2008; Nestler & others, 2010). Errors in judging the future's foreseeability and in remembering our past combine to create **hindsight bias** (also called the *I-knew-it-all-along phenomenon*).

Thus, after elections or stock market shifts, most commentators find the turn of events unsurprising: "The market was due for a correction." After the 2010 Gulf oil disaster, it seemed obvious—in hindsight—that BP employees had taken some shortcuts and ignored warnings, and that government oversight was lax. As the Danish philosopher–theologian Søren Kierkegaard put it, "Life is lived forwards, but understood backwards."

If hindsight bias is pervasive, you may now be feeling that you already knew about this phenomenon. Indeed, almost any conceivable result of a psychological experiment can seem like common sense—*after* you know the result.

You can demonstrate the phenomenon yourself. Take a group of people and tell half of them one psychological finding and the other half the opposite result. For example, tell half as follows:

> Social psychologists have found that, whether choosing friends or falling in love, we are most attracted to people whose traits are different from our own. There seems to be wisdom in the old saying "Opposites attract."

Tell the other half:

> Social psychologists have found that, whether choosing friends or falling in love, we are most attracted to people whose traits are similar to our own. There seems to be wisdom in the old saying "Birds of a feather flock together."

Ask the people first to explain the result. Then ask them to say whether it is "surprising" or "not surprising." Virtually all will find a good explanation for whichever result they were given and will say it is "not surprising."

Indeed, we can draw on our stockpile of proverbs to make almost any result seem to make sense. If a social psychologist reports that separation intensifies romantic attraction, John Q. Public responds, "You get paid for this? Everybody knows that 'absence makes the heart grow fonder.'" Should it turn out that separation *weakens* attraction, John will say, "My grandmother could have told you, 'Out of sight, out of mind.'"

Karl Teigen (1986) must have had a few chuckles when he asked University of Leicester (England) students to evaluate actual proverbs and their opposites. When given the proverb "Fear is stronger than love," most rated it as true. But so did students who were given its reversed form, "Love is stronger than fear." Likewise, the genuine proverb "He that is fallen cannot help him who is down" was rated highly; but so too was "He that is fallen can help him who is down." My favorites, however, were two highly rated proverbs: "Wise men make proverbs and fools repeat them" (authentic) and its made-up counterpart, "Fools make proverbs and wise men repeat them."

The hindsight bias creates a problem for many psychology students. Sometimes results are genuinely surprising (for example, that Olympic *bronze* medalists take more joy in their achievement than do silver medalists). More often, when you read the results of experiments in your textbooks, the material seems easy, even obvious. When you later take a multiple-choice test on which you must choose among several plausible conclusions, the task may become surprisingly difficult. "I don't know what happened," the befuddled student later moans. "I thought I knew the material."

The I-knew-it-all-along phenomenon can have unfortunate consequences. It is conducive to arrogance—an overestimation of our own intellectual powers. Moreover, because outcomes seem as if they should have been foreseeable, we are more likely to blame decision makers for what are in retrospect "obvious" bad choices than to praise them for good choices, which also seem "obvious."

Starting *after* the morning of 9/11 and working backward, signals pointing to the impending disaster seemed obvious. A U.S. Senate investigative report listed the missed or misinterpreted clues (Gladwell, 2003): The CIA knew that al Qaeda operatives had entered the country. An FBI agent sent a memo to headquarters that began by warning "the Bureau and New York of the possibility of a coordinated effort by Osama bin Laden to send students to the United States to attend civilian aviation universities and colleges." The FBI ignored that accurate warning and failed to relate it to other reports that terrorists were planning to use planes as weapons. The president received a daily briefing titled "Bin Laden Determined to Strike Inside the United States" and stayed on holiday. "The dumb fools!" it seemed to hindsight critics. "Why couldn't they connect the dots?"

But what seems clear in hindsight is seldom clear on the front side of history. The intelligence community is overwhelmed with "noise"—piles of useless information surrounding the rare shreds of useful information. Analysts must therefore be selective in deciding which to pursue, and only when a lead is pursued does it stand a chance of being connected to another lead. In the 6 years before 9/11, the FBI's counterterrorism unit could never have pursued all 68,000 uninvestigated leads. In hindsight, the few useful ones are now obvious.

In the aftermath of the 2008 world financial crisis, it seemed obvious that government regulators should have placed safeguards against the ill-fated bank lending practices. But what was obvious in hindsight was unforeseen by the chief American regulator, Alan Greenspan, who found himself "in a state of shocked disbelief" at the economic collapse.

We sometimes blame ourselves for "stupid mistakes"—perhaps for not having handled a person or a situation better. Looking back, we see how we should have handled it. "I should have known how busy I would be at the semester's end and started that paper earlier." But sometimes we are too hard on ourselves. We forget that what is obvious to us *now* was not nearly so obvious at the time.

Physicians who are told both a patient's symptoms and the cause of death (as determined by autopsy) sometimes wonder how an incorrect diagnosis could have been made. Other physicians, given only the symptoms, do not find the diagnosis nearly so obvious (Dawson & others, 1988). Would juries be slower to assume malpractice if they were forced to take a foresight rather than a hindsight perspective?

What do we conclude—that common sense is usually wrong? Sometimes it is. At other times, conventional wisdom is right—or it falls on both sides of an issue: Does happiness come from knowing the truth, or from preserving illusions? From being with others, or from living in peaceful solitude? Opinions are a dime a dozen. No matter what we find, there will be someone who foresaw it. (Mark Twain jested that Adam was the only person who, when saying a good thing, knew that nobody had said it before.) But which of the many competing ideas best fit reality? Research can specify the circumstances under which a commonsense truism is valid.

The point is not that common sense is predictably wrong. Rather, common sense usually is right—*after the fact.* We therefore easily deceive ourselves into thinking that we know and knew more than we do and did. And that is precisely why we need science to help us sift reality from illusion and genuine predictions from easy hindsight.

CONCEPTS TO REMEMBER

hindsight bias   The tendency to exaggerate, after learning an outcome, one's ability to have foreseen how something turned out. Also known as the *I-knew-it-all-along phenomenon.*

PART TWO

❖

Social Thinking

This book unfolds around its definition of social psychology: the scientific study of how we *think about* (Part Two), *influence* (Part Three), and *relate to* (Part Four) one another.

These modules on social thinking examine the interplay between our sense of self and our social worlds, for example, by showing how self-interest colors our social judgments.

Succeeding modules explore the amazing and sometimes rather amusing ways we form beliefs about our social worlds. We have quite remarkable powers of intuition (or what social psychologists call *automatic information processing*), yet in at least a half-dozen ways, our intuition often fails us. Knowing these ways not only beckons us to humility but also can help us sharpen our thinking, keeping it more closely in touch with reality.

We will explore the links between attitudes and behaviors: Do our attitudes determine our behaviors? Do our behaviors determine our attitudes? Or does it work both ways?

Finally, we will apply these concepts and findings to clinical psychology, by showing where clinical intuition may go astray but also how social psychologists might assist a clinician's explanation and treatment of depression, loneliness, and anxiety.

MODULE

3*

❖

Self-Concept: Who Am I?

No topic in psychology today is more heavily researched than the self. In 2011, the word *self* appeared in 21,693 book and article summaries in *PsycINFO* (the online archive of psychological research)—more than 20 times the number that appeared in 1970. How, and how accurately, do we know ourselves? What determines our self-concept?

AT THE CENTER OF OUR WORLDS: OUR SENSE OF SELF

You have many ways to complete the sentence "I am _____." (What five answers might you give?) Taken together, your answers define your **self-concept.**

The most important aspect of yourself is your self. The elements of your self-concept, the specific beliefs by which you define yourself, are your **self-schemas** (Markus & Wurf, 1987). *Schemas* are mental templates by which we organize our worlds. Our *self*-schemas—our perceiving ourselves as athletic, overweight, smart, or whatever—powerfully affect how

www.mhhe.com/myerssspsc

Activity 3.1

* Modules 3 to 5 were coauthored by Jean Twenge, professor of psychology at San Diego State University. Professor Twenge's research on social rejection and on generational changes in personality and the self has been published in many articles and books, including *Generation Me: Why Today's Young Americans Are More Confident, Assertive, Entitled—and More Miserable Than Ever Before* (2006) and *The Narcissism Epidemic: Living in the Age of Entitlement* (with W. Keith Campbell, 2009).

we perceive, remember, and evaluate other people and ourselves. If athletics is central to your self-concept (if being an athlete is one of your self-schemas), then you will tend to notice others' bodies and skills. You will quickly recall sports-related experiences. And you will welcome information that is consistent with your self-schema (Kihlstrom & Cantor, 1984). If your friend's birthday is close to yours, you'll be more likely to remember it (Kesebir & Oishi, 2010). The self-schemas that make up our self-concepts help us organize and retrieve our experiences.

Our sense of self is central to our lives—so much so that we tend to see ourselves on center stage and to overestimate the extent to which others notice us. Because of this **spotlight effect,** we intuitively overestimate the extent to which others' attention is aimed at us.

Timothy Lawson (2010) explored the spotlight effect by having college students change into a sweatshirt with "American Eagle" printed on the front before meeting a group of peers. Nearly 40 percent were sure the other students would remember what the shirt said, but only 10 percent actually did. Most observers did not even notice that the students changed sweatshirts after leaving the room for a few minutes. In another experiment, even noticeably embarrassing clothes, such as a T-shirt with singer Barry Manilow on it, provoked only 23 percent of observers to notice—many fewer than the 50 percent estimated by the unfortunate students sporting the 1970's soft rock warbler on their chests (Gilovich & others, 2000).

What's true of our dorky clothes and bad hair is also true of our emotions: our anxiety, irritation, disgust, deceit, or attraction (Gilovich & others, 1998). Fewer people notice than we presume. Keenly aware of our own emotions, we often have the illusion that they are present to others. The same goes for our social blunders and public mental slips. But research shows that what we agonize over, others may hardly notice and soon forget (Savitsky & others, 2001). The more self-conscious we are, the more we believe this *illusion of transparency* (Vorauer & Ross, 1999).

SELF AND CULTURE

How did you complete the "I am _____" statement on page 19? Did you give information about your personal traits, such as "I am honest," "I am tall," or "I am outgoing"? Or did you also describe your social identity, such as "I am a Pisces," "I am a MacDonald," or "I am a Muslim"?

For some people, especially those in industrialized Western cultures, **individualism** prevails. Identity is self-contained. Adolescence is a time of separating from parents, becoming self-reliant, and defining one's personal, *independent self.* One's identity—as a unique individual with particular abilities, traits, values, and dreams—remains fairly constant.

The psychology of Western cultures assumes that your life will be enriched by believing in your power of personal control. Western literature, from *The Iliad* to *The Adventures of Huckleberry Finn*, celebrates the self-reliant individual. Movie plots feature rugged heroes who buck the establishment. Songs proclaim "I Gotta Be Me," declare that "The Greatest Love of All" is loving oneself (Schoeneman, 1994), and state without irony that "I Believe the World Should Revolve Around Me." Individualism flourishes when people experience affluence, mobility, urbanism, and mass media (Freeman, 1997; Marshall, 1997; Triandis, 1994).

Most cultures native to Asia, Africa, and Central and South America place a greater value on **collectivism,** by respecting one's groups and identifying oneself accordingly. They nurture what Shinobu Kitayama and Hazel Markus (1995) call the *interdependent self*. In these cultures, people are more self-critical and have less need for positive self-regard (Heine & others, 1999). Malaysians, Indians, Koreans, Japanese, and traditional Kenyans such as the Maasai, for example, are much more likely than Australians, Americans, and the British to complete the "I am" statement with their group identities (Kanagawa & others, 2001; Ma & Schoeneman, 1997). When speaking, people using the languages of collectivist countries say "I" less often (Kashima & Kashima, 1998, 2003). A person might say "Went to the movie" rather than "I went to the movie." Compared with U.S. church websites, Korean church websites place more emphasis on social connections and participation and less on personal spiritual growth and self-betterment (Sasaki & Kim, 2011).

Pigeonholing cultures as solely individualist or collectivist oversimplifies, because within any culture individualism varies from person to person (Oyserman & others, 2002a, 2002b). There are individualist Chinese and collectivist Americans, and most of us sometimes behave communally, sometimes individualistically (Bandura, 2004). Individualism–collectivism also varies across a country's regions and political views. In the United States, Native Hawaiians and people living in the deep South exhibit greater collectivism than do those in Mountain West states such as Oregon and Montana (Plaut & others, 2002; Vandello & Cohen, 1999). Conservatives tend to be economic individualists ("don't tax or regulate me") and moral collectivists ("legislate against immorality"). Liberals tend to be economic collectivists (supporting national health care) and moral individualists ("keep your laws off my body"). Despite individual and subcultural variations, researchers continue to regard individualism and collectivism as genuine cultural variables (Schimmack & others, 2005).

Growing Individualism within Cultures

Cultures can also change over time, and many seem to be growing more individualistic. New economic opportunities have challenged traditional collectivistic ways in India. Chinese citizens younger than 25 are more likely than those older than 25 to agree with individualistic statements such as "make a name for yourself" and "live a life that suits your tastes"

(Arora, 2005). Chinese citizens who are younger, more urban, more affluent, and only children—all modern attributes—are also more likely to endorse self-centered statements (Cai & others, 2011). In the United States, younger generations report significantly more positive self-feelings than young people did in the 1960s and 1970s (Gentile & others, 2010; Twenge & Campbell, 2008; Twenge & others, 2011; but for an opposing view, see Trzesniewski & Donnellan, 2010). One study found that popular song lyrics became more likely to use "I" and "me" and less likely to use "we" and "us" between 1980 and 2007 (DeWall & others, 2011), with the norm shifting from the sappy love song of the 1980s ("Endless Love," 1981) to the self-celebration of the 2000s (Justin Timberlake singlehandedly bringing "Sexy Back," 2006).

Even your name might show the shift toward individualism: American parents are now less likely to give their children common names and more likely to help them stand out with an unusual name. While nearly 20 percent of boys born in 1990 received one of the 10 most common names, only 8 percent received such a common name by 2010, with the numbers similar for girls (Twenge & others, 2010). Today, you don't have to be the child of a celebrity to get a name as unique as Shiloh, Suri, Knox, or Apple.

Americans and Australians, most of whom are descended from those who struck out on their own to emigrate, are more likely than Europeans to give their children uncommon names. Parents in the western United States and Canada, descended from independent pioneers, are also more likely than those in the more established East to give their children uncommon names (Varnum & Kitayama, 2011). The more individualistic the time or the place, the more children receive unique names.

These changes demonstrate something that goes deeper than a name: the interaction between individuals and society. Did the culture focus on uniqueness first and cause the parents' name choices, or did individual parents decide they wanted their children to be unique, thus creating the culture? A similar chicken-and-egg question applies to the song lyrics: Did a more self-focused population listen to more self-focused songs, or did listening to more self-focused songs make people more self-focused? The answer, though not yet fully understood, is probably both (Markus & Kitayama, 2010).

If you grew up in a Western culture, you were probably told to "express yourself"—through writing, the choices you make, the products you buy, and perhaps through your tattoos or piercings. When asked about the purpose of language, American students were more likely to explain that it allows self-expression, whereas Korean students focused on how language allows communication with others. American students were also more likely to see their choices as expressions of themselves and to evaluate their personal choices more favorably (Kim & Sherman, 2007). The individualized latté—"decaf, single shot, skinny, extra hot"—that seems just right at a North American coffee shop would seem strange in Seoul, note Kim and Hazel Markus (1999). In Korea, people place less value on expressing their uniqueness and more on tradition and shared practices

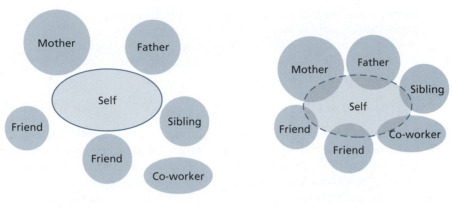

Independent view of self   Interdependent view of self

FIGURE 3-1
Self-construal as independent or interdependent. The independent self acknowledges relationships with others. But the interdependent self is more deeply embedded in others (Markus & Kitayama, 1991).

(Choi & Choi, 2002). Korean advertisements tend to feature people together, whereas American advertisements highlight personal choice or
freedom (Markus, 2001; Morling & Lamoreaux, 2008).

Activity
3.1

With an *inter*dependent self, one has a greater sense of belonging. If
they were uprooted and cut off from family, colleagues, and loyal friends,
interdependent people would lose the social connections that define who
they are. When Chinese participants were asked to think about their
mothers, a brain region associated with the self became activated—an
area that lit up for Western participants only when they thought about
themselves (Zhu & others, 2007). Interdependent selves have not one self
but many selves: self-with-parents, self-at-work, self-with-friends (Cross
& others, 1992). As Figure 3-1 and Table 3-1 suggest, the interdependent
self is embedded in social memberships. Conversation is less direct and

TABLE 3-1 SELF-CONCEPT: INDEPENDENT OR INTERDEPENDENT

	Independent	*Interdependent*
Identity is	Personal, defined by individual traits and goals	Social, defined by connections with others
What matters	Me—personal achievement and fulfillment; my rights and liberties	We—group goals and solidarity; our social responsibilities and relationships
Disapproves of	Conformity	Egotism
Illustrative motto	"To thine own self be true"	"No one is an island"
Cultures that support	Individualistic Western	Collectivistic Asian and Third World

more polite (Holtgraves, 1997), and people focus more on gaining social approval (Lalwani & others, 2006). In an interdependent culture, the goal of social life is to harmonize with and support one's communities, not—as it is in more individualistic societies—to enhance one's individual self and make choices independently.

Culture and Self-Esteem

Self-esteem in collectivist cultures correlates closely with "what others think of me and my group." Self-concept in these cultures is malleable (context-specific) rather than stable (enduring across situations). In one study, four in five Canadian students but only one in three Chinese and Japanese students agreed that "the beliefs that you hold about who you are (your inner self) remain the same across different activity domains" (Tafarodi & others, 2004).

For those in individualistic cultures, self-esteem is more personal and less relational. Threaten our *personal* identity and we'll feel angrier and gloomier than when someone threatens our collective identity (Gaertner & others, 1999).

So when, do you suppose, are university students in collectivist Japan and individualist United States most likely to report positive emotions such as happiness and elation? For Japanese students, happiness comes with positive social engagement—with feeling close, friendly, and respectful. For American students, it more often comes with disengaged emotions—with feeling effective, superior, and proud (Kitayama & Markus, 2000). Conflict in collectivist cultures often takes place between groups; individualist cultures breed more conflict (and crime and divorce) between individuals (Triandis, 2000).

When Kitayama (1999), after 10 years of teaching and researching in America, visited his Japanese alma mater, Kyoto University, graduate students were "astounded" when he explained the Western idea of the independent self. "I persisted in explaining this Western notion of self-concept—one that my American students understood intuitively—and finally began to persuade them that, indeed, many Americans do have such a disconnected notion of self. Still, one of them, sighing deeply, said at the end, 'Could this *really* be true?'"

SELF-KNOWLEDGE

"Know thyself," admonished an ancient Greek oracle. We certainly try. We readily form beliefs about ourselves, and we in Western cultures don't hesitate to explain why we feel and act as we do. But how well do we actually know ourselves?

"There is one thing, and only one in the whole universe which we know more about than we could learn from external observation," noted

C. S. Lewis (1952, pp. 18–19). "That one thing is [ourselves]. We have, so to speak, inside information; we are in the know." Indeed. Yet sometimes we *think* we know, but our inside information is wrong. That is the unavoidable conclusion of some fascinating research.

Explaining Our Behavior

Why did you choose where to go to college? Why did you lash out at your roommate? Why did you fall in love with that special person? Sometimes we know. Sometimes we don't. Asked why we have felt or acted as we have, we produce plausible answers. Yet, when causes are subtle, our self-explanations are often wrong. We may dismiss factors that matter and inflate others that don't. People may misattribute their rainy-day gloom to life's emptiness (Schwarz & Clore, 1983). And people routinely deny being influenced by the media, which, they readily acknowledge, affects *others.*

Also thought provoking are studies in which people have recorded their moods every day for 2 or 3 months (Stone & others, 1985; Weiss & Brown, 1976; Wilson & others, 1982). They also recorded factors that might affect their moods: the day of the week, the weather, the amount they slept, and so forth. At the end of each study, the people judged how much each factor had affected their moods. Even with their attention on their daily moods, there was little relationship between their perceptions of how well a factor predicted their mood and how well it really did. For example, people thought they would experience more negative moods on Mondays, but in fact their moods were no more negative on Mondays than on other weekdays. This raises a disconcerting question: How much insight do we really have into what makes us happy or unhappy? As Daniel Gilbert (2007, 2011) notes, not much: We are remarkably bad predictors of what will make us happy. "We seem to know less about the worlds inside our heads than about the world our heads are inside."

Predicting Our Behavior

People also err when predicting their behavior. Dating couples tend to predict the longevity of their relationships through rose-colored glasses. Their friends and family often know better, report Tara MacDonald and Michael Ross (1997). Among University of Waterloo students, their roommates were better predictors of whether their romances would survive than they were. Medical residents weren't very good at predicting whether they would do well on a surgical skills exam, but their peers in the program predicted each other's performance with startling accuracy (Lutsky & others, 1993). So if you're in love and want to know whether it will last, don't listen to your heart—ask your roommate. And if you want to predict your routine daily behaviors—how much time you will spend laughing, on the phone, or watching TV, for example—your close friends' estimates will likely prove at least as accurate as your own (Vazire & Mehl, 2008).

One of the most common errors in behavior prediction is underestimating how long it will take to complete a task (called the **planning fallacy**). The Big Dig freeway construction project in Boston was supposed to take 10 years and actually took 20 years. The Sydney Opera House was supposed to be completed in 6 years; it took 16. In one study, college students writing a senior thesis paper were asked to predict when they would complete the project. On average, students finished 3 weeks later than their "most realistic" estimate—and a week later than their "worst-case scenario" estimate (Buehler & others, 2002). However, friends and teachers were able to predict just how late these papers would be. Just as you should ask your friends how long your relationship is likely to survive, if you want to know when you will finish your term paper, ask your roommate or your mom. You could also do what Microsoft does: Managers automatically add 30 percent onto a software developer's estimate of completion—and 50 percent if the project involves a new operating system (Dunning, 2006).

So, how can you improve your self-predictions? The best way is to be more realistic about how long tasks took in the past. Apparently people underestimate how long something will take because they misremember previous tasks as taking less time than they in fact did (Roy & others, 2005).

Predicting Our Feelings

Many of life's big decisions involve predicting our future feelings. Would marrying this person lead to lifelong contentment? Would entering this profession make for satisfying work? Would going on this vacation produce a happy experience? Or would the likelier results be divorce, job burnout, and holiday disappointment?

Sometimes we know how we will feel—if we fail that exam, win that big game, or soothe our tensions with a half-hour jog. We know what exhilarates us and what makes us anxious or bored. Other times we may mispredict our responses. Asked how they would feel if asked sexually harassing questions on a job interview, most women studied by Julie Woodzicka and Marianne LaFrance (2001) said they would feel angry. When actually asked such questions, however, women more often experienced fear.

Studies of "affective forecasting" reveal that people have greatest difficulty predicting the *intensity* and the *duration* of their future emotions (Wilson & Gilbert, 2003). People have mispredicted how they would feel some time after a romantic breakup, receiving a gift, losing an election, winning a game, and being insulted (Gilbert & Ebert, 2002; Loewenstein & Schkade, 1999). Some examples:

- When young men are sexually aroused by erotic photographs, then exposed to a passionate date scenario in which their date asks them to "stop," they admit that they might not stop. If not shown sexually arousing pictures first, they more often deny the possibility of being sexually aggressive. When not aroused, one easily mispredicts how one will feel and act when aroused—a phenomenon that leads to unexpected professions of love during lust, to unintended pregnancies, and to repeat offenses among sex abusers who have sincerely vowed "never again."

- Hungry shoppers do more impulse buying ("Those doughnuts would be delicious!") than do shoppers who have just enjoyed a quarter-pound blueberry muffin (Gilbert & Wilson, 2000). When we are hungry, we mispredict how gross those deep-fried dough-nuts will seem when we are sated. When stuffed, we may under-estimate how yummy a doughnut might be with a late-night glass of milk—a purchase whose appeal quickly fades when we have eaten one or two.

- When natural disasters like hurricanes occur, people predict that their sadness will be greater if more people are killed. But after Hurricane Katrina struck in 2005, students' sadness was similar whether it was believed that 50 people had been killed or 1,000 had been killed (Dunn & Ashton-James, 2008). What *did* influence how sad people felt? Seeing pictures of victims. No wonder poi-gnant images on TV have so much influence on us after disasters.

- People overestimate how much their well-being would be af-fected by both bad events (a romantic breakup, failing to reach an athletic goal [Eastwick & others, 2007a; van Dijk & others, 2008]) and good events (weight loss, more television channels, more free time). Even extreme events, such as winning a state lottery or suf-fering a paralyzing accident, affect long-term happiness less than most people suppose.

Our intuitive theory seems to be: We want. We get. We are happy. If that were true, this chapter would have fewer words. In reality, note Daniel Gilbert and Timothy Wilson (2000), we often "miswant." People who imagine an idyllic desert island holiday with sun, surf, and sand may be disappointed when they discover "how much they require daily struc-ture, intellectual stimulation, or regular infusions of Pop Tarts." We think that if our candidate or team wins we will be delighted for a long while. But multiple studies reveal that the emotional traces of such good tidings evaporate more rapidly than we expect.

Moreover, we are especially prone to impact bias after *negative* events. When Gilbert and colleagues (1998) asked assistant professors to predict their happiness a few years after achieving tenure or not, most believed a favorable outcome was important for their future happiness: "Losing my job would crush my life's ambitions. It would be terrible." Yet when surveyed several years after the event, those denied tenure were about as happy as those who received it. Impact bias is important, say Wilson and Gilbert (2005), because people's affective forecasts— their predictions of their future emotions—influence their decisions. If people overestimate the intensity and the duration of the pleasure they will gain from purchasing a new car or undergoing cosmetic surgery, then they may make ill-advised investments in that new Mercedes or extreme makeover.

Let's make this personal. Gilbert and Wilson invite us to imagine how we might feel a year after losing our nondominant hands. Compared with today, how happy would you be?

Thinking about that, you perhaps focused on what the calamity would mean: no clapping, no shoe tying, no competitive basketball, no speedy keyboarding. Although you likely would forever regret the loss, your general happiness some time after the event would be influenced by "two things: (a) the event, and (b) everything else" (Gilbert & Wilson, 2000). In focusing on the negative event, we discount the importance of everything else that contributes to happiness and so overpredict our enduring misery. "Nothing that you focus on will make as much difference as you think," write researchers David Schkade and Daniel Kahneman (1998).

Moreover, say Wilson and Gilbert (2003), people neglect the speed and the power of their psychological immune system, which includes their strategies for rationalizing, discounting, forgiving, and limiting emotional trauma. Being largely ignorant of the speed and strength of our psychological immune system (a phenomenon Gilbert and Wilson call *immune neglect*), we adapt to disabilities, romantic breakups, exam failures, tenure denials, and personal and team defeats more readily than we would expect. Ironically, as Gilbert and colleagues report (2004), major negative events (which activate our psychological defenses) can be less enduringly distressing than minor irritations (which don't activate our defenses). We are, under most circumstances, amazingly resilient.

The Wisdom and Illusions of Self-Analysis

To a striking extent, then, our intuitions are often dead wrong about what has influenced us and what we will feel and do. But let's not overstate the case. When the causes of our behavior are conspicuous and the correct explanation fits our intuition, our self-perceptions will be accurate (Gavanski & Hoffman, 1987). When the causes of behavior are obvious to an observer, they are usually obvious to us as well.

We are unaware of much that goes on in our minds. Perception and memory studies show that we are more aware of the *results* of our thinking than of its process. For example, we experience the results of our mind's unconscious workings when we set a mental clock to record the passage of time or to awaken us at an appointed hour, or when we somehow achieve a spontaneous creative insight after a problem has unconsciously "incubated." Similarly, creative scientists and artists often cannot report the thought processes that produced their insights, although they have superb knowledge of the results.

Timothy Wilson (1985, 2002) offers a bold idea: The mental processes that *control* our social behavior are distinct from the mental processes through which we *explain* our behavior. Our rational explanations may therefore omit the unconscious attitudes that actually guide our behavior. In nine experiments, Wilson and colleagues (1989, 2008) found that the attitudes people consciously expressed toward things or people usually predicted their subsequent behavior reasonably well. Their attitude reports became useless, however, if the participants were first asked to *analyze* their feelings. For example, dating couples' level of happiness with their relationship accurately predicted whether they would still be dating several months later. But participants who first listed all the reasons they could think of why their relationship was good or bad before rating their happiness were misled—their happiness ratings were useless in predicting the future of the relationship! Apparently, the process of dissecting the relationship drew attention to easily verbalized factors that were actually not as important as harder-to-verbalize happiness. We are often "strangers to ourselves," Wilson concluded (2002).

Such findings illustrate that we have a **dual attitude system,** say Wilson and colleagues (2000). Our automatic *implicit* attitudes regarding someone or something often differ from our consciously controlled, *explicit* attitudes (Gawronski & Bodenhausen, 2006; Nosek, 2007). From childhood, for example, we may retain a habitual, automatic fear or dislike of people for whom we now consciously verbalize respect and appreciation. Although explicit attitudes may change with relative ease, notes Wilson, "implicit attitudes, like old habits, change more slowly." With repeated practice, however, new habitual attitudes can replace old ones.

This research on the limits of our self-knowledge has two practical implications. The first is for psychological inquiry. *Self-reports are often untrustworthy.* Errors in self-understanding limit the scientific usefulness of subjective personal reports.

The second implication is for our everyday lives. The sincerity with which people report and interpret their experiences is no guarantee of the validity of those reports. Personal testimonies are powerfully persuasive. But they may also be wrong. Keeping this potential for error in mind can help us feel less intimidated by others and be less gullible.

CONCEPTS TO REMEMBER

self-concept   What we know and believe about ourselves.

self-schema   Beliefs about self that organize and guide the processing of self-relevant information.

spotlight effect   The belief that others are paying more attention to our appearance and behavior than they really are.

individualism   The concept of giving priority to one's own goals over group goals and defining one's identity in terms of personal attributes rather than group identifications.

collectivism   Giving priority to the goals of one's groups (often one's extended family or work group) and defining one's identity accordingly.

planning fallacy   The tendency to underestimate how long it will take to complete a task.

dual attitude system   Differing implicit (automatic) and explicit (consciously controlled) attitudes toward the same object. Verbalized explicit attitudes may change with education and persuasion; implicit attitudes change slowly, with practice that forms new habits.

4*

❖

Self-Serving Bias

Most of us have a good reputation with ourselves. In studies of self-esteem, even low-scoring people respond in the midrange of possible scores. (A low-self-esteem person responds to statements such as "I have good ideas" with a qualifying adjective, such as "somewhat" or "sometimes.") In a study of self-esteem across 53 nations, the average self-esteem score was above the midpoint in every country (Schmitt & Allik, 2005). In recent samples of U.S. college students, the most common score on a self-esteem measure was the maximum—in effect, "perfect" self-esteem (Gentile & others, 2010). One of social psychology's most provocative yet firmly established conclusions concerns the potency of **self-serving bias**—a tendency to perceive oneself favorably.

Activity 4.1

EXPLAINING POSITIVE AND NEGATIVE EVENTS

Many dozens of experiments have found that people accept credit when told they have succeeded. They attribute the success to their ability and effort, but they attribute failure to external factors such as bad luck or the problem's inherent "impossibility" (Campbell & Sedikides, 1999). Similarly, in explaining their victories, athletes commonly credit themselves,

---

*This module benefits from the input of Jean Twenge, professor of psychology at San Diego State University. Professor Twenge's research on social rejection and on generational changes in personality and the self has been published in many articles and books, including *Generation Me: Why Today's Young Americans Are More Confident, Assertive, Entitled—and More Miserable Than Ever Before* (2006), and *The Narcissism Epidemic: Living in the Age of Entitlement* (with W. Keith Campbell, 2009).

but they attribute losses to something else: bad breaks, bad referee calls, or the other team's super effort or dirty play (Grove & others, 1991; Lalonde, 1992; Mullen & Riordan, 1988). And how much responsibility do you suppose car drivers tend to accept for their accidents? On insurance forms, drivers have described their accidents in words such as these: "An invisible car came out of nowhere, struck my car, and vanished"; "As I reached an intersection, a hedge sprang up, obscuring my vision, and I did not see the other car"; and "A pedestrian hit me and went under my car" (*Toronto News*, 1977).

Self-serving explanations contribute to marital discord, worker dissatisfaction, and bargaining impasses (Kruger & Gilovich, 1999). Small wonder that divorced people usually blame their partner for the breakup (Gray & Silver, 1990), or that managers often blame poor performance on workers' lack of ability or effort (Imai, 1994; Rice, 1985). (Workers are more likely to blame something external—supplies, excessive workload, difficult co-workers, or ambiguous assignments.) Small wonder, too, that people evaluate pay raises as fairer when they receive a bigger raise than most of their co-workers (Diekmann & others, 1997).

We help maintain our positive self-images by associating ourselves with success and distancing ourselves from failure. For example, "I got an A on my econ test" versus "The prof gave me a C on my history exam." Blaming failure or rejection on something external, even another's prejudice, is less depressing than seeing oneself as undeserving (Major & others, 2003). We will, however, acknowledge our distant past failings—those by our "former" self, note Anne Wilson and Michael Ross (2001). Describing their old precollege selves, their University of Waterloo students offered nearly as many negative as positive statements. When describing their present selves, they offered three times more positive statements. "I've learned and grown, and I'm a better person today," most people surmise. Chumps yesterday, champs today.

Ironically, we are even biased against seeing our own bias. People claim they avoid self-serving bias themselves but readily acknowledge that others commit this bias (Pronin & others, 2002). This "bias blind spot" can have serious consequences during conflicts. If you're negotiating with your roommate over who does household chores and you believe your roommate has a biased view of the situation, you're much more likely to become angry (Pronin & Ross, 2006). Apparently we see ourselves as objective and everyone else as biased.

*C*AN WE ALL BE BETTER THAN AVERAGE?

Self-serving bias also appears when people compare themselves with others. If the sixth-century B.C. Chinese philosopher Lao-tzu was right that "at no time in the world will a man who is sane over-reach himself, over-spend himself, over-rate himself," then most of us are a little insane. For on *subjective, socially desirable,* and *common dimensions,* most people see themselves as better than the average person. Compared with people in general, most people see themselves as more ethical, more competent at their job, friendlier, more intelligent, better looking, less prejudiced, healthier, and even more insightful and less biased in their self-assessments. (See "Focus On: Self-Serving Bias—How Do I Love Me? Let Me Count the Ways.")

Every community, it seems, is like Garrison Keillor's fictional Lake Wobegon, where "all the women are strong, all the men are good-looking, and all the children are above average." Many people believe that they will become even more above average in the future—if I'm good now, I will be even better soon, they seem to think (Kanten & Teigen, 2008). One of Freud's favorite jokes was of the husband who told his wife, "If one of us should die, I think I would go live in Paris."

The self-serving bias is also common in marriages. In a 2008 survey, 49 percent of married men said they did half to most of the child care. But only 31 percent of wives said their husbands did this much. In the same survey, 70 percent of women said they do most of the cooking, but 56 percent of the men said *they* do most of the cooking (Galinsky & others, 2009). The general rule: Group members' estimates of how much they contribute to a joint task typically sum to more than 100 percent (Savitsky & others, 2005).

www.mhhe.com/myerseasp8e

Activity
4.2

Focus On: Self-Serving Bias—How Do I Love Me? Let Me Count the Ways

"The one thing that unites all human beings, regardless of age, gender, religion, economic status, or ethnic background," notes columnist Dave Barry (1998), "is that deep down inside, we all believe that we are above average drivers." We also believe we are above average on most any other subjective and desirable trait. Among the many faces of self-serving bias are these:

- *Ethics.* Most businesspeople see themselves as more ethical than the average businessperson (Baumhart, 1968; Brenner & Molander, 1977). One national survey asked, "How would you rate your own morals and values on a scale from 1 to 100 (100 being perfect)?" Fifty percent of people rated themselves 90 or above; only 11 percent said 74 or less (Lovett, 1997).

- *Professional competence.* In one survey, 90 percent of business managers rated their performance as superior to their average peer (French, 1968). In Australia, 86 percent of people rated their job performance as above average, and only 1 percent as below average (Headey & Wearing, 1987). Most surgeons believe *their* patients' mortality rate to be lower than average (Gawande, 2002).

- *Virtues.* In The Netherlands, most high school students rate themselves as more honest, persistent, original, friendly, and reliable than the average high school student (Hoorens, 1993, 1995).

- *Intelligence.* Most people perceive themselves as more intelligent, better looking, and much less prejudiced than their average peer (*Public Opinion*, 1984; Watt & Larkin, 2010; Wylie, 1979). When someone outperforms them, people tend to think of the other as a genius (Lassiter & Munhall, 2001).

- *Parental support.* Most adults believe they support their aging parents more than do their siblings (Lerner & others, 1991).

- *Health.* Los Angeles residents view themselves as healthier than most of their neighbors, and most college students believe they will outlive their actuarially predicted age of death by approximately 10 years (Larwood, 1978; Snyder, 1978).

- *Attractiveness.* Is it your experience, as it is mine, that most photos of you seem not to do you justice? One experiment showed people a lineup of faces—one their own, the others being their face morphed into those of less and more attractive faces (Epley & Whitchurch, 2008). When asked which was their actual face, people tended to identify an attractively enhanced version of their face.

- *Driving.* Most drivers—even most drivers who have been hospitalized for accidents—believe themselves to be safer and more skilled than the average driver (Guerin, 1994; McKenna & Myers, 1997; Svenson, 1981). Dave Barry was right.

My wife and I used to pitch our laundry on the floor next to our bedroom clothes hamper. In the morning, one of us would put it in. When she suggested that I take more responsibility for this, I thought, "Huh? I already do it 75 percent of the time." So I asked her how often she thought she picked up the clothes. "Oh," she replied, "about 75 percent of the time."

Within commonly considered domains, subjective behavioral dimensions (such as "disciplined") trigger even greater self-serving bias

© Jean Sorensen.

than observable behavioral dimensions (such as "punctual"). Subjective qualities give us leeway in constructing our own definition of success (Dunning & others, 1989, 1991). Rating my "athletic ability," I ponder my basketball play, not the agonizing weeks I spent as a Little League baseball player hiding in right field. Assessing my "leadership ability," I conjure up an image of a great leader whose style is similar to mine. By defining ambiguous criteria in our own terms, each of us can see ourselves as relatively successful. In one College Entrance Examination Board survey of 829,000 high school seniors, *none* rated themselves below average in "ability to get along with others" (a subjective, desirable trait), 60 percent rated themselves in the top 10 percent, and 25 percent saw themselves among the top 1 percent! In 2012, 77 percent of incoming college students described themselves as above average in their "drive to achieve," another subjective and desirable trait (Pryor & others, 2012).

Researchers have wondered: Do people really believe their above-average self-estimates? Is their self-serving bias partly a function of how the questions are phrased (Krizan & Suls, 2008)? When Elanor Williams and Thomas Gilovich (2008) had people bet real money when estimating their relative performance on tests, they found that, yes, "people truly believe their self-enhancing self-assessments."

*U*NREALISTIC OPTIMISM

Optimism predisposes a positive approach to life. "The optimist," notes H. Jackson Brown (1990, p. 79), "goes to the window every morning and says, 'Good morning, God.' The pessimist goes to the window and says, 'Good God, morning.'"

Studies of more than 90,000 people across 22 cultures reveal that most humans are more disposed to optimism than pessimism (Fischer & Chalmers, 2008). Indeed, many of us have what researcher Neil Weinstein (1980, 1982) terms "an unrealistic optimism about future life events." In a 2006–2008 worldwide poll, most people expected their lives to improve more in the next 5 years than they did in the past 5 years (Deaton, 2009)— an especially striking expectation considering the worldwide recession that followed. Partly because of their relative pessimism about others' fates (Hoorens & others, 2008; Shepperd, 2003), students perceive themselves as far more likely than their classmates to get a good job, draw a good salary, and own a home. They also see themselves as far *less* likely to experience negative events, such as developing a drinking problem, having a heart attack before age 40, or being fired. Adult women are much more likely to be unduly optimistic than pessimistic about their relative risk of breast cancer (Waters & others, 2011). Football fans believe their favorite team has a 77 percent chance of winning their first game. Even after 4 months when (on average) their team won only half the time, they still hold out hope and predict a 70 percent chance of their team winning (Massey & others, 2011).

Parents extend their unrealistic optimism to their children, assuming their child is less likely to drop out of college, become depressed, or get lung cancer than the average child. According to a study (Lench & others, 2006), parents assumed their children would be more likely to complete college, remain healthy, and stay happy.

Illusory optimism increases our vulnerability. Believing ourselves immune to misfortune, we do not take sensible precautions. Sexually active undergraduate women who don't consistently use contraceptives perceived themselves, compared with other women at their university, as much *less* vulnerable to unwanted pregnancy (Burger & Burns, 1988). Elderly drivers who rated themselves as "above average" were four times more likely than more modest drivers to flunk a driving test and be rated "unsafe" (Freund & others, 2005). Students who enter university with inflated assessments of their academic ability often suffer deflating self-esteem and well-being and are more likely to drop out (Robins & Beer, 2001). For illusory optimism, we often pay a price.

Those who cheerfully deny the effects of smoking or stumble into ill-fated relationships remind us that blind optimism, like pride, may go before a fall. When gambling, optimists persist longer than pessimists, even when piling up losses (Gibson & Sanbonmatsu, 2004). If those who deal in the stock market or in real estate perceive their business intuition as superior to that of their competitors, they, too, may be in for disappointment. Even the seventeenth-century economist Adam Smith, a defender of human economic rationality, foresaw that people would overestimate their chances of gain. This "absurd presumption in their own good fortune," he said, arises from "the overweening conceit which the greater part of men have of their own abilities" (Spiegel, 1971, p. 243).

Unrealistic optimism appears to be on the rise. In the 1970s, half of American high school seniors predicted that they would be "very good" workers as adults—the highest rating available, and thus the equivalent of giving themselves five stars out of five. By 2006, two-thirds of teens believed they would achieve this stellar outcome (Twenge & Campbell, 2008). Even more striking, half of high school seniors in 2000 believed that they would earn a graduate degree—even though only 9 percent were likely to actually do so (Reynolds & others, 2006). Although aiming high has benefits for success, those who aim too high may struggle with depression as they learn to adjust their goals to more realistic heights (Wrosch & Miller, 2009).

Optimism definitely beats pessimism in promoting self-efficacy, health, and well-being (Armor & Taylor, 1996; Segerstrom, 2001). As natural optimists, most people believe they will be happier with their lives in the future—a belief that surely helps create happiness in the present (Robinson & Ryff, 1999). If our optimistic prehistoric ancestors were more likely than their pessimistic neighbors to surmount challenges and survive, then small wonder that we are disposed to optimism (Haselton & Nettle, 2006).

Yet a dash of realism—or what Julie Norem (2000) calls *defensive pessimism*—can sometimes save us from the perils of unrealistic optimism. Defensive pessimism anticipates problems and motivates effective coping. As a Chinese proverb says, "Be prepared for danger while staying in peace." Students who exhibit excess optimism (as many students destined for low grades do) benefit from some self-doubt, which motivates study (Prohaska, 1994; Sparrell & Shrauger, 1984). Students who are overconfident tend to underprepare, whereas their equally able but less confident peers study harder and get higher grades (Goodhart, 1986; Norem & Cantor, 1986; Showers & Ruben, 1987). Viewing things in a more immediate, realistic way often helps. Students in one experiment were wildly optimistic in predicting their test performance when the test was hypothetical, but they were surprisingly accurate when the test was imminent (Armor & Sackett, 2006). Believing you're great when nothing can prove you wrong is one thing, but with an evaluation fast approaching, best not to look like a bragging fool.

It's also important to listen to criticism. "One gentle rule I often tell my students," writes David Dunning (2006), "is that if two people independently give them the same piece of negative feedback, they should at least consider the possibility that it might be true." So, there is a power to negative as well as positive thinking. The moral: Success in school and beyond requires enough optimism to sustain hope and enough pessimism to motivate concern.

FALSE CONSENSUS AND UNIQUENESS

We have a curious tendency to enhance our self-images by overestimating or underestimating the extent to which others think and act as we do. On matters of *opinion*, we find support for our positions by overestimating the extent to which others agree—a phenomenon called the **false consensus effect** (Krueger & Clement, 1994b; Marks & Miller, 1987; Mullen & Goethals, 1990). Sharad Goel, Winter Mason, and Duncan Watts (2010) found that Facebook users were 90 percent accurate in guessing when they agreed with their friends on political and other issues, but they were only 41 percent accurate in guessing disagreement. In other words, most of the time they thought their friends agreed with them when they didn't. Business students asked to make decisions about ethical dilemmas overestimated how many other students made the same choice (Flynn & Wiltermuth, 2010). White Australians prejudiced against Aborigines were more likely to believe that other Whites were also prejudiced (Watt & Larkin, 2010). The sense we make of the world seems like common sense.

When we behave badly or fail in a task, we reassure ourselves by thinking that such lapses also are common. After one person lies to another, the liar begins to perceive the *other* person as dishonest (Sagarin & others, 1998). If we feel sexual desire toward another, we may overestimate the other's reciprocal desire. We guess that others think and act as we do: "I lie, but doesn't everyone?" If we cheat on our income taxes, smoke, or enhance our appearance, we are likely to overestimate the number of other people who do likewise. As former *Baywatch* actor David Hasselhoff said, "I have had Botox. Everyone has!" "We don't see things as they are," says a proverb. "We see things as we are."

Robyn Dawes (1990) proposed that this false consensus may occur because we generalize from a limited sample, which prominently includes ourselves. Lacking other information, why not "project" ourselves; why not impute our own knowledge to others and use our responses as a clue to their likely responses? Most people are in the majority; so when people assume they are in the majority they are usually right. Also, we're more likely to spend time with people who share our attitudes and behaviors and, consequently, to judge the world from the people we know. Small wonder that Germans tend to think that the typical European looks rather German, whereas the Portuguese see Europeans as looking more Portuguese (Imhoff & others, 2011).

On matters of *ability* or when we behave well or successfully, however, a **false uniqueness effect** more often occurs (Goethals & others, 1991).

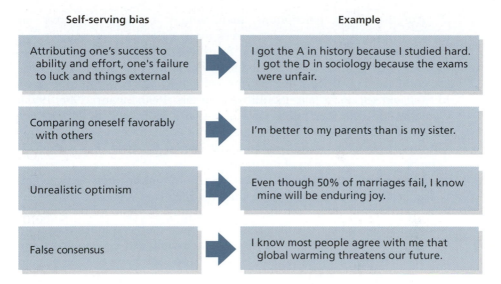

Self-serving bias   **Example**

Attributing one's success to   I got the A in history because I studied hard.
ability and effort, one's failure   I got the D in sociology because the exams
to luck and things external   were unfair.

Comparing oneself favorably
with others   I'm better to my parents than is my sister.

Unrealistic optimism   Even though 50% of marriages fail, I know
                                     mine will be enduring joy.

False consensus   I know most people agree with me that
                                     global warming threatens our future.

FIGURE 4-1
How self-serving bias works.

We serve our self-image by seeing our talents and moral behaviors as relatively unusual. Dutch college students preferred being part of a larger group in matters of opinion such as politics (false consensus) but wanted to be part of a smaller group in matters of taste such as musical preferences (false uniqueness; Spears & others, 2009). After all, a band isn't cool anymore if too many people like it.

To sum up, self-serving bias appears as self-serving attributions, self-congratulatory comparisons, illusory optimism, and false consensus for one's failings (Figure 4-1).

SELF-ESTEEM MOTIVATION

Why do people perceive themselves in self-enhancing ways? One explanation sees the self-serving bias as a by-product of how we process and remember information about ourselves. Comparing ourselves with others requires us to notice, assess, and recall their behavior and ours. Thus, there are multiple opportunities for flaws in our information processing (Chambers & Windschitl, 2004). In one study, married people gave themselves credit for doing more housework than their spouses did. Might that not be due, as Michael Ross and Fiore Sicoly (1979) believed, to our greater recall for what we've actively done and our lesser recall for what we've not done or merely observed our partner doing? I could easily picture myself picking up the laundry off the bedroom floor, but I was less aware of the times when I absentmindedly overlooked it.

Are the biased perceptions, then, simply a perceptual error, an emotion-free glitch in how we process information? Or are self-serving *motives* also involved? It's now clear from research that we have multiple motives. Questing for self-knowledge, we're motivated to *assess our competence* (Dunning, 1995). Questing for self-confirmation, we're motivated to *verify our self-conceptions* (Sanitioso & others, 1990; Swann, 1996, 1997). Questing for self-affirmation, we're especially motivated to *enhance our self-image* (Sedikides, 1993). Self-esteem motivation, then, helps power our self-serving bias. As social psychologist Daniel Batson (2006) surmises, "The head is an extension of the heart."

Most people are extremely motivated to maintain their self-esteem. In fact, a study found that college students preferred a boost to their self-esteem to eating their favorite food, engaging in their favorite sexual activity, seeing a best friend, drinking alcohol, or receiving a paycheck (Bushman & others, 2011). So, somewhat incredibly, self-esteem was more important than sex, pizza, and beer! What happens when your self-esteem is threatened—for example, by a failure or an unflattering comparison with someone else? When brothers have markedly different ability levels—for example, one is a great athlete and the other is not—they report not getting along well (Tesser, 1988).

Self-esteem threats also occur among friends, whose success can be more threatening than that of strangers (Zuckerman & Jost, 2001). Your level of self-esteem also makes a difference: High self-esteem people usually react to a self-esteem threat by compensating for it (blaming someone else or trying harder next time). These reactions help them preserve their positive feelings about themselves. Low self-esteem people, however, are more likely to "break" by blaming themselves or giving up (VanDellen & others, 2011).

What underlies the motive to maintain or enhance self-esteem? Mark Leary (1998, 2004b, 2007) believes that our self-esteem feelings are like a fuel gauge. Relationships enable surviving and thriving. Thus, the self-esteem gauge alerts us to threatened social rejection, motivating us to act with greater sensitivity to others' expectations. Studies confirm that social rejection lowers our self-esteem and makes us more eager for approval. Spurned or jilted, we feel unattractive or inadequate. Like a blinking dashboard light, this pain can motivate action—self-improvement and a search for acceptance and inclusion elsewhere.

REFLECTIONS ON SELF-ESTEEM AND SELF-SERVING BIAS

If you are like some readers, by now you are finding self-serving bias either depressing or contrary to your own occasional feelings of inadequacy. Even people who exhibit the self-serving bias may feel inferior—to those who are a step or two higher on the ladder of success, attractiveness, or skill. Moreover, not everyone operates with a self-serving bias. Some people *do* suffer from low self-esteem. Positive self-esteem does have some benefits.

The Self-Serving Bias as Adaptive

Self-esteem has its dark side, but also its bright side. When good things happen, people with high self-esteem are more likely to savor and sustain the good feelings (Wood & others, 2003). "Believing one has more talents and positive qualities than one's peers allows one to feel good about oneself and to enter the stressful circumstances of daily life with the resources conferred by a positive sense of self," noted Shelley Taylor and co-researchers (2003b).

Self-serving bias and its accompanying excuses also help protect people from depression (Snyder & Higgins, 1988; Taylor & others, 2003a). Nondepressed people usually exhibit self-serving bias. They excuse their failures on laboratory tasks or perceive themselves as being more in control than they are. Depressed people's self-appraisals and their appraisals of how others really view them are not inflated.

Self-serving bias additionally helps buffer stress. George Bonanno and colleagues (2005) assessed the emotional resiliency of workers who escaped from the World Trade Center or its environs on September 11, 2001. They found that those who displayed self-enhancing tendencies were the most resilient.

In their *terror management theory*, Jeff Greenberg, Sheldon Solomon, and Tom Pyszczynski (1997; Greenberg, 2008) propose another reason why positive self-esteem is adaptive: It buffers anxiety, including anxiety related to our certain death. In childhood, we learn that when we meet the standards taught us by our parents, we are loved and protected; when we don't, love and protection may be withdrawn. We therefore come to associate viewing ourselves as good with feeling secure. Greenberg and colleagues argue that positive self-esteem—viewing oneself as good and secure—even protects us from feeling terror over our eventual death. Their research shows that reminding people of their mortality (for example, by writing a short essay on dying) motivates them to affirm their self-worth. When facing such threats, self-esteem buffers anxiety. In 2004, a year after the U.S. invasion, Iraqi teens who felt their country was under threat reported the highest self-esteem (Carlton-Ford & others, 2008).

As research on depression and anxiety suggests, there is practical wisdom in self-serving perceptions. It may be strategic to believe we are smarter, stronger, and more socially successful than we are. Cheaters may give a more convincing display of honesty if they believe themselves honorable. Belief in our superiority can also motivate us to achieve—creating a self-fulfilling prophecy—and can sustain our hope through difficult times (Willard & Gramzow, 2009).

The Self-Serving Bias as Maladaptive

Although self-serving pride may help protect us from depression, it can also be maladaptive. People who blame others for their social difficulties are often unhappier than people who can acknowledge their mistakes (Anderson & others, 1983; Newman & Langer, 1981; Peterson & others, 1981).

Research by Barry Schlenker (1976; Schlenker & Miller, 1977a, 1977b) has also shown how self-serving perceptions can poison a group. As a rock band guitarist during his college days, Schlenker noted that "rock band members typically overestimated their contributions to a group's success and underestimated their contributions to failure. I saw many good bands disintegrate from the problems caused by these self-glorifying tendencies." In his later life as a University of Florida social psychologist, Schlenker explored group members' self-serving perceptions. In nine experiments, he had people work together on some task. He then falsely informed them that their group had done either well or poorly. In every one of those studies, the members of successful groups claimed more responsibility for their group's performance than did members of groups that supposedly failed at the task.

If most group members believe they are underpaid and underappreciated relative to their better-than-average contributions, disharmony and envy are likely. College presidents and academic deans will readily recognize the phenomenon. Ninety percent or more of college faculty members have rated themselves as superior to their average colleague (Blackburn & others, 1980; Cross, 1977). It is therefore inevitable that when merit salary raises are announced and half receive an average raise or less, many will feel themselves victims of injustice.

Self-serving biases also inflate people's judgments of their groups. When groups are comparable, most people consider their own group superior (Codol, 1976; Jourden & Heath, 1996; Taylor & Doria, 1981).

- Most university sorority members perceive those in their sorority as far less likely to be conceited and snobbish than those in other sororities (Biernat & others, 1996).
- Fifty-three percent of Dutch adults rate their marriage or partnership as better than that of most others; only 1 percent rate it as worse than most (Buunk & van der Eijnden, 1997).
- Sixty-six percent of Americans give their oldest child's public school a grade of A or B. But nearly as many—64 percent—give the nation's public schools a grade of C or D (Whitman, 1996).

That people see themselves and their groups with a favorable bias is hardly new. The tragic flaw portrayed in ancient Greek drama was *hubris,* or pride. Like the subjects of our experiments, the Greek tragic figures were not self-consciously evil; they merely thought too highly of themselves. In literature, the pitfalls of pride are portrayed again and again. In theology, pride has long been first among the "seven deadly sins."

If pride is akin to the self-serving bias, then what is humility? Is it self-contempt? Humility is not handsome people believing they are ugly and smart people trying to believe they are slow-witted. False modesty can actually be a cover for pride in one's better-than-average humility. (James Friedrich [1996] reports that most students congratulate themselves on being better than average at not thinking themselves better than average!) True humility is more like self-forgetfulness than false modesty. It leaves us free to recognize accurately and rejoice in our special talents and, with the same honesty, to recognize the talents of others.

CONCEPTS TO REMEMBER

self-serving bias   The tendency to perceive oneself favorably.

false consensus effect   The tendency to overestimate the commonality of one's opinions and one's undesirable or unsuccessful behaviors.

false uniqueness effect   The tendency to underestimate the commonality of one's abilities and one's desirable or successful behaviors.

MODULE

5*

❖

The Power of Positive Thinking

We have considered a potent self-serving bias uncovered by social psychologists. When most people see themselves as more moral and deserving than others, conflict among people and nations is a natural result.

Studies of the self-serving bias expose deep truths about human nature. But single truths seldom tell the whole story, because the world is complex. Indeed, there is an important complement to these truths. High self-esteem—a sense of self-worth—is adaptive. Compared with those with low self-esteem, people with high self-esteem are happier, less neurotic, less troubled by ulcers and insomnia, and less prone to drug and alcohol addictions (Brockner & Hulton, 1978; Brown, 1991). Many clinical psychologists report that underneath much human despair is an impoverished self-acceptance.

Albert Bandura (1986) merges much of this research into a concept called **self-efficacy**, a scholarly version of the wisdom behind the power of positive thinking. An optimistic belief in our own competence and effectiveness pays dividends (Bandura & others, 1999; Maddux and Gosselin, 2003). Children and adults with strong feelings of self-efficacy are more persistent, less anxious, and less depressed. They also live healthier lives and are more academically successful.

---

*This module benefits from the input of Jean Twenge, professor of psychology at San Diego State University. Professor Twenge's research on social rejection and on generational changes in personality and the self has been published in many articles and books, including *Generation Me: Why Today's Young Americans Are More Confident, Assertive, Entitled—and More Miserable Than Ever Before* (2006) and *The Narcissism Epidemic: Living in the Age of Entitlement* (with W. Keith Campbell, 2009).

Your self-efficacy is how competent you feel to do something. If you believe you can do something, will this belief necessarily make a difference? That depends on a second factor: Do you have control over your outcomes? You may, for example, feel like an effective driver (high self-efficacy), yet feel endangered by drunken drivers (low control). You may feel like a competent student or worker but, fearing discrimination based on your age, gender, or appearance, you may think your prospects are dim.

*L*OCUS OF CONTROL

"I have no social life," complained a 40-something single man to student therapist Jerry Phares. At Phares's urging, the patient went to a dance, where several women danced with him. "I was just lucky," he later reported. "It would never happen again." When Phares reported this to his mentor, Julian Rotter, it crystallized an idea he had been forming. In Rotter's experiments and in his clinical practice, some people seemed to persistently "feel that what happens to them is governed by external forces of one kind or another, while others feel that what happens to them is governed largely by their own efforts and skills" (quoted by Hunt, 1993, p. 334).

What do you think about your own life? Are you more often in charge of your destiny or a victim of circumstance? Rotter called this dimension **locus of control.** With Phares, he developed 29 paired statements to measure a person's locus of control. Imagine taking this test. Which statements do you more strongly believe?

a. In the long run, people get the respect they deserve in this world.	or	**b.** Unfortunately, people's worth passes unrecognized no matter how hard they try.
a. What happens to me is my own doing.	or	**b.** Sometimes I feel that I don't have enough control over the direction my life is taking.
a. The average person can have an influence in government decisions.	or	**b.** This world is run by the few people in power, and there is not much the little guy can do about it.

If your answers to these questions (from Rotter, 1973) were mostly "a," you probably believe you control your own destiny (*internal* locus of control). If your answers were mostly "b," you probably feel chance or outside forces determine your fate (*external* locus of control). Those who see themselves as *internally* controlled are more likely to do well in school, be more productive at work, make more money, successfully stop smoking, maintain a healthy weight, deal with marital problems directly, be more satisfied with life, and achieve long-term goals (Findley & Cooper, 1983; Gale & others, 2008; Miller & others, 1986; Wang & others, 2010).

*L*EARNED HELPLESSNESS VERSUS SELF-DETERMINATION

The benefits of feelings of control also appear in animal research. In research done before today's greater concern for animal welfare, dogs confined in a cage and taught that they could not escape shocks learned a sense of helplessness. Later, these dogs cowered passively in other situations when they *could* escape punishment. Dogs that learned personal control (by successfully escaping their first shocks) adapted easily to a new situation. Researcher Martin Seligman (1975, 1991) noted similarities to this **learned helplessness** in human situations. Depressed or oppressed people, for example, become passive because they believe their efforts have no effect. Helpless dogs and depressed people both suffer paralysis of the will, passive resignation, and even motionless apathy (Figure 5-1).

On the other hand, people benefit by training their self-control "muscles." College students who practiced self-control by sticking with an exercise program or reducing their impulse-buying also ate less junk food, cut down on alcohol, and studied more (Oaten & Cheng, 2006a, 2006b). So if you learn how to exert willpower in one area of your life, resisting temptation in other areas becomes easier too.

Ellen Langer and Judith Rodin (1976) tested the importance of personal control by treating elderly patients in a highly rated Connecticut nursing home in one of two ways. With one group, the benevolent caregivers emphasized "our responsibility to make this a home you can be proud of and happy in." They gave the patients their normal well-intentioned, sympathetic care and allowed them to assume a passive care-receiving role. Three weeks later, most of these patients were rated by themselves, by interviewers, and by nurses as further debilitated. Langer and Rodin's other treatment promoted personal control. It emphasized opportunities for choice, the possibilities for influencing nursing-home policy, and the

FIGURE 5-1
Learned helplessness. When animals and people experience uncontrollable bad events, they learn to feel helpless and resigned.

person's responsibility "to make of your life whatever you want." These patients were given small decisions to make and responsibilities to fulfill. During the ensuing 3 weeks, 93 percent of this group showed improved alertness, activity, and happiness.

Studies confirm that systems of governing or managing people that promote personal control will indeed promote health and happiness (Deci & Ryan, 1987). Here are some additional examples:

- Prisoners given some control over their environments—by being able to move chairs, control TV sets, and operate the lights— experience less stress, exhibit fewer health problems, and commit less vandalism (Ruback & others, 1986; Wener & others, 1987).

- Workers given leeway in carrying out tasks and making decisions experience improved morale (Miller & Monge, 1986). So do tele-commuting workers who have more flexibility in balancing their work and personal life (Valcour, 2007).

- In all countries studied, people who perceive themselves as hav-ing free choice experience greater satisfaction with their lives. And countries where people experience more freedom have more satis-fied citizens (Inglehart & others, 2008).

The Costs of Excess Choice

Can there ever be too much of a good thing such as freedom and self-determination? Barry Schwartz (2000, 2004) contends that individu-alistic modern cultures indeed have "an excess of freedom," causing decreased life satisfaction and increased rates of clinical depression. Too many choices can lead to paralysis, or what Schwartz calls "the tyranny of freedom." After choosing from among 30 kinds of jams or chocolates, people express less satisfaction with their choices than those choosing from among 6 options (Iyengar & Lepper, 2000). Making choices is also tiring. Students who read the catalog and chose which classes they would take during the upcoming semester—versus those who simply read it but made no choices—were later less likely to study for an important test and more likely to procrastinate by playing video games and reading magazines. In another study, students who chose among an array of consumer products were later less able to consume an unsavory but healthy drink (Vohs & others, 2008). So after choosing among the 19,000 possible beverage combinations at Starbucks or the 40,000 items at the average supermarket, you might be less satisfied with your choices and more likely to go home and eat ice cream straight from the container.

Christopher Hsee and Reid Hastie (2006) illustrate how choice may enhance regret. Give employees a free trip to either Paris or Hawaii and they will be happy. But give them a choice between the two and they may be less happy. People who choose Paris may regret that it lacks the warmth and the ocean. Those who choose Hawaii may regret the lack of great museums.

In other experiments, people have expressed greater satisfaction with irrevocable choices (such as those made in an "all purchases final" sale) than with reversible choices (as when allowing refunds or exchanges). Ironically, people like and will pay for the freedom to reverse their choices. Yet, note Daniel Gilbert and Jane Ebert (2002), that same freedom "can inhibit the psychological processes that manufacture satisfaction."

That principle may help explain a curious social phenomenon (Myers, 2000a): National surveys show that people expressed more satisfaction with their marriages several decades ago when marriage was more irrevocable ("all purchases final"). Today, despite greater freedom to escape bad marriages and try new ones, people tend to express somewhat less satisfaction with the marriage that they have.

REFLECTIONS ON SELF-EFFICACY

The Power of Positive Thinking

Although psychological research on perceived self-control is relatively new, the emphasis on taking charge of one's life and realizing one's potential is not. The you-can-do-it theme of rags-to-riches is an enduring idea. We find it in Norman Vincent Peale's 1950s best-seller, *The Power of Positive Thinking*: "If you think in positive terms you will get positive results. That is the simple fact." We find it in the many self-help books and videos that urge people to succeed through positive mental attitudes.

Research on self-control gives us greater confidence in traditional virtues such as perseverance and hope. Bandura (2004) acknowledges that self-efficacy is fed by social persuasion ("You have what it takes to succeed") and by self-persuasion ("I think I can, I think I can"). Modeling—seeing similar others succeed with effort—helps, too. But the biggest source of self-efficacy, he says, is *mastery experiences*. "Successes build a robust belief in one's efficacy." If your initial efforts to lose weight, stop smoking, or improve your grades succeed, your self-efficacy increases.

A team of researchers led by Roy Baumeister (Baumeister & others, 2003) concurs with Bandura's conclusion about mastery experiences. "Praising all the children just for being themselves," they contend, "simply devalues praise." Better to praise and bolster self-esteem "in recognition of good performance. . . . As the person performs or behaves better, self-esteem is encouraged to rise, and the net effect will be to reinforce both good behavior and improvement. Those outcomes are conducive to both the happiness of the individual and the betterment of society."

"*This gives my confidence a real boost.*"

Confidence and feelings of self-efficacy grow from successes.
© Edward Koren/The New Yorker Collection/www.cartoonbank.com

So there is a power to positive thinking. But let us remember the point at which we began our consideration of self-efficacy: Any truth, separated from its complementary truth, is a half-truth. The truth embodied in the concept of self-efficacy can encourage us to not resign ourselves to bad situations, to persist despite initial failures, to exert effort without being overly distracted by self-doubts. But lest the pendulum swing too far toward this truth, we had best remember that it, too, is not the whole story. If positive thinking can accomplish anything, then if we are unhappily married, poor, or depressed, we have only ourselves to blame. For shame! If only we had tried harder, been more disciplined, less stupid. Failing to appreciate that difficulties sometimes reflect the oppressive power of social situations can tempt us to blame people for their problems and failures, or even to blame ourselves too harshly for our own. Ironically, life's greatest disappointments, as well as its highest achievements, are born of the highest expectations. The bigger we dream, the more we might attain—and the more we risk falling short.

The "Dark Side" of Self-Esteem

People with low self-esteem often have problems in life—they make less money, abuse drugs, and are more likely to be depressed (Salmela-Aro & Nurmi, 2007; Trzesniewski & others, 2006). However, a correlation between two variables is sometimes caused by a third factor. Maybe people low in self-esteem also faced poverty as children, experienced sexual abuse, or had parents who used drugs—all possible causes of later struggling. Sure enough, a study that controlled for these factors found that the link between self-esteem and negative outcomes disappeared (Boden & others, 2008). In other words, low self-esteem was not the cause of these young adults' problems—the seeming cause, instead, was that many could not escape their tough childhoods.

High self-esteem does have some benefits—it fosters initiative, resilience, and pleasant feelings (Baumeister & others, 2003). Yet teen males who engage in sexual activity at an "inappropriately young age" tend to have *higher* than average self-esteem. So do teen gang leaders, extreme ethnocentrists, terrorists, and men in prison for committing violent crimes (Bushman & Baumeister, 2002; Dawes, 1994, 1998). "Hitler had very high self-esteem," note Baumeister and co-authors (2003).

Narcissism: Self-Esteem's Conceited Sister
High self-esteem becomes especially problematic if it crosses over into narcissism, or having an inflated sense of self. Most people with high self-esteem value both individual achievement and relationships with others. Narcissists usually have high self-esteem, but they are missing the piece about caring for others (Campbell & others, 2002). Although narcissists are often outgoing and charming early on, their self-centeredness often leads to relationship problems in the long run (Campbell, 2005).

In a series of experiments conducted by Brad Bushman and Roy Baumeister (1998), undergraduate volunteers wrote essays and received rigged feedback that said, "This is one of the worst essays I've read!" Those who scored high on narcissism were much more likely to retaliate, blasting painful noise into the headphones of the student they believed had criticized them. Narcissists weren't aggressive toward someone who praised them ("great essay!"). It was the insult that set them off. But what about self-esteem? Maybe only the "insecure" narcissists—those low in self-esteem—would lash out. But that's not how it turned out—instead, the students high in both self-esteem and narcissism were the most aggressive. The same was true in a classroom setting—those who were high in both self-esteem and narcissism were the most likely to retaliate against a classmate's criticism by giving him or her a bad grade (Bushman & others, 2009; Figure 5-2). Narcissists can be charming and entertaining. But as one wit has said, "God help you if you cross them."

It's also possible to have too much narcissistic pride in your group, not just yourself. Polish undergraduates who displayed a "collective narcissism," believing their country was superior to others, were more prejudiced against Jewish people. Mexican undergraduates high in collective narcissism were more likely to view the construction of a U.S.–Mexico border wall as an insult and to endorse a boycott of U.S.

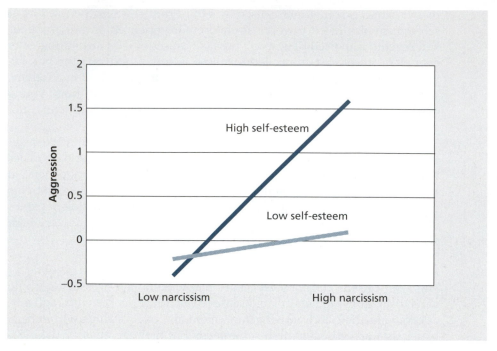

FIGURE 5-2
Narcissism, self-esteem, and aggression. Narcissism and self-esteem interact to influence aggression. In an experiment by Brad Bushman and colleagues (2009), the recipe for retaliation against a critical classmate required both narcissism and high self-esteem.

products in retaliation (Golec deZavala & others, 2009). So whether someone has excessive pride in themselves or their group, others may end up suffering.

"The enthusiastic claims of the self-esteem movement mostly range from fantasy to hogwash," says Baumeister (1996), who suspects he has "probably published more studies on self-esteem than anybody else. . . . The effects of self-esteem are small, limited, and not all good." Folks with high self-esteem, he reports, are more likely to be obnoxious, to interrupt, and to talk at people rather than with them (in contrast to the more shy, modest, self-folks with low self-esteem). "My conclusion is that self-control is worth 10 times as much as self-esteem."

What about the idea that an overinflated ego is just a cover for deep-seated insecurity? Do narcissistic people actually hate themselves "deep down inside"? Recent studies show that the answer is *no*. People who score high on measures of narcissistic personality traits also score high on measures of self-esteem. In case narcissists were claiming high self-esteem just for show, researchers also asked undergraduates to play a computer game where they had to press a key as quickly as possible to match the word "me" with words such as "good," "wonderful," "great," and "right," and words such as "bad," "awful," "terrible," and "wrong." High scorers on the narcissism scale were faster than others to associate themselves with good words, and slower than others to pair themselves with bad words (Campbell & others, 2007). And narcissists were even faster to identify with words such as "outspoken," "dominant," and "assertive." Although it might be comforting to think that an arrogant classmate is just covering for his insecurity, chances are that deep down inside he thinks he's *awesome*.

After tracking self-importance across the past several decades, psychologist Jean Twenge (2006; Twenge & others, 2008) reports that today's young generation—*Generation Me*, she calls it—express more narcissism (by agreeing with statements such as "If I ruled the world, it would be a better place" or "I think I am a special person"). Narcissism scores rose over time on college campuses from Alabama to Maryland to California (Stewart & Bernhardt, 2010; Twenge & Foster, 2008, 2010). Narcissism correlates with materialism, the desire to be famous, inflated expectations, fewer committed relationships and more "hooking up," more gambling, and more cheating, all of which have also risen as narcissism has increased. Narcissism is also linked to a lack of empathy—the ability to take someone else's perspective and be concerned about their problems—and empathy has dropped precipitously among college students (Konrath & others, 2011). The researchers speculate that today's generation may be so wrapped up in online interaction that their in-person interaction skills have atrophied. Or, they say, empathy might have declined because young people today are "feeling too busy on their paths to success," single-mindedly concentrating on their own achievement because the world is now so competitive. Yet, ironically, those high in narcissism and low in empathy are less—not more—successful in the long run, making lower grades in college and performing poorly at work (Judge & others, 2006; Robins & Beer, 2001).

Low Versus Secure Self-Esteem

The findings linking a highly positive self-concept with negative behavior exist in tension with the findings that people expressing low self-esteem are more vulnerable to assorted clinical problems, including anxiety, loneliness, and eating disorders. When feeling bad or threatened, low-self-esteem people often take a negative view of everything. They notice and remember others' worst behaviors and think their partners don't love them (Murray & others, 1998, 2002; Ybarra, 1999).

Secure self-esteem—one rooted more in feeling good about who one is than in grades, looks, money, or others' approval—is conducive to long-term well-being (Kernis, 2003; Schimel & others, 2001). Jennifer Crocker and colleagues (Crocker, 2002; Crocker and Luhtanen, 2003; Crocker and Park, 2004; Crocker and Knight, 2005) confirmed this in studies with

University of Michigan students. Those whose self-worth was most frag-ile—most contingent on external sources—experienced more stress, anger, relationship problems, drug and alcohol use, and eating disorders than did those whose sense of self-worth was rooted more in internal sources, such as personal virtues.

Ironically, note Crocker and Lora Park (2004), those who pursue self-esteem, perhaps by seeking to become beautiful, rich, or popular, may lose sight of what really makes for quality of life. Moreover, if feeling good about ourselves is our goal, then we may become less open to criticism, more likely to blame than empathize with others, and more pressured to succeed at activities rather than enjoy them. Over time, such pursuit of self-esteem can fail to satisfy our deep needs for competence, relationship, and autonomy, note Crocker and Park. To focus less on one's self-image, and more on developing one's talents and relationships, eventually leads to greater well-being. Kristin Neff (2011) suggests we label this approach self-compassion—leaving behind comparisons with others and instead treating ourselves with kindness. As an Indian proverb puts it, "There is nothing noble in being superior to some other person. The true nobility is in being superior to your previous self."

CONCEPTS TO REMEMBER

self-efficacy   A sense that one is competent and effective, distinguished from self-esteem, which is one's sense of self-worth. A sharpshooter in the military might feel high self-efficacy and low self-esteem.

locus of control   The extent to which people perceive outcomes as internally control-lable by their own efforts or as externally controlled by chance or outside forces.

learned helplessness   The sense of hopelessness and resignation learned when a human or ani-mal perceives no control over repeated bad events.

6

❖

The Fundamental Attribution Error

As later modules will reveal, social psychology's most important lesson concerns the influence of our social environment. At any moment, our internal state, and therefore what we say and do, depends on the situation as well as on what we bring to the situation. In experiments, a slight difference between two situations sometimes greatly affects how people respond. As a professor, I have seen this when teaching the same subject at both 8:30 A.M. and 7:00 P.M. Silent stares would greet me at 8:30; at 7:00, I had to break up a party. In each situation, some individuals were more talkative than others, but the difference between the two situations exceeded the individual differences.

Attribution researchers have found a common problem with our attributions. When explaining someone's behavior, we often underestimate the impact of the situation and overestimate the extent to which it reflects the individual's traits and attitudes. Thus, even knowing the effect of the time of day on classroom conversation, I found it terribly tempting to assume that the people in the 7:00 P.M. class were more extraverted than the "silent types" who came at 8:30 A.M. Likewise, we may infer that people fall because they're clumsy rather than because they were tripped; that people smile because they're happy rather than faking friendliness, and that people speed past us on the highway because they're aggressive rather than late for an important meeting.

This discounting of the situation, dubbed by Lee Ross (1977) the **fundamental attribution error**, appears in many experiments. In the first such study, Edward Jones and Victor Harris (1967) had Duke University students read debaters' speeches supporting or attacking Cuba's then leader,

Video
6.1

55

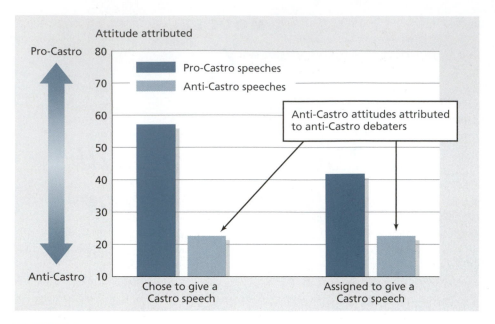

FIGURE 6-1
The fundamental attribution error. When people read a debate speech supporting or attacking Fidel Castro, they attributed corresponding attitudes to the speechwriter, even when the debate coach assigned the writer's position.   Source: Data from Jones & Harris (1967).

Fidel Castro. When told that the debater chose which position to take, the students logically enough assumed it reflected the person's own attitude. But what happened when the students were told that the debate coach had assigned the position? People who are merely feigning a position write more forceful statements than you'd expect (Allison & others, 1993; Miller & others, 1990). Thus, even knowing that the debater had been told to take a pro- or anti-Castro position did not prevent students from inferring that the debater in fact had the assigned leanings (Figure 6-1). People seemed to think, "Yeah, I know he was assigned that position, but, you know, I think he really believes it."

We commit the fundamental attribution error when we explain other people's behavior. Our own behavior we often explain in terms of the situation. So Ian might attribute his behavior to the situation ("I was angry because everything was going wrong"), whereas Rosa might think, "Ian was hostile because he is an angry person." When referring to ourselves, we typically use verbs that describe our actions and reactions ("I get annoyed when . . ."). Referring to someone else, we more often describe what that person is ("He is nasty") (Fiedler & others, 1991); McGuire & McGuire, 1986; White & Younger, 1988). Husbands who attribute their wives' criticism to her being "mean and cold" are more likely to become violent (Schweinle & others, 2002). When she expresses distress about their relationship, he hears the worst and reacts angrily.

THE FUNDAMENTAL ATTRIBUTION ERROR IN EVERYDAY LIFE

If we know the checkout cashier is taught to say, "Thank you and have a nice day," do we nevertheless automatically conclude that the cashier is a friendly, grateful person? We certainly know how to discount behavior that we attribute to ulterior motives (Fein & others, 1990). Yet consider what happened when Williams College students talked with a supposed clinical psychology graduate student who acted either warm and friendly or aloof and critical. Researchers David Napolitan and George Goethals (1979) told half the students beforehand that her behavior would be spontaneous. They told the other half that for purposes of the experiment, she had been instructed to feign friendly (or unfriendly) behavior. The effect of the information? None. If she acted friendly, they assumed she really was a friendly person; if she acted unfriendly, they assumed she was an unfriendly person. As when viewing a dummy on the ventriloquist's lap or a movie actor playing a "good-guy" or "bad-guy" role, we find it difficult to escape the illusion that the scripted behavior reflects an inner disposition. Perhaps this is why Leonard Nimoy, who played Mr. Spock on the original *Star Trek*, entitled his book *I Am Not Spock.*

The discounting of social constraints was evident in a thought-provoking experiment by Lee Ross and collaborators (Ross & others, 1977). The experiment re-created Ross's firsthand experience of moving from graduate student to professor. His doctoral oral exam had proved a humbling experience as his apparently brilliant professors quizzed him on topics they specialized in. Six months later, *Dr.* Ross was himself an examiner, now able to ask penetrating questions on *his* favorite topics. Ross's hapless student later confessed to feeling exactly as Ross had a half-year before—dissatisfied with his ignorance and impressed with the apparent brilliance of the examiners.

In the experiment, with Teresa Amabile and Julia Steinmetz, Ross set up a simulated quiz game. He randomly assigned some Stanford University students to play the role of questioner, some to play the role of contestant, and others to observe. The researchers invited the questioners to make up difficult questions that would demonstrate their wealth of knowledge. Any one of us can imagine such questions using one's own domain of competence: "Where is Bainbridge Island?" "How did Mary, Queen of Scots, die?" "Which has the longer coastline, Europe or Africa?"

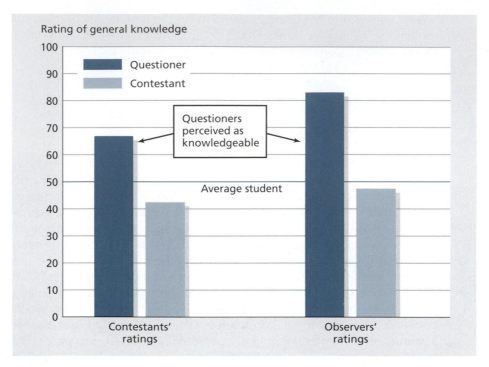

FIGURE 6-2
Both contestants and observers of a simulated quiz game assumed that a person who had been randomly assigned the role of questioner was far more knowledgeable than the contestant. Actually, the assigned roles of questioner and contestant simply made the questioner seem more knowledgeable. The failure to appreciate this illustrates the fundamental attribution error.   Source: Data from Ross & others (1977).

If even those few questions have you feeling a little uninformed, then you will appreciate the results of this experiment.*

Everyone had to know that the questioners would have the advantage. Yet both contestants and observers (but not the questioners) came to the erroneous conclusion that the questioners *really were* more knowledgeable than the contestants (Figure 6-2). Follow-up research shows that these misimpressions are hardly a reflection of low social intelligence. If anything, college students and other intelligent and socially competent people are *more* likely to make the attribution error (Bauman & Skitka, 2010; Block & Funder, 1986).

In real life, those with social power usually initiate and control conversations, which often leads underlings to overestimate their knowledge

---

*Bainbridge Island is across Puget Sound from Seattle. Mary was ordered beheaded by her cousin Queen Elizabeth I. Although the African continent is more than double the area of Europe, Europe's coastline is longer. (It is more convoluted, with many harbors and inlets, a geographical fact that contributed to its role in the history of maritime trade.)

and intelligence. Medical doctors, for example, are often presumed to be experts on all sorts of questions unrelated to medicine. Similarly, students often overestimate the brilliance of their teachers. (As in the experiment, teachers are questioners on subjects of their special expertise.) When some of these students later become teachers, they are usually amazed to discover that teachers are not so brilliant after all.

To illustrate the fundamental attribution error, most of us need look no further than our own experiences. Determined to make some new friends, Bev plasters a smile on her face and anxiously plunges into a party. Everyone else seems quite relaxed and happy as they laugh and talk with one another. Bev wonders to herself, "Why is everyone always so at ease in groups like this while I'm feeling shy and tense?" Actually, everyone else is feeling nervous, too, and making the same attribution error in assuming that Bev and the others *are* as they *appear*—confidently convivial.

WHY DO WE MAKE THE ATTRIBUTION ERROR?

So far we have seen a bias in the way we explain other people's behavior: We often ignore powerful situational determinants. Why do we tend to underestimate the situational determinants of others' behavior but not of our own?

Perspective and Situational Awareness

Differing Perspectives

Attribution theorists have pointed out that we observe others from a different perspective than we observe ourselves (Jones, 1976; Jones & Nisbett, 1971). When we act, the *environment* commands our attention. When we watch another person act, that *person* occupies the center of our attention and the environment becomes relatively invisible. If I'm mad, it's the situation that's making me angry. But someone I see getting mad may seem like an ill-tempered person.

From his analysis of 173 studies, Bertram Malle (2006) concluded that the actor–observer difference is actually minimal. When our action feels intentional and admirable, we attribute it to our own good reasons, not to the situation. It's only when we behave badly that we're more likely to attribute our behavior to the situation, while someone observing us may spontaneously infer a trait.

In some experiments, people have viewed a videotape of a suspect confessing during a police interview. If they viewed the confession through a camera focused on the suspect, they perceived the confession as genuine. If they viewed it through a camera focused on the detective, they perceived it as more coerced (Lassiter & Irvine, 1986; Lassiter & others, 2005, 2007). The camera perspective influenced people's guilt judgments even when the judge instructed them not to allow this to happen (Lassiter & others, 2002).

In courtrooms, most confession videotapes focus on the confessor. As we might expect, noted Daniel Lassiter and Kimberly Dudley (1991), such tapes yield a nearly 100 percent conviction rate when played by prosecutors. Aware of this research, reports Lassiter, New Zealand has made it a national policy that police interrogations be filmed with equal focus on the officer and the suspect, such as by filming them with side profiles of both.

Perspectives Change with Time

As the once-visible person recedes in their memory, observers often give more and more credit to the situation. As we saw previously in the ground-breaking attribution error experiment by Edward Jones and Victor Harris (1967), immediately after hearing someone argue an assigned position, people assume that's how the person really felt. Jerry Burger and M. L. Palmer (1991) found that a week later they are much more ready to credit the situational constraints. The day after a presidential election, Burger and Julie Pavelich (1994) asked voters why the election turned out as it did. Most attributed the outcome to the candidates' personal traits and positions (the winner from the incumbent party was likable). When they asked other voters the same question a year later, only a third attributed the verdict to the candidates. More people now credited circumstances, such as the country's good mood and the robust economy.

Let's make this personal: Are you generally quiet, talkative, or does it depend on the situation? "Depends on the situation" is a common answer. But when asked to describe a friend—or to describe what they were like 5 years ago—people more often ascribe trait descriptions. When recalling our past, we become like observers of someone else, note researchers Emily Pronin and Lee Ross (2006). For most of us, the "old you" is some-one other than today's "real you." We regard our distant past selves (and our distant future selves) almost as if they were other people occupying our body.

Activity
6.1

These experiments point to a reason for the attribution error: *We find causes where we look for them.* To see this in your own experience, consider: Would you say your social psychology instructor is a quiet or a talkative person?

My guess is you inferred that he or she is fairly outgoing. But con-sider: Your attention focuses on your instructor while he or she behaves in a public context that demands speaking. The instructor also observes his or her own behavior in many different situations—in the classroom, in meetings, at home. "Me talkative?" your instructor might say. "Well, it all depends on the situation. When I'm in class or with good friends, I'm rather outgoing. But at conventions and in unfamiliar situations I feel and act rather shy." Because we are acutely aware of how our behavior varies with the situation, we see ourselves as more variable than other people (Baxter & Goldberg, 1987; Kammer, 1982; Sande & others, 1988). "Nigel is uptight, Fiona is relaxed. With me it varies."

Cultural Differences

Cultures also influence attribution error (Ickes, 1980; Watson, 1982). A Western worldview predisposes people to assume that people, not situations, cause events. Internal explanations are more socially approved (Jellison & Green, 1981). "You can do it!" we are assured by the pop psychology of positive-thinking Western culture. You get what you deserve and deserve what you get.

As children grow up in Western culture, they learn to explain behavior in terms of the other's personal characteristics (Rholes & others, 1990; Ross, 1981). As a first-grader, one of my sons unscrambled the words "gate the sleeve caught Tom on his" into "The gate caught Tom on his sleeve." His teacher, applying the Western cultural assumptions of the curriculum materials, marked that wrong. The "right" answer located the cause within Tom: "Tom caught his sleeve on the gate."

The fundamental attribution error occurs across varied cultures (Krull & others, 1999). Yet people in Eastern Asian cultures are somewhat more sensitive than Westerners are to the importance of situations. Thus, when aware of the social context, they are less inclined to assume that others' behavior corresponds to their traits (Choi & others, 1999; Farwell & Weiner, 2000; Masuda & Kitayama, 2004).

Some languages promote external attributions. Instead of "I was late," Spanish idiom allows one to say, "The clock caused me to be late." In collectivist cultures, people less often perceive others in terms of personal dispositions (Lee & others, 1996; Zebrowitz-McArthur, 1988). They are less likely to spontaneously interpret a behavior as reflecting an inner trait (Newman, 1993). When told of someone's actions, Hindus in India are less likely than Americans to offer dispositional explanations ("She is kind") and more likely to offer situational explanations ("Her friends were with her") (Miller, 1984).

*H*OW FUNDAMENTAL IS THE FUNDAMENTAL ATTRIBUTION ERROR?

The fundamental attribution error is *fundamental* because it colors our explanations in basic and important ways. Researchers in Britain, India, Australia, and the United States have found that people's attributions predict their attitudes toward the poor and the unemployed (Furnham, 1982; Pandey & others, 1982; Skitka, 1999; Wagstaff, 1983; Weiner & others, 2011). Those who attribute poverty and unemployment to personal dispositions ("They're just lazy and undeserving") tend to adopt political positions unsympathetic to such people (Figure 6-3). This *dispositional attribution* ascribes behavior to the person's disposition and traits. Those who make *situational attributions* ("If you or I were to live with the same overcrowding, poor education, and discrimination, would we be any better off?") tend to

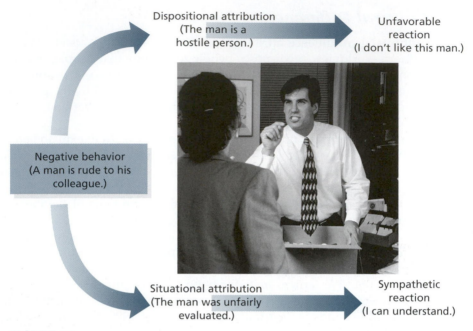

Dispositional attribution
(The man is a hostile person.)

Unfavorable reaction
(I don't like this man.)

Negative behavior
(A man is rude to his colleague.)

Situational attribution
(The man was unfairly evaluated.)

Sympathetic reaction
(I can understand.)

FIGURE 6-3
Attributions and reactions. How we explain someone's negative behavior determines how we feel about it.

adopt political positions that offer more direct support to the poor. Tell me your attributions for poverty and I will guess your politics.

Can we benefit from being aware of the attribution error? I once assisted with some interviews for a faculty position. One candidate was interviewed by six of us at once; each of us had the opportunity to ask two or three questions. I came away thinking, "What a stiff, awkward person he is." The second candidate I met privately over coffee, and we immediately discovered we had a close, mutual friend. As we talked, I became increasingly impressed by what a "warm, engaging, stimulating person she is." Only later did I remember the fundamental attribution error and reassess my analysis. I had attributed his stiffness and her warmth to their dispositions; in fact, I later realized, such behavior resulted partly from the difference in their interview situations.

$\mathcal{C}$ONCEPTS TO REMEMBER

fundamental attribution error   The tendency for observers to underestimate situational influences and overestimate dispositional influences upon others' behavior. (Also called *correspondence bias*, because we so often see behavior as corresponding to a disposition.)

❖

The Powers and Perils of Intuition

What are our powers of intuition—of immediately knowing something without reasoning or analysis? Advocates of "intuitive management" believe we should tune into our hunches. When judging others, they say, we should plug into the nonlogical smarts of our "right brain." When hiring, firing, and investing, we should listen to our premonitions. In making judgments, we should trust the force within.

Are the intuitionists right that important information is immediately available apart from our conscious analysis? Or are the skeptics correct in saying that intuition is "our knowing we are right, whether we are or not"?

Activity 7.1

Priming research hints that the unconscious indeed controls much of our behavior. As John Bargh and Tanya Chartrand (1999) explain, "Most of a person's everyday life is determined not by their conscious intentions and deliberate choices but by mental processes that are put into motion by features of the environment and that operate outside of conscious awareness and guidance." When the light turns red, we react and hit the brake before consciously deciding to do so. Indeed, reflect Neil Macrae and Lucy Johnston (1998), "to be able to do just about anything at all (e.g., driving, dating, dancing), action initiation needs to be decoupled from the inefficient (i.e., slow, serial, resource-consuming) workings of the conscious mind, otherwise inaction inevitably would prevail."

*T*HE POWERS OF INTUITION

"The heart has its reasons which reason does not know," observed seventeenth-century philosopher-mathematician Blaise Pascal. Three centuries later, scientists have proved Pascal correct. We know more than we know we know. Studies of our unconscious information processing confirm our limited access to what's going on in our minds (Bargh & Ferguson, 2000; Greenwald & Banaji, 1995; Strack & Deutsch, 2004). Our thinking is partly *controlled* (reflective, deliberate, and conscious) and—more than psychologists once supposed—partly *automatic* (impulsive, effortless, and without our awareness). Automatic, intuitive thinking occurs not "on-screen" but off-screen, out of sight, where reason does not go. Consider these examples of automatic thinking:

- *Schemas* are mental concepts that intuitively guide our perceptions and interpretations. Whether we hear someone speaking of religious *sects* or *sex* depends not only on the word spoken but also on how we automatically interpret the sound.

- *Emotional reactions* are often nearly instantaneous, happening before there is time for deliberate thinking. One neural shortcut takes information from the eye or the ear to the brain's sensory switchboard (the thalamus) and out to its emotional control center (the amygdala) before the thinking cortex has had any chance to intervene (LeDoux, 2002). Our ancestors who intuitively feared a sound in the bushes were usually fearing nothing. But when the sound was made by a dangerous predator, they became more likely to survive to pass their genes down to us than their more deliberative cousins.

- Given sufficient *expertise*, people may intuitively know the answer to a problem. Many skills, from piano playing to swinging a golf club, begin as a controlled, deliberate process of following rules and gradually become automatic and intuitive (Kruglanski & Gigerenzer, 2011). Master chess players intuitively recognize meaningful patterns that novices miss and often make their next move with only a glance at the board, as the situation cues information stored in their memory. Similarly, without knowing quite how, we recognize a friend's voice after the first spoken word of a phone conversation.

- Faced with a decision but lacking the expertise to make an informed snap judgment, our *unconscious thinking* may guide us toward a satisfying choice. That's what Dutch psychologist Ap Dijksterhuis and co-workers (Dijksterhuis & Nordgren, 2006; Dijksterhuis & others, 2006; Strick & others, 2010) discovered after showing people, for example, a dozen pieces of information about each of four potential apartments. Compared with people who made instant decisions or were given time to analyze the information, the most satisfying decisions were made by those who were distracted and unable to focus consciously on the problem. Although these findings are controversial (González-Vallejo & others, 2008; Lassiter & others, 2009; Newell & others, 2008), this much seems true: When facing a tough decision, it often pays to take our time—even to sleep on it—and to await the intuitive result of our out-of-sight information processing (Sio & Ormerod, 2009).

Some things—facts, names, and past experiences—we remember explicitly (consciously). But other things—skills and conditioned dispositions—we remember *implicitly,* without consciously knowing or declaring that we know. It's true of us all but most strikingly evident in people with brain damage who cannot form new explicit memories. One such person never could learn to recognize her physician, who would need to reintroduce himself with a handshake each day. One day, the physician affixed a tack to his hand, causing the patient to jump with pain. When the physician next returned, he was still unrecognized (explicitly). But the patient, retaining an implicit memory, would not shake his hand.

Equally dramatic are the cases of *blindsight.* Having lost a portion of the visual cortex to surgery or stroke, people may be functionally blind in part of their field of vision. Shown a series of sticks in the blind field, they report seeing nothing. After correctly guessing whether the sticks are vertical or horizontal, the patients are astounded when told, "You got them all right." Like the patient who "remembered" the painful handshake, these people know more than they know they know.

Consider your own taken-for-granted capacity to recognize a face. As you look at it, your brain breaks the visual information into subdimensions such as color, depth, movement, and form and works on each aspect simultaneously before reassembling the components. Finally, using automatic processing, your brain compares the perceived image with previously stored images. Voilà! Instantly and effortlessly, you recognize your grandmother. If intuition is immediately knowing something without reasoned analysis, then perceiving is intuition par excellence.

So, many routine cognitive functions occur automatically, unintentionally, without awareness. We might remember how automatic processing helps us get through life by picturing our minds as functioning like large corporations. Our CEO—our controlled consciousness—attends to many of the most important, complex, and novel issues, while subordinates deal with routine affairs and matters requiring instant action. Like a CEO, consciousness sets goals and priorities, often with little knowledge of operational activities in the underlying departments. This delegation of resources enables us to react to many situations quickly and efficiently. The bottom line: Our brain knows much more than it tells us.

*T*HE LIMITS OF INTUITION

We have seen how automatic, intuitive thinking can "make us smart" (Gigerenzer, 2007, 2010). Elizabeth Loftus and Mark Klinger (1992) nevertheless spoke for other cognitive scientists in having doubts about the brilliance of intuition. They reported "a general consensus that the unconscious may not be as smart as previously believed." For example, although subliminal stimuli can trigger a weak, fleeting response—enough to evoke a feeling if not conscious awareness—there is no evidence that commercial subliminal tapes can "reprogram your unconscious mind" for success. In fact, a significant body of evidence indicates that they can't (Greenwald, 1992).

Social psychologists have explored not only our error-prone hindsight judgments but also our capacity for illusion—for perceptual misinterpretations, fantasies, and constructed beliefs. Michael Gazzaniga (1992, 1998, 2008) reports that patients whose brain hemispheres have been surgically separated will instantly fabricate—and believe—explanations of their own puzzling behaviors. If the patient gets up and takes a few steps after the experimenter flashes the instruction "walk" to the patient's nonverbal right hemisphere, the verbal left hemisphere will instantly provide the patient with a plausible explanation ("I felt like getting a drink").

Illusory intuition also appears in the vast new literature on how we take in, store, and retrieve social information. As perception researchers study visual illusions for what they reveal about our normal perceptual mechanisms, social psychologists study illusory thinking for what it reveals about normal information processing. These researchers want to give us a map of everyday social thinking, with the hazards clearly marked.

As we examine some of these efficient thinking patterns, remember this: Demonstrations of how people create counterfeit beliefs do not prove that all beliefs are counterfeit (although to recognize counterfeiting, it helps to know how it's done).

*W*E OVERESTIMATE THE ACCURACY OF OUR JUDGMENTS

So far we have seen that our cognitive systems process a vast amount of information efficiently and automatically. But our efficiency has a trade-off; as we interpret our experiences and construct memories, our automatic intuitions sometimes err. Usually, we are unaware of our flaws.

To explore this **overconfidence phenomenon**, Daniel Kahneman and Amos Tversky (1979) gave people factual statements and asked them to fill in the blanks, as in the following sentence: "I feel 98 percent certain that the air distance between New Delhi and Beijing is more than _____ miles but less than _____ miles."* Most individuals were overconfident: Approximately 30 percent of the time, the correct answers lay outside the range they felt 98 percent confident about.

To find out whether overconfidence extends to social judgments, David Dunning and associates (1990) created a game show. They asked Stanford University students to guess a stranger's answers to a series of questions, such as "Would you prepare for a difficult exam alone or with others?" and "Would you rate your lecture notes as neat or messy?" Knowing the type of question but not the actual questions, the participants first interviewed their target person about background, hobbies, academic interests, aspirations, astrological sign—anything they thought might be helpful. Then, while the targets privately answered 20 of the two-choice questions, the interviewers predicted their target's answers and rated their own confidence in the predictions.

The interviewers guessed right 63 percent of the time, beating chance by 13 percent. But, on average, they *felt* 75 percent sure of their predictions. When guessing their own roommates' responses, they were 68 percent correct and 78 percent confident. Moreover, the most confident people were most likely to be overconfident. People also are markedly overconfident when judging whether someone is telling the truth or when estimating things such as the sexual history of their dating partner or the activity preferences of their roommates (DePaulo & others, 1997; Swann & Gill, 1997).

Ironically, *incompetence feeds overconfidence.* It takes competence to recognize what competence is, note Justin Kruger and David Dunning (1999). Students who score at the bottom on tests of grammar, humor, and logic are most prone to overestimating their gifts at such. Those who don't know what good logic or grammar is are often unaware that they lack it. If you make a list of all the words you can form out of the letters in "psychology," you may feel brilliant—but then stupid when a friend starts naming the ones you missed. Deanna Caputo and Dunning (2005) re-created this phenomenon in experiments, confirming that our ignorance of our ignorance sustains our self-confidence. Follow-up studies indicate that this "ignorance of one's incompetence" occurs mostly on relatively easy-seeming tasks. On very difficult tasks, poor performers more often appreciate their lack of skill (Burson & others, 2006).

Ignorance of one's incompetence helps explain David Dunning's (2005) startling conclusion from employee assessment studies that "what others see in us . . . tends to be more highly correlated with objective outcomes than what we see in ourselves." In one study, participants watched someone walk into a room, sit, read a weather report, and walk out (Borkenau & Liebler, 1993). Based on nothing more than that, their estimate of the

---

*The distance between New Delhi and Beijing is 2,500 miles.

person's intelligence correlated with the person's intelligence score about as well as did the person's own self-estimate (.30 vs. .32)! If ignorance can beget false confidence, then—yikes!—where, we may ask, are you and I unknowingly deficient?

Activity
7.2

Are people better at predicting their own *behavior?* To find out, Robert Vallone and colleagues (1990) had college students predict in September whether they would drop a course, declare a major, elect to live off campus next year, and so forth. Although the students felt, on average, 84 percent sure of those self-predictions, they were wrong nearly twice as often as they expected to be. Even when feeling 100 percent sure of their predictions, they erred 15 percent of the time.

In estimating their chances for success on a task, such as a major exam, people's confidence runs highest when the moment of truth is off in the future. By exam day, the possibility of failure looms larger and confidence typically drops (Gilovich & others, 1993; Shepperd & others, 2005). Roger Buehler and colleagues (1994, 2010) report that most students also confidently underestimate how long it will take them to complete papers and other major assignments. They are not alone:

- *The "planning fallacy."* How much free time do you have today? How much free time do you expect you will have a month from today? Most of us overestimate how much we'll be getting done, and therefore how much free time we will have (Zauberman & Lynch, 2005). Professional planners, too, routinely underestimate the time and expense of projects. In 1969, Montreal Mayor Jean Drapeau proudly announced that a $120 million stadium with a retractable roof would be built for the 1976 Olympics. The roof was completed in 1989 and cost $120 million by itself. In 1985, officials estimated that Boston's "Big Dig" highway project would cost $2.6 billion and take until 1998. The cost ballooned to $14.6 billion and the project took until 2006.

- *Stockbroker overconfidence.* Investment experts market their services with the confident presumption that they can beat the stock market average, forgetting that for every stockbroker or buyer saying "Sell!" at a given price, there is another saying "Buy!" A stock's price is the balance point between those mutually confident judgments. Thus, incredible as it may seem, economist Burton Malkiel (2011) reports that mutual fund portfolios selected by investment analysts have not outperformed randomly selected stocks.

- *Political overconfidence.* Overconfident decision makers can wreak havoc. It was a confident Adolf Hitler who from 1939 to 1945 waged war against the rest of Europe. It was a confident Lyndon Johnson who in the 1960s invested U.S. weapons and soldiers in the effort to salvage democracy in South Vietnam.

What produces overconfidence? Why doesn't experience lead us to a more realistic self-appraisal? For one thing, people tend to recall their mistaken judgments as times when they were *almost* right. Philip Tetlock (1998a, 1998b, 1999, 2005) observed this after inviting various academic and government experts to project—from their viewpoint in the late 1980s—the future governance of the Soviet Union, South Africa, and Canada. Five years later, communism had collapsed, South Africa had become a multiracial democracy, and Canada's French-speaking minority had not seceded. Experts who had felt more than 80 percent confident were right in predicting these turns of events less than 40 percent of the time. Yet, reflecting on their judgments, those who erred believed they were still basically right. I was "almost right," said many. "The hardliners almost succeeded in their coup attempt against Gorbachev." "The Quebecois separatists almost won the secessionist referendum." "But for the coincidence of de Klerk and Mandela, there would have been a much bloodier transition to black majority rule in South Africa." The Iraq War was a good idea, just badly executed, excused many of those who had supported it. Among political experts—and also stock market forecasters, mental health workers, and sports prognosticators—overconfidence is hard to dislodge.

People also tend not to seek information that might disprove what they believe. P. C. Wason (1960) demonstrated this, as you can, by giving participants a sequence of three numbers—2, 4, 6—that conformed to a rule he had in mind. (The rule was simply *any three ascending numbers*.) To enable the participants to discover the rule, Wason invited each person to generate additional sets of three numbers. Each time, Wason told the person whether or not the set conformed to his rule. As soon as participants were sure they had discovered the rule, they were to stop and announce it.

The result? Seldom right but never in doubt: 23 of the 29 participants convinced themselves of a wrong rule. They typically formed some erroneous belief about the rule (for example, counting by two's) and then searched for *confirming* evidence (for example, by testing 8, 10, 12) rather than attempting to *disconfirm* their hunches. We are eager to verify our beliefs but less inclined to seek evidence that might disprove them, a phenomenon called the **confirmation bias.**

Remedies for Overconfidence

What lessons can we draw from research on overconfidence? One lesson is to be wary of other people's dogmatic statements. Even when people are sure they are right, they may be wrong. Confidence and competence need not coincide.

Three techniques have successfully reduced the overconfidence bias. One is *prompt feedback* (Lichtenstein & Fischhoff, 1980). In everyday life, weather forecasters and those who set the odds in horse racing both receive clear, daily feedback. And experts in both groups do quite well at estimating their probable accuracy (Fischhoff, 1982).

To reduce "planning fallacy" overconfidence, people can be asked to *unpack a task*—to break it down into its subcomponents—and estimate the time required for each. Justin Kruger and Matt Evans (2004) report that doing so leads to more realistic estimates of completion time.

When people think about why an idea *might* be true, it begins to seem true (Koehler, 1991). Thus, a third way to reduce overconfidence is to get people to think of one good reason *why* their judgments *might be wrong;* that is, force them to consider disconfirming information (Koriat & others, 1980). Managers might foster more realistic judgments by insisting that all proposals and recommendations include reasons why they might *not* work.

Still, we should be careful not to undermine people's reasonable self-confidence or to destroy their decisiveness. In times when their wisdom is needed, those lacking self-confidence may shrink from speaking up or making tough decisions. Overconfidence can cost us, but realistic self-confidence is adaptive.

CONSTRUCTING MEMORIES OF OURSELVES AND OUR WORLDS

Activity
7.3

Do you agree or disagree with this statement?

> Memory can be likened to a storage chest in the brain into which we deposit material and from which we can withdraw it later if needed. Occasionally, something is lost from the "chest," and then we say we have forgotten.

Approximately 85 percent of college students said they agreed (Lamal, 1979). As one magazine ad put it, "Science has proven the accumulated experience of a lifetime is preserved perfectly in your mind."

Actually, psychological research has proved the opposite. Our memories are not exact copies of experiences that remain on deposit in a memory bank. Rather, we construct memories at the time of withdrawal. Like a paleontologist inferring the appearance of a dinosaur from bone fragments, we reconstruct our distant past by using our current feelings and expectations to combine information fragments. Thus, we can easily (although unconsciously) revise our memories to suit our current knowledge. When one of my sons complained, "The June issue of *Cricket* never came," and was then shown where it was, he delightedly responded, "Oh good, I knew I'd gotten it."

Reconstructing Our Past Attitudes

Five years ago, how did you feel about nuclear power? About your country's president or prime minister? About your parents? If your attitudes have changed, what do you think is the extent of the change?

Activity
7.4

Experimenters have explored such questions, and the results have been unnerving. People whose attitudes have changed often insist that they have always felt much as they now feel. Daryl Bem and Keith McConnell (1970) conducted a survey among Carnegie Mellon University students. Buried in it was a question concerning student control over the university curriculum. A week later, the students agreed to write an essay opposing student control. After doing so, their attitudes shifted toward greater opposition to student control. When asked to recall how they had answered the question before writing the essay, the students "remembered" holding the opinion that they *now* held and denied that the experiment had affected them.

After observing Clark University students similarly denying their former attitudes, researchers D. R. Wixon and James Laird (1976) commented, "The speed, magnitude, and certainty" with which the students revised their own histories "was striking." As George Vaillant (1977) noted after following adults through time, "It is all too common for caterpillars to become butterflies and then to maintain that in their youth they had been little butterflies. Maturation makes liars of us all."

The construction of positive memories brightens our recollections. Terence Mitchell, Leigh Thompson, and colleagues (1994, 1997) report that people often exhibit *rosy retrospection*—they recall mildly pleasant events more favorably than they experienced them. College students on a 3-week bike trip, older adults on a guided tour of Austria, and undergraduates on vacation all reported enjoying their experiences as they were having them. But they later recalled such experiences even more fondly, minimizing the unpleasant or boring aspects and remembering the high points. Thus, the pleasant times during which I have sojourned in Scotland I now (back in my office facing deadlines and interruptions) romanticize as pure bliss. The drizzle and the pesky midges are but dim memories. The spectacular scenery and the fresh sea air and the favorite tea rooms are still with me. With any positive experience, some of our pleasure resides in the anticipation, some in the actual experience, and some in the rosy retrospection.

Cathy McFarland and Michael Ross (1985) found that as our relationships change, we also revise our recollections of other people. They had university students rate their steady dating partners. Two months later, they rated them again. Students who were more in love than ever had a tendency to overestimate their first impressions—it was "love at first sight." Those who had broken up were more likely to *underestimate* their earlier liking—recalling the partner as somewhat selfish and bad-tempered.

Diane Holmberg and John Holmes (1994) discovered the phenomenon also operating among 373 newlywed couples, most of whom reported being very happy. When resurveyed 2 years later, those whose marriages had soured recalled that things had always been bad. The results are "frightening," say Holmberg and Holmes: "Such biases can lead to a dangerous downward spiral. The worse your current view of your partner is, the worse your memories are, which only further confirms your negative attitudes."

It's not that we are totally unaware of how we used to feel, just that when memories are hazy, current feelings guide our recall. When widows and widowers try to recall the grief they felt on their spouse's death 5 years earlier, their current emotional state colors their memories (Safer & others, 2001). When patients recall their previous day's headache pain, their current feelings sway their recollections (Eich & others, 1985). Parents of every generation bemoan the values of the next generation, partly because they misrecall their youthful values as being closer to their current values. And teens of every generation recall their parents as—depending on their current mood—wonderful or woeful (Bornstein & others, 1991).

Reconstructing Our Past Behavior

Memory construction enables us to revise our own histories. Michael Ross, Cathy McFarland, and Garth Fletcher (1981) exposed some University of Waterloo students to a message convincing them of the desirability of toothbrushing. Later, in a supposedly different experiment, these students recalled brushing their teeth more often during the preceding 2 weeks than did students who had not heard the message. Likewise, judging from surveys, people report smoking many fewer cigarettes than are actually sold (Hall, 1985). And they recall casting more votes than were actually recorded (Bureau of the Census, 1993).

Social psychologist Anthony Greenwald (1980) noted the similarity of such findings to happenings in George Orwell's novel *1984*—in which it was "necessary to remember that events happened in the desired manner." Indeed, argued Greenwald, we all have "totalitarian egos" that revise the past to suit our present views. Thus, we underreport bad behavior and overreport good behavior.

Sometimes our present view is that we've improved—in which case we may misrecall our past as more unlike the present than it actually was. This tendency resolves a puzzling pair of consistent findings: Those who participate in psychotherapy and self-improvement programs for weight control, smoking cessation, and exercise show only modest improvement on average. Yet they often claim considerable benefit. Michael Conway and Michael Ross (1986) explain why: Having expended so much time, effort, and money on self-improvement, people may think, "I may not be perfect now, but I was worse before; this did me a lot of good."

CONCEPTS TO REMEMBER

overconfidence phenomenon The tendency to be more confident than correct—to overestimate the accuracy of one's beliefs.

confirmation bias A tendency to search for information that confirms one's preconceptions.

8

❖

Reasons for Unreason

What good fortune for those in power that people do not think.

Adolph Hitler

What species better deserves the name *Homo sapiens*—wise humans? Our cognitive powers outstrip the smartest computers in recognizing patterns, handling language, and processing abstract information. Our information processing is also wonderfully efficient. With such precious little time to process so much information, we specialize in mental shortcuts. Scientists marvel at the speed and ease with which we form impressions, judgments, and explanations. In many situations, our snap generalizations—"That's dangerous!"—are adaptive. They promote our survival.

But our adaptive efficiency has a trade-off; snap generalizations sometimes err. Our helpful strategies for simplifying complex information can lead us astray. To enhance our own powers of critical thinking, let's consider four reasons for unreason—common ways in which people form or sustain false beliefs:

1. Our preconceptions control our interpretations.
2. We often are swayed more by anecdotes than by statistical facts.
3. We misperceive correlation and control.
4. Our beliefs can generate their own conclusions.

OUR PRECONCEPTIONS CONTROL OUR INTERPRETATIONS

It is a significant fact about the human mind: Our preconceptions guide how we perceive and interpret information. We interpret the world through belief-tinted glasses. "Sure, preconceptions matter," people will agree; yet they fail to realize how great the effect is on themselves.

An experiment by Robert Vallone, Lee Ross, and Mark Lepper (1985) reveals just how powerful preconceptions can be. They showed pro-Israeli and pro-Arab students six network news segments describing the 1982 killing of civilian refugees at two camps in Beirut, Lebanon. As Figure 8-1 illustrates, each group perceived the networks as hostile to its side.

The phenomenon is commonplace: Sports fans perceive referees as partial to the other side. Political candidates and their supporters nearly always view the news media as unsympathetic to their cause (Richardson & others, 2008).

It's not just fans and politicians. People everywhere perceive mediators and media as biased against their position. "There is no subject about which people are less objective than objectivity," noted one media commentator (Poniewozik, 2003). Indeed, people's perceptions of bias can

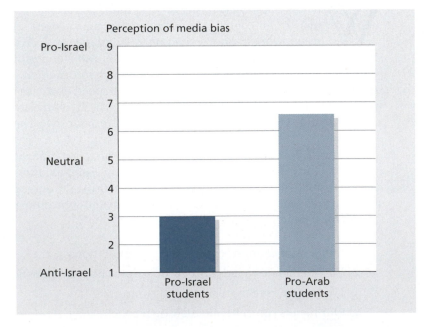

FIGURE 8-1
Pro-Israeli and pro-Arab students who viewed network news descriptions of the "Beirut massacre" believed the coverage was biased against their point of view.   Source: Data from Vallone & others (1985).

be used to assess their attitudes (Saucier & Miller, 2003). Tell me where you see bias, and you will signal your attitudes.

Our assumptions about the world can even make contradictory evidence seem supportive. For example, Ross and Lepper assisted Charles Lord (1979) in asking two groups of students to evaluate the results of two supposedly new research studies. Half the students favored capital punishment and half opposed it. Of the studies they evaluated, one confirmed and the other disconfirmed the students' beliefs about the deterrent effect of the death penalty. The results: Both proponents and opponents of capital punishment readily accepted evidence that confirmed their belief but were sharply critical of disconfirming evidence. Showing the two sides an *identical* body of mixed evidence had not lessened their disagreement but *increased* it.

Is that why, in politics, religion, and science, ambiguous information often fuels conflict? Presidential debates in the United States have mostly reinforced predebate opinions. By nearly a 10-to-1 margin, those who already favored one candidate or the other perceived their candidate as having won (Kinder & Sears, 1985). Thus, report Geoffrey Munro and colleagues (1997), people on both sides may become even more supportive of their respective candidates after viewing a presidential debate.

Other experiments have manipulated people's preconceptions—with astonishing effects upon their interpretations and recollections. Myron Rothbart and Pamela Birrell (1977) had University of Oregon students assess the facial expression of a man (Figure 8-2). Those told he was a

FIGURE 8-2
Judge for yourself. Is this person's expression cruel or kind? If told he was a Nazi, would your reading of his face differ?

Gestapo leader responsible for barbaric medical experiments on concentration camp inmates intuitively judged his expression as cruel. (Can you see that barely suppressed sneer?) Those told he was a leader in the anti-Nazi underground movement whose courage saved thousands of Jewish lives judged his facial expression as warm and kind. (Just look at those caring eyes and that almost smiling mouth.)

Filmmakers control people's perceptions of emotion by manipulating the setting in which they see a face. They call this the "Kulechov effect" after a Russian film director who would skillfully guide viewers' inferences by manipulating their assumptions. Kulechov demonstrated the phenomenon by creating three short films that presented identical footage of the face of an actor with a neutral expression after viewers had first been shown one of three different scenes: a dead woman, a bowl of soup, or a girl playing. As a result, in the first film the actor seemed sad, in the second thoughtful, and in the third happy.

WE ARE MORE SWAYED BY MEMORABLE EVENTS THAN FACTS

Consider the following: Do more people live in Iraq or in Tanzania? (See page 80 for the answer.)

You probably answered according to how readily Iraqis and Tanzanians come to mind. If examples are readily *available* in our memory—as Iraqis tend to be—then we presume that other such examples are commonplace. Usually this is true, so we are often well served by this cognitive rule, called the **availability heuristic**. Said simply, the more easily we recall something, the more likely it seems.

But sometimes the rule deludes us. If people hear a list of famous people of one sex (Oprah Winfrey, Lady Gaga, and Hillary Clinton) intermixed with an equal-size list of unfamous people of the other sex (Donald Scarr, William Wood, and Mel Jasper), the famous names will later be more cognitively available. Most people will subsequently recall having heard more (in this instance) women's names (McKelvie, 1995, 1997; Tversky & Kahneman, 1973). Likewise, media attention to gay–lesbian issues makes gays and lesbians cognitively available. Thus, the average U.S. adult in a 2011 Gallup poll estimated that 25 percent of Americans are gay or lesbian (Morales, 2011b)—some seven times the number who, in surveys, actually self-identify as gay, lesbian, or bisexual (Gates, 2011). Even fictional happenings in novels, television, and movies leave images that later penetrate our judgments (Gerrig & Prentice, 1991; Green & others, 2002; Mar & Oatley, 2008).

Or consider this: Order these four cities according to their crime rates: Atlanta, Los Angeles, New York, St. Louis. If, with available images from TV crime dramas in mind, you thought New York and Los Angeles are the most crime-ridden, guess again; they're the least crime-ridden of the four (Federal Bureau of Investigation, 2011).

Our use of the availability heuristic highlights a basic principle of social thinking: People are slow to deduce particular instances from a general truth, but they are remarkably quick to infer general truth from a vivid instance. No wonder that after hearing and reading stories of rapes, robberies, and beatings, 9 out of 10 Canadians overestimated—usually by a considerable margin—the percentage of crimes that involved violence (Doob & Roberts, 1988). And no wonder that South Africans, after a series of headline-grabbing gangland robberies and slayings, estimated that violent crime had almost doubled between 1998 and 2004, when actually it had decreased substantially (Wines, 2005).

The availability heuristic explains why vivid, easy-to-imagine events, such as shark attacks or diseases with easy-to-picture symptoms, may seem more likely to occur than harder-to-picture events (MacLeod & Campbell, 1992; Sherman & others, 1985). Likewise, powerful anecdotes can be more compelling than statistical information. We fret over extremely rare child abduction, even if we don't buckle our children in the backseat. We dread terrorism but are indifferent to global climate change—"Armageddon in slow motion." Especially after the 2011 Japanese tsunami and nuclear power catastrophe, we fear nuclear power, with little concern for the many more deaths related to mining and burning coal (von Hippel, 2011). In short, we worry about remote possibilities while ignoring higher probabilities, a phenomenon that Cass Sunstein (2007b) calls our "probability neglect."

Because news footage of airplane crashes is a readily available memory for most of us—especially since September 11, 2001—we often suppose we are more at risk traveling in commercial airplanes than in cars. Actually, from 2003 to 2005, U.S. travelers were 230 times more likely to die in a car crash than on a commercial flight covering the same distance (National Safety Council, 2008). In 2006, reports the Flight Safety Foundation, there was one airliner accident for every 4.2 million flights by Western-built commercial jets (Wald, 2008). For most air travelers, the most dangerous part of the journey is the drive to the airport.

Soon after 9/11, as many people abandoned air travel and took to the roads, I estimated that if Americans flew 20 percent less and instead drove those unflown miles, we could expect an additional 800 traffic deaths in the ensuing year (Myers, 2001). It took a curious German researcher (why didn't I think of this?) to check that prediction against accident data, which confirmed an excess of some 350 deaths in the last 3 months of 2001 compared with the 3-month average in the preceding 5 years (Gigerenzer, 2004). The 9/11 terrorists appear to have killed more people unnoticed—on America's roads—than they did with the 266 fatalities on those four planes.

By now it is clear that our naive statistical intuitions, and our resulting fears, are driven not by calculation and reason but by emotions attuned to the availability heuristic. After this book is published, there likely will be

Vivid, memorable—and therefore cognitively available—events influence our perception of the social world. The resulting "probability neglect" often leads people to fear the wrong things, such as fearing flying or terrorism more than smoking, driving, or climate change. If four jumbo jets filled with children crashed every day—approximating the number of childhood diarrhea deaths resulting from the rotavirus—something would have been done about it.   Reprinted courtesy of Dave Bohn.

another dramatic natural or terrorist event, which will again propel our fears, vigilance, and resources in a new direction. Terrorists, aided by the media, may again achieve their objective of capturing our attention, draining our resources, and distracting us from the mundane, undramatic, insidious risks that, over time, devastate lives, such as the rotavirus that each day claims the equivalent of four 747s filled with children (Parashar & others, 2006). But then again, dramatic events can also serve to awaken us to real risks. That, say some scientists, is what happened when the extreme floods, droughts, snows, tornadoes, and hurricanes of 2011 and 2012 raised concern that global climate change, is destined to become nature's own weapon of mass destruction. For Australians and Americans, a temporary hot day can prime people to believe more in global warming (Li & others, 2011). Even feeling hot in an *indoor* room increases people's belief in global warming (Risen & Critcher, 2011).

WE MISPERCEIVE CORRELATION AND CONTROL

Another influence on everyday thinking is our search for order in random events, a tendency that can lead us down all sorts of wrong paths.

Illusory Correlation

It is easy to see a correlation where none exists. When we expect to find significant relationships, we easily associate random events, perceiving

Answer to Question on page 78:   *Tanzania's 43 million people greatly outnumber Iraq's 31 million. Most people, having more vivid images of Iraqis, guess wrong.*

an **illusory correlation**. William Ward and Herbert Jenkins (1965) showed people the results of a hypothetical 50-day cloud-seeding experiment. They told participants which of the 50 days the clouds had been seeded and which days it rained. The information was nothing more than a random mix of results: Sometimes it rained after seeding; sometimes it didn't. Participants nevertheless became convinced—in conformity with their ideas about the effects of cloud seeding—that they really had observed a relationship between cloud seeding and rain.

Other experiments confirm the principle: *People easily misperceive random events as confirming their beliefs* (Crocker, 1981; Jennings & others, 1982; Trolier & Hamilton, 1986). If we believe a correlation exists, we are more likely to notice and recall confirming instances. If we believe that premonitions correlate with events, we notice and remember any joint occurrence of the premonition and the event's later occurrence. If we believe that overweight women are unhappier, we perceive that we have witnessed such a correlation even when we have not (Viken & others, 2005). We ignore or forget all the times unusual events do not coincide. If, after we think about a friend, the friend calls us, we notice and remember that coincidence. We don't notice all the times we think of a friend without any ensuing call, or receive a call from a friend about whom we've not been thinking.

Illusion of Control

Our tendency to perceive random events as related feeds an **illusion of control**—the idea that *chance events are subject to our influence*. This keeps gamblers going and makes the rest of us do all sorts of unlikely things.

Gambling

Ellen Langer (1977) demonstrated the illusion of control in betting experiments. Compared with those given an assigned lottery number, people who chose their own number demanded four times as much money when asked if they would sell their ticket. When playing a game of chance against an awkward and nervous person, they bet significantly more than when playing against a dapper, confident opponent. Being the person who throws the dice or spins the wheel increases people's confidence (Wohl & Enzle, 2002). In these and other ways, more than 50 experiments have consistently found people acting as if they can predict or control chance events (Presson & Benassi, 1996; Thompson & others, 1998).

Observations of real-life gamblers confirm these experimental findings. Dice players may throw softly for low numbers and hard for high numbers (Henslin, 1967). The gambling industry thrives on gamblers' illusions. Gamblers attribute wins to their skill and foresight. Losses become "near misses" or "flukes," or for the sports gambler, a bad call by the referee or a freakish bounce of the ball (Gilovich & Douglas, 1986).

Stock traders also like the "feeling of empowerment" that comes from being able to choose and control their own stock trades, as if their being in control can enable them to outperform the market average. One ad declared that online investing "is about control." Alas, the illusion of control breeds overconfidence and frequent losses after stock market trading costs are subtracted (Barber & Odean, 2001a, 2001b).

People like feeling in control, and so when experiencing a lack of control, will act to create a sense of predictability. In experiments, loss of control has led people to form illusory correlations in stock market information, to perceive nonexistent conspiracies, and to develop superstitions (Whitson & Galinsky, 2008).

Regression Toward the Average

Tversky and Kahneman (1974) noted another way by which an illusion of control may arise: We fail to recognize the statistical phenomenon of **regression toward the average.** Because exam scores fluctuate partly by chance, most students who get extremely high scores on an exam will get lower scores on the next exam. If their first score is at the ceiling, their second score is more likely to fall back ("regress") toward their own average than to push the ceiling even higher. That is why a student who does consistently good work, even if never the best, will sometimes end a course at the top of the class. Conversely, the lowest scoring students on the first exam are likely to improve. If those who scored lowest go for tutoring after the first exam, the tutors are likely to feel effective when the student improves, even if the tutoring had no effect.

Indeed, when things reach a low point, we will try anything, and whatever we try—going to a psychotherapist, starting a new diet-exercise plan, reading a self-help book—is more likely to be followed by improvement than by further deterioration. Sometimes we recognize that events are not likely to continue at an unusually good or bad extreme. (When we're extremely high or low, we tend to fall back toward our normal average.)

OUR BELIEFS CAN GENERATE THEIR OWN CONFIRMATION

Our intuitive beliefs resist reality for another reason: They sometimes lead us to act in ways that produce their apparent confirmation. Our beliefs about other people can therefore become **self-fulfilling prophecies.** In his well-known studies of *experimenter bias*, Robert Rosenthal (1985, 2006) found that research participants sometimes live up to what they believe experimenters expect of them. In one study, experimenters asked individuals to judge the success of people in various photographs. The experimenters read the same instructions to all their participants and showed them the same photos. Nevertheless, experimenters who expected their participants to see the photographed people as successful obtained higher ratings than did those who expected their participants to see the people as failures. Even more startling—and controversial—are reports that teachers' beliefs about their students similarly serve as self-fulfilling prophecies. If a teacher believes a student is good at math, will the student do well in the class? Let's examine this.

Do Teacher Expectations Affect Student Performance?

Teachers do have higher expectations for some students than for others. Perhaps you have detected this after having a brother or sister precede you in school, after receiving a label such as "gifted" or "learning disabled," or after being tracked with "high-ability" or "average-ability" students. Perhaps conversation in the teachers' lounge sent your reputation ahead of you. Or perhaps your new teacher scrutinized your school file or discovered your family's social status.

But how big is the effect of such expectations? By Rosenthal's own count, in only approximately 4 in 10 of the nearly 500 published experiments did expectations significantly affect performance (Rosenthal, 1991, 2002). Low expectations do not doom a capable child, nor do high expectations magically transform a slow learner into a valedictorian. Human nature is not so pliable.

High expectations do, however, seem to boost low achievers, for whom a teacher's positive attitude may be a hope-giving breath of fresh air (Madon & others, 1997). How are such expectations transmitted? Rosenthal and other investigators report that teachers look, smile, and nod more at "high-potential students." Teachers also may teach more to their "gifted" students, set higher goals for them, call on them more, and give them more time to answer (Cooper, 1983; Harris & Rosenthal, 1985, 1986; Jussim, 1986).

Reading the experiments on teacher expectations makes me wonder about the effect of *students'* expectations upon their teachers. You no doubt begin many of your courses having heard "Professor Smith is interesting" and "Professor Jones is a bore." Robert Feldman and Thomas Prohaska (1979; Feldman & Theiss, 1982) found that such expectations can affect both student and teacher. Students in a learning experiment who expected to be taught by an excellent teacher perceived their teacher (who was unaware of their expectations) as more competent and interesting than did students with low expectations. Furthermore, the students actually learned more. In a later experiment, women who were led to expect their male instructor to be sexist had a less positive experience with him, performed worse, and rated him as less competent than did women not given the sexist expectation (Adams & others, 2006).

Were these results due entirely to the students' perceptions or also to a self-fulfilling prophecy that affected the teacher? In a follow-up experiment, Feldman and Prohaska videotaped teachers and had observers rate their performances. Teachers were judged most capable when assigned a student who nonverbally conveyed positive expectations.

To see whether such effects might also occur in actual classrooms, a research team led by David Jamieson (Jamieson & others, 1987) experimented with four Ontario high school classes taught by a newly transferred teacher. During individual interviews, they told students in two of the classes that both other students and the research team rated the teacher very highly. Compared with the control classes, students who were given positive expectations paid better attention during class. At the end of the teaching unit, they also got better grades and rated the teacher as clearer in her teaching. The attitudes that a class has toward its teacher are as important, it seems, as the teacher's attitude toward the students.

Do We Get from Others What We Expect?

So the expectations of experimenters and teachers, although usually reasonably accurate, occasionally act as self-fulfilling prophecies. How widespread are self-fulfilling prophecies? Do we get from others what we expect of them? Studies show that our perceptions of others are more accurate than biased (Jussim, 2012). Self-fulfilling prophecies have "less than extraordinary power." Yet sometimes, self-fulfilling prophecies do operate in work settings (with managers who have high or low expectations), in courtrooms (as judges instruct juries), and in simulated police contexts (as interrogators with guilty or innocent expectations interrogate and pressure suspects) (Kassin & others, 2003; Rosenthal, 2003, 2006).

Do self-fulfilling prophecies color our personal relationships? There are times when negative expectations of someone lead us to be extra nice to that person, which induces him or her to be nice in return—thus *dis*confirming our expectations. But a more common finding in studies of social interaction is that, yes, we do to some extent get what we expect (Olson & others, 1996).

In laboratory games, hostility nearly always begets hostility: People who perceive their opponents as noncooperative will readily induce them to be noncooperative (Kelley & Stahelski, 1970). Each party's perception of the other as aggressive, resentful, and vindictive induces the other to display those behaviors in self-defense, thus creating a vicious self-perpetuating circle. Likewise, whether I expect my wife to be in a bad mood or in a loving mood may affect how I relate to her, thereby inducing her to confirm my belief.

So, do intimate relationships prosper when partners idealize each other? Are positive illusions of the other's virtues self-fulfilling? Or are they more often self-defeating, by creating high expectations that can't be met? Among University of Waterloo dating couples followed by Sandra Murray and associates (1996a, 1996b, 2000), positive ideals of one's partner were good omens. Idealization helped buffer conflict, bolster satisfaction, and turn self-perceived frogs into princes or princesses. When someone loves and admires us, it helps us become more the person he or she imagines us to be.

When dating couples deal with conflicts, hopeful optimists and their partners tend to perceive each other as engaging constructively. Compared to those with more pessimistic expectations, they then feel more supported and more satisfied with the outcome (Srivastava & others, 2006). Among married couples, too, those who worry that their partner doesn't love and accept them interpret slight hurts as rejections, which motivates them to devalue the partner and distance themselves. Those who presume their partner's love and acceptance respond less defensively, read less into stressful events, and treat the partner better (Murray & others, 2003). Love helps create its presumed reality.

Several experiments conducted by Mark Snyder (1984) at the University of Minnesota show how, once formed, erroneous beliefs about the social world can induce others to confirm those beliefs, a phenomenon called **behavioral confirmation.** In a classic study, Snyder, Elizabeth Tanke, and Ellen Berscheid (1977) had male students talk on the telephone with women they thought (from having been shown a picture) were either attractive or unattractive. Analysis of just the women's comments during the conversations revealed that the supposedly attractive women spoke more warmly than the supposedly unattractive women. The men's erroneous beliefs had become a self-fulfilling prophecy by leading them to act in a way that influenced the women to fulfill the men's stereotype that beautiful people are desirable people.

Expectations influence children's behavior, too. After observing the amount of litter in three classrooms, Richard Miller and colleagues (1975) had the teacher and others repeatedly tell one class that they should be neat and tidy. This persuasion increased the amount of litter placed in wastebaskets from 15 to 45 percent, but only temporarily. Another class, which also had been placing only 15 percent of its litter in wastebaskets, was repeatedly congratulated for being so neat and tidy. After 8 days of hearing this, and still 2 weeks later, these children were fulfilling the expectation by putting more than 80 percent of their litter in wastebaskets. Tell children they are hardworking and kind (rather than lazy and mean), and they may live up to their labels.

These experiments help us understand how social beliefs, such as stereotypes about people with disabilities or about people of a particular race or sex, may be self-confirming. How others treat us reflects how we and others have treated them.

*C*ONCLUSIONS

We have reviewed reasons why people sometimes form false beliefs. We cannot easily dismiss these experiments: Most of their participants were intelligent people, often students at leading universities. Moreover, people's intelligence scores are uncorrelated with their vulnerability to many different thinking biases (Stanovich & West, 2008). One can be very smart and exhibit seriously bad judgment.

Trying hard also doesn't eliminate thinking biases. These predictable distortions and biases occurred even when payment for right answers motivated people to think optimally. As one researcher concluded, the illusions "have a persistent quality not unlike that of perceptual illusions" (Slovic, 1972).

Research in cognitive social psychology thus mirrors the mixed review given humanity in literature, philosophy, and religion. Many research psychologists have spent lifetimes exploring the awesome capacities of the human mind. We are smart enough to have cracked our own genetic code, to have invented talking computers, and to have sent people to the moon. Three cheers for human reason.

Well, two cheers—because the mind's premium on efficient judgment makes our intuition more vulnerable to misjudgment than we suspect. With remarkable ease, we form and sustain false beliefs. Led by our preconceptions, feeling overconfident, persuaded by vivid anecdotes, perceiving correlations and control even where none may exist, we construct our social beliefs and then influence others to confirm them. "The naked intellect," observed novelist Madeleine L'Engle, "is an extraordinarily inaccurate instrument."

CONCEPTS TO REMEMBER

availability heuristic   A cognitive rule that judges the likelihood of things in terms of their availability in memory. If instances of something come readily to mind, we presume them to be commonplace.

illusory correlation   Perception of a relationship where none exists, or perception of a stronger relationship than actually exists.

illusion of control   Perception of uncontrollable events as subject to one's control or as more controllable than they are.

regression toward the average   The statistical tendency for extreme scores or extreme behavior to return toward one's average.

self-fulfilling prophecy   A belief that leads to its own fulfillment.

behavioral confirmation   A type of self-fulfilling prophecy whereby people's social expectations lead them to behave in ways that cause others to confirm their expectations.

9

❖

Behavior and Belief

The ancestor of every action is a thought.

Ralph Waldo Emerson, *Essays, First Series*, 1841

Which comes first, belief or behavior? Inner attitude or outer action? Character or conduct? What is the relationship between who we *are* (on the inside) and what we *do* (on the outside)?

Opinions on this chicken-and-egg question vary. "The ancestor of every action is a thought," wrote American essayist Ralph Waldo Emerson in 1841. To the contrary, said British prime minister Benjamin Disraeli, "Thought is the child of Action." Most people side with Emerson. Underlying our teaching, preaching, and counseling is the assumption that private beliefs determine public behavior: If we want to alter people's actions, we therefore need to change their hearts and minds.

*D*O ATTITUDES INFLUENCE BEHAVIOR?

Attitudes are beliefs and feelings that can influence our reactions. If we *believe* that someone is threatening, we might *feel* dislike and therefore *act* unfriendly. Presuming that attitudes guide behavior, social psychologists during the 1940s and 1950s studied factors that influence attitudes. Thus they were shocked when dozens of studies during the 1960s revealed that what people say they think and feel often has little to do with how they act (Wicker, 1971). In these studies, students' attitudes toward cheating bore little relation to the likelihood of their actually cheating. People's attitudes toward the church were only modestly linked with church attendance on any given Sunday. Self-described racial attitudes predicted little of the variation in behavior that occurred when people faced an actual interracial situation. People, it seemed, weren't walking the talk.

This realization stimulated more studies during the 1970s and 1980s, which revealed that our attitudes *do* influence our actions, especially when three conditions are met:

1. *When external influences on our actions are minimal.* Sometimes we adjust our attitude reports to please our listeners. This was vividly demonstrated when the U.S. House of Representatives once overwhelmingly passed a salary increase for itself in an off-the-record vote, and then moments later overwhelmingly defeated the same bill on a roll-call vote. At other times social pressure diverts our behavior from the dictates of our attitudes (leading good people sometimes to harm people they do not dislike). When external pressures do not blur the link between our attitudes and actions, we can see that link more clearly.

2. *When the attitude is specific to the behavior.* People readily profess honesty while cheating in reporting their taxes, cherish a clean environment while not recycling, or applaud good health while smoking and not exercising. But their more specific attitudes toward jogging better predict whether they jog (Olson & Zanna, 1981), their attitudes toward recycling do predict whether they recycle (Oskamp, 1991), and their attitudes toward contraception predict their contraceptive use (Morrison, 1989).

3. *When we are conscious of our attitudes.* Attitudes can lie dormant as we act out of habit or as we flow with the crowd. For our attitudes to guide our actions, we must pause to consider them. Thus, when we are self-conscious, perhaps after looking in a mirror, or reminded of how we feel, we act truer to our convictions (Fazio, 1990). Likewise, attitudes formed through a significant experience are more often remembered and acted upon.

So, an attitude will influence our behavior *if* other influences are minimal, *if* the attitude specifically relates to the behavior, and *if* the attitude is potent, perhaps because something brings it to mind. Under these conditions, we *will* stand up for what we believe.

DOES BEHAVIOR INFLUENCE ATTITUDES?

Do we also come to believe in what we've stood up for? Indeed. One of social psychology's big lessons is that we are likely not only to think ourselves into a way of acting but also to act ourselves into a way of thinking. Many streams of evidence confirm that *attitudes follow behavior*.

Role Playing

The word **role** is borrowed from the theater and, as in the theater, refers to actions expected of those who occupy a particular social position. When enacting new social roles, we may at first feel phony. But our unease seldom lasts.

Think of a time when you stepped into some new role—perhaps your first days on a job or at college. That first week on campus, for example, you may have been supersensitive to your new social situation and tried valiantly to act mature and to suppress your high school behavior. At such times you may have felt self-conscious. You observed your new speech and actions because they weren't natural to you. Then one day something amazing happened: Your pseudo-intellectual talk no longer felt forced. The role began to fit as comfortably as your old jeans and T-shirt.

Activity
9.1

In one famous study, college men volunteered to spend time in a simulated prison constructed in Stanford's psychology department by Philip Zimbardo (1971; Haney & Zimbardo, 1998, 2009). Zimbardo wanted to find out: Is prison brutality a product of evil prisoners and malicious guards? Or do the institutional roles of guard and prisoner embitter and harden even compassionate people? Do the people make the place violent? Or does the place make the people violent?

Video
9.1

By a flip of a coin, Zimbardo designated some students as guards. He gave them uniforms, billy clubs, and whistles and instructed them to enforce the rules. The other half, the prisoners, were locked in cells and made to wear humiliating hospital-gown-like outfits. After a jovial first day of "playing" their roles, the guards and the prisoners, and even the experimenters, got caught up in the situation. The guards began to disparage the prisoners, and some devised cruel and degrading routines. The prisoners broke down, rebelled, or became apathetic. There developed, reported Zimbardo (1972), a "growing confusion between reality and illusion, between role-playing and self-identity. . . . This prison which we had created . . . was absorbing us as creatures of its own reality." Observing the emerging social pathology, Zimbardo was forced to call off the planned two-week simulation after only six days.

The point is not that we are powerless to resist imposed roles. In Zimbardo's prison simulation, in Abu Ghraib Prison (where guards degraded Iraq war prisoners), and in other atrocity-producing situations, some people become sadistic and others do not (Haslam & Reicher, 2007; Mastroianni & Reed, 2006; Zimbardo, 2007). In water, salt dissolves and sand does not. So also, notes John Johnson (2007), when placed in a rotten barrel, some people become bad apples and others do not. Behavior is a product of both the individual person and the situation, and the prison study appears to have attracted volunteers who were prone to aggressiveness (McFarland & Carnahan, 2009).

After the Abu Ghraib degradation of Iraqi prisoners, Philip Zimbardo (2004a, 2004b) noted "direct and sad parallels between similar behavior of the 'guards' in the Stanford Prison Experiment." Such behavior, he contends, is attributable to a toxic situation that can make good people into perpetrators of evil. "It's not that we put bad apples in a good barrel. We put good apples in a bad barrel. The barrel corrupts anything that it touches."

The deeper lesson of the role-playing studies is not that we are powerless machines. Rather, it concerns how what is unreal (an artificial role) can subtly morph into what is real. In a new career—as teacher, soldier, or businessperson, for example—we enact a role that shapes our attitudes.

Saying Becomes Believing

People often adapt what they say to please their listeners. They are quicker to tell people good news than bad, and they adjust their message toward their listener's position (Manis & others, 1974; Tesser & others, 1972; Tetlock, 1983). When induced to give spoken or written support to something they doubt, people will often feel bad about their deceit. Nevertheless, they begin to believe what they are saying—*provided* they weren't bribed or coerced into doing so. When there is no compelling external explanation for one's words, saying becomes believing (Klaas, 1978).

Tory Higgins and his colleagues (Higgins & McCann, 1984; Higgins & Rholes, 1978) illustrated how saying becomes believing. They had university students read a personality description of someone and then summarize it for someone else, who was believed either to like or to dislike that person. The students wrote a more positive description when the recipient liked the person. Having said positive things, they also then liked the person more themselves. Asked to recall what they had read, they remembered the description as more positive than it was. In short, people tend to adjust their messages to their listeners, and, having done so, to believe the altered message.

The Foot-in-the-Door Phenomenon

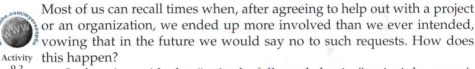

Activity
9.2

Most of us can recall times when, after agreeing to help out with a project or an organization, we ended up more involved than we ever intended, vowing that in the future we would say no to such requests. How does this happen?

In keeping with the "attitude follows behavior" principle, experiments suggest that if you want people to do a big favor for you, an effective strategy is to get them to do a small favor first. In the best-known demonstration of this **foot-in-the-door phenomenon**, researchers posing as drive-safely volunteers asked Californians to permit the installation of huge, poorly lettered "Drive Carefully" signs in their front yards. Only 17 percent consented. Others were first approached with a small request: Would they display three-inch "Be a safe driver" window signs? Nearly all readily agreed. When approached two weeks later to allow the large, ugly signs in their front yards, 76 percent consented (Freedman & Fraser, 1966). One project helper who went from house to house later recalled that, not knowing who had been previously visited, "I was simply stunned at how easy it was to convince some people and how impossible to convince others" (Ornstein, 1991).

Other researchers have confirmed the foot-in-the-door phenomenon with altruistic behaviors.

- Angela Lipsitz and others (1989) report that ending blood-drive reminder calls with, "We'll count on seeing you then, OK? [pause for response]" increased the show-up rate from 62 to 81 percent.

- In Internet chat rooms, Paul Markey and his colleagues (2002) requested help ("I can't get my e-mail to work. Is there any way I can get you to send me an e-mail?"). Help increased—from 2 to 16 percent—by including a smaller prior request ("I am new to this whole computer thing. Is there any way you can tell me how to look at someone's profile?").

- Nicolas Guéguen and Céline Jacob (2001) tripled the rate of French Internet users contributing to child land-mine victims organizations (from 1.6 to 4.9 percent) by first inviting them to sign a petition against land mines.

Note that in these experiments, as in many of the 100+ other foot-in-the-door experiments, the initial compliance—stating one's intention, signing a petition—was voluntary (Burger & Guadagno, 2003). We will see again and again that when people commit themselves to public behaviors *and* perceive those acts to be their own doing, they come to believe more strongly in what they have done.

Social psychologist Robert Cialdini is a self-described "patsy." "For as long as I can recall, I've been an easy mark for the pitches of peddlers, fund-raisers, and operators of one sort or another." To better understand why one person says yes to another, he spent three years as a trainee in various sales, fund-raising, and advertising organizations, discovering how they exploit "the weapons of influence." He also put those weapons to the test in simple experiments. In one, Cialdini and his collaborators (1978) explored a variation of the foot-in-the-door phenomenon by experimenting with the **lowball technique**. After the customer agrees to buy a new car because of its bargain price and begins completing the sales forms, the salesperson removes the price advantage by charging for options or by checking with a boss who disallows the deal because "we'd be losing money." Folklore has it that more lowballed customers now stick with the higher-priced purchase than would have agreed to it at the outset. Airlines and hotels use the tactic by attracting inquiries with great deals available on only a few seats or rooms; then, when those aren't available, they hope the customer will agree to a higher-priced option.

Marketing researchers and salespeople have found that the principle works even when we are aware of a profit motive (Cialdini, 1988). A harmless initial commitment—returning a postcard for more information and a "free gift," agreeing to listen to an investment possibility—often moves us toward a larger commitment. Because salespeople sometimes exploited the power of those small commitments by trying to bind people to purchase agreements, many states now have laws that allow customers a few days to think over their purchases and cancel. To counter the effect of these laws, many companies use what the sales-training program of one company calls "a very important psychological aid in preventing customers from backing out of their contracts" (Cialdini, 1988, p. 78). They simply have the customer, rather than the salesperson, fill out the agreement. Having written it themselves, people usually live up to their commitment.

The foot-in-the-door phenomenon is a lesson worth remembering. Someone trying to seduce us—financially, politically, or sexually—will often use this technique to create a momentum of compliance. The practical lesson: Before agreeing to a small request, think about what may follow.

Evil Acts and Attitudes

The attitudes-follow-behavior principle works with immoral acts as well. Evil sometimes results from gradually escalating commitments. A trifling evil act can whittle down one's moral sensitivity, making it easier to perform a worse act. To paraphrase La Rochefoucauld's 1665 book of *Maxims,* it is not as difficult to find a person who has never succumbed to a given temptation as to find a person who has succumbed only once. After telling a "white lie" and thinking, "Well, that wasn't so bad," the person may go on to tell a bigger lie.

Another way in which evil acts influence attitudes is the paradoxical fact that we tend not only to hurt those we dislike but also to dislike those we hurt. Several studies (Berscheid & others, 1968; Davis & Jones, 1960; Glass, 1964) found that harming an innocent victim—by uttering hurtful comments or delivering electric shocks—typically leads aggressors to disparage their victims, thus helping them justify their cruel behavior. This is especially so when we are coaxed into it, not coerced. When we agree to a deed voluntarily, we take more responsibility for it.

The phenomenon appears in wartime. Prisoner-of-war camp guards would sometimes display good manners to captives in their first days on the job, but not for long. Soldiers ordered to kill may initially react with revulsion to the point of sickness over their act. But not for long (Waller, 2002). Before long, they will denigrate their enemies with nicknames. People tend to dehumanize their enemies and humanize their pets.

Attitudes also follow behavior in peacetime. A group that holds another in slavery will likely come to perceive the slaves as having traits that justify their oppression. Prison staff who participate in executions experience "moral disengagement" by coming to believe (more strongly than do other prison staff) that their victims deserve their fate (Osofsky & others, 2005). Actions and attitudes feed each other, sometimes to the point of moral numbness. The more one harms another and adjusts one's attitudes, the easier it becomes to do harm. Conscience is corroded.

To simulate the "killing begets killing" process, Andy Martens and his collaborators (2007) asked University of Arizona students to kill some bugs. They wondered: Would killing initial bugs in a "practice" trial increase students' willingness to kill more bugs later? To find out, they asked some students to look at one small bug in a container, then to dump

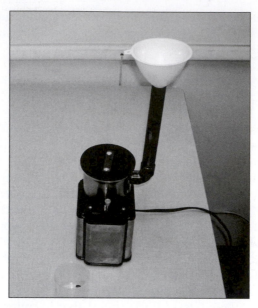

FIGURE 9-1
Killing begets killing. Students who initially
perceived themselves as killing several bugs,
by dropping them in this apparent killing
machine, later killed an increased number of
bugs during a self-paced killing period. (In
reality, no bugs were harmed.)

it into the coffee grinding machine shown in Figure 9-1, and then to press
the "on" button for 3 seconds. (No bugs were actually killed. An unseen
stopper at the base of the insert tube prevented the bug from actually entering the opaque killing machine, which had torn bits of paper to simulate the sound of a killing.) Others, who initially killed five bugs (or so
they thought), went on to "kill" significantly more bugs during an ensuing 20-second period.

Harmful acts shape the self, but so, thankfully, do moral acts. Our
character is reflected in what we do when we think no one is looking.
Researchers have tested character by giving children temptations when
it seems no one is watching. Consider what happens when children resist the temptation. In a dramatic experiment, Jonathan Freedman (1965)
introduced elementary school children to an enticing battery-controlled
robot, instructing them not to play with it while he was out of the room.
Freedman used a severe threat with half the children and a mild threat
with the others. Both were sufficient to deter the children.

Several weeks later a different researcher, with no apparent relation to the earlier events, left each child to play in the same room with

the same toys. Of the children who had been given the severe threat, three-fourths now freely played with the robot; of those given the mild deterrent, two-thirds still *resisted* playing with it. Apparently, the deterrent was strong enough to elicit the desired behavior yet mild enough to leave them with a sense of choice. Having earlier chosen consciously *not* to play with the toy, the mildly deterred children internalized their decisions. Moral action, especially when chosen rather than coerced, affects moral thinking.

Moreover, positive behavior fosters liking for the person. Doing a favor for an experimenter or another participant, or tutoring a student, usually increases liking of the person helped (Blanchard & Cook, 1976). People who pray for a romantic partner (even in controlled experiments) thereafter exhibit greater commitment and fidelity to the partner (Fincham & others, 2010). It is a lesson worth remembering: If you wish to love someone more, act as if you do.

In 1793 Benjamin Franklin tested the idea that doing a favor engenders liking. As clerk of the Pennsylvania General Assembly, he was disturbed by opposition from another important legislator. So Franklin set out to win him over:

> I did not . . . aim at gaining his favour by paying any servile respect to him but, after some time, took this other method. Having heard that he had in his library a certain very scarce and curious book I wrote a note to him expressing my desire of perusing that book and requesting he would do me the favour of lending it to me for a few days. He sent it immediately and I return'd it in about a week, expressing strongly my sense of the favour. When we next met in the House he spoke to me (which he had never done before), and with great civility; and he ever after manifested a readiness to serve me on all occasions, so that we became great friends and our friendship continued to his death. (quoted by Rosenzweig, 1972, p. 769)

Interracial Behavior and Racial Attitudes

If moral action feeds moral attitudes, will positive interracial behavior reduce racial prejudice—much as mandatory seat belt use has produced more favorable seat belt attitudes? That was part of social scientists' testimony before the U.S. Supreme Court's 1954 decision to desegregate schools. Their argument ran like this: If we wait for the heart to change—through preaching and teaching—we will wait a long time for racial justice. But if we legislate moral action, we can, under the right conditions, indirectly affect heartfelt attitudes.

That idea runs counter to the presumption that "you can't legislate morality." Yet attitude change has, as some social psychologists predicted, followed desegregation. Consider the following:

- Following the Supreme Court decision, the percentage of White Americans favoring integrated schools jumped and now includes nearly everyone. (For other examples of old and current racial attitudes, see Module 23.)

- In the 10 years after the Civil Rights Act of 1964, the percentage of White Americans who described their neighborhoods, friends, co-workers, or other students as all-White declined by about 20 percent for each of those measures. Interracial behavior was increasing. During the same period, the percentage of White Americans who said that Blacks should be allowed to live in any neighborhood increased from 65 percent to 87 percent (*ISR Newsletter*, 1975). Attitudes were changing, too.

- More uniform national standards against discrimination were followed by decreasing differences in racial attitudes among people of differing religions, classes, and geographic regions. As Americans came to act more alike, they came to think more alike (Greeley & Sheatsley, 1971; Taylor & others, 1978).

*B*RAINWASHING

Many people assume that the most potent social indoctrination comes through *brainwashing,* a term coined to describe what happened to American prisoners of war (POWs) during the 1950s Korean War. Although the "thought-control" program was not as irresistible as "brainwashing" suggests, the results still were disconcerting. Hundreds of prisoners cooperated with their captors. Twenty-one chose to remain after being granted permission to return to America. And many of those who did return came home believing "although communism won't work in America, I think it's a good thing for Asia" (Segal, 1954).

Edgar Schein (1956) interviewed many of the POWs and reported that the captors' methods included a gradual escalation of demands. The captors always started with trivial requests and gradually worked up to more significant ones. "Thus after a prisoner had once been 'trained' to speak or write out trivia, statements on more important issues were demanded." Moreover, they always expected active participation, be it just copying something or participating in group discussions, writing self-criticism, or uttering public confessions. Once a prisoner had spoken or written a statement, he felt an inner need to make his beliefs consistent with his acts. That often drove prisoners to persuade themselves of what they had done wrong. The "start small and build" tactic was an effective application of the foot-in-the-door technique, and it continues to be so today in the socialization of terrorists and torturers.

The effect of a society's behavior on its racial attitudes suggests the possibility of employing the same idea for political socialization on a mass scale. For many Germans during the 1930s, participation in Nazi rallies, displaying the Nazi flag, and especially the public greeting "Heil Hitler" established a profound inconsistency between behavior and belief. Historian Richard Grunberger (1971) reports that for those who had their doubts about Hitler, "the 'German greeting' was a powerful conditioning device. Having once decided to intone it as an outward token of conformity, many experienced . . . discomfort at the contradiction between their words and their feelings. Prevented from saying what they believed, they tried to establish their psychic equilibrium by consciously making themselves believe what they said" (p. 27).

From these observations—of the effects of role playing, the foot-in-the-door experience, moral and immoral acts, interracial behavior, and brainwashing—there is a powerful practical lesson: If we want to change ourselves in some important way, it's best not to wait for insight or inspiration. Sometimes we need to act—to begin writing that paper, to make those phone calls, to see that person—even if we don't feel like acting. To strengthen our convictions, it helps to enact them. In this way, faith and love are alike; if we keep them to ourselves, they shrivel. If we enact and express them, they grow.

Now let me ask you, before reading further, to play theorist. Ask yourself: Why in these studies and real-life examples did attitudes follow behavior? Why might playing a role or making a speech influence your attitude?

WHY DOES BEHAVIOR AFFECT OUR ATTITUDES?

Social psychologists agree: Our actions influence our attitudes, sometimes turning foes into friends, captives into collaborators, and doubters into believers. Social psychologists debate: Why?

One idea is that, wanting to make a good impression, people might merely express attitudes that *appear* consistent with their actions. Let's be honest with ourselves. We do care about appearances—why else would we spend so much on clothes, cosmetics, and weight control? To manage the impression we're creating, we might adjust what we say to please rather than offend. To appear consistent we might at times feign attitudes that harmonize with our actions.

But this isn't the whole story. Experiments suggest that some genuine attitude change follows our behavior commitments. Cognitive dissonance theory and self-perception theory offer two explanations.

Cognitive dissonance theory, developed by the late Leon Festinger (1957), proposes that we feel tension or a lack of harmony ("dissonance"), when two simultaneously accessible thoughts or beliefs ("cognitions") are psychologically inconsistent. Festinger argued that to reduce this unpleasant arousal, we often adjust our thinking. This simple idea, and some surprising predictions derived from it, have spawned more than 2,000 studies (Cooper, 1999).

www.mhhe.com/myersocialpsychology

Activity
9.3

One way people minimize dissonance, Festinger believed, is through **selective exposure** to agreeable information. Studies have asked people about their views on various topics, and then invited them to choose whether they wanted to view information supporting or opposing their viewpoint. By about a two to one ratio, people (less secure and open-minded people, especially) preferred supporting rather than challenging information (Fischer & Greitemeyer, 2010; Hart & others, 2009; Sweeny & others, 2010). Thus, reported a bipartisan U.S. Senate (2004) intelligence committee, the belief that Iraq had weapons of mass destruction led government leaders to welcome information supporting their assumption and to downplay contradictory information, and thus to launch a war. People are especially keen on reading information that supports their political, religious, and ethical views—a phenomenon that most of us can illustrate from our own favorite news and blog sources. On more practical and less values-relevant topics, "accuracy motives" are more likely to drive us. Thus, we welcome a home inspection before buying or a second opinion before surgery.

Dissonance theory pertains mostly to discrepancies between behavior and attitudes. We are aware of both. Thus, if we sense some inconsistency, perhaps some hypocrisy, we feel pressure for change. That helps explain why British and U.S. cigarette smokers have been much less likely than nonsmokers to believe that smoking is dangerous (Eiser & others, 1979; Saad, 2002).

After the 2003 Iraq War, noted the director of the Program of International Policy Attitudes, some Americans struggled to reduce their "experience of cognitive dissonance" (Kull, 2003). The war's main premise had been that Saddam Hussein, unlike most other brutal dictators whom the world was tolerating, had weapons of mass destruction. As the war began, only 38 percent of Americans said the war was justified even if Iraq did not have weapons of mass destruction (Gallup, 2003). Nearly four in five Americans believed their invading troops would find such, and a similar percentage supported the just-launched war (Duffy, 2003; Newport & others, 2003).

When no such weapons were found, the war-supporting majority experienced dissonance, which was heightened by their awareness of the war's financial and human costs, by scenes of Iraq in chaos, by surging anti-American attitudes in Europe and in Muslim countries, and by inflamed pro-terrorist attitudes. To reduce their dissonance, noted the Program of International Policy Attitudes, some Americans revised their memories of their government's primary rationale for going to war. The reasons now became liberating an oppressed people from tyrannical and genocidal rule and laying the groundwork for a more peaceful and democratic Middle East. Three months after the war began, the once-minority opinion became, for a time, the majority view: 58 percent of Americans now supported the war even if there were none of the proclaimed weapons of mass destruction (Gallup, 2003). "Whether or not they find weapons of mass destruction doesn't matter," suggested Republican pollster Frank Luntz (2003), "because the rationale for the war changed."

In *Mistakes Were Made (But Not By Me): Why We Justify Foolish Beliefs, Bad Decisions, and Hurtful Acts,* social psychologists Carol Tavris and Elliot Aronson (2007, p. 7) illustrate dissonance reduction by leaders of various political parties when faced with clear evidence that a decision they made or a course of action they chose turned out to be wrong, even disastrous. This human phenomenon is nonpartisan, note Tavris and Aronson: "A president who has justified his actions to himself, believing that he has *the truth*, becomes impervious to self-correction." For example, Democratic President Lyndon Johnson's biographer described him as someone who held to his beliefs, even when sinking in the quagmire of Vietnam, regardless "of the facts in the matter." And Republican president George W. Bush, in the years after launching the Iraq war, said that "knowing what I know today, I'd make the decision again" (2005), that "I've never been more convinced that the decisions I made are the right decisions" (2006), and that "this war has . . . come at a high cost in lives and treasure, but those costs are necessary" (2008).

Cognitive dissonance theory assumes that our need to maintain a consistent and positive self-image motivates us to adopt attitudes that justify our actions. Assuming no such motive, **self-perception theory** says simply that when our attitudes are unclear to us, we observe our behaviors and then infer our attitudes from them. As Anne Frank wrote in her diary, "I can watch myself and my actions just like an outsider." Having done so—having noted how we acted toward that person knocking at our door—we infer how we felt about the person.

Dissonance theory best explains what happens when our actions openly contradict our well-defined attitudes. When, say, we hurt someone we like, we feel tension, which we might reduce by viewing the other as a jerk. Self-perception theory best explains what happens when we are unsure of our attitudes: We infer them by observing ourselves. If we lend our new neighbors, whom we neither like nor dislike, a cup of sugar, our helpful behavior can lead us to infer that we like them.

In proposing self-perception theory, Daryl Bem (1972) assumed that when we're unsure of our attitudes, we infer them, much as we make inferences about others' attitudes. So it goes as we observe our own behavior. What we freely say and do can be self-revealing. To paraphrase an old saying, How do I know what I think until I hear what I say or see what I do?

The debate over how to explain the attitudes-follow-behavior effect has inspired hundreds of experiments that reveal the conditions under which dissonance and self-perception processes operate. As often happens in science, each theory provides a partial explanation of a complex reality. If only human nature were simple, one simple theory could describe it. Alas, but thankfully, we are not simple creatures, and that is why there are many miles to go before psychological researchers can sleep.

CONCEPTS TO REMEMBER

attitude   A belief and feeling that can predispose our response to something or someone.

role   A set of norms that defines how people in a given social position ought to behave.

foot-in-the-door phenomenon   The tendency for people who have first agreed to a small request to comply later with a larger request.

lowball technique   A tactic for getting people to agree to something. People who agree to an initial request will often still comply when the requester ups the ante. People who receive only the costly request are less likely to comply with it.

cognitive dissonance   Tension that arises when one is simultaneously aware of two inconsistent cognitions. For example, dissonance may occur when we realize that we have, with little justification, acted contrary to our attitudes or made a decision favoring one alternative despite reasons favoring another.

selective exposure   The tendency to seek information and media that agree with one's views and to avoid dissonant information.

self-perception theory   The theory that when we are unsure of our attitudes, we infer them much as would someone observing us—by looking at our behavior and the circumstances under which it occurs.

MODULE

10

❖

Clinical Intuition

Is Susan suicidal? Should John be committed to a mental hospital? If released, will Tom be a homicide risk? Facing such questions, clinical psychologists struggle to make accurate judgments, recommendations, and predictions.

Such clinical judgments are also *social* judgments and thus vulnerable to illusory correlations, overconfidence bred by hindsight, and self-confirming diagnoses (Maddux, 1993). Let's see why alerting mental health workers to how people form impressions (and *mis*impressions) might help avert serious misjudgments.

*I*LLUSORY CORRELATIONS

As we noted in Module 8, it's tempting to see correlations where none exist. If we expect two things to be associated—if, for example, we believe that premonitions predict events—it's easy to perceive illusory correlations. Even when shown random data, we may notice and remember instances when premonitions and events are coincidentally related and soon forget all the instances when premonitions aren't borne out and when events happen without a prior premonition.

Clinicians, like all of us, may perceive illusory correlations. Imagine that Mary, a mental health worker, expects particular responses to Rorschach inkblots to be more common among people with a sexual disorder. Might she, in reflecting on her experience, believe she has witnessed such associations?

To discover when such a perception is an illusory correlation, psychological science offers a simple method: Have one clinician administer and interpret the test. Have another clinician assess the same person's traits or symptoms. Repeat this process with many people. Are test outcomes in fact correlated with reported symptoms? Some tests are indeed predictive. Others, such as the Rorschach inkblots and the Draw-a-Person test, have correlations far weaker than their users suppose (Lilienfeld & others, 2000, 2005).

Why, then, do clinicians continue to express confidence in uninformative or ambiguous tests? Pioneering experiments by Loren Chapman and Jean Chapman (1969, 1971) helped us see why. They invited college students and professional clinicians to study some test performances and diagnoses. If the students or clinicians *expected* a particular association, they generally *perceived* it, regardless of whether the data were supportive. For example, clinicians who believed that only suspicious people draw peculiar eyes on the Draw-a-Person test perceived such a relationship—even when shown cases in which suspicious people drew peculiar eyes less often than nonsuspicious people. If they believed in a connection, they were more likely to notice confirming instances. To believe is to see.

*H*INDSIGHT

If someone we know commits suicide, how do we react? One common reaction is to think that we, or those close to the person, should have been able to predict and therefore to prevent the suicide: "We should have known!" In hindsight, we can see the suicidal signs and the pleas for help. One experiment gave participants a description of a depressed person. Some participants were told that the person subsequently committed suicide; other participants were not told this. Compared with those not informed of the suicide, those who had been informed became more likely to say they "would have expected" it (Goggin & Range, 1985). Moreover, they viewed the victim's family more negatively. After a tragedy, an I-should-have-known-it-all-along phenomenon can leave family, friends, and therapists feeling guilty.

David Rosenhan (1973) and seven associates provided a striking example of error-prone after-the-fact explanations. To test mental health workers' clinical insights, they each made an appointment with a different mental hospital admissions office and complained of "hearing voices." Apart from giving false names and vocations, they reported their life histories and emotional states honestly and exhibited no further symptoms. Most were diagnosed with schizophrenia and remained hospitalized for two to three weeks. Hospital clinicians then searched for early incidents in the pseudopatients' life histories and hospital behavior that "confirmed" and "explained" the diagnosis. Rosenhan tells of one pseudopatient who truthfully explained to the interviewer that he had a close childhood relationship with his mother but was rather remote from his father. During adolescence and beyond, however, his father became a close friend while his relationship with his mother cooled. His present relationship with his wife was characteristically close and warm. Apart from occasional angry exchanges, friction was minimal. The children had rarely been spanked.

The interviewer, "knowing" the person suffered schizophrenia, explained the problem this way:

> This white 39-year-old male . . . manifests a long history of considerable ambivalence in close relationships, which begins in early childhood. A warm relationship with his mother cools during his adolescence. A distant relationship to his father is described as becoming very intense. Affective stability is absent. His attempts to control emotionality with his wife and children are punctuated by angry outbursts and, in the case of the children, spankings. And while he says that he has several good friends, one senses considerable ambivalence embedded in those relationships also.

Rosenhan later told some staff members (who had heard about his controversial experiment but doubted such mistakes could occur in their hospital) that during the next three months one or more pseudopatients would seek admission to their hospital. After the three months, he asked the staff to guess which of the 193 patients admitted during that time were really pseudopatients. Of the 193 new patients, 41 were believed by at least one staff member to be pseudopatients. Actually, there were none.

SELF-CONFIRMING DIAGNOSES

So far we've seen that mental health clinicians sometimes perceive illusory correlations and that hindsight explanations can err. A third possible problem with clinical judgment is that it may prod patients to produce evidence that seems to support it: the client fits into the therapist's expectations. To get a feel for how this phenomenon might be tested experimentally, imagine yourself on a blind date with someone who has been told that you are an uninhibited, outgoing person. To see whether this is true, your date slips questions into the conversation, such as "Have you ever done anything crazy in front of other people?" As you answer such questions, will you reveal a different "you" than if your date had been told you were shy and reserved?

In a clever series of experiments, Mark Snyder (1984), in collaboration with William Swann and others, gave University of Minnesota students some hypotheses to test concerning individuals' traits. Their finding: People often test for a trait by looking for information that confirms it. As in the blind-date example, if people are trying to find out if someone is an extravert, they often solicit instances of extraversion

("What would you do if you wanted to liven things up at a party?"). Testing for introversion, they are more likely to ask, "What factors make it hard for you to really open up to people?" In response, those probed for extraversion *seem* more sociable, and those probed for introversion seem more shy. Our assumptions about another help elicit the behavior we expect.

At Indiana University, Russell Fazio and his colleagues (1981) reproduced this finding and also discovered that those asked the "extraverted" questions later perceived themselves as actually more outgoing than those asked the introverted questions. Moreover, they really became noticeably more outgoing. An accomplice of the experimenter later met each participant in a waiting room and 70 percent of the time guessed correctly from the person's behavior which condition the person had come from.

Given such experiments, can you see why the behaviors of people undergoing psychotherapy come to fit their therapists' theories (Whitman & others, 1963)? When Harold Renaud and Floyd Estess (1961) conducted life-history interviews of 100 healthy, successful adult men, they were startled to discover that their subjects' childhood experiences were loaded with "traumatic events," tense relations with certain people, and bad decisions by their parents—the very factors usually used to explain psychiatric problems. If therapists go fishing for traumas in early childhood experiences, they will often find them. Thus, surmised Snyder (1981):

> The psychiatrist who believes (erroneously) that adult gay males had bad childhood relationships with their mothers may meticulously probe for recalled (or fabricated) signs of tension between their gay clients and their mothers, but neglect to so carefully interrogate their heterosexual clients about their maternal relationships. No doubt, any individual could recall some friction with his or her mother, however minor or isolated the incidents.

Nineteenth-century poet Robert Browning anticipated Snyder's conclusion: "As is your sort of mind, so is your sort of search: You'll find what you desire."

CLINICAL VERSUS STATISTICAL PREDICTION

Not surprisingly, given these hindsight- and diagnosis-confirming tendencies, most clinicians and interviewers express more confidence in their intuitive assessments than in statistical data (such as using past grades and aptitude scores to predict success in graduate or professional school). Yet when researchers pit statistical prediction against intuitive prediction, the statistics usually win. Statistical predictions are indeed unreliable. But human intuition—even expert intuition—is even more unreliable (Faust & Ziskin, 1988; Meehl, 1954; Swets & others, 2000).

Three decades after demonstrating the superiority of statistical over intuitive prediction, Paul Meehl (1986) found the evidence stronger than ever:

> There is no controversy in social science which shows [so many] studies coming out so uniformly in the same direction as this one . . . When you are pushing 90 investigations, predicting everything from the outcome of football games to the diagnosis of liver disease and when you can hardly come up with a half dozen studies showing even a weak tendency in favor of the clinician, it is time to draw a practical conclusion.

Why then do so many clinicians continue to interpret Rorschach inkblot tests and offer intuitive predictions about parolees, suicide risks, and likelihood of child abuse? Partly out of sheer ignorance, said Meehl, but also partly out of "mistaken conceptions of ethics":

> If I try to forecast something important about a college student, or a criminal, or a depressed patient by inefficient rather than efficient means, meanwhile charging this person or the taxpayer 10 times as much money as I would need to achieve greater predictive accuracy, that is not a sound ethical practice. That it feels better, warmer, and cuddlier to me as predictor is a shabby excuse indeed.

Such words are shocking. Did Meehl (who did not completely dismiss clinical expertise) underestimate experts' intuitions? To see why his findings are apparently valid, consider the assessment of human potential by graduate admissions interviewers. Dawes (1976) explained why statistical prediction is so often superior to an interviewer's intuition when predicting certain outcomes such as graduate school success:

Activity
10.1

> What makes us think that we can do a better job of selection by interviewing (students) for a half hour, than we can by adding together relevant (standardized) variables, such as undergraduate GPA, GRE score, and perhaps ratings of letters of recommendation? The most reasonable explanation to me lies in our overevaluation of our cognitive capacity. And it is really cognitive conceit. Consider, for example, what goes into a GPA. Because for most graduate applicants it is based on at least 3½ years of undergraduate study, it is a composite measure arising from a minimum of 28 courses and possibly, with the popularity of the quarter system, as many as 50 . . . Yet you and I, looking at a folder or interviewing someone for a half hour, are supposed to be able to form a better impression than one based on 3½ years of the cumulative evaluations of 20–40 different professors. . . . Finally, if we do wish to ignore GPA, it appears that the only reason for doing so is believing that the candidate is particularly brilliant even though his or her record may not show it. What better evidence for such brilliance can we have than a score on a carefully devised aptitude test? Do we really think we are better equipped to assess such aptitude than is the Educational Testing Service, whatever its faults?

The bottom line, contends Dawes (2005) after three decades pressing his point, is that, lacking evidence, using clinical intuition rather than statistical prediction "is simply unethical."

*I*MPLICATIONS FOR BETTER CLINICAL PRACTICE

For mental health workers, this module suggests four implications:

1. To reduce the risk of being fooled by illusory correlations, beware of the tendency to see relationships that you expect to see or that are supported by striking examples readily available in your memory.
2. To reduce the risk of being fooled by hindsight bias, realize that it can lead you to feel overconfident and sometimes to judge yourself too harshly for not having foreseen outcomes.
3. To reduce the risk of being fooled by self-confirming diagnoses, guard against the tendency to ask questions that assume your preconceptions are correct; remember that clients' verbal agreement with what you say does not prove its validity; consider opposing ideas and test them, too (Garb, 1994).
4. Harness the powers of statistical prediction.

Clinical Therapy: The Powers of Social Cognition

If you are a typical college student, you may occasionally feel mildly depressed. Perhaps you have at times felt dissatisfied with life, discouraged about the future, sad, lacking appetite and energy, unable to concentrate, perhaps even wondering if life is worth living. Maybe disappointing grades have seemed to jeopardize your career goals. Perhaps the breakup of a relationship has left you in despair. At such times, you may fall into self-focused brooding that only worsens your feelings. In one survey of American collegians, 31 percent reported that during the last school year they had at some point felt "so depressed it was difficult to function" (ACHA, 2009). For 13 percent of adult American men and 22 percent of women, life's down times are not just temporary blue moods in response to bad events; rather, they define a major depressive episode that lasts for weeks without any obvious cause—and thus, at some point, a diagnosis of depression (Pelham, 2009).

Activity
11.1

One of psychology's most intriguing research frontiers concerns the cognitive processes that accompany psychological disorders. What are the memories, attributions, and expectations of depressed, lonely, shy, or illness-prone people? In the case of depression, the most heavily researched disorder, dozens of studies are providing some answers.

SOCIAL COGNITION AND DEPRESSION

People who feel depressed tend to think in negative terms. They view life through dark-colored glasses. With seriously depressed people—those who are feeling worthless, lethargic, indifferent toward friends and family, and unable to sleep or eat normally—the negative thinking is self-defeating. Their intensely pessimistic outlook leads them to magnify every bad experience and minimize every good one. They may view advice to "count your blessings" or "look on the bright side" as hopelessly unrealistic. As one depressed young woman reported, "The real me is worthless and inadequate. I can't move forward with my work because I become frozen with doubt" (Burns, 1980, p. 29).

Distortion or Realism?

Are all depressed people unrealistically negative? To find out, Lauren Alloy and Lyn Abramson (1979; Alloy & others, 2004) studied college students who were either mildly depressed or not depressed. They had the students press a button and observe whether the button controlled a light coming on. Surprisingly, the depressed students were quite accurate in estimating their degree of control. It was the nondepressives whose judgments were distorted; they exaggerated their control. Despite their self-preoccupation, mildly depressed people also are more attuned to others' feelings (Harkness & others, 2005).

This surprising phenomenon of **depressive realism**, nicknamed the "sadder-but-wiser effect," shows up in various judgments of one's control or skill (Ackermann & DeRubeis, 1991; Alloy & others, 1990). Shelley Taylor (1989, p. 214) explains:

> Normal people exaggerate how competent and well liked they are. Depressed people do not. Normal people remember their past behavior with a rosy glow. Depressed people [unless severely depressed] are more even-handed in recalling their successes and failures. Normal people describe themselves primarily positively. Depressed people describe both their positive and their negative qualities. Normal people take credit for successful outcomes and tend to deny responsibility for failure. Depressed people accept responsibility for both success and failure. Normal people exaggerate the control they have over what goes on around them. Depressed people are less vulnerable to the illusion of control. Normal people believe to an unrealistic degree that the future holds a bounty of good things and few bad things. Depressed people are more realistic in their perceptions of the future. In fact, on virtually every point on which normal people show enhanced self-regard, illusions of control, and unrealistic visions of the future, depressed people fail to show the same biases. "Sadder but wiser" does indeed appear to apply to depression.

Underlying the thinking of depressed people are their attributions of responsibility. Consider: If you fail an exam and blame yourself, you may conclude that you are stupid or lazy; consequently, you may feel depressed. If you attribute the failure to an unfair exam or to other circumstances beyond your control, you may feel angry. In over 100 studies involving 15,000 subjects, depressed people have been more likely than nondepressed people to exhibit a negative **explanatory style**

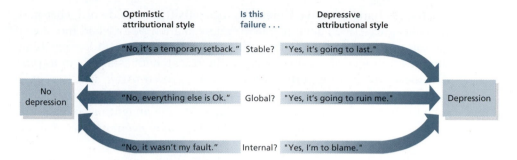

FIGURE 11-1
Depressive explanatory style. Depression is linked with a negative, pessimistic way of explaining and interpreting failures.

(Haeffel & others, 2008; Peterson & Steen, 2002; Sweeney & others, 1986). As shown in Figure 11-1, this explanatory style attributes failure and setbacks to causes that are *stable* ("It's going to last forever"), *global* ("It's going to affect everything I do"), and *internal* ("It's all my fault"). The result of this pessimistic, overgeneralized, self-blaming thinking, say Abramson and her colleagues (1989), is a depressing sense of hopelessness.

Is Negative Thinking a Cause or a Result of Depression?

The cognitive accompaniments of depression raise a chicken-and-egg question: Do depressed moods cause negative thinking, or does negative thinking cause depression?

Depressed Moods Cause Negative Thinking

Without a doubt our moods color our thinking. When we *feel* happy, we *think* happy. We see and recall a good world. But let our mood turn gloomy, and our thoughts switch to a different track. Off come the rose-colored glasses; on come the dark glasses. Now the bad mood primes our recollections of negative events (Bower, 1987; Johnson & Magaro, 1987). Our relationships seem to sour, our self-images tarnish, our hopes dim, others seem more sinister (Brown & Taylor, 1986; Mayer & Salovey, 1987). As depression increases, memories and expectations plummet; when depression lifts, thinking brightens (Barnett & Gotlib, 1988; Kuiper & Higgins, 1985). Thus, *currently* depressed people recall their parents as having been rejecting and punitive. But *formerly* depressed people recall their parents in the same positive terms as do never-depressed people (Lewinsohn & Rosenbaum, 1987). Thus, when you hear depressed people trashing their parents, remember: *Moods modify memories.*

By studying Indiana University basketball fans, Edward Hirt and his colleagues (1992) demonstrated that even a temporary bad mood can darken our thinking. After the fans were either depressed by watching their team lose or elated by a victory, the researchers asked them to predict the team's future performance, and their own. After a loss, people offered bleaker assessments not only of the team's future but also of their own likely performance at throwing darts, solving anagrams, and getting a date. When things aren't going our way, it may seem as though they never will.

A depressed mood also affects behavior. When depressed, we tend to be withdrawn, glum, and quick to complain. Stephen Strack and James Coyne (1983) found that depressed people were realistic in thinking that others didn't appreciate their behavior; their pessimism and bad moods can even trigger social rejection (Carver & others, 1994). Depressed behavior can also trigger reciprocal depression in others. College students who have depressed roommates tend to become a little depressed themselves (Burchill & Stiles, 1988; Joiner, 1994; Sanislow & others, 1989). In dating couples, too, depression is often contagious (Katz & others, 1999). (Better news comes from a study that followed nearly 5,000 residents of one Massachussetts city for 20 years. Happiness also is contagious. When surrounded by happy people, people become more likely to be happy in the future [Fowler & Christakis, 2008].)

Negative Thinking Causes Depressed Moods

Depression is natural when experiencing severe stress—losing a job, getting divorced or rejected, or suffering any experience that disrupts our sense of who we are and why we are worthy human beings. The brooding that comes with this short-term depression can be adaptive. Much as nausea and pain protect the body from toxins, so depression protects us, by slowing us down, causing us to reassess, and then redirecting our energy in new ways (Andrews & Thomson, 2009, 2010; Watkins, 2008). Insights gained during times of depressed inactivity may later result in better strategies for interacting with the world. But depression-prone people respond to bad events with intense rumination and self-blame (Mor & Winquist, 2002; Pyszczynski & others, 1991). Their self-esteem fluctuates more rapidly up with boosts and down with threats (Butler & others, 1994).

Why are some people so affected by *minor* stresses? Evidence suggests that when stress-induced rumination is filtered through a negative explanatory style, the frequent outcome is depression (Robinson & Alloy, 2003). Colin Sacks and Daphne Bugental (1987) asked some young women to get acquainted with a stranger who sometimes acted cold and unfriendly, creating an awkward social situation. Unlike optimistic women, those with a pessimistic explanatory style—who characteristically offer stable, global, and internal attributions for bad events—reacted to the social failure by feeling depressed. Moreover, they then behaved more antagonistically toward the next people they met. Their negative thinking led to a negative mood, which led to negative behavior.

Such depressing rumination is more common among women, reported Susan Nolen-Hoeksema (2003). When trouble strikes, men tend to act, women tend to think—and often to "overthink," she reports. And that helps explain why, beginning in adolescence, women have, compared with men, a doubled risk of depression (Hyde & others, 2008).

Outside the laboratory, studies of children, teenagers, and adults confirm that those with the pessimistic explanatory style more often become depressed when bad things happen. One study monitored university students every six weeks for two-and-a-half years (Alloy & others, 1999). One percent of those who began college with optimistic thinking styles had a first depressive episode, as did 17 percent of those with pessimistic thinking styles. "A recipe for severe depression is preexisting pessimism encountering failure," notes Martin Seligman (1991, p. 78).

Researcher Peter Lewinsohn and his colleagues (1985) have assembled these findings into a coherent psychological understanding of depression. The negative self-image, attributions, and expectations of a depressed person are, they report, an essential link in a vicious circle that is triggered by negative experience—perhaps academic or vocational failure, family conflict, or social rejection (Figure 11-2). Such ruminations create a depressed mood that alters how a person thinks and acts, which then fuels further negative experiences, self-blame, and depressed mood. In experiments, mildly depressed people's moods brighten when a task diverts their attention to something external (Nix & others, 1995). Depression is therefore *both* a cause and a result of negative cognitions.

Martin Seligman (1991, 1998, 2002) believes that self-focus and self-blame help explain the near-epidemic levels of depression in the Western world today. In North America, for example, young adults today are three times as likely as their grandparents to have suffered

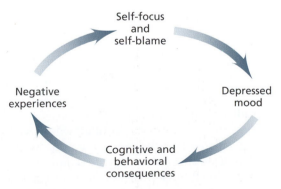

FIGURE 11-2
The vicious circle of depression.

depression—despite their grandparents' experiencing a lower standard of living and greater hardship (Cross-National Collaborative Group, 1992; Swindle & others, 2000). Seligman believes that the decline of religion and family, plus the growth of individualism, breeds hopelessness and self-blame when things don't go well. Failed courses, careers, and marriages produce despair when we stand alone, with nothing and no one to fall back on. If, as a macho *Fortune* ad declared, you can "make it on your own," on "your own drive, your own guts, your own energy, your own ambition," then whose fault is it if you *don't* make it? In non-Western cultures, where close-knit relationships and cooperation are the norm, major depression is less common and less tied to guilt and self-blame over perceived personal failure. In Japan, for example, depressed people instead tend to report feeling shame over letting down their family or co-workers (Draguns, 1990).

These insights into the thinking style linked with depression have prompted social psychologists to study thinking patterns associated with other problems. How do those who are plagued with excessive loneliness, shyness, or substance abuse view themselves? How well do they recall their successes and their failures? And to what do they attribute their ups and downs?

SOCIAL COGNITION AND LONELINESS

If depression is the common cold of psychological disorders, then loneliness is the headache. Loneliness, whether chronic or temporary, is a painful awareness that our social relationships are less numerous or meaningful than we desire. In modern cultures, close social relationships *are* less numerous. One national survey revealed a one-third drop, over two decades, in the number of people with whom Americans can discuss "important matters." Moreover, the number of Americans living alone is up 30 percent since 1980 (Miller, 2011). Reflecting on such findings, Robert Putnam (2006) reported that his data likewise reveal "sharp generational differences—baby boomers are more socially marooned than their parents, and the boomers' kids are lonelier still. Is it because of two-career families? Ethnic diversity? The Internet? Suburban sprawl? Everyone has a favorite culprit. Mine is TV, but the jury is still out."

In a study of Dutch adults, Jenny de Jong-Gierveld (1987) documented the loneliness that unmarried and unattached people are likely to experience. She speculated that the modern emphasis on individual fulfillment and the depreciation of marriage and family life may be "loneliness-provoking" (as well as depression-provoking). Job-related mobility also makes for fewer long-term family and social ties, and increased loneliness (Dill & Anderson, 1999).

But loneliness need not coincide with aloneness. One can feel lonely in the middle of a party. "In America, there is loneliness but no solitude," lamented Mary Pipher (2002). "There are crowds but no community." In Los Angeles, observed her daughter, "There are 10 million people around me but nobody knows my name." Lacking social connections, and feeling lonely (or when made to feel so in an experiment), people may compensate by seeing humanlike qualities in things, animals, and supernatural beings, with which they find companionship (Epley & others, 2008).

One can be utterly alone—as I am while writing these words in the solitude of an isolated turret office at a British university 5,000 miles from home—without feeling lonely. To feel lonely is to feel excluded from a group, unloved by those around you, unable to share your private concerns, different and alienated from those in your surroundings (Beck & Young, 1978; Davis & Franzoi, 1986). Having lonely acquaintances increases the chance that you feel lonely (Cacioppo & others, 2009). Loneliness tends to run in social clusters, as its negative thoughts and behaviors spread.

Loneliness also increases the risk of health problems. In *Loneliness: Human Nature and the Need for Social Connection,* John Cacioppo and William Patrick (2008) explain that loneliness affects stress hormones and immune activity. Loneliness therefore puts people at increased risk not only for depression and suicide, but also high blood pressure, heart disease, cognitive decline, and sleep impairment (Hawkley & Cacioppo, 2010; Shankar & others, 2011; VanderWeele & others, 2011). A digest of data from more than 300,000 people in 148 studies showed that social isolation increased the risk of death about as much as smoking, and more than obesity or inactivity (Holt-Lunstad & others, 2010).

Loneliness—which may be evoked by an icy stare or a cold shoulder—even feels, quite literally, cold. When recalling an experience of exclusion, people estimate a lower room temperature than when thinking of being included. After being excluded in a little ball game, people show a heightened preference for warm foods and drinks (Zhong & Leonardelli, 2008).

Loneliness can be adaptive. Such feelings signal people to seek social connections, which facilitate survival. Even when loneliness triggers nostalgia—a longing for the past—it serves to remind people of their social connections (Zhou & others, 2008).

Like depressed people, chronically lonely people seem caught in a vicious circle of self-defeating social thinking and social behaviors. They have some of the negative explanatory style of the depressed; they perceive their interactions as making a poor impression, blame themselves for their poor social relationships, and see most things as beyond their control (Anderson & others, 1994; Christensen & Kashy, 1998; Snodgrass, 1987). Moreover, they perceive others in negative ways. When paired with a stranger of the same gender or with a first-year college roommate, lonely students are more likely to perceive the other person negatively (Jones & others, 1981; Wittenberg & Reis, 1986). Ironically, report Danu Stinson and

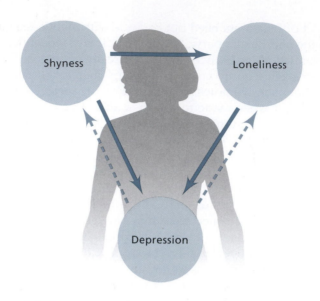

FIGURE 11-3
The interplay of chronic shyness, loneliness, and depression. Solid arrows indicate primary cause-effect direction, as summarized by Jody Dill and Craig Anderson (1999). Dotted lines indicate additional effects.

her co-researchers (2011), socially insecure people therefore often behave in ways that produce the very social rejection they fear. As Figure 11-3 illustrates, loneliness, depression, and shyness sometimes feed one another.

These negative views may both reflect and color the lonely person's experience. Believing in their social unworthiness and feeling pessimistic about others inhibit lonely people from acting to reduce their loneliness. Lonely people often find it hard to introduce themselves, make phone calls, and participate in groups (Nurmi & others, 1996, 1997; Rook, 1984; Spitzberg & Hurt, 1987). Yet, like mildly depressed people, they are attuned to others and skilled at recognizing emotional expression (Gardner & others, 2005).

SOCIAL COGNITION AND ANXIETY

Shyness is a form of social anxiety characterized by self-consciousness and worry about what others think (Anderson & Harvey, 1988; Asendorpf, 1987; Carver & Scheier, 1986). Being interviewed for a much-wanted job, dating someone for the first time, stepping into a roomful of strangers, performing before an important audience, or giving a speech (one of the most common phobias) can make almost anyone feel anxious. But some people feel anxious in almost any situation in which they may feel they are being evaluated, even having lunch with a co-worker. For these people, anxiety is more a personality trait than a temporary state.

What causes us to feel anxious in social situations? Why are some people shackled in the prison of their own social anxiety? Barry Schlenker and Mark Leary (1982, 1985; Leary & Kowalski, 1995) answer those questions by applying self-presentation theory. Self-presentation theory assumes that we are eager to present ourselves in ways that make a good impression. The implications for social anxiety are straightforward: *We feel anxious when we are motivated to impress others but have self-doubts.* This simple principle helps explain a variety of research findings, each of which may ring true in your own experience. We feel most anxious when we are

- with powerful, high-status people—people whose impressions of us matter.
- in an evaluative context, such as when making a first impression on the parents of one's fiancé.
- self-conscious (as shy people often are), with our attention focused on ourselves and how we are coming across.
- focused on something central to our self-image, as when a college professor presents ideas before peers at a professional convention.
- in novel or unstructured situations, such as a first school dance or first formal dinner, where we are unsure of the social rules.

For most people, the tendency in all such situations is to be cautiously self-protective: to talk less; to avoid topics that reveal one's ignorance; to be guarded about oneself; to be unassertive, agreeable, and smiling.

Compared with unshy people, shy, self-conscious people (whose numbers include many adolescents) see incidental events as somehow relevant to themselves (Fenigstein, 1984; Fenigstein & Vanable, 1992). Shy, anxious people overpersonalize situations, a tendency that breeds anxious concern and, in extreme cases, paranoia. They also overestimate the extent to which other people are watching and evaluating them. If their hair won't comb right or they have a facial blemish, they assume everyone else notices and judges them accordingly. Shy people may even be conscious of their self-consciousness. They wish they could stop worrying about blushing, about what others are thinking, or about what to say next.

To reduce social anxiety, some people turn to alcohol. Alcohol lowers anxiety and reduces self-consciousness (Hull & Young, 1983). Thus, chronically self-conscious people are especially likely to drink following a failure. If recovering from alcoholism, they are more likely than those low in self-consciousness to relapse when they again experience stress or failure.

Symptoms as diverse as anxiety and alcohol abuse can serve a self-handicapping function. Labeling oneself as anxious, shy, depressed, or under the influence of alcohol can provide an excuse for failure (Snyder & Smith, 1986). Behind a barricade of symptoms, the person's ego stands secure. "Why don't I date? Because I'm shy, so people don't easily get to know the real me." The symptom is an unconscious strategic ploy to explain away negative outcomes.

What if we were to remove the need for such a ploy by providing people with a handy alternative explanation for their anxiety and therefore for possible failure? Would a shy person no longer need to be shy? That is precisely what Susan Brodt and Philip Zimbardo (1981) found when they brought shy and not-shy college women to the laboratory and had them converse with a handsome male who posed as another participant. Before the conversation, the women were cooped up in a small chamber and blasted with loud noise. Some of the shy women (but not others) were told that the noise would leave them with a pounding heart, a common symptom of social anxiety. Thus, when these women later talked with the man, they could attribute their pounding hearts and any conversational difficulties to the noise, not to their shyness or social inadequacy. Compared with the shy women who were not given this handy explanation for their pounding hearts, these women were no longer so shy. They talked fluently once the conversation got going and asked questions of the man. In fact, unlike the other shy women (whom the man could easily spot as shy), these women were to him indistinguishable from the not-shy women.

SOCIAL-PSYCHOLOGICAL APPROACHES TO TREATMENT

We have considered patterns of thinking that are linked with problems ranging from serious depression to extreme shyness to physical illness. Do these maladaptive thought patterns suggest any treatments? There is no social-psychological therapy. But therapy is a social encounter, and social psychologists have suggested how their principles might be integrated into existing treatment techniques (Forsyth & Leary, 1997; Strong & others, 1992). Consider two approaches discussed below.

Inducing Internal Change through External Behavior

In Module 9 we reviewed a broad range of evidence for a simple but powerful principle: Our actions affect our attitudes. The roles we play, the things we say and do, and the decisions we make influence who we are.

Consistent with this attitudes-follow-behavior principle, several psychotherapy techniques prescribe action:

- Behavior therapists try to shape behavior on the theory that the client's inner disposition will also change after the behavior changes.
- In assertiveness training, the individual may first role-play assertiveness in a supportive context, then gradually implement assertive behaviors in everyday life.
- Rational-emotive therapy assumes that we generate our own emotions; clients receive "homework" assignments to talk and act in new ways that will generate new emotions: Challenge that overbearing relative. Stop telling yourself you're an unattractive person and ask someone out.
- Self-help groups subtly induce participants to behave in new ways in front of the group—to express anger, cry, act with high self-esteem, express positive feelings.

All these techniques share a common assumption: If we cannot directly control our feelings by sheer willpower, we can influence them indirectly through our behavior.

Experiments confirm that what we say about ourselves can affect how we feel. In one experiment, students were induced to write self-laudatory essays (Mirels & McPeek, 1977). These students, more than others who wrote essays about a current social issue, later expressed higher self-esteem when rating themselves privately for a different experimenter. In several more experiments, Edward Jones and his associates (1981; Rhodewalt & Agustsdottir, 1986) influenced students to present themselves to an interviewer in either self-enhancing or self-deprecating ways. Again, the public displays—whether upbeat or downbeat—carried over to later self-esteem. Saying is believing, even when we talk about ourselves.

Breaking Vicious Circles

If depression, loneliness, and social anxiety maintain themselves through a vicious circle of negative experiences, negative thinking, and self-defeating behavior, it should be possible to break the circle at any of several points—by changing the environment, by training the person to behave more constructively, or by reversing negative thinking. And it is. Several therapy methods help free people from depression's vicious circle.

Social Skills Training

Depression, loneliness, and shyness are not just problems in someone's mind. To be around a depressed person for any length of time can be irritating and depressing. As lonely and shy people suspect, they may indeed come across poorly in social situations. How ironic that the more self-preoccupied people seek to make a good impression, the more their effort may backfire (Lun & others, 2011). Those who instead focus on supporting others more often enjoy others' regard in return. In these cases, social skills training may help. By observing and then practicing new behaviors in safe situations, the person may develop the confidence to behave more effectively in other situations. As the person begins to enjoy the rewards of behaving more skillfully, a more positive self-perception develops. Frances Haemmerlie and Robert Montgomery (1982, 1984, 1986) demonstrated this in several heartwarming studies with shy, anxious college students. Those who are inexperienced and nervous around those of the other sex may say to themselves, "I don't date much, so I must be socially inadequate, so I shouldn't try reaching out to anyone." To reverse this negative sequence, Haemmerlie and Montgomery enticed such students into pleasant interactions with people of the other sex.

In one experiment, college men completed social anxiety questionnaires and then came to the laboratory on two different days. Each day they enjoyed 12-minute conversations with each of six young women. The men thought the women were also participants. Actually, the women were confederates who had been asked to carry on a natural, positive, friendly conversation with each of the men.

The effect of these two-and-a-half hours of conversation was remarkable. As one participant wrote afterward, "I had never met so many girls that I could have a good conversation with. After a few girls, my confidence grew to the point where I didn't notice being nervous like I once did." Such comments were supported by a variety of measures. Unlike men in a control condition, those who experienced the conversations reported considerably less female-related anxiety when retested one week and six months later. Placed alone in a room with an attractive female stranger, they also became much more likely to start a conversation. Outside the laboratory they actually began occasional dating.

Haemmerlie and Montgomery note that not only did all this occur without any counseling, it may very well have occurred *because* there was no counseling. Having behaved successfully on their own, the men could now perceive themselves as socially competent. Although seven months later the researchers did debrief the participants, by that time the men had presumably enjoyed enough social success to maintain their internal attributions for success. "Nothing succeeds like success," concluded Haemmerlie (1987)— "as long as there are no external factors present that the client can use as an excuse for that success!"

Explanatory Style Therapy
The vicious circles that maintain depression, loneliness, and shyness can be broken by social skills training, by positive experiences that alter self-perceptions, *and* by changing negative thought patterns. Some people

have good social skills, but their experiences with hypercritical friends and family have convinced them otherwise. For such people it may be enough to help them reverse their negative beliefs about themselves and their futures. Among the cognitive therapies with this aim is an *explanatory style therapy* proposed by social psychologists (Abramson, 1988; Gillham & others, 2000; Masi & others, 2011).

One such program taught depressed college students to change their typical attributions. Mary Anne Layden (1982) first explained the advantages of making attributions more like those of the typical nondepressed person (by accepting credit for successes and seeing how circumstances can make things go wrong). After assigning a variety of tasks, she helped the students see how they typically interpreted success and failure. Then came the treatment phase: Layden instructed them to keep a diary of daily successes and failures, noting how they contributed to their own successes and noting external reasons for their failures. When retested after a month of this attributional retraining and compared with an untreated control group, their self-esteem had risen and their attributional style had become more positive. The more their explanatory style improved, the more their depression lifted. By changing their attributions, they had changed their emotions.

Having emphasized what changed behavior and thought patterns can accomplish, we do well to remind ourselves of their limits. Social skills training and positive thinking cannot transform us into consistent winners who are loved and admired by everyone. Furthermore, temporary depression, loneliness, and shyness are perfectly appropriate responses to profoundly bad events. It is when such feelings exist chronically and without any discernible cause that there is reason for concern and a need to change the self-defeating thoughts and behaviors.

CONCEPTS TO REMEMBER

depressive realism The tendency of mildly depressed people to make accurate rather than self-serving judgments, attributions, and predictions.

explanatory style One's habitual way of explaining life events.

A negative, pessimistic, depressive explanatory style attributes failure to stable, global, and internal causes.

PART THREE

❖

Social Influence

S ocial psychologists study not only how we think about one another—our topic in the preceding modules—but also how we influence and relate to one another. In Modules 12 through 21 we probe social psychology's central concern: the powers of social influence.

What are these unseen social forces that push and pull us? How powerful are they? Research on social influence helps illuminate the invisible strings by which our social worlds move us about. This unit reveals these subtle powers, especially the cultural sources of gender attitudes, the forces of social conformity, the routes to persuasion, and the consequences of being with others and participating in groups.

When we see how these influences operate in everyday situations, we can better understand why people feel and act as they do. And we can ourselves become less vulnerable to unwanted manipulation, and more adept at pulling our own strings.

12

❖

Human Nature and Cultural Diversity

How do we humans differ? How are we alike? These questions are central to a world where social diversity has become, as historian Arthur Schlesinger (1991) said, "the explosive problem of our times." In a world ripped apart by ethnic, cultural, and gender differences, can we learn to accept our diversity, value our cultural identities, *and* recognize the extent of our human kinship? I believe we can. To see why, let's consider the evolutionary and cultural roots of our humanity.

*E*VOLUTION AND BEHAVIOR

In many important ways, we are more alike than different. As members of one great family with common ancestors, they share not only a common biology but also common behavior tendencies. Each of them sleeps and wakes, feels hunger and thirst, and develops language through identical mechanisms. We prefer sweet tastes to sour and fear snakes more than sparrows. They both divide the visual spectrum into similar colors and divide time into past, present, and future. They and their kin across the globe all know how to read one another's frowns and smiles.

Humans everywhere are intensely social. We join groups, conform, and recognize distinctions of social status. We return favors, punish offenses, and grieve a child's death. As children, beginning at about 8 months of age, we displayed fear of strangers, and as adults we favor members of our own groups. Confronted by those with dissimilar attitudes or attributes, we react warily or negatively. Anthropologist Donald Brown (1991, 2000) identified several hundred such universal behavior and language patterns.

To sample among just those beginning with "v," all human societies have verbs, violence, visiting, and vowels.

Even much of our morality is common across cultures and eras. Before they can walk, babies will display a moral sense by disapproving what's wrong or naughty (Bloom, 2010). People old and young, female and male, whether living in Tokyo, Tehran, or Toledo, all respond negatively when asked, "If a lethal gas is leaking into a vent and is headed toward a room with seven people, is it okay to push someone into the vent—saving the seven but killing the one?" And they respond more approvingly when asked if it's okay to allow someone to fall into the vent, again sacrificing one life but saving seven (Hauser, 2006, 2009).

The universal behaviors that define human nature arise from our biological similarity. We may say, "My ancestors came from Ireland" or "My roots are in China" or "I'm Italian," but anthropologists tell us that if we could trace our ancestors back 100,000 or more years, we would see that we are all Africans (Shipman, 2003). In response to climate change and the availability of food, those early hominids migrated across Africa into Asia, Europe, the Australian subcontinent and, eventually, the Americas. As they adapted to their new environments, early humans developed differences that, measured on anthropological scales, are recent and superficial. Those who stayed in Africa had darker skin pigment—what Harvard psychologist Steven Pinker (2002) calls "sunscreen for the tropics"—and those who went far north of the equator evolved lighter skins capable of synthesizing vitamin D in less direct sunlight. Still, historically, we all are Africans.

We were Africans recently enough that "there has not been much time to accumulate many new versions of the genes," notes Pinker (2002, p. 143). Indeed, biologists who study our genes have found that we humans are strikingly similar, like members of one tribe. We may be more numerous than chimpanzees, but chimps are more genetically varied.

To explain the traits of our species, and all species, the British naturalist Charles Darwin (1859) proposed an evolutionary process. Follow the genes, he advised. Darwin's idea, to which philosopher Daniel Dennett (2005) would give "the gold medal for the best idea anybody ever had," was that **natural selection** enables evolution.

The idea, simplified, is this:

- Organisms have many and varied offspring.
- Those offspring compete for survival in their environment.
- Certain biological and behavioral variations increase their chances of reproduction and survival in that environment.
- Those offspring that do survive are more likely to pass their genes to ensuing generations.
- Thus, over time, population characteristics may change.

Natural selection implies that certain genes—those that predisposed traits that increased the odds of surviving long enough to reproduce and nurture descendants—became more abundant. In the snowy Arctic environment, for example, genes programming a thick coat of camouflaging white fur have won the genetic competition in polar bears.

Natural selection, long an organizing principle of biology, has recently become an important principle for psychology as well. **Evolutionary psychology** studies how natural selection predisposes not just physical traits suited to particular contexts—polar bears' coats, bats' sonar, humans' color vision—but also psychological traits and social behaviors that enhance the preservation and spread of one's genes (Buss, 2005, 2007, 2009). We humans are the way we are, say evolutionary psychologists, because nature selected those who had our traits—those who, for example, preferred the sweet taste of nutritious, energy-providing foods and who disliked the bitter or sour flavors of foods that are toxic. Those lacking such preferences were less likely to survive to contribute their genes to posterity.

As mobile gene machines, we carry not only the physical legacy but also the psychological legacy of our ancestors' adaptive preferences. We long for whatever helped them survive, reproduce, and nurture their offspring to survive and reproduce. Even negative emotions—anxiety, loneliness, depression, anger—are nature's way of motivating us to cope with survival challenges. "The purpose of the heart is to pump blood," notes evolutionary psychologist David Barash (2003). "The brain's purpose," he adds, is to direct our organs and our behavior "in a way that maximizes our evolutionary success. That's it."

The evolutionary perspective highlights our universal human nature. We not only share certain food preferences but we also share answers to social questions, such as, Whom should I trust? Whom should I help? When, and with whom, should I mate? Who may dominate me, and whom may I control? Evolutionary psychologists contend that our emotional and behavioral answers to those questions are the same answers that worked for our ancestors.

And what should we fear? Mostly, we fear dangers faced by our distant ancestors. We fear foes, unfamiliar faces, and heights—and thus, possible terrorists, the ethnically different, and airplanes. We fear what's immediate and sudden more than greater, gradual harms from historically newer threats, such as smoking or climate change.

Because our social tasks are common to people everywhere, humans everywhere tend to agree on the answers. For example, all humans rank others by authority and status. And all have ideas about economic justice (Fiske, 1992). Evolutionary psychologists highlight these universal characteristics that have evolved through natural selection. Cultures, however, provide the specific rules for working out these elements of social life.

CULTURE AND BEHAVIOR

Perhaps our most important similarity, the hallmark of our species, is our capacity to learn and adapt. Our genes enable an adaptive human brain—a cerebral hard drive that receives the culture's software. Evolution has prepared us to live creatively in a changing world and to thrive in environments from equatorial jungles to arctic ice fields. Compared with bees, birds, and bulldogs, nature has humans on a looser genetic leash. Ironically, our shared human biology enables our cultural diversity. It enables those in one **culture** to value promptness, welcome frankness, or accept premarital sex, whereas those in another culture do not. As social psychologist Roy Baumeister (2005, p. 29) observes, "Evolution made us for culture."

Evolutionary psychology incorporates environmental influences. It recognizes that nature and nurture interact in forming us. Genes are not fixed blueprints; their expression depends on the environment, much as the tea I am now drinking was not "expressed" until meeting a hot water environment. One study of New Zealand young adults revealed a gene variation that put people at risk for depression, but only if they had also experienced major life stresses such as a marital breakup (Caspi & others, 2003). Neither the stress nor the gene alone produced depression, but the two interacting did.

We humans have been selected not only for big brains and biceps but also for culture. We come prepared to learn language and to bond and cooperate with others in securing food, caring for young, and protecting ourselves. Nature therefore predisposes us to learn whatever culture we are born into. The cultural perspective highlights human adaptability. People's "natures are alike," said Confucius; "it is their habits that carry them far apart." And far apart we still are, note world culture researchers Ronald Inglehart and Christian Welzel (2005). Despite increasing education, "we are not moving toward a uniform global culture: cultural convergence is not taking place. A society's cultural heritage is remarkably enduring" (p. 46).

Cultural Diversity

The diversity of our languages, customs, and expressive behaviors confirms that much of our behavior is socially programmed, not hardwired. The genetic leash is long. As sociologist Ian Robertson (1987) has noted:

> Americans eat oysters but not snails. The French eat snails but not locusts. The Zulus eat locusts but not fish. The Jews eat fish but not pork. The Hindus eat pork but not beef. The Russians eat beef but not snakes. The Chinese eat snakes but not people. The Jalé of New Guinea find people delicious. (p. 67)

If we all lived as homogeneous ethnic groups in separate regions of the world, as some people still do, cultural diversity would be less relevant to our daily living. In Japan, where 98.5 percent of people are Japanese (CIA, 2011), internal cultural differences are minimal. In contrast, these differences are encountered many times each day by most residents of New York City, where more than one-third of the 8 million residents are foreign-born.

Increasingly, cultural diversity surrounds us. More and more we live in a global village, connected to our fellow villagers by electronic social networks, jumbo jets, and international trade.

Confronting another culture is sometimes a startling experience. American males may feel uncomfortable when Middle Eastern heads of state greet the U.S. president with a kiss on the cheek. A German student, accustomed to speaking to "Herr Professor" only on rare occasions, considers it strange that at my institution most faculty office doors are open and students stop by freely. An Iranian student on her first visit to an American McDonald's restaurant fumbles around in her paper bag looking for the eating utensils until she sees the other customers eating their french fries with, of all things, their hands. In many areas of the globe, your best manners and mine are serious breaches of etiquette. Foreigners visiting Japan often struggle to master the rules of the social game—when to take off their shoes, how to pour the tea, when to give and open gifts, how to act toward someone higher or lower in the social hierarchy.

Migration and refugee evacuations are mixing cultures more than ever. "East is East and West is West, and never the twain shall meet," wrote the nineteenth-century British author Rudyard Kipling. But today, East and West, and North and South, meet all the time. Italy is home to many Albanians, Germany to Turks, England (where Mohammed in its various spellings is now the most frequent name given to newborn boys [Cohen, 2011]) to Pakistanis. The result is both friendship and conflict. One in 5 Canadians and 1 in 8 Americans is an immigrant. As we work, play, and live with people from diverse cultural backgrounds, it helps to understand how our cultures influence us and how our cultures differ. In a conflict-laden world, achieving peace requires a genuine appreciation for both our genuine differences and our deep similarities.

As etiquette rules illustrate, all cultures have their accepted ideas about appropriate behavior. We often view these social expectations, or **norms**, as a negative force that imprisons people in a blind effort to perpetuate tradition. Norms do restrain and control us—so successfully and so subtly that we hardly sense their existence. Like fish in the ocean, we are all so immersed in our cultures that we must leap out of them to understand their influence. "When we see other Dutch people behaving in what foreigners would call a Dutch way," noted Dutch psychologists Willem Koomen and Anton Dijker (1997), "we often do not realize that the behavior is typically Dutch."

There is no better way to learn the norms of our culture than to visit another culture and see that its members do things *that* way, whereas we do them *this* way. When living in Scotland, I acknowledged to my children that, yes, Europeans eat meat with the fork facing down in the left hand. "But we Americans consider it good manners to cut the meat and then transfer the fork to the right hand. I admit it's inefficient. But it's the way *we* do it."

To those who don't accept them, such norms may seem arbitrary and confining. To most in the Western world, the Muslim woman's veil seems arbitrary and confining, but not to most in Muslim cultures. Just as a stage play moves smoothly when the actors know their lines, so social behavior occurs smoothly when people know what to expect. Norms grease the social machinery. In unfamiliar situations, when the norms may be unclear, we monitor others' behavior and adjust our own accordingly.

Cultures vary in their norms for expressiveness, punctuality, rule-breaking, and personal space. Consider the following:

Expressiveness

To someone from a relatively formal northern European culture, a person whose roots are in an expressive Mediterranean culture may seem "warm, charming, inefficient, and time-wasting." To the Mediterranean person, the northern European may seem "efficient, cold, and overconcerned with time" (Beaulieu, 2004; Triandis, 1981).

Punctuality

Latin American business executives who arrive late for a dinner engagement may be mystified by how obsessed their North American counterparts are with punctuality. North American tourists in Japan may wonder about the lack of eye contact from passing pedestrians.

Rule-Breaking

When people see social norms being violated, such as banned graffiti on a wall, they become more likely to follow the rule-breaking norm by violating other rules, such as littering. In six experiments, a Dutch research team led by Kees Keizer (2008) found people more than doubly likely to disobey social rules when it appeared that others were doing so. For example, when useless flyers were put on bike handles, one-third of cyclists tossed the flyer on the ground as litter when there was no graffiti on the adjacent wall. But more than two-thirds did so when the wall was covered with graffiti (Figure 12-1).

Personal Space

Personal space is a sort of portable bubble or buffer zone that we like to maintain between ourselves and others. As the situation changes, the

FIGURE 12-1
Degraded surroundings can degrade behavior. In a University of Groningen study, people mostly did not litter the ground with an unwanted flyer when an adjacent wall was clean, but *did* litter when the wall was graffiti laden.

bubble varies in size. With strangers, most Americans maintain a fairly large personal space, keeping 4 feet or more between us. On uncrowded buses, or in restrooms or libraries, we protect our space and respect others' space. We let friends come closer (Novelli & others, 2010).

Individuals differ: Some people prefer more personal space than others (Smith, 1981; Sommer, 1969; Stockdale, 1978). Groups differ, too: Adults maintain more distance than children. Men keep more distance from one another than do women. For reasons unknown, cultures near the equator prefer less space and more touching and hugging. Thus, the British and the Scandinavians prefer more distance than the French and the Arabs; North Americans prefer more space than Latin Americans.

To see the effect of encroaching on another's personal space, play space invader. Stand or sit a foot or so from a friend and strike up a conversation. Does the person fidget, look away, back off, show other signs of discomfort? These are the signs of arousal noted by space-invading researchers (Altman & Vinsel, 1978).

Cultures differ not only in their norms for such behaviors, but also in the strength of their norms. One 33-nation study asked people to rate the appropriateness of various behaviors (such as eating or crying) in different situations (such as at a bank or a party). Societies exposed to threats such as territorial conflict or resource scarcity tend to be "tighter" cultures, with strong, enforced norms (Gelfand & others, 2011).

Cultural Similarity

Thanks to human adaptability, cultures differ. Yet beneath the veneer of cultural differences, cross-cultural psychologists see "an essential universality" (Lonner, 1980). As members of one species, we find that the processes that underlie our differing behaviors are much the same everywhere. At ages 4 to 5, for example, children across the world begin to exhibit a "theory of mind" that enables them to infer what others are thinking (Norenzayan & Heine, 2005). If they witness a toy being moved while another child isn't looking, they become able—no matter their culture—to infer that the other child will *think* it still is where it was.

Universal Friendship Norms

People everywhere have some common norms for friendship. From studies conducted in Britain, Italy, Hong Kong, and Japan, Michael Argyle and Monika Henderson (1985) noted several cultural variations in the norms that define the role of friend. For example, in Japan it's especially important not to embarrass a friend with public criticism. But there are also some apparently universal norms: Respect the friend's privacy; make eye contact while talking; don't divulge things said in confidence.

Universal Status Norms

Roger Brown (1965, 1987; Kroger & Wood, 1992) has studied another universal norm. Wherever people form status hierarchies, they also talk to higher-status people in the respectful way they often talk to strangers. And they talk to lower-status people in the more familiar, first-name way they speak to friends. Patients call their physician "Dr. So and So"; the physician may reply using the patients' first names. Students and professors typically address one another in a similarly nonmutual way.

Most languages have two forms of the English pronoun "you": a respectful form and a familiar form (for example, *Sie* and *du* in German, *vous* and *tu* in French, *usted* and *tu* in Spanish). People typically use the familiar form with intimates and subordinates—with close friends and family members but also in speaking to children and pets. A German adolescent receives a boost when strangers begin addressing him or her as "Sie" instead of "du."

This first aspect of Brown's universal norm—that *forms of address communicate not only social distance but also social status*—correlates with a second aspect: *Advances in intimacy are usually suggested by the higher-status person.* In Europe, where most twosomes begin a relationship with the polite, formal "you" and may eventually progress to the more intimate "you," someone obviously has to initiate the increased intimacy. Who do you suppose does so? On some congenial occasion, the elder or richer or more distinguished of the two is the one to say, "Let's say 'du' to each other."

This norm extends beyond language to every type of advance in intimacy. It is more acceptable to borrow a pen from or put a hand on the shoulder of one's intimates and subordinates than to behave in such a casual way with strangers or superiors. Similarly, the president of my college invites faculty to his home before they invite him to theirs. In the progression toward intimacy, the higher-status person is typically the pacesetter.

The Incest Taboo

The best-known universal norm is the taboo against incest: Parents are not to have sexual relations with their children, nor siblings with one another. Although the taboo apparently is violated more often than psychologists once believed, the norm is still universal. Every society disapproves of incest. Given the biological penalties for inbreeding (through the emergence of disorders linked to recessive genes), evolutionary psychologists can easily understand why people everywhere are predisposed against incest.

Norms of War

Humans even have cross-cultural norms for conducting war. In the midst of killing one's enemy, there are agreed-upon rules that have been honored for centuries. You are to wear identifiable uniforms, surrender with a gesture of submission, and treat prisoners humanely. (If you can't kill them before they surrender, you should feed them thereafter.) However, although cross-cultural, these norms are not universal. During the Iraq War that began under the George W. Bush administration, Iraqi forces violated these norms by showing surrender flags and then attacking, and by dressing soldiers as liberated civilians to set up ambushes. A U.S. military spokesperson complained that "both of these actions are among the most serious violations of the laws of war" (Clarke, 2003).

So, some norms are culture-specific, others are universal. The force of culture appears in varying norms, whereas it is largely our genetic predispositions—our human nature—that account for the universality of some norms. Thus, we might think of nature as universal and nurture as culture-specific.

CONCEPTS TO REMEMBER

natural selection   The evolutionary process by which heritable traits that best enable organisms to survive and reproduce in particular environments are passed to ensuing generations.

evolutionary psychology   The study of the evolution of cognition and behavior using principles of natural selection.

culture   The enduring behaviors, ideas, attitudes, and traditions shared by a large group of people and transmitted from one generation to the next.

norms   Standards for accepted and expected behavior. Norms prescribe "proper" behavior. (In a different sense of the word, norms also describe what most others do—what is *normal*.)

personal space   The buffer zone we like to maintain around our bodies. Its size depends on our familiarity with whoever is near us.

13

❖

Gender, Genes, and Culture

T here are many obvious dimensions of human diversity—height, weight, hair color, to name a few. But for people's self-concepts and social relationships, the two dimensions that matter most—and that people first attune to—are race and, especially, gender (Stangor & others, 1992). When you were born, the first thing people wanted to know about you was, "Is it a boy or a girl?" It's believed to be either one or the other, and not a matter left to choice. When a Canadian couple in 2011 vowed to keep secret the gender of their baby, "Storm," so that the child could later develop its own gender identity without having to meet gender expectations, a storm of criticism erupted (AP, 2011).

GENDER AND GENES

Later we will consider how race and sex affect the way others regard and treat us. For now, let's consider **gender**—the characteristics people associate with male and female. What behaviors are characteristic and expected of males? of females?

"Of the 46 chromosomes in the human genome, 45 are unisex," noted Judith Rich Harris (1998). Females and males are therefore similar in many physical traits and developmental milestones, such as the age of sitting up, teething, and walking. They also are alike in many psychological traits, such as overall vocabulary, creativity, intelligence, self-esteem, and happiness. Women and men feel the same emotions and longings, both dote on their children, and they have similar-appearing brains (although, on average, men have more neurons and women have more neural connections). Indeed, noted Janet Shibley Hyde (2005) from her review of 46 meta-analyses (each a statistical digest of dozens of studies), the common result for most variables studied is *gender similarity*. Your "opposite sex" is actually your nearly identical sex.

So shall we conclude that men and women are essentially the same, except for a few anatomical oddities that hardly matter apart from special occasions? Actually, some differences do exist, and it is these differences, not the many similarities, that capture attention and make news. In both science and everyday life, differences excite interest—enough to have stimulated some 18,000 studies comparing females and males (Ellis & others, 2008). Compared with males, the average female

- has 70 percent more fat, has 40 percent less muscle, is 5 inches shorter, and weighs 40 pounds less.
- is more sensitive to smells and sounds.
- is doubly vulnerable to anxiety disorders and depression.

Compared with females, the average male is

- slower to enter puberty (by about two years) but quicker to die (by four years, worldwide).
- three times more likely to be diagnosed with ADHD (attention deficit/hyperactivity disorder), four times more likely to commit suicide, and five times more likely to be killed by lightning.
- more capable of wiggling the ears.

During the 1970s, many scholars worried that studies of such gender differences might reinforce stereotypes. Would gender differences be construed as women's deficits? Although the findings confirm some stereotypes of women—as less physically aggressive, more nurturant, and more socially sensitive—those traits are not only celebrated by many feminists but also preferred by most people, whether male or female (Prentice & Carranza, 2002; Swim, 1994). Small wonder, then, that most people rate their beliefs and feelings regarding women as more *favorable* than their feelings regarding men (Eagly, 1994; Haddock & Zanna, 1994).

*G*ENDER DIFFERENCES

Let's compare men's and women's social connections, dominance, aggressiveness, and sexuality. After we have described these few differences, we can then consider how the evolutionary and cultural perspectives might explain them. Do gender differences reflect natural selection? Are they culturally constructed—a reflection of the roles that men and women often play and the situations in which they act? Or do genes and culture together bend the genders?

Independence versus Connectedness

Individual men display outlooks and behavior that vary from fierce competitiveness to caring nurturance. So do individual women. Without denying that, several late-twentieth-century feminist psychologists contended that women more than men give priority to close, intimate relationships (Chodorow, 1978, 1989; Gilligan, 1982; Gilligan & others, 1990; Miller, 1986). Consider the evidence:

Play

Compared with boys, girls talk more intimately and play less aggressively, noted Eleanor Maccoby (2002) from her decades of research on gender development. They also play in smaller groups, often talking with one friend. Boys more often do larger group activities (Rose & Rudolph, 2006). And as they each interact with their own gender, their differences from girls grow.

Friendship

As adults, women in individualist cultures describe themselves in more relational terms, welcome more help, experience more relationship-linked emotions, and are more attuned to others' relationships (Addis & Mahalik, 2003; Gabriel & Gardner, 1999; Tamres & others, 2002; Watkins & others, 1998, 2003). In conversation, men more often focus on tasks and on connections with large groups, whereas women focus on personal relationships (Tannen, 1990). "Perhaps because of their greater desire for intimacy," report Joyce Benenson and colleagues (2009), during their first year of college, women are twice as likely as men to change roommates.

On the phone, women's conversations last longer, and girls send more than twice as many text messages as do boys (Friebel & Seabright, 2011; Lenhart, 2010; Smoreda & Licoppe, 2000). On the computer, women also spend more time sending e-mails, in which they express more emotion (Crabtree, 2002; Thomson & Murachver, 2001). And they spend more time on social networking sites (Pryor & others, 2010).

When in groups, women share more of their lives and offer more support (Dindia & Allen, 1992; Eagly, 1987). When facing stress, men tend to respond with "fight or flight"; often, their response to a threat is combat. In nearly all studies, notes Shelley Taylor (2002), women who are under stress more often "tend and befriend"; they turn to friends and family for support. Among first-year college students, 5 in 10 males and 7 in 10 females say it is *very* important to "help others who are in difficulty" (Sax & others, 2002).

Vocations
In general, report Felicia Pratto and her colleagues (1997), men gravitate disproportionately to jobs that enhance inequalities (prosecuting attorney, corporate advertising); women gravitate to jobs that reduce inequalities (public defender, advertising work for a charity). Studies of 640,000 people's job preferences reveal that men more than women value earnings, promotion, challenge, and power; women more than men value good hours, personal relationships, and opportunities to help others (Konrad & others, 2000; Pinker, 2008). Indeed, in most of the North American caregiving professions, such as social worker, teacher, and nurse, women outnumber men. Worldwide, women's vocational interests, compared with men's, usually relate more to people and less to things (Diekman & others, 2010; Eagly, 2009; Lippa, 2008a).

Family Relations
Women's connections as mothers, daughters, sisters, and grandmothers bind families (Rossi & Rossi, 1990). Following their child's birth, parents (women especially) become more traditional in their gender-related attitudes and behaviors (Ferriman & others, 2009; Katz-Wise, 2010). Women spend more time caring for both preschoolers and aging parents (Eagly & Crowley, 1986). Compared with men, they buy three times as many gifts and greeting cards, write two to four times as many personal letters, and make 10 to 20 percent more long-distance calls to friends and family (Putnam, 2000). Asked to provide photos that portray who they are, women include more photos of parents and of themselves with others (Clancy & Dollinger, 1993).

Empathy
When surveyed, women are far more likely to describe themselves as having **empathy**, or being able to feel what another feels—to rejoice with those who rejoice and weep with those who weep. To a lesser extent, the empathy difference extends to laboratory studies:

- Shown slides or told stories, girls react with more empathy (Hunt, 1990).
- Given upsetting experiences in the laboratory or in real life, women more than men express empathy for others enduring similar experiences (Batson & others, 1996).
- Observing another receiving pain after misbehaving, women's empathy-related brain circuits display elevated activity even when men's do not—after the other had misbehaved (Singer & others, 2006).
- Women are more likely to cry or report feeling distressed at another's distress (Eisenberg & Lennon, 1983). In a 2003 Gallup poll, 12 percent of American men and 43 percent of women reported having cried as a result of the war in Iraq.

All these differences help to explain why, compared with male friendships, both men and women report friendships with women to be more intimate, enjoyable, and nurturing (Rubin, 1985; Sapadin, 1988). When you want empathy and understanding, someone to whom you can disclose your joys and hurts, to whom do you turn? Most men and women usually turn to women.

One explanation for this male–female empathy difference is that women tend to outperform men at reading others' emotions. In her analysis of 125 studies of men's and women's sensitivity to nonverbal cues, Judith Hall (1984, 2006) discerned that women are generally superior at decoding others' emotional messages. For example, shown a 2-second silent film clip of the face of an upset woman, women guess more accurately whether she is criticizing someone or discussing her divorce. Women also are more often strikingly better than men at recalling others' appearance, report Marianne Schmid Mast and Judith Hall (2006). In experiments, high-status people are less accurate in reading others' emotions (Kraus & others, 2010).

Finally, women are more skilled at *expressing* emotions nonverbally, says Hall. This is especially so for positive emotion, report Erick Coats and Robert Feldman (1996). They had people talk about times they had been happy, sad, and angry. When shown 5-second silent video clips of those reports, observers could much more accurately discern women's than men's emotions when recalling happiness. Men, however, were slightly more successful in conveying anger.

Social Dominance

Imagine two people: One is "adventurous, autocratic, coarse, dominant, forceful, independent, and strong." The other is "affectionate, dependent, dreamy, emotional, submissive, and weak." If the first person sounds more to you like a man and the second like a woman, you are not alone, report John Williams and Deborah Best (1990, p. 15). From Asia to Africa and Europe to Australia, people rate men as more dominant, driven, and aggressive. Moreover, studies of nearly 80,000 people across 70 countries show that men more than women rate power and achievement as important (Schwartz & Rubel, 2005).

These perceptions and expectations correlate with reality. In essentially every society, men *are* socially dominant (Pratto, 1996). As Peter Hegarty and his colleagues (2010) have observed, across time, men's names have come first: "King and Queen," "his and hers," "Mr. and Mrs.," "Bill and Hillary." Shakespeare never wrote plays with titles such as *Juliet and Romeo* or *Cleopatra and Antony.*

As we will see, gender differences vary greatly by culture, and gender differences are shrinking in many industrialized societies as women assume more managerial and leadership positions. Yet

- Women in 2011 were but 19 percent of the world's legislators (IPU, 2011).

- Men more than women are concerned with social dominance and are more likely to favor conservative political candidates and programs that preserve group inequality (Eagly & others, 2004; Sidanius & Pratto, 1999).

- Men are half of all jurors but have been 90 percent of elected jury leaders; men are also the leaders of most ad hoc laboratory groups (Colarelli & others, 2006; Davis & Gilbert, 1989; Kerr & others, 1982).

- In Britain, men hold 87 percent of top-100 company board positions (BIS, 2011).

Across many studies, people *perceive* leaders as having more culturally masculine traits—as being more confident, forceful, independent, and outspoken (Koenig & others, 2011). When writing letters of recommendation, people more often use such "agentic" adjectives when describing male candidates, and more "communal" adjectives (helpful, kind, sympathetic, nurturing, tactful) when describing women candidates (Madera & others, 2009). The net effect may be to disadvantage women applying for leadership roles.

Men's style of communicating undergirds their social power. In situations where roles aren't rigidly scripted, men tend to be more autocratic, women more democratic (Eagly & Carli, 2007). In leadership roles, men tend to excel as directive, task-focused leaders; women excel more often in the "transformational" leadership that is favored by more and more organizations, with inspirational and social skills that build team spirit. Men more than women place priority on winning, getting ahead, and dominating others (Sidanius & others, 1994). This may explain why people's preference for a male leader is greater for competitions between groups, such as when countries are at war, than when conflicts occur within a group (Van Vugt & Spisak, 2008).

Men also act more impulsively and take more risks (Byrnes & others, 1999; Cross & others, 2011). One study of data from 35,000 stockbroker accounts found that "men are more overconfident than women" and therefore made 45 percent more stock trades (Barber & Odean, 2001a). Because trading costs money, and because men's trades proved no more successful, their results underperformed the stock market by 2.65 percent, compared with women's 1.72 percent underperformance. The men's trades were riskier—and the men were the poorer for it.

In writing, women tend to use more communal prepositions ("with"), fewer quantitative words, and more present tense. One computer program, which taught itself to recognize gender differences in word usage and sentence structure, successfully identified the author's gender in 80 percent of 920 British fiction and nonfiction works (Koppel & others, 2002).

In conversation, men's style reflects their concern for independence, women's for connectedness. Men are more likely to act as powerful people often do—talking assertively, interrupting intrusively, touching with the hand, staring more, smiling less (Leaper & Robnett, 2011). Stating the results from a female perspective, women's influence style tends to be more indirect—less interruptive, more sensitive, more polite, less cocky, and more qualified and hedged.

So is it right to declare (in the title words of one 1990s bestseller), *Men Are from Mars, Women Are from Venus?* Actually, note Kay Deaux and Marianne LaFrance (1998), men's and women's conversational styles vary with the social context. Much of the style we attribute to men is typical of people (men and women) in positions of status and power (Hall & others, 2006). For example, students nod more when speaking with professors than when speaking with peers, and women nod more than men (Helweg-Larsen & others, 2004). Men—and people in high-status roles—tend to talk louder and to interrupt more (Hall & others, 2005). Moreover, individuals vary; some men are hesitant, some women assertive. To suggest that women and men are from different emotional planets greatly oversimplifies.

Aggression

By **aggression**, psychologists mean behavior intended to hurt. Throughout the world, hunting, fighting, and warring are primarily male activities (Wood & Eagly, 2007). In surveys, men admit to more aggression than do women. In laboratory experiments, men indeed exhibit more physical aggression, for example, by administering what they believe are hurtful electric shocks (Knight & others, 1996). In Canada, the male-to-female arrest ratio is 8 to 1 for murder (Statistics Canada, 2010). In the United States, where 92 percent of prisoners are male, it is 9 to 1 (FBI, 2009). Almost all suicide terrorists have been young men (Kruglanski & Golec de Zavala, 2005). So also are nearly all battlefield deaths and death row inmates.

But again the gender difference fluctuates with the context. When there is provocation, the gender gap shrinks (Bettencourt & Kernahan, 1997; Richardson, 2005). And within less assaultive forms of aggression—for instance, slapping a family member, throwing something, or verbally attacking someone—women are no less aggressive than men (Björkqvist, 1994; White & Kowalski, 1994). Indeed, says John Archer (2000, 2004, 2007, 2009) from his statistical digests of dozens of studies, women may be slightly more likely to commit indirect aggressive acts, such as spreading malicious gossip. But all across the world and at all ages, men much more often injure others with physical aggression.

Sexuality

There is also a gender gap in sexual attitudes and assertiveness (Petersen & Hyde, 2010). It's true that in their physiological and subjective responses to sexual stimuli, women and men are "more similar than different" (Griffitt, 1987). Yet consider the following:

Activity
13.1

- "I can imagine myself being comfortable and enjoying 'casual' sex with different partners," agreed 48 percent of men and 12 percent of women in an Australian survey (Bailey & others, 2000). One 48-nation study showed country-by-country variation in acceptance of unrestricted sexuality, ranging from relatively promiscuous Finland to relatively monogamous Taiwan (Schmitt, 2005). But in every country studied, it was the men who expressed more desire for unrestricted sex. Likewise, when the BBC surveyed more than 200,000 people in 53 nations, men everywhere more strongly agreed that "I have a strong sex drive" (Lippa, 2008b).

- The American Council on Education's recent survey of a quarter of a million first-year college students offers a similar finding. "If two people really like each other, it's all right for them to have sex even if they've known each other for only a very short time," agreed 58 percent of men but only 34 percent of women (Pryor & others, 2005).

- In a survey of 3,400 randomly selected 18- to 59-year-old Americans, half as many men (25 percent) as women (48 percent) cited affection for the partner as a reason for first intercourse. How often do they think about sex? "Every day" or "several times a day," said 19 percent of women and 54 percent of men (Laumann & others, 1994). Canadians concur, with 11 percent of women and 46 percent of men saying "several times a day" (Fischstein & others, 2007).

The gender difference in sexual attitudes carries over to behavior. "With few exceptions anywhere in the world," reported cross-cultural psychologist Marshall Segall and his colleagues (1990, p. 244), "males are more likely than females to initiate sexual activity."

Compared with lesbians, gay men also report more interest in uncommitted sex, more frequent sex, more interest in pornography, more responsiveness to visual stimuli, and more concern with partner attractiveness (Peplau & Fingerhut, 2007; Rupp & Wallen, 2008; Schmitt, 2007). The 47 percent of coupled American lesbians is double the 24 percent of gay men who are coupled (Doyle, 2005). Among those electing civil unions in Vermont and same-sex marriage in Massachusetts, two-thirds have been female couples (Belluck, 2008; Rothblum, 2007). "It's not that gay men are oversexed," observed Steven Pinker (1997). "They are simply men whose male desires bounce off other male desires rather than off female desires."

Indeed, not only do men fantasize more about sex, have more permissive attitudes, and seek more partners, they also are more quickly aroused, desire sex more often, masturbate more frequently, use more pornography, are less successful at celibacy, refuse sex less often, take more risks, expend more resources to gain sex, and prefer more sexual variety (Baumeister & others, 2001; Baumeister & Vohs, 2004; Petersen & Hyde, 2011). In one sample of 18- to 25-year-old collegians, the median man thought about sex about once per hour, the median woman about once every two hours, albeit with great individual differences (Fisher & others, 2011). One survey asked 16,288 people from 52 nations how many sexual partners they desired in the next month. Among those unattached, 29 percent of men and 6 percent of women wanted more than one partner (Schmitt, 2003, 2005). These results were identical for straight and gay people (29 percent of gay men and 6 percent of lesbians desired more than one partner).

"Everywhere sex is understood to be something females have that males want," offered anthropologist Donald Symons (1979, p. 253). Small wonder, say Baumeister and Vohs, that cultures everywhere attribute greater value to female than male sexuality, as indicated in gender asymmetries in prostitution and courtship, where men generally offer money, gifts, praise, or commitment in implicit exchange for a woman's sexual engagement. In human sexual economics, they note, women rarely if ever pay for sex. Like labor unions opposing "scab labor" as undermining the value of their own work, most women oppose other women's offering "cheap sex," which reduces the value of their own sexuality. Across 185 countries, the scarcer the available men, the *higher* is the teen pregnancy rate—because when men are scarce "women compete against each other by offering sex at a lower price in terms of commitment" (Barber, 2000; Baumeister & Vohs, 2004). When women are scarce, as is increasingly the case in China and India, the market value of their sexuality rises, and they are able to command greater commitment.

Sexual fantasies, too, express the gender difference (Ellis & Symons, 1990). In male-oriented erotica, women are unattached and lust driven. In romance novels, whose primary market is women, a tender male is emotionally consumed by his devoted passion for the heroine. Social scientists aren't the only ones to have noticed. "Women can be fascinated by a four-hour movie with subtitles wherein the entire plot consists of a man and a woman yearning to have, but never actually having a relationship," observes humorist Dave Barry (1995). "Men HATE that. Men can take maybe 45 seconds of yearning, and they want everybody to get naked. Followed by a car chase. A movie called 'Naked People in Car Chases' would do really well among men."

*E*VOLUTION AND GENDER: DOING WHAT COMES NATURALLY?

Mindful of the evidence, gender researcher Diane Halpern (2010) describes "consistent findings of sex differences that hold up across studies, across species, and across cultures." But why? "What do you think is the main reason men and women have different personalities, interests, and abilities?" asked the Gallup Organization (1990) in a national survey. "Is it mainly because of the way men and women are raised, or are the differences part of their biological makeup?" Among the 99 percent who answered the question (apparently without questioning its assumptions), about the same percentage answered "upbringing" as said "biology."

There are, of course, certain salient biological sex differences. Men's genes predispose the muscle mass to hunt game; women's the capability to breastfeed infants. Are biological sex differences limited to such obvious distinctions in reproduction and physique? Or do men's and women's genes, hormones, and brains differ in ways that also contribute to behavioral differences?

Gender and Mating Preferences

Noting the worldwide persistence of gender differences in aggressiveness, dominance, and sexuality, evolutionary psychologist Douglas Kenrick (1987) suggested, as have many others since, that "we cannot change the evolutionary history of our species, and some of the differences between us are undoubtedly a function of that history." Evolutionary psychology predicts no sex differences in all those domains in which the sexes faced similar adaptive challenges (Buss, 1995b, 2009). Both sexes regulate heat with sweat. The two have similar taste preferences to nourish their bodies. And they both grow calluses where the skin meets friction. But evolutionary psychology does predict sex differences in behaviors relevant to mating and reproduction.

Consider, for example, the male's greater sexual initiative. The average male produces many trillions of sperm in his lifetime, making sperm cheap compared with eggs. (If you happen to be an average man, you will make more than 1,000 sperm while reading this sentence.) Moreover, while a female brings one fetus to term and then nurses it, a male can spread his genes by fertilizing many females. Women's investment in childbearing is, just for starters, 9 months; men's investment may be 9 seconds.

Thus, say evolutionary psychologists, females invest their reproductive opportunities carefully, by looking for signs of resources and commitment. Males compete with other males for chances to win the genetic sweepstakes by sending their genes into the future, and thus look for healthy, fertile soil in which to plant their seed. Women want to find men who will help them tend the garden—resourceful and monogamous dads rather than wandering cads. Women seek to reproduce wisely, men widely. Or so the theory goes.

Video 13.1

Moreover, evolutionary psychology suggests, physically dominant males excelled in gaining access to females, which over generations enhanced male aggression and dominance as the less-aggressive males had fewer chances to reproduce. Exposing men to images of attractive women primes increased support for international aggression, which is consistent with the theory that mating desires may be one motivation for war (Chang & others, 2011). Whatever genes helped Montezuma II to become Aztec king were also given to his offspring, along with those from many of the 4,000 women in his harem (Wright, 1998). If our ancestral mothers benefited from being able to read their infants' and suitors' emotions, then natural selection may have similarly favored emotion-detecting ability in females. Underlying all these presumptions is a principle: *Nature selects traits that help send one's genes into the future.*

Little of this process is conscious. Few people in the throes of passion stop to think, "I want to give my genes to posterity." Rather, say evolutionary psychologists, our natural yearnings are our genes' way of making more genes. Emotions execute evolution's dispositions, much as hunger executes the body's need for nutrients.

Evolutionary psychology also predicts that men will strive to offer what women will desire—external resources and physical protection. Male peacocks strut their feathers; male humans, their abs, Audis, and assets (Sundie & others, 2011). In one experiment, teen males rated "having lots of money" as more important after they were put alone in a room with a teen female (Roney, 2003). In one Cardiff, Wales, study, men rated a woman as equally attractive whether she was at the wheel of a humble Ford Fiesta or a swanky Bentley; women found the man more attractive if seen in the luxury car (Dunn & Searle, 2010). "Male achievement is ultimately a courtship display," says Glenn Wilson (1994).

To attract men, women may balloon their breasts, Botox their wrinkles, and liposuction their fat to offer men the youthful, healthy appearance (connoting fertility) that men desire—while, in some experiments, demeaning the success and appearance of other attractive women (Agthe & others, 2008; Vukovic & others, 2008). Women's and men's mate preferences confirm these observations. Studies in 37 cultures, from Australia to Zambia, reveal that men everywhere feel attracted to women whose physical features, such as youthful faces and forms, suggest fertility. Women everywhere feel attracted to men whose wealth, power, and ambition promise resources for protecting and nurturing offspring. But there are gender similarities, too: Whether residing on an Indonesian island or in urban São Paulo, both women and men desire kindness, love, and mutual attraction.

Monthly fertility also matters. Women's behaviors, scents, and voices provide subtle clues to their ovulation, which men can detect (Haselton &

Gildersleeve, 2011). When at peak fertility, women express greater preference for masculine faces, greater apprehensiveness of potentially threatening men, and greater ability to detect men's sexual orientation (Eastwick, 2009; Little & others, 2008; Navarrete & others, 2009; Rule & others, 2011).

Reflecting on those findings, Buss (1999) reports feeling somewhat astonished "that men and women across the world differ in their mate preferences in precisely the ways predicted by the evolutionists. Just as our fears of snakes, heights, and spiders provide a window for viewing the survival hazards of our evolutionary ancestors, our mating desires provide a window for viewing the resources our ancestors needed for reproduction. We all carry with us today the desires of our successful forebears."

REFLECTIONS ON EVOLUTIONARY PSYCHOLOGY

Without disputing natural selection—nature's process of selecting physical and behavioral traits that enhance gene survival—critics see a problem with evolutionary explanations. Evolutionary psychologists sometimes start with an effect (such as the male-female difference in sexual initiative) and then work backward to construct an explanation for it. That approach is reminiscent of functionalism, a dominant theory in psychology during the 1920s, whose logic went like this: "Why does that behavior occur? Because it serves such and such a function." As biologists Paul Ehrlich and Marcus Feldman (2003) have pointed out, the evolutionary theorist can hardly lose when employing hindsight. Today's evolutionary psychology is like yesterday's Freudian psychology, say such critics: Either theory can be retrofitted to whatever happens.

The way to overcome the hindsight bias is to imagine things turning out otherwise. Let's try it. Imagine that women were stronger and more physically aggressive than men. "But of course!" someone might say, "all the better for protecting their young." And if human males were never known to have extramarital affairs, might we not see the evolutionary wisdom behind their fidelity? There is more to bringing offspring to maturity than merely depositing sperm, so men and women both gain by investing jointly in their children. Males who are loyal to their mates and offspring are more apt to ensure that their young will survive to perpetuate their genes. Monogamy also increases men's certainty of paternity. (These are, in fact, evolutionary explanations—again based on hindsight—for why humans, and certain other species whose young require a heavy parental investment, tend to pair off and be monogamous).

Evolutionary psychologists reply that criticisms of their theories as being hindsight-based are "flat-out wrong." They argue that hindsight plays no less a role in cultural explanations: Why do women and men differ? Because their culture *socializes* their behavior! When people's roles vary across time and place, "culture" *describes* those roles better than it explains them. And far from being mere hindsight conjecture, say evolutionary psychologists, their field is an empirical science that tests evolutionary predictions with data from animal behavior, cross-cultural observations, and hormonal and genetic studies. As in many scientific fields, observations inspire a theory that generates new, testable predictions. The predictions alert us to unnoticed phenomena and allow us to confirm, refute, or revise the theory. Thus, evolutionary psychologists take credit for predicting—and confirming—that

- gender generates jealousy (Levy & Kelly, 2010). Men more often than women experience sexual jealousy (concern about their partner's physical relationship with another). Women more than men experience emotional jealousy (concern about their partner's emotional involvement with another).
- we favor others who share our genes, such as family members, or can return our favors.
- our memories tend to retain survival-relevant information, such as food location (Confer & others, 2010).

Evolutionary psychology's critics acknowledge that evolution helps explain both our commonalities and our differences (a certain amount of diversity aids survival). But they contend that our common evolutionary heritage does not, by itself, predict the enormous cultural variation in human marriage patterns (from one spouse to a succession of spouses to multiple wives to multiple husbands to spouse swapping). Nor does it explain cultural changes in behavior patterns over mere decades of time. The most significant trait that nature has endowed us with, it seems, is the capacity to adapt—to learn and to change. Evolution is *not* genetic determinism, say its defenders, because evolution has prepared us to adapt to varied environments (Confer & others, 2010). As everyone agrees, cultures vary and cultures change.

Gender and Hormones

If genes predispose gender-related traits, they must do so by their effects on our bodies. In male embryos, the genes direct the formation of testes, which begin to secrete testosterone, the male sex hormone that influences masculine appearance. Studies indicate that girls who were exposed to excess testosterone during fetal development tend to exhibit more tomboyish play behavior than other girls (Hines, 2004). Other case studies have followed males who, having been born without penises, are reared as girls (Reiner & Gearhart, 2004). Despite their being put in dresses and treated as girls, most exhibit male-typical play and eventually—in most cases, not without emotional distress—come to have a male identity.

The gender gap in aggression also seems influenced by testosterone. In various animals, administering testosterone heightens aggressiveness. In humans, violent male criminals have higher than normal testosterone levels; so do National Football League players and boisterous fraternity members (Dabbs, 2000). Moreover, for both humans and monkeys, the gender difference in aggression appears early in life (before culture has much effect) and wanes as testosterone levels decline during adulthood. No one of these lines of evidence is conclusive. Taken together, they convince many scholars that sex hormones matter. But so, as we will see, does culture.

CULTURE AND GENDER

Culture, as we noted earlier, is what's shared by a large group and transmitted across generations—ideas, attitudes, behaviors, and traditions. Like biological creatures, cultures vary and compete for resources and thus evolve over time (Mesoudi, 2009). Cultures evolve through a "culture cycle," noted Hazel Markus and Alana Conner (2011): "1) people create the cultures to which they later adapt, and 2) cultures shape people so that they act in ways that perpetuate their cultures." Humans are culturally shaped culture shapers.

We can see the shaping power of culture in ideas about how men and women should behave. And we can see culture in the disapproval they endure when they violate those expectations (Kite, 2001). In countries everywhere, girls spend more time helping with housework and child care, and boys spend more time in unsupervised play (Edwards, 1991; Kalenkoski & others, 2009; United Nations, 2010). Even in contemporary, dual-career, North American marriages, men do most of the household repairs, and women arrange the child care (Bianchi & others, 2000; Fisher & others, 2007). Such behavior expectations for males and females—of who should cook, wash dishes, hunt game, and lead companies and countries—define **gender roles.**

Does culture construct these gender roles? Or do gender roles merely reflect men's and women's natural behavior tendencies? The variety of gender roles across cultures and over time shows that culture indeed helps construct our gender roles.

Gender Roles Vary with Culture and Time

Despite gender role inequalities, the majority of the world's people would ideally like to see more parallel male and female roles. A 2003 Pew Global Attitudes survey asked 38,000 people whether life was more satisfying when both spouses work and share child care, or when women stay home and care for the children while the husband provides. In 41 of 44 countries, most chose the first answer.

However, big country-to-country differences exist. Egyptians disagreed with the world majority opinion by 2 to 1, whereas Vietnamese concurred by 11 to 1. When jobs are scarce, should men have more right to a job? Yes, agreed about 1 in 8 people in Britain, Spain, and the United States—and 4 in 5 people in Indonesia, Pakistan, and Nigeria (Pew, 2010, July 10).

In the last half-century—a thin slice of our long history—gender roles have changed dramatically. In 1938, just 1 in 5 Americans approved "of a married woman earning money in business or industry if she has a husband capable of supporting her." By 1996, 4 in 5 approved (Niemi & others, 1989; NORC, 1996). In 1967, 57 percent of first-year American collegians agreed that "the activities of married women are best confined to the home and family." In 2005, when the question was last asked, only 20 percent agreed (Astin & others, 1987; Pryor & others, 2005).

Behavioral changes have accompanied this attitude shift. In 1965 the Harvard Business School had never granted a degree to a woman. In 2010, 38 percent of its graduates were women. From 1960 to 2011, women rose from 6 percent to 47 percent of U.S. medical students and from 3 percent to 50 percent of law students (AMA, 2010; ABA, 2011; Hunt, 2000). In the mid-1960s American married women devoted *seven times* as many hours to housework as did their husbands (Bianchi & others, 2000). By 2010, the gender gap had shrunk, yet persisted: 20 percent of men and 49 percent of women did housework in an average day; with women averaging 2.6 hours on their housework days and men 2.1 hours on theirs (BLS, 2011).

The changing male-female roles cross many cultures, as illustrated by women's gradually increasing representation in the parliaments of most nations (Inglehart & Welzel, 2005; IPU, 2011). Such changes, across cultures and over a remarkably short time, signal that evolution and biology do not fix gender roles: Time also bends the genders.

CONCLUSIONS: BIOLOGY *AND* CULTURE

We needn't think of evolution and culture as competitors. Cultural norms subtly yet powerfully affect our attitudes and behavior. But they don't do so independent of biology. Everything social and psychological is ultimately biological. If others' expectations influence us, that is part of our biological programming. Moreover, what our biological heritage initiates, culture may accentuate. Genes and hormones predispose males to be more physically aggressive than females. But culture amplifies that difference through norms that expect males to be tough and females to be the kinder, gentler sex.

Biology and culture may also **interact.** Advances in genetic science indicate how experience uses genes to change the brain (Quartz & Sejnowski, 2002). Environmental stimuli can activate genes that produce new brain cell branching receptors. Visual experience activates genes that develop the brain's visual area. Parental touch activates genes that help offspring cope with future stressful events. Genes are not set in stone; they respond adaptively to our experiences.

A new field of *epigenetics* (meaning "in addition to" genetics) explores the molecular mechanisms by which environments trigger genetic expression. Experience may attach complex molecules to parts of DNA molecules, thereby preventing any genes in that stretch of DNA from producing the proteins coded by that gene. Diet, drugs, and stress, including child abuse, can all produce the epigenetic molecules that regulate gene expression (Champagne & others, 2003; Champagne & Mashoodh, 2009; McGowan & others, 2010).

Biology and experience interact when biological traits influence how the environment reacts. Men, being 8 percent taller and averaging almost double the proportion of muscle mass, are bound to experience life differently from women. Or consider this: A very strong cultural norm dictates that males should be taller than their female mates. In one U.S. study, only 1 in 720 married couples violated that norm (Gillis & Avis, 1980). With hindsight, we can speculate a psychological explanation: Perhaps being taller helps men perpetuate their social power over women. But we can also speculate evolutionary wisdom that might underlie the cultural norm: If people preferred partners of their own height, tall men and short women would often be without partners. As it is, evolution dictates that men tend to be taller than women, and culture dictates the same for couples. So the height norm might well be a result of biology *and* culture.

Alice Eagly (2009) and Wendy Wood (Wood & Eagly, 2007) theorize how biology and culture interact (Figure 13-1). They believe that a variety of factors, including biological influences and childhood socialization, predispose a sexual division of labor. In adult life the immediate causes of

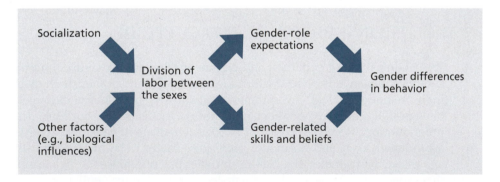

FIGURE 13-1
A social-role theory of gender differences in social behavior. Various influences, including childhood experiences and factors, bend males and females toward differing roles. It is the expectations and the skills and beliefs associated with these differing roles that affect men's and women's behavior.   Source: Adapted from Eagly (1987, 2009) and Eagly & Wood (1991).

gender differences in social behavior are the *roles* that reflect this sexual division of labor. Men, because of their biologically endowed strength and speed, tend to be found in roles demanding physical power. Women's capacity for childbearing and breastfeeding inclines them to more nurturant roles. Each sex then tends to exhibit the behaviors expected of those who fill such roles and to have their skills and beliefs shaped accordingly. Nature and nurture are a "tangled web." As role assignments become more equal, Eagly predicts that gender differences "will gradually lessen."

CONCEPTS TO REMEMBER

gender In psychology, the characteristics, whether biological or socially influenced, by which people define male and female.

empathy The vicarious experience of another's feelings; putting oneself in another's shoes.

aggression Physical or verbal behavior intended to hurt someone. In laboratory experiments, this might mean delivering electric shocks or saying something likely to hurt another's feelings.

gender role A set of behavior expectations (norms) for males and females.

interaction A relationship in which the effect of one factor (such as biology) depends on another factor (such as environment).

14

❖

How Nice People Get Corrupted

Y ou have surely experienced the phenomenon: As a controversial speaker or a music concert finishes, the adoring fans near the front leap to their feet, applauding. The approving folks just behind them follow their example and join the standing ovation. Now the wave of people standing reaches people who, unprompted, would merely be giving polite applause from their comfortable seats. Seated among them, part of you wants to stay seated ("this speaker was nothing exciting"). But as the wave of standing people sweeps by, will you alone stay seated? It's not easy being a minority of one. Unless you heartily dislike what you've just heard, you will probably rise to your feet, at least briefly.

Researchers who study **conformity** construct miniature social worlds—laboratory microcultures that simplify and simulate important features of everyday social influence. Consider two noted sets of experiments. Each provides a method for studying conformity—and some startling findings.

*A*SCH'S STUDIES OF CONFORMITY

From his boyhood, Solomon Asch (1907–1996) recalled a traditional Jewish seder at Passover:

> I asked my uncle, who was sitting next to me, why the door was being opened. He replied, "The prophet Elijah visits this evening every Jewish home and takes a sip of wine from the cup reserved for him."
> I was amazed at this news and repeated, "Does he really come? Does he really take a sip?"

My uncle said, "If you watch very closely, when the door is opened you will see—you watch the cup—you will see that the wine will go down a little."
        And that's what happened. My eyes were riveted upon the cup of wine. I was determined to see whether there would be a change. And to me it seemed . . . that indeed something was happening at the rim of the cup, and the wine did go down a little. (Aron & Aron, 1989, p. 27)

Activity
14.1

Years later, social psychologist Asch recreated his boyhood experience in his laboratory. Imagine yourself as one of Asch's volunteer subjects. You are seated sixth in a row of seven people. The experimenter explains that you will be in a study of perceptual judgments, and then asks you to say which of the three lines in Figure 14-1 matches the standard line. You can easily see that it's line 2. So it's no surprise when the five people responding before you all say, "Line 2."
        The next comparison proves as easy, and you settle in for what seems a simple test. But the third trial startles you. Although the correct answer seems just as clear-cut, the first person gives a wrong answer. When the second person gives the same wrong answer, you sit up in your chair and stare at the cards. The third person agrees with the first two. Your jaw drops; you start to perspire. "What is this?" you ask yourself. "Are they blind? Or am I?" The fourth and fifth people agree with the others. Then the experimenter looks at you. Now you are experiencing an epistemological dilemma: "What is true? Is it what my peers tell me or what my eyes tell me?"
        Dozens of college students experienced that conflict in Asch's experiments. Those in a control condition who answered alone were correct more than 99 percent of the time. Asch wondered: If several others (confederates

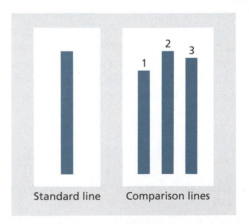

FIGURE 14-1
Sample comparison from Solomon Asch's conformity procedure. The participants judged which of three comparison lines matched the standard.

coached by the experimenter) gave identical wrong answers, would people declare what they would otherwise have denied? Although some people never conformed, three-quarters did so at least once. All told, 37 percent of the responses were conforming (or should we say *"trusting* of others").

Of course, that means 63 percent of the time people did *not* conform. The experiments show that most people "tell the truth even when others do not," note Bert Hodges and Anne Geyer (2006). Despite the independence shown by many of his participants, Asch's (1955) feelings about the conformity were as clear as the correct answers to his questions: "That reasonably intelligent and well-meaning young people are willing to call white black is a matter of concern. It raises questions about our ways of education and about the values that guide our conduct."

Asch's procedure became the standard for hundreds of later experiments. Those experiments lacked what Chapter 1 called the "mundane realism" of everyday conformity, but they did have "experimental realism." People became emotionally involved in the experience. The Sherif and Asch results are startling because they involved no obvious pressure to conform—there were no rewards for "team play," no punishments for individuality.

Other experiments have explored conformity in everyday situations. One study engaged soccer referees. In many sports, from figure skating to soccer football, referees make instantaneous decisions amid crowd noise. When rating a skating performance or deciding whether a soccer player collision merits a yellow card, does the crowd noise—which increases when an opposing player commits a seeming infraction—make a difference? To find out, Christian Unkelbach and Daniel Memmert (2010) examined 1,530 soccer matches across five seasons in Germany's premier league. On average, home teams received 1.89 yellow cards and away

In one of Asch's conformity experiments, subject number 6 experienced uneasiness and conflict after hearing five people before him give a wrong answer.

teams 2.35. Moreover, the difference was greater in louder soccer stadiums where fans were not separated from the field by a running track. And in laboratory experiments, professional referees who judged filmed foul scenes awarded more yellow cards when a scene was accompanied by high-volume noise.

If people are that conforming in response to such minimal pressure, how compliant will they be if they are directly coerced? Could someone force the average North American or European to perform cruel acts? I would have guessed not: Their humane, democratic, individualistic values would make them resist such pressure. Besides, the easy verbal pronouncements of those experiments are a giant step away from actually harming someone; you and I would never yield to coercion to hurt another. Or would we? Social psychologist Stanley Milgram wondered.

*M*ILGRAM'S OBEDIENCE EXPERIMENTS

Milgram's (1965, 1974) experiments—"the most famous, or infamous, stud[ies] in the annals of scientific psychology" (Benjamin & Simpson, 2009)—tested what happens when the demands of authority clash with the demands of conscience. "Perhaps more than any other empirical contributions in the history of social science," noted Lee Ross (1988), "they have become part of our society's shared intellectual legacy—that small body of historical incidents, biblical parables, and classic literature that serious thinkers feel free to draw on when they debate about human nature or contemplate human history."

Video 14.1

Here is the scene staged by Milgram, a creative artist who wrote stories and stage plays, and who used trial-and-error pilot testing to hone this drama for maximum impact (Russell, 2011): Two men come to Yale University's psychology laboratory to participate in a study of learning and memory. A stern experimenter in a lab coat explains that this is a pioneering study of the effect of punishment on learning. The experiment requires one of them to teach a list of word pairs to the other and to punish errors by delivering shocks of increasing intensity. To assign the roles, they draw slips out of a hat. One of the men (a mild-mannered, 47-year-old accountant who is actually the experimenter's confederate) says that his slip says "learner" and is ushered into an adjacent room. The other man (a volunteer who has come in response to a newspaper ad) is assigned to the role of "teacher." He takes a mild sample shock and then looks on as the experimenter straps the learner into a chair and attaches an electrode to his wrist.

Teacher and experimenter then return to the main room (Figure 14-2), where the teacher takes his place before a "shock generator" with switches ranging from 15 to 450 volts in 15-volt increments. The switches are labeled "Slight Shock," "Very Strong Shock," "Danger: Severe Shock," and

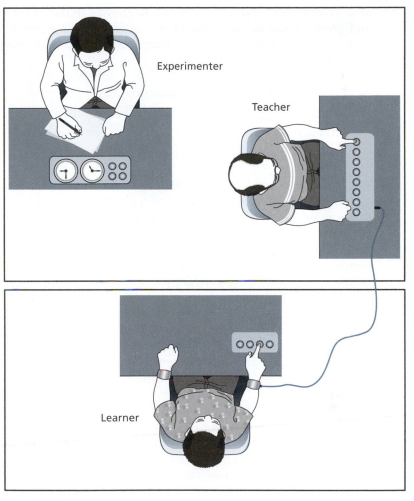

FIGURE 14-2
Milgram's obedience experiment.   Source: en.wikipedia.org/wiki/
Milgram_experiment

so forth. Under the 435- and 450-volt switches appears "XXX." The experimenter tells the teacher to "move one level higher on the shock generator"
each time the learner gives a wrong answer. With each flick of a switch,
lights flash, relay switches click, and an electric buzzer sounds.

If the participant complies with the experimenter's requests, he hears
the learner grunt at 75, 90, and 105 volts. At 120 volts the learner shouts
that the shocks are painful. And at 150 volts he cries out, "Experimenter,
get me out of here! I won't be in the experiment anymore! I refuse to go
on!" By 270 volts his protests have become screams of agony, and his
pleas to be let out continue. At 300 and 315 volts, he screams his refusal to

answer. After 330 volts he falls silent. In answer to the teacher's inquiries and pleas to end the experiment, the experimenter states that the non-responses should be treated as wrong answers. To keep the participant going, he uses four verbal prods:

Prod 1: Please continue (or Please go on).

Prod 2: The experiment requires that you continue.

Prod 3: It is absolutely essential that you continue.

Prod 4: You have no other choice; you must go on.

How far would you go? Milgram described the experiment to 110 psychiatrists, college students, and middle-class adults. People in all three groups guessed that they would disobey by about 135 volts; none expected to go beyond 300 volts. Recognizing that self-estimates may reflect self-serving bias, Milgram asked them how far they thought *other* people would go. Virtually no one expected anyone to proceed to XXX on the shock panel. (The psychiatrists guessed about one in a thousand.)

But when Milgram conducted the experiment with 40 men—a vocational mix of 20- to 50-year-olds—26 of them (65 percent) progressed all the way to 450 volts. Those who stopped often did so at the 150-volt point, when the learner's protestations became more compelling (Packer, 2008).

Wondering if people today would similarly obey, Jerry Burger (2009) replicated Milgram's experiment—though only to the 150-volt point. At that point, 70 percent of participants were still obeying, a slight reduction from Milgram's result. (In Milgram's experiment, most who were obedient to this point continued to the end. In fact, all who reached 450 volts complied with a command to *continue* the procedure until, after two further trials, the experimenter called a halt.)

Having expected a low rate of **obedience**, and with plans to replicate the experiment in Germany and assess the culture difference, Milgram was disturbed (A. Milgram, 2000). So instead of going to Germany, Milgram next made the learner's protests even more compelling. As the learner was strapped into the chair, the teacher heard him mention his "slight heart condition" and heard the experimenter's reassurance that "although the shocks may be painful, they cause no permanent tissue damage." The learner's anguished protests were to little avail; of 40 new men in this experiment, 25 (63 percent) fully complied with the experimenter's demands (Figure 14-3). Ten later studies that included women found that women's compliance rates were similar to men's (Blass, 1999).

The obedience of his subjects disturbed Milgram. The procedures he used disturbed many social psychologists (Miller, 1986). The "learner" in these experiments actually received no shock (he disengaged himself from the electric chair and turned on a tape recorder that delivered the protests). Nevertheless, some critics said that Milgram did to his participants

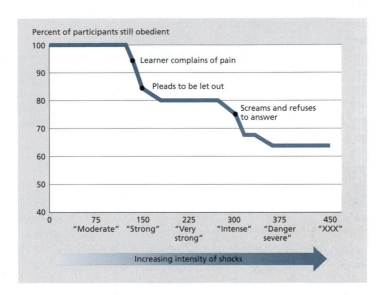

FIGURE 14-3
The Milgram obedience experiment. Percentage of participants
complying despite the learner's cries of protest and failure to
respond.   Source: From Milgram, 1965.

what they assumed they were doing to their victims: He stressed them
against their will. Indeed, like Nazi executioners in the early days of the
Holocaust (Brooks, 2011), many of the "teachers" did experience agony.
They sweated, trembled, stuttered, bit their lips, groaned, or even broke
into uncontrollable nervous laughter. A *New York Times* reviewer complained that the cruelty inflicted by the experiments "upon their unwitting subjects is surpassed only by the cruelty that they elicit from them"
(Marcus, 1974).

Critics also argued that the participants' self-concepts may have been
altered. One participant's wife told him, "You can call yourself Eichmann"
(referring to Nazi death camp administrator Adolf Eichmann). CBS television depicted the results and the controversy in a two-hour dramatiza-
tion. "A world of evil so terrifying no one dares penetrate its secret. Until
Now!" declared a *TV Guide* ad for the program (Elms, 1995).

In his own defense, Milgram pointed to the important lessons taught
by his nearly two-dozen experiments with a diverse sample of more than
1,000 participants. He also reminded critics of the support he received
from the participants after the deception was revealed and the experiment
explained. When surveyed afterward, 84 percent said they were glad to
have participated; only 1 percent regretted volunteering. A year later,
a psychiatrist interviewed 40 of those who had suffered most and concluded that, despite the temporary stress, none was harmed.

The ethical controversy was "terribly overblown," Milgram believed:

> There is less consequence to subjects in this experiment from the standpoint of effects on self-esteem, than to university students who take ordinary course examinations, and who do not get the grades they want. . . . It seems that [in giving exams] we are quite prepared to accept stress, tension, and consequences for self-esteem. But in regard to the process of generating new knowledge, how little tolerance we show. (Quoted by Blass, 1996.)

What Breeds Obedience?

Milgram did more than reveal the extent to which people will obey an authority; he also examined the conditions that breed obedience. When he varied the social conditions, compliance ranged from 0 to 93 percent fully obedient. Four factors that determined obedience were the victim's emotional distance, the authority's closeness and legitimacy, whether or not the authority was part of a respected institution, and the liberating effects of a disobedient fellow participant.

Emotional Distance of the Victim

Milgram's participants acted with greatest obedience and least compassion when the "learners" could not be seen (and could not see them). When the victim was remote and the "teachers" heard no complaints, nearly all obeyed calmly to the end. That situation minimized the learner's influence relative to the experimenter's. But what if we made the learner's pleas and the experimenter's instructions more equally visible? When the learner was in the same room, "only" 40 percent obeyed to 450 volts. Full compliance dropped to a still-astonishing 30 percent when teachers were required to force the learner's hand into contact with a shock plate. In a reenacted Milgram experiment—with videotaped actors who were either hidden or seen on a computer screen and known to be feigning hurt—participants were, again, much less obedient when the victim was visible (Dambrun & Vatiné, 2010).

In everyday life, too, it is easiest to abuse someone who is distant or depersonalized. People who might never be cruel to someone in person may be nasty when posting comments to anonymous people on Internet discussion boards. Throughout history, executioners have often depersonalized those being executed by placing hoods over their heads. The ethics of war allow one to bomb a helpless village from 40,000 feet but not to shoot an equally helpless villager. In combat with an enemy they can see, many soldiers either do not fire or do not aim. Such disobedience is rare among those given orders to kill with the more distant artillery or aircraft weapons (Padgett, 1989).

On the positive side, people act most compassionately toward those who are personalized. That is why appeals for the unborn, for the hungry, or for animal rights are nearly always personalized with a compelling photograph or description. When queried by researchers John Lydon and Christine Dunkel-Schetter (1994), expectant women expressed more commitment to their pregnancies if they had seen ultrasound pictures of their fetuses that clearly displayed body parts.

Closeness and Legitimacy of the Authority

The physical presence of the experimenter also affected obedience. When Milgram's experimenter gave the commands by telephone, full obedience dropped to 21 percent (although many lied and said they were obeying). Other studies confirm that when the one making the command is physically close, compliance increases. Given a light touch on the arm, people are more likely to lend a dime, sign a petition, or sample a new pizza (Kleinke, 1977; Smith & others, 1982; Willis & Hamm, 1980).

The authority, however, must be perceived as legitimate. In another twist on the basic experiment, the experimenter received a rigged telephone call that required him to leave the laboratory. He said that since the equipment recorded data automatically, the "teacher" should just go ahead. After the experimenter left, another person, who had been assigned a clerical role (actually a second confederate), assumed command. The clerk "decided" that the shock should be increased one level for each wrong answer and instructed the teacher accordingly. Now 80 percent of the teachers refused to comply fully. The confederate, feigning disgust at this defiance, sat down in front of the shock generator and tried to take over the teacher's role. At that point most of the defiant participants protested. Some tried to unplug the generator. One large man lifted the zealous confederate from his chair and threw him across the room. This rebellion against an illegitimate authority contrasted sharply with the deferential politeness usually shown the experimenter.

It also contrasts with the behavior of hospital nurses who in one study were called by an unknown physician and ordered to administer an obvious drug overdose (Hofling & others, 1966). The researchers told one group of nurses and nursing students about the experiment and asked how they would react. Nearly all said they would not have followed the order. One said she would have replied, "I'm sorry, sir, but I am not authorized to give any medication without a written order, especially one so large over the usual dose and one that I'm unfamiliar with. If it were possible, I would be glad to do it, but this is against hospital policy and my own ethical standards." Nevertheless, when 22 other nurses were actually given the phoned-in overdose order, all but one obeyed without delay (until being intercepted on their way to the patient). Although not all nurses are so compliant (Krackow & Blass, 1995; Rank & Jacobson, 1977), these nurses were following a familiar script: Doctor (a legitimate authority) orders; nurse obeys.

Compliance with legitimate authority was also apparent in the strange case of the "rectal earache" (Cohen & Davis, 1981). A doctor ordered eardrops for a patient suffering infection in the right ear. On the prescription, the doctor abbreviated "place in right ear" as "place in R ear." Reading the order, the compliant nurse put the required drops in the compliant patient's rectum.

Institutional Authority

If the prestige of the authority is that important, then perhaps the institutional prestige of Yale University legitimized the Milgram experiment commands. In postexperimental interviews, many participants said that had it not been for Yale's reputation, they would not have obeyed. To see whether that was true, Milgram moved the experiment to less prestigious Bridgeport, Connecticut. He set himself up in a modest commercial building as the "Research Associates of Bridgeport." When the "learner-has-a-heart-condition" experiment was run with the same personnel, what percentage of the men do you suppose fully obeyed? Although the obedience rate (48 percent) was still remarkably high, it was significantly lower than the 65 percent rate at Yale.

Although no expert came, another police officer, unaware of the drama, happened onto the scene, took out his power bullhorn, and yelled at the assembled cliffside group: "Who's the ass who left that Pontiac station wagon double-parked out there in the middle of the road? I almost hit it. Move it *now*, whoever you are." Hearing the message, Alfred obediently got down at once, moved the car, and then without a word got into the police cruiser for a trip to the nearby hospital.

The Liberating Effects of Group Influence

These classic experiments give us a negative view of conformity. But conformity can also be constructive. The heroic firefighters who rushed into the flaming World Trade Center towers were "incredibly brave," note social psychologists Susan Fiske, Lasana Harris, and Amy Cuddy (2004), but they were also "partly obeying their superiors, partly conforming to extraordinary group loyalty." Consider, too, the occasional liberating effect of conformity. Perhaps you can recall a time you felt justifiably angry at an unfair teacher but you hesitated to object. Then one or two other students spoke up about the unfair practices, and you followed their example, which had a liberating effect. Milgram captured this liberating effect of conformity by placing the teacher with two confederates who were to help conduct the procedure. During the experiment, both confederates defied the experimenter, who then ordered the real participant to continue alone. Did he? No. Ninety percent liberated themselves by conforming to the defiant confederates.

REFLECTIONS ON THE CLASSIC STUDIES

The common response to Milgram's results is to note their counterparts in the "I was only following orders" defenses of Adolf Eichmann, in Nazi Germany; of American Lieutenant William Calley, who in 1968 directed the unprovoked slaughter of hundreds of Vietnamese in the village of My Lai; and of the "ethnic cleansings" occurring in Iraq, Rwanda, Bosnia, and Kosovo.

Soldiers are trained to obey superiors. Thus, one participant in the My Lai massacre recalled:

> [Lieutenant Calley] told me to start shooting. So I started shooting, I poured about four clips into the group. . . . They were begging and saying, "No, no." And the mothers were hugging their children and. . . . Well, we kept right on firing. They was waving their arms and begging. (Wallace, 1969)

The "safe" scientific contexts of the obedience experiments differ from the wartime contexts. Moreover, much of the mockery and brutality of war and genocide goes beyond obedience (Miller, 2004).

The obedience experiments also differ from the other conformity experiments in the strength of the social pressure: Obedience is explicitly commanded. Yet both the Asch and the Milgram experiments share certain commonalities. They showed how compliance can take precedence over moral sense. They succeeded in pressuring people to go against their own consciences. They did more than teach an academic lesson; they sensitized us to moral conflicts in our own lives. And they illustrated and affirmed two familiar social psychological principles: the link between *behavior and attitudes* and the *power of the situation*.

Behavior and Attitudes

Module 9 noted a situation in which attitudes fail to determine behavior: when external influences override inner convictions. These experiments vividly illustrate that principle. When responding alone, Asch's participants nearly always gave the correct answer. It was another matter when they stood alone against a group.

In the obedience experiments, a powerful social pressure (the experimenter's commands) overcame a weaker one (the remote victim's pleas). Torn between the pleas of the victim and the orders of the experimenter, between the desire to avoid doing harm and the desire to be a good participant, a surprising number of people chose to obey.

Why were the participants unable to disengage themselves? Imagine yourself as the teacher in yet another version of Milgram's experiment (one he never conducted). Assume that when the learner gives the first wrong answer, the experimenter asks you to zap him with 330 volts. After flicking the switch, you hear the learner scream, complain of a heart disturbance, and plead for mercy. Do you continue?

I think not. Recall the step-by-step entrapment of the foot-in-the-door phenomenon (Module 9) as we compare this hypothetical experiment to what Milgram's participants experienced. Their first commitment was mild—15 volts—and it elicited no protest. By the time they delivered 75 volts and heard the learner's first groan, they already had complied 5 times, and the next request was to deliver only slightly more. By the time they delivered 330 volts, the participants had complied 22 times and reduced some of their dissonance. They were therefore in a different psychological state from that of someone beginning the experiment at that point. The same thing occurred with the fast-food restaurant managers in the strip-search scam, after they had complied with initially reasonable-seeming orders from a supposed authority. As we saw in Module 9, external behavior and internal disposition can feed each other, sometimes in an escalating spiral. Thus, reported Milgram (1974, p. 10):

> Many subjects harshly devalue the victim as a consequence of acting against him. Such comments as, "He was so stupid and stubborn he deserved to get shocked," were common. Once having acted against the victim, these subjects found it necessary to view him as an unworthy individual, whose punishment was made inevitable by his own deficiencies of intellect and character.

During the early 1970s, Greece's military junta used this "blame-the-victim" process to train torturers (Haritos-Fatouros, 1988, 2002; Staub, 1989, 2003). There, as in the earlier training of SS officers in Nazi Germany, the military selected candidates based on their respect for and submission to authority. But such tendencies alone do not a torturer make. Thus, they would first assign the trainee to guard prisoners, then to participate in arrest squads, then to hit prisoners, then to observe torture, and only then to practice it. Step by step, an obedient but otherwise decent person evolved into an agent of cruelty. Compliance bred acceptance. If we focus on the end point—450 volts of torture administered—we are aghast at the evil conduct. If we consider how one gets there—in tiny steps—we understand.

As a Holocaust survivor, University of Massachusetts social psychologist Ervin Staub knows too well the forces that can transform citizens into agents of death. From his study of human genocide across the world, Staub (2003) shows where gradually increasing aggression can lead. Too often, criticism produces contempt, which licenses cruelty, which, when justified, leads to brutality, then killing, then systematic killing. Evolving attitudes both follow and justify actions. Staub's disturbing conclusion: "Human beings have the capacity to come to experience killing other people as nothing extraordinary" (1989, p. 13).

But humans also have a capacity for heroism. During the Nazi Holocaust, the French village of Le Chambon sheltered 5,000 Jews and other refugees destined for deportation to Germany. The villagers were mostly Protestants whose own authorities, their pastors, had taught them to "resist whenever our adversaries will demand of us obedience contrary to the orders of the Gospel" (Rochat, 1993; Rochat & Modigliani, 1995). Ordered to divulge the locations of sheltered Jews, the head pastor modeled disobedience: "I don't know of Jews, I only know of human beings." Without knowing how terrible the war would be, the resisters, beginning in 1940, made an initial commitment and then—supported by their beliefs, by their own authorities, and by one another—remained defiant till the village's liberation in 1944. Here and elsewhere, the ultimate response to Nazi occupation came early. Initial helping heightened commitment, leading to more helping.

The Power of the Situation

The most important lesson of Module 13 (that culture is a powerful shaper of lives) and this module's most important lesson (that immediate situational forces are just as powerful) reveal the strength of the social context. To feel this for yourself, imagine violating some minor norms: standing up in the middle of a class; singing out loud in a restaurant; playing golf in a suit. In trying to break with social constraints, we suddenly realize how strong they are.

The students in one Pennsylvania State University experiment found it surprisingly difficult to violate the norm of being "nice" rather than confrontational. Participants imagined themselves discussing with three others whom to select for survival on a desert island. They were asked to imagine one of the others, a man, injecting three sexist comments, such as, "I think we need more women on the island to keep the men satisfied." How would they react to such sexist remarks? Only 5 percent predicted they would ignore each of the comments or wait to see how others reacted. But when Janet Swim and Lauri Hyers (1999) engaged other students in discussions where such comments were actually made by a male confederate, 55 percent (not 5 percent) said nothing. Likewise, although people predict they would be upset by witnessing a person making a racial slur—and would avoid picking the racist person as a partner in an experiment—those actually experiencing such an event typically exhibit indifference (Kawakami & others, 2009). These experiments demonstrate the power of normative pressures and how hard it is to predict behavior, even our own behavior.

How ironic that in 2011, the human struggle with confrontation should play out at Swim and Hyers' university—Penn State—in a public debate about how its revered football coach and other university officials should have responded to learning that a fellow coach had sexually abused boys.

(The coaches reportedly did pass on the reports to superiors, but allowed the alleged abuser to continue using university facilities.) Commentators were outraged; they presumed that *they* themselves would have acted more strongly. But the lessons of history, of bystander response (see Chapter 12), and of these experiments remind us that *saying* what we would do in a hypothetical situation is often easier than *doing* it in a real situation.

Milgram's experiments also offer a lesson about evil. In horror movies and suspense novels, evil results from a few bad apples, a few depraved killers. In real life we similarly think of Hitler's extermination of Jews or of Osama bin Laden's terrorist plot. But evil also results from social forces—from the heat, humidity, and disease that help make a whole barrel of apples go bad. The American military police, whose abuse of Iraqi prisoners at Abu Ghraib prison horrified the world, were under stress, taunted by many they had come to save, angered by comrades' deaths, overdue to return home, and under lax supervision—an evil situation that produced evil behavior (Fiske, 2004; Lankford, 2009). Situations can induce ordinary people to capitulate to cruelty.

This is especially true when, as happens often in complex societies, the most terrible evil evolves from a sequence of small evils. German civil servants surprised Nazi leaders with their willingness to handle the paperwork of the Holocaust. They were not killing Jews, of course; they were merely pushing paper (Silver & Geller, 1978). When fragmented, evil becomes easier. Milgram studied this compartmentalization of evil by involving yet another 40 men more indirectly. With someone else triggering the shock, they had only to administer the learning test. Now, 37 of the 40 fully complied.

So it is in our everyday lives: The drift toward evil usually comes in small increments, without any conscious intent to do evil. Procrastination involves a similar unintended drift, toward self-harm (Sabini & Silver, 1982). A student knows the deadline for a term paper weeks ahead. Each diversion from work on the paper—a video game here, a TV program there—seems harmless enough. Yet gradually the student veers toward not doing the paper without ever consciously deciding not to do it.

It is tempting to assume that Eichmann and the Auschwitz death camp commanders were uncivilized monsters. Indeed, their evil was fueled by virulent anti-Semitism. And the social situation alone does not explain why, in the same neighborhood or death camp, some personalities displayed vicious cruelty and others heroic kindness. Still, the commanders would not have stood out to us as monsters. After a hard day's work, they would relax by listening to Beethoven and Schubert. Of the 14 men who formulated the Final Solution leading to the Nazi Holocaust, 8 had European university doctorates (Patterson, 1996). Like most other Nazis, Eichmann himself was outwardly indistinguishable from common people with ordinary jobs (Arendt, 1963; Zillmer & others, 1995). Mohamed Atta, the leader of the 9/11 attacks, reportedly had been a "good boy" and an excellent student from a healthy family. Zacarias Moussaoui, the would-be twentieth 9/11 attacker, had been very polite when applying for flight lessons and buying knives. He called women "ma'am." The pilot of the second plane to hit the World Trade Center was said to be an amiable, "laid-back" fellow, much like the "intelligent, friendly, and 'very courteous' " pilot of the plane that dove into the Pentagon. If these men had lived next door to us, they would hardly have fit our image of evil monsters. They were "unexceptional" people (McDermott, 2005).

As Milgram noted (1974, p. 6), "The most fundamental lesson of our study is that ordinary people, simply doing their jobs, and without any particular hostility on their part, can become agents in a terrible destructive process." As Mister Rogers often reminded his preschool television audience, "Good people sometimes do bad things." Under the sway of evil forces, even nice people are sometimes corrupted as they construct moral rationalizations for immoral behavior (Tsang, 2002). So it is that ordinary soldiers may, in the end, follow orders to shoot defenseless civilians; admired political leaders may lead their citizens into ill-fated wars; ordinary employees may follow instructions to produce and distribute harmful, degrading products; and ordinary group members may heed commands to brutally haze initiates.

CONCEPTS TO REMEMBER

conformity A change in behavior or belief as the result of real or imagined group pressure.

obedience Acting in accord with a direct order.

15

❖

Two Routes to Persuasion

Persuasion, whether it be education or propaganda, is everywhere—
at the heart of politics, marketing, courtship, parenting, negotiation,
evangelism, and courtroom decision making. Social psychologists
therefore seek to understand what leads to effective, long-lasting attitude
change. What factors affect persuasion? As persuaders, how can we most
effectively "educate" others?

Imagine that you are a marketing or advertising executive. Or imagine
that you are a preacher, trying to increase love and charity among your
parishioners. Or imagine that you want to restrain climate change, to encourage breast-feeding, or to campaign for a political candidate. What
could you do to make yourself and your message persuasive? And if you
are wary of being influenced, to what tactics should you be alert?

To answer such questions, social psychologists usually study persuasion the way some geologists study erosion—by observing the effects
of various factors in brief, controlled experiments. The effects are small
and are most potent on weak attitudes that don't touch our values. Yet
they enable us to understand how, given enough time, such factors could
produce big effects.

*T*HE TWO ROUTES

In choosing tactics, you must first decide: Should you focus mostly
on building strong *central arguments*? Or should you make your message appealing by associating it with favorable *peripheral cues*, such as
sex appeal? Persuasion researchers Richard Petty and John Cacioppo

Video
15.1

(Cass-ee-OH-poh) (1986; Petty & others, 2005) and Alice Eagly and Shelly Chaiken (1993) report that persuasion is likely to occur via either a central or peripheral route. When people are motivated and able to think about an issue, they are likely to take the **central route to persuasion**—focusing on the arguments. If those arguments are strong and compelling, persuasion is likely. If the message offers only weak arguments, thoughtful people will notice that the arguments aren't very compelling and will counterargue.

But sometimes the strength of the arguments doesn't matter. Sometimes we're not motivated or able to think carefully. If we're distracted, uninvolved, or just plain busy, we may not take the time to reflect on the message's content. Rather than analyzing whether the arguments are compelling, we might follow the **peripheral route to persuasion**—focusing on cues that trigger automatic acceptance without much thinking. Smart advertisers adapt ads to their consumers' thinking. They do so for good reason. Much of consumer behavior—such as one's spontaneous decision, while shopping, to pick up some ice cream of a particular brand—is made unthinkingly (Dijksterhuis & others, 2005). Something as minor as German music may lead customers to buy German wine, whereas others, hearing French music, reach for French wine (North & others, 1997). Billboards and television commercials—media that consumers are able to take in for only brief amounts of time—therefore use the peripheral route, with visual images as peripheral cues. Instead of providing arguments in favor of smoking, cigarette ads associate the product with images of beauty and pleasure. So do soft-drink ads that promote "the real thing" with images of youth, vitality, and happy polar bears. On the other hand, magazine computer ads (which interested, logical consumers may pore over for some time) seldom feature Hollywood stars or great athletes. Instead, they offer customers information on competitive features and prices.

These two routes to persuasion—one explicit and reflective, the other more implicit and automatic—were a forerunner to today's "dual processing" models of the human mind. Central route processing often swiftly changes explicit attitudes. Peripheral route processing more slowly builds implicit attitudes, through repeated associations between an attitude object and an emotion (Jones & others, 2009; Petty & Briñol, 2008; Walther & others, 2011).

None of us has the time to thoughtfully analyze all issues. Often we take the peripheral route, by using simple rule-of-thumb heuristics, such as "trust the experts" or "long messages are credible" (Chaiken & Maheswaran, 1994). Residents of my community once voted on a complicated issue involving the legal ownership of our local hospital. I didn't have the time or the interest to study that question myself (I had this book to write). But I noted that referendum supporters were all people I either liked or regarded as experts. So I used a simple heuristic—friends and experts can be

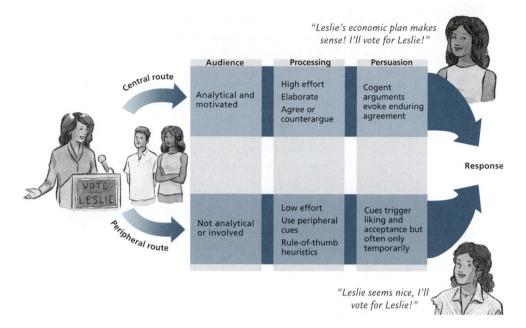

FIGURE 15-1
The central and peripheral routes to persuasion. Computer ads typically take the central route, by assuming their audience wants to systematically compare features and prices. Soft-drink ads usually take the peripheral route, by merely associating their product with glamour, pleasure, and good moods. Central route processing more often produces enduring attitude change.

trusted—and voted accordingly. We all make snap judgments using such heuristics: If a speaker is articulate and appealing, has apparently good motives, and has several arguments (or better, if the different arguments come from different sources), we usually take the easy peripheral route and accept the message without much thought (Figure 15-1).

THE ELEMENTS OF PERSUASION

Among the ingredients of persuasion explored by social psychologists are these four: (1) the communicator, (2) the message, (3) how the message is communicated, and (4) the audience. In other words, *who* says *what*, by what *method*, to *whom*?

Who Says? The Communicator

Imagine the following scene: I. M. Wright, a middle-aged American, is watching the evening news. In the first segment, a small group of radicals is shown burning an American flag. As they do, one shouts through a bullhorn that whenever any government becomes oppressive, "it is the Right of the People to alter or to abolish it. . . . It is their right, it is their duty, to throw off such government!" Angered, Mr. Wright mutters to his wife, "It's sickening to hear them spouting that Communist line." In the next segment, a presidential candidate speaking before an antitax rally declares, "Thrift should be the guiding principle in our government expenditure. It should be made clear to all government workers that corruption and waste are very great crimes." An obviously pleased Mr. Wright relaxes and smiles: "Now that's the kind of good sense we need. That's my kinda guy."

Now switch the scene. Imagine Mr. Wright hearing the same revolutionary line about "the Right of the People" at a July 4 oration of the Declaration of Independence (from which the line comes) and hearing a Communist speaker read the thrift sentence from *Quotations from Chairman Mao Zedong* (from which it comes). Would he now react differently?

Social psychologists have found that who is saying something does affect how an audience receives it. In one experiment, when the Socialist and Liberal leaders in the Dutch parliament argued identical positions using the same words, each was most effective with members of his own party (Wiegman, 1985). "Accepting that there are differences between people" sounds sensible to most of us—unless we hear those words spoken by former South African prime minister Hendrik Verwoerd (1958), explaining his government's segregationist apartheid policy. It's not just the message that matters, but also who says it. What makes one communicator more persuasive than another?

Credibility

Any of us would find a statement about the benefits of exercise more believable if it came from the Royal Society or National Academy of Sciences rather than from a tabloid newspaper. But the effects of source **credibility** (perceived expertise and trustworthiness) diminish after a month or so. If a credible person's message is persuasive, its impact may fade as its source is forgotten or dissociated from the message. And the impact of a noncredible person may correspondingly increase over time if people remember the message better than the reason for discounting it (Cook & Flay, 1978; Kumkale & Albarracin, 2004; Pratkanis & others, 1988). This delayed persuasion, after people forget the source or its connection with the message, is called the **sleeper effect**.

Attractiveness

Most of us deny that endorsements by star athletes and entertainers affect us. We know that stars are seldom knowledgeable about the products they endorse. Besides, we know the intent is to persuade us; we don't just accidentally eavesdrop on Jennifer Lopez discussing clothes or fragrances. Such ads are based on another characteristic of an effective communicator: **attractiveness**.

We may think we are not influenced by attractiveness or likability, but researchers have found otherwise. We're more likely to respond to those we like, a phenomenon well-known to those organizing charitable solicitations and candy sales. Even a mere fleeting conversation with someone is enough to increase our liking for that person and our responsiveness to his or her influence (Burger & others, 2001). Our liking may open us up to the communicator's arguments (central route persuasion), or it may trigger positive associations when we see the product later (peripheral route persuasion).

Attractiveness comes in several forms. *Physical attractiveness* is one. Arguments, especially emotional ones, are often more influential when they come from people we consider beautiful (Chaiken, 1979; Dion & Stein, 1978; Pallak & others, 1983).

Similarity also makes for attractiveness. As Module 26 will emphasize, we tend to like people who are like us. We also are influenced by them, a fact that was harnessed by a successful antismoking campaign that featured youth appealing to other youth through ads that challenged the tobacco industry about its destructiveness and its marketing practices (Krisberg, 2004). People who *act* as we do, subtly mimicking our postures, are likewise more influential. Thus, salespeople are sometimes taught to "mimic and mirror": If the customer's arms or legs are crossed, cross yours; if she smiles, smile back.

Another example: Theodore Dembroski, Thomas Lasater, and Albert Ramirez (1978) gave African American junior high students an audiotaped appeal for proper dental care. When a dentist assessed the cleanliness of their teeth the next day, those who heard the appeal from an African American dentist (whose face they were shown) had cleaner teeth. As a general rule, people respond better to a message that comes from someone in their group (Van Knippenberg & Wilke, 1992; Wilder, 1990).

What Is Said? The Message Content

It matters not only who says something but also *what* that person says. If you were to help organize an appeal to get people to vote for school taxes or to stop smoking or to give money to world hunger relief, you might wonder how best to promote central route persuasion. Common sense could lead you to either side of these questions:

- Is a logical message more persuasive—or one that arouses emotion?
- Will you get more opinion change by advocating a position only slightly discrepant from the listeners' existing opinions or by advocating an extreme point of view?

- Should the message express your side only, or should it acknowledge and refute the opposing views?

- If people are to present both sides—say, in successive talks at a community meeting or in a political debate—is there an advantage to going first or last?

Let's take these questions one at a time.

Reason Versus Emotion

Suppose you were campaigning in support of world hunger relief. Would you best itemize your arguments and cite an array of impressive statistics? Or would you be more effective presenting an emotional approach—perhaps the compelling story of one starving child? In my community, supporters of a proposed antidiscrimination ordinance protecting gay people wondered: To what extent might opinions be swayed by reason and evidence related to sexual orientation, and to what extent by emotion? Is what matters more *what* people know or their feelings toward *whom* they know? Of course, an argument can be both reasonable and emotional. You can marry passion and logic. Still, which is *more* influential—reason or emotion? Was Shakespeare's Lysander right: "The will of man is by his reason sway'd"? Or was Lord Chesterfield's advice wiser: "Address yourself generally to the senses, to the heart, and to the weaknesses of mankind, but rarely to their reason"?

The answer: It depends on the audience. Well-educated or analytical people are responsive to rational appeals (Cacioppo & others, 1983, 1996; Hovland & others, 1949). Thoughtful, involved audiences often travel the central route; they are more responsive to reasoned arguments. Uninterested audiences more often travel the peripheral route; they are more affected by their liking of the communicator (Chaiken, 1980; Petty & others, 1981).

To judge from interviews before major elections, many voters are uninvolved. As we might therefore expect, Americans' voting preferences have been more predictable from emotional reactions to the candidates than from their beliefs about the candidates' traits and likely behaviors (Abelson & others, 1982). What matters is not just candidates' positions (which candidate embodies your views) but their likeability (who you want to spend time with).

The Effect of Good Feelings

Messages also become more persuasive through association with good feelings. Irving Janis and colleagues (1965; Dabbs & Janis, 1965) found that Yale students were more convinced by persuasive messages if they were allowed to enjoy peanuts and Pepsi while reading the messages. Similarly, Mark Galizio and Clyde Hendrick (1972) found that Kent State University students were more persuaded by folk-song lyrics accompanied by pleasant guitar music than they were by unaccompanied lyrics. There is, it seems, something to be gained from conducting business over sumptuous lunches with soft background music.

Good feelings often enhance persuasion, partly by enhancing positive thinking and partly by linking good feelings with the message (Petty & others, 1993). As noted previously, people who are in a good mood view the world through rose-colored glasses. But they also make faster, more impulsive decisions; they rely more on peripheral cues (Bodenhausen, 1993; Braverman, 2005; Moons & Mackie, 2007). Unhappy people ruminate more before reacting, so they are less easily swayed by weak arguments. (They also *produce* more cogent persuasive messages [Forgas, 2007].) Thus, if you can't make a strong case, you might want to put your audience in a good mood and hope they'll feel good about your message without thinking too much about it.

Knowing that humor can put people in a good mood, a Dutch research team led by Madelijn Strick (Strick & others, 2009) invited people to view ads in the vicinity of either funny cartoons (Figure 15-2) or the same cartoons altered to be unfunny. Their finding: Products associated with humor were better liked, as measured by an implicit attitude test, and were more often chosen.

FIGURE 15-2
In experiments at Radboud University Nijmegen, humor (as on the left) enhanced people's liking for products such as these. © Sun Media Corporation. Reprinted by permission.

The Effect of Arousing Fear

Messages can also be effective by evoking negative emotions. When persuading people to cut down on smoking, get a tetanus shot, or drive carefully, a fear-arousing message can be potent (de Hoog & others, 2007; Muller & Johnson, 1990). By requiring cigarette makers to include graphic representations of the hazards of smoking on each pack of cigarettes, more than three dozen other governments have assumed—correctly, it turns out—that showing cigarette smokers the horrible things that can happen to smokers adds to persuasiveness (O'Hegarty & others, 2007; Peters & others, 2007; Stark & others, 2008). If its courts will allow, the United States will follow the example of other nations in requiring graphic photo warnings (Reardon, 2011; Wilson, 2011).

But how much fear should you arouse? Should you evoke just a little fear, lest people become so frightened that they tune out your painful message? Or should you try to scare the daylights out of them? Experiments show that, often, the more frightened and vulnerable people feel, the more they respond (de Hoog & others, 2007; Leventhal, 1970; Robberson & Rogers, 1998).

The effectiveness of fear-arousing communications has been applied in ads discouraging not only smoking but also risky sexual behaviors and drinking and driving. When Claude Levy-Leboyer (1988) found that attitudes toward alcohol and drinking habits among French youth were changed effectively by fear-arousing pictures, the French government incorporated such pictures into its TV spots.

One effective antismoking ad campaign offered graphic "truth" ads. In one, vans pull up outside an unnamed corporate tobacco office. Teens pile out and unload 1,200 body bags covering two city blocks. As a curious corporate suit peers out a window above, a teen shouts into a loudspeaker: "Do you know how many people tobacco kills every day? . . . We are going to leave these here for you, so you can see what 1,200 people actually look like" (Nicholson, 2007). Unlike teens who viewed a simultaneous cerebral Philip Morris ad (lecturing, "Think. Don't Smoke") and were not less likely to smoke, those viewing the more dramatic and edgy ad became significantly less inclined to smoke (Farrelly & others, 2002, 2008).

Fear-arousing communications have also been used to increase breast cancer detection behaviors, such as getting mammograms or doing breast self-exams, and checking for signs of skin cancer. Sara Banks, Peter Salovey, and colleagues (1995) had women aged 40–66 years who had not obtained mammograms view an educational video on mammography. Of those who received a positively framed message (emphasizing that getting a mammogram can save your life through early detection), only half got a mammogram within 12 months. Of those who received a fear-framed message (emphasizing that not getting a mammogram can cost you your life), two-thirds got a mammogram within 12 months.

Playing on fear works best if a message leads people not only to fear the severity and likelihood of a threatened event but also to perceive a solution and feel capable of implementing it (DeVos-Comby & Salovey, 2002; Maddux & Rogers, 1983; Ruiter & others, 2001). Many ads designed to reduce sexual risks will aim both to arouse fear—"AIDS kills"—and to offer a protective strategy: Abstain, wear a condom, or save sex for a committed relationship. Also, "gain-framed" messages are often equally effective as "loss-framed" messages (O'Keefe & Jensen, 2011). Gain-framed messages focus on the advantages of healthy behavior (for example, "If you wear sunscreen, you'll have attractive skin" rather than "If you don't wear sunscreen, you'll have unattractive skin"). Thus, a global climate change article that ends by describing future catastrophic consequences is less persuasive to many skeptics than one that concludes by discussing possible solutions (Feinberg & Willer, 2010).

Vivid stories can also, however, be used for good, especially when what's most memorable conveys the central message rather than distracting from it (Guadagno & others, 2011). After the genocidal conflict between Rwanda's Hutus and Tutsi, a yearlong field experiment explored the impact of a radio soap opera that featured stories of prejudice, conflict, communication, reconciliation, and even love across group lines in two fictional communities. Compared with a control group exposed to a health-related radio soap opera, listeners became more accepting of empathy, cooperation, trauma healing, and even intermarriage (Paluck, 2009). Fiction fostered forbearance.

To Whom Is It Said? The Audience

It also matters who *receives* a message. Let's consider two audience characteristics: age and thoughtfulness.

How Old Are They?

As evident during the 2008 U.S. presidential campaign—with John McCain the decided favorite of older voters and Barack Obama of younger voters—people's social and political attitudes correlate with their age. Social psychologists offer two possible explanations for age differences:

- A *life cycle explanation:* Attitudes change (for example, become more conservative) as people grow older.
- A *generational explanation:* Attitudes do *not* change; older people largely hold onto the attitudes they adopted when they were

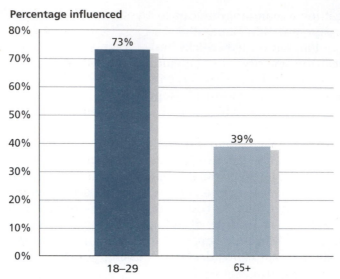

Percentage influenced

Percentage favoring gay marriage, by age

FIGURE 15-3

A generation gap in 2012 U.S. attitudes regarding same-sex marriage, as reported by Gallup (Newport, 2012). A "life cycle" explanation of generational differences in attitudes suggests that people become more conservative with age. A "generational explanation" suggests that each generation tends to hold on to attitudes formed during the adolescent and early adults years.

young. Because these attitudes are different from those being adopted by young people today, a generation gap develops. (Figure 15-3 offers one example of a large generation gap.).

The evidence mostly supports the generational explanation. In surveys and resurveys of groups of younger and older people over several years, the attitudes of older people usually show less change than do those of young people. As David Sears (1979, 1986) put it, researchers have "almost invariably found generational rather than life cycle effects."

The teens and early twenties are important formative years (Koenig & others, 2008; Krosnick & Alwin, 1989). Attitudes are changeable then, and the attitudes formed tend to stabilize through middle adulthood. Gallup interviews of more than 120,000 people suggest that political attitudes formed at age 18—relatively Republican-favoring during the popular Reagan era, and more Democratic-favoring during the unpopular George W. Bush era—tend to last (Silver, 2009).

Young people might therefore be advised to choose their social influences—the groups they join, the media they imbibe, the roles they adopt—carefully. In analyzing National Opinion Research Center archives, James Davis (2004) discovered, for example, that Americans reaching age 16 during the 1960s have, ever since, been more politically liberal than average. Much as tree rings can, years later, reveal the telltale marks laid down by a drought, so attitudes decades later may reveal the events, such as the Vietnam War and civil rights era of the 1960s, that shaped the adolescent and early twenties mind. For many people, these years are a critical period for the formation of attitudes and values.

Adolescent and early adult experiences are formative partly because they make deep and lasting impressions. When Howard Schuman and Jacqueline Scott (1989) asked people to name the one or two most important national or world events of the previous half-century, most recalled events from their teens or early twenties. For those who experienced the Great Depression or World War II as 16- to 24-year-olds, those events overshadowed the civil rights movement and the Kennedy assassination of the early sixties, the Vietnam War and moon landing of the late sixties, and the women's movement of the seventies—all of which were imprinted on the minds of younger people who experienced them as 16- to 24-year-olds. We may therefore expect that today's young adults will include events such as 9/11 and the Iraq war or the ensuing economic recession as memorable turning points.

That is not to say that older adults are inflexible. Studies conducted by Norval Glenn in 1980 and 1981 found that most people in their fifties and sixties had more liberal sexual and racial attitudes than they had in their thirties and forties. Given the "sexual revolution" that began in the 1960s and became mainstream in the 1970s, these middle-aged people had apparently changed with the times. Few of us are utterly uninfluenced by changing cultural norms. Moreover, near the end of their lives, older adults may again become more susceptible to attitude change, perhaps because of a decline in the strength of their attitudes (Visser & Krosnick, 1998). Or perhaps, as some research suggests, resistance to attitude change peaks in midlife because that's when people tend to occupy higher power social roles, which call forth resoluteness (Eaton & others, 2009).

What Are They Thinking?

The crucial aspect of central route persuasion is not the message but the responses it evokes in a person's mind. Our minds are not sponges that soak up whatever pours over them. If a message summons favorable thoughts, it persuades us. If it provokes us to think of contrary arguments, we remain unpersuaded.

Forewarned Is Forearmed—If You Care Enough to Counterargue.

What circumstances breed counterargument? One is knowing that someone is going to try to persuade you. If you had to tell your family that you wanted to drop out of school, you would likely anticipate their pleading with you to stay. So you might develop a list of arguments to counter every conceivable argument they might make.

Jonathan Freedman and David Sears (1965) demonstrated the difficulty of trying to persuade people under such circumstances. They warned one group of California high schoolers that they were going to hear a talk: "Why Teenagers Should Not Be Allowed to Drive." Those forewarned did not budge in their opinions. Others, not forewarned, did budge. In courtrooms, too, defense attorneys sometimes forewarn juries about prosecution evidence to come. With mock juries, such "stealing thunder" neutralizes its impact (Dolnik & others, 2003).

Distraction Disarms Counterarguing.   Persuasion is also enhanced by a distraction that inhibits counterarguing (Festinger & Maccoby, 1964; Keating & Brock, 1974; Osterhouse & Brock, 1970). Political ads often use this technique. The words promote the candidate, and the visual images keep us occupied so we don't analyze the words. Distraction is especially effective when the message is simple (Harkins & Petty, 1982; Regan & Cheng, 1973). Sometimes, though, distraction precludes our processing an ad. That helps explain why ads viewed during violent or sexual TV programs are so often unremembered and ineffective (Bushman, 2005, 2007).

Uninvolved Audiences Use Peripheral Cues.   Recall the two routes to persuasion—the central route of systematic thinking and the peripheral route of heuristic cues. Like a road that winds through a small town, the central route has starts and stops as the mind analyzes arguments and formulates responses. Like the freeway that bypasses the town, the peripheral route speeds people to their destination. Analytical people—those with a high *need for cognition*—enjoy thinking carefully and prefer central routes (Cacioppo & others, 1996). People who like to conserve their mental resources—those with a low need for cognition—are quicker to respond to such peripheral cues as the communicator's attractiveness and the pleasantness of the surroundings.

This simple theory—that *what we think in response to a message is crucial,* especially if we are motivated and able to think about it—has generated many predictions, most of which have been confirmed by Petty, Cacioppo, and others (Axsom & others, 1987; Haddock & others, 2008; Harkins & Petty, 1987). Many experiments have explored ways to stimulate people's thinking

- by using *rhetorical questions.*
- by presenting *multiple speakers* (for example, having each of three speakers give one argument instead of one speaker giving three).
- by making people *feel responsible* for evaluating or passing along the message.

- by *repeating* the message.
- by getting people's *undistracted attention.*

The consistent finding with each of these techniques: *Stimulating thinking makes strong messages more persuasive and* (because of counterarguing) *weak messages less persuasive.*

The theory also has practical implications. Effective communicators care not only about their images and their messages but also about how their audience is likely to react. The best instructors get students to think actively. They ask rhetorical questions, provide intriguing examples, and challenge students with difficult problems. Such techniques foster the central route to persuasion. In classes in which the instruction is less engaging, you can still provide your own central processing. If you think about the material and elaborate on the arguments, you are likely to do better in the course.

During the final days of a closely contested 1980 U.S. presidential campaign, Ronald Reagan effectively used rhetorical questions to stimulate desired thoughts in voters' minds. His summary statement in the presidential debate began with two potent rhetorical questions that he repeated often during the campaign's remaining week: "Are you better off than you were four years ago? Is it easier for you to go and buy things in the stores than it was four years ago?" Most people answered no, and Reagan, thanks partly to the way he prodded people to take the central route, won by a bigger-than-expected margin.

THE TWO ROUTES TO PERSUASION IN THERAPY

One constructive use of persuasion is in counseling and psychotherapy, which social-counseling psychologist Stanley Strong views "as a branch of applied social psychology" (1978, p. 101). By the 1990s, more and more psychologists had accepted the idea that social influence, one person affecting another, is at the heart of therapy.

Early analyses of psychotherapeutic influence focused on how therapists establish credible expertise and trustworthiness and how their credibility enhances their influence (Strong, 1968). Later analyses focused less on the therapist than on how the interaction affects the client's thinking (Cacioppo & others, 1991; McNeill & Stoltenberg, 1988; Neimeyer & others, 1991). Peripheral cues, such as therapist credibility, may open the door for ideas that the therapist can now get the client to think about. But the thoughtful central route to persuasion provides the most enduring attitude and behavior change. Therapists should therefore aim not to elicit a client's superficial agreement with their expert judgment but to change the client's own thinking.

Fortunately, most clients entering therapy are motivated to take the central route—to think deeply about their problems under the therapist's guidance. The therapist's task is to offer arguments and raise questions calculated to elicit favorable thoughts. The therapist's insights matter less than the thoughts they evoke in the client. The therapist needs to put things in ways that a client can hear and understand, comments that will prompt agreement rather than counterargument, and that will allow time and space for the client to reflect. Questions such as "How do you respond to what I just said?" can stimulate the client's thinking.

Martin Heesacker (1989) illustrated how a therapist can help a client reflect with the case of Dave, a 35-year-old male graduate student. Having seen what Dave denied—an underlying substance abuse problem—the counselor drew on his knowledge of Dave, an intellectual person who liked hard evidence, in persuading him to accept the diagnosis and join a treatment-support group. The counselor said, "OK, if my diagnosis is wrong, I'll be glad to change it. But let's go through a list of the characteristics of a substance abuser to check out my accuracy." The counselor then went through each criterion slowly, giving Dave time to think about each point. As he finished, Dave sat back and exclaimed, "I don't believe it: I'm a damned alcoholic."

In his 1620 Pensées, the philosopher Pascal foresaw this principle: "People are usually more convinced by reasons they discover themselves than by those found by others." It's a principle worth remembering.

CONCEPTS TO REMEMBER

persuasion   The process by which a message induces change in beliefs, attitudes, or behaviors.

central route to persuasion   Occurs when interested people focus on the arguments and respond with favorable thoughts.

peripheral route to persuasion   Occurs when people are influenced by incidental cues, such as a speaker's attractiveness.

credibility   Believability. A credible communicator is perceived as both expert and trustworthy.

sleeper effect   A delayed impact of a message that occurs when an initially discounted message becomes effective, such as we remember the message but forget the reason for discounting it.

attractiveness   Having qualities that appeal to an audience. An appealing communicator (often someone similar to the audience) is most persuasive on matters of subjective preference.

16

❖

Indoctrination and Inoculation

Many of life's powers can either harm or help us. Nuclear power enables us to light up homes or wipe out cities. Sexual power helps us to express committed love or to seek selfish gratification. Similarly, persuasion's power enables us to promote health or to sell addiction, to advance peace or stir up hate, to enlighten or deceive. And such powers are great. Consider the following:

- *The spread of weird beliefs:* About 1 American in 5 thinks the sun revolves around the earth (Dean, 2005). About 1 in 5 have expressed belief that President Obama is a Muslim and 1 in 4 that he was born outside the United States (Blanton, 2011; Pew, 2010). Others deny that the moon landing and the Holocaust happened.

- *Climate change skepticism:* The scientific community, represented by various national academies of science and the Intergovernmental Panel on Climate Change, is in a virtual consensus about three facts of life: (1) Atmospheric greenhouse gases are accumulating; (2) diminishing sea ice and rising temperatures confirm the world's warming; and (3) this climate change will almost certainly produce rising sea levels and more extreme weather, including record floods, tornadoes, droughts, and high temperatures. "Climate change is occurring, is caused largely by human activities, and poses significant risks," declares the U.S. National Research Council (2010). Nevertheless, as the past decade was ending, popular climate *skepticism* was growing. The number of Americans who believed global warming has been happening declined from 84 to 74 percent between 2007 and 2010, as concern diminished—and then rebounded in 2012 in the aftermath of record heat, drought, and hurricane damage (Krosnick, 2010; Pew, 2012). In Britain, the proportion who believed climate change was not only happening but also "now established as largely manmade" dropped from 41 percent in 2009 to 26 percent in 2010. And the number of Germans fearing global warming dropped to 42 percent, from 62 percent 4 years earlier (Rosenthal, 2010). Researchers wondered: Why was the scientific consensus failing to persuade and to motivate action? And what might be done?

- *Promoting healthier living:* Due partly to health-promotion campaigns, the Centers for Disease Control and Prevention reports that the American cigarette smoking rate has plunged to 21 percent, half the rate of 40 years ago. *Statistics Canada* reports a similar smoking decline in Canada. And the rate of new U.S. collegians reporting abstinence from beer has increased—from 26 percent in 1982 to 62 percent in 2010 (Pryor & others, 2007, 2010).

As the previous examples show, efforts to persuade are sometimes diabolical, sometimes controversial, and sometimes beneficial. Persuasion is neither inherently good nor bad. It is a message's purpose and content that elicit judgments of good or bad. The bad we call "propaganda." The good we call "education." Education is more factually based and less coercive than propaganda. Yet generally we call it "education" when we believe it, "propaganda" when we don't (Lumsden & others, 1980).

CULT INDOCTRINATION

On March 22, 1997, in California, Marshall Herff Applewhite and 37 of his disciples decided the time had come to shed their bodies—mere "containers"—and be whisked up to a UFO trailing the Hale–Bopp Comet, en route to heaven's gate. So they put themselves to sleep by mixing phenobarbital into pudding or applesauce, washing it down with vodka, and then fixing plastic bags over their heads so they would suffocate in their slumber. On that same day, a cottage in the Quebec village of St. Casimir exploded in an inferno, consuming 5 people—the latest of 74 members of the Order of the Solar Temple to have committed suicide in Canada, Switzerland, and France. All were hoping to be transported to the star Sirius, nine light-years away.

The question on many minds: What persuades people to leave behind their former beliefs and join these mental chain gangs? Should we attribute their strange behaviors to strange personalities? Or do their experiences illustrate the common dynamics of social influence and persuasion?

Bear two things in mind. First, this is hindsight analysis. It uses persuasion principles to explain, after the fact, a curious social phenomenon. Second, explaining *why* people believe something says nothing about the *truth* of their beliefs. That is a logically separate issue. A psychology of religion might tell us *why* a theist believes in God and an atheist disbelieves, but it cannot tell us who is right. Explaining either belief does nothing to change its validity. Remember that if someone tries to discount your beliefs by saying, "You just believe that because . . . ," you might recall Archbishop William Temple's reply to a questioner who challenged: "Well, of course, Archbishop, the point is that you believe what you believe because of the way you were brought up." To which the archbishop replied: "That is as it may be. But the fact remains that you believe I believe what I believe because of the way I was brought up, because of the way you were brought up."

In recent decades, several **cults**—which some social scientists prefer to call *new religious movements*—have gained much publicity: Sun Myung Moon's Unification Church, Jim Jones's People's Temple, David Koresh's Branch Davidians, and Marshall Applewhite's Heaven's Gate.

Sun Myung Moon's mixture of Christianity, anticommunism, and glorification of Moon himself as a new messiah attracted a worldwide following. In response to Moon's declaration "What I wish must be your wish," many people committed themselves and their incomes to the Unification Church.

In 1978 in Guyana, 914 disciples of Jim Jones, who had followed him there from San Francisco, shocked the world when they died by following his order to down a suicidal grape drink laced with tranquilizers, painkillers, and a lethal dose of cyanide.

In 1993, high-school dropout David Koresh used his talent for memorizing Scripture and mesmerizing people to seize control of a faction of the Branch Davidian sect. Over time, members were gradually relieved of their bank accounts and possessions. Koresh also persuaded the men to live celibately while he slept with their wives and daughters, and he convinced his 19 "wives" that they should bear his children. Under siege after a shootout that killed 6 members and 4 federal agents, Koresh told his followers they would soon die and go with him straight to heaven. Federal agents rammed the compound with tanks, hoping to inject tear gas. By the end of the assault, 86 people were consumed in a fire.

Marshall Applewhite was not similarly tempted to command sexual favors. Having been fired from two music teaching jobs for affairs with students, he sought sexless devotion by castration, as had 7 of the other 17 Heaven's Gate men who died with him (Chua-Eoan, 1997; Gardner, 1997). While in a psychiatric hospital in 1971, Applewhite had linked up with nurse and astrology dabbler Bonnie Lu Nettles, who gave the intense and charismatic Applewhite a cosmological vision of a route to "the next level." Preaching with passion, he persuaded his followers to renounce families, sex, drugs, and personal money with promises of a spaceship voyage to salvation.

How could these things happen? What persuaded these people to give such total allegiance? Shall we make dispositional explanations—by blaming the victims? Shall we dismiss them as gullible or unbalanced? Or can familiar principles of conformity, compliance, dissonance, persuasion, and group influence explain their behavior—putting them on common ground with the rest of us who in our own ways are shaped by such forces?

Attitudes Follow Behavior

As we saw in Module 9's discussion of behavior and belief, people usually internalize commitments made voluntarily, publicly, and repeatedly. Cult leaders seem to know this.

Compliance Breeds Acceptance

New converts soon learn that membership is no trivial matter. They are quickly made active members of the team. Behavioral rituals, public recruitment, and fund-raising strengthen the initiates' identities as members. Those in social psychological experiments come to believe in what they bear witness to (Aronson & Mills, 1959; Gerard & Mathewson, 1966), and cult initiates likewise become committed advocates. The greater the personal commitment, the more the need to justify it.

The Foot-in-the-Door Phenomenon

How are people induced to make a commitment to such a drastic life change? Seldom by an abrupt, conscious decision. One does not just decide, "I'm through with mainstream religion. I'm gonna find a cult." Nor do cult recruiters approach people on the street with, "Hi. I'm a Moonie. Care to join us?" Rather, the recruitment strategy exploits the foot-in-the-door principle. Unification Church recruiters, for example, would invite people to a dinner and then to a weekend of warm fellowship and discussions of philosophies of life. At the weekend retreat, they would encourage the attenders to join them in songs, activities, and discussion. Potential converts were then urged to sign up for longer training retreats. The pattern in cults is for the activities to become gradually more arduous, culminating in having recruits solicit contributions and attempt to convert others.

Once converts have entered the cult, they find that monetary offerings are at first voluntary, then mandatory. Jim Jones eventually inaugurated a required 10-percent-of-income contribution, which soon increased to 25 percent. Finally, he ordered members to turn over to him everything they owned. Workloads also became progressively more demanding. Former cult member Grace Stoen recalls the gradual progress:

> Nothing was ever done drastically. That's how Jim Jones got away with so much. You slowly gave up things and slowly had to put up with more, but it was always done very gradually. It was amazing, because you would sit up sometimes and say, wow, I really have given up a lot. I really am putting up with a lot. But he did it so slowly that you figured, I've made it this far, what the hell is the difference? (Conway & Siegelman, 1979, p. 236)

Persuasive Elements

We can also analyze cult persuasion using the factors discussed in Module 15: *Who* (the communicator) said *what* (the message) to *whom* (the audience)?

The Communicator

Successful cults typically have a charismatic leader—someone who attracts and directs the members. As in experiments on persuasion, a credible communicator is someone the audience perceives as expert and trustworthy—for example, as "Father" Moon.

Jim Jones used "psychic readings" to establish his credibility. Newcomers were asked to identify themselves as they entered the church before services. Then one of his aides would quickly call the person's home and say, "Hi. We're doing a survey, and we'd like to ask you some questions." During the service, one ex-member recalled, Jones would call out the person's name and say

> Have you ever seen me before? Well, you live in such and such a place, your phone number is such and such, and in your living room you've got this, that, and the other, and on your sofa you've got such and such a pillow. . . . Now do you remember me ever being in your house? (Conway & Siegelman, 1979, p. 234)

Trust is another aspect of credibility. Cult researcher Margaret Singer (1979) noted that middle-class Caucasian youths are more vulnerable to recruitment because they are more trusting. They lack the "street smarts" of lower-class youths (who know how to resist a hustle) and the wariness of upper-class youths (who have been warned of kidnappers since childhood). Many cult members have been recruited by friends or relatives, people they trust (Stark & Bainbridge, 1980).

The Message

The vivid, emotional messages and the warmth and acceptance with which the group showers lonely or depressed people can be strikingly appealing: Trust the master, join the family; we have the answer, the "one way." The message echoes through channels as varied as lectures, small-group discussions, and direct social pressure.

The Audience

Recruits are often young people under 25 years old, still at that comparatively open age before attitudes and values stabilize. Some, such as the followers of Jim Jones, are less educated people who like the message's simplicity and find it difficult to counterargue. But most are educated, middle-class people who, taken by the ideals, overlook the contradictions in those who profess selflessness and practice greed, who pretend concern and behave callously.

Potential converts are often at turning points in their lives, facing personal crises, or vacationing or living away from home. They have needs; the cult offers them an answer (Lofland & Stark, 1965; Singer, 1979). Gail Maeder joined Heaven's Gate after her T-shirt shop had failed. David Moore joined when he was 19, just out of high school, and searching for direction. Times of social and economic upheaval are especially conducive to someone who can make apparent simple sense out of the confusion (O'Dea, 1968; Sales, 1972).

Most of those who have carried out suicide bombings in the Middle East (and other places such as Bali, Madrid, and London) were, likewise, young men at the transition between adolescence and adult maturity. Like cult recruits, they come under the influence of authoritative, religiously oriented communicators. These compelling voices indoctrinate them into seeing themselves as "living martyrs" whose fleeting moment of self-destruction will be their portal into bliss and heroism. To overcome the will to survive, each candidate makes public commitments—creating a will, writing good-bye letters, making a farewell video—that create a psychological point of no return (Kruglanski & Golec de Zavala, 2005). All of this typically transpires in the relative isolation of small cells, with group influences that fan hatred for the enemy.

Group Effects

Cults also illustrate the next module's theme: the power of a group to shape members' views and behavior. The cult typically separates members from their previous social support systems and isolates them with other cult members. There may then occur what Rodney Stark and William Bainbridge (1980) call a "social implosion": External ties weaken until the group collapses inward socially, each person engaging only with other group members. Cut off from families and former friends, they lose access to counterarguments. The group now offers identity and defines reality. Because the cult frowns on or punishes disagreements, the apparent consensus helps eliminate any lingering doubts. Moreover, stress and emotional arousal narrow attention, making people "more susceptible to poorly supported arguments, social pressure, and the temptation to derogate nongroup members" (Baron, 2000).

Marshall Applewhite and Bonnie Nettles at first formed their own group of two, reinforcing each other's aberrant thinking—a phenomenon that psychiatrists call *folie à deux* (French for "insanity of two"). As others joined them, the group's social isolation facilitated peculiar thinking. Internet conspiracy groups can likewise foster paranoia. Heaven's Gate was skilled in Internet recruiting.

These techniques—increasing behavioral commitments, persuasion, and group isolation—do not, however, have unlimited power. The Unification Church successfully recruited fewer than 1 in 10 people who attended its workshops (Ennis & Verrilli, 1989). Most who joined Heaven's Gate left before that fateful day. David Koresh ruled with a mix of persuasion, intimidation, and violence. As Jim Jones made his demands more extreme, he, too, increasingly had to control people with intimidation. He used threats of harm to those who fled the community, beatings for noncompliance, and drugs to neutralize disagreeable members. By the end, he was as much an arm twister as a mind bender.

Some of these cult influence techniques bear similarities to techniques used by more benign, widely accepted groups. Buddhist and Catholic monasteries, for example, have cloistered adherents with kindred spirits. Fraternity and sorority members have reported that the initial "love bombing" of potential cult recruits is not unlike their own "rush" period. Members lavish prospective pledges with attention and make them feel special. During the pledge period, new members are somewhat isolated, cut off from old friends who did not pledge. They spend time studying the history and rules of their new group. They suffer and commit time on its behalf. They are expected to comply with all its demands. The result is usually a committed new member.

Much the same is true of some therapeutic communities for recovering drug and alcohol abusers. Zealous self-help groups form a cohesive "social cocoon," have intense beliefs, and exert a profound influence on members' behavior (Galanter, 1989, 1990).

I choose the examples of fraternities, sororities, self-help groups, and psychotherapy not to disparage them but to illustrate two concluding observations. First, if we attribute new religious movements to the leader's mystical force or to the followers' peculiar weaknesses, we may delude ourselves into thinking we are immune to social control techniques. In truth, our own groups—and countless political leaders, educators, and other persuaders—successfully use many of these same tactics on us. Between education and indoctrination, enlightenment and propaganda, conversion and coercion, therapy and mind control, there is but a blurry line.

Second, the fact that Jim Jones and other cult leaders abused the power of persuasion does not mean persuasion is intrinsically bad. Knowing that persuasive power, like nuclear power, can be harnessed for evil purposes should alert us, as scientists and citizens, to guard against its immoral use. But the power itself is neither inherently evil nor inherently good; it is how we use it that determines whether its effect is destructive or constructive. Condemning persuasion because of deceit is like condemning eating because of gluttony.

RESISTING PERSUASION: ATTITUDE INOCULATION

This consideration of persuasive influences has perhaps made you wonder if it is possible to resist unwanted persuasion.

Blessed with logic, information, and motivation, we do resist falsehoods. If the credible-seeming repair person's uniform and the doctor's title have intimidated us into unthinking agreement, we can rethink our habitual responses to authority. We can seek more information before committing time or money. We can question what we don't understand.

Stimulate Commitment

There is another way to resist: Before encountering others' judgments, make a public commitment to your position. Having stood up for your convictions, you will become less susceptible (or, should we say, less "open") to what others have to say.

Challenging Beliefs

How might we stimulate people to commit themselves? Charles Kiesler (1971) offered one possible way: Mildly attack their position. Kiesler found that when committed people were attacked strongly enough to cause them to react, but not so strongly as to overwhelm them, they became even more committed. Kiesler explained: "When you attack committed people and your attack is of inadequate strength, you drive them to even more extreme behaviors in defense of their previous commitment" (p. 88). Perhaps you can recall that happening in an argument, as those involved escalated their rhetoric, committing themselves to increasingly extreme positions.

Developing Counterarguments

There is a second reason a mild attack might build resistance. Like inoculations against disease, even weak arguments will prompt counterarguments, which are then available for a stronger attack. William McGuire (1964) documented this in some famous experiments. McGuire wondered: Could we inoculate people against persuasion much as we inoculate them against a virus? Is there such a thing as **attitude inoculation?** Could we take people raised in a "germ-free ideological environment"—people who hold some unquestioned belief—and stimulate their mental defenses? And would subjecting them to a small dose of belief-threatening material inoculate them against later persuasion?

A "poison parasite" ad.

That is what McGuire did. First, he found some cultural truisms, such as "It's a good idea to brush your teeth after every meal if at all possible." He then showed that people were vulnerable to a powerful, credible assault upon those truisms (for example, prestigious authorities were said to have discovered that too much toothbrushing can damage one's gums). If, however, before having their belief attacked, they were "immunized" by first receiving a small challenge to their belief, *and* if they read or wrote an essay in refutation of this mild attack, then they were better able to resist the powerful attack.

Robert Cialdini and colleagues (2003) agree that appropriate counterarguments are a great way to resist persuasion. But they wondered how to bring them to mind in response to an opponent's ads. The answer, they suggest, is a "poison parasite" defense—one that combines a poison (strong counterarguments) with a parasite (retrieval cues that bring those arguments to mind when seeing the opponent's ads). In their studies, participants who viewed a familiar political ad were least persuaded by it when they had earlier seen counterarguments overlaid on a replica of the ad. Seeing the ad again thus also brought to mind the puncturing counterarguments. Antismoking ads have effectively done this, for example, by re-creating a "Marlboro Man" commercial set in the rugged outdoors but now showing a coughing, decrepit cowboy.

Real-Life Applications: Inoculation Programs

Inoculating Children Against Peer Pressure to Smoke
Consider how laboratory research findings can lead to practical applications. One research team had high school students "inoculate" seventh-graders against peer pressures to smoke (McAlister & others, 1980). The

seventh-graders were taught to respond to advertisements implying that liberated women smoke by saying, "She's not really liberated if she is hooked on tobacco." They also acted in role plays in which, after being called "chicken" for not taking a cigarette, they answered with statements such as "I'd be a real chicken if I smoked just to impress you." After several of these sessions during the seventh and eighth grades, the inoculated students were half as likely to begin smoking as were uninoculated students at another junior high school—one that had an identical parental smoking rate (Figure 16-1).

Other research teams have confirmed that inoculation procedures, sometimes supplemented by other life skill training, reduce teen smoking (Botvin & others, 1995, 2008; Evans & others, 1984; Flay & others, 1985). Most newer efforts emphasize strategies for resisting social pressure. One study exposed sixth- to eighth-graders to antismoking films or to information about smoking, together with role plays of student-generated ways of refusing a cigarette (Hirschman & Leventhal, 1989). A year and a half later, 31 percent of those who watched the antismoking films had taken up smoking. Among those who role-played refusing, only 19 percent had begun smoking.

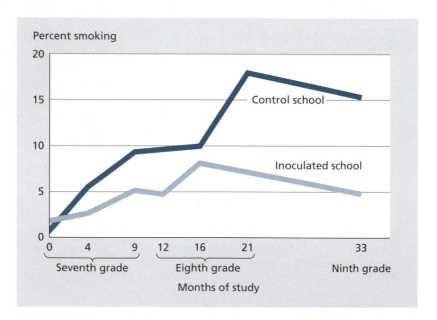

FIGURE 16-1
The percentage of cigarette smokers at an "inoculated" junior high school was much less than at a matched control school using a more typical smoking education program.   Source: Data from McAlister & others (1980), Telch & others (1981).

Antismoking and drug education programs apply other persuasion principles, too. They use attractive peers to communicate information. They trigger the students' own cognitive processing ("Here's something you might want to think about"). They get the students to make a public commitment (by making a rational decision about smoking and then announcing it, along with their reasoning, to their classmates). Some of these smoking-prevention programs require only 2–6 hours of class, using prepared printed materials or videotapes. Today, any school district or teacher wishing to use the social psychological approach to smoking prevention can do so easily, inexpensively, and with the hope of significant reductions in future smoking rates and associated health costs.

Inoculating Children Against the Influence of Advertising

Belgium, Denmark, Greece, Ireland, Italy, and Sweden all restrict advertising that targets children (McGuire, 2002). In the United States, notes Robert Levine in *The Power of Persuasion: How We're Bought and Sold,* the average child sees more than 10,000 commercials a year. "Two decades ago," he notes, "children drank twice as much milk as soda. Thanks to advertising, the ratio is now reversed" (2003, p. 16).

Smokers often develop an "initial brand choice" in their teens, stated a 1981 report from researchers at Philip Morris (Federal Trade Commission, 2003). "Today's teenager is tomorrow's potential regular customer, and the overwhelming majority of smokers first begin to smoke while still in their teens" (Lichtblau, 2003). That explains why some cigarette and smokeless tobacco companies aggressively market to college and university students, by advertising, by sponsoring parties, and by offering free cigarettes (usually in situations in which students are also drinking), all as part of their marketing of nicotine to "entry level" smokers (Farrell, 2005).

Hoping to restrain advertising's influence, researchers have studied how to immunize young children against the effects of television commercials. Their research was prompted partly by studies showing that children, especially those under age 8 years, (1) have trouble distinguishing commercials from programs and fail to grasp their persuasive intent, (2) trust television advertising rather indiscriminately, and (3) desire and badger their parents for advertised products (Adler & others, 1980; Feshbach, 1980; Palmer & Dorr, 1980). Children, it seems, are an advertiser's dream: gullible, vulnerable, and an easy sell.

Armed with these findings, citizens' groups have given the advertisers of such products a chewing out (Moody, 1980): "When a sophisticated advertiser spends millions to sell unsophisticated, trusting children an unhealthy product, this can only be called exploitation." In "Mothers' Statement to Advertisers" (Motherhood Project, 2001), a broad coalition of women echoed this outrage:

> For us, our children are priceless gifts. For you, our children are customers, and childhood is a "market segment" to be exploited. . . . The line between

meeting and creating consumer needs and desire is increasingly being crossed, as your battery of highly trained and creative experts study, analyze, persuade, and manipulate our children. . . . The driving messages are "You deserve a break today," "Have it your way," "Follow your instincts. Obey your thirst," "Just Do It," "No Boundaries," "Got the Urge?" These [exemplify] the dominant message of advertising and marketing: that life is about selfishness, instant gratification, and materialism.

On the other side are the commercial interests. They claim that ads allow parents to teach their children consumer skills and, more important, finance children's television programs. In the United States, the Federal Trade Commission has been in the middle, pushed by research findings and political pressures while trying to decide whether to place new constraints on TV ads for unhealthy foods and for R-rated movies aimed at underage youth.

Meanwhile, researchers have found that inner-city seventh-graders who are able to think critically about ads—who have "media resistance skills"—also better resist peer pressure as eighth-graders and are less likely to drink alcohol as ninth-graders (Epstein & Botvin, 2008). Researchers have also wondered whether children can be taught to resist deceptive ads. In one such effort, a team of investigators led by Norma Feshbach (1980; S. Cohen, 1980) gave small groups of Los Angeles–area elementary schoolchildren three half-hour lessons in analyzing commercials. The children were inoculated by viewing ads and discussing them. For example, after viewing a toy ad, they were immediately given the toy and challenged to make it do what they had just seen in the commercial. Such experiences helped breed a more realistic understanding of commercials.

Implications of Attitude Inoculation

The best way to build resistance to brainwashing probably is not just stronger indoctrination into one's current beliefs. If parents are worried that their children might become members of a cult, they might better teach their children about the various cults and prepare them to counter persuasive appeals.

For the same reason, religious educators should be wary of creating a "germ-free ideological environment" in their churches and schools. People who live amid diverse views become more discerning and more likely to modify their views only in response to credible arguments (Levitan & Visser, 2008). Also, a challenge to one's views, if refuted, is more likely to solidify one's position than to undermine it, particularly if the threatening material can be examined with like-minded others (Visser & Mirabile, 2004). Cults apply this principle by forewarning members of how families and friends will attack the cult's beliefs. When the expected challenge comes, the member is armed with counterarguments.

Another implication is that, for the persuader, an ineffective appeal can be worse than none. Can you see why? Those who reject an appeal are inoculated against further appeals. Consider an experiment in which Susan Darley and Joel Cooper (1972) invited students to write essays advocating a strict dress code. Because that was against the students' own positions and the essays were to be published, all chose *not* to write the essay—even those offered money to do so. After turning down the money, they became even more extreme and confident in their anti–dress code opinions. Those who have rejected initial appeals to quit smoking may likewise become immune to further appeals. Ineffective persuasion, by stimulating the listener's defenses, may be counterproductive. It may "harden the heart" against later appeals.

To be critical thinkers, we might take a cue from inoculation research. Do you want to build your resistance to false messages without becoming closed to valid messages? Be an active listener. Force yourself to counterargue. Don't just listen; react. After hearing a political speech, discuss it with others. If the message cannot withstand careful analysis, so much the worse for it. If it can, its effect on you will be that much more enduring.

www.mhhe.com/myersesp6e

Activity
16.1

CONCEPTS TO REMEMBER

cult (also called new religious movement)   A group typically characterized by (1) distinctive rituals and beliefs related to its devotion to a god or a person, (2) isolation from the surrounding "evil" culture, and (3) a charismatic leader.

(A sect, by contrast, is a spin-off from a major religion.)

attitude inoculation   Exposing people to weak attacks upon their attitudes so that when stronger attacks come, they will have refutations available.

❖

17

The Mere Presence
of Others

Our world contains not only 7 billion individuals but also 196 nation-states, 4 million local communities, 20 million economic organizations, and hundreds of millions of other formal and informal groups—couples having dinner, housemates hanging out, soldiers plotting strategy. How do such groups influence individuals?

Let's explore social psychology's most elementary question: Are we affected by the mere presence of another person—by people who are not competing, do not reward or punish, and in fact do nothing except be present as a passive audience or as **co-actors?**

THE MERE PRESENCE OF OTHERS

More than a century ago, Norman Triplett (1898), a psychologist interested in bicycle racing, noticed that cyclists' times were faster when they raced together than when each one raced alone against the clock. Before he peddled his hunch (that others' presence boosts performance), Triplett conducted one of social psychology's first laboratory experiments. Children told to wind string on a fishing reel as rapidly as possible wound faster when they worked with competing co-actors than when they worked alone. "The bodily presence of another contestant . . . serves to liberate latent energy," concluded Triplett.

A modern reanalysis of Triplett's data revealed that the difference did not reach statistical significance (Stroebe, 2012; Strube, 2005). But ensuing experiments did find that others' presence improves the speed with which people do simple multiplication problems and cross out designated letters. It

195

also improves the accuracy with which people perform simple motor tasks, such as keeping a metal stick in contact with a dime-sized disk on a moving turntable (F. H. Allport, 1920; Dashiell, 1930; Travis, 1925). This **social facilitation** effect also occurs with animals. In the presence of others of their species, ants excavate more sand, chickens eat more grain, and sexually active rat pairs mate more often (Bayer, 1929; Chen, 1937; Larsson, 1956).

But wait: Other studies revealed that on some tasks the presence of others *hinders* performance. In the presence of others, cockroaches, para-keets, and green finches learn mazes more slowly (Allee & Masure, 1936; Gates & Allee, 1933; Klopfer, 1958). This disruptive effect also occurs with people. Others' presence diminishes efficiency at learning nonsense syllables, completing a maze, and performing complex multiplication problems (Dashiell, 1930; Pessin, 1933; Pessin & Husband, 1933).

Saying that the presence of others sometimes facilitates performance and sometimes hinders it is about as satisfying as the typical Scottish weather forecast—predicting that it might be sunny but then again it might rain. By 1940, social facilitation research ground to a halt, and it lay dormant for 25 years until awakened by the touch of a new idea.

Social psychologist Robert Zajonc (1923–2008, pronounced *Zy-ence*, rhymes with *science*) wondered whether these seemingly contradictory findings could be reconciled. As often happens at creative moments in science, Zajonc (1965) used one field of research to illuminate another. The illumination came from a well-established experimental psychology principle: Arousal enhances whatever response tendency is dominant. Increased arousal enhances performance on easy tasks for which the most likely— "dominant"—response is correct. People solve easy anagrams, such as *akec,* fastest when aroused. On complex tasks, for which the correct answer is not dominant, increased arousal promotes *incorrect* responding. On more difficult anagrams, such as *theloacco,* people do worse when aroused.

Could this principle solve the mystery of social facilitation? It seemed reasonable to assume that others' presence will arouse or energize people (Mullen & others, 1997); most of us can recall feeling tense or excited in front of an audience. If social arousal facilitates dominant responses, it should *boost performance on easy tasks* and *hurt performance on difficult tasks.*

With that explanation, the confusing results made sense. Winding fishing reels, doing simple multiplication problems, and eating were all easy tasks for which the responses were well learned or naturally dominant. Sure enough, having others around boosted performance. Learning new material, doing a maze, and solving complex math problems were more difficult tasks for which the correct responses were initially less probable. In these cases, the presence of others increased the number of *incorrect* responses on these tasks. The same general rule—*arousal facilitates dominant responses*—worked in both cases (Figure 17-1). Suddenly, what had looked like contradictory results no longer seemed contradictory.

Zajonc's solution, so simple and elegant, left other social psychologists thinking what Thomas H. Huxley thought after first reading Darwin's *On*

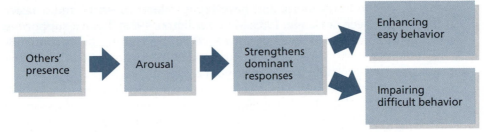

FIGURE 17-1
The effects of social arousal. Robert Zajonc reconciled apparently conflicting findings by proposing that arousal from others' presence strengthens dominant responses (the correct responses only on easy or well-learned tasks).

the Origin of Species: "How extremely stupid not to have thought of that!" It seemed obvious—once Zajonc had pointed it out. Perhaps, however, the pieces fit so neatly only through the spectacles of hindsight. Would the solution survive direct experimental tests?

After almost 300 studies, conducted with the help of more than 25,000 volunteers, the solution has survived (Bond & Titus, 1983; Guerin, 1993, 1999). Social arousal facilitates dominant responses, whether right or wrong. For example, Peter Hunt and Joseph Hillery (1973) found that in others' presence, students took less time to learn a simple maze and more time to learn a complex one (just as the cockroaches do!). And James Michaels and collaborators (1982) found that good pool players in a student union (who had made 71 percent of their shots while being unobtrusively observed) did even better (80 percent) when four observers came up to watch them play. Poor shooters (who had previously averaged 36 percent) did even worse (25 percent) when closely observed.

Athletes, actors, and musicians perform well-practiced skills, which helps explain why they often perform best when energized by the responses of a supportive audience. Studies of more than a quarter million college and professional athletic events worldwide reveal that home teams win approximately 6 in 10 games (somewhat fewer for baseball and football, somewhat more for basketball and soccer, but consistently more than half). The home advantage may, however, also stem from the players' familiarity with their home environment, less travel fatigue, feelings of dominance derived from territorial control, or increased team identity when cheered by fans (Zillmann & Paulus, 1993).

CROWDING: THE PRESENCE OF MANY OTHERS

So people do respond to others' presence. But does the presence of observers always arouse people? In times of stress, a comrade can be comforting. Nevertheless, with others present, people perspire more, breathe faster, tense their muscles more, and have higher blood pressure and a faster heart rate (Geen & Gange, 1983; Moore & Baron, 1983). Even a supportive audience may elicit poorer performance on challenging tasks (Butler & Baumeister, 1998). Having your entire extended family attend your first piano recital probably won't boost your performance.

The effect of others' presence increases with their number (Jackson & Latané, 1981; Knowles, 1983). Sometimes the arousal and self-conscious attention created by a large audience interferes even with well-learned, automatic behaviors, such as speaking. Given *extreme* pressure, we're vulnerable to "choking." Stutterers tend to stutter more in front of larger audiences than when speaking to just one or two people (Mullen, 1986).

Being *in* a crowd also intensifies positive or negative reactions. When they sit close together, friendly people are liked even more, and *dis*liked even more (Schiffenbauer & Schiavo, 1976; Storms & Thomas, 1977). In experiments with Columbia University students and with Ontario Science Center visitors, Jonathan Freedman and co-workers (1979, 1980) had an accomplice listen to a humorous tape or watch a movie with other participants. When they all sat close together, the accomplice could more readily induce the individuals to laugh and clap. As theater directors and sports fans know, and as researchers have confirmed, a "good house" is a full house (Aiello & others, 1983; Worchel & Brown, 1984).

Perhaps you've noticed that a class of 35 students feels more warm and lively in a room that seats just 35 than when spread around a room that seats 100. When others are close by, we are more likely to notice and join in their laughter or clapping. But crowding also enhances arousal, as Gary Evans (1979) found. He tested 10-person groups of University of Massachusetts students, either in a room 20 by 30 feet or in one 8 by 12 feet. Compared with those in the large room, those densely packed had higher pulse rates and blood pressure (indicating arousal). On difficult tasks they made more errors, an effect of crowding replicated by Dinesh Nagar and Janak Pandey (1987) with university students in India. Crowding, then, has a similar effect to being observed by a crowd: it enhances arousal, which facilitates dominant responses.

WHY ARE WE AROUSED IN THE PRESENCE OF OTHERS?

What you do well, you will be energized to do best in front of others (unless you become hyperaroused and self-conscious). What you find difficult may seem impossible in the same circumstances. What is it about other people that creates arousal? Evidence supports three possible factors (Aiello & Douthitt, 2001; Feinberg & Aiello, 2006): evaluation apprehension, distraction, and mere presence.

Evaluation Apprehension

Nickolas Cottrell surmised that observers make us apprehensive because we wonder how they are evaluating us. To test whether **evaluation apprehension** exists, Cottrell and associates (1968) blindfolded observers, supposedly in preparation for a perception experiment. In contrast to the effect of the watching audience, the mere presence of these blindfolded people did *not* boost well-practiced responses.

Other experiments confirmed Cottrell's conclusion: The enhancement of dominant responses is strongest when people think they are being evaluated. In one experiment, individuals running on a University of California at Santa Barbara jogging path sped up as they came upon a woman seated on the grass—*if* she was facing them rather than sitting with her back turned (Worringham & Messick, 1983).

The self-consciousness we feel when being evaluated can also interfere with behaviors that we perform best automatically (Mullen & Baumeister, 1987). If self-conscious basketball players analyze their body movements while shooting critical free throws, they are more likely to miss.

Driven by Distraction

Glenn Sanders, Robert Baron, and Danny Moore (1978; Baron, 1986) carried evaluation apprehension a step further. They theorized that when we wonder how co-actors are doing or how an audience is reacting, we become distracted. This *conflict* between paying attention to others and paying attention to the task overloads our cognitive system, causing arousal. We are "driven by distraction." This arousal comes not just from the presence of another person but even from a nonhuman distraction, such as bursts of light (Sanders, 1981a, 1981b).

Mere Presence

Zajonc, however, believed that the mere presence of others produces some arousal even without evaluation apprehension or arousing distraction. Recall that facilitation effects also occur with nonhuman animals. This hints at an innate social arousal mechanism common to much of the zoological world. (Animals probably are not consciously worrying about how other animals are evaluating them.) At the human level, most runners are energized when running with someone else, even one who neither competes nor evaluates.

This is a good time to remind ourselves that a good theory is a scientific shorthand: It simplifies and summarizes a variety of observations. Social facilitation theory does this well. It is a simple summary of many research findings. A good theory also offers clear predictions that (1) help confirm or modify the theory, (2) guide new exploration, and (3) suggest practical applications. Social facilitation theory has definitely generated the first two types of prediction: (1) The basics of the theory (that the presence of others is arousing and that this social arousal enhances dominant responses) have been confirmed, and (2) the theory has brought new life to a long-dormant field of research.

Are there (3) some practical applications? We can make some educated guesses. Many new office buildings have replaced private offices with large, open areas divided by low partitions. Might the resulting awareness of others' presence help boost the performance of well-learned tasks but disrupt creative thinking on complex tasks? Can you think of other possible applications?

CONCEPTS TO REMEMBER

co-actors Co-participants working individually on a noncompetitive activity.

social facilitation   (1) Original meaning: the tendency of people to perform simple or well-learned tasks better when others are present. (2) Current meaning: the strengthening of dominant (prevalent, likely) responses in the presence of others.

evaluation apprehension Concern for how others are evaluating us.

18

❖

Many Hands Make Diminished Responsibility

In a team tug-of-war, will eight people on a side exert as much force as the sum of their best efforts in individual tugs-of-war? If not, why not?

Social facilitation usually occurs when people work toward individual goals and when their efforts, whether winding fishing reels or solving math problems, can be individually evaluated. These situations parallel some everyday work situations. But what about those in which people pool their efforts toward a *common* goal and where individuals are *not* accountable for their efforts? A team tug-of-war provides one such example. Organizational fund-raising—pooling candy sale proceeds to pay for the class trip—provides another. So does a class group project on which all students get the same grade. On such "additive tasks"—tasks where the group's achievement depends on the sum of the individual efforts—will team spirit boost productivity? Will bricklayers lay bricks faster when working as a team than when working alone? One way to attack such questions is with laboratory simulations.

MANY HANDS MAKE LIGHT WORK

Nearly a century ago, French engineer Max Ringelmann (reported by Kravitz & Martin, 1986) found that the collective effort of tug-of-war teams was but half the sum of the individual efforts. Contrary to the presumption that "in unity there is strength," this suggested that group members may actually be *less* motivated when performing additive tasks. Maybe, though, poor performance stemmed from poor coordination—people

FIGURE 18-1
The rope-pulling apparatus. People in the first position pulled less hard when they thought people behind them were also pulling.   Source: Data from Ingham, Levinger, Graves, & Peckham, 1974. Photo by Alan G. Ingham.

pulling a rope in slightly different directions at slightly different times. A group of Massachusetts researchers led by Alan Ingham (1974) cleverly eliminated that problem by making individuals think others were pulling with them, when in fact they were pulling alone. Blindfolded participants were assigned the first position in the apparatus shown in Figure 18-1 and told, "Pull as hard as you can." They pulled 18 percent harder when they knew they were pulling alone than when they believed that behind them two to five people were also pulling.

Researchers Bibb Latané, Kipling Williams, and Stephen Harkins (1979; Harkins & others, 1980) kept their ears open for other ways to investigate this diminished effort, which they labeled **social loafing.** They observed that the noise produced by six people shouting or clapping "as loud as you can" was less than three times that produced by one person alone. Like the tug-of-war task, however, noisemaking is vulnerable to group inefficiency. So Latané and associates followed Ingham's example by leading their Ohio State University participants to believe others were shouting or clapping with them, when in fact they were doing so alone.

Their method was to blindfold six people, seat them in a semicircle, and have them put on headphones, over which they were blasted with the sound of people shouting or clapping. People could not hear their own shouting or clapping, much less that of others. On various trials they were instructed to shout or clap either alone or along with the group. People who were told about this experiment guessed the participants would shout louder when with others, because they would be less inhibited (Harkins, 1981). The actual result? Social loafing: When the participants believed five others were also either shouting or clapping, they produced one-third less noise than when they thought themselves alone. Social loafing occurred even when the participants were high school cheerleaders who believed themselves to be cheering together rather than alone (Hardy & Latané, 1986).

John Sweeney (1973), a political scientist interested in the policy implications of social loafing, observed the phenomenon in a cycling experiment. University of Texas students pumped exercise bicycles more energetically (as measured by electrical output) when they knew they were being individually monitored than when they thought their output was being pooled with that of other riders. In the group condition, people were tempted to **free-ride** on the group effort.

In this and 160 other studies (Karau & Williams, 1993), we see a twist on one of the psychological forces that makes for social facilitation: evaluation apprehension. In the social loafing experiments, individuals believed they were evaluated only when they acted alone. The group situation (rope pulling, shouting, and so forth) *decreased* evaluation apprehension. When people are not accountable and cannot evaluate their own efforts, responsibility is diffused across all group members (Harkins & Jackson, 1985; Kerr & Bruun, 1981). By contrast, the social facilitation experiments *increased* exposure to evaluation. When made the center of attention, people self-consciously monitor their behavior (Mullen & Baumeister, 1987). So, when being observed *increases* evaluation concerns, social facilitation occurs; when being lost in a crowd *decreases* evaluation concerns, social loafing occurs (Figure 18-2).

To motivate group members, one strategy is to make individual performance identifiable. Some football coaches do this by filming and evaluating each player individually. Whether in a group or not, people exert more effort when their outputs are individually identifiable: University swim team members swim faster in intrasquad relay races when someone monitors and announces their individual times (Williams & others, 1989).

SOCIAL LOAFING IN EVERYDAY LIFE

Activity
18.1

How widespread is social loafing? In the laboratory, the phenomenon occurs not only among people who are pulling ropes, cycling, shouting, and clapping but also among those who are pumping water or air, evaluating poems or editorials, producing ideas, typing, and detecting signals. Do these consistent results generalize to everyday worker productivity?

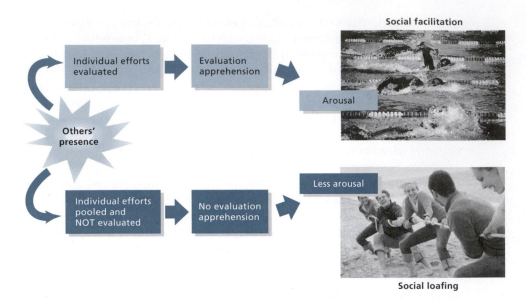

FIGURE 18-2
Social facilitation or social loafing? When individuals cannot be evaluated or held accountable, loafing becomes more likely. An individual swimmer is evaluated on her ability to win the race. In tug-of-war, no single person on the team is held accountable, so any one member might relax or loaf.

In one small experiment, assembly-line workers produced 16 percent more product when their individual output was identified, even though they knew their pay would not be affected (Faulkner & Williams, 1996). And consider: A key job in a pickle factory once was picking the right size dill pickle halves off the conveyor belt and stuffing them into jars. Unfortunately, workers were tempted to stuff any size pickle in, because their output was not identifiable (the jars went into a common hopper before reaching the quality-control section). Williams, Harkins, and Latané (1981) note that research on social loafing suggests "making individual production identifiable, and raises the question: 'How many pickles could a pickle packer pack if pickle packers were only paid for properly packed pickles?'"

Researchers have also found evidence of social loafing in varied cultures, particularly by assessing agricultural output in formerly communist countries. On their collective farms under communism, Russian peasants worked one field one day, another field the next, with little direct responsibility for any given plot. For their own use, they were given small private plots. One analysis found that the private plots occupied 1 percent of the agricultural land, yet produced 27 percent of the Soviet farm output (H. Smith, 1976). In communist Hungary, private plots accounted for only 13 percent of the farmland but produced one-third of the output (Spivak, 1979). When China began allowing farmers to sell food grown in excess of that owed to the state, food production jumped 8 percent per year—2.5 times the annual increase in the preceding 26 years (Church, 1986). In an effort to tie rewards to productive effort, today's Russia is "decollectivizing" many of its farms (Kramer, 2008).

What about collectivist cultures under noncommunist regimes? Latané and co-researchers (Gabrenya & others, 1985) repeated their sound-production experiments in Japan, Thailand, Taiwan, India, and Malaysia. Their findings? Social loafing was evident in all those countries, too. Seventeen later studies in Asia reveal that people in collectivist cultures do, however, exhibit less social loafing than do people in individualist cultures (Karau & Williams, 1993; Kugihara, 1999). As we noted, loyalty to family and work groups runs strong in collectivist cultures. Likewise, women tend to be less individualistic than men—and to exhibit less social loafing.

In North America, workers who do not pay dues or volunteer time to their unions or professional associations nevertheless are usually happy to accept the benefits those organizations provide. So, too, are public television viewers who don't respond to their station's fund drives. This hints at another possible explanation of social loafing. When rewards are divided equally, regardless of how much one contributes to the group, any individual gets more reward per unit of effort by free-riding on the group. So people may be motivated to slack off when their efforts are not individually monitored and rewarded. Situations that welcome free riders can therefore be, in the words of one commune member, a "paradise for parasites."

But surely collective effort does not always lead to slacking off. Sometimes the goal is so compelling and maximum output from everyone is so essential that team spirit maintains or intensifies effort. In an Olympic crew race, will the individual rowers in an eight-person crew pull their oars with less effort than those in a one- or two-person crew?

The evidence assures us they will not. People in groups loaf less when the task is *challenging, appealing,* or *involving* (Karau & Williams, 1993; Tan & Tan, 2008). On challenging tasks, people may perceive their efforts as indispensable (Harkins & Petty, 1982; Kerr, 1983; Kerr & others, 2007). When people see others in their group as unreliable or as unable to contribute much, they work harder (Plaks & Higgins, 2000; Williams & Karau, 1991). But, in many situations, so do less capable individuals as they strive to keep up with others' greater productivity (Weber & Hertel, 2007). Adding incentives or challenging a group to strive for certain standards also promotes collective effort (Harkins & Szymanski, 1989; Shepperd & Wright, 1989).

Groups also loaf less when their members are *friends* or they feel identified with or indispensable to their group (Davis & Greenlees, 1992; Gockel & others, 2008; Karau & Williams, 1997; Worchel & others, 1998). Even just expecting to interact with someone again serves to increase effort on team projects (Groenenboom & others, 2001). Collaborate on a class project with others whom you will be seeing often and you will probably feel more motivated than you would if you never expected to see them again. Cohesiveness intensifies effort.

These findings parallel those from studies of everyday work groups. When groups are given challenging objectives, when they are rewarded for group success, and when there is a spirit of commitment to the "team," group members work hard (Hackman, 1986). Keeping work groups small can also help members believe their contributions are indispensable (Comer, 1995). Although social loafing is common when group members work without individual accountability, many hands need not always make light work.

*C*ONCEPTS TO REMEMBER

social loafing   The tendency for people to exert less effort when they pool their efforts toward a common goal than when they are individually accountable.

free riders   People who benefit from the group but give little in return.

19

❖

Doing Together What We Would Not Do Alone

In April 2003, in the wake of American troops entering Iraq's cities, looters—"liberated" from the scrutiny of Saddam Hussein's police—ran rampant. Hospitals lost beds. The National Library lost tens of thousands of old manuscripts and lay in smoldering ruins. Universities lost computers, chairs, even lightbulbs. The National Museum in Baghdad lost 15,000 stolen objects—most of what had not previously been removed to safekeeping (Burns, 2003a, 2003b; Lawler, 2003c; Polk & Schuster, 2005). "Not since the Spanish conquistadors ravaged the Aztec and Inca cultures has so much been lost so quickly," reported *Science* (Lawler, 2003a). "They came in mobs: A group of 50 would come, then would go, and another would come," explained one university dean (Lawler, 2003b).

Such reports—and those of the 2011 arson and looting that occurred in London and other English cities—had the rest of the world wondering: What happened to the looters' sense of morality? Why did such behavior erupt? And why was it not anticipated?

Their behavior even left many of the rioters later wondering what possessed them. In court, some of the arrested rioters seemed bewildered by their behavior (Smith, 2011). The mother of one of them, a recent university graduate, explained that her daughter had been sobbing in her bedroom since her arrest over a stolen television. "She doesn't even know why she took it. She doesn't need a telly." An engineering student, arrested after looting a supermarket while he was walking home, was said by his lawyer to having "got caught up in the moment" and was now "incredibly ashamed" (Somaiya, 2011).

DEINDIVIDUATION

Social facilitation experiments show that groups can arouse people, and social loafing experiments show that groups can diffuse responsibility. When arousal and diffused responsibility combine, and normal inhibitions diminish, the results may be startling. People may commit acts that range from a mild lessening of restraint (throwing food in the dining hall, snarling at a referee, screaming during a rock concert) to impulsive self-gratification (group vandalism, orgies, thefts) to destructive social explosions (police brutality, riots, lynchings).

These unrestrained behaviors have something in common: They are somehow provoked by the power of a group. Groups can generate a sense of excitement, of being caught up in something bigger than one's self. It is harder to imagine a single rock fan screaming deliriously at a private rock concert, or a single police officer beating a defenseless offender or suspect. It's in group situations that people are more likely to abandon normal restraints, to forget their individual identity, to become responsive

Apparently acting without their normal conscience, people looted Iraqi institutions after the toppling of Saddam Hussein's regime.

to group or crowd norms—in a word, to become what Leon Festinger, Albert Pepitone, and Theodore Newcomb (1952) labeled **deindividuated.** What circumstances elicit this psychological state?

Group Size

A group has the power not only to arouse its members but also to render them unidentifiable. The snarling crowd hides the snarling basketball fan. A lynch mob enables its members to believe they will not be prosecuted; they perceive the action as the *group's.* Looters, made faceless by the mob, are freed to loot. In an analysis of 21 instances in which crowds were present as someone threatened to jump from a building or a bridge, Leon Mann (1981) found that when the crowd was small and exposed by daylight, people usually did not try to bait the person with cries of "Jump!" But when a large crowd or the cover of night gave people anonymity, the crowd usually did bait and jeer.

Brian Mullen (1986) reported a similar effect associated with lynch mobs: The bigger the mob, the more its members lose self-awareness and become willing to commit atrocities, such as burning, lacerating, or dismembering the victim.

In each of these examples, from sports crowds to lynch mobs, evaluation apprehension plummets. People's attention is focused on the situation, not on themselves. And because "everyone is doing it," all can attribute their behavior to the situation rather than to their own choices.

Anonymity

How can we be sure that the effect of crowds means greater anonymity? We can't. But we can experiment with anonymity to see if it actually lessens inhibitions. Philip Zimbardo (1970, 2002) got the idea for such an experiment from his undergraduate students, who questioned how good boys in William Golding's *Lord of the Flies* could so suddenly become monsters after painting their faces. To experiment with such anonymity, he dressed New York University women in identical white coats and hoods, rather like Ku Klux Klan members (Figure 19-1). Asked to deliver electric shocks to a woman, they pressed the shock button twice as long as did women who were unconcealed and wearing large name tags. Even dimmed lighting or wearing sunglasses increases people's perceived anonymity, and thus their willingness to cheat or behave selfishly (Zhong & others, 2010).

The Internet offers similar anonymity. Millions of those who were aghast at the looting by the Baghdad mobs were on those very days anonymously pirating music tracks using file-sharing software. With so many doing it, and with so little concern about being caught, downloading someone's copyright-protected property and then offloading it to an MP3

FIGURE 19-1
In Philip Zimbardo's deindividuation research, anonymous women delivered more shock to helpless victims than did identifiable women.

player just didn't seem terribly immoral. Internet bullies who would never to someone's face say, "Get a life, you phony," will hide behind their anonymity. Facebook, to its credit, requires people to use their real names, which constrains bullying, hate-filled, inflammatory comments.

On several occasions, anonymous online bystanders have egged on people threatening suicide, sometimes with live video feeding the scene to scores of people. Online communities "are like the crowd outside the building with the guy on the ledge," noted one analyst of technology's social effects (quoted by Stelter, 2008). Sometimes a caring person tried to talk the person down, while others, in effect, chanted, "Jump, jump." "The anonymous nature of these communities only emboldens the meanness or callousness of the people on these sites."

Testing deindividuation on the streets, Patricia Ellison, John Govern, and their colleagues (1995) had a confederate driver stop at a red light and wait for 12 seconds whenever she was followed by a convertible or a 4 × 4 vehicle. While enduring the wait, she recorded any horn-honking (a mild aggressive act) by the car behind. Compared with drivers of convertibles and 4 × 4s with the car tops down, those who were relatively anonymous (with the tops up) honked one-third sooner, twice as often, and for nearly twice as long. Anonymity feeds incivility.

A research team led by Ed Diener (1976) cleverly demonstrated the effect both of being in a group and of being physically anonymous. At Halloween, they observed 1,352 Seattle children trick-or-treating. As the children, either alone or in groups, approached 1 of 27 homes scattered

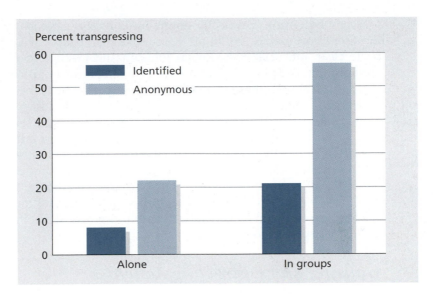

FIGURE 19-2
Children were more likely to transgress by taking extra Halloween candy
when in a group, when anonymous, and, especially, when deindividuated
by the combination of group immersion and anonymity.   Source: Data from
Diener & others (1976).

throughout the city, an experimenter greeted them warmly, invited them
to "take *one* of the candies," and then left the candy unattended. Hidden
observers noted that children in groups were more than twice as likely to
take extra candy as solo children. Also, children who had been asked their
names and where they lived were less than half as likely to transgress as
those who were left anonymous. As Figure 19-2 shows, the transgression
rate varied dramatically with the situation. When they were deindividuated both by group immersion and by anonymity, most children stole
extra candy.

Those studies make me wonder about the effect of wearing uniforms.
Preparing for battle, warriors in some tribal cultures (like some rabid
sports fans) depersonalize themselves with body and face paints or special masks. After the battle, some cultures kill, torture, or mutilate any
remaining enemies; other cultures take prisoners alive. Robert Watson
(1973) scrutinized anthropological files and discovered this: The cultures
with depersonalized warriors were also the cultures that brutalized their
enemies. In Northern Ireland, 206 of 500 violent attacks studied by Andrew
Silke (2003) were conducted by attackers who wore masks, hoods, or other
face disguises. Compared with undisguised attackers, these anonymous
attackers inflicted more serious injuries, attacked more people, and committed more vandalism.

Does becoming physically anonymous *always* unleash our worst impulses? Fortunately, no. In all these situations, people were responding to clear antisocial cues. Robert Johnson and Leslie Downing (1979) point out that the Klan-like outfits worn by Zimbardo's participants may have been stimulus cues for hostility. In an experiment at the University of Georgia, women put on nurses' uniforms before deciding how much shock someone should receive. When those wearing the nurses' uniforms were made anonymous, they became *less* aggressive in administering shocks than when their names and personal identities were stressed. From their analysis of 60 deindividuation studies, Tom Postmes and Russell Spears (1998; Reicher & others, 1995) concluded that being anonymous makes one less self-conscious, more group-conscious, and more responsive to cues present in the situation, whether negative (Klan uniforms) or positive (nurses' uniforms).

Arousing and Distracting Activities

Aggressive outbursts by large groups are often preceded by minor actions that arouse and divert people's attention. Group shouting, chanting, clapping, or dancing serve both to hype people up and to reduce self-consciousness.

Ed Diener's experiments (1976, 1979) have shown that activities such as throwing rocks and group singing can set the stage for more disinhibited behavior. There is a self-reinforcing pleasure in acting impulsively while observing others doing likewise. When we see others act as we are acting, we think they feel as we do, which reinforces our own feelings (Orive, 1984). Moreover, impulsive group action absorbs our attention. When we yell at the referee, we are not thinking about our values; we are reacting to the immediate situation. Later, when we stop to think about what we have done or said, we sometimes feel chagrined. Sometimes. At other times we *seek* deindividuating group experiences—dances, worship experiences, team sports—where we can enjoy intense positive feelings and closeness to others.

*D*IMINISHED SELF-AWARENESS

Group experiences that diminish self-consciousness tend to disconnect behavior from attitudes. Research by Ed Diener (1980) and Steven Prentice-Dunn and Ronald Rogers (1980, 1989) revealed that unselfconscious, deindividuated people are less restrained, less self-regulated, more likely to act without thinking about their own values, and more responsive to the situation. Those findings complement and reinforce the experiments on **self-awareness.**

Self-awareness is the opposite of deindividuation. Those made self-aware, by acting in front of a mirror or a TV camera, exhibit *increased* self-control, and their actions more clearly reflect their attitudes. In front of a mirror, people taste-testing cream cheese varieties eat less of the high-fat variety (Sentyrz & Bushman, 1998).

People made self-aware are also less likely to cheat (Beaman & others, 1979; Diener & Wallbom, 1976). So are those who generally have a strong sense of themselves as distinct and independent (Nadler & others, 1982). In Japan, where (mirror or no mirror) people more often imagine how they might look to others, people are no more likely to cheat when not in front of a mirror (Heine & others, 2008). The principle: People who are self-conscious, or who are temporarily made so, exhibit greater consistency between their words outside a situation and their deeds in it.

We can apply those findings to many situations in everyday life. Circumstances that decrease self-awareness, as alcohol consumption does, increase deindividuation (Hull & others, 1983). Deindividuation decreases in circumstances that increase self-awareness: mirrors and cameras, small towns, bright lights, large name tags, undistracted quiet, individual clothes and houses (Ickes & others, 1978). When a teenager leaves for a party, a parent's parting advice could well be "Have fun, and remember who you are." In other words, enjoy being with the group, but be self-aware; maintain your personal identity; be wary of deindividuation.

CONCEPTS TO REMEMBER

deindividuation Loss of self-awareness and evaluation apprehension; occurs in group situations that foster responsiveness to group norms, good or bad.

self-awareness A self-conscious state in which attention focuses on oneself. It makes people more sensitive to their own attitudes and dispositions.

20

❖

How Do Groups Intensify Decisions?

Many conflicts grow as people on both sides talk mostly with like-minded others. Which effect—good or bad—does group interaction more often have? Police brutality and mob violence demonstrate its destructive potential. Yet support-group leaders, management consultants, and educational theorists proclaim group interaction's benefits, and social and religious movements urge their members to strengthen their identities by fellowship with like-minded others.

Studies of people in small groups have produced a principle that helps explain both bad and good outcomes: Group discussion often strengthens members' initial inclinations. The unfolding of this research on **group polarization** illustrates the process of inquiry—how an interesting discovery often leads researchers to hasty and erroneous conclusions, which ultimately are replaced with more accurate conclusions. This is a scientific mystery I can discuss firsthand, having been one of the detectives.

THE CASE OF THE "RISKY SHIFT"

Activity
20.1

More than 300 studies began with a surprising finding by James Stoner (1961), then an MIT graduate student. For his master's thesis in management, Stoner tested the commonly held belief that groups are more cautious than individuals. He posed decision dilemmas in which the participant's task was to advise imagined characters how much risk to

215

take. Put yourself in the participant's shoes: What advice would you give the character in this situation?[1]

> Helen is a writer who is said to have considerable creative talent but who so far has been earning a comfortable living by writing cheap westerns. Recently she has come up with an idea for a potentially significant novel. If it could be written and accepted, it might have considerable literary impact and be a big boost to her career. On the other hand, if she cannot work out her idea or if the novel is a flop, she will have expended considerable time and energy without remuneration.
>
> Imagine that you are advising Helen. Please check the *lowest* probability that you would consider acceptable for Helen to attempt to write the novel.
>
> Helen should attempt to write the novel if the chances that the novel will be a success are at least

_____ 1 in 10	_____ 7 in 10
_____ 2 in 10	_____ 8 in 10
_____ 3 in 10	_____ 9 in 10
_____ 4 in 10	_____ 10 in 10 (Place a check here if you think
_____ 5 in 10	Helen should attempt the novel only if it is certain that the novel will be a success.)
_____ 6 in 10	

After making your decision, guess what this book's average reader would advise.

Having marked their advice on a dozen items, five or so individuals would then discuss and reach agreement on each item. How do you think the group decisions compared with the average decision before the discussions? Would the groups be likely to take greater risks, be more cautious, or stay the same?

To everyone's amazement, the group decisions were usually riskier. This "risky shift phenomenon" set off a wave of group risk-taking studies. These revealed that risky shift occurs not only when a group decides by consensus; after a brief discussion, individuals, too, will alter their decisions. What is more, researchers successfully repeated Stoner's finding with people of varying ages and occupations in a dozen nations.

During discussion, opinions converged. Curiously, however, the point toward which they converged was usually a lower (riskier) number than their initial average. Here was a delightful puzzle. The small risky shift effect was reliable, unexpected, and without any

---

[1] This item, constructed for my own research, illustrates the sort of decision dilemma posed by Stoner.

immediately obvious explanation. What group influences produce such an effect? And how widespread is it? Do discussions in juries, business committees, and military organizations also promote risk taking? Does this explain why teenage reckless driving, as measured by death rates, nearly doubles when a 16- or 17-year-old driver has two teenage passengers rather than none (Chen & others, 2000)? Does it explain stock bubbles, as people discuss why stocks are rising, thus creating an informational cascade that drives stocks even higher (Sunstein, 2009)?

After several years of study, we discovered that the risky shift was not universal. We could write decision dilemmas on which people became more *cautious* after discussion. One of these featured "Roger," a young married man with two school-age children and a secure but low-paying job. Roger can afford life's necessities but few of its luxuries. He hears that the stock of a relatively unknown company may soon triple in value if its new product is favorably received or decline considerably if it does not sell. Roger has no savings. To invest in the company, he is considering selling his life insurance policy.

Can you see a general principle that predicts both the tendency to give riskier advice after discussing Helen's situation and more cautious advice after discussing Roger's? If you are like most people, you would advise Helen to take a greater risk than Roger, even before talking with others. It turns out there is a strong tendency for discussion to accentuate these initial leanings; groups discussing the "Roger" dilemma became more risk-averse than they were before discussion.

*D*O GROUPS INTENSIFY OPINIONS?

Realizing that this group phenomenon was not a consistent shift toward increased risk, we reconceived the phenomenon as a tendency for group discussion to *enhance* group members' initial leanings. This idea led investigators to propose what French researchers Serge Moscovici and Marisa Zavalloni (1969) called group polarization: *Discussion typically strengthens the average inclination of group members.*

Group Polarization Experiments

This new view of the group-induced changes prompted experimenters to have people discuss attitude statements that most of them favored, or that most of them opposed. Would talking in groups enhance their shared initial inclinations? In groups, would risk takers take bigger risks, bigots become more hostile, and givers become more generous? That's what the group polarization hypothesis predicts (Figure 20-1).

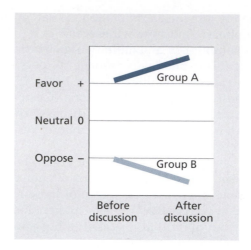

FIGURE 20-1
Group polarization. The group polarization hypothesis predicts that discussion
will strengthen an attitude shared by
group members.

Dozens of studies confirm group polarization.

- Moscovici and Zavalloni (1969) observed that discussion enhanced French students' initially positive attitude toward their
  president and negative attitude toward Americans.
- Mititoshi Isozaki (1984) found that Japanese university students
  gave more pronounced judgments of "guilty" after discussing
  a traffic case. When jury members are inclined to award damages,
  the group award similarly tends to exceed that preferred by the
  median jury member (Sunstein, 2007a).
- Markus Brauer and co-workers (2001) found that French students'
  dislike for certain other people was exacerbated after discussing
  their shared negative impressions.

Another research strategy has been to pick issues on which opinions
are divided and then isolate people who hold the same view. Does discussion with like-minded people strengthen shared views? Does it magnify
the attitude gap that separates the two sides?

George Bishop and I wondered. So we set up groups of relatively
prejudiced and unprejudiced high school students and asked them to
respond—before and after discussion—to issues involving racial attitudes,
such as property rights versus open housing (Myers & Bishop, 1970).
We found that the discussions among like-minded students did indeed
increase the initial gap between the two groups (Figure 20-2).

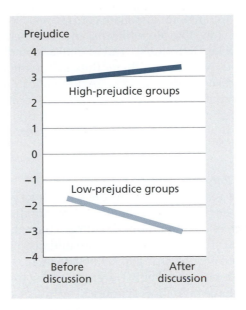

FIGURE 20-2
Discussion increased polarization
between homogeneous groups of high-
and low-prejudice high school students.
Talking over racial issues increased
prejudice in a high-prejudice group
and decreased it in a low-prejudice
group.   Source: Data from Myers &
Bishop (1970).

Studies in Britain and Australia confirm that group discussion can magnify both negative and positive tendencies. When people share negative impressions of a group, such as an immigrant group, discussion supports their negativity and increases their willingness to discriminate (Smith & Postmes, 2011). And when people share concern about an injustice, discussion amplifies their moral concern (Thomas & McGarty, 2009).

Group Polarization in Everyday Life

In everyday life, people associate mostly with others whose attitudes are similar to their own. (Just look at your own circle of friends.) Does everyday group interaction with like-minded friends intensify shared attitudes? Do nerds become nerdier and jocks jockier?

It happens. The self-segregation of boys into all-male groups and of girls into all-female groups accentuates over time their initially modest gender differences, notes Eleanor Maccoby (2002). Boys with boys become gradually more competitive and action oriented in their play and fictional fare. Girls with girls become more relationally oriented.

On U.S. federal appellate court cases, "Republican-appointed judges tend to vote like Republicans and Democratic-appointed judges tend to vote like Democrats," David Schkade and Cass Sunstein (2003) have observed. No surprise there. But such tendencies are accentuated when among like-minded judges. "A Republican appointee sitting with two other Republicans votes far more conservatively than when the same judge sits with at least one Democratic appointee. A Democratic appointee, meanwhile, shows the same tendency in the opposite ideological direction."

Group Polarization in Schools

Another real-life parallel to the laboratory phenomenon is what education researchers have called the "accentuation" effect: Over time, initial differences among groups of college students become accentuated. If the first-year students at college X are initially more intellectual than the students at college Y, that gap is likely to increase by the time they graduate. Likewise, compared with fraternity and sorority members, independents tend to have more liberal political attitudes, a difference that grows with time in college (Pascarella & Terenzini, 1991). Researchers believe this results partly from group members reinforcing shared inclinations.

Group Polarization in Communities

Polarization also occurs in communities, as people self-segregate. "Crunchy places . . . attract crunchy types and become crunchier," observes David Brooks (2005). "Conservative places . . . attract conservatives and become more so." Neighborhoods become echo chambers, with opinions ricocheting off kindred-spirited friends.

Show social psychologists a like-minded group that interacts mostly among themselves and they will show you a group that may become more extreme. One experiment assembled small groups of Coloradoans in liberal Boulder and conservative Colorado Springs. The discussions increased agreement within small groups about global warming, affirmative action, and same-sex unions. Nevertheless, those in Boulder generally converged further left and those in Colorado Springs further right (Schkade & others, 2007).

With communities serving as political echo chambers, the United States is increasingly polarized. The percentage of landslide counties— those voting 60 percent or more for one presidential candidate—nearly doubled between 1976 and 2008 (Bishop, 2008). The percentage of entering collegians declaring themselves as politically "middle of the road" dropped from 60 percent in 1983 to 46 in 2010, with corresponding increases in those declaring themselves on the right or the left (Pryor & others, 2005, 2010).

In laboratory studies, the competitive relationships and mistrust that individuals often display when playing games with one another often worsen when the players are groups (Winquist & Larson, 2004). During actual community conflicts, like-minded people associate increasingly with one another, amplifying their shared tendencies. Gang delinquency emerges from a process of mutual reinforcement within neighborhood gangs, whose members share attributes and hostilities (Cartwright, 1975). If "a second out-of-control 15-year-old moves in [on your block]," surmises David Lykken (1997), "the mischief they get into as a team is likely to be more than merely double what the first would do on his own. . . . A gang is more dangerous than the sum of its individual parts." Indeed, "unsupervised peer groups" are "the strongest predictor" of a neighborhood's crime victimization rate, report Bonita Veysey and Steven Messner (1999). Moreover, experimental interventions that take delinquent adolescents and group them with other delinquents actually—no surprise to any group polarization researcher—increase the rate of problem behavior (Dishion & others, 1999).

Group Polarization on the Internet
E-mail, blogs, and electronic chat rooms offer a potential new medium for like-minded people to find one another and for group interaction that increases social fragmentation and polarization. Facebook offers tens of thousands of groups of kindred spirits discussing religion, politics, hobbies, cars, music, and you name it. The Internet's countless virtual groups enable peacemakers and neo-Nazis, geeks and goths, conspiracy schemers and cancer survivors to isolate themselves with like-minded others and find support for their shared concerns, interests, and suspicions (Gerstenfeld & others, 2003; McKenna & Bargh, 1998, 2000; Sunstein, 2001, 2009). Indeed, most of us read blogs that reinforce rather than challenge our views, and those blogs link mostly to like-minded blogs—connecting liberals with liberals, conservatives with conservatives—like having conversations with the bathroom mirror (Lazer & others, 2009). Will such discussions produce group polarization? Will socially networked birds of a feather find support for their shared beliefs, values, and suspicions? Will peacemakers become more pacifistic and militia members more terror prone? E-mail, Google, and chat rooms "make it much easier for small groups to rally like-minded people, crystallize diffuse hatreds, and mobilize lethal force," observes Robert Wright (2003). As broadband spreads, Internet-spawned polarization will increase, he speculates. According to one University of Haifa analysis, terrorist websites—which grew from a dozen in 1997 to some 4,700 at the end of 2005—increased more than four times faster than the total number of websites (Ariza, 2006).

Group Polarization in Terrorist Organizations
From their analysis of terrorist organizations throughout the world, Clark McCauley and Mary Segal (1987; McCauley, 2002) note that terrorism does not erupt suddenly. Rather, it arises among people whose shared grievances bring them together and fans their fire. As they interact in isolation

from moderating influences, they become progressively more extreme. The social amplifier brings the signal in more strongly. The result is violent acts that the individuals, apart from the group, would never have committed.

For example, the 9/11 terrorists were bred by a long process that engaged the polarizing effect of interaction among the like-minded. The process of becoming a terrorist, noted a National Research Council panel, isolates individuals from other belief systems, dehumanizes potential targets, and tolerates no dissent (Smelser & Mitchell, 2002). Group members come to categorize the world as "us" and "them" (Moghaddam, 2005; Qirko, 2004). Ariel Merari (2002), an investigator of Middle Eastern and Sri Lankan suicide terrorism, believes the key to creating a terrorist suicide is the group process. "To the best of my knowledge, there has not been a single case of suicide terrorism which was done on a personal whim."

According to one analysis of terrorists who were members of the Salafi Jihad—an Islamic fundamentalist movement, including al Qaeda—70 percent joined while living as expatriates. After moving to foreign places in search of jobs or education, they became keenly mindful of their Muslim identity and often gravitated to mosques and moved in with other expatriate Muslims, who sometimes recruited them into cell groups that provided "mutual emotional and social support" and "development of a common identity" (Sageman, 2004).

Massacres, similarly, have been found to be group phenomena. The violence is enabled and escalated by the killers egging one another on, noted Robert Zajonc (2000), who knew violence as a survivor of a World War II Warsaw air raid that killed both his parents (Burnstein, 2009). It is difficult to influence someone once "in the pressure cooker of the terrorist group," notes Jerrold Post (2005) after interviewing many accused terrorists. "In the long run, the most effective antiterrorist policy is one that inhibits potential recruits from joining in the first place."

*E*XPLAINING GROUP POLARIZATION

Why do groups adopt stances that are more exaggerated than that of their average individual member? Researchers hoped that solving the mystery of group polarization might provide some insights into group influence. Solving small puzzles sometimes provides clues for solving larger ones.

Among several proposed theories of group polarization, two have survived scientific scrutiny. One deals with the *arguments* presented during a discussion and is an example of *informational influence* (influence that results from accepting evidence about reality). The other concerns how members of a group view themselves vis-à-vis the other members, an example of *normative influence* (influence based on a person's desire to be accepted or admired by others).

Informational Influence

According to the best-supported explanation, group discussion elicits a pooling of ideas, most of which favor the dominant viewpoint. Some discussed ideas are common knowledge to group members (Gigone & Hastie, 1993; Larson & others, 1994; Stasser, 1991). Other ideas may include persuasive arguments that some group members had not previously considered. When discussing Helen the writer, someone may say, "Helen should go for it, because she has little to lose. If her novel flops, she can always go back to writing cheap westerns." Such statements often entangle information about the person's *arguments* with cues concerning the person's *position* on the issue. But when people hear relevant arguments without learning the specific stands other people assume, they still shift their positions (Burnstein & Vinokur, 1977; Hinsz & others, 1997). *Arguments,* in and of themselves, matter.

Normative Influence

A second explanation of polarization involves comparison with others. As Leon Festinger (1954) argued in his influential theory of **social comparison,** we humans want to evaluate our opinions and abilities by comparing our views with others'. We are most persuaded by people in our "reference groups"—groups we identify with (Abrams & others, 1990; Hogg & others, 1990). Moreover, wanting people to like us, we may express stronger opinions after discovering that others share our views.

When we ask people (as I asked you earlier) to predict how others would respond to items such as the "Helen" dilemma, they typically exhibit *pluralistic ignorance:* They don't realize how strongly others support the socially preferred tendency (in this case, writing the novel). A typical person will advise writing the novel even if its chance of success is only 4 in 10 but will estimate that most other people would require 5 or 6 in 10. (This finding is reminiscent of the self-serving bias: People tend to view themselves as better-than-average embodiments of socially desirable traits and attitudes.) When the discussion begins, most people discover they are not outshining the others as they had supposed. In fact, some others are ahead of them, having taken an even stronger position in favor of writing the novel. No longer restrained by a misperceived group norm, they are liberated to voice their preferences more strongly.

Perhaps you can recall a time when you and someone else wanted to go out with each other but each of you feared to make the first move, presuming the other probably did not have a reciprocal interest. Such pluralistic ignorance impedes the start-up of relationships (Vorauer & Ratner, 1996).

Or perhaps you can recall when you and others were guarded and reserved in a group, until someone broke the ice and said, "Well, to be perfectly honest, I think. . . ." Soon you were all surprised to discover strong support for your shared views.

Social comparison theory prompted experiments that exposed people to others' positions but not to their arguments. This is roughly the experience we have when reading the results of an opinion poll or of exit polling on election day. When people learn others' positions—without prior commitment and without discussion or sharing of arguments—will they adjust their responses to maintain a socially favorable position (Myers, 1978)? This comparison-based polarization is usually less than that produced by a lively discussion. Still, it's surprising that instead of simply conforming to the group average, people often go it one better.

Merely learning others' choices also contributes to the bandwagon effect that creates blockbuster songs, books, and movies. Sociologist Matthew Salganik and colleagues (2006) experimented with the phenomenon by engaging 14,341 Internet participants in listening to and, if they wished, downloading previously unknown songs. The researchers randomly assigned some participants to a condition that disclosed previous participants' download choices. Among those given that information, popular songs became more popular and unpopular songs became less popular.

Group polarization research illustrates the complexity of social-psychological inquiry. Much as we like our explanations of a phenomenon to be simple, one explanation seldom accounts for all the data. Because people are complex, more than one factor frequently influences an outcome. In group discussions, persuasive arguments predominate on issues that have a factual element ("Is she guilty of the crime?"). Social comparison sways responses on value-laden judgments ("How long a sentence should she serve?") (Kaplan, 1989). On the many issues that have both factual and value-laden aspects, the two factors work together. Discovering that others share one's feelings (social comparison) unleashes arguments (informational influence) supporting what everyone secretly favors.

*G*ROUPTHINK

Do the social psychological phenomena we have been considering in these first 20 modules occur in sophisticated groups such as corporate boards or the president's cabinet? Is there likely to be self-justification? Self-serving bias? A cohesive "we feeling" promoting conformity and stifling dissent? Public commitment producing resistance to change? Group polarization? Social psychologist Irving Janis (1971, 1982) wondered whether such phenomena might help explain good and bad group decisions made by some twentieth-century American presidents and their advisers. To find out, he analyzed the decision-making procedures that led to several major fiascos:

- *Pearl Harbor.* In the weeks preceding the December 1941 Pearl Harbor attack that put the United States into World War II, military commanders in Hawaii received a steady stream of information about Japan's preparations for an attack on the United States somewhere in the Pacific. Then military intelligence lost radio contact with Japanese aircraft carriers, which had begun moving straight for Hawaii. Air reconnaissance could have spotted the carriers or at least provided a few minutes' warning. But complacent commanders decided against such precautions. The result: No alert was sounded until the attack on a virtually defenseless base was under way. The loss: 18 ships, 170 planes, and 2,400 lives.

- *The Bay of Pigs Invasion.* In 1961, President John Kennedy and his advisers tried to overthrow Fidel Castro by invading Cuba with 1,400 CIA-trained Cuban exiles. Nearly all the invaders were soon killed or captured, the United States was humiliated, and Cuba allied itself more closely with the former U.S.S.R. After learning the outcome, Kennedy wondered aloud, "How could we have been so stupid?"

- *The Vietnam War.* From 1964 to 1967, President Lyndon Johnson and his "Tuesday lunch group" of policy advisers escalated the war in Vietnam on the assumption that U.S. aerial bombardment, defoliation, and search-and-destroy missions would bring North Vietnam to the peace table with the appreciative support of the South Vietnamese populace. They continued the escalation despite warnings from government intelligence experts and nearly all U.S. allies. The resulting disaster cost more than 58,000 American and 1 million Vietnamese lives, polarized Americans, drove the president from office, and created huge budget deficits that helped fuel inflation in the 1970s.

Janis believed those blunders were bred by the tendency of decision-making groups to suppress dissent in the interest of group harmony, a phenomenon he called **groupthink.** In work groups, team spirit is good for morale and boosts productivity (Mullen & Copper, 1994). But when making decisions, close-knit groups may pay a price. Janis believed that the soil from which groupthink sprouts includes

- an amiable, *cohesive* group.
- relative *isolation* of the group from dissenting viewpoints.
- a *directive leader* who signals what decision he or she favors.

When planning the ill-fated Bay of Pigs invasion, the newly elected President Kennedy and his advisers enjoyed a strong esprit de corps. Arguments critical of the plan were suppressed or excluded, and the president soon endorsed the invasion.

SYMPTOMS OF GROUPTHINK

From historical records and the memoirs of participants and observers, Janis identified eight groupthink symptoms. These symptoms are a collective form of dissonance reduction as group members try to maintain their positive group feeling when facing a threat (Turner & Pratkanis, 1994; Turner & others, 1992).

The first two groupthink symptoms lead group members to *overestimate their group's might and right.*

- *An illusion of invulnerability.* The groups Janis studied all developed an excessive optimism that blinded them to warnings of danger. Told that his forces had lost radio contact with the Japanese carriers, Admiral Kimmel, the chief naval officer at Pearl Harbor, joked that maybe the Japanese were about to round Honolulu's Diamond Head. They actually were, but Kimmel's laughing at the idea dismissed the very possibility of its being true.

- *Unquestioned belief in the group's morality.* Group members assume the inherent morality of their group and ignore ethical and moral issues. The Kennedy group knew that adviser Arthur Schlesinger, Jr., and Senator J. William Fulbright had moral reservations about invading a small, neighboring country. But the group never entertained or discussed those moral qualms.

Group members also become *closed-minded.*

- *Rationalization.* The groups discount challenges by collectively justifying their decisions. President Johnson's Tuesday lunch group spent far more time rationalizing (explaining and justifying) than reflecting upon and rethinking prior decisions to escalate. Each initiative became an action to defend and justify.

- *Stereotyped view of opponent.* Participants in these groupthink tanks consider their enemies too evil to negotiate with or too weak and unintelligent to defend themselves against the planned initiative. The Kennedy group convinced itself that Castro's military was so weak and his popular support so shallow that a single brigade could easily overturn his regime.

Finally, the group suffers from pressures toward *uniformity.*

- *Conformity pressure.* Group members rebuffed those who raised doubts about the group's assumptions and plans, at times not by argument but by personal sarcasm. Once, when President Johnson's assistant Bill Moyers arrived at a meeting, the president derided him with, "Well, here comes Mr. Stop-the-Bombing." Faced with such ridicule, most people fall into line.

- *Self-censorship.* To avoid uncomfortable disagreements, members withheld or discounted their misgivings. In the months following the Bay of Pigs invasion, Arthur Schlesinger (1965, p. 255) reproached himself "for having kept so silent during those crucial discussions in the Cabinet Room, though my feelings of guilt were tempered by the knowledge that a course of objection would have accomplished little save to gain me a name as a nuisance."

- *Illusion of unanimity.* Self-censorship and pressure not to puncture the consensus create an illusion of unanimity. What is more, the apparent consensus confirms the group's decision. This appearance of consensus was evident in the Pearl Harbor, Bay of Pigs, and Vietnam fiascos and in other fiascos before and since. Albert Speer (1971), an adviser to Adolf Hitler, described the atmosphere around Hitler as one where pressure to conform suppressed all deviation. The absence of dissent created an illusion of unanimity:

  In normal circumstances people who turn their backs on reality are soon set straight by the mockery and criticism of those around them, which makes them aware they have lost credibility. In the Third Reich there were no such correctives . . . . No external factors disturbed the uniformity of hundreds of unchanging faces, all mine. (p. 379)

- *Mindguards.* Some members protect the group from information that would call into question the effectiveness or morality of its decisions. Before the Bay of Pigs invasion, Robert Kennedy took Schlesinger aside and told him, "Don't push it any further." Secretary of State Dean Rusk withheld diplomatic and intelligence experts' warnings against the invasion. They thus served as the president's "mindguards," protecting him from disagreeable facts rather than physical harm.

Groupthink in Action

Groupthink symptoms can produce a failure to seek and discuss contrary information and alternative possibilities (Figure 20-3). When a leader promotes an idea and when a group insulates itself from dissenting views, groupthink may produce defective decisions (McCauley, 1989).

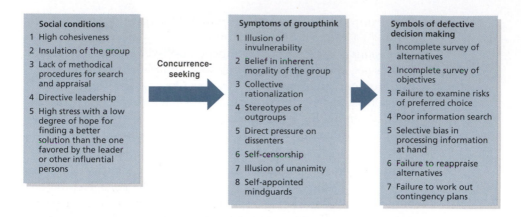

FIGURE 20-3
Theoretical analysis of groupthink.   Source: Janis & Mann (1977, p. 132).

British psychologists Ben Newell and David Lagnado (2003) believe groupthink symptoms may have also contributed to the Iraq War. They and others contended that both Saddam Hussein and George W. Bush surrounded themselves with like-minded advisers and intimidated opposing voices into silence. Moreover, they each received filtered information that mostly supported their assumptions—Iraq's expressed assumption that the invading force could be resisted; and the United States' assumption that Iraq had weapons of mass destruction, that its people would welcome invading soldiers as liberators, and that a short, peaceful occupation would soon lead to a thriving democracy.

PREVENTING GROUPTHINK

Flawed group dynamics help explain many failed decisions; sometimes too many cooks spoil the broth. However, given open leadership, a cohesive team spirit can improve decisions. Sometimes two or more heads are better than one.

In search of conditions that breed good decisions, Janis also analyzed two successful ventures: the Truman administration's formulation of the Marshall Plan for getting Europe back on its feet after World War II and the Kennedy administration's handling of the former U.S.S.R.'s attempts to install missile bases in Cuba in 1962. Janis's (1982) recommendations for preventing groupthink incorporate many of the effective group procedures used in both cases:

- Be impartial—do not endorse any position. Don't start group discussions by having people state their positions; doing so suppresses information sharing and degrades the quality of decisions (Mojzisch & Schulz-Hardt, 2010).

- Encourage critical evaluation; assign a "devil's advocate." Better yet, welcome the input of a genuine dissenter, which does even more to stimulate original thinking and to open a group to opposing views, report Charlan Nemeth and colleagues (2001a, 2001b).
- Occasionally subdivide the group, then reunite to air differences.
- Welcome critiques from outside experts and associates.
- Before implementing, call a "second-chance" meeting to air any lingering doubts.

When such steps are taken, group decisions may take longer to make, yet ultimately prove less defective and more effective.

CONCEPTS TO REMEMBER

group polarization   Group-produced enhancement of members' preexisting tendencies; a strengthening of the members' average tendency, not a split within the group.

social comparison   Evaluating one's opinions and abilities by comparing oneself with others.

groupthink   "The mode of thinking that persons engage in when concurrence-seeking becomes so dominant in a cohesive in-group that it tends to override realistic appraisal of alternative courses of action."—Irving Janis (1971)

MODULE

21

❖

Power to the Person

"There are trivial truths and great truths," declared the physicist Niels Bohr. "The opposite of a trivial truth is plainly false. The opposite of a great truth is also true." Each chapter in this unit on social influence teaches a great truth: *the power of the situation*. This great truth about the power of external pressures would explain our behavior if we were passive, like tumbleweeds. But, unlike tumbleweeds, we are not just blown here and there by the situations in which we find ourselves. We act; we react. We respond, and we get responses. We can resist the social situation and sometimes even change it. For that reason, I've chosen to conclude each of these "social influence" chapters by calling attention to the opposite of the great truth: *the power of the person.*

Perhaps stressing the power of culture leaves you somewhat uncomfortable. Do external forces determine your behavior? Most of us see ourselves as free beings, as the originators of our actions (well, at least of our good actions). We worry that cultural explanations for our actions might lead to what philosopher Jean-Paul Sartre called "bad faith"—evading responsibility by blaming something or someone for one's fate.

Actually, social control (the power of the situation) and personal control (the power of the person) no more compete with each other than do biological and cultural explanations. Social and personal explanations are both valid, for at any moment we are both the creatures and the creators of our social worlds. We may well be the products of the interplay of our genes and environment. But it is also true that the future is coming, and it is our job to decide where it is going. Our choices today determine our environment tomorrow.

INTERACTING PERSONS AND SITUATIONS

Social situations do profoundly influence individuals. But individuals also influence social situations. The two *interact.* Asking whether external situations or inner dispositions determine behavior is like asking whether length or width determines a room's area.

The interaction occurs in at least three ways (Snyder & Ickes, 1985).

- *A given social situation often affects different people differently.* Because our minds do not see reality identically or objectively, we respond to a situation as we construe it. And some people (groups as well as individuals) are more sensitive and responsive to social situations than others (Snyder, 1983). The Japanese, for example, are more responsive to social expectations than the British (Argyle & others, 1978).

- *People often choose their situations* (Ickes & others, 1997). Given a choice, sociable people elect situations that evoke social interaction. When you chose your college, you were also choosing to expose yourself to a specific set of social influences. Ardent political liberals are unlikely to choose to live in suburban Dallas, join the Chamber of Commerce, and watch Fox News. They are more likely to live in San Francisco or Toronto, join Greenpeace, and read the *Huffington Post*—in other words, to choose a social world that reinforces their inclinations.

- *People often create their situations.* Recall again that our preconceptions can be self-fulfilling: If we expect someone to be extraverted, hostile, intelligent, or sexy, our actions toward the person may induce the very behavior we expect. What, after all, makes a social situation but the people in it? A conservative environment is created by conservatives. What takes place in the sorority or fraternity is created by its members. The social environment is not like the weather—something that just happens to us. It is more like our homes—something we make for ourselves.

Thus, power resides both in persons and in situations. *We create and are created by our cultural worlds.*

The reciprocal causation between situations and persons allows us to see people as either *reacting to* or *acting upon* their environment. Each perspective is correct, for we are both the products and the architects of our social worlds. But is one perspective wiser? In one sense, it is wise to see ourselves as the creatures of our environments (lest we become too proud of our achievements and blame ourselves too much for our problems) and to see others as free actors (lest we become paternalistic and manipulative).

Perhaps, however, we would do well more often to assume the reverse—to view ourselves as free agents and to view others as situationally influenced. We would then assume self-efficacy as we view ourselves, and we would seek understanding and social reform as we relate to others. Most religions, in fact, encourage us to take responsibility for ourselves but to refrain from judging others. Is that because our natural inclination is the opposite: to excuse our own failures while blaming others for theirs?

RESISTING SOCIAL PRESSURE

Social psychology offers other reminders of the power of the person. We are not just billiard balls moving where pushed. We may act according to our own values, independently of the forces that push upon us. Knowing that someone is trying to coerce us may even prompt us to react in the *opposite* direction.

Reactance

Activity 21.1

Individuals value their sense of freedom and self-efficacy. When blatant social pressure threatens their sense of freedom, they often rebel. Think of Romeo and Juliet, whose love was intensified by their families' opposition. Or think of children asserting their freedom and independence by doing the opposite of what their parents ask. Savvy parents therefore offer their children choices instead of commands: "It's time to clean up: Do you want a bath or a shower?"

The theory of psychological **reactance**—that people act to protect their sense of freedom—is supported by experiments showing that attempts to restrict a person's freedom often produce an anticonformity "boomerang effect" (Brehm & Brehm, 1981; Nail & others, 2000). In one field experiment, many nongeeky students stopped wearing a "Livestrong" wristband when nearby geeky academic students started wearing the band (Berger & Heath, 2008). Likewise, rich Brits stopped wearing Burberry caps after the caps caught on among soccer hooligans (Clevstrom & Passariello, 2006).

Reactance may contribute to underage drinking. A survey of 18- to 24-year-olds by the Canadian Centre on Substance Abuse (1997) revealed that 69 percent of those over the legal drinking age (21) had been drunk in the last year, as had 77 percent of those *under* 21. In the United States, a survey of students on 56 campuses revealed a 25 percent rate of alcohol abstinence among students of legal drinking age (21) but only a 19 percent abstinence rate among students under 21 (Engs & Hanson, 1989).

Asserting Uniqueness

Imagine a world of complete conformity, where there were no differences among people. Would such a world be a happy place? If nonconformity can create discomfort, can sameness create comfort?

People feel uncomfortable when they appear too different from others. But in individualistic Western cultures they also feel uncomfortable when they appear exactly like everyone else. As experiments by C. R. Snyder and Howard Fromkin (1980) have shown, people feel better when they see themselves as moderately unique. Moreover, they act in ways that will assert their individuality. In one experiment, Snyder (1980) led Purdue University students to believe that their "10 most important attitudes" were either distinct from or nearly identical to the attitudes of 10,000 other students. When they next participated in a conformity experiment, those deprived of their feeling of uniqueness were the ones most likely to assert their individuality by nonconformity. Moreover, individuals who have the highest "need for uniqueness" tend to be the least responsive to majority influence (Imhoff & Erb, 2009).

Both social influence and the desire for uniqueness appear in popular baby names. People seeking less commonplace names often hit upon the same ones at the same time. Among the top 10 U.S. girls' baby names for 2007 were Isabella (2), Madison (5), and Olivia (7). Those who in the 1960s broke out of the pack by naming their baby Rebecca, thinking they were bucking convention, soon discovered their choice was part of a new pack, noted Peggy Orenstein (2003). Hillary, a popular late '80s, early '90s name, became less original-seeming and less frequent (even among her admirers) after Hillary Clinton became famous. Although the popularity of such names then fades, observes Orenstein, it may resurface with a future generation. Max, Rose, and Sophie sound like the roster of a retirement home—or a primary school.

Seeing oneself as unique also appears in people's "spontaneous self-concepts." William McGuire and his Yale University colleagues (McGuire & others, 1979; McGuire & Padawer-Singer, 1978) invited children to "tell us about yourself." In reply, the children mostly mentioned their distinctive attributes. Foreign-born children were more likely than others to mention their birthplace. Redheads were more likely than black- and brown-haired children to volunteer their hair color. Light and heavy children were the most likely to refer to their body weight. Minority children were the most likely to mention their race.

Likewise, we become more keenly aware of our gender when we are with people of the other gender (Cota & Dion, 1986). When I attended an American Psychological Association meeting with 10 others—all women, as it happened—I immediately was aware of my gender. As we took a break at the end of the second day, I joked that the line would be short at my bathroom, triggering the woman sitting next to me to notice what hadn't crossed her mind—the group's gender makeup.

The principle, says McGuire, is that "one is conscious of oneself insofar as, and in the ways that, one is different." Thus, "If I am a Black woman in a group of White women, I tend to think of myself as a Black; if I move to a group of Black men, my blackness loses salience and I become more conscious of being a woman" (McGuire & others, 1978). This insight helps us understand why White people who grow up amid non-White people tend to have a strong White identity, why gays may be more conscious of their sexual identity than straights, and why any minority group tends to be conscious of its distinctiveness and how the surrounding culture relates to it (Knowles & Peng, 2005). The majority group, being less conscious of race, may see the minority group as hypersensitive. When occasionally living in Scotland, where my American accent marks me as a foreigner, I become conscious of my national identity and sensitive to how others react to it.

When the people of two cultures are nearly identical, they still will notice their differences, however small. Even trivial distinctions may provoke scorn and conflict. Jonathan Swift satirized the phenomenon in *Gulliver's Travels* with the story of the Little-Endians' war against the Big-Endians. Their difference: The Little-Endians preferred to break their eggs on the small end, the Big-Endians on the large end. On a world scale, the differences may not seem great between Sunni and Shia. But anyone who reads the news knows that these small differences have meant big conflicts (Rothbart & Taylor, 1992). Rivalry is often most intense when the other group closely resembles you.

So, although we do not like being greatly deviant, we are, ironically, all alike in wanting to feel distinctive and in noticing how we are distinctive. (In thinking you are different, you are like everyone else.) But as research on the self-serving bias makes clear, it is not just any kind of distinctiveness we seek but distinctiveness in the right direction. Our quest is not merely to be different from the average, but *better* than average.

MINORITY INFLUENCE

We have seen that

- cultural situations mold us, but we also help create and choose these situations.

- pressures to conform sometimes overwhelm our better judgment, but blatant pressure motivates reactance as we assert our individuality and freedom.

- persuasive forces are powerful, but we can resist persuasion by making public commitments and by anticipating persuasive appeals.

Consider, finally, how individuals can influence their groups. In most social movements, a small minority will sway, and then eventually become, the majority. "All history," wrote Ralph Waldo Emerson, "is a record of the power of minorities, and of minorities of one." Think of Copernicus and Galileo, of Martin Luther King, Jr., of Susan B. Anthony, of Nelson Mandela. The American civil rights movement was ignited by the refusal of one African American woman, Rosa Parks, to relinquish her seat on a bus in Montgomery, Alabama. Technological history has also been made by innovative minorities. As Robert Fulton developed his steamboat—"Fulton's Folly"—he endured constant derision: "Never did a single encouraging remark, a bright hope, a warm wish, cross my path" (Cantril & Bumstead, 1960). Indeed, if minority viewpoints never prevailed, history would be static and nothing would ever change.

What makes a minority persuasive? What might Arthur Schlesinger have done to get the Kennedy group to consider his doubts about the Bay of Pigs invasion? Experiments initiated by Serge Moscovici in Paris have identified several determinants of minority influence: *consistency, self-confidence,* and *defection.*

Consistency

More influential than a minority that wavers is a minority that sticks to its position. Moscovici and associates (1969; Moscovici, 1985) found that if a minority of participants consistently judges blue slides as green, members of the majority will occasionally agree. But if the minority wavers, saying "blue" to one-third of the blue slides and "green" to the rest, virtually no one in the majority will ever agree with "green."

Experiments show—and experience confirms—that nonconformity, especially persistent nonconformity, is often painful, and that being a minority in a group can be unpleasant (Levine, 1989; Lücken & Simon, 2005). That helps explain a *minority slowness effect*—a tendency for people with minority views to express them less quickly than do people in the majority (Bassili, 2003). If you set out to be Emerson's minority of one, prepare yourself for ridicule—especially when you argue an issue that's personally relevant to the majority and when the group wants to settle an issue by reaching consensus (Kameda & Sugimori, 1993; Kruglanski & Webster, 1991; Trost & others, 1992). Even when people in the majority know that the disagreeing person is factually or morally right, they may still, unless they change their position, dislike the person (Chan & others, 2010).

People may attribute your dissent to psychological peculiarities (Papastamou & Mugny, 1990). When Charlan Nemeth (1979, 2011) planted a minority of two within a simulated jury and had them oppose the majority's opinions, the duo was inevitably disliked. Nevertheless, the majority acknowledged that the persistence of the two did more than anything else to make them rethink their positions. Compared to majority influence that often triggers unthinking agreement, minority influence stimulates a deeper processing of arguments, often with increased creativity (Kenworthy & others, 2008; Martin & others, 2007, 2008).

University students who have racially diverse friends, or who are exposed to racial diversity in discussion groups, display less simplistic thinking (Antonio & others, 2004). With dissent from within one's own group, people take in more information, think about it in new ways, and often make better decisions (Page, 2007). Believing that one need not win friends to influence people, Nemeth quotes Oscar Wilde: "We dislike arguments of any kind; they are always vulgar, and often convincing."

Some successful companies have recognized the creativity and innovation sometimes stimulated by minority perspectives, which may contribute new ideas and stimulate colleagues to think in fresh ways. 3M, which has been famed for valuing "respect for individual initiative," has welcomed employees spending time on wild ideas. The Post-it note's adhesive was a failed attempt by Spencer Silver to develop a super-strong glue. Art Fry, after having trouble marking his church choir hymnal with pieces of paper, thought, "What I need is a bookmark with Spence's adhesive along the edge." Even so, this was a minority view that eventually won over a skeptical marketing department (Nemeth, 1997).

Self-Confidence

Consistency and persistence convey self-confidence. Furthermore, Nemeth and Joel Wachtler (1974) reported that any behavior by a minority that conveys self-confidence—for example, taking the head seat at the table—tends to raise self-doubts among the majority. By being firm and forceful, the minority's apparent self-assurance may prompt the majority to reconsider its position. This is especially so on matters of opinion rather than fact. Using their research at Italy's University of Padova, Anne Maass and colleagues (1996) report that minorities are less persuasive when answering a question of fact ("from which country does Italy import most of its raw oil?") than attitude ("from which country should Italy import most of its raw oil?").

Defections from the Majority

A persistent minority punctures any illusion of unanimity. When a minority consistently doubts the majority wisdom, majority members become freer to express their own doubts and may even switch to the minority position. But what about a lone defector, someone who initially agreed with the majority but then reconsidered and dissented? In research with University of Pittsburgh students, John Levine (1989) found that a minority person who had defected from the majority was even more persuasive than a consistent minority voice. Nemeth's jury-simulation experiments found that once defections begin, others often soon follow, initiating a snowball effect.

Are these factors that strengthen minority influence unique to minorities? Sharon Wolf and Bibb Latané (1985; Wolf, 1987) and Russell Clark (1995) have argued that the same social forces work for both majorities and minorities. Informational influence (via persuasive arguments) and normative influence (via social comparison) fuel both group polarization and minority influence. And if consistency, self-confidence, and defections from the other side strengthen the minority, such variables also strengthen a majority. The social impact of any position, majority or minority, depends on the strength, immediacy, and number of those who support it.

There is a delightful irony in this new emphasis on how individuals can influence the group. Until recently, the idea that the minority could sway the majority was itself a minority view in social psychology. Nevertheless, by arguing consistently and forcefully, Moscovici, Nemeth, Maass, Clark, and others convinced the majority of group influence researchers that minority influence is a phenomenon worthy of study. And the way that several of these minority influence researchers came by their interests should, perhaps, not surprise us. Anne Maass (1998) became interested in how minorities could effect social change after growing up in postwar Germany and hearing her grandmother's personal accounts of fascism. Charlan Nemeth (1999) developed her interest while she was a visiting professor in Europe "working with Henri Tajfel and Serge Moscovici. The three of us were 'outsiders'—I an American Roman Catholic female in Europe, they having survived World War II as Eastern European Jews. Sensitivity to the value and the struggles of the minority perspective came to dominate our work."

*I*S LEADERSHIP MINORITY INFLUENCE?

Activity
21.2

In 1910, the Norwegians and the English engaged in an epic race to the South Pole. The Norwegians, effectively led by Roald Amundsen, made it. The English, ineptly led by Robert Falcon Scott, did not; Scott and three team members died. Amundsen illustrated the power of **leadership,** the process by which individuals mobilize and guide groups.

Some leaders are formally appointed or elected; others emerge informally as the group interacts. What makes for good leadership often depends on the situation. The best person to lead the engineering team may not make the best leader of the sales force. Some people excel at *task leadership*—at organizing work, setting standards, and focusing on goal attainment. Others excel at *social leadership*—at building teamwork, mediating conflicts, and being supportive.

Task leaders generally have a directive style—one that can work well if the leader is bright enough to give good orders (Fiedler, 1987). Being goal oriented, such leaders also keep the group's attention and effort focused on its mission. Experiments show that the combination of specific, challenging goals and periodic progress reports helps motivate high achievement (Locke & Latham, 1990, 2002, 2009).

Social leaders generally have a democratic style—one that delegates authority, welcomes input from team members, and, as we have seen, helps prevent groupthink. Data amassed from 118 studies reveal that women are much more egalitarian than men; they are more opposed to social hierarchies (Lee & others, 2011). Many experiments reveal that social leadership is good for morale. Group members usually feel more satisfied when they participate in making decisions (Spector, 1986; Vanderslice & others, 1987). Given control over their tasks, workers also become more motivated to achieve (Burger, 1987).

The once-popular "great person" theory of leadership—that all great leaders share certain traits—has fallen into disrepute. Effective leadership styles, we now know, are less about the big "I" than the big "we." Effective leaders represent, enhance, and champion a group's identity (Haslam & others, 2010). Effective leadership also varies with the situation. Subordinates who know what they are doing may resent working under task leadership, whereas those who don't may welcome it. Recently, however, social psychologists have again wondered if there might be qualities that mark a good leader in many situations (Hogan & others, 1994). British social psychologists Peter Smith and Monir Tayeb (1989) report that studies done in India, Taiwan, and Iran have found that the most effective supervisors in coal mines, banks, and government offices scored high on tests of *both* task and social leadership. They are actively concerned with how work is progressing *and* sensitive to the needs of their subordinates.

Studies also reveal that many effective leaders of laboratory groups, work teams, and large corporations exhibit the behaviors that help make a minority view persuasive. Such leaders engender trust by *consistently* sticking to their goals. And they often exude a *self-confident* charisma that kindles the allegiance of their followers (Bennis, 1984; House & Singh, 1987). Effective leaders typically have a compelling *vision* of some desired state of affairs, especially during times of collective stress (Halevy & others, 2011). They also have an ability to *communicate* that vision to others in clear and simple language, and enough optimism and faith in their group to *inspire* others to follow. Socially dominant, influential individuals also seem competent (whether they are or not) because they act as if they were—by talking a lot (Anderson & Kilduff, 2009).

In one analysis of 50 Dutch companies, the highest morale was at firms with chief executives who most inspired their colleagues "to transcend their own self-interests for the sake of the collective" (de Hoogh & others, 2004). Leadership of this kind—**transformational leadership**—motivates others to identify with and commit themselves to the group's mission. Transformational leaders—many of whom are charismatic, energetic, self-confident extraverts—articulate high standards, inspire people to share their vision, and offer personal attention (Bono & Judge, 2004). In organizations, the frequent result of such leadership is a more engaged, trusting, and effective workforce (Turner & others, 2002).

To be sure, groups also influence their leaders. Sometimes those at the front of the herd have simply sensed where it is already heading. Political candidates know how to read the opinion polls. Someone who typifies the group's views is more likely to be selected as a leader; a leader who deviates too radically from the group's standards may be rejected (Hogg & others, 1998). Smart leaders usually remain with the majority and spend their influence prudently. In rare circumstances, the right traits matched with the right situation yield history-making greatness, notes Dean Keith Simonton (1994). To have a Winston Churchill or a Margaret Thatcher, a Thomas Jefferson or a Karl Marx, a Napoleon or an Adolf Hitler, an Abraham Lincoln or a Martin Luther King, Jr., takes the right person in the right place at the right time. When an apt combination of intelligence, skill, determination, self-confidence, and social charisma meets a rare opportunity, the result is sometimes a championship, a Nobel Prize, or a social revolution.

*C*ONCEPTS TO REMEMBER

reactance A motive to protect or restore one's sense of freedom. Reactance arises when someone threatens our freedom of action.

leadership The process by which certain group members motivate and guide the group.

transformational leadership Leadership that, enabled by a leader's vision and inspiration, exerts significant influence.

❖

PART FOUR

Social Relations

Having explored how we do social psychology (Part I), and how we think about (Part II) and influence (Part III) one another, we come to social psychology's fourth facet—how we relate to one another. Our feelings and actions toward other people are sometimes negative, sometimes positive.

The upcoming modules on prejudice, aggression, and conflict examine the unpleasant aspects of human relations: Why do we dislike, even despise, one another? Why and when do we hurt one another?

Then in the modules on conflict resolution, liking, loving, and helping, we explore the more pleasant aspects: How can social conflicts be justly and amicably resolved? Why do we like or love particular people? When will we offer help to others?

Finally, Module 31 asks what social psychological principles might contribute to help avert an ecological holocaust, triggered by increasing population, consumption, and climate change.

MODULE

22

❖

The Reach of Prejudice

Prejudice comes in many forms—for our own group and against some other group.

Consider some striking examples:

- *Religion.* In the aftermath of 9/11 and the Iraq and Afghanistan wars, Americans with a strong national identity expressed the most disdain for Arab immigrants (Lyons & others, 2010). And if told a job applicant is Muslim, many managers are not inclined to hire or pay well (Park & others, 2009). "Muslims are one of the last minorities in the U.S. that it is still possible to demean openly," observed columnist Nicholas Kristof (2010) as antagonism toward Islamic mosques flared. In Europe, most non-Muslims express concern about "Islamic extremism" and perceive poor Muslim-Western relations (Pew, 2011). Middle Eastern Muslims reciprocate the negativity toward "greedy" and "immoral" Westerners and frequently report not believing that Arabs carried out the 9/11 attacks (Wike & Grim, 2007; Pew, 2011).

- *Obesity.* When seeking love and employment, overweight people—especially White women—face slim prospects. In correlational studies, overweight people marry less often, gain entry to less-desirable jobs, and make less money (Swami & others, 2008). Weight discrimination, in fact, exceeds racial or gender discrimination and occurs at every employment stage—hiring, placement, promotion, compensation, discipline, and discharge (Roehling, 2000). Negative assumptions about and discrimination against

243

overweight people help explain why overweight women and obese men seldom (relative to their numbers in the general population) become the CEOs of large corporations or get elected to office (Roehling & others, 2008, 2009, 2010). As children, the obese are more often bullied, and as adults, they are more often depressed (de Wit & others, 2010; Lumeng & others, 2010; Luppino & others, 2010; Mendes, 2010).

- *Sexual orientation.* Many gay youth—two-thirds of gay secondary school students in one national British survey—have reported experiencing homophobic bullying (Hunt & Jensen, 2007). The U.S. National Longitudinal Study of Adolescent Health revealed that gay and lesbian teens are much more likely to be harshly punished by schools and courts than are their straight peers, despite being less likely to engage in serious wrongdoing (Himmelstein & Brückner, 2011). Among adults, one in five British lesbians and gays report having been victimized by aggressive harassment, insults, or physical assaults (Dick, 2008). In a U.S. national survey, 20 percent of gay, lesbian, and bisexual persons reported having experienced a personal or property crime owing to their sexual orientation, and half reported experiencing verbal harassment (Herek, 2009).

- *Age.* People's perceptions of the elderly—as generally kind but frail, incompetent, and unproductive—predispose patronizing behavior, such as baby-talk speech that leads elderly people to feel less competent and act less capably (Bugental & Hehman, 2007).

- *Immigrants.* A fast-growing research literature documents anti-immigrant prejudice among Germans toward Turks, the French toward North Africans, the British toward West Indians and Pakistanis, and Americans toward Latin American immigrants (Pettigrew, 2006). As we will see, the same factors that feed racial and gender prejudice also feed dislike of immigrants (Pettigrew & others, 2008; Zick & others, 2008).

WHAT IS PREJUDICE?

Activity
22.1

Prejudice, stereotyping, discrimination, racism, sexism—the terms often overlap. Let's clarify them. Each of the situations just described involved a negative evaluation of some group. And that is the essence of **prejudice:** a preconceived negative judgment of a group and its individual members.

Prejudice is an attitude which is a distinct combination of feelings, inclinations to act, and beliefs. A prejudiced person may *dislike* those different from self and *behave* in a discriminatory manner, *believing* them ignorant and dangerous.

The negative evaluations that mark prejudice often are supported by negative beliefs, called **stereotypes.** To stereotype is to generalize. To simplify the world, we generalize: The British are reserved. Americans are outgoing. Professors are absentminded.

Such generalizations can be more or less true (and are not always negative). The elderly are stereotyped as more frail, which, despite individual differences, they are. "Stereotypes," note Lee Jussim, Clark McCauley, and Yueh-Ting Lee (1995), "may be positive or negative, accurate or inaccurate." An accurate stereotype may even be desirable. We call it "sensitivity to diversity" or "cultural awareness in a multicultural world." To stereotype the British as more concerned about punctuality than Mexicans is to understand what to expect and how to get along with others in each culture. "Accuracy dominates bias," notes Lee Jussim (2012). "The social perception glass (of people judging others) is about 90 percent full."

The 10 percent problem with stereotypes arises when they are *overgeneralized* or just plain wrong. To presume that most American welfare clients are African American is to overgeneralize, because it just isn't so. To presume that single people are less conscientious and more neurotic than partnered people, as did people in one German study, was wrong, because it just wasn't so (Greitemeyer, 2009). To presume that people with disabilities are incompetent and asexual, as did Oregonians in another study, misrepresents reality (Nario-Redmond, 2010). To stigmatize the obese as slow, lazy, and undisciplined is inaccurate (Puhl & Heuer, 2009, 2010). To presume that Muslims are terrorists, priests are pedophiles, and evangelicals hate homosexuals overgeneralizes from the worst examples of each.

Prejudice is a negative *attitude;* **discrimination** is negative *behavior.* Discriminatory behavior often has its source in prejudicial attitudes (Dovidio & others, 1996; Wagner & others, 2008). Such was evident when researchers analyzed the responses to 1,115 identically worded e-mails sent to Los Angeles area landlords regarding vacant apartments. Encouraging replies came back to 89 percent of notes signed "Patrick McDougall," to 66 percent from "Said Al-Rahman," and to 56 percent from "Tyrell Jackson" (Carpusor & Loges, 2006). Other researchers have followed suit. When 4,859 U.S. state legislators received e-mails shortly before the 2008 election asking how to register to vote, "Jake Mueller" received more replies than "DeShawn Jackson," though fewer from minority legislators (Butler & Broockman, 2011). Likewise, Jewish Israeli students were less likely to alert the sender to a misaddressed e-mail that came from an Arab name and town ("Muhammed Yunis of Ashdod") rather than from one of their own group ("Yoav Marom of Tel Aviv") (Tykocinski & Bareket-Bojmel, 2009).

Activity
22.2

Attitudes and behavior are often loosely linked. Prejudiced attitudes need not breed hostile acts, nor does all oppression spring from prejudice. **Racism** and **sexism** are institutional practices that discriminate, even when there is no prejudicial intent. If word-of-mouth hiring practices in an all-White business have the effect of excluding potential non-White employees, the practice could be called racist—even if an employer intended no discrimination. When job ads for male-dominated vocations feature words associated with male stereotypes ("We are a dominant engineering firm seeking individuals who can perform in a competitive environment"), and job ads for female-dominated vocations feature the opposite ("We seek people who will be sensitive to clients' needs and can develop warm client relationships"), the result may be institutional sexism. Without intending any prejudice, the gendered wording helps sustain gender inequality (Gaucher & others, 2011).

Prejudice: Implicit and Explicit

Prejudice provides one of the best examples of our *dual attitude* system. We can have different explicit (conscious) and implicit (automatic) attitudes toward the same target, as shown by 500 studies using the Implicit Association Test (Carpenter, 2008). The test, which has been taken online by some 6 million people, assesses "implicit cognition"—what you know without knowing that you know (Greenwald & others, 2008). It does so by measuring people's speed of associations. Much as we more quickly associate a hammer with a nail than with a pail, so the test can measure how speedily we associate "White" with "good" versus "Black" with "good." Thus, people may retain from childhood a habitual, automatic fear or dislike of people for whom they now express respect and admiration. Although explicit attitudes may change dramatically with education, implicit attitudes may linger, changing only as we form new habits through practice (Kawakami & others, 2000).

A raft of experiments—by researchers at Ohio State University and the University of Wisconsin (Devine & Sharp, 2008), Yale and Harvard universities (Banaji, 2004), Indiana University (Fazio, 2007), the University of Colorado (Wittenbrink, 2007; Wittenbrink & others, 1997), the University of Washington (Greenwald & others, 2000), the University of Virginia (Nosek & others, 2007), and New York University (Bargh & Chartrand, 1999)—have confirmed that prejudiced and stereotypic evaluations can occur outside people's awareness. Some of these studies briefly flash words or faces that "prime" (automatically activate) stereotypes for some racial, gender, or age group. Without their awareness, the participants' activated stereotypes may then bias their behavior. Having been primed with images associated with African Americans, for example, they may then react with more hostility to an experimenter's (intentionally) annoying request.

Critics contend that the Implicit Association Test lacks sufficient validity to assess or label individuals (Blanton & others, 2006, 2009). The test is more appropriate for research, which has shown, for example, that implicit biases predict behaviors ranging from acts of friendliness to work evaluations (Greenwald & others, 2009). In the 2008 U.S. presidential election, both implicit and explicit prejudice predicted voters' support for Barack Obama, and his election in turn led to some reduction in implicit prejudice (Bernstein & others, 2010; Payne & others, 2010).

Keeping in mind the distinction between conscious, explicit prejudice and unconscious, implicit prejudice, let's examine two common forms of prejudice: racial prejudice and gender prejudice.

Racial Prejudice

In the context of the world, every race is a minority. Non-Hispanic Whites, for example, are only one-fifth of the world's people and will be one-eighth within another half-century. Thanks to mobility and migration over the past two centuries, the world's races now intermingle, in relations that are sometimes hostile, sometimes amiable.

To a molecular biologist, skin color is a trivial human characteristic, one controlled by a minuscule genetic difference. Moreover, nature doesn't cluster races in neatly defined categories. It is people, not nature, who label Barack Obama, the son of a White woman, as "Black."

Most folks see prejudice—in other people. In one Gallup poll, White Americans estimated 44 percent of their peers to be high in prejudice (5 or higher on a 10-point scale). How many gave themselves a high score? Just 14 percent (Whitman, 1998).

Is Racial Prejudice Disappearing?

Which is right: people's perceptions of high prejudice in others, or their perceptions of low prejudice in themselves? And is racial prejudice becoming a thing of the past?

Explicit prejudicial attitudes can change very quickly.

- In 1942, most Americans agreed, "There should be separate sections for Negroes on streetcars and buses" (Hyman & Sheatsley, 1956). Today the question would seem bizarre, because such blatant prejudice has nearly disappeared.
- In 1942, fewer than a third of all Whites (only 1 in 50 in the South) supported school integration; by 1980, support for it was 90 percent.
- In 1958, 4 percent of Americans of all races approved of Black-White marriages—as did 86 percent in 2011 (Jones, 2011).

Considering what a thin slice of history is covered by the years since 1942, or even since slavery was practiced, the changes are dramatic. In Britain, overt racial prejudice, as expressed in opposition to interracial marriage or having an ethnic minority boss, has similarly plummeted, especially among younger adults (Ford, 2008).

African Americans' attitudes also have changed since the 1940s, when Kenneth Clark and Mamie Clark (1947) demonstrated that many African Americans held anti-Black prejudices. In making its historic 1954 decision declaring segregated schools unconstitutional, the Supreme Court found it noteworthy that when the Clarks gave African American children a choice between Black dolls and White dolls, most chose the White. In studies from the 1950s through the 1970s, Black children were increasingly likely to prefer Black dolls. And adult Blacks came to view Blacks and Whites as similar in such traits as intelligence, laziness, and dependability (Jackman & Senter, 1981; Smedley & Bayton, 1978).

Shall we conclude, then, that racial prejudice is extinct in countries such as the United States, Britain, and Canada? Not if we consider the 6,604 reported hate crime incidents during 2009 (FBI, 2008, 2009). Not if we consider the small proportion of Whites who, as Figure 22-1 shows, would not vote for a Black presidential candidate. Not if we consider the 6 percent greater support that Obama would likely have received in 2008, according to one statistical analysis of voter racial and political attitudes, if there had been no White racial prejudice (Fournier & Tompson, 2008).

So, how great is the progress toward racial equality? In the United States, Whites tend to contrast the present with the oppressive past, perceiving swift and radical progress. Blacks tend to contrast the present with their ideal world, which has not yet been realized, and perceive somewhat less progress (Eibach & Ehrlinger, 2006).

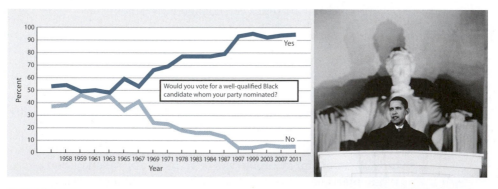

FIGURE 22-1
Changing racial attitudes of White Americans from 1958 to 2011. Abraham Lincoln's ghostly embrace of Barack Obama visualized the Obama mantra: "Change we can believe in." Two days later, Obama stood on steps built by the hands of slaves, placed his hand on a Bible last used in Lincoln's own inauguration, and spoke "a most sacred oath"—in a place, he reflected, where his "father less than 60 years ago might not have been served at a local restaurant."   Source: Data from Gallup Polls (brain.gallup.com).

Subtle Forms of Prejudice

Prejudice in subtle forms is even more widespread than blatant, overt prejudice. Modern prejudice often appears subtly, in our preferences for what is familiar, similar, and comfortable (Dovidio & others, 1992; Esses & others, 1993a; Gaertner & Dovidio, 2005).

Some experiments have assessed people's *behavior* toward Blacks and Whites. Whites are equally helpful to any person in need—except when the needy person is remote (for instance, a wrong-number caller with an apparent Black accent who needs a message relayed). Likewise, when asked to use electric shocks to "teach" a task, White people have given no more (if anything, less) shock to a Black than to a White person—except when they were angered or when the recipient couldn't retaliate or know who did it (Crosby & others, 1980; Rogers & Prentice-Dunn, 1981).

Thus, prejudiced attitudes and discriminatory behavior surface when they can hide behind the screen of some other motive. In Australia, Britain, France, Germany, and the Netherlands, blatant prejudice has been replaced by subtle prejudice (exaggerating ethnic differences, feeling less admiration and affection for immigrant minorities, rejecting them for supposedly nonracial reasons) (Pedersen & Walker, 1997; Tropp & Pettigrew, 2005a). Some researchers call such subtle prejudice "modern racism" or "cultural racism."

Modern prejudice even appears as a race sensitivity that leads to exaggerated reactions to isolated minority persons—overpraising their accomplishments, overcriticizing their mistakes, and failing to warn Black students, as they would White students, about potential academic difficulty (Crosby & Monin, 2007; Fiske, 1989; Hart & Morry, 1997; Hass & others, 1991).

It also appears as patronization. For example, Kent Harber (1998) gave White students at Stanford University a poorly written essay to evaluate. When the students thought the writer was Black, they rated it *higher* than when they were led to think the author was White, and they rarely offered harsh criticisms. The evaluators, perhaps wanting to avoid the appearance of bias, patronized the Black essayists with lower standards. Such "inflated praise and insufficient criticism" may hinder minority student achievement, Harber noted. In follow-up research, Harber and his colleagues (2010) found that Whites concerned about appearing biased not only rate and comment more favorably on weak essays attributed to Black students, they also recommend less time for skill development. To protect their own self-image as unprejudiced, they bend over backward to give positive and unchallenging feedback.

Automatic Prejudice

How widespread are automatic prejudiced reactions to African Americans? Experiments have shown such reactions in varied contexts. For example, in clever experiments by Anthony Greenwald and his colleagues

(1998, 2000), 9 in 10 White people took longer to identify pleasant words (such as *peace* and *paradise*) as "good" when associated with Black rather than White faces. The participants consciously expressed little or no prejudice; their bias was unconscious and unintended. Moreover, report Kurt Hugenberg and Galen Bodenhausen (2003), the more strongly people exhibit such implicit prejudice, the readier they are to perceive anger in Black faces.

Critics note that unconscious *associations* may only indicate cultural assumptions, perhaps without *prejudice* (which involves negative feelings and action tendencies). But some studies find that implicit bias can leak into behavior:

- In a Swedish study, a measure of implicit biases against Arab-Muslims predicted the likelihood of 193 corporate employers not interviewing applicants with Muslim names (Rooth, 2007).

- In a medical study of 287 physicians, those exhibiting the most implicit racial bias were the least likely to recommend clot-busting drugs for a Black patient described as complaining of chest pain (Green & others, 2007).

- In a study of 44 Australian drug and alcohol nurses, those displaying the most implicit bias against drug users were also the most likely, when facing job stress, to want a different job (von Hippel & others, 2008).

In some situations, automatic, implicit prejudice can have life or death consequences. In separate experiments, Joshua Correll and his co-workers (2002, 2006, 2007) and Anthony Greenwald and his co-workers (2003) invited people to press buttons quickly to "shoot" or "not shoot" men who suddenly appeared onscreen holding either a gun or a harmless object such as a flashlight or a bottle. The participants (both Blacks and Whites, in one of the studies) more often mistakenly shot harmless targets who were Black. (Follow-up computerized simulations revealed that it's Black *male* suspects—not females, whether Black or White—that are more likely to be associated with threat and to be shot [Plant & others, 2011].)

In the aftermath of London police shooting dead a man who *looked* Muslim, researchers also found Australians more ready to shoot someone wearing Muslim headgear (Unkelbach & others, 2008). If we implicitly associate a particular ethnic group with danger, then faces from that group will tend to capture our attention and trigger arousal (Donders & others, 2008; Dotsch & Wigboldus, 2008; Trawalter & others, 2008).

In a related series of studies, Keith Payne (2001, 2006) and Charles Judd and colleagues (2004) found that when primed with a Black rather than a White face, people think guns: They more quickly recognize a gun and they more often mistake a tool, such as a wrench, for a gun. Even when race does not bias perception, it may bias reaction—as people require more or less evidence before firing (Klauer & Voss, 2008).

Jennifer Eberhardt and her colleagues (2004) demonstrated that the reverse effect can occur as well. Exposing people to weapons makes them pay more attention to faces of African Americans and even makes police officers more likely to judge stereotypical-looking African Americans as criminals. These studies help explain why in 1999, Amadou Diallo (a Black immigrant in New York City) was shot 41 times by police officers for removing his wallet from his pocket.

It also appears that different brain regions are involved in automatic and consciously controlled stereotyping (Correll & others, 2006; Cunningham & others, 2004; Eberhardt, 2005). Pictures of outgroups that elicit the most disgust (such as drug addicts and the homeless) elicit brain activity in areas associated with disgust and avoidance (Harris & Fiske, 2006). This suggests that automatic prejudices involve primitive regions of the brain associated with fear, such as the amygdala.

Even the social scientists who study prejudice seem vulnerable to automatic prejudice, note Anthony Greenwald and Eric Schuh (1994). They analyzed biases in authors' citations of social science articles by people with selected non-Jewish names (Erickson, McBride, etc.) and Jewish names (Goldstein, Siegel, etc.). Their analysis of nearly 30,000 citations, including 17,000 citations of prejudice research, found something remarkable: Compared with Jewish authors, non-Jewish authors had 40 percent higher odds of citing non-Jewish names. (Greenwald and Schuh could not determine whether Jewish authors were overciting their Jewish colleagues or whether non-Jewish authors were overciting their non-Jewish colleagues, or both.)

Gender Prejudice

How pervasive is prejudice against women? In Module 13 we examined gender-role norms—people's ideas about how women and men *ought* to behave. Here we consider gender *stereotypes*—people's beliefs about how women and men *do* behave. Norms are *pre*scriptive; stereotypes are *de*scriptive.

Gender Stereotypes

From research on stereotypes, two conclusions are indisputable: Strong gender stereotypes exist, and, as often happens, members of the stereotyped group accept the stereotypes. Men and women agree that you *can* judge the book by its sexual cover. In one survey, Mary Jackman and Mary Senter (1981) found that gender stereotypes were much stronger than racial stereotypes. For example, only 22 percent of men thought the two sexes equally "emotional." Of the remaining 78 percent, those who believed females were more emotional outnumbered those who thought males were more emotional by 15 to 1. And what did the women believe? To within 1 percentage point, their responses were identical.

Remember that stereotypes are generalizations about a group of people and may be true, false, or overgeneralized from a kernel of truth. In Module 13 we noted that the average man and woman do differ somewhat in social connectedness, empathy, social power, aggressiveness, and sexual initiative (though not in intelligence). Do we then conclude that gender stereotypes are accurate? Sometimes stereotypes exaggerate differences. But not always, observed Janet Swim (1994). She found that Pennsylvania State University students' stereotypes of men's and women's restlessness, nonverbal sensitivity, aggressiveness, and so forth were reasonable approximations of actual gender differences.

Gender stereotypes have persisted across time and culture. Averaging data from 27 countries, John Williams and his colleagues (1999, 2000) found that people everywhere perceive women as more agreeable, and men as more outgoing. The persistence and omnipresence of gender stereotypes have led some evolutionary psychologists to believe they reflect innate, stable reality (Lueptow & others, 1995).

Stereotypes (beliefs) are not prejudices (attitudes). Stereotypes may support prejudice. Yet one might believe, without prejudice, that men and women are "different yet equal." Let's therefore see how researchers probe for gender prejudice.

Sexism: Benevolent and Hostile

Judging from what people tell survey researchers, attitudes toward women have changed as rapidly as racial attitudes have. As Figure 22-2 shows, the percentage of Americans willing to vote for a female presidential candidate has roughly paralleled the increased percentage willing to vote for a Black candidate. In 1967, 56 percent of first-year American college students agreed that "the activities of married women are best confined to the home and family"; by 2002, only 22 percent agreed (Astin & others, 1987; Sax & others, 2002). Thereafter, the home–family question no longer seemed worth asking.

Alice Eagly and her associates (1991) and Geoffrey Haddock and Mark Zanna (1994) also report that people don't respond to women with gut-level negative emotions as they do to certain other groups. Most people like women more than men. They perceive women as more understanding, kind, and helpful. A *favorable* stereotype, which Eagly (1994) dubs the *women-are-wonderful effect,* results in a favorable attitude.

But gender attitudes often are ambivalent, report Peter Glick, Susan Fiske, and their colleagues (1996, 2007) from their surveys of 15,000 people in 19 nations. Gender attitudes frequently mix a *benevolent sexism* ("Women have a superior moral sensibility") with *hostile sexism* ("Once a man commits, she puts him on a tight leash").

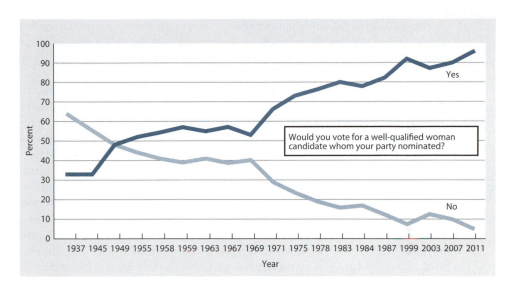

FIGURE 22-2
Changing Gender Attitudes from 1958 to 2011.   Source: Data from Gallup Polls (gallup
.com/poll/4729/presidency.aspx).

Peter Glick and Susan Fiske's distinction between "hostile" and "benevolent" sexism extends to other prejudices. We see other groups as competent
or as likable, but often not as both. These two culturally universal dimensions of social perception—likability (warmth) and competence—were
illustrated by one European's comment that "Germans love Italians, but
don't admire them. Italians admire Germans, but don't love them" (Cuddy
& others, 2009). We typically respect the competence of those high in status
and like those who agreeably accept a lower status.

Gender Discrimination
Being male isn't all roses. Compared to women, men are three times more
likely to commit suicide and be murdered. They are nearly all the battlefield and death row casualties. They die five years sooner. And males represent the majority with mental retardation or autism, as well as students
in special education programs (Baumeister, 2007; S. Pinker, 2008).

Is gender bias fast becoming extinct in Western countries? Has the
women's movement nearly completed its work? As with racial prejudice,
blatant gender prejudice is dying, but subtle bias lives.

Violate gender stereotypes, and people may react. People take notice
of a cigar-smoking woman and a tearful man, and denigrate a White
rapper (Phelan & Rudman, 2010). A woman whom people see as power
hungry suffers more voter backlash than does a similarly power-hungry
man (Okimoto & Brescoll, 2010).

In the world beyond democratic Western countries, gender discrimination is not subtle. Two-thirds of the world's unschooled children are girls (United Nations, 1991). In some countries, discrimination extends to violence, even prosecuting rape victims for adultery (UN, 2006).

But the biggest violence against women may occur prenatally. Around the world, people tend to prefer having baby boys. In the United States, in 1941, 38 percent of expectant parents said they preferred a boy if they could have only one child; 24 percent preferred a girl; and 23 percent said they had no preference. In 2011, the answers were virtually unchanged, with 40 percent still preferring a boy (Newport, 2011). With the widespread use of ultrasound to determine the sex of a fetus and the growing availability of abortion, these preferences are, in some countries, affecting the number of boys and girls. In China, where 95 percent of orphanage children are girls (Webley, 2009), the 118 boys born for every 100 girls has led to an excess of 32 million under-20 males. These are tomorrow's "bare branches," as the Chinese think of them—bachelors who will have trouble finding mates (Hvistendahl, 2009, 2010, 2011; Zhu & others, 2009). This "gender genocide" is not found only in China. Taiwan, Singapore, India, and South Korea likewise have millions of "missing women" (Abrevaya, 2009). In response, China has made sex-selective abortions a criminal offense.

To conclude, overt prejudice against people of color and against women is far less common today than it was in the mid-twentieth century. Nevertheless, techniques that are sensitive to subtle prejudice still detect widespread bias. And in parts of the world, gender prejudice makes for misery. Therefore, we need to look carefully and closely at the social, emotional, and cognitive sources of prejudice.

*C*ONCEPTS TO REMEMBER

prejudice   A preconceived negative judgment of a group and its individual members.

stereotype   A belief about the personal attributes of a group of people. Stereotypes are sometimes overgeneralized, inaccurate, and resistant to new information (and sometimes accurate).

discrimination   Unjustified negative behavior toward a group or its members.

racism   (1) An individual's prejudicial attitudes and discriminatory behavior toward people of a given race, or (2) institutional practices (even if not motivated by prejudice) that subordinate people of a given race.

sexism   (1) An individual's prejudicial attitudes and discriminatory behavior toward people of a given sex, or (2) institutional practices (even if not motivated by prejudice) that subordinate people of a given sex.

MODULE

23

❖

The Roots of Prejudice

Prejudice springs from several sources. It may arise from differences in social status and people's desires to justify and maintain those differences. It may also be learned from our parents as they socialize us about what differences they believe matter between people. Our social institutions, too, may maintain and support prejudice. Consider first how prejudice can function to defend self-esteem and social position.

SOCIAL SOURCES OF PREJUDICE

A principle to remember: *Unequal status breeds prejudice.* Masters view slaves as lazy, irresponsible, lacking ambition—as having exactly those traits that justify the slavery. Historians debate the forces that create unequal status. But after those inequalities exist, prejudice helps justify the economic and social superiority of those who have wealth and power. Tell me the economic relationship between two groups, and I'll predict the intergroup attitudes. Upper-class individuals are more likely than those in poverty to see people's fortunes as the outcomes they have earned, thanks to skill and effort, and not as the result of having connections, money, and good luck (Kraus & others, 2011).

Historical examples abound. Where slavery was practiced, prejudice ran strong. Nineteenth-century politicians justified imperial expansion by describing exploited colonized people as "inferior," "requiring protection," and a "burden" to be borne (G. W. Allport, 1958, pp. 204–205). Six decades ago, sociologist Helen Mayer Hacker (1951) noted how stereotypes of Blacks and women helped rationalize the inferior status of each: Many people thought

255

both groups were mentally slow, emotional and primitive, and "contented" with their subordinate role. Blacks were "inferior"; women were "weak." Blacks were all right in their place; women's place was in the home.

Theresa Vescio and her colleagues (2005) tested that reasoning. They found that powerful men who stereotype their female subordinates give them plenty of praise, but fewer resources, thus undermining their performance. This sort of patronizing allows the men to maintain their positions of power. In the laboratory, too, patronizing benevolent sexism (statements implying that women, as the weaker sex, need support) has undermined women's cognitive performance by planting intrusive thoughts—self-doubts, preoccupations, and decreased self-esteem (Dardenne & others, 2007).

Socialization

Prejudice springs from unequal status and from other social sources, including our acquired values and attitudes. The influence of family socialization appears in children's prejudices, which often mirror those perceived in their mothers (Castelli & others, 2007). Even children's implicit racial attitudes reflect their parents' explicit prejudice (Sinclair & others, 2004). Our families and cultures pass on all kinds of information—how to find mates, drive cars, and divide the household labors, and whom to distrust and dislike.

The Authoritarian Personality

In the 1940s, University of California, Berkeley, researchers—two of whom had fled Nazi Germany—set out on an urgent research mission: to uncover the psychological roots of the poisonous right-wing anti-Semitism that caused the slaughter of millions of Jews in Nazi Germany. In studies of American adults, Theodor Adorno and his colleagues (1950) discovered that hostility toward Jews often coexisted with hostility toward other minorities. In those who were strongly prejudiced, prejudice appeared to be not specific to one group but an entire way of thinking about those who are "different." Moreover, these judgmental, **ethnocentric** people shared certain tendencies: an intolerance for weakness, a punitive attitude, and a submissive respect for their group's authorities, as reflected in their agreement with such statements as "Obedience and respect for authority are the most important virtues children should learn." From those findings, Adorno and his colleagues (1950) surmised that these tendencies define an **authoritarian personality** that is particularly prone to engage in prejudice and stereotyping.

More recent inquiry into authoritarian people's early lives has revealed that, as children, they often face harsh discipline. Militant extremism, on both the political left and the right, shares some common themes, such as catastrophizing, desiring vengeance, and dehumanizing the enemy (Saucier & others, 2009). This extremism supposedly leads the individuals affected to repress their hostilities and impulses, which they project onto outgroups. Research into authoritarianism also suggests that the insecurity of authoritarian individuals predisposes them toward an excessive concern with power and status and an inflexible right-wrong way of thinking that makes ambiguity difficult to tolerate. Such people therefore tend to be submissive to those with power over them and aggressive or punitive toward those whom they consider lower in status than themselves. In other words, "My way or the highway."

Scholars have criticized research into the authoritarian personality for focusing on right-wing authoritarianism and overlooking similarly dogmatic authoritarianism of the left. Still, contemporary studies of right-wing authoritarians by University of Manitoba psychologist Bob Altemeyer (1988, 1992) confirmed that there *are* individuals whose fears and hostilities surface as prejudice. Their feelings of moral superiority may go hand in hand with brutality toward perceived inferiors. Altemeyer also concludes that right-wing authoritarians tend to be "equal opportunity bigots." Different forms of prejudice—toward Blacks, gays and lesbians, women, Muslims, immigrants, the homeless—*do* tend to coexist in the same individuals (Zick & others, 2008). Moreover, authoritarian tendencies, sometimes reflected in ethnic tensions, surge during threatening times of economic recession and social upheaval (Cohrs & Ibler, 2009; Doty & others, 1991; Sales, 1973).

Religion and Prejudice

Those who benefit from social inequalities while avowing that "all are created equal" need to justify keeping things the way they are. What could be a more powerful justification than to believe that God has ordained the existing social order? For all sorts of cruel deeds, noted William James, "piety is the mask" (1902, p. 264).

In almost every country, leaders invoke religion to sanctify the present order. The use of religion to support injustice helps explain a consistent pair of findings concerning North American Christianity: (1) White church members express more racial prejudice than nonmembers, and (2) those professing fundamentalist beliefs express more prejudice than those professing more progressive beliefs (Hall & others, 2010; Johnson & others, 2011).

If religion causes prejudice, then more religious church members should also be more prejudiced. But three other findings consistently indicate otherwise.

- Among church members, faithful church attenders were, in 24 out of 26 comparisons, less prejudiced than occasional attenders (Batson & Ventis, 1982).
- Gordon Allport and Michael Ross (1967) found that those for whom religion is an end in itself (those who agree, for example, with the statement "My religious beliefs are what really lie behind my whole approach to life") express *less* prejudice than those for

whom religion is more a means to other ends (who agree "A primary reason for my interest in religion is that my church is a congenial social activity"). And those who score highest on Gallup's "spiritual commitment" index are more welcoming of a person of another race moving in next door (Gallup & Jones, 1992).

- Protestant ministers and Roman Catholic priests gave more support to the U.S. civil rights movement than did laypeople (Fichter, 1968; Hadden, 1969). In Germany, 45 percent of clergy in 1934 had aligned themselves with the Confessing Church, which was organized to oppose Nazi influence on the German Protestant Church (Reed, 1989).

What, then, is the relationship between religion and prejudice? The answer we get depends on *how* we ask the question. If we define religiousness as church membership or willingness to agree at least superficially with traditional religious beliefs, then the more religious people are the more racially prejudiced. Bigots often rationalize bigotry with religion. But if we assess depth of religious commitment in any of several other ways, then the very devout are less prejudiced—hence the religious roots of the modern civil rights movement, among whose leaders were many ministers and priests. It was Thomas Clarkson and William Wilberforce's faith-inspired values ("Love your neighbor as yourself") that, two centuries ago, motivated their successful campaign to end the British Empire's slave trade and the practice of slavery. As Gordon Allport concluded, "The role of religion is paradoxical. It makes prejudice and it unmakes prejudice" (1958, p. 413).

Conformity

Once established, prejudice is maintained largely by inertia. If prejudice is socially accepted, many people will follow the path of least resistance and conform to the fashion. They will act not so much out of a need to hate as out of a need to be liked and accepted. Thus, people become more likely to favor (or oppose) discrimination after hearing someone else do so, and they are less supportive of women after hearing sexist humor (Ford & others, 2008; Zitek & Hebl, 2007).

During the 1950s, Thomas Pettigrew (1958) studied Whites in South Africa and the American South. His discovery: Those who conformed most to other social norms were also most prejudiced; those who were less conforming mirrored less of the surrounding prejudice.

The price of nonconformity was painfully clear to the ministers of Little Rock, Arkansas, where the U.S. Supreme Court's 1954 school desegregation decision was implemented. Most ministers privately favored integration but feared that advocating it openly would decrease membership and financial contributions (Campbell & Pettigrew, 1959).

Conformity also maintains gender prejudice. "If we have come to think that the nursery and the kitchen are the natural sphere of a woman," wrote George Bernard Shaw in an 1891 essay, "we have done so exactly as English children come to think that a cage is the natural sphere of a parrot—because they have never seen one anywhere else." Children who *have* seen women elsewhere—children of employed women—have expressed less stereotyped views of men and women (Hoffman, 1977). Women students exposed to female science, technology, engineering, and mathematics (STEM) experts likewise express more positive implicit attitudes toward STEM studies and display more effort on STEM tests (Stout & others, 2011).

In all this, there is a message of hope. If prejudice is not deeply ingrained in personality, then as fashions change and new norms evolve, prejudice can diminish. And so it has.

MOTIVATIONAL SOURCES OF PREJUDICE

Various kinds of motivations underlie the hostilities of prejudice. Motivations can also lead people to avoid prejudice.

Frustration and Aggression: The Scapegoat Theory

Frustration (the blocking of a goal) often evoke hostility. When the cause of our frustration is intimidating or unknown, we often redirect our hostility. This phenomenon of "displaced aggression" may have contributed to the lynchings of African Americans in the South after the Civil War. Between 1882 and 1930, more lynchings occurred in years when cotton prices were low and economic frustration was therefore presumably high (Hepworth & West, 1988; Hovland & Sears, 1940). Hate crimes seem not to have fluctuated with unemployment in recent decades (Falk & others, 2011; Green & others, 1998). However, when living standards are rising, societies tend to be more open to diversity and to the passage and enforcement of antidiscrimination laws (Frank, 1999). Ethnic peace is easier to maintain during prosperous times.

Targets for displaced aggression vary. Following their defeat in World War I and their country's subsequent economic chaos, many Germans saw Jews as villains. Long before Hitler came to power, one German leader explained: "The Jew is just convenient. . . . If there were no Jews, the anti-Semites would have to invent them" (quoted by G. W. Allport, 1958, p. 325). In earlier centuries people vented their fear and hostility on witches, whom they sometimes burned or drowned in public. In our time, Americans who reacted to 9/11 with more anger than fear expressed greater intolerance toward immigrants and Middle Easterners (Skitka & others, 2004). Passions provoke prejudice. Special individuals who experience no negative emotional response to social threats—namely, children with the genetic disorder called Williams syndrome—display a notable lack of racial stereotypes and prejudice (Santos et al., 2010). No passion, no prejudice.

Competition is an important source of frustration that can fuel prejudice. When two groups compete for jobs, housing, or social prestige, one group's goal fulfillment can become the other group's frustration. Thus, the **realistic group conflict theory** suggests that prejudice arises when groups compete for scarce resources (Maddux & others, 2008; Pereira & others, 2010; Sassenberg & others, 2007). A corresponding ecological principle, Gause's law, states that maximum competition will exist between species with identical needs.

Consider how this has played out across the world:

- In Western Europe, economically frustrated people express relatively high levels of blatant prejudice toward ethnic minorities (Pettigrew & others, 2008, 2010).

- In Canada, opposition to immigration since 1975 has gone up and down with the unemployment rate (Palmer, 1996).

- In the United States, concerns about immigrants taking jobs are greatest among those with the lowest incomes (AP/Ipsos, 2006; Pew, 2006).

- In South Africa, dozens of African immigrants were killed by mobs and 35,000 people were hounded from squatter camps by poor South Africans who resented the economic competition. "These foreigners have no IDs, no papers, and yet they get the jobs," said one unemployed South African, noting that "They are willing to work for 15 rand [about $2] a day" (Bearak, 2010). When interests clash, prejudice may be the result.

Social Identity Theory: Feeling Superior to Others

Humans are a group-bound species. Our ancestral history prepares us to feed and protect ourselves—to live—in groups. Humans cheer for their groups, kill for their groups, die for their groups. Evolution prepares us, when encountering strangers, to make a quick judgment: friend or foe? Those from our group, those who look like us, even those who *sound* like us—with accents like our own—we instantly tend to like (Gluszek & Dovidio, 2010; Kinzler & others, 2009).

Not surprisingly, as noted by Australian social psychologists John Turner (1981, 2000), Michael Hogg (1992, 2008, 2010), and their colleagues, we also define ourselves by our groups. Self-concept—our sense of who we are—contains not just a *personal identity* (our sense of our personal attributes and attitudes) but also a **social identity** (Chen & others, 2006). Fiona identifies herself as a woman, an Aussie, a Labourite, a University of New South Wales student, a MacDonald family member. We carry such social identities like playing cards, playing them when appropriate. Prime American students to think of themselves as "Americans," and they will display heightened anger and disrespect toward Muslims; prime their "student" identity, and they will instead display heightened anger toward police (Ray & others, 2008).

Working with the late British social psychologist Henri Tajfel, a Polish native who lost family and friends in the Holocaust and then devoted much of his career to studying ethnic hatred, Turner (1947–2011) proposed *social identity theory.* Turner and Tajfel observed the following:

- *We categorize:* We find it useful to put people, ourselves included, into categories. To label someone as a Hindu, a Scot, or a bus driver is a shorthand way of saying some other things about the person.
- *We identify:* We associate ourselves with certain groups (our **ingroups**) and gain self-esteem by doing so.
- *We compare:* We contrast our groups with other groups (**outgroups**), with a favorable bias toward our own group.

We humans naturally divide others into those inside and those out-side our group. We also evaluate ourselves partly by our group member-ships. Having a sense of "we-ness" strengthens our self-concepts. It *feels* good. We seek not only *respect* for ourselves but also *pride* in our groups (Smith & Tyler, 1997). Moreover, seeing our groups as superior helps us feel even better. It's as if we all think, "I am an X [name your group]. X is good. Therefore, I am good."

Lacking a positive personal identity, people often seek self-esteem by identifying with a group. Thus, many disadvantaged youths find pride, power, security, and identity in gang affiliations. When people's personal and social identities become fused—when the boundary between self and group blurs—they become more willing to fight or die for their group (Gómez & others, 2011; Swann & others, 2009). Many superpatriots, for example, define themselves by their national identities (Staub, 1997, 2005). And many people at loose ends find identity in their associations with new religious movements, self-help groups, or fraternal clubs (Figure 23-1).

Because of our social identifications, we conform to our group norms. We sacrifice ourselves for team, family, nation. And the more important our social identity and the more strongly attached we feel to a group, the more we react prejudicially to threats from another group (Crocker & Luhtanen, 1990; Hinkle & others, 1992).

Ingroup Bias

The group definition of who you are—your gender, race, religion, marital status, academic major—implies a definition of who you are not. The circle that includes "us" (the ingroup) excludes "them" (the outgroup). The more

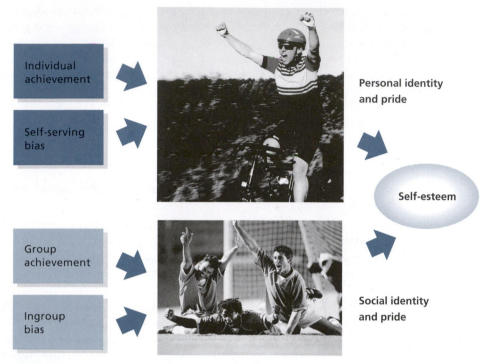

FIGURE 23-1
Personal identity and social identity together feed self-esteem.

that ethnic Turks in the Netherlands see themselves as Turks or as Muslims, the less they see themselves as Dutch (Verkuyten & Yildiz, 2007).

The mere experience of being formed into groups may promote **ingroup bias.** Ask children, "Which are better, the children in your school or the children at [another school nearby]?" Virtually all will say their own school has the better children.

For adults, too, the closer to home, the better things seem. More than 80 percent of both Whites and Blacks say race relations are generally good in their own neighborhoods, but fewer than 60 percent see relations as generally good in the country as a whole (Sack & Elder, 2000). Merely sharing a birthday with someone creates enough of a bond to evoke heightened cooperation in a laboratory experiment (Miller & others, 1998).

Ingroup Bias Expresses and Supports a Positive Self-Concept   Ingroup bias is one more example of the human quest for a positive self-concept. Most people have a positive self-image, which they project to their ingroups more than to outgroups (DiDonato & others, 2011). Their ingroup bias expresses their positive self-concept, but it also supports their self-concept. When our group has been successful, we can make ourselves feel better by identifying more strongly with it. College students whose team has just been victorious frequently report, "*We* won." After their team's defeat, students are more likely to say, "*They* lost." Basking in the reflected glory of a successful ingroup is strongest among those who have just experienced an ego blow, such as learning they did poorly on a "creativity test" (Cialdini & others, 1976). We can also bask in the reflected glory of a friend's achievement—except when the friend outperforms us on something pertinent to our identity (Tesser & others, 1988). If you think of yourself as an outstanding psychology student, you will likely take more pleasure in a friend's excellence in mathematics.

Ingroup Bias Feeds Favoritism   We are so group conscious that, given any excuse to think of ourselves as a group, we will do so—and we will then exhibit ingroup bias. Even forming conspicuous groups on no logical basis—for instance, merely by composing groups X and Y with the flip of a coin—will produce some ingroup bias (Billig & Tajfel, 1973; Brewer & Silver, 1978; Locksley & others, 1980). In Kurt Vonnegut's novel *Slapstick,* computers gave everyone a new middle name; all "Daffodil-11s" then felt unity with one another and distance from "Raspberry-13s." The self-serving bias rides again, enabling people to achieve a more positive social identity: "We" are better than "they," even when "we" and "they" are defined randomly!

In a series of experiments, Tajfel and Michael Billig (1974; Tajfel, 1970, 1981, 1982) further explored how little it takes to provoke favoritism toward *us* and unfairness toward *them*. In one study, Tajfel and Billig had individual British teenagers evaluate modern abstract paintings and then told them that they and some other teens had favored the art of Paul Klee over that of Wassily Kandinsky, while others favored Kandinsky. Finally, without ever meeting the other members of their Klee-favoring group, each teen divided some money among members of the Klee- and Kandinsky-favoring groups. In this and other experiments, defining groups even in this trivial way produced ingroup favoritism. David Wilder (1981) summarized the typical result: "When given the opportunity to divide 15 points [worth money], subjects generally award 9 or 10 points to their own group and 5 or 6 points to the other group."

We are more prone to ingroup bias when our group is small and lower in status relative to the outgroup (Ellemers & others, 1997; Mullen & others, 1992). When we're part of a small group surrounded by a larger group, we are more conscious of our group membership. When our ingroup is the majority, we think less about it. To be a foreign student, to be gay or lesbian, or to be of a minority race or gender at some social gathering is to feel one's social identity more keenly and to react accordingly.

Need for Status, Self-Regard and Belonging
Status is relative: To perceive ourselves as having status, we need people below us. Thus, one psychological benefit of prejudice, or of any status

system, is a feeling of superiority. Most of us can recall a time when we took secret satisfaction in another's failure—perhaps seeing a brother or sister punished or a classmate failing a test. In Europe and North America, prejudice is often greater among those low or slipping on the socioeconomic ladder and among those whose positive self-image is threatened (Lemyre & Smith, 1985; Pettigrew & others, 1998; Thompson & Crocker, 1985). In one study, members of lower-status sororities were more disparaging of competing sororities than were members of higher-status sororities (Crocker & others, 1987). If our status is secure, we have less need to feel superior.

In study after study, thinking about your own mortality—by writing a short essay on dying and the emotions aroused by thinking about death—provokes enough insecurity to intensify ingroup favoritism and outgroup prejudice (Greenberg & others, 1990, 2009; Harmon-Jones & others, 1996; Schimel & others 1999). One study found that among Whites, thinking about death can even promote liking for racists who argue for their group's superiority (Greenberg & others, 2001, 2008). With death on their minds, people exhibit **terror management.** They shield themselves from the threat of their own death by derogating those who further arouse their anxiety by challenging their worldviews. When people are already feeling vulnerable about their mortality, prejudice helps bolster a threatened belief system. Thinking about death can also heighten communal feelings, such as ingroup identification, togetherness, and altruism (McGregor & others, 2001; Sani & others, 2009).

Reminding people of their death can also affect support for important public policies. Before the 2004 presidential election, giving people cues

"It's not enough that we succeed. Cats must also fail."

© Leo Cullum/ The New Yorker Collection/www .cartoonbank.com

related to death—including asking them to recall their emotions related to the 9/11 attack, or subliminally exposing them to 9/11 related pictures—increased support for President George W. Bush and his antiterrorism policies (Landau & others, 2004). In Iran, reminders of death increased college students' support for suicide attacks against the United States (Pyszczynski & others, 2006).

Despising outgroups can also serve to strengthen the ingroup. As we will explore further in Module 29, the perception of a common enemy unites a group. School spirit is seldom so strong as when the game is with the archrival. The sense of comradeship among workers is often highest when they all feel a common antagonism toward management. To solidify the Nazi hold over the Germany people, Hitler threatened them with the "Jewish menace."

*C*OGNITIVE SOURCES OF PREJUDICE

How does the way we think about the world influence our stereotypes? And how do our stereotypes affect our judgments? Fueled by a surge in studies of stereotyping (Figure 23-2), new approaches to prejudice apply new research on social thinking. Stereotyped beliefs and prejudiced attitudes exist not only because of social conditioning and because they

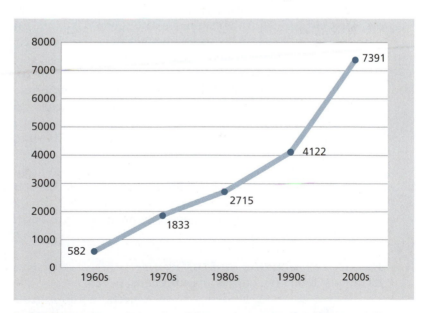

FIGURE 23-2
Number of psychological articles mentioning "stereotypes" (or derivative word), by decade.   Source: PsycINFO.

enable people to displace hostilities, but also as by-products of normal thinking processes. Many stereotypes spring less from malice of the heart than from the machinery of the mind. Like perceptual illusions, by-products of our knack for interpreting the world, stereotypes can be by-products of how we simplify our complex worlds.

Categorization: Classifying People into Groups

One way we simplify our environment is to *categorize*—to organize the world by clustering objects into groups (Macrae & Bodenhausen, 2000, 2001). A biologist classifies plants and animals. A human classifies people. Having done so, we think about them more easily. If persons in a group share some similarities—if most MENSA members are smart, and most basketball players are tall—knowing their group memberships can provide useful information with minimal effort (Macrae & others, 1994). Stereotypes sometimes offer "a beneficial ratio of information gained to effort expended" (Sherman & others, 1998). Stereotypes represent cognitive efficiency. They are energy-saving schemes for making speedy judgments and predicting how others will think and act. Thus, they served as "ultimate, evolutionary functions," by enabling our ancestors to cope and survive (Navarette & others, 2010).

Spontaneous Categorization
Ethnicity and sex are powerful ways of categorizing people. Imagine Tom, a 45-year-old African American real-estate agent in Atlanta. I suspect that your image of "Black male" predominates over the categories "middle-aged," "businessperson," and "American southerner."

Experiments expose our spontaneous categorization of people by race. Much as we organize what is actually a color continuum into what we perceive as distinct colors, such as red, blue, and green, so our "discontinuous minds" (Dawkins, 1993) cannot resist categorizing people into groups. We label people of widely varying ancestry as simply "Black" or "White," as if such categories were black and white. When individuals view different people making statements, they often forget who said what but remember the race of the person who made each statement (Hewstone & others, 1991; Stroessner & others, 1990; Taylor & others, 1978). By itself, such categorization is not prejudice, but it does provide a foundation for prejudice.

Perceived Similarities and Differences
Picture the following objects: apples, chairs, pencils.

There is a strong tendency to see objects within a group as being more uniform than they really are. Were your apples all red? Your chairs all straight-backed? Your pencils all yellow? Once we classify two days in the same month, they seem more alike, temperature-wise, than the same interval across months. People guess the 8-day average temperature difference between, for instance, November 15 and 23 to be less than the 8-day difference between November 30 and December 8 (Krueger & Clement, 1994).

It's the same with people. When we assign people to groups—athletes, drama majors, math professors—we are likely to exaggerate the similarities within the groups and the differences between them (S. E. Taylor, 1981; Wilder, 1978). We assume that other groups are more homogeneous than our own. Mere division into groups can create an **outgroup homogeneity effect**—a sense that *they* are "all alike" and different from "us" and "our" group (Ostrom & Sedikides, 1992). We generally like people we perceive as similar to us and dislike those we perceive as different, so the result is ingroup bias (Byrne & Wong, 1962; Rokeach & Mezei, 1966; Stein & others, 1965).

When the group is our own, we are more likely to see diversity:

- Many non-Europeans see the Swiss as a fairly homogeneous people. But to the people of Switzerland, the Swiss are diverse, encompassing French-, German-, Italian-, and Romansh-speaking groups.

- Many Anglo Americans lump "Latinos" together. Mexican Americans, Cuban Americans, and Puerto Ricans—among others—see important differences (Huddy & Virtanen, 1995).

- Sorority sisters perceive the members of any other sorority as less diverse than the members of their own (Park & Rothbart, 1982).

Perhaps you have noticed: *They*—the members of any racial group other than your own—even *look* alike. Many of us can recall embarrassing ourselves by confusing two people of another racial group, prompting the person we've misnamed to say, "You think we all look alike." Experiments in the United States, Scotland, and Germany reveal that people of other races do in fact *seem* to look more alike than do people of one's own race (Chance & Goldstein, 1981, 1996; Ellis, 1981; Meissner & Brigham, 2001; Sporer & Horry, 2011). When White students are shown faces of a few White and a few Black individuals and then asked to pick those individuals out of a photographic lineup, they show an **own-race bias:** They more accurately recognize the White faces than the Black ones, and they often falsely recognize Black faces never before seen.

As Figure 23-3 illustrates, Blacks more easily recognize another Black than they do a White (Bothwell & others, 1989). Hispanics, Blacks, and Asians all recognize faces from their own races better than from one another's (Gross, 2009). Likewise, British South Asians are quicker than White Brits to recognize South Asian faces (Walker & Hewstone, 2008). And 10- to 15-year-old Turkish children are quicker than Austrian children

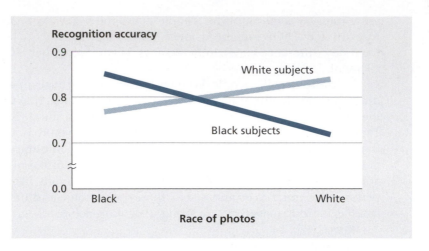

FIGURE 23-3
The own-race bias. White subjects more accurately recognize the faces of
Whites than of Blacks; Black subjects more accurately recognize the faces of
Blacks than of Whites.   Source: From P. G. Devine & R. S. Malpass, 1985.

to recognize Turkish faces (Sporer & others, 2007). Even infants as young
as 9 months display better own-race recognition of faces (Kelly & others,
2005, 2007).

It's true outside the laboratory as well, as Daniel Wright and his colleagues (2001) found after either a Black or a White researcher approached
Black and White people in South African and English shopping malls. When
later asked to identify the researcher from lineups, people better recognized
those of their own race. It's not that we cannot perceive differences among
faces of another group. Rather, when looking at a face from another racial
group we often attend, first, to group ("that man is Black") rather than to
individual features. When viewing someone of our own group, we are
less attentive to the race category and more attentive to individual details
(Bernstein & others, 2007; Hugenberg & others, 2010; Shriver & others, 2008;
Young & others, 2010).

Distinctiveness: Perceiving People Who Stand Out

Other ways we perceive our worlds also breed stereotypes. Distinctive
people and vivid or extreme occurrences often capture attention and distort judgments.

Distinctive People
Have you ever found yourself in a situation where you were the only
person of your gender, race, or nationality? If so, your difference from
the others probably made you more noticeable and the object of more

attention. A Black in an otherwise White group, a man in an otherwise female group, or a woman in an otherwise male group seems more prominent and influential and to have exaggerated good and bad qualities (Crocker & McGraw, 1984; S. E. Taylor & others, 1979). When someone in a group is made conspicuous, we tend to see that person as causing whatever happens (Taylor & Fiske, 1978). If we are positioned to look at Joe, even if Joe is merely an average group member, Joe will seem to have a greater-than-average influence on the group.

Have you noticed that people also define you by your most distinctive traits and behaviors? Tell people about someone who is a skydiver and a tennis player, report Lori Nelson and Dale Miller (1995), and they will think of the person as a skydiver. Asked to choose a gift book for the person, they will pick a skydiving book over a tennis book. A person who has both a pet snake and a pet dog is seen more as a snake owner than a dog owner.

People also take note of those who violate expectations (Bettencourt & others, 1997). "Like a flower blooming in winter, intellect is more readily noticed where it is not expected," reflected Stephen Carter (1993, p. 54) on his own experience as an African American intellectual. Such perceived distinctiveness makes it easier for highly capable job applicants from low-status groups to get noticed, although they also must work harder to prove that their abilities are genuine (Biernat & Kobrynowicz, 1997).

Ellen Langer and Lois Imber (1980) cleverly demonstrated the attention paid to distinctive people. They asked Harvard students to watch a video of a man reading. The students paid closer attention when they were led to think he was out of the ordinary—a cancer patient, a homosexual, or a millionaire. They noticed characteristics that other viewers ignored, and their evaluation of him was more extreme. Those who thought the man was a cancer patient noticed distinctive facial characteristics and bodily movements and thus perceived him to be much more "different from most people" than did the other viewers. The extra attention we pay to distinctive people creates an illusion that they differ from others more than they really do. If people thought you had the IQ of a genius, they would probably notice things about you that otherwise would pass unnoticed.

Distinctiveness Feeds Self-Consciousness   When surrounded by Whites, Blacks sometimes detect people reacting to their distinctiveness. Many report being stared or glared at, being subject to insensitive comments, and receiving bad service (Swim & others, 1998). Sometimes, however, we misperceive others as reacting to our distinctiveness. Researchers Robert Kleck and Angelo Strenta (1980) discovered this when they led Dartmouth College women to feel disfigured. The women thought the purpose of the experiment was to assess how someone would react to a facial scar created with theatrical makeup; the scar was on the right cheek, running from the ear to the mouth. Actually, the purpose was to see how the women themselves, when made to feel deviant, would perceive others' behavior toward them. After applying the makeup, the experimenter gave each woman a small hand mirror so she could see the authentic-looking scar. When she put the mirror down, he then applied some "moisturizer" to "keep the makeup from cracking." What the "moisturizer" really did was remove the scar.

The scene that followed was poignant. A young woman, feeling terribly self-conscious about her supposedly disfigured face, talked with another woman who saw no such disfigurement and knew nothing of what had gone on before. If you have ever felt similarly self-conscious— perhaps about a physical handicap, acne, even just a bad hair day—then perhaps you can sympathize with the self-conscious woman. Compared with women who were led to believe their conversational partners merely thought they had an allergy, the "disfigured" women became acutely sensitive to how their partners were looking at them. They rated their partners as more tense, distant, and patronizing. Observers who later analyzed videotapes of how the partners treated "disfigured" persons could find no such differences in treatment. Self-conscious about being different, the "disfigured" women had misinterpreted mannerisms and comments they would otherwise not have noticed.

Self-conscious interactions between a majority and a minority person can therefore feel tense even when both are well intentioned (Devine & others, 1996). Tom, who is known to be gay, meets tolerant Bill, who is straight and wants to respond without prejudice. But feeling unsure of himself, Bill holds back a bit. Tom, expecting negative attitudes from most people, misreads Bill's hesitancy as hostility and responds with a seeming chip on his shoulder.

Vivid Cases

Our minds also use distinctive cases as a shortcut to judging groups. Are the Japanese good baseball players? "Well, there's Ichiro Suzuki and Hideki Matsui and Kosuke Fukudome. Yeah, I'd say so." Note the thought processes at work here: Given limited experience with a particular social group, we recall examples of it and generalize from those (Sherman, 1996). Moreover, encountering an example of a negative stereotype (for instance, a hostile Black) can prime the stereotype, leading us to minimize contact with the group (Henderson-King & Nisbett, 1996).

Such generalizing from a single case can cause problems. Vivid instances, though more available in memory, seldom represent the larger group. Exceptional athletes, though distinctive and memorable, are not the best basis for judging the distribution of athletic talent among an entire group.

Those in a numerical minority, being more distinctive, also may be numerically overestimated by the majority. What proportion of your country's population would you say is Muslim? People in non-Muslim countries often overestimate this proportion. (In the United States, a Pew

Research Center [2011] study reported that 0.8 percent of the population were Muslim.)

Consider a 2011 Gallup survey, in which the average American guessed that 25 percent of people are exclusively homosexual (Morales, 2011). The best evidence suggests that about 3 percent of men and 1 or 2 percent of women have a same-sex orientation (Chandra & others, 2011; Herbenick & others, 2010).

Distinctive Events

Stereotypes assume a correlation between group membership and individuals' presumed characteristics ("Italians are emotional," "Jews are shrewd," "Accountants are perfectionists"). Often, people's stereotypes are accurate (Jussim, 2012). But sometimes our attentiveness to unusual occurrences creates illusory correlations. Because we are sensitive to distinctive events, the co-occurrence of two such events is especially noticeable—more noticeable than each of the times the unusual events do *not* occur together.

David Hamilton and Robert Gifford (1976) demonstrated illusory correlation in a classic experiment. They showed students slides in which various people, members of "Group A" or "Group B," were said to have done something desirable or undesirable. For example, "John, a member of Group A, visited a sick friend in the hospital." Twice as many statements described members of Group A as Group B. But both groups did nine desirable acts for every four undesirable behaviors. Since both Group B and the undesirable acts were less frequent, their co-occurrence—for example, "Allen, a member of Group B, dented the fender of a parked car and didn't leave his name"—was an unusual combination that caught people's attention. The students therefore overestimated the frequency with which the "minority" group (B) acted undesirably, and they judged Group B more harshly.

Remember, Group A members outnumbered Group B members two to one, and Group B members committed undesirable acts in the same *proportion* as Group A members (thus, they committed only half as many). Moreover, the students had no preexisting biases for or against Group B, and they received the information more systematically than daily experience ever offers it. Although researchers debate why it happens, they agree that illusory correlation occurs and provides yet another source for the formation of racial stereotypes (Berndsen & others, 2002). Thus, the features that most distinguish a minority from a majority are those that become associated with it (Sherman & others, 2009). Your ethnic or social group may be like other groups in most ways, but people will notice how it differs.

In experiments, even single co-occurrences of an unusual act by someone in an atypical group—"Ben, a Jehovah's Witness, owns a pet sloth"—can embed illusory correlations in people's minds (Risen & others, 2007). This enables the mass media to feed illusory correlations. When a self-described homosexual person murders or sexually abuses someone, homosexuality is often mentioned. When a heterosexual does the same, the person's sexual orientation is seldom mentioned. Such reporting adds to the illusion of a large correlation between (1) violent tendencies and (2) homosexuality.

Attribution: Is It a Just World?

In explaining others' actions, we frequently commit the fundamental attribution error that was discussed in Module 6. We attribute others' behavior so much to their inner dispositions that we discount important situational forces. The error occurs partly because our attention focuses on the person, not on the situation. A person's race or sex is vivid and gets attention; the situational forces working upon that person are usually less visible. Slavery was often overlooked as an explanation for slave behavior; the behavior was instead attributed to the slaves' own nature. Until recently, the same was true of how we explained the perceived differences between women and men. Because gender-role constraints were hard to see, we attributed men's and women's behavior solely to their presumed innate dispositions. The more people assume that human traits are fixed dispositions, the stronger are their stereotypes and the greater their acceptance of racial inequities (Levy & others, 1998; Williams & Eberhardt, 2008).

Activity
23.1

In a series of experiments conducted at the universities of Waterloo and Kentucky, Melvin Lerner and his colleagues (Lerner, 1980; Lerner & Miller, 1978) discovered that merely *observing* another innocent person being victimized is enough to make the victim seem less worthy.

Lerner (1980) noted that such disparaging of hapless victims results from the need to believe that "I am a just person living in a just world, a world where people get what they deserve." From early childhood, he argues, we are taught that good is rewarded and evil punished. Hard work and virtue pay dividends; laziness and immorality do not. From this it is but a short leap to assuming that those who flourish must be good and those who suffer must deserve their fate.

Numerous studies have confirmed this **just-world phenomenon** (Hafer & Bègue, 2005). Imagine that you, along with some others, are participating in one of Lerner's studies—supposedly on the perception of emotional cues (Lerner & Simmons, 1966). One of the participants, a confederate, is selected by lottery to perform a memory task. This person receives painful shocks whenever she gives a wrong answer. You and the others note her emotional responses.

After watching the victim receive these apparently painful shocks, the experimenter asks you to evaluate her. How would you respond? With compassionate sympathy? We might expect so. As Ralph Waldo Emerson wrote, "The martyr cannot be dishonored." On the contrary, in these experiments the martyrs *were* dishonored. When observers were powerless to alter the victim's fate, they often rejected and devalued the victim. Juvenal, the Roman satirist, anticipated these results: "The Roman mob follows after Fortune . . . and hates those who have been condemned." And the more ongoing the suffering, as with Jews even after the Holocaust, the greater the dislike of the victims (Imhoff & Banse, 2009).

Linda Carli and her colleagues (1989, 1999) report that the just-world phenomenon colors our impressions of rape victims. Carli had people read detailed descriptions of interactions between a man and a woman. In one scenario, a woman and her boss meet for dinner, go to his home, and each have a glass of wine. Some read this scenario with a happy ending: "Then he led me to the couch. He held my hand and asked me to marry him." In hindsight, people find the ending unsurprising and admire the man's and woman's character traits. Others read the same scenario with a terrible ending: "But then he became very rough and pushed me onto the couch. He held me down on the couch and raped me." Given this ending, people see the rape as inevitable and blame the woman for provocative behavior that seems faultless in the first scenario.

This line of research suggests that people are indifferent to social injustice not because they have no concern for justice but because they see no injustice. Those who assume a just world believe that rape victims must have behaved seductively (Borgida & Brekke, 1985), that battered spouses must have provoked their beatings (Summers & Feldman, 1984), that poor people don't deserve better (Furnham & Gunter, 1984), and that sick people are responsible for their illnesses (Gruman & Sloan, 1983). When researchers activate the concept of choice by having people record others' choices, participants (in the United States) display less empathy for disadvantaged individuals, engage in more victim-blaming, and show reduced support for social policies such as affirmative action (Savani & others, 2011).

Such beliefs enable successful people to reassure themselves that they, too, deserve what they have. The wealthy and healthy can see their own good fortune, and others' misfortune, as justly deserved. Linking good fortune with virtue and misfortune with moral failure enables the fortunate to feel pride and to avoid responsibility for the unfortunate.

People loathe a loser even when the loser's misfortune quite obviously stems substantially from bad luck. Children, for example, tend to view lucky others—such as someone who has found money on a sidewalk—as more likely than unlucky children to do good things and be a nice person (Olson & others, 2008). Adults *know* that gambling outcomes are just good or bad luck and should not affect their evaluations of the gambler. Still, they can't resist playing Monday-morning quarterback—judging people by their results. Ignoring the fact that reasonable decisions can bring bad results, they judge losers as less competent (Baron & Hershey, 1988). Lawyers and stock market investors may similarly judge themselves by their outcomes, becoming smug after successes and self-reproachful after failures. Talent and initiative matter. But the just-world assumption discounts the uncontrollable factors that can derail good efforts even by talented people.

Just-world thinking also leads people to justify their culture's familiar social systems (Jost & others, 2009; Kay & others, 2009). The way things are, we're inclined to think, is the way things ought to be. Such natural conservatism makes it difficult to pass new social policies, such as voting rights laws or tax or health care reform. But after a new policy is in place, our "system justification" works to sustain it. Thus, Canadians mostly approve of their government policies, such as national health care, strict gun control, and no capital punishment, whereas Americans likewise mostly support differing policies to which they are accustomed.

THE CONSEQUENCES OF PREJUDICE

How can stereotypes create their own reality? How can prejudice undermine people's performance? Prejudice has consequences as well as causes.

Self-Perpetuating Prejudgments

Prejudice involves preconceived judgments. Prejudgments are inevitable: None of us is a dispassionate bookkeeper of social happenings, tallying evidence for and against our biases.

Prejudgments guide our attention and our memories. People who accept gender stereotypes often misrecall their own school grades in stereotype-consistent ways. For example, women often recall receiving worse math grades and better arts grades than were actually the case (Chatard & others, 2007).

Moreover, after we judge an item as belonging to a category such as a particular race or sex, our memory for it later shifts toward the features we associate with that category. Johanne Huart and his colleagues (2005) demonstrated this by showing Belgian university students a face that was a blend of 70 percent of the features of a typical male and 30 percent female (or vice versa). Later, those shown the 70 percent male face recalled seeing a male (as you might expect), but also misrecalled the face as being even more prototypically male.

Prejudgments Are Self-Perpetuating

Whenever a member of a group behaves as expected, we duly note the fact; our prior belief is confirmed. When a member of a group behaves inconsistently with our expectation, we may interpret or explain away the behavior as due to special circumstances (Crocker & others, 1983). The contrast to a stereotype can also make someone seem exceptional. Telling some people that "Maria played basketball" and others that "Mark played basketball" may make Maria seem more athletic than Mark (Biernat, 2003). Stereotypes therefore influence how we construe someone's behavior. Prime White folks with negative media images of Black folks (for example, looting after Hurricane Katrina), and the activated stereotype may be poisonous. In one experiment, such images produced reduced empathy for other Black people in need (Johnson & others, 2008).

Perhaps you, too, can recall a time when, try as you might, you could not overcome someone's opinion of you, when no matter what you did you were misinterpreted. Misinterpretations are likely when someone *expects* an unpleasant encounter with you (Wilder & Shapiro, 1989). William Ickes and his colleagues (1982) demonstrated this in an experiment with pairs of college-age men. As the men arrived, the experimenters falsely forewarned one member of each pair that the other person was "one of the unfriendliest people I've talked to lately." The two were then introduced and left alone together for five minutes. Students in another condition of the experiment were led to think the other participant was exceptionally friendly.

Those in both conditions were friendly to the new acquaintance. In fact, those who expected him to be *un*friendly went out of their way to be friendly, and their friendly behavior elicited a warm response. But unlike the positively biased students, those expecting an unfriendly person attributed this reciprocal friendliness to their own "kid-gloves" treatment of him. They afterward expressed more mistrust and dislike for the person and rated his behavior as less friendly. Despite their partner's actual friendliness, the negative bias induced these students to "see" hostilities lurking beneath his "forced smiles." They would never have seen it if they hadn't believed it.

We do notice information that is strikingly inconsistent with a stereotype, but even that information has less impact than might be expected. When we focus on an atypical example, we can salvage the stereotype by splitting off a new category (Brewer & Gaertner, 2004; Hewstone, 1994; Kunda & Oleson, 1995, 1997). The positive image that British schoolchildren form of their friendly school police officers (whom they perceive as a special category) doesn't improve their image of police officers in general (Hewstone & others, 1992). This **subtyping**—seeing people who deviate as exceptions—helps maintain the stereotype that police officers are unfriendly and dangerous.

A different way to accommodate the inconsistent information is to form a new stereotype for those who don't fit. Recognizing that the stereotype does not apply for everyone in the category, homeowners who have "desirable" Black neighbors can form a new and different stereotype of "professional, middle-class Blacks." This **subgrouping**—forming a subgroup stereotype—tends to lead to modest change in the stereotype as the stereotype becomes more differentiated (Richards & Hewstone, 2001). Subtypes are *exceptions* to the group; subgroups are acknowledged as a *part* of the overall group.

Discrimination's Impact: The Self-Fulfilling Prophecy

Attitudes may coincide with the social hierarchy not only as a rationalization for it but also because discrimination affects its victims. "One's reputation," wrote Gordon Allport, "cannot be hammered, hammered, hammered into one's head without doing something to one's character"

(1958, p. 139). If we could snap our fingers and end all discrimination, it would be naive for the White majority to say to Blacks, "The tough times are over, folks! You can now all be attaché-carrying executives and professionals." When the oppression ends, its effects linger, like a societal hangover.

In *The Nature of Prejudice*, Allport catalogued 15 possible effects of victimization. Allport believed these reactions were reducible to two basic types—those that involve blaming oneself (withdrawal, self-hate, aggression against one's own group) and those that involve blaming external causes (fighting back, suspiciousness, increased group pride). If victimization takes a toll—for instance, higher rates of crime—people can use the result to justify the discrimination: "If we let those people in our nice neighborhood, property values will plummet."

Does discrimination indeed affect its victims? We must be careful not to overstate the point. The soul and style of Black culture is for many a proud heritage, not just a response to victimization (Jones, 2003). Nevertheless, social beliefs *can* be self-confirming, as demonstrated in a clever pair of experiments by Carl Word, Mark Zanna, and Joel Cooper (1974). In the first experiment, Princeton University White male volunteers interviewed White and Black research assistants posing as job applicants. When the applicant was Black, the interviewers sat farther away, ended the interview 25 percent sooner, and made 50 percent more speech errors than when the applicant was White. Imagine being interviewed by someone who sat at a distance, stammered, and ended the interview rather quickly. Would it affect your performance or your feelings about the interviewer?

To find out, the researchers conducted a second experiment in which trained interviewers treated people as the interviewers in the first experiment had treated either the White or the Black applicants. When videotapes of the interviews were later rated, those who were treated like the Blacks in the first experiment seemed more nervous and less effective. Moreover, the interviewees could themselves sense a difference; those treated the way the Blacks had been treated judged their interviewers to be less adequate and less friendly. The experimenters concluded that part of "the 'problem' of Black performance resides . . . within the interaction setting itself." As with other self-fulfilling prophecies, prejudice affects its targets.

Stereotype Threat

Just being sensitive to prejudice is enough to make us self-conscious when living as a numerical minority—perhaps as a Black person in a White community or as a White person in a Black community. As with other circumstances that siphon off our mental energy and attention, the result can be diminished mental and physical stamina (Inzlicht &

others, 2006). Placed in a situation where others expect you to perform poorly, your anxiety may also cause you to confirm the belief. I am a short guy in my 60s. When I join a pickup basketball game with bigger, younger players, I presume that they expect me to be a detriment to their team, and that tends to undermine my confidence and performance. Claude Steele and his colleagues call this phenomenon **stereotype threat**—a self-confirming apprehension that one will be evaluated based on a negative stereotype (Steele, 2010; Steele & others, 2002; see also reducingstereotypethreat.org).

In several experiments, Steven Spencer, Claude Steele, and Diane Quinn (1999) gave a very difficult math test to men and women students who had similar math backgrounds. When told that there were *no* gender differences on the test and no evaluation of any group stereotype, the women's performance consistently equaled the men's. Told that there *was* a gender difference, the women dramatically confirmed the stereotype. Frustrated by the extremely difficult test questions, they apparently felt added apprehension, which undermined their performances. For female engineering students, interacting with a sexist man likewise undermines test performance (Logel & others, 2009). Even before exams, stereotype threat can also hamper women's learning math rules and operations (Rydell & others, 2010).

The media can provoke stereotype threat. Paul Davies and his colleagues (2002, 2005) had women and men watch a series of commercials while expecting that they would be tested for their memory of details. For half the participants, the commercials contained only neutral stimuli; for the other half, some of the commercials contained images of "airheaded" women. After seeing the stereotypic images, women not only performed worse than men on a math test but also reported less interest in obtaining a math or science major or entering a math or science career.

Might racial stereotypes be similarly self-fulfilling? Steele and Joshua Aronson (1995) gave difficult verbal abilities tests to Whites and Blacks. Blacks underperformed Whites only when taking the tests under conditions high in stereotype threat. A similar stereotype threat effect has occurred with Hispanic Americans (Nadler & Clark, 2011).

Jeff Stone and his colleagues (1999) report that stereotype threat affects athletic performance, too. Blacks did worse than usual when a golf task was framed as a test of "sports intelligence," and Whites did worse when it was a test of "natural athletic ability." "When people are reminded of a negative stereotype about themselves—'White men can't jump' or 'Black men can't think'—it can adversely affect performance," Stone (2000) surmised.

If you tell students they are at risk of failure (as is often suggested by minority support programs), the stereotype may erode their performance, says Steele (1997). It may cause them to "disidentify" with school and seek

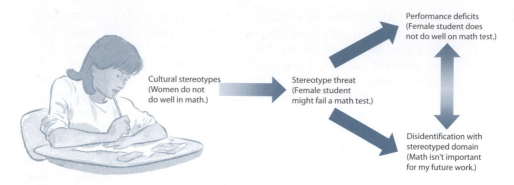

FIGURE 23-4
Stereotype threat. Threat from facing a negative stereotype can produce performance deficits and disidentification.

self-esteem elsewhere (Figure 23-4). Indeed, as African American students move from eighth to tenth grade, there has been a weakening connection between their school performance and self-esteem (Osborne, 1995). Moreover, students who are led to think they have benefited from gender- or race-based preferences in gaining admission to a college or an academic group tend to underperform those who are led to feel competent (Brown & others, 2000).

Better, therefore, to challenge students to believe in their potential, observes Steele. In another of his research team's experiments, Black students responded well to criticism of their writing when also told, "I wouldn't go to the trouble of giving you this feedback if I didn't think, based on what I've read in your letter, that you are capable of meeting the higher standard that I mentioned" (Cohen & others, 1999).

Social psychologists have been more successful in explaining prejudice than in alleviating it. Because prejudice results from many interrelated factors, no simple remedy exists. Nevertheless, we can now anticipate techniques for reducing prejudice (discussed further in chapters to come): If unequal status breeds prejudice, we can seek to create cooperative, equal-status relationships. If prejudice rationalizes discriminatory behavior, we can mandate nondiscrimination. If social institutions support prejudice, we can pull out those supports (for example, with media that model interracial harmony). If outgroups seem more homogeneous than they really are, we can make efforts to personalize their members. If automatic prejudices lead us to engage in behaviors that make us feel guilty, we can use that guilt to motivate ourselves to break the prejudice habit.

Since the end of World War II in 1945, a number of those antidotes have been applied, and racial and gender prejudices have indeed diminished. Social-psychological research also has helped break down discriminatory barriers.

CONCEPTS TO REMEMBER

ethnocentric Believing in the superiority of one's own ethnic and cultural group, and having a corresponding disdain for all other groups.

authoritarian personality A personality that is disposed to favor obedience to authority and intolerance of outgroups and those lower in status.

realistic group conflict theory The theory that prejudice arises from competition between groups for scarce resources.

social identity The "we" aspect of our self-concept; the part of our answer to "Who am I?" that comes from our group memberships.

ingroup "Us"—a group of people who share a sense of belonging, a feeling of common identity.

outgroup "Them"—a group that people perceive as distinctively different from or apart from their ingroup.

ingroup bias The tendency to favor one's own group.

terror management According to "terror management theory," people's self-protective emotional and cognitive responses (including adhering more strongly to their cultural worldviews and prejudices) when confronted with reminders of their mortality.

outgroup homogeneity effect Perception of outgroup members as more similar to one another than are ingroup members. Thus "they are alike; we are diverse."

own-race bias The tendency for people to more accurately recognize faces of their own race. (Also called the *cross-race effect* or *other-race effect*.)

just-world phenomenon The tendency of people to believe that the world is just and that people therefore get what they deserve and deserve what they get.

subtyping Accommodating individuals who deviate from one's stereotype by thinking of them as "exceptions to the rule."

subgrouping Accommodating individuals who deviate from one's stereotype by forming a new stereotype about this subset of the group.

stereotype threat A disruptive concern, when facing a negative stereotype, that one will be evaluated based on a negative stereotype. Unlike self-fulfilling prophecies that hammer one's reputation into one's self-concept, stereotype threat situations have immediate effects.

24

❖

*The Nature and Nurture of Aggression**

Activity
24.1

During the past century, some 250 wars killed 110 million people, enough to populate a "nation of the dead" with more than the combined population of France, Belgium, the Netherlands, Denmark, Finland, Norway, and Sweden. The tolls came not only from the two world wars but also from genocides, including the 1915 to 1923 genocide of 1 million Armenians by the Ottoman Empire, the slaughter of some 250,000 Chinese in Nanking after it had surrendered to Japanese troops in 1937, the 1971 Pakistani genocide of 3 million Bangladeshis, and the 1.5 million Cambodians murdered in a reign of terror starting in 1975 (Dutton & others, 2005; Sternberg, 2003). As Hitler's genocide of millions of Jews, Stalin's genocide of millions of Russians, Mao's genocide of millions of Chinese, and the genocide of millions of Native Americans from the time of Columbus through the nineteenth century make plain, the human potential for extraordinary cruelty crosses cultures.

Even outside of war, and in recent times, human beings have an extraordinary capacity for harming one another. Although violent crime declined since the 1990s, 15,241 people were murdered in the United States

---

*Modules 24 and 25, based on *Social Psychology*, 11th Edition content, are co-authored by Jean Twenge, professor of psychology at San Diego State University. Professor Twenge's research on social rejection and on generational changes in personality and the self has been published in many articles and books, including *Generation Me: Why Today's Young Americans Are More Confident, Assertive, Entitled—and More Miserable Than Ever Before* (2006) and *The Narcissism Epidemic: Living in the Age of Entitlement* (with W. Keith Campbell, 2009).

in 2009; 88,097 were forcibly raped; and an incredible 806,843—nearly a million—were shot, stabbed, or assaulted with another weapon (FBI, 2011). In the decade after 9/11, the United States spent $2.6 trillion on the Iraq and Afghanistan wars that claimed well over 100,000 lives.

Less severe, but still harmful, aggression is even more common. In a survey of children across 35 countries, more than 1 out of 10 reported being bullied at school (Craig & Harel, 2004). Among a sample of Canadian middle- and high-school students, half said they had been bullied online in the previous three months. Their experiences included being called names, having rumors spread about them, or having their private pictures distributed without their consent (Mishna & others, 2010).

To a social psychologist, **aggression** is physical or verbal behavior intended to cause harm. This definition excludes unintentional harm, such as auto accidents or sidewalk collisions; it also excludes actions that may involve pain as an unavoidable side effect of helping someone, such as dental treatments or—in the extreme—assisted suicide. It includes kicks and slaps, threats and insults, even gossip or snide "digs" (as in online bullying).

Instrumental aggression aims to injure, too—but only as a means to some other end. Most terrorism is instrumental aggression. "What nearly all suicide terrorist campaigns have in common is a specific secular and strategic goal," concludes Robert Pape (2003) after studying all suicide bombings from 1980 to 2001. That goal is "to compel liberal democracies to withdraw military forces from territory that the terrorists consider to be their homeland." Terrorism is rarely committed by someone with a psychological pathology, note Arie Kruglanski and his colleagues (2009); instead, terrorists seek personal significance through, for example, attaining hero or martyr status. Terrorism is also a strategic tool used during conflict. In explaining the aim of the 9/11 attacks, Osama bin Laden noted that for a cost of only $500,000 they inflicted $500 billion worth of damage to the American economy (Zakaria, 2008).

Most wars are instrumental aggression. In 2003, American and British leaders justified attacking Iraq not as a hostile effort to kill Iraqis but as an instrumental act of liberation and of self-defense against presumed weapons of mass destruction. Adolescents who bully others—either verbally or physically—are also engaged in instrumental aggression, because they often seek to demonstrate their dominance and high status. In the strange hierarchy of adolescence, being mean and disliked can sometimes make you popular and revered (Salmivalli, 2009).

THEORIES OF AGGRESSION

Is Aggression an Instinct?

Philosophers have debated whether our human nature is fundamentally that of a benign, contented, "noble savage" or that of a brute. The first view, argued by the eighteenth-century French philosopher Jean-Jacques Rousseau (1712–1778), blames society, not human nature, for social evils. The second idea, associated with the English philosopher Thomas Hobbes (1588–1679), credits society for restraining the human brute. In the twentieth century, the "brutish" view—that aggressive drive is inborn and thus inevitable—was argued by Sigmund Freud, the founder of psychoanalysis, in Vienna and Konrad Lorenz, an animal behavior expert, in Germany.

Freud speculated that human aggression springs from a self-destructive impulse. It redirects toward others the energy of a primitive death urge (the "death instinct"). Lorenz, an animal behavior expert, saw aggression as adaptive rather than self-destructive. The two agreed that aggressive energy is instinctive (innate, unlearned, and universal). If not discharged, it supposedly builds up until it explodes or until an appropriate stimulus "releases" it, like a mouse releasing a mousetrap.

The idea that aggression is an instinct collapsed as the list of supposed human instincts grew to include nearly every conceivable human behavior and scientists became aware how much behavior varies from person to person and culture to culture. Yet, biology clearly does influence behavior just as nurture works upon nature. Our experiences interact with the nervous system engineered by our genes.

Neural Influences

Because aggression is a complex behavior, no one spot in the brain controls it. But researchers have found brain neural systems in both animals and humans that facilitate aggression. When the scientists activate these brain areas, hostility increases; when they deactivate them, hostility decreases. Docile animals can thus be provoked into rage, and raging animals into submission.

In one experiment, researchers placed an electrode in an aggression-inhibiting area of a domineering monkey's brain. A smaller monkey, given a button that activated the electrode, learned to push it every time the tyrant monkey became intimidating. Brain activation works with humans, too. After receiving painless electrical stimulation in her amygdala (a part of the brain core), one woman became enraged and smashed her guitar against the wall, barely missing her psychiatrist's head (Moyer, 1976, 1983).

Does this mean that violent people's brains are in some way abnormal? To find out, Adrian Raine and his colleagues (1998, 2000, 2005, 2008) used brain scans to measure brain activity in murderers and to measure the amount of gray matter in men with antisocial conduct disorder. They found that the prefrontal cortex, which acts like an emergency brake on deeper brain areas involved in aggressive behavior, was 14 percent less active than normal in murderers (excluding those who had been abused by their parents) and 15 percent smaller in the antisocial men. As other studies of murderers and death-row inmates confirm, abnormal brains can contribute to abnormally aggressive behavior (Davidson & others, 2000; Lewis, 1998; Pincus, 2001).

Genetic Influences

Heredity influences the neural system's sensitivity to aggressive cues. It has long been known that animals can be bred for aggressiveness. Sometimes this is done for practical purposes (the breeding of fighting cocks). Sometimes breeding is done for research. Finnish psychologist Kirsti Lagerspetz (1979) took normal albino mice and bred the most aggressive ones together; she did the same with the least aggressive ones. After repeating the procedure for 26 generations, she had one set of fierce mice and one set of placid mice.

Aggressiveness also varies among individuals (Asher, 1987; Bettencourt & others, 2006; Denson & others, 2006; Olweus, 1979). Our temperaments— how intense and reactive we are—are partly brought with us into the world, influenced by our sympathetic nervous system's reactivity (Kagan, 1989; Wilkowski & Robinson, 2008). A person's temperament, observed in infancy, usually endures (Larsen & Diener, 1987; Wilson & Matheny, 1986). A 3-year-old who exhibits little conscientiousness and self-control is more vulnerable to substance abuse and arrest by age 32 (Moffitt & others, 2011). A child who is nonaggressive at age 8 will very likely still be a nonaggressive person at age 48 (Huesmann & others, 2003).

In a study examining 12.5 million residents of Sweden, those with a genetic sibling convicted of a violent crime were 4 times as likely to be convicted themselves. Rates were much lower for adopted siblings, suggesting a strong genetic component and a more modest environmental influence (Frisell & others, 2011).

Blood Chemistry

Blood chemistry also influences neural sensitivity to aggressive stimulation.

Alcohol

Both laboratory experiments and police data indicate that alcohol unleashes aggression when people are provoked (Bushman, 1993; Taylor & Chermack, 1993; Testa, 2002). Consider the following:

- The Australian city of Melbourne saw a marked upswing in assaults during the 2000s, fueled primarily by alcohol consumption late at night (Eckersley & Reeder, 2008).

- When asked to think back on relationship conflicts, intoxicated people administer stronger shocks and feel angrier than do sober people during lab experiments (MacDonald & others, 2000).

- In 65 percent of homicides and 55 percent of in-home fights and assaults, the assailant and/or the victim had been drinking (American Psychological Association, 1993). Four in 10 prisoners convicted of a violent crime were drinking when they committed murder, assault, robbery, or sexual assault (Karberg & James, 2005).

Alcohol enhances aggressiveness by reducing people's self-awareness, by focusing their attention on a provocation, and by people's mentally associating alcohol with aggression (Bartholow & Heinz, 2006; Giancola & Corman, 2007; Ito & others, 1996). Alcohol also predisposes people to interpret ambiguous acts (such as a bump in a crowd) as provocations (Begue & others, 2010). Alcohol deindividuates, and it disinhibits.

Testosterone

Hormonal influences appear to be much stronger in lower animals than in humans. But human aggressiveness does correlate with the male sex hormone testosterone. Consider the following:

- Drugs that diminish testosterone levels in violent human males will subdue their aggressive tendencies.

- After men reach age 25, their testosterone levels and rates of violent crime decrease together.

- Testosterone levels tend to be higher among prisoners convicted of planned and unprovoked violent crimes than of nonviolent crimes (Dabbs, 1992; Dabbs & others, 1995, 1997, 2001).

Young, male, and restless. In the 2011 riots that swept English cities, those arrested overwhelmingly shared one genetic characteristic—a Y chromosome—and were testosterone-fueled teens or people in their early 20s.   Source: *The Guardian*, 2011.

- Among the normal range of teen boys and adult men, those with high testosterone levels are more prone to delinquency, hard drug use, and aggressive responses to provocation (Archer, 1991; Dabbs & Morris, 1990; Olweus & others, 1988).

- After handling a gun, men's testosterone levels rise; and the more their testosterone rises, the more aggressive they are toward others (Klinesmith & others, 2006).

- In men, testosterone increases the facial width-to-height ratio. Sure enough, in the laboratory, men with relatively wider faces display more aggression. The same is true in the hockey rink, where collegiate and professional hockey players with relatively wide faces spend more time in the penalty box (Carré & McCormick, 2008). Other people also correctly guessed that wide-faced men would be more aggressive, and they were less likely to trust them (Carré & others, 2009; Stirrat & Perrett, 2010).

Testosterone, said James Dabbs (2000), "is a small molecule with large effects." Injecting a man with testosterone won't automatically make him aggressive, yet men with low testosterone are somewhat less likely to react aggressively when provoked (Geen, 1998). Testosterone is roughly like battery power. Only if the battery levels are very low will things noticeably slow down.

Poor Diet

When British researcher Bernard Gesch first tried to study the effect of diet on aggression, he stood in front of hundreds of inmates at an English prison—but no matter how loudly he talked, none of them would listen. Finally, he talked privately to the "daddy"—the inmates' "tough guy" leader—and 231 inmates signed on to receive nutritional supplements or a placebo. Prisoners who got the extra nutrition were involved in 35 percent fewer violent incidents (Gesch & others, 2002). Such programs may eventually help people outside of prison as well, because many people have diets deficient in important nutrients, such as omega-3 fatty acids (found in fish and important for brain function) and calcium (which guards against impulsivity).

PSYCHOLOGICAL INFLUENCES ON AGGRESSION

There exist important neural, genetic, and biochemical influences on aggression. Biological influences predispose some people more than others to react aggressively to conflict and provocation. But there is more to the story.

Frustration and Aggression

It is a warm evening. Tired and thirsty after two hours of studying, you borrow some change from a friend and head for the nearest soft-drink machine.

Britsh actor Jamie Waylett, best known for playing Draco Malfoy's aggressive sidekick Vincent Crabbe in the Harry Potter movies, exemplifies the association between wide faces and aggressive behavior. The association held true in real life: In 2012, Waylett was sentenced to two years in jail for participating in the 2011 London riots.

As the machine devours the change, you can almost taste the cold, refreshing cola. But when you push the button, nothing happens. You push it again. Then you flip the coin return button. Still nothing. Again, you hit the buttons. You slam the machine. Alas, no money and no drink. You stomp back to your studies, empty-handed and shortchanged. Should your roommate beware? Are you now more likely to say or do something hurtful?

One of the first psychological theories of aggression, the popular frustration-aggression theory, answered yes (Dollard, 1939). **Frustration** is anything (such as the malfunctioning vending machine) that blocks us from attaining a goal. Frustration grows when our motivation to achieve a goal is very strong, when we expected gratification, and when the blocking is complete. When Rupert Brown and his colleagues (2001) surveyed British ferry passengers heading to France, they found much higher than normal aggressive attitudes on a day when French fishing boats blockaded the port, preventing their travel. Blocked from obtaining their goal, the passengers became more likely (in responding to various vignettes) to agree with an insult toward a French person who had spilled coffee.

The aggressive energy need not explode directly against its source. Most people learn to inhibit direct retaliation, especially when others might disapprove or punish; instead, we *displace*, or redirect, our hostilities to safer targets. **Displacement** occurs in an old anecdote about a man who, humiliated by his boss, berates his wife, who yells at their son, who kicks the dog, which bites the mail carrier (who goes home and berates his wife . . .). In experiments and in real life, displaced aggression is most likely when the target shares some similarity to the instigator and does some minor irritating act that unleashes the displaced aggression (Marcus-Newhall & others, 2000; Miller & others, 2003; Pedersen & others, 2000, 2008). When someone is harboring anger from a prior provocation, even a trivial offense may elicit an explosive overreaction (as you may realize if you have ever yelled at your roommate after losing money in a malfunctioning vending machine).

In one experiment, Eduardo Vasquez and his co-researchers (2005) provoked some University of Southern California students (but not others) by having an experimenter insult their performance on an anagram-solving test. Shortly afterward, the students had to decide how long another supposed student should be required to immerse his or her hand in painful cold water while completing a task. When the supposed student committed a trivial offense—by giving a mild insult—the previously provoked participants responded punitively, by recommending a longer cold-water treatment. This phenomenon of displaced aggression helps us understand, notes Vasquez, why a previously provoked and still-angry person might respond to mild highway offenses with road rage, or react to spousal criticism with spouse abuse. It also helps explain why frustrated major league baseball pitchers, in one analysis of nearly 5 million at-bats from 74,197 games since 1960, were most likely to hit batters after the batter hit a home run the last time at bat, or after the previous batter did so (Timmerman, 2007).

Outgroup targets are especially vulnerable to displaced aggression (Pedersen & others, 2008). Opposites attack. Various commentators have observed that the understandably intense American anger over 9/11 contributed to the eagerness to attack Iraq. Americans were looking for an outlet for their rage and found one in an evil tyrant, Saddam Hussein, who was once their ally. "The 'real reason' for this war," noted Thomas Friedman (2003), "was that after 9/11 America needed to hit someone in the Arab-Muslim world. . . . We hit Saddam for one simple reason: because we could, and because he deserved it, and because he was right in the heart of that world." One of the war's advocates, Vice President Richard Cheney (2003), seemed to concur. When asked why most others in the world disagreed with America's war, he replied, "They didn't experience 9/11."

Laboratory tests of the frustration-aggression theory have produced mixed results: Sometimes frustration increased aggressiveness, sometimes not. For example, if the frustration was understandable—if, as in one experiment, a confederate disrupted a group's problem solving because his hearing aid malfunctioned (rather than just because he wasn't paying attention)—frustration led to irritation, not aggression (Burnstein & Worchel, 1962).

Leonard Berkowitz (1978, 1989) realized that the original theory overstated the frustration-aggression connection, so he revised it. Berkowitz theorized that frustration produces *anger,* an emotional readiness to aggress. Anger arises when someone who frustrates us could have chosen to act otherwise (Averill, 1983; Weiner, 1981).

A frustrated person is especially likely to lash out when aggressive cues pull the cork, releasing bottled-up anger. Sometimes the cork will blow without such cues. But, as we will see, cues associated with aggression amplify aggression (Carlson & others, 1990).

Berkowitz (1968, 1981, 1995) and others found that the sight of a weapon is such a cue. In one experiment, children who had just played with toy guns became more willing to knock down another child's blocks. In another, angered University of Wisconsin men gave more electric shocks to their tormenter when a rifle and a revolver (supposedly left over from a previous experiment) were nearby than when badminton rackets had been left behind (Berkowitz & LePage, 1967). Guns prime hostile thoughts and punitive judgments (Anderson & others, 1998; Dienstbier & others, 1998). What's within sight is within mind. This is especially so when a weapon is perceived as an instrument of violence rather than a recreational item. For hunters, seeing a hunting rifle does not prime aggressive thoughts, though it does for nonhunters (Bartholow & others, 2004).

Berkowitz was not surprised that in the United States, a country with some 200 million privately owned guns, half of all murders are committed with handguns, or that handguns in homes are far more likely to kill household members than intruders. "Guns not only permit violence," he reported, "they can stimulate it as well. The finger pulls the trigger, but the trigger may also be pulling the finger."

Berkowitz was further unsurprised that countries that ban handguns have lower murder rates. Compared with the United States, Britain has one-fourth as many people and one-sixteenth as many murders. The United States has 10,000 handgun homicides a year; Australia has about a dozen, Britain two dozen, and Canada 100. When Washington, D.C., adopted a law restricting handgun possession, the numbers of gun-related murders and suicides each abruptly dropped about 25 percent. No changes occurred in other methods of murder and suicide, nor did adjacent areas outside the reach of this law experience any such declines (Loftin & others, 1991).

Guns not only serve as aggression cues but also put psychological distance between aggressor and victim. As Milgram's obedience studies taught us, remoteness from the victim facilitates cruelty. A knife can kill someone, but a knife attack requires a great deal more personal contact than pulling a trigger from a distance.

The Learning of Aggression

Theories of aggression based on instinct and frustration assume that hostile urges erupt from inner emotions, which naturally "push" aggression from within. Social psychologists also contend that learning "pulls" aggression out of us.

The Rewards of Aggression

By experience and by observing others, we learn that aggression often pays. Experiments have transformed animals from docile creatures into ferocious fighters. Severe defeats, on the other hand, create submissiveness (Ginsburg & Allee, 1942; Kahn, 1951; Scott & Marston, 1953).

People, too, can learn the rewards of aggression. A child whose aggressive acts successfully intimidate other children will likely become increasingly aggressive (Patterson & others, 1967). Aggressive hockey players—the ones sent most often to the penalty box for rough play—score more goals than nonaggressive players (McCarthy & Kelly, 1978a, 1978b). Canadian teenage hockey players whose fathers applaud physically aggressive play show the most aggressive attitudes and style of play (Ennis & Zanna, 1991). In the waters off Somalia, paying ransom to hijackers of ships—a reported $150 million in 2008 (BBC, 2008)—rewarded the pirates, thus fueling further hijackings. In such cases, aggression is instrumental in achieving certain rewards.

The same is true of terrorist acts, which enable powerless people to garner widespread attention. "The primary targets of suicide-bombing attacks are not those who are injured but those who are made to witness it through media coverage," note Paul Marsden and Sharon Attia (2005). Terrorism's purpose is, with the help of media amplification, to terrorize. "Kill one, frighten ten thousand," asserts an ancient Chinese proverb. Deprived of what Margaret Thatcher called "the oxygen of publicity," terrorism would surely diminish, concluded Jeffrey Rubin (1986). It's like the 1970s incidents of naked spectators "streaking" onto football fields for a few seconds of television exposure. After the networks decided to ignore the incidents, the phenomenon ended.

Observational Learning

Albert Bandura (1997) proposed a **social learning theory** of aggression. He believes that we learn aggression not only by experiencing its payoffs but also by observing others. As with most social behaviors, we acquire aggression by watching others act and noting the consequences.

Picture this scene from one of Bandura's experiments (Bandura & others, 1961). A preschool child is put to work on an interesting art activity. An adult is in another part of the room, where there are Tinker Toys, a mallet, and a big, inflated "Bobo" doll. After a minute of working with the Tinker Toys, the adult gets up and for almost 10 minutes attacks the inflated doll. She pounds it with the mallet, kicks it, and throws it, while yelling, "Sock him in the nose. . . . Knock him down. . . . Kick him."

After observing this outburst, the child is taken to a different room with many very attractive toys. But after two minutes the experimenter interrupts, saying these are her best toys and she must "save them for the other children." The frustrated child now goes into yet another room with various toys designed for aggressive and nonaggressive play, two of which are a Bobo doll and a mallet.

Children who were not exposed to the aggressive adult model rarely displayed any aggressive play or talk. Although frustrated, they nevertheless played calmly. Those who had observed the aggressive adult were many times more likely to pick up the mallet and lash out at the doll. Watching the adult's aggressive behavior lowered their inhibitions. Moreover, the children often reproduced the model's specific acts and said her words. Observing aggressive behavior had both lowered their inhibitions and taught them ways to aggress.

A peaceable kingdom. In 2008, a man was convicted of murder in Scotland's Orkney Islands—only the second murder conviction since the 1800s.

Bandura (1979) believes that everyday life exposes us to aggressive models in the family, in one's subculture, and, as we will see, in the mass media. Physically aggressive children tend to have had physically punitive parents, who disciplined them by modeling aggression with screaming, slapping, and beating (Patterson & others, 1982). These parents often had parents who were themselves physically punitive (Bandura & Walters, 1959; Straus & Gelles, 1980). Such punitive behavior may escalate into abuse, and although most abused children do not become criminals or abusive parents, 30 percent do later abuse their own children—four times the general population rate (Kaufman & Zigler, 1987; Widom, 1989). Even more mild physical punishment, such as spanking, is linked to later aggression (Gershoff, 2002). Violence often begets violence.

The social environment outside the home also provides models. In communities where "macho" images are admired, aggression is readily transmitted to new generations (Cartwright, 1975; Short, 1969). The violent subculture of teenage gangs, for instance, provides its junior members with aggressive models. Among Chicago adolescents who are otherwise equally at risk for violence, those who have observed gun violence were twice as likely to be violent (Bingenheimer & others, 2005).

The broader culture also matters. Show social psychologists a man from a nondemocratic culture that has great economic inequality, that prepares men to be warriors, and that has engaged in war, and they will show you someone who is predisposed to aggressive behavior (Bond, 2004).

Richard Nisbett (1990, 1993) and Dov Cohen (1996, 1998) have explored the effect of a subculture on attitudes toward violence. They report that the American South, settled by Scots-Irish sheep herders ever wary of threats to their flocks, has a "culture of honor," which maintains that insults deserve retaliation (Henry, 2009). After squeezing by another man in a hallway and hearing him mutter an insult, White Southern men expressed more aggressive thoughts and experienced a surge in testosterone. White Northern men were more likely to find the encounter funny (Cohen & others, 1996). To the present day, American cities populated by southerners have higher than average White homicide rates (Vandello & others, 2008). More students in "culture of honor" states bring weapons to school, and these states have had three times as many school shootings as others (Brown & others, 2009).

People learn aggressive responses both by experience and by observing aggressive models. But when will aggressive responses actually occur? Bandura (1979) contended that aggressive acts are motivated by a variety of aversive experiences—frustration, pain, insults. Such experiences arouse us emotionally. But whether we act aggressively depends on the consequences we anticipate. Aggression is most likely when we are aroused and it seems safe *and* rewarding to aggress.

Environmental Influences on Aggression

Social learning theory offers a perspective from which we can examine specific influences on aggression. Under what conditions do we aggress? What environmental influences pull our trigger?

Painful Incidents

Researcher Nathan Azrin (1967) was doing experiments with laboratory rats in a cage wired to deliver electric shocks to the animals' feet. Azrin wanted to know if switching off the shocks would reinforce two rats' positive interactions with each other. He planned to turn on the shock and then, when the rats approached each other, cut off the pain. To his great surprise, the experiment proved impossible. As soon as the rats felt pain, they attacked each other, before the experimenter could switch off the shock. The greater the shock (and pain), the more violent the attack. The same effect occurred across a long list of species, including cats, turtles, and snakes. The animals were not selective about their targets. They would attack animals of their own species and those of a different species, or stuffed dolls, or even tennis balls.

The researchers also varied the source of pain. They found that not only shocks induced attack; intense heat and "psychological pain"—for example, suddenly not rewarding hungry pigeons that have been trained to expect a grain reward after pecking at a disk—brought the same reaction as shocks. This "psychological pain" is, of course, frustration.

Pain heightens aggressiveness in humans, too. Many of us can recall such a reaction after stubbing a toe or suffering a headache. Leonard Berkowitz and his associates demonstrated this by having University of Wisconsin students hold one hand in either lukewarm water or painfully cold water. Those whose hands were submerged in the cold water reported feeling more irritable and more annoyed, and they were more willing to blast another person with unpleasant noise. In view of such results, Berkowitz (1983, 1989, 1998) proposed that aversive stimulation rather than frustration is the basic trigger of hostile aggression. Frustration is certainly one important type of unpleasantness. But any aversive event, whether a dashed expectation, a personal insult, or physical pain, can incite an emotional outburst. Even the torment of a depressed state increases the likelihood of hostile, aggressive behavior.

Heat

An uncomfortable environment also heightens aggressive tendencies. Offensive odors, cigarette smoke, and air pollution have all been linked with aggressive behavior (Rotton & Frey, 1985). But the most-studied environmental irritant is heat. William Griffitt (1970; Griffitt & Veitch, 1971) found that compared with students who answered questionnaires in a room with a normal temperature, those who did so in an uncomfortably

hot room (over 90°F) reported feeling more tired and aggressive and expressed more hostility toward a stranger. Follow-up experiments revealed
that heat also triggers retaliation in response to an attack or injury (Bell,
1980; Rule & others, 1987).

Does uncomfortable heat increase aggression in the real world as well
as in the laboratory? Consider the following:

- In heat-stricken Phoenix, Arizona, the drivers of cars without air-
conditioning were more likely to honk at a stalled car (Kenrick &
MacFarlane, 1986).

- In an analysis of 57,293 Major League Baseball games since 1952,
batters were more likely to be hit by a pitch during hot weather—
nearly 50% more likely when the temperature was 90 degrees or
above (versus 59 degrees or below) and when three of the pitch-
er's teammates had previously been hit (Larrick & others, 2011).
Pitchers weren't wilder on hot days—they had no more walks or
wild pitches. They just clobbered more batters.

- Studies in six cities have found that when the weather is hot, violent
crimes are more likely (Anderson & Anderson, 1984; Cohn, 1993;
Cotton, 1981, 1986; Harries & Stadler, 1988; Rotton & Cohn, 2004).

- Across the Northern Hemisphere, it is not only hotter days that
have more violent crimes, but also hotter seasons of the year, hotter
summers, hotter years, hotter cities, and hotter regions (Anderson & Delisi, 2010). Anderson and his colleagues project that if a
4-degree-Fahrenheit (about 2°C) global warming occurs, the United
States alone will see at least 50,000 more serious assaults annually.

Attacks

Being attacked or insulted by another is especially conducive to aggression. Several experiments, including one at Osaka University by Kennichi
Ohbuchi and Toshihiro Kambara (1985), confirm that intentional attacks
breed retaliatory attacks. In most of these experiments, one person competes with another in a reaction-time contest. After each test trial, the winner chooses how much shock to give the loser. Actually, each person is
playing a programmed opponent, who steadily escalates the amount of
shock. Do the real participants respond charitably? Hardly. Extracting "an
eye for an eye" is the more likely response.

Crowding

Crowding—the subjective feeling of not having enough space—is stressful. Crammed in the back of a bus, trapped in slow-moving freeway traffic, or living three to a small room in a college dorm diminishes one's
sense of control (Baron & others, 1976; McNeel, 1980). Might such experiences also heighten aggression?

The stress experienced by animals allowed to overpopulate a confined environment does heighten aggressiveness (Calhoun, 1962; Christian & others, 1960). But it is a rather large leap from rats in an enclosure or deer on an island to humans in a city. Nevertheless, it's true that dense urban areas do experience higher rates of crime and emotional distress (Fleming & others, 1987; Kirmeyer, 1978). Even when they don't suffer higher crime rates, residents of crowded cities may *feel* more fearful. Toronto's crime rate has been four times higher than Hong Kong's. Yet compared with Toronto people, people from safer Hong Kong—which is four times more densely populated—have reported feeling more fearful on their city's streets (Gifford & Peacock, 1979).

REDUCING AGGRESSION

Can we reduce aggression? Here we look at how theory and research suggest ways to control it.

Catharsis?

"Youngsters should be taught to vent their anger," surmised advice columnist Ann Landers (1969). If a person "bottles up his rage, we have to find an outlet. We have to give him an opportunity of letting off steam," asserted the once prominent psychiatrist Fritz Perls (1973). "Some expression of prejudice . . . lets off steam . . . it can siphon off conflict through words, rather than actions," argued Andrew Sullivan (1999) in a *New York Times Magazine* article on hate crimes. Such statements assume the "hydraulic model," which implies accumulated aggressive energy, like dammed-up water, needs a release.

The concept of **catharsis** is usually credited to Aristotle. Although Aristotle actually said nothing about aggression, he did argue that we can purge emotions by experiencing them and that viewing the classic tragedies therefore enabled a catharsis (purging) of pity and fear. To have an emotion excited, he believed, is to have that emotion released (Butcher, 1951). The catharsis hypothesis has been extended to include the emotional release supposedly obtained not only by observing drama but also through our recalling and reliving past events, through our expressing emotions, and through our actions.

Researcher Brad Bushman (2002) notes, "Venting to reduce anger is like using gasoline to put out a fire." For example, Robert Arms and his associates report that Canadian and American spectators of football, wrestling, and hockey games exhibit *more* hostility after viewing the event than before (Arms & others, 1979; Goldstein & Arms, 1971; Russell, 1983).

In laboratory tests of catharsis, Brad Bushman (2002) invited angered participants to hit a punching bag while either ruminating about someone who angered them or thinking about becoming physically fit. A third group did not hit the punching bag. When given a chance to administer loud blasts of noise to the person who angered them, people in the punching bag plus rumination condition felt angrier and were most aggressive. Moreover, doing nothing at all more effectively reduced aggression than did "blowing off steam" by hitting the bag.

In some real-life experiments, too, aggressing has led to heightened aggression. Ebbe Ebbesen and his co-researchers (1975) interviewed 100 engineers and technicians shortly after they were angered by layoff notices. Some were asked questions that gave them an opportunity to vent hostility against their employer or supervisors—for example, "What instances can you think of where the company has not been fair with you?" Did the opportunity to express their hostility reduce it? To the contrary, their hostility increased. Expressing hostility bred more hostility.

Sound familiar? Recall from Module 9 that cruel acts beget cruel attitudes. Furthermore, as we noted in analyzing Stanley Milgram's obedience experiments, little aggressive acts can breed their own justification. People derogate their victims, rationalizing further aggression.

Retaliation may, in the short run, reduce tension and even provide pleasure (Ramirez & others, 2005). But in the long run it fuels more negative feelings. When people who have been provoked hit a punching bag, even when they believe it will be cathartic, the effect is the opposite—leading them to exhibit *more* cruelty, report Bushman and his colleagues (1999, 2000, 2001). "It's like the old joke," reflected Bushman (1999). "How do you get to Carnegie Hall? Practice, practice, practice. How do you become a very angry person? The answer is the same. Practice, practice, practice."

Should we therefore bottle up anger and aggressive urges? Silent sulking is hardly more effective, because it allows us to continue reciting our grievances as we conduct conversations in our heads. Fortunately, there are nonaggressive ways to express our feelings and to inform others how their behavior affects us. Across cultures, those who reframe accusatory "you" messages as "I" messages—"I feel angry about what you said," or, "I get irritated when you leave dirty dishes"—communicate their feelings in a way that better enables the other person to make a positive response (Kubany & others, 1995). We can be assertive without being aggressive.

A Social Learning Approach

If aggressive behavior is learned, then there is hope for its control. Let us briefly review factors that influence aggression and speculate how to counteract them.

Aversive experiences such as frustrated expectations and personal attacks predispose hostile aggression. So it is wise to refrain from planting false, unreachable expectations in people's minds. Anticipated rewards and costs influence instrumental aggression. This suggests that we should reward cooperative, nonaggressive behavior.

In experiments, children become less aggressive when caregivers ignore their aggressive behavior and reinforce their nonaggressive behavior (Hamblin & others, 1969).

Moreover, there are limits to punishment's effectiveness. Most homicides are impulsive, hot aggression—the result of an argument, an insult, or an attack. If mortal aggression were cool and instrumental, we could hope that waiting until it happens and severely punishing the criminal afterward would deter such acts. In that world, states that impose the death penalty might have a lower murder rate than states without the death penalty. But in our world of hot homicide, that is not so (Costanzo, 1998). As John Darley and Adam Alter (2009) note, "A remarkable amount of crime is committed by impulsive individuals, frequently young males, who are frequently drunk or high on drugs, and who often are in packs of similar and similarly mindless young men." No wonder, they say, that trying to reduce crime by increasing sentences has proven so fruitless, whereas on-the-street policing that produces more arrests has produced encouraging results, such as a 50 percent drop in gun-related crimes in some cities.

Thus, we must *prevent* aggression before it happens. We must teach nonaggressive conflict-resolution strategies. When psychologists Sandra Jo Wilson and Mark Lipsey (2005) assembled data from 249 studies of school violence prevention programs, they found encouraging results, especially for programs focused on selected "problem" students. After being taught problem-solving skills, emotion-control strategies, and conflict resolution techniques, the typical 20 percent of students engaging in some violent or disruptive behavior in a typical school year was reduced to 13 percent.

To foster a gentler world, we could model and reward sensitivity and cooperation from an early age, perhaps by training parents how to discipline without violence. Training programs encourage parents to reinforce desirable behaviors and to frame statements positively ("When you finish cleaning your room, you can go play," rather than, "If you don't clean your room, you're grounded"). One "aggression-replacement program" has kept many juvenile offenders and gang members from being arrested again by teaching the youths and their parents communication skills, training them to control anger, and raising their level of moral reasoning (Goldstein & others, 1998).

If observing aggressive models lowers inhibitions and elicits imitation, we might also reduce brutal, dehumanizing portrayals in films and on television—steps comparable to those already taken to reduce racist and sexist portrayals. We can also inoculate children against the effects of media violence. Wondering if the TV networks would ever "face the facts and change their programming," Eron and Huesmann (1984) taught 170 Oak Park, Illinois, children that television portrays the world unrealistically, that aggression is less common and less effective than TV suggests, and that aggressive behavior is undesirable. (Drawing upon attitude research, Eron and Huesmann encouraged children to draw these inferences themselves and to attribute their expressed criticisms of television to their own convictions.) When restudied two years later, these children were less influenced by TV violence than were untrained children. In a more recent study, Stanford University used 18 classroom lessons to persuade children to simply reduce their TV watching and video game-playing (Robinson & others, 2001). They reduced their TV viewing by a third—and the children's aggressive behavior at school dropped 25 percent compared with children in a control school. Even music can help reduce aggression when it models the right attitude: German students who were randomly assigned to hear prosocial music like "We Are the World" and "Help" behaved less aggressively than those who heard neutral music (Greitemeyer, 2011).

Suggestions such as these can help us minimize aggression. But given the complexity of aggression's causes and the difficulty of controlling them, who can feel the optimism expressed by Andrew Carnegie's forecast that in the twentieth century, "To kill a man will be considered as disgusting as we in this day consider it disgusting to eat one." Since Carnegie uttered those words in 1900, some 200 million human beings have been killed. It is a sad irony that although today we understand human aggression better than ever before, humanity's inhumanity endures.

CULTURE CHANGE AND WORLD VIOLENCE

Nevertheless, cultures can change. "The Vikings slaughtered and plundered," notes science writer Natalie Angier. "Their descendants in Sweden haven't fought a war in nearly 200 years." Indeed, as psychologist Steven Pinker (2011) documents, across centuries, humans have become more civilized and all forms of violence—including wars, genocide, and murders—have declined. We've graduated from plundering neighboring tribes to economic interdependence, from a world in which Western European countries initiated two new wars per year over 600 years to, for the past seven decades, zero wars. Surprisingly, to those of us who love modern British murder mysteries, "a contemporary Englishman has about a 50-fold less chance of being murdered than his compatriot in the Middle Ages," notes Pinker. In all but one western democracy, the death penalty has been abolished. And the sole exception—the United States—no longer practices it for witchcraft, counterfeiting, and horse theft, and has seen declines in, or the disappearance of, lynchings, hate crimes, rapes, corporal punishment, and antigay attitudes and intimidation. We can, he concludes, be grateful "for the institutions of civilization and enlightenment [economic trade, education, government policing and justice] that have made it possible."

CONCEPTS TO REMEMBER

aggression   Physical or verbal behavior intended to hurt someone.

instrumental aggression   Aggression that aims to injure, but only as a means to some other end.

frustration   The blocking of goal-directed behavior.

displacement   The redirection of aggression to a target other than the source of the frustration. Generally, the new target is a safer or more socially acceptable target.

social learning theory   The theory that we learn social behavior by observing and imitating and by being rewarded and punished.

crowding   A subjective feeling that there is not enough space per person.

catharsis   Emotional release. The catharsis view of aggression is that aggressive drive is reduced when one "releases" aggressive energy, either by acting aggressively or by fantasizing aggression.

Do the Media Influence Social Behavior?

C an viewing or role-playing violence be an additional influence on aggressive behavior—perhaps by triggering imitation, by desensitizing viewers to aggression, or by altering their perceptions of reality? Research on viewer responses to pornography, television violence, and violent video games offers some insights.

PORNOGRAPHY AND SEXUAL VIOLENCE

Pornography is now a bigger business in the United States than professional football, basketball, and baseball combined, thanks to some $13 billion a year spent on the industry's cable and satellite networks, theaters and pay-per-view movies, and in-room hotel movies, phone sex, sex magazines, and Internet sites (D'Orlando, 2011; Richtel, 2007). The easy availability of pornography on the Internet has accelerated its popularity. In a recent survey of 18- to 26-year-old American men, 87 percent said they viewed pornography at least once a month, and nearly half used it at least once a week (Carroll & others, 2008). However, only 31 percent of women reported viewing pornography at all. Social psychological research on pornography has focused mostly on depictions of sexual violence, which is commonplace in popular recent adult videos (Sun & others, 2008). A typical sexually violent episode finds a man forcing himself upon a woman. She at first resists and tries to fight off her attacker. Gradually she becomes sexually aroused, and her resistance melts. By the end she is in ecstasy, pleading for more. We have all viewed or read nonpornographic versions of this sequence: She resists, he persists. Dashing man grabs and forcibly kisses protesting woman. Within moments, the arms that were pushing him away are clutching him tight, her resistance overwhelmed by her unleashed passion. The problem, of course, is that women do not actually respond this way to rape.

Social psychologists report that viewing such fictional scenes of a man overpowering and arousing a woman can (a) distort one's perceptions of how women actually respond to sexual coercion and (b) increase men's aggression against women.

Distorted Perceptions of Sexual Reality

Does viewing sexual violence reinforce the "rape myth"—that some women would welcome sexual assault and that "no doesn't really mean no"? Researchers have observed a correlation between the amount of TV viewing and rape myth acceptance (Kahlor & Morrison, 2007). To explore the relationship experimentally, Neil Malamuth and James Check (1981) showed University of Manitoba men either two nonsexual movies or two movies depicting a man sexually overcoming a woman. A week later, when surveyed by a different experimenter, those who saw the films with mild sexual violence were more accepting of violence against women.

Other studies confirm that exposure to pornography increases acceptance of the rape myth (Oddone-Paolucci & others, 2000). For example, while spending three evenings watching sexually violent movies, men became progressively less bothered by the raping and slashing (Mullin & Linz, 1995). Compared with men not exposed to the films, three days later they expressed less sympathy for domestic violence victims, and they rated the victims' injuries as less severe. In fact, said researchers Edward Donnerstein, Daniel Linz, and Steven Penrod (1987), what better way for an evil character to get people to react calmly to the torture and mutilation of women than to show a gradually escalating series of such films?

Aggression Against Women

Evidence also suggests that pornography contributes to men's actual aggression toward women (Kingston & others, 2009). Nathaniel Lambert and his colleagues (2011) asked male and female college students, "Approximately how many times in the past 30 days have you viewed a pornographic website?" Even after taking gender into account, those who had viewed porn more frequently were also more likely to physically assault friends and romantic partners over the next three weeks, and were more aggressive toward another student in a lab experiment. When given the chance to stick pins into a doll representing their relationship partner, those who viewed more Internet porn symbolically stabbed their partner with more pins. Pornography also affects the children who see it. Among 1,000 10- to 15-year-old boys and girls, those who saw movies, magazines, or websites with violent sexual content were 6 times more likely to be sexually aggressive toward others (defined as "kissed, touched, or done anything sexual with another person when that person did not want you to do so"), even after adjusting for factors such as gender, aggressive traits, and family background (Ybarra & others, 2011).

Canadian and American sexual offenders commonly acknowledge pornography use. Among 155 men arrested for Internet-based child pornography, 85 percent admitted they had molested a child at least once, and the average offender had 13 victims (Bourke & Hernandez, 2009). The reverse is also true: rapists, serial killers, and child molesters report using pornography at unusually high rates (Bennett, 1991; Kingston & others, 2008; Marshall, 1989; Ressler & others, 1988). Among university men, high pornography consumption has predicted sexual aggressiveness even after controlling for other predictors of antisocial behavior, such as general hostility (Vega & Malamuth, 2007).

But perhaps pornography doesn't actually cause violence but instead, violent men like violent pornography. To rule out this explanation, it is necessary to perform an experiment—for example, to randomly assign some people to watch pornography. In one such experiment, 120 University of Wisconsin men watched a neutral, erotic, or aggressive-erotic (rape) film. Then the men, supposedly as part of another experiment, "taught" a male or female confederate some nonsense syllables by choosing how much shock to administer for incorrect answers. The men who had watched the rape film administered markedly stronger shocks, especially when angered and with a female victim (Donnerstein, 1980). A consensus statement by 21 leading social scientists summed up the results of experiments in this area: "Exposure to violent pornography increases punitive behavior toward women" (Koop, 1987).

If the ethics of conducting such experiments trouble you, rest assured that these researchers appreciate the controversial and powerful experience they are giving participants. Only after giving their knowing consent do people participate. Moreover, after the experiment, researchers effectively debunk any myths the films communicated (Check & Malamuth, 1984). Another experiment avoided the ethical dilemma by asking college students who usually consumed pornography to abstain from consumption for a month. Compared with those who instead gave up a favorite food, those who had dialed back on their porn consumption were less aggressive (Lambert & others, 2011).

Justification for this experimentation is not only scientific but also humanitarian. In a nationally representative survey of 9,684 American adults, 11 percent of women reported experiencing forced sex at some time in their lives (Basile & others, 2007; CDC, 2008).

Surveys in other industrialized countries offer similar results. Three in four stranger rapes and nearly all acquaintance rapes went unreported to police. Thus, the official rape rate greatly underestimates the actual rape rate.

Media Awareness Education

As most Germans in the 1930s and 1940s quietly tolerated the degrading anti-Semitic images that fed the Nazi Holocaust, so most people today tolerate media images of women that feed sexual harassment, abuse, and rape. Should such portrayals that demean or violate women be restrained by law?

In the contest of individual versus collective rights, most people in Western nations side with individual rights. As an alternative to censorship, many psychologists favor "media awareness training." Pornography researchers have successfully resensitized and educated participants to women's actual responses to sexual violence. Could educators similarly promote critical viewing skills? By sensitizing people to the portrayal of women that predominates in pornography and to issues of sexual harassment and violence, it should be possible to debunk the myth that women enjoy being coerced. "Our utopian and perhaps naive hope," wrote Edward Donnerstein, Daniel Linz, and Steven Penrod (1987, p. 196), "is that in the end the truth revealed through good science will prevail and the public will be convinced that these images not only demean those portrayed but also those who view them."

Is such a hope naive? Consider this: Without a ban on cigarettes, U.S. adult smokers dropped from 42 percent in 1965 to 19 percent in 2010 (CDC, 2012). Without censorship of racism, once-common media images of African Americans as childlike, superstitious buffoons have nearly disappeared. As public consciousness changed, scriptwriters, producers, and media executives shunned exploitative images of minorities. Will we one day look back with embarrassment on the time when movies entertained people with scenes of mayhem, mutilation, and sexual coercion?

TELEVISION AND THE INTERNET

We have seen that watching an aggressive model attack a Bobo doll can unleash children's aggressive urges and teach them new ways to aggress. And we have seen that after viewing movies depicting sexual violence, many angry men will act more violently toward women. Does everyday television viewing have any similar effects?

Today, in much of the industrialized world, nearly all households (99.2 percent in Australia, for example) have a TV set, more than have telephones (Trewin, 2001). Most homes have more than one set, which helps explain why parents and children often give differing reports of what the children are watching (Donnerstein, 1998).

In the average U.S. home, the TV is on eight hours a day, with individual teens averaging about four hours and adults three hours (Robinson & Martin, 2009; Strasburger & others, 2010). Thanks to digital video recorders (DVRs) that allow people to "time shift" their TV watching, Americans in 2008 watched more TV than ever before (Nielsen, 2008a, 2008b).

During all those hours, what social behaviors are modeled? From 1994 to 1997, bleary-eyed employees of the National Television Violence Study (1997) analyzed some 10,000 programs from the major networks and cable channels. Their findings? Six in 10 programs contained violence ("physically compelling action that threatens to hurt or kill, or actual hurting or killing").

What does it add up to? All told, television beams its electromagnetic waves into children's eyeballs for more growing-up hours than they spend in school. More hours, in fact, than they spend in any other waking activity. By the end of elementary school, the average child has witnessed some 8,000 TV murders and 100,000 other violent acts (Huston & others, 1992). According to one content analysis, American prime-time violence increased 75 percent between 1998 and the 2005–2006 season, which averaged 4.41 violent events per hour (PTC, 2007). Reflecting on his 22 years of cruelty counting, media researcher George Gerbner (1994) lamented: "Humankind has had more bloodthirsty eras but none as filled with *images* of violence as the present. We are awash in a tide of violent representations the world has never before seen . . . drenching every home with graphic scenes of expertly choreographed brutality."

Television's Effects on Behavior

Do viewers imitate violent models? Examples abound of actual criminals reenacting television crimes. In one survey of 208 prison convicts, 9 of 10 admitted learning new criminal tricks by watching crime programs. Four out of 10 said they had attempted specific crimes seen on television (*TV Guide*, 1977).

Correlating TV Viewing and Behavior

Stories of TV-inspired crime are not scientific evidence. Researchers therefore use correlational and experimental studies to examine the effects of viewing violence. One technique, commonly used with schoolchildren, correlates their TV watching with their aggressiveness. The frequent result: The more violent the content of the child's TV viewing, the more aggressive the child (Eron, 1987; Turner & others, 1986). The relationship is modest but consistently found in North America, Europe, and Australia. And it extends to devious "indirect aggression." British girls who most often view programs that model gossiping, backbiting, and social exclusion also more often display such behavior (Coyne & Archer, 2005).

Can we conclude, then, that a diet of violent TV fuels aggression? Perhaps you are already thinking that because this is a correlational study, the cause-effect relation could also work in the opposite direction. Maybe aggressive children prefer aggressive programs. Or maybe some underlying third factor, such as lower intelligence, predisposes some children to prefer both aggressive programs and aggressive behavior.

Researchers have developed two ways to test these alternative explanations. They test the "hidden third factor" explanation by statistically pulling out the influence of some of these possible factors. For example, William Belson (1978; Muson, 1978) studied 1,565 London boys. Compared with those who watched little violence, those who watched a great deal (especially realistic rather than cartoon violence) admitted to 50 percent more violent acts during the preceding six months (for example, vandalizing a public telephone). Belson also examined 22 likely third factors, such as family size. The "heavy violence" and "light violence" viewers still differed after the researchers equated them with respect to potential third factors. So Belson surmised that the heavy viewers were indeed more violent *because* of their TV exposure.

Similarly, Leonard Eron and Rowell Huesmann (1980, 1985) found that violence viewing among 875 8-year-olds correlated with aggressiveness even after statistically pulling out several obvious possible third factors. Moreover, when they restudied those individuals as 19-year-olds, they discovered that viewing violence at age 8 modestly predicted aggressiveness at age 19, but that aggressiveness at age 8 did *not* predict viewing violence at age 19. Aggression followed viewing, not the reverse. Moreover, by age 30, those who had watched the most violence in childhood were more likely than others to have been convicted of a crime (Figure 25-1).

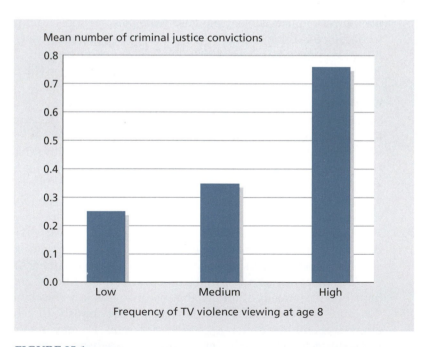

FIGURE 25-1
Children's television viewing and later criminal activity. Violence viewing at age 8 was a predictor of a serious criminal offense by age 30.   Source: Data from Eron and Huesmann (1984).

Follow-up studies have confirmed these findings in various ways, including the following:

- Correlating 8-year-olds' violence viewing with their later likelihood of adult spouse abuse (Huesmann & others, 1984, 2003)
- Correlating adolescents' violence viewing with their later likelihood of assault, robbery, and threats of injury (Johnson & others, 2002)
- Correlating elementary schoolchildren's violent media exposure with how often they got into fights when restudied 2 to 6 months later (Gentile & others, 2004)

In all these studies, the investigators were careful to adjust for likely "third factors," such as preexisting lower intelligence or hostility.

Many people now spend more screen time in front of their computers than in front of the television. In many ways, the Internet allows an even greater variety of options for viewing violence than television does, including violent videos, violent pictures, and hate-group websites (Donnerstein, 2011). It also allows people to create and distribute violent media themselves, and to bully others through e-mail, instant messaging, or on social networking websites (Donnerstein, 2011). In a survey of European adolescents, one-third reported seeing violent or hateful content online (Livingstone & Haddon, 2009). Among U.S. youth, those who frequently visited violent websites were 5 times more likely to report engaging in violent behavior (Ybarra & others, 2008).

Notice that these studies illustrate how researchers are using correlational findings to *suggest* cause and effect. Yet an infinite number of possible third factors could be creating a merely coincidental relation between viewing violence and practicing aggression. Fortunately, the experimental method can control these extraneous factors. If we randomly assign some children to watch a violent film and others a nonviolent film, any later aggression difference between the two groups will be due to the only factor that distinguishes them: what they watched.

TV Viewing Experiments

Video 25.1

The trailblazing Bobo-doll experiments by Albert Bandura and Richard Walters (1963) sometimes had young children view the adult pounding the inflated doll on film instead of observing it live—with much the same effect. Then Leonard Berkowitz and Russell Geen (1966) found that angered college students who viewed a violent film acted more aggressively than did similarly angered students who viewed nonaggressive films. These laboratory experiments, coupled with growing public concern, were sufficient to prompt the U.S. Surgeon General to commission 50 new research studies during the early 1970s. By and large, those studies, and more than 100 later ones, confirmed that viewing violence amplifies aggression (Anderson & others, 2003).

For example, research teams led by Ross Parke (1977) in the United States and Jacques Leyens (1975) in Belgium showed institutionalized American and Belgian delinquent boys a series of either aggressive or nonaggressive commercial films. Their consistent finding: "Exposure to movie violence . . . led to an increase in viewer aggression." Compared with the week preceding the film series, physical attacks increased sharply in cottages where boys were viewing violent films. Dolf Zillmann and James Weaver (1999) similarly exposed men and women, on four consecutive days, to violent or nonviolent feature films. When participating in a different project on the fifth day, those exposed to the violent films were more hostile to the research assistant.

The aggression provoked in these experiments is not assault and battery; it's more on the scale of a shove in the lunch line, a cruel comment, or a threatening gesture. Nevertheless, the convergence of evidence is striking. "The irrefutable conclusion," said a 1993 American Psychological Association youth violence commission, is "that viewing violence increases violence." This is especially so among people with aggressive tendencies and when an attractive person commits justified, realistic violence that goes unpunished and that shows no pain or harm (Comstock, 2008; Gentile & others, 2007; Zillmann & Weaver, 2007).

All in all, conclude researchers Brad Bushman and Craig Anderson (2001), the evidence for media effects on aggression is now "overwhelming." The research base is large, the methods diverse, and the overall findings consistent, echo a National Institute of Mental Health task force of leading media violence researchers (Anderson & others, 2003). "Our in-depth review . . . reveals unequivocal evidence that exposure to media violence can increase the likelihood of aggressive and violent behavior in both immediate and long-term contexts."

Why Does TV Viewing Affect Behavior?

Given the convergence of correlational and experimental evidence, researchers have explored *why* viewing violence has this effect. Consider three possibilities (Geen & Thomas, 1986). One is the *arousal* it produces (Mueller & others, 1983; Zillmann, 1989). As we noted earlier, arousal tends to spill over: One type of arousal energizes other behaviors.

Other research shows that viewing violence *disinhibits*. In Bandura's experiment, the adult's punching of the Bobo doll seemed to make outbursts legitimate and to lower the children's inhibitions. Viewing violence primes the viewer for aggressive behavior by activating violence-related thoughts (Berkowitz, 1984; Bushman & Geen, 1990; Josephson, 1987). Listening to music with sexually violent lyrics seems to have a similar effect (Barongan & Hall, 1995; Johnson & others, 1995; Pritchard, 1998).

Media portrayals also evoke *imitation*. The children in Bandura's experiments reenacted the specific behaviors they had witnessed. The commercial television industry is hard-pressed to dispute that television leads viewers to imitate what they have seen: Its advertisers model consumption. Are media executives right, however, to argue that TV merely holds a mirror to a violent society, that art imitates life, and that the "reel" world therefore shows us the real world? Actually, on TV programs, acts of assault have outnumbered affectionate acts four to one. In other ways as well, television models an unreal world.

But there is good news here, too. If the ways of relating and problem solving modeled on television do trigger imitation, especially among young viewers, then TV modeling of **prosocial behavior** should be socially beneficial. In Module 30 we will explore how television's subtle influence can indeed teach children positive lessons in behavior.

In one such study, researchers Lynette Friedrich and Aletha Stein (1973; Stein & Friedrich, 1972) showed preschool children *Mister Rogers' Neighborhood* episodes each day for 4 weeks as part of their nursery school program. (*Mister Rogers' Neighborhood* aimed to enhance young children's social and emotional development.) During the viewing period, children from less-educated homes became more cooperative, helpful, and likely to state their feelings. In a follow-up study, kindergartners who viewed four Mister Rogers' programs were able to state the show's prosocial content, both on a test and in puppet play (Friedrich & Stein, 1975; also Coates & others, 1976).

MEDIA INFLUENCES: VIDEO GAMES

The scientific debate over the effects of media violence "is basically over," contend Douglas Gentile and Craig Anderson (2003; Anderson & Gentile, 2008). Researchers are now shifting their attention to video games, which are extremely popular among teens and can be extremely violent. Educational research shows that "video games are excellent teaching tools," note Gentile and Anderson. "If health video games can successfully teach health behaviors, and flight simulator video games can teach people how to fly, then what should we expect violent murder-simulating games to teach?"

The Games Kids Play

In 2012, the video-game industry celebrated its fortieth birthday. Since the first video game in 1972, we have moved from electronic Ping-Pong to splatter games (Anderson & others, 2007). In one poll, 97 percent of 12- to 17-year-olds said they play video games. Half had played a video game the day before. Many of these games were violent—half of the teens said they played first-person shooter games, such as *Halo* or *Counter-Strike*, and 2 out of 3 played action games that often involve violence, such as *Grand Theft Auto* (Pew Research Center, 2008). Younger children are also playing violent games: In one survey of fourth-graders, 59 percent of girls and 73 percent of boys reported that their favorite games were violent ones (Anderson, 2003, 2004). The Federal Trade Commission found that in four out of five attempts, underage children could easily purchase "M" (mature) games, supposedly intended for sale only to those 17 and older (Pereira, 2003).

In the popular *Grand Theft Auto: San Andreas*, youth are invited to play the role of a psychopath, notes Gentile (2004). "You can run down pedestrians with the car, you can do carjackings, you can do drive-by shootings, you can run down to the red-light district, pick up a prostitute, have sex with her in your car, and then kill her to get your money back." In effective 3D graphics, you can knock people over, stomp on them until they cough up blood, and watch them die.

Effects of the Games Kids Play

Concerns about violent video games heightened after teen assassins in separate incidents in Kentucky, Arkansas, Colorado, and Connecticut enacted the horrific violence they had so often played onscreen; concerns emerged again after the 2011 slaughter of Norwegians by an avid World of Warcraft gamer. People wondered: What do youth learn from endless hours of role-playing attacking and dismembering people? And was anything accomplished when some Norwegian stores responded to the killings by pulling violent games from their shelves (Anderson, 2011)?

Most smokers don't die of lung cancer. Most abused children don't become abusive. And most people who spend hundreds of hours rehearsing human slaughter live gentle lives. This enables video-game defenders, like tobacco and TV interests, to say their products are harmless. "There is absolutely no evidence, none, that playing a violent game leads to aggressive behavior," contended Doug Lowenstein (2000), president of the Interactive Digital Software Association.

Gentile and Anderson offer some reasons why violent game playing *might* have a more toxic effect than watching violent television. With game playing, players

- identify with, and play the role of, a violent character.
- actively rehearse violence, instead of passively watching it.
- engage in the whole sequence of enacting violence—selecting victims, acquiring weapons and ammunition, stalking the victim, aiming the weapon, pulling the trigger.
- are engaged with continual violence and threats of attack.
- repeat violent behaviors over and over.
- are rewarded for violent acts.

For such reasons, military organizations often prepare soldiers to fire in combat by engaging them with attack-simulation games.

But do people who play violent video games go on to behave aggressively outside the game? "I play violent video games," some may protest, "And I'm not aggressive." As columnist Roger Simon (2011) wrote about research showing that media violence leads to real-life aggression, "Such claims bewilder me. I grew up playing with toy guns and have never shot anybody (though I know plenty who deserve it)." The problem with this common argument is that one isolated example proves nothing—it's not a scientific study. A better approach is to examine large samples of people to find out if, on average, violent video games increase aggression.

A number of experiments suggest that playing violent video games does, on average, increase aggressive behavior, thoughts, and feelings. Combining data from 381 studies with 130,296 participants, Craig Anderson and his colleagues (2010) found a clear effect: Violent video-game playing increased aggression—for children, adolescents, and young adults; in North America, Japan, and Western Europe; and across three research designs (correlational, experimental, and longitudinal). That means violent video games caused aggression even when participants were randomly assigned to play them (vs. a nonviolent game), which rules out the possibility that (for example) aggressive people like to play aggressive games. Longitudinal studies, which follow people over time, produce similar results: among German adolescents, today's violent game playing predicted later aggression, but today's aggression did not predict future violent game playing (Moller & Krahe, 2008).

Playing violent video games has an array of effects including the following:

- *Increases in aggressive behaviors:* After violent game play, children and youth play more aggressively with their peers, get into more arguments with their teachers, and participate in more fights. The effect occurs inside and outside the laboratory, across self-reports, teacher reports, and parent reports, and for the reasons illustrated in Figure 25-2. Even among young adolescents low in hostility, 10 times more of the heavy violent gamers got into fights compared with their nongaming counterparts. And after they started playing the violent games, previously nonhostile kids became more likely to have fights (Gentile & others, 2004). In Japan, too, playing violent video games early in a school year predicts physical aggressiveness later in the year, even after controlling for gender and prior aggressiveness (Anderson & others, 2008).

- *Increases in aggressive thoughts.* After playing a violent game, students became more likely to guess that a man whose car was just rear-ended would respond aggressively by using abusive

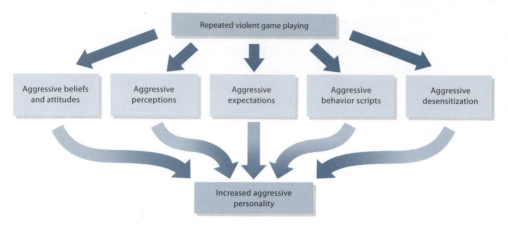

FIGURE 25-2
Violent video-game influences on aggressive tendencies.   Source: Adapted from Craig
A. Anderson and Brad J. Bushman (2001).

language, kicking out a window, or starting a fight (Bushman &
Anderson, 2002).

- *Increases in aggressive feelings,* including hostility, anger, or revenge.
- *Decreases in helping others and in empathy for others.* Students
  randomly assigned to play a violent or nonviolent video game
  later overheard a loud fight that ended with one person writhing
  on the floor in pain from a sprained ankle. Students who had just
  played a violent game took more than 1 minute on average to
  come to the person's aid, almost 4 times as long as those who had
  played a nonviolent game (Bushman & Anderson, 2009).

After violent video-game playing, people become more likely to exploit rather than to trust and cooperate with a partner (Sheese & Graziano,
2005). They also become *desensitized* to violence, showing decreased brain
activity associated with emotion (Bartholow & others, 2006; Carnagey
& others, 2007). Tobias Greitemeyer and Neil McLatchie (2011) explored
a specific kind of desensitization: Seeing other people as less human.
Among British university students, those randomly assigned to play a
violent game were more likely to describe in nonhuman terms someone
who had insulted them. And the less human they saw the person, the
more aggressive they were.

Moreover, the more violent the games that are played, the bigger the
effects. The bloodier the game (for example, the higher the blood level
setting in one experiment with *Mortal Combat* players) the greater the
gamer's after-game hostility and arousal (Barlett & others, 2008). More-
realistic games—showing violence more likely to happen in real life—also

produced more aggressive feelings than less-realistic games (Bartlett & Rodeheffer, 2009). Video games *have* become more violent in the past few years, which helps explain why newer studies find the biggest effects. Although much remains to be learned, these studies challenge the catharsis hypothesis—the idea that violent games allow people to safely express their aggressive tendencies and "get their anger out" (Kutner & Olson, 2008). Practicing violence breeds rather than releases violence, say catharsis critics. Yet the idea that games might relieve angry feelings is one of the main draws of violent video games for angry people (Bushman & Whitaker, 2010). Unfortunately, say critics, this strategy is likely to backfire, leading to more anger and aggression.

In 2005, California State Senator Leland Yee proposed a law banning the sale of violent video games to those under 18. The bill was signed into law, but video game manufacturers immediately sued, and it never went into effect. The U.S. Supreme Court heard the case in 2010, and more than 100 social scientists signed a statement in support of the law, writing that "Overall, the research data conclude that exposure to violent video games causes an increase in the likelihood of aggressive behavior." In 2011, the Supreme Court struck down the law, primarily citing the First Amendment's guarantee of free speech but also expressing doubts that the research showed "a direct causal link between playing violent video games and actual harm to minors" (Scalia, 2011).

Similarly, academic researchers are not unanimous in the view that violent video games have meaningful effects on real-world behavior. Christopher Ferguson and John Kilburn (2010), for example, signed a statement to the Supreme Court criticizing the California law. They point out that from 1996 to 2006, when violent video game sales were increasing, real-life youth violence was decreasing. Ferguson and Kilburn also argue that the effects of violent video games on aggression are small—only some people who play violent video games will act aggressively in real life. Their skepticism helped persuade the Australian Attorney General's Department (2010) that research on violent video game effects "is contested and inconclusive." Brad Bushman and his colleagues (2010) argue that the violent gaming effect is larger than the toxic effects of asbestos or the effect of secondhand smoke on lung cancer. Not everyone exposed to asbestos or secondhand smoke will develop cancer, they point out, but they are still considered public health dangers.

Of course, video games are not all bad—not all of them are violent, and even the violent games improve hand-eye coordination and reaction time (Dye & others, 2009). Moreover, game-playing is focused fun that helps satisfy basic needs for a sense of competence, control, and social connection (Przyblski et al., 2010). No wonder an experiment that randomly assigned 6- to 9-year-old boys to receive a game system found them spending an average of 40 minutes a day on it over the next few months. The downside: They spent less time on schoolwork, resulting in lower reading and writing scores than the control group that did not get a game system (Weis & Cerankosky, 2010).

What about playing prosocial games in which people help each other—the conceptual opposite of violent games? In three studies with children and adults in Singapore, Japan, and the United States, those who played prosocial video games helped others, shared, and cooperated more in real-life situations (Gentile & others, 2009). As Douglas Gentile and Craig Anderson (2011) conclude, "Video games are excellent teachers." Educational games teach children reading and math, prosocial games teach prosocial behavior, and violent games teach violence, they note. We do what we're taught to do, whether that's to help or to hurt.

As a concerned scientist, Craig Anderson (2003, 2004) therefore encourages parents to discover what their kids are ingesting and to ensure that their media diet, as least in their own home, is healthy. Parents may not be able to control what their child watches, plays, and eats in someone else's home. Nor can they control the media's effect on their children's peer culture. (That is why advising parents to "just say no" is naive.) But parents can oversee consumption in their own home and provide increased time for alternative activities. Networking with other parents can build a kid-friendly neighborhood. And schools can help by providing media-awareness education.

CONCEPTS TO REMEMBER

prosocial behavior Positive, constructive, helpful social behavior; the opposite of antisocial behavior.

MODULE

26

❖

Who Likes Whom?

In your beginning there very likely was an attraction—the attraction between a particular man and a particular woman.

What predisposes one person to like, or to love, another? So much has been written about liking and loving that almost every conceivable explanation—and its opposite—has already been proposed. For most people—and for you—what factors nurture liking and loving? Does absence make the heart grow fonder? Or is someone who is out of sight also out of mind? Is it likes that attract? Or opposites?

Consider a simple but powerful reward theory of attraction: Those who reward us, or whom we associate with rewards, we like. Friends reward each other. Without keeping score, they do favors for each other.

Likewise, we develop a liking for those with whom we associate pleasant happenings and surroundings. Thus, surmised Elaine Hatfield and William Waltser (1978), "Romantic dinners, trips to the theatre, evenings at home together, and vacations never stop being important. . . . If your relationship is to survive, it's important that you *both* continue to associate your relationship with good things."

But as with most sweeping generalizations, the reward theory of attraction leaves many questions unanswered. What, precisely, *is* rewarding? Is it usually more rewarding to be with someone who differs from us or someone who is similar to us? to be lavishly flattered or constructively criticized? What factors have fostered *your* close relationships?

PROXIMITY

One powerful predictor of whether any two people are friends is sheer **proximity.** Proximity can also breed hostility; most assaults and murders involve people living close together. But much more often, proximity prompts liking. Mitja Back and his University of Leipzig colleagues (2008) confirmed this by randomly assigning students to seats at their first class meeting and then having each make a brief self-introduction to the whole class. One year after this one-time seating assignment, students reported greater friendship with those who just happened, during that first class gathering, to be seated next to or near them.

Though it may seem trivial to those pondering the mysterious origins of romantic love, sociologists long ago found that most people marry someone who lives in the same neighborhood, or works at the same company or job, or sits in the same class, or visits the same favorite place (Bossard, 1932; Burr, 1973; Clarke, 1952; McPherson & others, 2001). In a Pew survey (2006) of people married or in long-term relationships, 38 percent met at work or at school, and some of the rest met when their paths crossed in their neighborhood, church, or gym or while growing up. Look around. If you marry, it may well be to someone who has lived or worked or studied within walking distance.

Interaction

Even more significant than geographic distance is "functional distance"— how often people's paths cross. We become friends with those who use the same entrances, parking lots, and recreation areas. Randomly assigned college roommates, who interact frequently, are far more likely to become good friends than enemies (Newcomb, 1961). At the college where I teach, men and women once lived on opposite sides of the campus. They understandably bemoaned the lack of cross-sex friendships. Now that they live in gender-integrated residence halls and share common sidewalks, lounges, and laundry facilities, friendships between men and women are far more frequent. Interaction enables people to explore their similarities, to sense one another's liking, and to perceive themselves as part of a social unit (Arkin & Burger, 1980).

So if you're new in town and want to make friends, try to get an apartment near the mailboxes, a desk near the coffeepot, a parking spot near the main buildings. Such is the architecture of friendship.

Why does proximity breed liking? One factor is availability; obviously there are fewer opportunities to get to know someone who attends a different school or lives in another town. But there is more to it. Most people like their roommates, or those one door away, better than those two doors away. Those just a few doors away, or even a floor below, hardly live at an inconvenient distance. Moreover, those close by are potential enemies as well as friends. So why does proximity encourage affection more often than animosity?

Anticipation of Interaction

Proximity enables people to discover commonalities and exchange rewards. But merely *anticipating* interaction also boosts liking. John Darley and Ellen Berscheid (1967) discovered this when they gave University of Minnesota women ambiguous information about two other women, one of whom they expected to talk with intimately. Asked how much they liked each one, the women preferred the person they expected to meet. Expecting to date someone similarly boosts liking (Berscheid & others, 1976). Even voters on the losing side of an election will find their opinions of the winning candidate—whom they are now stuck with—rising (Gilbert & others, 1998).

The phenomenon is adaptive. Anticipatory liking—expecting that someone will be pleasant and compatible—increases the chance of forming a rewarding relationship (Klein & Kunda, 1992; Knight & Vallacher, 1981; Miller & Marks, 1982). How good that we are biased to like those we often see, for our lives are filled with relationships with people whom we may not have chosen but with whom we need to have continuing interactions—roommates, siblings, grandparents, teachers, classmates, co-workers. Liking such people is surely conducive to better relationships and to happier, more productive living.

Mere Exposure

Proximity leads to liking not only because it enables interaction and anticipatory liking but also for a simpler reason: More than 200 experiments reveal that, contrary to an old proverb, familiarity does not breed contempt. Rather, it fosters fondness (Bornstein, 1989, 1999). **Mere exposure** to all sorts of novel stimuli—nonsense syllables, Chinese calligraphy characters, musical selections, faces—boosts people's ratings of them. Do the supposed Turkish words *nansoma, saricik,* and *afworbu* mean something better or something worse than the words *iktitaf, biwojni,* and *kadirga?* University of Michigan students tested by Robert Zajonc (1968, 1970) preferred whichever of these words they had seen most frequently. The more times they had seen a meaningless word or a Chinese ideograph, the more likely they were to say it meant something good (Figure 26-1). I've tested this idea with my own students. Periodically flash certain nonsense words on a screen. By the end of the semester, students will rate those "words" more positively than other nonsense words they have never before seen.

Or consider: What are your favorite letters of the alphabet? People of differing nationalities, languages, and ages prefer the letters appearing in their own names and those that frequently appear in their own languages (Hoorens & Nuttin, 1993; Hoorens & others, 1990; Kitayama & Karasawa, 1997; Nuttin, 1987). French students rate capital W, the least frequent letter in French, as

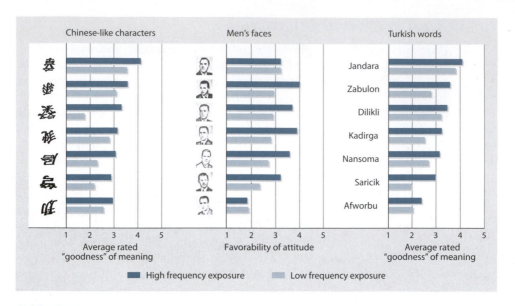

FIGURE 26-1
The mere-exposure effect. Students rated stimuli—a sample of which is shown here—more positively after being shown them repeatedly.   Source: From Zajonc (1968).

their least favorite letter. In an endowment management exercise, American business students preferred to buy stocks that shared the same first letter as their name (Knewtson & Sias, 2010). Japanese students prefer not only letters from their names but also numbers corresponding to their birth dates. This "name letter effect" reflects more than mere exposure, however—see "Focus On: Liking Things Associated with Oneself" on page 319.

The mere-exposure effect violates the commonsense prediction of boredom—*decreased* interest—regarding repeatedly heard music or tasted foods (Kahneman & Snell, 1992). Unless the repetitions are incessant ("Even the best song becomes tiresome if heard too often," says a Korean proverb), familiarity usually doesn't breed contempt, it increases liking. When completed in 1889, the Eiffel Tower in Paris was mocked as grotesque (Harrison, 1977). Today, it is the beloved symbol of Paris.

The mere-exposure effect has "enormous adaptive significance," notes Zajonc (1998). It is a "hardwired" phenomenon that predisposes our attractions and attachments. It helped our ancestors categorize things and people as either familiar and safe or unfamiliar and possibly dangerous. The more two strangers interact, the more attractive they tend to find each other (Reis & others, 2011).

The phenomenon's negative side is our wariness of the unfamiliar—which may explain the automatic, unconscious prejudice people often feel when confronting those who are different. Infants as young as 3 months exhibit an own-race preference: If surrounded by others of their race, they

Focus On: Liking Things Associated with Oneself

We humans love to feel good about ourselves, and generally we do. Not only are we prone to self-serving bias (Module 4), we also exhibit what Brett Pelham, Matthew Mirenberg, and John Jones (2002) call *implicit egotism:* We like what we associate with ourselves.

That includes the letters of our name, but also the people, places, and things that we unconsciously connect with ourselves (Jones & others, 2002; Koole & others, 2001). If a stranger's or politician's face is morphed to include features of our own, we like the new face better (Bailenson & others, 2009; DeBruine, 2004). Thanks to natural inbreeding avoidance, women with brothers tend to trust unfamiliar men whose faces are morphed with their own but do not feel attracted to them; they find self-resembling men's faces to be "trustworthy but not lust-worthy" (DeBruine & others, 2011). We are also more attracted to people whose arbitrary experimental code number resembles our birth date, and we are even disproportionately likely to marry someone whose first or last name resembles our own, such as by starting with the same letter (Jones & others, 2004).

Such preferences appear to subtly influence other major life decisions as well, including our locations and careers, report Pelham and colleagues. Philadelphia, being larger than Jacksonville, has 2.2 times as many men named Jack. But it has 10.4 times as many people named Philip. Likewise, Virginia Beach has a disproportionate number of people named Virginia.

Does this merely reflect the influence of one's place when naming one's baby? Are people in Georgia, for example, more likely to name their babies George or Georgia? That may be so, but it doesn't explain why states tend to have a relative excess of people whose *last* names are similar to the state names. California, for example, has a disproportionate number of people whose names begin with Cali (as in Califano). Likewise, major Canadian cities tend to have larger-than-expected numbers of people whose last names overlap with the city names. Toronto has a marked excess of people whose names begin with Tor.

Moreover, St. Louis has a 49 percent excess (relative to the national proportion) of men named Louis, and people named Hill, Park, Beach, Lake, or Rock are disproportionately likely to live in cities with names (such as Park City) that include their names. "People are attracted to places that resemble their names," surmise Pelham, Mirenberg, and Jones.

Weirder yet—I am not making this up—people seem to prefer careers related to their names. Across the United States, Jerry, Dennis, and Walter are equally popular names (0.42 percent of people carry each of these names). Yet America's dentists are almost twice as likely to be named Dennis as Jerry or Walter. There also are 2.5 times as many dentists named Denise as there are with the equally popular name Beverly or Tammy. People named George or Geoffrey are overrepresented among geoscientists (geologists, geophysicists, and geochemists). And in the 2000 presidential campaign, people with last names beginning with B and G were disproportionately likely to contribute to the campaigns of Bush and Gore, respectively.

The implicit egotism phenomenon does have its skeptics. Uri Simonsohn (2011a, 2011b) acknowledges that implicit egotism occurs in the laboratory, and he was able to replicate the associations between people's names, occupations, and places. But he argues that "reverse causality" sometimes is the explanation. For example, streets are often named after their residents, and towns are often named after their founders (Williams founded Williamsburg). And founders' descendants may stick around. In reply, Pelham and Mauricio Carvallo (2011) grant that some of the effects—especially for career choice—are modest. But they contend that implicit egotism is a real, though subtle, unconscious judgmental bias.

Reading about implicit egotism-based preferences gives me pause: Has this anything to do with why I enjoyed that trip to Fort Myers? Why I've written about moods, the media, and marriage? Why I collaborated with Professor Murdoch? If so, does this also explain why it was Suzie who sold seashells by the seashore?

prefer to gaze at faces of their own familiar race (Bar-Haim & others, 2006; Kelly & others, 2005, 2007).

We even like ourselves better the way we're used to seeing ourselves. In a delightful experiment, Theodore Mita, Marshall Dermer, and Jeffrey Knight (1977) photographed women students at the University of Wisconsin, Milwaukee, and later showed each one her actual picture along with its mirror image. Asked which picture they liked better, most preferred their mirror image—the image they were used to seeing. (No wonder our photographs never look quite right.) When close friends of the women were shown the same two pictures, they preferred the true picture—the image *they* were used to seeing.

Advertisers and politicians exploit this phenomenon. When people have no strong feelings about a product or a candidate, repetition alone can increase sales or votes (McCullough & Ostrom, 1974; Winter, 1973). After endless repetition of a commercial, shoppers often have an unthinking,

The mere-exposure effect. If she is like most of us, German chancellor Angela Merkel may prefer her familiar mirror-image (left), which she sees each morning while brushing her teeth, to her actual image (right).

automatic, favorable response to the product. If candidates are relatively unknown, those with the most media exposure usually win (Patterson, 1980; Schaffner & others, 1981). Political strategists who understand the mere-exposure effect have replaced reasoned argument with brief ads that hammer home a candidate's name and sound-bite message.

The respected chief of the Washington State Supreme Court, Keith Callow, learned this lesson when in 1990 he lost to a seemingly hopeless opponent, Charles Johnson. Johnson, an unknown attorney who handled minor criminal cases and divorces, filed for the seat on the principle that judges "need to be challenged." Neither man campaigned, and the media ignored the race. On election day, the two candidates' names appeared without any identification—just one name next to the other. The result: a 53 percent to 47 percent Johnson victory. "There are a lot more Johnsons out there than Callows," offered the ousted judge afterward to a stunned legal community. Indeed, the state's largest newspaper counted 27 Charles Johnsons in its local phone book. There was Charles Johnson, the local judge. And, in a nearby city, there was television anchorman Charles Johnson, whose broadcasts were seen on statewide cable TV. Forced to choose between two unknown names, many voters preferred the comfortable, familiar name of Charles Johnson.

*P*HYSICAL ATTRACTIVENESS

What do (or did) you seek in a potential date? Sincerity? Character? Humor? Good looks? Sophisticated, intelligent people are unconcerned with such superficial qualities as good looks; they know "beauty is only skin deep" and "you can't judge a book by its cover." At least, they know that's how they *ought* to feel. As Cicero counseled, "Resist appearance."

The belief that looks are unimportant may be another instance of how we deny real influences upon us, for there is now a file cabinet full of research studies showing that appearance matters. The consistency and pervasiveness of this effect is astonishing. Good looks are an asset.

Attractiveness and Dating

Like it or not, a young woman's physical attractiveness is a moderately good predictor of how frequently she dates, and a young man's attractiveness is a modestly good predictor of how frequently he dates (Berscheid & others, 1971; Krebs & Adinolfi, 1975; Reis & others, 1980, 1982; Walster & others, 1966). However, women more than men say they would prefer a mate who's homely and warm over one who's attractive and cold (Fletcher & others, 2004). In a worldwide BBC Internet survey of nearly 220,000 people, men more than women ranked attractiveness as important in a mate, whereas women more than men assigned importance to honesty, humor, kindness, and dependability (Lippa, 2007).

Do such self-reports imply, as many have surmised, that women are better at following Cicero's advice? Or that nothing has changed since 1930, when the English philosopher Bertrand Russell (1930, p. 139) wrote, "On the whole women tend to love men for their character while men tend to love women for their appearance"? Or does it merely reflect the fact that men more often do the inviting? If women were to indicate their preferences among various men, would looks be as important to them as to men?

To determine whether men are indeed more influenced by looks, researchers have provided heterosexual male and female students with information about someone of the other sex, including the person's picture. Or they have briefly introduced a man and a woman and later asked each about their interest in dating the other. In such experiments, men have put somewhat more value on opposite-sex physical attractiveness (Feingold, 1990, 1991; Sprecher & others, 1994). Perhaps sensing this, women worry more about their appearance and constitute 92 percent of American cosmetic surgery patients (American Society for Aesthetic Plastic Surgery, 2011). Women also better recall others' appearance, as when asked "Was the person on the right wearing black shoes?" or when asked to recall someone's clothing or hair (Mast & Hall, 2006).

Do women respond to men's looks? In one ambitious study, Elaine Hatfield and co-workers (1966) matched 752 University of Minnesota first-year students for a "Welcome Week" matching dance. The researchers gave each student personality and aptitude tests but then matched the couples randomly. On the night of the dance, the couples danced and talked for 2½ hours and then took a brief intermission to evaluate their dates. How well did the personality and aptitude tests predict attraction? Did people like someone better who was high in self-esteem, or low in anxiety, or different from themselves in outgoingness? The researchers examined a long list of possibilities. But so far as they could determine, only one thing mattered: how physically attractive the person was (as previously rated by the researchers). The more attractive a woman was, the more the man liked her and wanted to date her again. And the more attractive the man was, the more the woman liked him and wanted to date him again. Pretty pleases.

Recent studies have gathered data from speed-dating evenings, during which people interact with a succession of potential dates for only a few minutes each and later indicate which ones they would like to see again (mutual "yes's" are given contact information). The procedure is rooted in research showing that we can form durable impressions of others based on seconds-long "thin slices" of their social behavior (Ambady & others, 2000). In speed-dating research by Paul Eastwick and Eli Finkel (2008a, 2008b), men more than women presumed the importance of a potential date's physical attractiveness; but in reality, a prospect's attractiveness was similarly important to both men and women.

Looks even influence voting, or so it seems from a study by Alexander Todorov and colleagues (2005; Todorov, 2011). They showed Princeton University students photographs of the two major candidates in 95 U.S. Senate races since 2000 and in 600 U.S. House of Representatives races. Based on looks alone, the students (by preferring competent-looking over more baby-faced candidates) correctly guessed the winners of 72 percent of the Senate and 67 percent of the House races. Follow-up studies have confirmed the finding that voters prefer competent-looking candidates (Antonakis & Dalgas, 2009; Chiao & others, 2008). But gender also mattered: Men were more likely to vote for physically attractive female candidates, and women were more likely to vote for approachable-looking male candidates. Likewise, heterosexual people display a positive bias toward attractive job candidates and university applicants—*if* they are of the other sex (Agthe & others, 2011).

To say that attractiveness is important, other things being equal, is not to say that physical appearance always outranks other qualities. Some people more than others judge people by their looks (Livingston, 2001). Moreover, attractiveness most affects first impressions. But first impressions are important—and have become more so as societies become increasingly mobile and urbanized and as contacts with people become more fleeting (Berscheid, 1981). Your Facebook self-presentation starts with . . . your face. In speed-dating experiments, the attractiveness effect is strongest when people's choices are superficially made—when meeting lots of people quickly (Lenton & Francesconi, 2010). That helps explain why attractiveness better predicts happiness and social connections for those in urban rather than rural settings (Plaut & others, 2009).

Though interviewers may deny it, attractiveness and grooming affect first impressions in job interviews—especially when the evaluator is of the other sex (Agthe & others, 2011; Cash & Janda, 1984; Mack & Rainey, 1990;

Marvelle & Green, 1980). People rate new products more favorably when they are associated with attractive inventors (Baron & others, 2006). Such impressions help explain why attractive people and tall people have more prestigious jobs and make more money (Engemann & Owyang, 2003; Persico & others, 2004).

Patricia Roszell and colleagues (1990) looked at the incomes of a national sample of Canadians whom interviewers had rated on a 1 (homely) to 5 (strikingly attractive) scale. They found that for each additional scale unit of rated attractiveness, people earned, on average, an additional $1,988 annually. Irene Hanson Frieze and associates (1991) did the same analysis with 737 MBA graduates after rating them on a similar 1-to-5 scale using student yearbook photos. For each additional scale unit of rated attractiveness, men earned an added $2,600 and women earned an added $2,150. In *Beauty Pays*, economist Daniel Hamermesh (2011) argues that, for a man, good looks have the earnings effect of another year and a half of schooling.

The Matching Phenomenon

Not everyone can end up paired with someone stunningly attractive. So how do people pair off? Judging from research by Bernard Murstein (1986) and others, they get real. They pair off with people who are about as attractive as they are. Studies have found a strong correspondence between the rated attractiveness of husbands and wives, of dating partners, and even of those within particular fraternities (Feingold, 1988; Montoya, 2008). People tend to select as friends, and especially to marry, those who are a "good match" not only to their level of intelligence, popularity, and self-worth but also to their level of attractiveness (Taylor & others, 2011).

Experiments confirm this **matching phenomenon.** When choosing whom to approach, knowing the other is free to say yes or no, people often approach and invest more in pursuing someone whose attractiveness roughly matches (or not too greatly exceeds) their own (Berscheid & others, 1971; Huston, 1973; Van Straaten & others, 2009). They seek out someone who seems desirable, but they are mindful of the limits of their own desirability. Good physical matches may be conducive to good relationships, reported Gregory White (1980) from a study of UCLA dating couples. Those who were most similar in physical attractiveness were most likely, 9 months later, to have fallen more deeply in love.

Perhaps this research prompts you to think of happy couples who differ in perceived "hotness." In such cases, the less attractive person often has compensating qualities. Each partner brings assets to the social marketplace, and the value of the respective assets creates an equitable match. Personal advertisements and self-presentations to online dating services exhibit this exchange of assets (Cicerello & Sheehan, 1995; Hitsch & others,

2006; Koestner & Wheeler, 1988; Rajecki & others, 1991). Men typically offer wealth or status and seek youth and attractiveness; women more often do the reverse: "Attractive, bright woman, 26, slender, seeks warm, professional male." Men who advertise their income and education, and women who advertise their youth and looks, receive more responses to their ads (Baize & Schroeder, 1995). The asset-matching process helps explain why beautiful young women often marry older men of higher social status (Elder, 1969; Kanazawa & Kovar, 2004). The richer the man, the younger and more beautiful the woman.

The Physical-Attractiveness Stereotype

Does the attractiveness effect spring entirely from sexual attractiveness? Clearly not, as Vicky Houston and Ray Bull (1994) discovered when they used a makeup artist to give an otherwise attractive accomplice an apparently scarred, bruised, or birthmarked face. When riding on a Glasgow commuter rail line, people of both sexes avoided sitting next to the accomplice when she appeared facially disfigured. Moreover, much as adults are biased toward attractive adults, young children are biased toward attractive children (Dion, 1973; Dion & Berscheid, 1974; Langlois & others, 2000). To judge from how long they gaze at someone, even 3-month-old infants prefer attractive faces (Langlois & others, 1987).

Adults show a similar bias when judging children. Margaret Clifford and Elaine Hatfield (Clifford & Walster, 1973) gave Missouri fifth-grade teachers identical information about a boy or a girl but with the photograph of an attractive or an unattractive child attached. The teachers perceived the attractive child as more intelligent and successful in school. Think of yourself as a playground supervisor having to discipline an unruly child. Might you, like the women studied by Karen Dion (1972), show less warmth and tact to an unattractive child? The sad truth is that most of us assume what we might call a "Bart Simpson effect"—that homely children are less able and socially competent than their beautiful peers.

What is more, we assume that beautiful people possess certain desirable traits. Other things being equal, we guess beautiful people are happier, sexually warmer, and more outgoing, intelligent, and successful—though not more honest or concerned for others (Eagly & others, 1991; Feingold, 1992b; Jackson & others, 1995). We are more eager to bond with attractive people, which motivates our projecting desirable attributes such as kindness and reciprocal interest into them (Lemay & others, 2010).

Added together, the findings define a **physical-attractiveness stereotype:** What is beautiful is good. Children learn the stereotype quite early—and one of the ways they learn it is through stories told to them by adults. "Disney movies promote the stereotype that what is beautiful is good," report Doris Bazzini and colleagues (2010) from an analysis of human characters in 21 animated films. Snow White and Cinderella are beautiful—and kind. The witch and the stepsisters are ugly—and wicked. "If you want to be loved by somebody who isn't already in your family, it doesn't hurt to be beautiful," surmised one 8-year-old girl. Or as one kindergarten girl put it when asked what it means to be pretty, "It's like to be a princess. Everybody loves you" (Dion, 1979).

If physical attractiveness is that important, then permanently changing people's attractiveness should change the way others react to them. But is it ethical to alter someone's looks? Such manipulations are performed millions of times a year by cosmetic surgeons and orthodontists. With teeth straightened and whitened, hair replaced and dyed, face lifted, fat liposuctioned, and breasts enlarged, lifted, or reduced, most self-dissatisfied people do express satisfaction with the results of their procedures, though some unhappy patients seek out repeat procedures (Honigman & others, 2004).

To examine the effect of such alterations on others, Michael Kalick (1977) had Harvard students rate their impressions of eight women based on profile photographs taken before or after cosmetic surgery. Not only did they judge the women as more physically attractive after the surgery but also as kinder, more sensitive, more sexually warm and responsive, more likable, and so on.

The speed with which first impressions form, and their influence on thinking, helps explain why pretty prospers. Even a .013-second exposure—too brief to discern a face—is enough to enable people to guess a face's attractiveness (Olson & Marshuetz, 2005). Moreover, when categorizing subsequent words as either good or bad, an attractive flashed face predisposes people to categorize good words faster. Pretty is perceived promptly and primes positive processing.

Do beautiful people indeed have desirable traits? For centuries, those who considered themselves serious scientists thought so when they sought to identify physical traits (shifty eyes, a weak chin) that would predict criminal behavior. Or, on the other hand, was Leo Tolstoy correct when he wrote that it's "a strange illusion . . . to suppose that beauty is goodness"? There is some truth to the stereotype. Attractive children and young adults are somewhat more relaxed, outgoing, and socially polished (Feingold, 1992b; Langlois & others, 2000). William Goldman and Philip Lewis (1977) demonstrated this by having 60 University of Georgia men call and talk for 5 minutes with each of three women students. Afterward, the men and women rated the most attractive of their unseen telephone partners as somewhat more socially skillful and likable. Physically attractive individuals tend also to be more popular, more outgoing, and more gender typed—more traditionally masculine if male, more feminine if female (Langlois & others, 1996).

These small average differences between attractive and unattractive people probably result from self-fulfilling prophecies. Attractive people are valued and favored, so many develop more social self-confidence. (Recall from Module 8 an experiment in which men evoked a warm response from unseen women they *thought* were attractive.) By that analysis, what's crucial to your social skill is not how you look but how people treat you and how you feel about yourself—whether you accept yourself, like yourself, and feel comfortable with yourself.

Who Is Attractive?

I have described attractiveness as if it were an objective quality like height, which some people have more of, some less. Strictly speaking, attractiveness is whatever the people of any given place and time find attractive. This, of course, varies. The beauty standards by which Miss Universe is judged hardly apply even to the whole planet. People in various places and times have pierced noses, lengthened necks, dyed hair, whitened teeth, painted skin, gorged themselves to become voluptuous, starved to become thin, and bound themselves with leather corsets to make their breasts seem small—or used silicone and padded bras to make them seem big. For cultures with scarce resources and for poor or hungry people, plumpness seems attractive; for cultures and individuals with abundant resources, beauty more often equals slimness (Nelson & Morrison, 2005). Moreover, attractiveness influences life outcomes less in cultures where relationships are based more on kinship or social arrangement than on personal choice (Anderson & others, 2008). Despite such variations, there remains "strong agreement both within and across cultures about who is and who is not attractive," note Judith Langlois and colleagues (2000).

To be really attractive is, ironically, to be *perfectly average* (Rhodes, 2006). Research teams led by Langlois and Lorri Roggman (Langlois & Roggman, 1990; Langlois & others, 1994) at the University of Texas and David Perrett (2010) at the University of St. Andrews have digitized multiple faces and averaged them using a computer. Inevitably, people find the composite faces more appealing than almost all the actual faces. Across 27 nations, even an average leg-length-to-body ratio looks more attractive than very short or long legs (Sorokowski & others, 2011). With both humans and animals, averaged looks best embody prototypes (for your typical man, woman, dog, or whatever) and thus are easy for the brain to process and categorize, notes Jamin Halberstadt (2006). Let's face it: Perfectly average is easy on the eyes (and brain).

Computer-averaged faces and bodies also tend to be perfectly *symmetrical*—another characteristic of strikingly attractive (and reproductively successful) people (Brown & others, 2008; Gangestad & Thornhill, 1997). Research teams led by Gillian Rhodes (Rhodes, 2006; Rhodes & others, 1999) and by Ian Penton-Voak (2001) have shown that if you could merge either half of your face with its mirror image—thus forming a perfectly symmetrical new face—you would boost your looks. With a few facial features excepted (Said & Todorov, 2011), averaging a number of such attractive, symmetrical faces produces an even better looking face.

Evolution and Attraction

Activity
26.1

Psychologists working from the evolutionary perspective explain the human preference for attractive partners in terms of reproductive strategy (Module 13). They assume that beauty signals biologically important information: health, youth, and fertility. And so it does, report Gordon Gallup and colleagues (2008). Men with attractive faces have higher quality sperm. Women with hourglass figures have more regular menstrual cycles and are more fertile. Over time, men who preferred fertile-looking women outreproduced those who were as happy to mate with postmenopausal females. That biological outcome of human history, David Buss (1989) believes, explains why the males he studied in 37 cultures—from Australia to Zambia—did indeed prefer youthful female characteristics that signify reproductive capacity.

Evolutionary psychologists also assume that evolution predisposes women to favor male traits that signify an ability to provide and protect resources. No wonder physically attractive females tend to marry high-status males, and men compete with such determination to display status by achieving fame and fortune. In screening potential mates, report Norman Li and fellow researchers (2002), men require a modicum of physical attractiveness, women require status and resources, and both welcome kindness and intelligence.

During ovulation, women show heightened preference for men with masculinized faces, voices, and bodies (Gallup & Frederick, 2010; Gangestad & others, 2004; Macrae & others, 2002). They show increased accuracy in judging male sexual orientation (Rule & others, 2011). And they show increased wariness of out-group men (McDonald & others, 2011). One study found that, when ovulating, young women tend to wear and prefer more revealing outfits than when infertile (Durante & others, 2008). In another study, ovulating lap dancers averaged $70 in tips per hour—double the $35 of those who were menstruating (Miller & others, 2007).

We are, evolutionary psychologists suggest, driven by primal attractions. Like eating and breathing, attraction and mating are too important to leave to the whims of culture.

The Contrast Effect

Although our mating psychology has biological wisdom, attraction is not all hardwired. What's attractive to you also depends on your comparison standards.

Douglas Kenrick and Sara Gutierres (1980) had male confederates interrupt Montana State University men in their dormitory rooms and explain, "We have a friend coming to town this week and we want to fix him up with a date, but we can't decide whether to fix him up with her or not, so we decided to conduct a survey. . . . We want you to give us your vote on how attractive you think she is . . . on a scale of 1 to 7." Shown a picture of an average young woman, those who had just been watching *Charlie's Angels* (a television show featuring three beautiful women) rated her less attractive than those who hadn't.

Laboratory experiments confirm this "contrast effect." To men who have recently been gazing at centerfolds, average women or even their own wives tend to seem less attractive (Kenrick & others, 1989). Viewing pornographic films simulating passionate sex similarly decreases satisfaction with one's own partner (Zillmann, 1989). Being sexually aroused may *temporarily* make a person of the other sex seem more attractive. But the lingering effect of exposure to perfect "10s," or of unrealistic sexual depictions, is to make one's own partner seem less appealing—more like a "6" than an "8."

It works the same way with our self-perceptions. After viewing a superattractive person of the same gender, people rate themselves as being *less* attractive than after viewing a homely person (Brown & others, 1992; Thornton & Maurice, 1997).

The Attractiveness of Those We Love

Let's conclude our discussion of attractiveness on an upbeat note. Not only do we perceive attractive people as likable but also we perceive likable people as attractive. Perhaps you can recall individuals who, as you grew to like them, became more attractive. Their physical imperfections were no longer so noticeable. Alan Gross and Christine Crofton (1977; see also Lewandowski & others, 2007) had students view someone's photograph after reading a favorable or an unfavorable description of the person's personality. Those portrayed as warm, helpful, and considerate also *looked* more attractive. It may be true, then, that "handsome is as handsome does." Discovering someone's similarities to us also makes the person seem more attractive (Beaman & Klentz, 1983; Klentz & others, 1987).

Moreover, love sees loveliness: The more in love a woman is with a man, the more physically attractive she finds him (Price & others, 1974). And the more in love people are, the less attractive they find all others of the opposite sex (Johnson & Rusbult, 1989; Simpson & others, 1990). "The grass may be greener on the other side," note Rowland Miller and Jeffry Simpson (1990), "but happy gardeners are less likely to notice." Beauty really *is*, to some extent, in the eye of the beholder.

SIMILARITY VERSUS COMPLEMENTARITY

From our discussion so far, one might surmise Leo Tolstoy was entirely correct: "Love depends . . . on frequent meetings, and on the style in which the hair is done up, and on the color and cut of the dress." Given time, however, other factors influence whether acquaintance develops into friendship.

Do Birds of a Feather Flock Together?

Of this much we may be sure: Birds that flock together are of a feather. Friends, engaged couples, and spouses are far more likely than randomly paired people to share common attitudes, beliefs, and values. Furthermore, the greater the similarity between husband and wife, the happier they are and the less likely they are to divorce (Byrne, 1971; Caspi & Herbener, 1990). Such correlational findings are intriguing. But cause and effect remain an enigma. Does similarity lead to liking? Or does liking lead to similarity?

Likeness Begets Liking

To discern cause and effect, we experiment. Imagine that at a campus party Lakesha gets involved in a long discussion of politics, religion, and personal likes and dislikes with Les and Lon. She and Les discover they agree on almost everything, she and Lon on few things. Afterward, she reflects: "Les is really intelligent . . . and so likable. I hope we meet again." In experiments, Donn Byrne (1971) and his colleagues captured the essence of Lakesha's experience. Over and over again, they found that the more similar someone's attitudes are to your own, the more you will like the person. Likeness produces liking not only for college students but also for children and the elderly, for people of various occupations, and for those in various cultures.

The likeness-leads-to-liking effect has been tested in real-life situations. At the University of Michigan, Theodore Newcomb (1961) studied two groups of 17 unacquainted male transfer students. After 13 weeks of boarding house life, those whose agreement was initially highest were most likely to have formed close friendships. One group of friends was composed of 5 liberal arts students, each a political liberal with strong intellectual interests. Another was made up of 3 conservative veterans who were all enrolled in the engineering college.

In various settings, people entering a room of strangers sit closer to those like themselves (Mackinnon & others, 2011). People with glasses sit closer to others with glasses. Long-haired people sit closer to people with long hair. Dark-haired people sit closer to people with dark hair (even after controlling for race and sex).

Whether in China or the Western world, similar attitudes, traits, and values help bring couples together and predict their satisfaction (Chen & others, 2009; Gaunt, 2006; Gonzaga & others, 2007). Speed-daters are drawn to those who share their speaking style (Ireland & others, 2011). Even morning and evening types tend to find one another (Randler & Kretz, 2011). One psychologist-founded Internet dating site claims to match singles using the similarities that mark happy couples (Carter & Snow, 2004; Warren, 2005).

So similarity breeds content. Birds of a feather *do* flock together. Surely you have noticed this upon discovering a person who shares your ideas, values, and desires; a special someone who likes the same foods, the same activities, the same music you do. (When liking the same music as another, people infer similar values as well [Boer & others, 2011].)

Do Opposites Attract?

Are we not also attracted to people who in some ways *differ* from ourselves? Researchers have explored that question by comparing not only friends' and spouses' attitudes and beliefs but also their ages, religions, races, smoking behaviors, economic levels, educations, height, intelligence, and appearance. In all these ways and more, similarity still prevails (Buss, 1985; Kandel, 1978). Smart birds flock together. So do rich birds, Protestant birds, tall birds, pretty birds.

Still we resist: Are we not attracted to people whose needs and personalities complement our own? Would a sadist and a masochist find true love? The *Reader's Digest* has told us that "opposites attract. . . . Socializers pair with loners, novelty-lovers with those who dislike change, free spenders with scrimpers, risk-takers with the very cautious" (Jacoby, 1986). Sociologist Robert Winch (1958) reasoned that the needs of an outgoing and domineering person would naturally complement those of someone who is shy and submissive. The logic seems compelling, and most of us can think of couples who view their differences as complementary: "My husband and I are perfect for each other. I'm Aquarius—a decisive person. He's Libra—can't make decisions. But he's always happy to go along with arrangements I make."

Some **complementarity** may evolve as a relationship progresses (even a relationship between identical twins). Yet people seem slightly more prone to like and to marry those whose needs and personalities are *similar* (Botwin & others, 1997; Buss, 1984; Fishbein & Thelen, 1981a, 1981b; Nias, 1979). Perhaps one day we will discover some ways (other than heterosexuality) in which differences commonly breed liking. Dominance/submissiveness may be one such way (Dryer & Horowitz, 1997; Markey & Kurtz, 2006). But as a general rule, opposites do not attract.

*L*IKING THOSE WHO LIKE US

With hindsight, the reward principle explains our conclusions so far:

- *Proximity* is rewarding. It costs less time and effort to receive friendship's benefits with someone who lives or works close by.
- We like *attractive* people because we perceive that they offer other desirable traits and because we benefit by associating with them.

- If others have *similar* opinions, we feel rewarded because we presume that they like us in return. Moreover, those who share our views help validate them. We especially like people if we have successfully converted them to our way of thinking (Lombardo & others, 1972; Riordan, 1980; Sigall, 1970).

- We like to be liked and love to be loved. Thus, liking is usually *mutual*. We like those who like us.

But does one person's liking another *cause* the other to return the appreciation? People's reports of how they fell in love suggest so (Aron & others, 1989). Discovering that an appealing someone really likes you seems to awaken romantic feelings. Experiments confirm it: Those told that certain others like or admire them usually feel a reciprocal affection (Berscheid & Walster, 1978). And all the better, one speed-dating experiment suggests, when someone likes *you* especially (Eastwick & others, 2007). A dash of uncertainty can also fuel desire. Thinking that someone probably likes you—but you aren't sure—tends to increase your thinking about, and feeling attracted to, another (Whitechurch & others, 2011).

And consider this finding by Ellen Berscheid and colleagues (1969): Students like another student who says eight positive things about them better than one who says seven positive things and one negative thing. We are sensitive to the slightest hint of criticism. Writer Larry L. King speaks for many in noting, "I have discovered over the years that good reviews strangely fail to make the author feel as good as bad reviews make him feel bad."

Whether we are judging ourselves or others, negative information carries more weight because, being less usual, it grabs more attention (Yzerbyt & Leyens, 1991). People's votes are more influenced by their impressions of presidential candidates' weaknesses than by their impressions of strengths (Klein, 1991), a phenomenon quickly grasped by those who design negative campaigns.

Our liking for those we perceive as liking us was recognized long ago. Observers from the ancient philosopher Hecato ("If you wish to be loved, love") to Ralph Waldo Emerson ("The only way to have a friend is to be one") to Dale Carnegie ("Dole out praise lavishly") anticipated the findings. What they did not anticipate was the precise conditions under which the principle works.

Self-Esteem and Attraction

Elaine Hatfield (Walster, 1965) wondered if another's approval is especially rewarding after we have been deprived of approval, much as eating is most rewarding when we're hungry. To test that idea, she gave some Stanford University women either very favorable or very unfavorable analyses of their personalities, affirming some and wounding others. Then she asked them to evaluate several people, including an attractive male confederate who just before the experiment had struck up a warm conversation with each woman and had asked each for a date. (Not one turned him down.) Which women do you suppose most liked the man? It was those whose self-esteem had been temporarily shattered and who were presumably hungry for social approval. After this experiment, Hatfield spent almost an hour talking with each woman explaining the experiment. She reports that, in the end, none remained disturbed by the temporary ego blow or the broken date.

Proximity, attractiveness, similarity, being liked—these are the factors known to influence our friendship formation. Sometimes friendship deepens into the passion and intimacy of love. What is love? And why does it sometimes flourish and sometimes fade? But to answer these questions, first we need to understand our deep need to belong.

OUR NEED TO BELONG

Aristotle called humans "the social animal." Indeed, we have what today's social psychologists call a **need to belong**—to connect with others in enduring, close relationships.

Social psychologists Roy Baumeister and Mark Leary (1995; Leary, 2010) illustrate the power of social attachments:

- For our ancestors, mutual attachments enabled group survival. When hunting game or erecting shelter, 10 hands were better than 2.

- For heterosexual women and men, the bonds of love can lead to children, whose survival chances are boosted by the nurturing of two bonded parents who support each other.

- For children and their caregivers, social attachments enhance survival. Unexplainably separated from each other, parent and toddler may both panic until reunited in a tight embrace. Reared under extreme neglect or in institutions without belonging to anybody, children become pathetic, anxious creatures.

- For university students, relationships consume much of life. How much of your waking life is spent talking with people? One sampling of 10,000 tape recordings of half-minute slices of students' waking hours (using belt-worn recorders) found them talking to someone 28 percent of the time—and that doesn't count the time they spent listening to someone (Mehl & Pennebaker, 2003).

- When not face-to-face, the world's 7 billion people connect by voice and texting through their more than 5 billion cell-phone subscriptions (International Telecommunication Union, 2010), or through social networks such as Facebook. In the United States, 9 in 10 college-bound high school seniors use social networking sites, with most visiting once or more a day (The College Board, 2011). Half of teens send 50 or more texts daily (Lenhart, 2010). Our need to belong motivates our investment in being continuously connected.

- For people everywhere (no matter their sexual orientation), actual and hoped-for close relationships can dominate thinking and emotions. Finding a supportive person in whom we can confide, we feel accepted and prized. Falling in love, we feel irrepressible joy. When relationships with partners, family, and friends are healthy, self-esteem—a barometer of our relationships—rides high (Denissen & others, 2008). Longing for acceptance and love, we spend billions on cosmetics, clothes, and diets. Even seemingly dismissive people relish being accepted (Carvallo & Gabriel, 2006).

- Exiled, imprisoned, or in solitary confinement, people ache for their own people and places. Rejected, we are at risk for depression (Nolan & others, 2003). Time passes more slowly and life seems less meaningful (Twenge & others, 2003).

- For the jilted, the widowed, and the sojourner in a strange place, the loss of social bonds triggers pain, loneliness, or withdrawal. Losing a close relationship, adults feel jealous, distraught, or bereaved, as well as mindful of death and life's fragility. After relocating, people—especially those with the strongest need to belong—typically feel homesick (Watt & Badger, 2009).

- Reminders of death in turn heighten our need to belong, to be with others, and to hold close those we love (Mikulincer & others, 2003; Wisman & Koole, 2003). Facing the terror of 9/11, millions of Americans called and connected with loved ones. Likewise, the shocking death of a classmate, a co-worker, or a family member brings people together, their differences no longer mattering.

We are, indeed, social animals. We need to belong. As with other motivations, thwarting the need to belong intensifies it; satisfying the need reduces the motivation (DeWall & others, 2009, 2011). When we do belong—when we feel supported by close, intimate relationships—we tend to be healthier and happier. Satisfy the need to belong in balance with two other human needs—to feel *autonomy* and *competence*—and the typical result is a deep sense of well-being (Deci & Ryan, 2002; Milyavskaya & others, 2009; Sheldon & Niemiec, 2006). Happiness is feeling connected, free, and capable.

Social psychologist Kipling Williams (2002, 2007, 2009, 2011) has explored what happens when our need to belong is thwarted by *ostracism* (acts of excluding or ignoring). Humans in all cultures, whether in schools, workplaces, or homes, use ostracism to regulate social behavior. Some of us know what it is like to be shunned—to be avoided, met with averted eyes, or given the silent treatment. Even just being among people speaking a language one doesn't know can leave one feeling excluded (Dotan-Eliaz & others, 2009).

People (women especially) respond to ostracism with depressed or numbed mood, anxiety, hurt feelings, efforts to restore relationships, and eventual withdrawal (Baumeister & others, 2009; Blackhart & others, 2009; Gerber & Wheeler, 2009a, 2009b). The silent treatment is "emotional abuse" and "a terrible, terrible weapon to use," say those who have experienced it from a family member or a co-worker. In experiments, people who are left out of a simple game of ball tossing feel deflated and stressed. Ostracism hurts, and the social pain is keenly felt—more than those who are not ostracized ever know (Nordgren & others, 2011). If only we better empathized with those rejected, there might be less tolerance of emotional bullying.

Sometimes deflation turns nasty, as people lash out at the very people whose acceptance they desire (Reijntjes & others, 2011). In several studies, Jean Twenge and collaborators (2001, 2002, 2007; DeWall & others, 2009; Leary & others, 2006) gave some people an experience of being socially included. Others experienced temporary exclusion: They were told (based on a personality test) either that they "were likely to end up alone later in life" or that others whom they'd met didn't want them in their group. Those led to feel excluded became not only more likely to engage in self-defeating behaviors, such as underperforming on an aptitude test, but also less able to regulate their behavior (they drank less of a healthy but bad-tasting drink and ate more unhealthy cookies). They also became more likely to disparage or deliver a blast of noise to someone who had insulted them. If a small laboratory experience of being "voted off the island" could produce such aggression, noted the researchers, one wonders what aggressive tendencies "might arise from a series of important rejections or chronic exclusion."

Williams and Steve Nida (2011) were surprised to discover that even "cyber-ostracism" by faceless people whom one will never meet takes a toll. (Perhaps you have experienced this when feeling ignored in a chat room or when your e-mail is not answered.) The researchers have had more than 5,000 participants from dozens of countries play a Web-based game of throwing a flying disk with two others (actually computer-generated fellow players). Those ostracized by the other players experienced poorer moods and became more likely to conform to others' wrong judgments on a subsequent perceptual task. Exclusion hurts longest for anxious people (Zadro & others, 2006). It hurts more for younger than older adults (Hawkley & others, 2011). And it hurts no less when it comes from a group that the rest of society spurns—Australian KKK members in one experiment (Gonsalkorale & Williams, 2006).

Williams and colleagues (2000) found ostracism stressful even when each of them was ignored for an agreed-upon day by the unresponsive four others. Contrary to their expectations that this would be a laughter-filled role-playing game, the simulated ostracism disrupted work, interfered with pleasant social functioning, and "caused temporary concern, anxiety, paranoia, and general fragility of spirit." To thwart our deep need to belong is to unsettle our life.

Ostracized people exhibit heightened activity in a brain cortex area that also activates in response to physical pain. Ostracism's social pain, much like physical pain, increases aggression (Riva & others, 2011). Hurt feelings are also embodied in a depressed heart rate (Moor & others, 2010). Heartbreak makes for heart brake.

Indeed, the pain of social rejection is so real that a pain-relieving Tylenol can reduce hurt feelings (DeWall & others, 2010, 2011). Ostracism's opposite—feeling love—activates brain reward systems. When looking at their beloved's picture, deeply in love university students feel markedly less thermal pain (Younger & others, 2010). Ostracism is a real pain. And love is a natural painkiller.

Asked to recall a time when they were socially excluded—perhaps left alone in the dorm when others went out—people in one experiment even perceived the room temperature as five degrees colder than did those asked to recall a social acceptance experience (Zhong & Leonardelli, 2008). Such recollections come easily: People remember and relive past social pain more easily than past physical pain (Chen & others, 2008).

Roy Baumeister (2005) finds a silver lining in the rejection research. When recently excluded people experience a safe opportunity to make a new friend, they "seem willing and even eager to take it." They become more attentive to smiling, accepting faces (DeWall & others, 2009). An exclusion experience also triggers increased mimicry of others' behavior as a nonconscious effort to build rapport (Lakin & others, 2008). And at a societal level, notes Baumeister, meeting the need to belong should pay dividends.

> My colleagues in sociology have pointed out that minority groups who feel excluded show many of the same patterns that our laboratory manipulations elicit: high rates of aggression and antisocial behavior, decreased willingness to cooperate and obey rules, poorer intellectual performance, more self-destructive acts, short-term focus, and the like. If we could promote a more inclusive society, in which more people feel themselves accepted as valued members, some of these tragic patterns might be reduced.

CONCEPTS TO REMEMBER

proximity   Geographical nearness. Proximity (more precisely, "functional distance") powerfully predicts liking.

mere-exposure effect   The tendency for novel stimuli to be liked more or rated more positively after the rater has been repeatedly exposed to them.

matching phenomenon   The tendency for men and women to choose as partners those who are a "good match" in attractiveness and other traits.

physical-attractiveness stereotype   The presumption that physically attractive people possess other socially desirable traits as well: What is beautiful is good.

complementarity   The popularly supposed tendency, in a relationship between two people, for each to complete what is missing in the other.

need to belong   A motivation to bond with others in relationships that provide ongoing, positive interactions.

❖

The Ups and Downs of Love

Loving is more complex than liking and thus more difficult to measure, more perplexing to study. People yearn for it, live for it, die for it.

Most attraction researchers have studied what is most easily studied—responses during brief encounters between strangers. The influences on our initial liking of another—proximity, attractiveness, similarity, being liked, and other rewarding traits—also influence our long-term, close relationships. The impressions that dating couples quickly form of each other therefore provide a clue to their long-term future (Berg, 1984; Berg & McQuinn, 1986). Indeed, if North American romances flourished *randomly,* without regard to proximity and similarity, then most Catholics (being a minority) would marry Protestants, most Blacks would marry Whites, and college graduates would be as apt to marry high school dropouts as fellow graduates.

So first impressions are important. Nevertheless, long-term loving is not merely an intensification of initial liking. Social psychologists therefore study enduring, close relationships.

PASSIONATE LOVE

The first step in scientifically studying romantic love, as in studying any variable, is to decide how to define and measure it. We have ways to measure aggression, altruism, prejudice, and liking—but how do we measure love?

"How do I love thee? Let me count the ways," wrote Elizabeth Barrett Browning. Social scientists have counted various ways. Psychologist

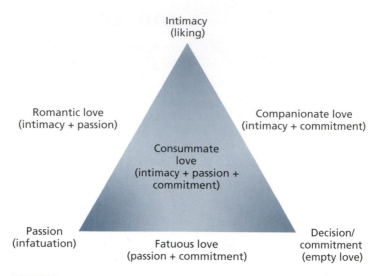

FIGURE 27-1
Robert Sternberg's (1988) conception of kinds of loving as combinations of three basic components of love.

Robert Sternberg (1998) views love as a triangle consisting of three components: passion, intimacy, and commitment (Figure 27-1).

Some elements of love are common to all loving relationships: mutual understanding, giving and receiving support, enjoying the loved one's company. Some elements are distinctive. If we experience passionate love, we express it physically, we expect the relationship to be exclusive, and we are intensely fascinated with our partner. You can see it in our eyes.

Zick Rubin (1973) confirmed this. He administered a love scale to hundreds of University of Michigan dating couples. Later, from behind a one-way mirror in a laboratory waiting room, he clocked eye contact among "weak-love" and "strong-love" couples. Other research indicates that mutual gaze conveys liking and averted eye gaze conveys ostracism (Wirth & others, 2010). So Rubin's result will not surprise you: The strong-love couples gave themselves away by gazing long into each other's eyes. When talking, they also nod their head, smile naturally, and lean forward (Gonzaga & others, 2001). When observing speed-daters, it takes but a few seconds to make a reasonably accurate guess as to whether one person is interested in another (Place & others, 2009).

Passionate love is emotional, exciting, intense. Elaine Hatfield (1988) defined it as *"a state of intense longing for union with another"* (p. 193). If reciprocated, one feels fulfilled and joyous; if not, one feels empty or despairing. Like other forms of emotional excitement, passionate love involves a roller coaster of elation and gloom, tingling exhilaration and dejected misery.

www.mhhe.com/myerssspe

Activity
27.1

A Theory of Passionate Love

To explain passionate love, Hatfield notes that a given state of arousal can be steered into any of several emotions, depending on how we attribute the arousal. An emotion involves both body and mind—both arousal and the way we interpret and label that arousal. Imagine yourself with pounding heart and trembling hands: Are you experiencing fear, anxiety, joy? Physiologically, one emotion is quite similar to another. You may therefore experience the arousal as joy if you are in a euphoric situation, anger if your environment is hostile, and passionate love if the situation is romantic. In this view, passionate love is the psychological experience of being biologically aroused by someone we find attractive.

If indeed passion is a revved-up state that's labeled "love," then whatever revs one up should intensify feelings of love. In several experiments, college men aroused sexually by reading or viewing erotic materials had a heightened response to a woman—for example, by scoring much higher on a love scale when describing their girlfriend (Carducci & others, 1978; Dermer & Pyszczynski, 1978; Stephan & others, 1971). Proponents of the **two-factor theory of emotion**, developed by Stanley Schachter and Jerome Singer (1962), argue that when the revved-up men responded to a woman, they easily misattributed some of their own arousal to her.

According to this theory, being aroused by *any* source should intensify passionate feelings—provided that the mind is free to attribute some of the arousal to a romantic stimulus. In a dramatic and famous demonstration of this phenomenon, Donald Dutton and Arthur Aron (1974) had an attractive young woman approach individual young men as they crossed a narrow, wobbly, 450-foot-long suspension walkway hanging 230 feet above British Columbia's rocky Capilano River. The woman asked each man to help her fill out a class questionnaire. When he had finished, she scribbled her name and phone number and invited him to call if he wanted to hear more about the project. Most accepted the phone number, and half who did so called. By contrast, men approached by the woman on a low, solid bridge, rarely called. Once again, physical arousal accentuated romantic responses.

Scary movies, roller-coaster rides, and physical exercise have the same effect, especially to those we find attractive (Foster & others, 1998; White & Kight, 1984).

As this suggests, passionate love is a biological as well as a psychological phenomenon. Research by social psychologist Arthur Aron and colleagues (2005) indicates that passionate love engages dopamine-rich brain areas associated with reward (Figure 27-2).

Love is also a social phenomenon. Love is more than lust, notes Ellen Berscheid (2010). Supplement sexual desire with a deepening friendship and the result is romantic love. Passionate love = lust + attachment.

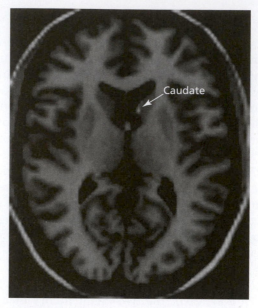

FIGURE 27-2
This is your brain on love. MRI scans from young adults intensely in love revealed areas, such as the caudate nucleus, that became more active when gazing at the loved-one's photo (but not when gazing at the photo of another acquaintance).
Source: Aron & others (2005).

Variations in Love: Culture and Gender

There is always a temptation to assume that most others share our feelings and ideas. We assume, for example, that love is a precondition for marriage. Most cultures—89 percent in one analysis of 166 cultures—do have a concept of romantic love, as reflected in flirtation or couples running off together (Jankowiak & Fischer, 1992). But in some cultures, notably those practicing arranged marriages, love tends to follow rather than to precede marriage. Even in the individualistic United States as recently as the 1960s, only 24 percent of college women and 65 percent of college men considered (as do nearly all collegians today) love to be the basis of marriage (Reis & Aron, 2008).

Gender

Do males and females differ in how they experience passionate love? Studies of men and women falling in and out of love reveal some surprises. Most people, including the writer of the following letter to a newspaper advice columnist, suppose that women fall in love more readily:

> Dear Dr. Brothers:
> Do you think it's effeminate for a 19-year-old guy to fall in love so hard it's like the whole world's turned around? I think I'm really crazy because this has happened several times now and love just seems to hit me on the head from nowhere. . . . My father says this is the way girls fall in love and that it doesn't happen this way with guys—at least it's not supposed to. I can't change how I am in this way but it kind of worries me.—P.T. (quoted by Dion & Dion, 1985)

P.T. would be reassured by the repeated finding that it is actually men who tend to fall in love more readily (Ackerman & others, 2011; Dion & Dion, 1985). Men also seem to fall out of love more slowly and are less likely than women to break up a premarital romance. In heterosexual relationships, it's men, not women, who most often are first to say "I love you" (Ackerman & others, 2011).

Once in love, however, women are typically as emotionally involved as their partners, or more so. They are more likely to report feeling euphoric and "giddy and carefree," as if they were "floating on a cloud." Women are also somewhat more likely than men to focus on the intimacy of the friendship and on their concern for their partner. Men are more likely than women to think about the playful and physical aspects of the relationship (Hendrick & Hendrick, 1995).

COMPANIONATE LOVE

Activity
27.2

Although passionate love burns hot, like a relationship booster rocket, it eventually simmers down once the relationship reaches a stable orbit. The high of romance may be sustained for a few months, even a couple of years. But no high lasts forever. "When you're in love it's the most glorious two-and-a-half days of your life," jested comedian Richard Lewis. The novelty, the intense absorption in the other, the tingly thrill of the romance, the giddy "floating on a cloud" feeling, fades. After 2 years of marriage, spouses express affection about half as often as when they were newlyweds (Huston & Chorost, 1994). About 4 years after marriage, the divorce rate peaks in cultures worldwide (Fisher, 1994). If a close relationship is to endure, it will settle to a steadier but still warm afterglow that Hatfield calls **companionate love**. The passion-facilitating hormones (testosterone, dopamine, adrenaline) subside, while the hormone oxytocin supports feelings of attachment and trust (Taylor & others, 2010).

Unlike the wild emotions of passionate love, companionate love is lower key; it's a deep, affectionate attachment. It activates different parts of the brain (Aron & others, 2005). And it is just as real. Nisa, a

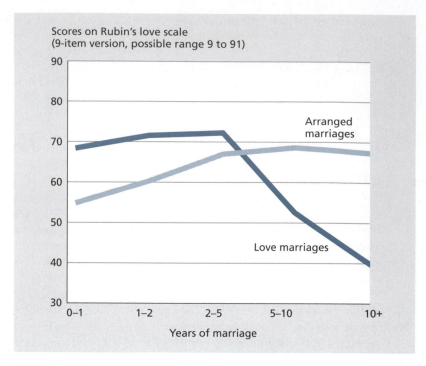

FIGURE 27-3
Romantic love between partners in arranged or love marriages in Jaipur, India. Source: Data from Gupta & Singh (1982).

!Kung San woman of the African Kalahari Desert, explains: "When two people are first together, their hearts are on fire and their passion is very great. After a while, the fire cools and that's how it stays. They continue to love each other, but it's in a different way—warm and dependable" (Shostak, 1981).

The cooling of passionate love over time and the growing importance of other factors, such as shared values, can be seen in the feelings of those who enter arranged versus love-based marriages in India. Usha Gupta and Pushpa Singh (1982) asked 50 couples in Jaipur, India, to complete a love scale. They found that those who married for love reported diminishing feelings of love after a 5-year newlywed period. By contrast, those in arranged marriages reported *more* love if their marriage was 5 or more years old (Figure 27-3; for other data on the seeming success of arranged marriages, see J. E. Myers & others [2005], Thakar & Epstein [2011], and Yelsma & Athappilly [1988]).

The cooling of intense romantic love often triggers a period of disillusion, especially among those who believe that romantic love is essential both for a marriage and for its continuation. Compared with North Americans, Asians tend to focus less on personal feelings and more on the practical aspects of social attachments (Dion & Dion, 1988; Sprecher & Toro-Morn, 2002; Sprecher & others, 1994). Thus, they are less vulnerable to disillusionment. Asians are also less prone to the self-focused individualism that in the long run can undermine a relationship and lead to divorce (Dion & Dion, 1991, 1996; Triandis & others, 1988).

The decline in intense mutual fascination may be natural and adaptive for species survival. The result of passionate love frequently is children, whose survival is aided by the parents' waning obsession with each other (Kenrick & Trost, 1987). Nevertheless, for those married more than 20 years, some of the lost romantic feeling is often renewed as the family nest empties and the parents are once again free to focus their attention on each other (Hatfield & Sprecher, 1986; White & Edwards, 1990). "No man or woman really knows what love is until they have been married a quarter of a century," said Mark Twain. If the relationship has been intimate, mutually rewarding, and rooted in a shared life history, companionate love deepens. But what is intimacy? And what is mutually rewarding?

MAINTAINING CLOSE RELATIONSHIPS

What factors influence the ups and downs of our close relationships? Let's consider two: equity and intimacy.

Equity

If each partner pursues his or her personal desires willy-nilly, the relationship will die. Therefore, our society teaches us to exchange rewards by what Elaine Hatfield, William Walster, and Ellen Berscheid (1978) have called an **equity** principle of attraction: What you and your partner get out of a relationship should be proportional to what you each put into it. If two people receive equal outcomes, they should contribute equally; otherwise one or the other will feel it is unfair. If both feel their outcomes correspond to the assets and efforts each contributes, then both perceive equity.

Strangers and casual acquaintances maintain equity by exchanging benefits: You lend me your class notes; later, I'll lend you mine. I invite you to my party; you invite me to yours. Those in an enduring relationship, including roommates and those in love, do not feel bound to trade similar benefits—notes for notes, parties for parties (Berg, 1984). They feel freer to maintain equity by exchanging a variety of benefits ("When you drop by to lend me your notes, why don't you stay for dinner?") and eventually to stop keeping track of who owes whom.

Long-Term Equity

Is it crass to suppose that friendship and love are rooted in an equitable exchange of rewards? Don't we sometimes give in response to a loved one's need, without expecting anything in return? Indeed, those involved in an equitable, long-term relationship are unconcerned with short-term equity. Margaret Clark and Judson Mills (1979, 1993; Clark, 1984, 1986) have argued that people even take pains to *avoid* calculating any exchange benefits. When we help a good friend, we do not want instant repayment. If someone invites us for dinner, we wait before reciprocating, lest the person attribute the motive for our return invitation to be merely paying off a social debt. True friends tune into one another's needs even when reciprocation is impossible (Clark & others, 1986, 1989). Similarly, happily married people tend not to keep score of how much they are giving and getting (Buunk & Van Yperen, 1991; Clark & others, 2010). As people observe their partners being self-giving, their sense of trust grows (Wieselquist & others, 1999).

Previously we noted an equity principle at work in the matching phenomenon: People usually bring equal assets to romantic relationships. Often, they are matched for attractiveness, status, and so forth. If they are mismatched in one area, such as attractiveness, they tend to be mismatched in some other area, such as status. But in total assets, they are an equitable match. No one says, and few even think, "I'll trade you my good looks for your big income." But especially in relationships that last, equity is the rule.

Perceived Equity and Satisfaction

In one Pew Research Center (2007b) survey, "sharing household chores" ranked third (after "faithfulness" and a "happy sexual relationship") among nine things that people saw as marks of successful marriages. Indeed, those in an equitable relationship are typically content (Fletcher & others, 1987; Hatfield & others, 1985; Van Yperen & Buunk, 1990). Those who perceive their relationship as inequitable feel discomfort: The one who has the better deal may feel guilty and the one who senses a raw deal may feel strong irritation. (Given the self-serving bias—most husbands perceive themselves as contributing more housework than their wives credit them for—the person who is "overbenefited" is less sensitive to the inequity.)

Robert Schafer and Patricia Keith (1980) surveyed several hundred married couples of all ages, noting those who felt their marriages were somewhat unfair because one spouse contributed too little to the cooking, housekeeping, parenting, or providing. Inequity took its toll: Those who perceived inequity also felt more distressed and depressed. During the child-rearing years, when wives often feel underbenefited and husbands overbenefited, marital satisfaction tends to dip. During the honeymoon and empty-nest stages, spouses are more likely to perceive equity and to feel satisfaction with their marriages (Feeney & others, 1994). When both partners freely give and receive, and make decisions together, the odds of sustained, satisfying love are good.

Self-Disclosure

Deep, companionate relationships are intimate. They enable us to be known as we truly are and to feel accepted. We discover this delicious experience in a good marriage or a close friendship—a relationship where trust displaces anxiety and where we are free to open ourselves without fear of losing the other's affection (Holmes & Rempel, 1989). Such relationships are characterized by what the late Sidney Jourard called **self-disclosure** (Derlega & others, 1993). As a relationship grows, self-disclosing partners reveal more and more of themselves to each other; their knowledge of each other penetrates to deeper levels. In relationships that flourish, much of this self-disclosure shares successes and triumphs, and mutual delight over good happenings (Gable & others, 2006). When a friend rejoices with us over good news, it not only increases our joy about the happy event but also helps us feel better about the friendship (Reis & others, 2010).

Experiments have probed both the *causes* and the *effects* of self-disclosure. When are people most willing to disclose intimate information concerning "what you like and don't like about yourself" or "what you're most ashamed and most proud of"? And what effects do such revelations have on those who reveal and receive them?

The most reliable finding is the **disclosure reciprocity** effect: Disclosure begets disclosure (Berg, 1987; Miller, 1990; Reis & Shaver, 1988). We reveal more to those who have been open with us. But intimate disclosure is seldom instant. (If it is, the person may seem indiscreet and unstable.) Appropriate intimacy progresses like a dance: I reveal a little, you reveal a little—but not too much. You then reveal more, and I reciprocate.

For those in love, deepening intimacy is exciting. "Rising intimacy will create a strong sense of passion," note Roy Baumeister and Ellen Bratslavsky (1999). This helps explain why those who remarry after the loss of a spouse tend to begin the new marriage with an increased frequency of sex, and why passion often rides highest when intimacy is restored following severe conflict.

Some people—most of them women—are especially skilled "openers"; they easily elicit intimate disclosures from others, even from those who normally don't reveal very much of themselves (Miller & others, 1983; Pegalis & others, 1994; Shaffer & others, 1996). Such people tend to be good listeners. During conversation, they maintain attentive facial expressions and appear to be comfortably enjoying themselves (Purvis & others, 1984). They may also express interest by uttering supportive phrases while their conversational partner is speaking. They are what psychologist Carl Rogers (1980) called " growth-promoting" listeners—people who are genuine in revealing their own feelings, who are accepting of others' feelings, and who are empathic, sensitive, reflective listeners.

What are the effects of such self-disclosure? Humanistic psychologist Sidney Jourard (1964) argued that dropping our masks, letting ourselves be known as we are, nurtures love. He presumed that it is gratifying to open up to another and then to receive the trust another implies by being open with us. People feel better on days when they have disclosed something significant about themselves, such as their being lesbian or gay, and feel worse when concealing their identity (Beals & others, 2009). Those whose days include more deep or substantive discussions, rather than just small talk, tend to be happier. That's what Mathias Mehl and co-researchers (2010) found after equipping 70 undergraduates with recording devices that snatched 30-second conversational snippets five times each hour over 4 days.

Having an intimate friend with whom we can discuss threats to our self-image seems to help us survive stress (Swann & Predmore, 1985). A true friendship is a special relationship that helps us cope with our other relationships. "When I am with my friend," reflected the Roman playwright Seneca, "methinks I am alone, and as much at liberty to speak anything as to think it." At its best, marriage is such a friendship, sealed by commitment.

Intimate self-disclosure is also one of companionate love's delights. The most self-revealing dating and married couples tend to enjoy the most satisfying and enduring relationships (Berg & McQuinn, 1986; Hendrick & others, 1988; Sprecher, 1987). For example, in a study of newlywed couples who were all equally in love, those who most deeply and accurately knew each other were most likely to enjoy enduring love (Neff & Karney, 2005). Married partners who most strongly agree that "I try to share my most intimate thoughts and feelings with my partner" tend to have the most satisfying marriages (Sanderson & Cantor, 2001). For very reticent people, marriage may not be as satisfying as it is for those more willing to share their feelings (Baker & McNulty, 2010).

In a Gallup national marriage survey, 75 percent of those who prayed with their spouses (and 57 percent of those who didn't) reported their marriages as very happy (Greeley, 1991). Among believers, shared prayer from the heart is a humbling, intimate, soulful exposure (Beach & others, 2011). Those who pray together also more often say they discuss their marriages together, respect their spouses, and rate their spouses as skilled lovers.

Researchers have also found that women are often more willing to disclose their fears and weaknesses than are men (Cunningham, 1981). As feminist writer Kate Millett (1975) put it, "Women express, men repress." Small wonder that both men and women report friendships with women to be more intimate, enjoyable, and nurturing, and that on social networks, both males and females seem to prefer female friends (Thelwall, 2008).

Nevertheless, men today, particularly men with egalitarian gender-role attitudes, seem increasingly willing to reveal intimate feelings and to enjoy the satisfactions that accompany a relationship of mutual trust and self-disclosure. And that, say Arthur Aron and Elaine Aron (1994), is the essence of love—two selves connecting, disclosing, and identifying with each other; two selves, each retaining their individuality, yet sharing activities, delighting in similarities, and mutually supporting. The result for many romantic partners is "self–other integration": intertwined self-concepts (Slotter & Gardner, 2009).

To promote self-disclosure in ongoing dating relationships, Richard Slatcher and James Pennebaker (2006) invited one member of 86 couples to spend 20 minutes on each of 3 days writing their deepest thoughts and feelings about the relationship (or, in a control condition, writing merely about their daily activities). Those who pondered and journaled their feelings expressed more emotion to their partners in the days following. Three months later, 77 percent were still dating (compared with 52 percent in the control group).

Does the Internet Create Intimacy or Isolation?

As a reader of this college text, you are almost surely one of the world's 2.3 billion (as of 2012) Internet users. It took the telephone seven decades to go from 1 percent to 75 percent penetration of North American households. Internet access reached 75 percent penetration in approximately 7 years (Putnam, 2000). You enjoy social networking, Web surfing, texting, and perhaps participating in listservs, news groups, or chat rooms (Internetworldstats.com).

www.mhhe.com/myerseesge

Activity
27.3

What do you think: Is computer-mediated communication within virtual communities a poor substitute for in-person relationships? Or is it a wonderful way to widen our social circles? Does the Internet do more to connect people or to drain time from face-to-face relationships? Consider the emerging debate.

Point The Internet, like the printing press and the telephone, expands communication, and communication enables relationships. Printing reduced face-to-face storytelling and the telephone reduced face-to-face chats, but both enable us to reach and be reached by people without limitations of time and distance. Social relations involve networking, and the Net is the ultimate network. It enables efficient networking with family, friends, and kindred spirits—including people we otherwise never would have found, be they fellow MS patients, St. Nicholas collectors, or Harry Potter fans.

Counterpoint True, but computer communication is impoverished. It lacks the nuances of eye-to-eye contact punctuated with nonverbal cues and physical touches. Except for simple emoticons—such as a :-) for an unnuanced smile—electronic messages are devoid of gestures, facial expressions, and tones of voice. No wonder it's so easy to misread them. The absence of expressive e-motion makes for ambiguous emotion.

For example, vocal nuances can signal whether a statement is serious, kidding, or sarcastic. Research by Justin Kruger and colleagues
(2006) shows that communicators often think their "just kidding" intent
is equally clear, whether e-mailed or spoken. Actually, when e-mailed, the
intent often isn't clear. Thanks also to one's anonymity in virtual discussions, the result is sometimes a hostile "flame war."

A Stanford University survey found that 25 percent of more than 4,000
adults surveyed reported that their time online had reduced time spent in
person and on the phone with family and friends (Nie & Erbring, 2000).
The Internet, like television, diverts time from real relationships. Internet
romances are not the developmental equivalent of real dating. Cybersex
is artificial intimacy. Individualized web-based entertainment displaces
getting together for bridge. Such artificiality and isolation is regrettable
because our ancestral history predisposes our needing real-time relationships, replete with smirks and smiles.

Point   But most folks don't perceive the Internet to be isolating. Another
national survey found that "Internet users in general—and online women
in particular—believe that their use of e-mail has strengthened their relationships and increased their contact with relatives and friends" (Pew
Research Center, 2000). Internet use may displace in-person intimacy, but
it also displaces television watching. If one-click cyber-shopping is bad for
your local bookstore, it frees time for relationships. Telecommuting does
the same, enabling people to work from home and thereby spend more
time with their families.

And why say that computer-formed relationships are unreal? On
the Internet, your looks and location cease to matter. Your appearance,
age, and race don't deter people from relating to you based on what's
more genuinely important—your shared interests and values. In workplace and professional networks, computer-mediated discussions are less
influenced by status and are therefore more candid and equally partici-
patory. Computer-mediated communication fosters more spontaneous
self-disclosure than face-to-face conversation (Joinson, 2001).

Most Internet flirtations go nowhere. "Everyone I know who has tried
online dating . . . agrees that we loathe spending (wasting?) hours gab-
bing to someone and then meeting him and realizing that he is a creep,"
observed one Toronto woman (Dicum, 2003). This experience would not
surprise Eli Finkel and his fellow social psychologists (2012). Nearly a century of research on romantic compatibility leads them to conclude that the
formulas of online matchmaking sites are unlikely to do what they claim.
The best predictors of relationship success, such as communication patterns and other indications of compatibility, emerge only *after* people meet
and get to know one another.

Nevertheless, friendships and romantic relationships that form on the
Internet are more likely than in-person relationships to last for at least

2 years, report Katelyn McKenna and John Bargh and their colleagues (Bargh & others, 2002; Bargh & McKenna, 2004; McKenna & Bargh, 1998, 2000; McKenna & others, 2002). In one experiment, they found that people disclosed more, with greater honesty and less posturing, when they met people online. They also felt more liking for people with whom they conversed online for 20 minutes than for those met for the same time face-to-face. This was true even when they unknowingly met the very same person in both contexts. People surveyed similarly feel that Internet friendships are as real, important, and close as offline relationships.

Counterpoint   The Internet allows people to be who they really are, but also to feign who they really aren't, sometimes in the interests of sexual exploitation. Internet sexual media, like other forms of pornography, likely serve to distort people's perceptions of sexual reality, decrease the attractiveness of their real-life partner, prime men to perceive women in sexual terms, make sexual coercion seem more trivial, provide mental scripts for how to act in sexual situations, increase arousal, and lead to disinhibition and imitation of loveless sexual behaviors.

Finally, suggests Robert Putnam (2000), the social benefits of computer-mediated communication are constrained by "cyberbalkanization." The Internet enables those of us with hearing loss to network, but it also enables White supremacists to find one another and thus contributes to social and political polarization.

As the debate over the Internet's social consequences continues, "the most important question," says Putnam (p. 180), will be "not what the Internet will do to us, but what we will do with it? . . . How can we harness this promising technology for thickening community ties? How can we develop the technology to enhance social presence, social feedback, and social cues? How can we use the prospect of fast, cheap communication to enhance the now fraying fabric of our real communities?"

*E*NDING RELATIONSHIPS

In 1971, a man wrote a love poem to his bride, slipped it into a bottle, and dropped it into the Pacific Ocean between Seattle and Hawaii. A decade later, a jogger found it on a Guam beach:

> If, by the time this letter reaches you, I am old and gray, I know that our love will be as fresh as it is today.
> It may take a week or it may take years for this note to find you. . . . If this should never reach you, it will still be written in my heart that I will go to extreme means to prove my love for you. Your husband, Bob.

The woman to whom the love note was addressed was reached by phone. When the note was read to her, she burst out laughing. And the more she heard, the harder she laughed. "We're divorced," she finally said, and slammed down the phone.

So it often goes. Smart brains can make dumb decisions. Comparing their unsatisfying relationship with the support and affection they imagine are available elsewhere, many relationships end. Each year, Canada and the United States record one divorce for every two marriages. As economic and social barriers to divorce weakened during the 1960s and 1970s, thanks partly to women's increasing employment, divorce rates rose. "We are living longer, but loving more briefly," quipped Os Guiness (1993, p. 309).

Britain's royal House of Windsor knows well the hazards of modern marriage. The fairy-tale marriages of Princess Margaret, Princess Anne, Prince Charles, and Prince Andrew all crumbled, smiles replaced with stony stares. Soon after her 1986 marriage to Prince Andrew, Sarah Ferguson gushed, "I love his wit, his charm, his looks. I worship him." Andrew reciprocated her euphoria: "She is the best thing in my life." Six years later, Andrew, having decided her friends were "philistines," and Sarah, having derided Andrew's boorish behavior as "terribly gauche," called it quits (*Time*, 1992).

Who Divorces?

To predict a culture's divorce rates, it helps to know its values (Triandis, 1994). Individualistic cultures (where love is a feeling and people ask, "What does my heart say?") have more divorce than do communal cultures (where love entails obligation and people ask, "What will other people say?"). Individualists marry "for as long as we both shall love," collectivists more often for life. Individualists expect more passion and personal fulfillment in a marriage, which puts greater pressure on the relationship (Dion & Dion, 1993). In one pair of surveys, "keeping romance alive" was rated as important to a good marriage by 78 percent of American women and 29 percent of Japanese women (*American Enterprise*, 1992).

Even in Western society, however, those who enter relationships with a long-term orientation and an intention to persist do experience healthier, less turbulent, and more durable partnerships (Arriaga, 2001; Arriaga & Agnew, 2001). Enduring relationships are rooted in enduring love and satisfaction, but also in fear of the termination cost, a sense of moral obligation, and inattention to possible alternative partners (Adams & Jones, 1997; Maner & others, 2009; Miller, 1997). For those determined that their marriage last, it usually does.

Those whose commitment to a union outlasts the desires that gave birth to it will endure times of conflict and unhappiness. One national survey found that 86 percent of those who were unhappily married but who stayed with the marriage were, when reinterviewed 5 years later, now mostly "very" or "quite" happy with their marriages (Popenoe, 2002).

By contrast, "narcissists"—those more focused on their own desires and image—enter relationships with less commitment and less likelihood of long-term relational success (Campbell & Foster, 2002).

Risk of divorce also depends on who marries whom (Fergusson & others, 1984; Myers, 2000a; Tzeng, 1992). People usually stay married if they

- married after age 20.
- both grew up in stable, two-parent homes.
- dated for a long while before marriage.
- are well and similarly educated.
- enjoy a stable income from a good job.
- live in a small town or on a farm.
- did not cohabit or become pregnant before marriage.
- are religiously committed.
- are of similar age, faith, and education.

None of those predictors, by itself, is essential to a stable marriage. Moreover, they are correlates of enduring marriages, not necessarily causes. But if none of those things is true for someone, marital breakdown is an almost sure bet. If all are true, they are very likely to stay together until death. The English perhaps had it right when, several centuries ago, they presumed that the temporary intoxication of passionate love was a foolish basis for permanent marital decisions. Better, they felt, to choose a mate based on stable friendship and compatible backgrounds, interests, habits, and values (Stone, 1977).

The Detachment Process

Our close relationships help define the social identity that shapes our self-concept (Slotter & others, 2010). Thus, much as we experience life's best moments when relationships begin—when having a baby, making a friend, falling in love—so we experience life's worst moments when relationships end, with death or a broken bond (Jaremka & others, 2011). Severing bonds produces a predictable sequence of agitated preoccupation with the lost partner, followed by deep sadness and, eventually, the beginnings of emotional detachment, a letting go of the old while focusing on someone new, and a renewed sense of self (Hazan & Shaver, 1994; Lewandowski & Bizzoco, 2007; Spielmann & others, 2009). Even newly separated couples who have long ago ceased feeling affection are often surprised at their desire to be near the former partner. Deep and long-standing attachments seldom break quickly; detaching is a process, not an event.

Among dating couples, the closer and longer the relationship and the fewer the available alternatives, the more painful the breakup

(Simpson, 1987). Surprisingly, Roy Baumeister and Sara Wotman (1992) report that, months or years later, people recall more pain over spurning someone's love than over having been spurned. Their distress arises from guilt over hurting someone, from upset over the heartbroken lover's persistence, or from uncertainty over how to respond. Among married couples, breakup has additional costs: shocked parents and friends, guilt over broken vows, anguish over reduced household income, and possibly restricted parental rights. Still, each year millions of couples are willing to pay such costs to extricate themselves from what they perceive as the greater costs of continuing a painful, unrewarding relationship. Such costs include, in one study of 328 married couples, a 10-fold increase in depression symptoms when a marriage is marked by discord rather than satisfaction (O'Leary & others, 1994). When, however, a marriage is "very happy," life as a whole usually seems "very happy" (Figure 27-4).

When relationships suffer, those without better alternatives or who feel invested in a relationship (through time, energy, mutual friends, possessions, and perhaps children) will seek alternatives to exiting the relationship. Caryl Rusbult and colleagues (1986, 1987, 1998) explored three ways of coping with a failing relationship. Some people exhibit *loyalty*— by waiting for conditions to improve. The problems are too painful to

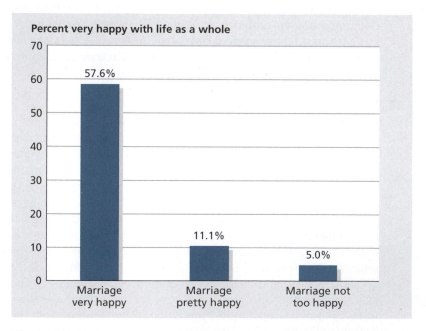

FIGURE 27-4
National opinion research center surveys of 23,076 married Americans, 1972–2004.

confront and the risks of separation are too great, so the loyal partner per-
severes, hoping the good old days will return. Others (especially men)
exhibit *neglect;* they ignore the partner and allow the relationship to dete-
riorate. With painful dissatisfactions ignored, an insidious emotional un-
coupling ensues as the partners talk less and begin redefining their lives
without each other. Still others will *voice* their concerns and take active
steps to improve the relationship by discussing problems, seeking advice,
and attempting to change.

Study after study—in fact, 115 studies of 45,000 couples—reveal that unhappy couples disagree, command, criticize, and put down. Happy couples
more often agree, approve, assent, and laugh (Karney & Bradbury, 1995;
Noller & Fitzpatrick, 1990). After observing 2,000 couples, John Gottman
(1994, 1998, 2005) noted that healthy marriages were not necessarily devoid
of conflict. Rather, they were marked by an ability to reconcile differences
and to overbalance criticism with affection. In successful marriages, positive interactions (smiling, touching, complimenting, laughing) outnumbered
negative interactions (sarcasm, disapproval, insults) by at least a five-to-one
ratio.

It's not distress and arguments that predict divorce, add Ted Huston
and colleagues (2001) from their following of newlyweds through time.
(Most newlyweds experience conflict.) Rather, it's coldness, disillusionment, and hopelessness that predict a dim marital future. This is especially
so, observed William Swann and associates (2003, 2006), when inhibited
men are coupled with critical women.

Successful couples have learned, sometimes aided by communication training, to restrain the poisonous put-downs and gut-level reactions and to think and behave more positively (McNulty, 2010). They
fight fairly (by stating feelings without insulting). They depersonalize
conflict with comments such as "I know it's not your fault" (Markman
& others, 1988; Notarius & Markman, 1993; Yovetich & Rusbult, 1994).
Would unhappy relationships get better if the partners agreed to *act* more
as happy couples do—by complaining and criticizing less? By affirming
and agreeing more? By setting aside times to voice their concerns? By
praying or playing together daily? As attitudes trail behaviors, do affec-
tions trail actions?

Joan Kellerman, James Lewis, and James Laird (1989) wondered.
They knew that among couples passionately in love, eye gazing is typically prolonged and mutual (Rubin, 1973). Would intimate eye gazing
similarly stir feelings between those not in love (much as 45 minutes of
escalating self-disclosure evoked feelings of closeness among those unacquainted students)? To find out, they asked unacquainted male–female
pairs to gaze intently for 2 minutes either at each other's hands or into
each other's eyes. When they separated, the eye gazers reported a tingle
of attraction and affection toward each other. Simulating love had begun
to stir it.

By enacting and expressing love, researcher Robert Sternberg (1988) believes the passion of initial romance can evolve into enduring love:

> "Living happily ever after" need not be a myth, but if it is to be a reality, the happiness must be based upon different configurations of mutual feelings at various times in a relationship. Couples who expect their passion to last forever, or their intimacy to remain unchallenged, are in for disappointment. . . . We must constantly work at understanding, building, and rebuilding our loving relationships. Relationships are constructions, and they decay over time if they are not maintained and improved. We cannot expect a relationship simply to take care of itself, any more than we can expect that of a building. Rather, we must take responsibility for making our relationships the best they can be.

Given the psychological ingredients of marital happiness—kindred minds, social and sexual intimacy, equitable giving and receiving of emotional and material resources—it becomes possible to contest the French saying "Love makes the time pass and time makes love pass." But it takes effort to stem love's decay. It takes effort to carve out time each day to talk over the day's happenings. It takes effort to forgo nagging and bickering and instead to disclose and hear each other's hurts, concerns, and dreams. It takes effort to make a relationship into "a classless utopia of social equality" (Sarnoff & Sarnoff, 1989), in which both partners freely give and receive, share decision making, and enjoy life together.

CONCEPTS TO REMEMBER

passionate love A state of intense longing for union with another. Passionate lovers are absorbed in each other, feel ecstatic at attaining their partner's love, and are disconsolate on losing it.

two-factor theory of emotion Arousal $\times$ its label = emotion

companionate love The affection we feel for those with whom our lives are deeply intertwined.

equity A condition in which the outcomes people receive from a relationship are proportional to what they contribute to it. Note: Equitable outcomes needn't always be equal outcomes.

self-disclosure Revealing intimate aspects of oneself to others.

disclosure reciprocity The tendency for one person's intimacy of self-disclosure to match that of a conversational partner.

MODULE

28

❖

Causes of Conflict

There is a speech that has been spoken in many languages by the leaders of many countries. It goes like this: "The intentions of our country are entirely peaceful. Yet, we are also aware that other nations, with their new weapons, threaten us. Thus we must defend ourselves against attack. By so doing, we shall protect our way of life and preserve the peace" (Richardson, 1960). Almost every nation claims concern only for peace but, mistrusting other nations, arms itself in self-defense. The result is a world that has been spending $5 billion per day on arms and armies while hundreds of millions die of malnutrition and untreated disease (SIPRI, 2011).

The elements of such **conflict** (a perceived incompatibility of actions or goals) are similar at many levels: conflict between nations in an arms race, between religious factions disputing points of doctrine, between corporate executives and workers disputing salaries, and between bickering spouses. Let's consider these conflict elements.

SOCIAL DILEMMAS

Several of the problems that most threaten our human future—nuclear arms, climate change, overpopulation, natural-resource depletion—arise as various parties pursue their self-interests, ironically, to their collective detriment. One individual may think, "It would cost me a lot to buy expensive greenhouse emission controls. Besides, the greenhouse gases I personally generate are trivial." Many others reason similarly, and the result is a warming climate, melting ice cover, rising seas, and more extreme weather. Thus, choices that are individually rewarding become collectively punishing. We therefore have a dilemma: How can we reconcile individual self-interest with communal well-being?

To isolate and study that dilemma, social psychologists have used laboratory games that expose the heart of many real social conflicts. "Social psychologists who study conflict are in much the same position as the astronomers," noted conflict researcher Morton Deutsch (1999). "We cannot conduct true experiments with large-scale social events. But we can identify the conceptual similarities between the large scale and the small, as the astronomers have between the planets and Newton's apple. That is why the games people play as subjects in our laboratory may advance our understanding of war, peace, and social justice."

Let's consider two laboratory games that are each an example of a **social trap:** the Prisoner's Dilemma and the Tragedy of the Commons.

The Prisoner's Dilemma

This dilemma derives from an anecdote concerning two suspects being questioned separately by the district attorney (DA) (Rapoport, 1960). The DA knows they are jointly guilty but has only enough evidence to convict them of a lesser offense. So the DA creates an incentive for each one to confess privately:

- If Prisoner A confesses and Prisoner B doesn't, the DA will grant immunity to A and will use A's confession to convict B of a maximum offense (and vice versa if B confesses and A doesn't).
- If both confess, each will receive a moderate sentence.
- If neither prisoner confesses, each will be convicted of a lesser crime and receive a light sentence.

The matrix of Figure 28-1 summarizes the choices. If you were a prisoner faced with such a dilemma, with no chance to talk to the other prisoner, would you confess?

Many people say they would confess to be granted immunity, even though mutual *non*confession elicits lighter sentences than mutual confession. Perhaps this is because (as shown in the Figure 28-1 matrix) no matter what the other prisoner decides, each is better off confessing than being convicted individually. If the other also confesses, the sentence is moderate rather than severe. If the other does not confess, one goes free.

University students have faced variations of the Prisoner's Dilemma, with the choices being to defect or to cooperate, and the outcomes not being prison terms but chips, money, or course points. On any given decision, a person is better off defecting (because such behavior exploits the other's cooperation or protects against the other's exploitation). However—and here's the rub—by not cooperating, both parties end up far worse off

Activity
28.1

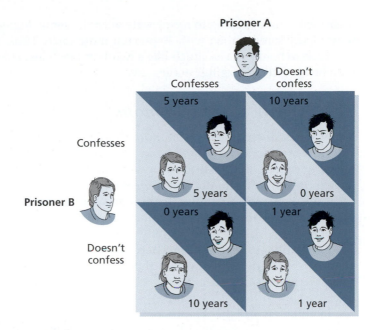

FIGURE 28-1
The classic prisoner's dilemma. In each box, the number above the diagonal is prisoner A's outcome. Thus, if both prisoners confess, both get five years. If neither confesses, each gets a year. If one confesses, that prisoner is set free in exchange for evidence used to convict the other of a crime bringing a 10-year sentence. If you were one of the prisoners, unable to communicate with your fellow prisoner, would you confess?

than if they had trusted each other and thus had gained a joint profit. This dilemma often traps each one in a maddening predicament in which both realize they *could* mutually profit. But unable to communicate, and mistrusting each other, they often become "locked in" to not cooperating. Outside the university, examples abound: seemingly intractable and costly conflicts between Israelis and Palestinians over borders, U.S. Republicans and Democrats over taxation and deficits, and professional athletes and team owners over pay.

Punishing another's lack of cooperation might seem like a smart strategy, but in the laboratory it can have counterproductive effects (Dreber & others, 2008). Punishment typically triggers retaliation, which means that those who punish tend to escalate conflict, worsening their outcomes, while nice guys finish first. What punishers see as a defensive reaction, recipients see as an aggressive escalation (Anderson & others, 2008). When hitting back, they may hit harder while seeing themselves as merely returning tit for tat. In one experiment, London volunteers used a mechanical device to press back on another's finger after receiving pressure on their own. While seeking to reciprocate with the same degree of pressure, they typically responded with 40 percent more force. Thus, touches soon escalated to hard presses, much like a child saying "I just *touched* him, and then he hit me!" (Shergill & others, 2003).

The Tragedy of the Commons

Many social dilemmas involve more than two parties. Climate change stems from deforestation and from the carbon dioxide emitted by vehicles, furnaces, and coal-fired power plants. Each gas-guzzling SUV contributes infinitesimally to the problem, and the harm each does is diffused over many people. To model such social predicaments, researchers have developed laboratory dilemmas that involve multiple people.

A metaphor for the insidious nature of social dilemmas is what ecologist Garrett Hardin (1968) called the Tragedy of the Commons. He derived the name from the centrally located grassy pasture in old English towns.

In today's world the "commons" can be air, water, fish, cookies, or any shared and limited resource. If all use the resource in moderation, it may replenish itself as rapidly as it's harvested. The grass will grow, the fish will reproduce, and the cookie jar will be restocked. If not, there occurs a tragedy of the commons. Imagine 100 farmers surrounding a commons capable of sustaining 100 cows. When each grazes one cow, the common feeding ground is optimally used. But then a farmer reasons, "If I put a second cow in the pasture, I'll double my output, minus the mere 1 percent overgrazing" and adds a second cow. So does each of the other farmers. The inevitable result? The Tragedy of the Commons—a mud field and famished cows.

Likewise, environmental pollution is the sum of many minor pollutions, each of which benefits the individual polluters much more than they could benefit themselves (and the environment) if they stopped polluting. We litter public places—dorm lounges, parks, zoos—while keeping our personal spaces clean. We deplete our natural resources because the immediate personal benefits of, for instance, taking a long, hot shower outweigh the seemingly inconsequential costs. Whalers knew others would exploit the whales if they didn't, and that taking a few whales would hardly diminish the species. Therein lies the tragedy. *Everybody's business (conservation) becomes nobody's business.*

Is such individualism uniquely American? Kaori Sato (1987) gave students in a more collective culture, Japan, opportunities to harvest—for actual money—trees from a simulated forest. The students shared equally the costs of planting the forest. The result was like those in Western cultures. More than half the trees were harvested before they had grown to the most profitable size.

Sato's forest reminds me of our home's cookie jar, which was restocked once a week. What we *should* have done was conserve cookies so that each day we could each enjoy two or three. But lacking regulation and fearing that other family members would soon deplete the resource, what we actually did was maximize our individual cookie consumption by downing one after the other. The result: Within 24 hours the cookie glut would often end, the jar sitting empty for the rest of the week.

The Prisoner's Dilemma and the Tragedy of the Commons games have several similar features. First, both games tempt people to *explain their own behavior situationally* ("I had to protect myself against exploitation by my opponent") and to explain their partners' behavior dispositionally ("she was greedy," "he was untrustworthy"). Most never realize that their counterparts are viewing them with the same fundamental attribution error (Gifford & Hine, 1997; Hine & Gifford, 1996). People with self-inflating, self-focused narcissistic tendencies are especially unlikely to empathize with others' perspectives (Campbell & others, 2005).

Second, *motives often change.* At first, people are eager to make some easy money, then to minimize their losses, and finally to save face and avoid defeat (Brockner & others, 1982; Teger, 1980). These shifting motives are strikingly similar to the shifting motives during the buildup of the 1960s Vietnam War. At first, President Johnson's speeches expressed concern for democracy, freedom, and justice. As the conflict escalated, his concern became protecting America's honor and avoiding the national humiliation of losing a war. A similar shift occurred during the war in Iraq, which was initially proposed as a response to Iraq's supposed weapons of mass destruction.

Third, most real-life conflicts, like the Prisoner's Dilemma and the Tragedy of the Commons, are **non-zero-sum games.** The two sides' profits and losses need not add up to zero. Both can win; both can lose. Each game pits the immediate interests of individuals against the well-being of the group. Each is a diabolical social trap that shows how, even when each individual behaves "rationally," harm can result. No malicious person planned for the earth's atmosphere to be warmed by a carbon dioxide blanket.

Not all self-serving behavior leads to collective doom. In a plentiful commons—as in the world of the eighteenth-century capitalist economist Adam Smith (1776, p. 18)—individuals who seek to maximize their own profit may also give the community what it needs: "It is not from the benevolence of the butcher, the brewer, or the baker, that we expect our dinner," he observed, "but from their regard to their own interest."

Resolving Social Dilemmas

Faced with social traps, how can we induce people to cooperate for their mutual betterment? Research with the laboratory dilemmas reveals several ways (Gifford & Hine, 1997).

Regulation

If taxes were entirely voluntary, how many would pay their full share? Modern societies do not depend on charity to pay for schools, parks, and social and military security. We also develop rules to safeguard our common good. Fishing and hunting have long been regulated by local seasons and limits; at the global level, an International Whaling Commission sets an agreed-upon "harvest" that enables whales to regenerate. Likewise, where fishing industries, such as the Alaskan halibut fishery, have implemented "catch shares"—guaranteeing each fisher a percentage of each year's allowable catch—competition and overfishing have been greatly reduced (Costello & others, 2008).

Small Is Beautiful

There is another way to resolve social dilemmas: Make the group small. In a small commons, each person feels more responsible and effective (Kerr, 1989). As a group grows larger, people become more likely to think, "I couldn't have made a difference anyway"—a common excuse for noncooperation (Kerr & Kaufman-Gilliland, 1997).

In small groups, people also feel more identified with a group's success. Residential stability also strengthens communal identity and procommunity behavior (Oishi & others, 2007). On the Pacific Northwest island where I grew up, our small neighborhood shared a communal water supply. On hot summer days when the reservoir ran low, a light came on, signaling our 15 families to conserve. Recognizing our responsibility to one another, and feeling that our conservation really mattered, each of us conserved. Never did the reservoir run dry. In a much larger commons—say, a city—voluntary conservation is less successful.

Communication

To resolve a social dilemma, people must communicate. In the laboratory as in real life, group communication sometimes degenerates into threats and name-calling (Deutsch & Krauss, 1960). More often, communication enables cooperation (Bornstein & others, 1988, 1989). Discussing the dilemma forges a group identity, which enhances concern for everyone's welfare. It devises group norms and expectations and pressures members to follow them. Especially when people are face-to-face, it enables them to commit themselves to cooperation (Bouas & Komorita, 1996; Drolet & Morris, 2000; Kerr & others, 1994, 1997; Pruitt, 1998).

Without communication, those who expect others not to cooperate will usually refuse to cooperate themselves (Messé & Sivacek, 1979; Pruitt & Kimmel, 1977). One who mistrusts is almost sure to be uncooperative (to protect against exploitation). Noncooperation, in turn, feeds further mistrust ("What else could I do? It's a dog-eat-dog world"). In experiments, communication reduces mistrust, enabling people to reach agreements that lead to their common betterment.

Changing the Payoffs

Laboratory cooperation rises when experimenters change the payoff matrix to reward cooperation and punish exploitation (Balliet & others, 2011). Changing payoffs also helps resolve actual dilemmas. In some cities, freeways clog and skies collect smog because people prefer the convenience of driving themselves directly to work. Each knows that one more car does not add noticeably to the congestion and pollution. To alter the personal cost-benefit calculations, many cities now give carpoolers incentives, such as designated freeway lanes or reduced tolls.

Appealing to Altruistic Norms

When cooperation obviously serves the public good, one can usefully appeal to the social-responsibility norm (Lynn & Oldenquist, 1986). In the 1960s struggle for civil rights, many marchers willingly agreed, for the sake of the larger group, to suffer harassment, beatings, and jail. In wartime, people make great personal sacrifices for the good of their group. As Winston Churchill said of the Battle of Britain, the actions of the Royal Air Force pilots were genuinely altruistic: A great many people owed a great deal to those who flew into battle knowing there was a high probability—70 percent for those on a standard tour of duty—that they would not return (Levinson, 1950).

To summarize, we can minimize destructive entrapment in social dilemmas by establishing rules that regulate self-serving behavior, by keeping groups small, by enabling people to communicate, by changing payoffs to make cooperation more rewarding, and by invoking compelling altruistic norms.

COMPETITION

In the module on prejudice, we noted that racial hostilities often arise when groups compete for scarce jobs, housing, or resources. When interests clash, conflict erupts.

But does competition by itself provoke hostile conflict? Real-life situations are so complex that it is hard to be sure. If competition is indeed responsible, then it should be possible to provoke in an experiment. We could randomly divide people into two groups, have the groups compete for a scarce resource, and note what happens. That is precisely what Muzafer Sherif (1966) and his colleagues did in a dramatic series of experiments with typical 11- and 12-year-old boys. The inspiration for those experiments dated back to Sherif's witnessing, as a teenager, Greek troops invading his Turkish province in 1919.

> They started killing people right and left. [That] made a great impression on me. There and then I became interested in understanding why these

things were happening among human beings. . . . I wanted to learn whatever science or specialization was needed to understand this intergroup savagery. (quoted by Aron & Aron, 1989, p. 131)

After studying the social roots of savagery, Sherif introduced the seeming essentials into several three-week summer camping experiences. In one study, he divided 22 unacquainted Oklahoma City boys into two groups, took them to a Boy Scout camp in separate buses, and settled them in bunkhouses about a half-mile apart at Oklahoma's Robber's Cave State Park. For most of the first week, each group was unaware of the other's existence. By cooperating in various activities—preparing meals, camping out, fixing up a swimming hole, building a rope bridge—each group soon became close-knit. They gave themselves names: "Rattlers" and "Eagles." Typifying the good feeling, a sign appeared in one cabin: "Home Sweet Home."

Group identity thus established, the stage was set for the conflict. Near the first week's end, the Rattlers discovered the Eagles "on 'our' baseball field." When the camp staff then proposed a tournament of competitive activities between the two groups (baseball games, tugs-of-war, cabin inspections, treasure hunts, and so forth), both groups responded enthusiastically. This was win-lose competition. The spoils (medals, knives) would all go to the tournament victor.

The result? The camp degenerated into open warfare. It was like a scene from William Golding's novel *Lord of the Flies*, which depicts the social disintegration of boys marooned on an island. In Sherif's study, the conflict began with each side calling the other names during the competitive activities. Soon it escalated to dining hall "garbage wars," flag burnings, cabin ransackings, even fistfights. Asked to describe the other group, the boys said they were "sneaky," "smart alecks," "stinkers," but referring to their own group as "brave," "tough," "friendly."

The win-lose competition had produced intense conflict, negative images of the outgroup, and strong ingroup cohesiveness and pride. Group polarization no doubt exacerbated the conflict. In competition-fostering situations, groups behave more competitively than do individuals (Wildschut & others, 2003, 2007). Even after hearing tolerance-advocating messages, ingroup discussion often exacerbates dislike of the conflicting group (Paluck, 2010).

All of this occurred without any cultural, physical, or economic differences between the two groups, and with boys who were their communities' "cream of the crop." Sherif noted that, had we visited the camp at that point, we would have concluded these "were wicked, disturbed, and vicious bunches of youngsters" (1966, p. 85). Actually, their evil behavior was triggered by an evil situation. Fortunately, as we will see in Module 29, Sherif not only made strangers into enemies; he then also made the enemies into friends.

PERCEIVED INJUSTICE

"That's unfair!" "What a ripoff!" "We deserve better!" Such comments typify conflicts bred by perceived injustice. But what is "justice"? According to some social-psychological theorists, people perceive justice as equity—the distribution of rewards in proportion to individuals' contributions (Walster & others, 1978). If you and I have a relationship (employer-employee, teacher-student, husband-wife, colleague-colleague), it is equitable if

$$\frac{\text{My outcomes}}{\text{My inputs}} = \frac{\text{Your outcomes}}{\text{Your inputs}}$$

If you contribute more and benefit less than I do, you will feel exploited and irritated; I may feel exploitative and guilty. Chances are, though, that you will be more sensitive to the inequity than I will be (Greenberg, 1986; Messick & Sentis, 1979).

We may agree with the equity principle's definition of justice yet disagree on whether our relationship is equitable. If two people are colleagues, what will each consider a relevant input? The older person may favor basing pay on seniority, the other on current productivity. Given such a disagreement, whose definition is likely to prevail? Those with social power usually convince themselves and others that they deserve what they're getting (Mikula, 1984). This has been called a "golden" rule: Whoever has the gold makes the rules.

MISPERCEPTION

Recall that conflict is a *perceived* incompatibility of actions or goals. Many conflicts contain but a small core of truly incompatible goals; the bigger problem is the misperceptions of the other's motives and goals. The Eagles and the Rattlers did indeed have some genuinely incompatible aims. But their perceptions subjectively magnified their differences (Figure 28-2).

In earlier modules we considered the seeds of such misperception:

- The *self-serving bias* leads individuals and groups to accept credit for their good deeds and shirk responsibility for bad deeds.
- A tendency to *self-justify* inclines people to deny the wrong of their evil acts. ("You call that hitting? I hardly touched him!")

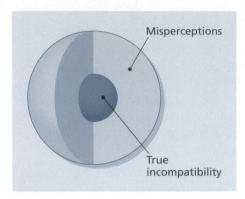

FIGURE 28-2
Many conflicts contain a core of truly
incompatible goals surrounded by a
larger exterior of misperceptions.

- Thanks to the *fundamental attribution error*, each side sees the other's hostility as reflecting an evil disposition.
- One then filters the information and interprets it to fit one's *preconceptions*.
- Groups frequently *polarize* these self-serving, self-justifying, biasing tendencies.
- One symptom of *groupthink* is the tendency to perceive one's own group as moral and strong, and the opposition as evil and weak. Acts of terrorism that in most people's eyes are despicable brutality are seen by others as "holy war."
- Indeed, the mere fact of being in a group triggers an *ingroup bias*.
- Negative *stereotypes* of the outgroup, once formed, are often resistant to contradictory evidence.

So it should not surprise us, though it should sober us, to discover that people in conflict—form distorted images of one another. Even the types of misperception are intriguingly predictable.

Mirror-Image Perceptions

To a striking degree, the misperceptions of those in conflict are mutual. People in conflict attribute similar virtues to themselves and vices to the other. When the American psychologist Urie Bronfenbrenner (1961) visited the Soviet Union in 1960 and conversed with many ordinary citizens in Russian, he was astonished to hear them saying the same things about America that Americans were saying about Russia. The Russians said that the U.S. government was militarily aggressive; that it exploited and deluded the American people; that in diplomacy, it was not to be trusted. "Slowly and painfully, it forced itself upon one that the Russians' distorted picture of us was curiously similar to our view of them—a mirror image."

When two sides have clashing perceptions, at least one of the two is misperceiving the other. And when such misperceptions exist, noted Bronfenbrenner, "It is a psychological phenomenon without parallel in the gravity of its consequences . . . for *it is characteristic of such images that they are self-confirming.*" If A expects B to be hostile, A may treat B in such a way that B fulfills A's expectations, thus beginning a vicious circle (Kennedy & Pronin, 2008). Morton Deutsch (1986) explained:

> You hear the false rumor that a friend is saying nasty things about you; you snub him; he then badmouths you, confirming your expectation. Similarly, if the policymakers of East and West believe that war is likely and either attempts to increase its military security vis-à-vis the other, the other's response will justify the initial move.

Negative **mirror-image perceptions** have been an obstacle to peace in many places:

- Both sides of the Arab-Israeli conflict insisted that "we" are motivated by our need to protect our security and our territory, whereas "they" want to obliterate us and gobble up our land. "We" are the indigenous people here, "they" are the invaders. "We" are the victims; "they" are the aggressors" (Bar-Tal, 2004; Heradstveit, 1979; Kelman, 2007). Given such intense mistrust, negotiation is difficult.

- At Northern Ireland's University of Ulster, Catholic and Protestant students viewed videos of a Protestant attack at a Catholic funeral and a Catholic attack at a Protestant funeral (Hunter & others, 1991). Most students attributed the other side's attack to "bloodthirsty" motives but its own side's attack to retaliation or self-defense.

- Terrorism is in the eye of the beholder. In the Middle East, a public opinion survey found 98 percent of Palestinians agreeing that the killing of 29 Palestinians by an assault-rifle-bearing Israeli at a mosque constituted terrorism, and 82 percent *dis*agreed that the killing of 21 Israeli youths by a Palestinian suicide-bombing constituted terrorism(Kruglanski & Fishman, 2006). Israelis likewise have responded to violence with intensified perceptions of Palestinian evil intent (Bar-Tal, 2004).

Such conflicts, notes Philip Zimbardo (2004a), engage "a two-category world—of good people, like US, and of bad people, like THEM." "In fact," note Daniel Kahneman and Jonathan Renshon (2007), all the biases uncovered in 40 years of psychological research are conducive to war. They "incline national leaders to exaggerate the evil intentions of adversaries, to misjudge how adversaries perceive them, to be overly sanguine when hostilities start, and overly reluctant to make necessary concessions in negotiations."

Opposing sides in a conflict tend to exaggerate their differences. On issues such as immigration and affirmative action, proponents aren't as liberal and opponents aren't as conservative as their adversaries suppose (Sherman & others, 2003). Opposing sides also tend to have a "bias blind spot," notes Cynthia McPherson Frantz (2006). They see their own understandings as not biased by their liking or disliking for others; but those who disagree with them seem unfair and biased.

John Chambers, Robert Baron, and Mary Inman (2006) confirmed misperceptions on issues related to abortion and politics. Partisans perceived exaggerated differences from their adversaries (who actually agreed with them more often than they supposed). From exaggerated perceptions of the other's position arise culture wars. Ralph White (1996, 1998) reports that the Serbs started the war in Bosnia partly out of an exaggerated fear of the relatively secularized Bosnian Muslims, whose beliefs they wrongly associated with Middle Eastern Islamic fundamentalism and fanatical terrorism. Resolving conflict involves abandoning such exaggerated perceptions and coming to understand the other's mind. But that isn't easy, notes Robert Wright (2003): "Putting yourself in the shoes of people who do things you find abhorrent may be the hardest moral exercise there is."

Destructive mirror-image perceptions also operate in conflicts between small groups and between individuals. As we saw in the dilemma games, both parties may say, "We want to cooperate. But *their* refusal to cooperate forces *us* to react defensively." When Kenneth Thomas and Louis Pondy (1977) asked executives to describe a significant recent conflict, only 12 percent felt the other party was cooperative; 74 percent perceived themselves as cooperative. The typical executive explained that he or she had "suggested," "informed," and "recommended," whereas the antagonist had "demanded," "disagreed with everything I said," and "refused."

Group conflicts are often fueled by an illusion that the enemy's top leaders are evil but their people, though controlled and manipulated, are pro-us. This *evil-leader–good people* perception characterized

Americans' and Russians' views of each other during the Cold War. The United States entered the Vietnam War believing that in areas dominated by the Communist Vietcong "terrorists," many of the people were allies-in-waiting. As suppressed information later revealed, those beliefs were mere wishful thinking. In 2003 the United States began the Iraq War presuming the existence of "a vast underground network that would rise in support of coalition forces to assist security and law enforcement" (Phillips, 2003). Alas, the network didn't materialize, and the resulting postwar security vacuum enabled looting, sabotage, persistent attacks on American forces, and increasing attacks from an insurgency determined to drive Western interests from the country.

Shifting Perceptions

If misperceptions accompany conflict, they should appear and disappear as conflicts wax and wane. And they do, with startling regularity. The same processes that create the enemy's image can reverse that image when the enemy becomes an ally. Thus, the "bloodthirsty, cruel, treacherous, buck-toothed little Japs" of World War II soon became—in North American minds (Gallup, 1972) and in the media—our "intelligent, hardworking, self-disciplined, resourceful allies."

The Germans, who after two world wars were hated, then admired, and then again hated, were once again admired—apparently no longer plagued by what earlier was presumed to be cruelty in their national character. So long as Iraq was attacking unpopular Iran, even while using chemical weapons to massacre its own Kurds, many nations supported it. Our enemy's enemy is our friend. When Iraq ended its war with Iran and invaded oil-rich Kuwait, Iraq's behavior suddenly became "barbaric." Images of our enemies change with amazing ease.

The extent of misperceptions during conflict provides a chilling reminder that people need not be insane or abnormally malicious to form distorted images of their antagonists. When we experience conflict with another nation, another group, or simply a roommate or a parent, we readily misperceive our own motives as good and the other's as evil. And just as readily, our antagonists form a mirror-image perception of us.

So, with antagonists trapped in a social dilemma, competing for scarce resources, or perceiving injustice, the conflict continues until something enables both parties to peel away their misperceptions and work at reconciling their actual differences. Good advice, then, is this: When in conflict, do not assume that the other fails to share your values and morality. Rather, compare perceptions, assuming that the other is likely perceiving the situation differently.

CONCEPTS TO REMEMBER

conflict   A perceived incompatibility of actions or goals.

social trap   A situation in which the conflicting parties, by each rationally pursuing its self-interest, become caught in mutually destructive behavior. Examples include the Prisoner's Dilemma and the Tragedy of the Commons.

non-zero-sum games   Games in which outcomes need not sum to zero. With cooperation, both can win; with competition, both can lose. (Also called *mixed-motive situations*.)

mirror-image perceptions   Reciprocal views of each other often held by parties in conflict; for example, each may view itself as moral and peace-loving and the other as evil and aggressive.

29

--- ❖ ---

Blessed Are the Peacemakers

We have seen how conflicts are ignited by social traps, competition, perceived injustices, and misperceptions. Although the picture is grim, it is not hopeless. Sometimes closed fists become open arms as hostilities evolve into friendship. Social psychologists have focused on four strategies for helping enemies become comrades. We can remember these as the four Cs of peacemaking: contact, cooperation, communication, and conciliation.

CONTACT

Might putting two conflicting individuals or groups into close contact enable them to know and like each other? Perhaps not. We have seen that proximity—and the accompanying interaction, anticipation of interaction, and mere exposure—boosts liking. We have noted how blatant racial prejudice declined following desegregation, showing that *attitudes follow behavior.*

Does Contact Predict Attitudes?

In general, contact predicts tolerance. In a painstakingly complete analysis, Linda Tropp and Thomas Pettigrew (2005a; Pettigrew & Tropp, 2008, 2011) assembled data from 516 studies of 250,555 people in 38 nations. In 94 percent of studies, *increased contact predicted decreased prejudice.* This is especially so for majority group attitudes toward minorities (Gibson & Claassen, 2010; Tropp & Pettigrew, 2005b).

Newer studies confirm the correlation between contact and positive attitudes:

- The more interracial contact South African Blacks and Whites have, the less prejudice they feel, and the more sympathetic their policy attitudes are to those of the other group (Dixon & others, 2007; Tredoux & Finchilescu, 2010).
- The more friendly contact Blacks and Whites have with one another, the better their attitudes toward one another—and toward other outgroups, such as Hispanics (Tausch & others, 2010).
- The more contact straight people have with gays and lesbians, the more accepting they become (Smith & others, 2009).
- The more contact Dutch adolescents have with Muslims, the more accepting of Muslims they are (González & others, 2008).
- Even vicarious indirect contact, via story reading or imagination, or through a friend's having an outgroup friend, tends to reduce prejudice (Cameron & Rutland, 2006; Crisp & others, 2011; Turner & others, 2007a, 2007b, 2008, 2010). This indirect contact effect, also called "the extended-contact effect," can spread more positive attitudes through a peer group (Christ & others, 2010).

In the United States, segregation and expressed prejudice have diminished together since the 1960s. But was interracial contact the *cause* of these improved attitudes? Were those who actually experienced desegregation affected by it?

Does Desegregation Improve Racial Attitudes?

School desegregation has produced measurable benefits, such as leading more Blacks to attend and succeed in college (Stephan, 1988). Does desegregation of schools, neighborhoods, and workplaces also produce favorable *social* results? The evidence is mixed.

On the one hand, many studies conducted during and shortly after desegregation found Whites' attitudes toward Blacks improving markedly. Whether the people were department store clerks and customers, merchant marines, government workers, police officers, neighbors, or students, racial contact led to diminished prejudice (Amir, 1969; Pettigrew, 1969). For example, near the end of World War II, the U.S. Army partially desegregated some of its rifle companies (Stouffer & others, 1949). When asked their opinions of such desegregation, 11 percent of the White soldiers in segregated companies approved. Of those in desegregated companies, 60 percent approved. They exhibited "system justification"—the human tendency to approve the way things are.

When Morton Deutsch and Mary Collins (1951) took advantage of a made-to-order natural experiment, they observed similar results. In accord with state law, New York City desegregated its public housing units; it assigned families to apartments without regard to race. In a similar development across the river in Newark, New Jersey, Blacks and Whites were assigned to separate buildings. When surveyed, White women in the desegregated development were far more likely to favor interracial housing and to say their attitudes toward Blacks had improved. Exaggerated stereotypes had wilted in the face of reality. As one woman put it, "I've really come to like it. I see they're just as human as we are."

Such findings influenced the Supreme Court's 1954 decision to desegregate schools and helped fuel the 1960s civil rights movement (Pettigrew, 1986, 2004). Yet initial studies of the effects of school desegregation were less encouraging. After reviewing all the available studies, Walter Stephan (1986) concluded that racial attitudes had been little affected by desegregation. For Blacks, the noticeable effect of desegregated schooling was less on attitudes than on their increased likelihood of attending integrated (or predominantly White) colleges, living in integrated neighborhoods, and working in integrated settings.

So, sometimes desegregation improves racial attitudes, and sometimes—especially when there is anxiety or perceived threat (Pettigrew, 2004)—it doesn't. Such disagreements excite the scientist's detective spirit. What explains the difference? So far, we've been lumping all kinds of desegregation together. Actual desegregation occurs in many ways and under vastly different conditions.

When Does Desegregation Improve Racial Attitudes?

Might exposure to other-race faces produce increased liking for other-race strangers? Indeed yes, Leslie Zebrowitz and her colleagues (2008) discovered, when exposing White participants to Asian and Black faces. Might the frequency of interracial contact also be a factor? It seems to be. Researchers have gone into dozens of desegregated schools and observed with whom children of a given race eat, talk, and loiter. Race influences contact. Whites disproportionately associate with Whites, Blacks with Blacks (Schofield, 1982, 1986). In one study of Dartmouth University e-mail exchanges, Black students, though only 7 percent of students, sent 44 percent of their e-mails to other Black students (Sacerdote & Marmaros, 2005).

The same self-imposed segregation was evident in a South African desegregated beach, as John Dixon and Kevin Durrheim (2003) discovered when they recorded the location of Black, White, and Indian beachgoers one midsummer (December 30th) afternoon (Figure 29-1). Desegregated neighborhoods, cafeterias, and restaurants, too, may fail to produce integrated interactions (Clack & others, 2005; Dixon & others, 2005a, 2005b). "Why are all the

FIGURE 29-1
Desegregation needn't mean contact. After this Scottburgh, South Africa, beach became "open" and desegregated in the new South Africa, Blacks (represented by black circles), Whites (gray circles), and Indians (white circles) tended to cluster with their own race.   Source: From Dixon & Durrheim, 2003.

Black kids sitting together?" people may wonder (a question that could as easily be asked of the White kids). One naturalistic study observed 119 class sessions of 26 University of Cape Town tutorial groups, which averaged 6 Black and 10 White students per group (Alexander & Tredoux, 2010). On average, the researchers calculated, 71 percent of Black students would have needed to change seats to achieve a fully integrated seating pattern.

In one study that tracked the attitudes of more than 1,600 European students, over time, contact did serve to reduce prejudice. But prejudice also minimized contact (Binder & others, 2009). Anxiety as well as prejudice helps explain why participants in interracial relationships (when students are paired as roommates or as partners in an experiment) may engage in less intimate self-disclosure than those in same-race relationships (Johnson & others, 2009; Trail & others, 2009).

Efforts to facilitate contact sometimes help, but sometimes fall flat. "We had one day when some of the Protestant schools came over," explained one Catholic youngster after a Northern Ireland school exchange (Cairns & Hewstone, 2002). "It was supposed to be like . . . mixing, but there was very little mixing. It wasn't because we didn't want to; it was just really awkward." The lack of mixing stems partly from "pluralistic ignorance." Many Whites and Blacks say they would like more contact but misperceive that the other does not reciprocate their feelings (Shelton & Richeson, 2005; Vorauer, 2001, 2005).

In contrast, the more encouraging older studies of store clerks, soldiers, and housing project neighbors involved considerable interracial contact, more than enough to reduce the anxiety that marks initial intergroup contact. Other studies show similar benefits when they involve prolonged, personal contact—between Black and White prison inmates, between Black and White girls in an interracial summer camp, between Black and White university roommates, and between Black, Colored, and White South Africans (Clore & others, 1978; Foley, 1976; Holtman & others, 2005; Van Laar & others, 2005). Among American students who have studied in Germany or in Britain, the more their contact with host country people, the more positive their attitudes (Stangor & others, 1996). Exchange students' hosts also are changed by the experience; they become more likely to see things from the other visitor culture's perspective (Vollhardt, 2010).

Those who form *friendships* with outgroup members develop more positive attitudes toward the outgroup (Page-Gould & others, 2010; Pettigrew & Tropp, 2000). It's not just head knowledge of other people that matters; it's also the *emotional* ties that form with intimate friendships and interracial roommate pairings that serve to reduce anxiety and increase empathy (Barlow & others, 2009; Pettigrew & Tropp, 2000, 2011; Shook & Fazio, 2008). For initially intolerant people, the anxiety-reducing effect of contact is especially strong (Hodson, 2011).

The diminishing anxiety that accompanies friendly outgroup interactions is a biological event: It is measurable as decreased stress hormone reactivity in cross-ethnic contexts (Page-Gould & others, 2008).

Surveys of nearly 4,000 Europeans reveal that friendship is a key to successful contact: If you have a minority group friend, you become much more likely to express sympathy and support for the friend's group, and even somewhat more support for immigration by that group. It's true of West Germans' attitudes toward Turks, French people's attitudes toward Asians and North Africans, Netherlanders' attitudes toward Surinamers and Turks, British attitudes toward West Indians and Asians, and Northern Ireland Protestants' and Catholics' attitudes toward each other (Brown & others, 1999; Hamberger & Hewstone, 1997; Paolini & others, 2004; Pettigrew, 1997).

The social psychologists who advocated desegregation never claimed that all contact would improve attitudes. They expected poor results when contacts were competitive, unsupported by authorities, and unequal (Pettigrew, 1988; Stephan, 1987). Before 1954 many prejudiced Whites had frequent contacts with Blacks—as shoeshine men and domestic workers. Such unequal contacts breed attitudes that merely justify the continuation of inequality. So it's important that the contact be **equal-status contact**, like that between the store clerks, the soldiers, the neighbors, the prisoners, and the summer campers.

*C*OOPERATION

Although equal-status contact can help, it is sometimes not enough. It didn't help when Muzafer Sherif stopped the Eagles versus Rattlers competition and brought the groups together for noncompetitive activities, such as watching movies, shooting off fireworks, and eating. By that time, their hostility was so strong that mere contact only provided opportunities for taunts and attacks. When an Eagle was bumped by a Rattler, his fellow Eagles urged him to "brush off the dirt." Desegregating the two groups hardly promoted their social integration.

Given entrenched hostility, what can a peacemaker do? Think back to the successful and the unsuccessful desegregation efforts. The army's racial mixing of rifle companies didn't just bring Blacks and Whites into equal-status contact, it made them interdependent. Together, they were fighting a common enemy, striving toward a shared goal.

Does that suggest a second factor that predicts whether the effect of desegregation will be favorable? Does competitive contact divide and *cooperative* contact unite? Consider what happens to people who together face a common predicament. In conflicts at all levels, from couples to rival teams to nations, shared threats and common goals breed unity.

Common External Threats Build Cohesiveness

Together with others, have you ever been caught in a blizzard, punished by a teacher, or persecuted and ridiculed because of your social, racial, or religious identity? If so, you may recall feeling close to those with whom you shared the predicament. Perhaps previous social barriers were dropped as you helped one another dig out of the snow or struggled to cope with your common enemy. Survivors of more extreme crises, such as a bombing, also often report a spirit of cooperation and solidarity rather than all-for-themselves panic (Drury & others, 2009).

Such friendliness is common among those who experience a shared threat. John Lanzetta (1955) observed this when he put four-man groups of naval ROTC cadets to work on problem-solving tasks and then began informing them over a loudspeaker that their answers were wrong, their productivity inexcusably low, their thinking stupid. Other groups did not receive this harassment. Lanzetta observed that the group members under duress became friendlier to one another, more cooperative, less argumentative, less competitive. They were in it together. And the result was a cohesive spirit.

Having a common enemy unified the groups of competing boys in Sherif's camping experiments—and in many subsequent experiments (Dion, 1979). Just being reminded of an outgroup (say, a rival school) heightens people's responsiveness to their own group (Wilder & Shapiro, 1984). When keenly conscious of who "they" are, we also know who "we" are.

When facing a well-defined external threat during wartime, we-feeling soars. The membership of civic organizations mushrooms (Putnam, 2000). Shared threats also produce a political "rally 'round the flag" effect (Lambert & others, 2010). After 9/11, "old racial antagonisms . . . dissolved," reported the *New York Times* (Sengupta, 2001). "I just thought of myself as Black," said 18-year-old Louis Johnson, reflecting on life before 9/11. "But now I feel like I'm an American, more than ever." In New York City, even divorce rates dropped in the aftermath of 9/11 (Hansel & others, 2011). One sampling of conversation on 9/11, and another of New York Mayor Giuliani's press conferences before and after 9/11, found a doubled rate of the word "we" (Liehr & others, 2004; Pennebaker & Lay, 2002).

Superordinate Goals Foster Cooperation

Closely related to the unifying power of an external threat is the unifying power of **superordinate goals**, goals that unite all in a group and require cooperative effort. To promote harmony among his warring campers, Sherif introduced such goals. He created a problem with the camp water supply, necessitating both groups' cooperation to restore the water. Given an opportunity to rent a movie, one expensive enough to require the joint resources of the two groups, they again cooperated. When a truck "broke down" on a camp excursion, a staff member casually left the tug-of-war rope nearby, prompting one boy to suggest that they all pull the truck to get it started. When it started, a backslapping celebration ensued over their victorious "tug-of-war against the truck."

After working together to achieve such superordinate goals, the boys ate together and enjoyed themselves around a campfire. Friendships sprouted across group lines. Hostilities plummeted. On the last day, the boys decided to travel home together on one bus. During the trip they no longer sat by groups. As the bus approached Oklahoma City and home, they, as one, spontaneously sang "Oklahoma" and then bade their friends farewell. With isolation and competition, Sherif made strangers into bitter enemies. With superordinate goals, he made enemies into friends.

Are Sherif's experiments mere child's play? Or can pulling together to achieve superordinate goals be similarly beneficial with adults in conflict? Robert Blake and Jane Mouton (1979) wondered. So in a series of two-week experiments involving more than 1,000 executives in 150 different groups, they re-created the essential features of the situation experienced by the Rattlers and the Eagles. Each group first engaged in activities by itself, then competed with another group, and then cooperated with the other group in working toward jointly chosen superordinate goals. Their results provided "unequivocal evidence that adult reactions parallel those of Sherif's younger subjects."

Extending those findings, John Dovidio, Samuel Gaertner, and their collaborators (2005, 2009) report that working cooperatively has especially favorable effects under conditions that lead people to define a new, inclusive group that dissolves their former subgroups. Old feelings of bias against another group diminish when members of the two groups sit alternately around a table (rather than on opposite sides), give their new group a single name, and then work together under conditions that foster a good mood. "Us" and "them" become "we."

Cooperative Learning Improves Racial Attitudes

So far we have noted the modest social benefits of desegregation if unaccompanied by the emotional bonds of friendship and by equal-status relationships. And we have noted the dramatic social benefits of successful, cooperative contacts between members of rival groups. Several research teams therefore wondered: Without compromising academic achievement, could we promote interracial friendships by replacing competitive learning situations with cooperative ones? Given the diversity of their methods—all involving students on integrated study teams, sometimes in competition with other teams—the results are striking and heartening.

One research team, led by Elliot Aronson (2004; Aronson & Gonzalez, 1988), elicited similar group cooperation with a "jigsaw" technique. In experiments in Texas and California elementary schools, the researchers assigned children to racially and academically diverse 6-member groups. The subject was then divided into six parts, with each student becoming the expert on his or her part. In a unit on Chile, one student might be the expert on Chile's history, another on its geography, another on its culture. First, the various "historians," "geographers," and so forth got together to master their material. Then they returned to the home groups to teach it to their classmates. Each group member held, so to speak, a piece of the jigsaw. Self-confident students therefore had to listen to and learn from reticent students who, in turn, soon realized they had something important to offer their peers.

With cooperative learning, students learn not only the material, but other lessons as well. Cross-racial friendships also begin to blossom. The exam scores of minority students improve (perhaps because academic achievement is now peer supported). After the experiments are over, many teachers continue using cooperative learning (D. W. Johnson & others, 1981; Slavin, 1990). "It is clear," wrote race-relations expert John McConahay (1981), that cooperative learning "is the most effective practice for improving race relations in desegregated schools that we know of to date."

To sum up, cooperative, equal-status contacts exert a positive influence on boy campers, industrial executives, college students, and schoolchildren. Does the principle extend to all levels of human relations? Are families unified by pulling together to farm the land, restore an old house, or sail a sloop? Are communal identities forged by barn raisings, group singing, or cheering on the football team? Is international understanding bred by international collaboration in science and space, by joint efforts to feed the world and conserve resources, by friendly personal contacts between people of different nations? Indications are that the answer to all of those questions is *yes* (Brewer & Miller, 1988; Desforges & others, 1991, 1997; Deutsch, 1985, 1994). Thus, an important challenge facing our divided world is to identify and agree on our superordinate goals and to structure cooperative efforts to achieve them.

COMMUNICATION

Conflicting parties have other ways to resolve their differences. When husband and wife, or labor and management, or nation X and nation Y disagree, they can **bargain** with each other directly. They can ask a third party to **mediate** by making suggestions and facilitating their negotiations. Or they can **arbitrate** by submitting their disagreement to someone who will study the issues and impose a settlement.

Bargaining

If you want to buy or sell a new car, are you better off adopting a tough bargaining stance—opening with an extreme offer so that splitting the difference will yield a favorable result? Or are you better off beginning with a sincere "good-faith" offer?

Experiments suggest no simple answer. On the one hand, those who demand more will often get more. Tough bargaining may lower the other party's expectations, making the other side willing to settle for less (Yukl, 1974). But toughness can sometimes backfire. Many a conflict is not over a pie of fixed size but over a pie that shrinks if the conflict continues. A time delay is often a lose-lose scenario. When a strike is prolonged, both labor and management lose. Being tough is another potential lose-lose scenario. If the other party responds with an equally tough stance, both may be locked into positions from which neither can back down without losing face. In the weeks before the 1991 Persian Gulf War, the first President Bush threatened, in the full glare of publicity, to "kick Saddam's ass." Saddam Hussein, no less macho, threatened to make "infidel" Americans "swim in their own blood." After such belligerent statements, it was difficult for each side to evade war and save face.

Mediation

A third-party mediator may offer suggestions that enable conflicting parties to make concessions and still save face (Pruitt, 1998). If my concession can be attributed to a mediator, who is gaining an equal concession from my antagonist, neither of us will be viewed as weakly caving in.

Turning Win-Lose into Win-Win

Mediators also help resolve conflicts by facilitating constructive communication. Their first task is to help the parties rethink the conflict and gain information about the others' interests. Typically, people on both sides have a competitive "win-lose" orientation: They are successful if their opponent is unhappy with the result, and unsuccessful if their opponent is pleased (Thompson & others, 1995). The mediator aims to replace this win-lose orientation with a cooperative "win-win" orientation, by prodding both sides to set aside their conflicting demands and instead to think about each other's underlying needs, interests, and goals. In experiments, Leigh Thompson (1990a, 1990b) found that, with experience, negotiators become better able to make mutually beneficial trade-offs and thus to achieve win-win resolutions.

A classic story of such a resolution concerns the two sisters who quarreled over orange (Follett, 1940). Finally they compromised and split the orange in half, whereupon one sister squeezed her half for juice while the other used the peel on her half to make a cake. If the sisters had each explained *why* they wanted the orange, they very likely would have agreed to share it, giving one sister all the juice and the other all the peel. This is an example of an **integrative agreement** (Pruitt & Lewis, 1975, 1977). Compared with compromises, in which each party sacrifices something important, integrative agreements are more enduring. Because they are mutually rewarding, they also lead to better ongoing relationships (Pruitt, 1986).

Unraveling Misperceptions with Controlled Communications

Communication often helps reduce self-fulfilling misperceptions. Perhaps you can recall experiences similar to that of this college student:

> Often, after a prolonged period of little communication, I perceive Martha's silence as a sign of her dislike for me. She, in turn, thinks that my quietness is a result of my being mad at her. My silence induces her silence, which makes me even more silent . . . until this snowballing effect is broken by some occurrence that makes it necessary for us to interact. And the communication then unravels all the misinterpretations we had made about one another.

The outcome of such conflicts often depends on *how* people communicate their feelings to one another. Roger Knudson and his colleagues (1980) invited married couples to come to the University of Illinois psychology laboratory and relive, through role playing, one of their past conflicts. Before, during, and after their conversation (which often generated as much emotion as the actual previous conflict), the couples were observed closely and questioned. Couples who evaded the issue—by failing to make their positions clear or failing to acknowledge their spouse's position—left with the illusion that they were more in harmony and agreement than they really were. Often, they came to believe they now agreed more when actually they agreed less. In contrast, those who engaged the issue—by making their positions clear and by taking one another's views into account—achieved more actual agreement and gained more accurate information about one another's perceptions. That helps explain why couples who communicate their concerns directly and openly are usually happily married (Grush & Glidden, 1987).

Conflict researchers report that a key factor is *trust* (Noor & others, 2008; Ross & Ward, 1995). If you believe the other person is well intentioned, you are more likely to divulge your needs and concerns. Lacking trust, you may fear that being open will give the other party information that might be used against you. Even simple behaviors can enhance trust. In experiments, negotiators who were instructed to mimic the others' mannerisms, as naturally empathic people in close relationships often do, elicited more trust and greater discovery of compatible interests and mutually satisfying deals (Maddux & others, 2008).

When the two parties mistrust each other and communicate unproductively, a third-party mediator—a marriage counselor, a labor mediator, a diplomat—sometimes helps. Often the mediator is someone trusted by both sides. In the 1980s it took an Algerian Muslim to mediate the conflict between Iran and Iraq, and the pope to resolve a geographical dispute between Argentina and Chile (Carnevale & Choi, 2000).

After coaxing the conflicting parties to rethink their perceived win-lose conflict, the mediator often has each party identify and rank its goals. When goals are compatible, the ranking procedure makes it easier for each to concede on less-important goals so that both achieve their chief goals (Erickson & others, 1974; Schulz & Pruitt, 1978). South Africa achieved internal peace when Black and White South Africans granted each other's top priorities—replacing apartheid with majority rule and safeguarding the security, welfare, and rights of Whites (Kelman, 1998).

When labor and management both believe that management's goal of higher productivity and profit is compatible with labor's goal of better wages and working conditions, they can begin to work for an integrative win-win solution.

When the parties then convene to communicate directly, they are usually not set loose in the hope that, eyeball-to-eyeball, the conflict will resolve itself. In the midst of a threatening, stressful conflict, emotions often disrupt the ability to understand the other party's point of view. Although happiness and gratitude can increase trust, anger decreases it (Dunn & Schweitzer, 2005). Communication may thus become most difficult just when it is most needed (Tetlock, 1985).

The mediator will often structure the encounter to help each party understand and feel understood by the other. The mediator may ask the conflicting parties to restrict their arguments to statements of fact, including statements of how they feel and how they respond when the other acts in a given way: "I enjoy music. But when you play it loud, I find it hard to concentrate. That makes me crabby." Also, the mediator may ask people to reverse roles and argue the other's position or to imagine and explain what the other person is experiencing. The mediator may have them restate one another's positions before replying with their own: "It annoys you when I play my music and you're trying to study."

Experiments show that taking the other's perspective and inducing empathy decreases stereotyping and increases cooperation (Batson & Moran, 1999; Galinsky & Moskowitz, 2000; Todd & others, 2011). It helps to humanize rather than demonize the other. Older people often find that easier to do, by having the wisdom to appreciate multiple perspectives and the limits of knowledge (Grossmann & others, 2010). Sometimes our elders are older, wiser, and better able to navigate social conflicts.

Neutral third parties may also suggest mutually agreeable proposals that would be dismissed—"reactively devalued"—if offered by either side. Constance Stillinger and her colleagues (1991) found that a nuclear disarmament proposal that Americans dismissed when attributed to the former Soviet Union seemed more acceptable when attributed to a neutral third party. Likewise, people will often reactively devalue a concession offered by an adversary ("they must not value it"); the same concession may seem more than a token gesture when suggested by a third party.

These peacemaking principles—based partly on laboratory experiments, partly on practical experience—have helped mediate both international and industrial conflicts (Blake & Mouton, 1962, 1979; Fisher, 1994; Wehr, 1979). One small team of Arab and Jewish Americans, led by social psychologist Herbert Kelman (1997, 2007, 2008), has conducted workshops bringing together influential Arabs and Israelis. Kelman and colleagues counter misperceptions and have participants seek creative solutions for their common good. Isolated, the participants are free to speak directly to their adversaries without fear that their constituents are second-guessing what they are saying. The result? Those from both sides typically come to understand the other's perspective and how the other side responds to their own group's actions.

Arbitration

Some conflicts are so intractable, the underlying interests so divergent, that a mutually satisfactory resolution is unattainable. Conflicting claims to Jerusalem as the capital of an independent Palestine versus a secure Israel have, so far, proven intractable. In a divorce dispute over custody of a child, both parents cannot enjoy full custody. In those and many other cases (disputes over tenants' repair bills, athletes' wages, and national territories), a third-party mediator may—or may not—help resolve the conflict.

If not, the parties may turn to *arbitration* by having the mediator or another third party *impose* a settlement. Disputants usually prefer to settle their differences without arbitration so that they retain control over the outcome. Neil McGillicuddy and others (1987) observed this preference in an experiment involving disputants coming to a dispute settlement center. When people knew they would face an arbitrated settlement if mediation failed, they tried harder to resolve the problem, exhibited less hostility, and thus were more likely to reach agreement.

In cases where differences seem large and irreconcilable, the prospect of arbitration may cause the disputants to freeze their positions, hoping to gain an advantage when the arbitrator chooses a compromise. To combat that tendency, some disputes, such as those involving salaries of individual baseball players, are settled with "final-offer arbitration," in which the third party chooses one of the two final offers. Final-offer arbitration motivates each party to make a reasonable proposal.

Typically, however, the final offer is not as reasonable as it would be if each party, free of self-serving bias, saw its own proposal through others' eyes. Negotiation researchers report that most disputants are made stubborn by "optimistic overconfidence" (Kahneman & Tversky, 1995). Successful mediation is hindered when, as often happens, both parties believe they have a two-thirds chance of winning a final-offer arbitration (Bazerman, 1986, 1990).

CONCILIATION

Sometimes tension and suspicion run so high that even communication, let alone resolution, becomes all but impossible. Each party may threaten, coerce, or retaliate against the other. Unfortunately, such acts tend to be reciprocated, escalating the conflict. So, would a strategy of appeasing the other party by being unconditionally cooperative produce a satisfying result? Often not. In laboratory games, those who are 100 percent cooperative often are exploited. Politically, a one-sided pacifism is usually out of the question.

Social psychologist Charles Osgood (1962, 1980) advocated a third alternative, one that is conciliatory yet strong enough to discourage exploitation. Osgood called it "graduated and reciprocated initiatives in tension reduction." He nicknamed it **GRIT,** a label that suggests the determination it requires. GRIT aims to reverse the "conflict spiral" by triggering reciprocal de-escalation. To do so, it draws upon social-psychological concepts, such as the norm of reciprocity and the attribution of motives.

GRIT requires one side to initiate a few small de-escalatory actions, after *announcing a conciliatory intent*. The initiator states its desire to reduce tension, declares each conciliatory act before making it, and invites the adversary to reciprocate. Such announcements create a framework that helps the adversary correctly interpret what otherwise might be seen as weak or tricky actions. They also bring public pressure to bear on the adversary to follow the reciprocity norm.

Next, the initiator establishes credibility and genuineness by carrying out, exactly as announced, several verifiable *conciliatory acts*. This intensifies the pressure to reciprocate. Making conciliatory acts diverse—perhaps offering medical help, closing a military base, and lifting a trade ban— keeps the initiator from making a significant sacrifice in any one area and leaves the adversary freer to choose its own means of reciprocation. If the adversary reciprocates voluntarily, its own conciliatory behavior may soften its attitudes.

GRIT *is* conciliatory. But it is not "surrender on the installment plan." The remaining aspects of the plan protect each side's self-interest by *maintaining retaliatory capability*. The initial conciliatory steps entail some small risk but do not jeopardize either one's security; rather, they are calculated to begin edging both sides down the tension ladder. If one side takes an aggressive action, the other side reciprocates in kind, making clear it will not tolerate exploitation. Yet the reciprocal act is not an overresponse that would re-escalate the conflict. If the adversary offers its own conciliatory acts, these, too, are matched or even slightly exceeded. Morton Deutsch (1993) captured the spirit of GRIT in advising negotiators to be " 'firm, fair, and friendly': *firm* in resisting intimidation, exploitation, and dirty tricks; *fair* in holding to one's moral principles and not reciprocating the other's immoral behavior despite his or her provocations; and *friendly* in the sense that one is willing to initiate and reciprocate cooperation."

Does GRIT really work? In a lengthy series of experiments at Ohio University, Svenn Lindskold and his associates (1976 to 1988) found "strong support for the various steps in the GRIT proposal." In laboratory games, announcing cooperative intent *does* boost cooperation. Repeated conciliatory or generous acts *do* breed greater trust (Klapwijk & Van Lange, 2009; Shapiro, 2010). Maintaining an equality of power *does* protect against exploitation.

GRIT-like strategies have occasionally been tried outside the laboratory, with promising results. To many, the most significant attempt at GRIT was the so-called Kennedy experiment (Etzioni, 1967). On June 10, 1963, President Kennedy gave a major speech, "A Strategy for Peace." He noted that "Our problems are man-made . . . and can be solved by man," and then announced his first conciliatory act: The United States was stopping all atmospheric nuclear tests and would not resume them unless another country did. Kennedy's entire speech was published in the Soviet press. Five days later Premier Khrushchev reciprocated, announcing he had halted production of strategic bombers. There soon followed further reciprocal gestures: The United States agreed to sell wheat to Russia, the Russians agreed to a "hot line" between the two countries, and the two countries soon achieved a test-ban treaty. For a time, these conciliatory initiatives eased relations between the two countries.

Might conciliatory efforts also help reduce tension between individuals? There is every reason to expect so. When a relationship is strained and communication nonexistent, it sometimes takes only a conciliatory gesture—a soft answer, a warm smile, a gentle touch—for both parties to begin easing down the tension ladder, to a rung where contact, cooperation, and communication again become possible.

CONCEPTS TO REMEMBER

equal-status contact Contact on an equal basis. Just as a relationship between people of unequal status breeds attitudes consistent with their relationship, so do relationships between those of equal status. Thus, to reduce prejudice, interracial contact should ideally be between persons equal in status.

superordinate goal A shared goal that necessitates cooperative effort; a goal that overrides people's differences from one another.

bargaining Seeking an agreement to a conflict through direct negotiation between parties.

mediation An attempt by a neutral third party to resolve a conflict by facilitating communication and offering suggestions.

arbitration Resolution of a conflict by a neutral third party who studies both sides and imposes a settlement.

integrative agreements Win-win agreements that reconcile both parties' interests to their mutual benefit.

GRIT Acronym for "graduated and reciprocated initiatives in tension reduction"—a strategy designed to de-escalate international tensions.

30

❖

When Do People Help?

On March 13, 1964, 28-year-old bar manager Kitty Genovese was set upon by a knife-wielding attacker as she returned from work to her Queens, New York, apartment house at 3:00 a.m. Her screams of terror and pleas for help—"Oh my God, he stabbed me! Please help me! Please help me!"—aroused some of her neighbors (38 of them, according to an initial *New York Times* report). Some supposedly came to their windows and caught fleeting glimpses as the attacker left and returned to attack again. Not until her attacker finally departed did anyone call the police. Soon after, Kitty Genovese died. A later analysis disputed the initial report that 38 witnesses observed the murder yet remained inactive (Manning & others, 2007). Nevertheless, the initial story helped inspire research on bystander inaction, which was illustrated in other incidents.

Eleanor Bradley tripped and broke her leg while shopping. Dazed and in pain, she pleaded for help. For 40 minutes, the stream of sidewalk pedestrians simply parted and flowed around her. Finally, a cab driver helped her to a doctor (Darley & Latané, 1968).

Or would we be heroes, like Everett Sanderson? Hearing the rumble of an approaching New York subway train, he leapt down onto the tracks and raced toward the approaching headlights to rescue Michelle De Jesus, a 4-year-old who had fallen from the platform. Three seconds before the train would have run her over, Sanderson flung Michelle into the crowd above. As the train roared in, he himself failed in his first effort to jump back to the platform. At the last instant, bystanders pulled him to safety (Young, 1977).

Or consider the hillside in Jerusalem, where hundreds of trees form the Garden of the Righteous. Beneath each tree is a plaque with the name of a European Christian who gave refuge to one or more Jews during the Nazi Holocaust. These "righteous Gentiles" knew that if the refugees were discovered, Nazi policy dictated that host and refugee would suffer a common fate. Many did (Hellman, 1980; Wiesel, 1985).

One hero who did not survive was Jane Haining, a Church of Scotland missionary who was matron at a school for 400 mostly Jewish girls. On the eve of war, the church, fearing her safety, ordered her to return home. She refused, saying, "If these children need me in days of sunshine, how much more do they need me in days of darkness?" (Barnes, 2008; Brown, 2008). She reportedly cut up her leather luggage to make soles for her girls' shoes. In April 1944, Haining accused a cook of eating sparse food rations intended for her girls. The cook, a Nazi party member, denounced her to the Gestapo, who arrested her for having worked among the Jews and having wept to see her girls forced to wear yellow stars. A few weeks later, she was sent to Auschwitz, where she suffered the same fate as millions of Jews.

In 2010, Victor Perez was standing outside his Fresno, California, house, talking with his cousin about the abduction of an 8-year-old girl the previous evening. As an older model, reddish-brown, white-striped Chevrolet truck drove by, Perez realized that it matched the abduction vehicle's description. "I decided to go after it while my cousin was dialing 911." Perez jumped into his own pickup and raced after the suspect truck. "He kept getting away. He kept going round my truck." The second time he caught up with him, "I saw the little girl and all fear was out the window. . . . I was just thinking we need to get that little girl to safety." On his fourth attempt, he forced the vehicle to stop, and the abductor, who was later apprehended, forced the traumatized and sexually abused girl out of the car. Afterward, the Fresno police chief reflected that, "If not for [Victor Perez] being as brave as he is, we may never have recovered her" (MSNBC, 2010).

Less dramatic acts of comforting, caring, and compassion abound: Without asking anything in return, people offer directions, donate money, give blood, volunteer time. Why, and when, will people help? What can be done to lessen indifference and increase helping?

Activity
30.1

Altruism is selfishness in reverse. An altruistic person is concerned and helpful even when no benefits are offered or expected in return. Jesus' parable of the Good Samaritan provides the classic illustration:

> A man was going down from Jerusalem to Jericho, and fell into the hands of robbers, who stripped him, beat him, and went away, leaving him half dead. Now by chance a priest was going down that road; and when he saw him, he passed by on the other side. So likewise a Levite, when he came to the place and saw him, passed by on the other side. But

a Samaritan while traveling came near him; and when he saw him, he was moved with pity. He went to him and bandaged his wounds, having poured oil and wine on them. Then he put him on his own animal, brought him to an inn, and took care of him. The next day he took out two denarii, gave them to the innkeeper, and said, "Take care of him; and when I come back, I will repay you whatever more you spend." (Luke 10:30–35, NRSV)

The Samaritan story illustrates altruism. Filled with compassion, he is motivated to give a stranger time, energy, and money while expecting neither repayment nor appreciation.

WHY DO PEOPLE HELP?

What motivates altruism? One idea, called **social-exchange theory**, is that we help after doing a cost-benefit analysis. As part of an exchange of benefits, helpers aim to maximize their rewards and minimize their costs. When donating blood, we weigh the costs (the inconvenience and discomfort) against the benefits (the social approval and noble feeling). If the anticipated rewards exceed the costs, we help.

You might object: Social-exchange theory takes the selflessness out of altruism. It seems to imply that a helpful act is never genuinely altruistic; we merely call it "altruistic" when the rewards are inconspicuous. If we know people are tutoring only to alleviate guilt or gain social approval, we hardly credit them for a good deed. We laud people for their altruism only when we can't otherwise explain it.

From babyhood onward, however, people sometimes exhibit a natural empathy, by feeling distress when seeing someone in distress and relief when their suffering ends. Loving parents (unlike child abusers and other perpetrators of cruelty) suffer when their children suffer and rejoice over their children's joys (Miller & Eisenberg, 1988). Although some helpful acts are indeed done to gain rewards or relieve guilt, experiments suggest that other helpful acts aim simply to increase another's welfare, producing satisfaction for oneself merely as a by-product (Batson, 1991). In these experiments, empathy often produces helping only when help-givers believe the other will actually receive the needed help and regardless of whether the recipient knows who helped.

Social norms also motivate helping. They prescribe how we *ought* to behave. We learn the **reciprocity norm**—that we should return help to those who have helped us. Thus we expect that those who receive favors (gifts, invitations, help) should later return them. The reciprocity norm is qualified by our awareness that some people are incapable of reciprocal giving and receiving. Thus we also feel a **social-responsibility**

norm—that we should help those who really need it, without regard to future exchanges. When we pick up the dropped books for the person on crutches, we expect nothing in return.

These suggested reasons for helping make biological sense. The empathy that parents feel for their children and other relatives promotes the survival of their shared genes. Likewise, say evolutionary psychologists, reciprocal altruism in small groups boosts everyone's survival.

WHEN DO PEOPLE HELP?

Social psychologists were curious and concerned about the bystanders' inaction. So they undertook experiments to identify when people will help in an emergency. Then they broadened the question to "Who is likely to help in non-emergencies—by such deeds as giving money, donating blood, or contributing time?" Among their answers: Helping often increases among people who are

- feeling guilty, thus providing a way to relieve the guilt or restore self-image;
- in a good mood; or
- deeply religious (evidenced by higher rates of charitable giving and volunteerism).

Social psychologists also study the *circumstances* that enhance helpfulness. The odds of our helping someone increase in these circumstances:

- We have just observed a helpful model.
- We are not hurried.
- The victim appears to need and deserve help.
- The victim is similar to us.
- We are in a small town or rural area.
- There are few other bystanders.

NUMBER OF BYSTANDERS

Bystander passivity during emergencies prompted social commentators to lament people's "alienation," "apathy," "indifference," and "unconscious sadistic impulses." By attributing the nonintervention to the bystanders' dispositions, we can reassure ourselves that, as caring people, we would have helped. But were the bystanders such inhuman characters?

Social psychologists Bibb Latané and John Darley (1970) were unconvinced. They staged ingenious emergencies and found that a single situational factor—the presence of other bystanders—greatly decreased intervention. By 1980, they had conducted four dozen experiments that compared help given by bystanders who perceived themselves to be either alone or with others. Given unrestricted communication among the bystanders, a person was at least as likely to be helped by a lone bystander as when observed by several bystanders (Latané & Nida, 1981; Stalder, 2008). In Internet communication, too, people are more likely to respond helpfully to a request for help (such as from someone seeking the link to the campus library) if they believe the request has come to them alone, and not to several others as well (Blair & others, 2005).

Sometimes the victim was actually less likely to get help when many people were around. When Latané, James Dabbs (1975), and 145 collaborators "accidentally" dropped coins or pencils during 1,497 elevator rides, they were helped 40 percent of the time when one other person was on the elevator and less than 20 percent of the time when there were six passengers.

Why does the presence of other bystanders sometimes inhibit helping? Latané and Darley surmised that as the number of bystanders increases, any given bystander is less likely to *notice* the incident, less likely to *interpret* the incident as a problem or an emergency, and less likely to *assume responsibility* for taking action (Figure 30-1).

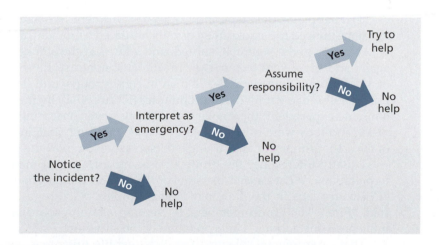

FIGURE 30-1
Latané and Darley's decision tree. Only one path up the tree leads to helping. At each fork of the path, the presence of other bystanders may divert a person down a branch toward not helping.   Source: Adapted from Darley & Latané (1968).

Noticing

Twenty minutes after Eleanor Bradley has fallen and broken her leg on a crowded city sidewalk, you come along. Your eyes are on the backs of the pedestrians in front of you (it is bad manners to stare at those you pass) and your private thoughts are on the day's events. Would you therefore be less likely to notice the injured woman than if the sidewalk were virtually deserted?

To find out, Latané and Darley (1968) had Columbia University men fill out a questionnaire in a room, either by themselves or with two strangers. While they were working (and being observed through a one-way mirror), there was a staged emergency: Smoke poured into the room through a wall vent. Solitary students, who often glanced idly about the room while working, noticed the smoke almost immediately—usually in less than 5 seconds. Those in groups kept their eyes on their work. It typically took them about 20 seconds to notice the smoke.

Interpreting

Once we notice an ambiguous event, we must interpret it. Put yourself in the room filling with smoke. Though worried, you don't want to embarrass yourself by appearing flustered. You glance at the others. They look calm, indifferent. Assuming everything must be okay, you shrug it off and go back to work. Then one of the others notices the smoke and, noting your apparent unconcern, reacts similarly. This is yet another example of informational influence.

So it happened in Latané and Darley's experiment. When those working alone noticed the smoke, they usually hesitated a moment, then got up, walked over to the vent, felt, sniffed, and waved at the smoke, hesitated again, and then went to report it. In dramatic contrast, those in groups of 3 did not move. Among the 24 men in eight groups, only 1 person reported the smoke within the first 4 minutes (Figure 30-2). By the end of the 6-minute experiment, the smoke was so thick it was obscuring the men's vision and they were rubbing their eyes and coughing. Still, in only three of the eight groups did even a single person leave to report the problem.

Equally interesting, the group's passivity affected its members' interpretations. What caused the smoke? "A leak in the air conditioning." "Chemistry labs in the building." "Steam pipes." "Truth gas." Not one said, "Fire." The group members, by serving as nonresponsive models, influenced one another's interpretation of the situation.

That experimental dilemma parallels real-life dilemmas we all face. Are the shrieks outside merely playful antics or the desperate screams of someone being assaulted? Is the boys' scuffling a friendly tussle or a vicious fight? Is the person slumped in the doorway sleeping, high on

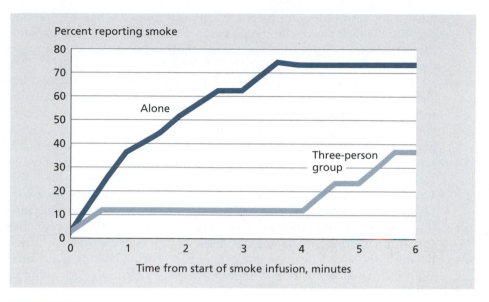

FIGURE 30-2
The smoke-filled-room experiment. Smoke pouring into the testing room was much more likely to be reported by individuals working alone than by three-person groups. Source: Data from Darley & Latané (1968).

drugs, or seriously ill, perhaps in a diabetic coma? That surely was the question confronting those who passed by Hugo Alfredo Tale-Yax as he lay on a Queens, New York, sidewalk, facedown and bleeding to death from multiple stab wounds. A surveillance video showed that for more than an hour, people walked by the homeless man, until finally one passerby shook him and then turned him over to reveal his wounds (*New York Times*, 2010).

In such dangerous situations with a perpetrator present and intervention requiring physical risk, the bystander effect is less (Fischer & others, 2011). Indeed, sometimes bystanders provide physical support in intervening. This was dramatically evident on 9/11 as passengers, led by Todd Beamer ("Let's roll!"), collectively intervened as four al Qaeda hijackers headed United Flight 93 toward its presumed target of the U.S. Capitol.

Assuming Responsibility

Misinterpretation is not the only cause of **bystander effect** (the inaction of strangers faced with ambiguous emergencies). Sometimes an emergency is obvious. According to initial reports, those who saw and heard

Kitty Genovese's pleas for help correctly interpreted what was happening. But the lights and silhouetted figures in neighboring windows told them that others were also watching. That diffused the responsibility for action.

Few of us have observed a murder. But all of us have at times been slower to react to a need when others were present. Passing a stranded motorist on a busy highway, we are less likely to offer help than on a country road. To explore bystander inaction in clear emergencies, Darley and Latané (1968) simulated the Genovese drama. They placed people in separate rooms from which the participants would hear a victim crying for help. To create that situation, Darley and Latané asked some New York University students to discuss their problems with university life over a laboratory intercom. The researchers told the students that to guarantee their anonymity, no one would be visible, nor would the experimenter eavesdrop. During the ensuing discussion, when the experimenter turned his microphone on, the participants heard one person lapse into a seizure. With increasing intensity and speech difficulty, he pleaded for someone to help.

Of those led to believe there were no other listeners, 85 percent left their room to seek help. Of those who believed four others also overheard the victim, only 31 percent went for help. Were those who didn't respond apathetic and indifferent? When the experimenter came in to end the experiment, most immediately expressed concern. Many had trembling hands and sweating palms. They believed an emergency had occurred but were undecided whether to act.

After their experiments, such as with the smoke-filled room, Latané and Darley asked the participants whether the presence of others had influenced them. We know the others had a dramatic effect. Yet the participants almost invariably denied the influence. They typically replied, "I was aware of the others, but I would have reacted just the same if they weren't there." That response reinforces a familiar point: *We often do not know why we do what we do.* That is why experiments are revealing. A survey of uninvolved bystanders following a real emergency would have left the bystander effect hidden.

These experiments raise an ethical issue. Is it right to force unwitting people to overhear someone's apparent collapse? Were the researchers in the seizure experiment ethical when they forced people to decide whether to interrupt their discussion to report the problem? Would you object to being in such a study? Note that it would have been impossible to get your "informed consent"; doing so would have destroyed the experiment's cover.

The researchers were always careful to debrief the laboratory participants. After explaining the seizure experiment, probably the most stressful, the experimenter gave the participants a questionnaire. One hundred percent said the deception was justified and that they would be willing to take part in similar experiments in the future. None reported feeling angry at the experimenter. Other researchers confirm that the overwhelming majority of participants in such experiments say that their participation was both instructive and ethically justified (Schwartz & Gottlieb, 1981). In field experiments, an accomplice assisted the victim if no one else did, thus reassuring bystanders that the problem was being dealt with.

Remember that the social psychologist has a twofold ethical obligation: to protect the participants and to enhance human welfare by discovering influences upon human behavior. Such discoveries can alert us to unwanted influences and show us how we might exert positive influences. The ethical principle seems to be: After protecting participants' welfare, social psychologists fulfill their responsibility to society by giving us insight into our behavior.

Will learning about the factors that inhibit altruism reduce their influence? Philip Zimbardo, whose "Heroism Project" aims to strengthen people's courage and compassion, contends that the first step to becoming a hero is recognizing social pressures that might deter your bystander action (Miller, 2011).

Experiments with University of Montana students by Arthur Beaman and colleagues (1978) revealed that once people understand why the presence of bystanders inhibits helping, they become more likely to help in group situations. The researchers used a lecture to inform some students how bystander inaction can affect the interpretation of an emergency and feelings of responsibility. Other students heard either a different lecture or no lecture at all. Two weeks later, as part of a different experiment in a different location, the participants found themselves walking (with an unresponsive confederate) past someone slumped over or past a person sprawled beneath a bicycle. Of those who had not heard the helping lecture, one-fourth paused to offer help; twice as many of those "enlightened" did so.

Having read this module, perhaps you, too, have changed. As you come to understand what influences people's responses, will your attitudes and your behavior be the same? Coincidentally, shortly before I wrote the last paragraph, a former student, now living in Washington, D.C., stopped by. She mentioned that she recently found herself part of a stream of pedestrians striding past a man lying unconscious on the sidewalk. "It took my mind back to our social psych class and the accounts of why people fail to help in such situations. Then I thought, 'Well, if I just walk by, too, who's going to help him?'" So she made a call to an emergency help number and waited with the victim—and other bystanders who now joined her—until help arrived.

So, how will learning about social influences upon good and evil affect you? Will the knowledge you've gained affect your actions? I hope so.

CONCEPTS TO REMEMBER

altruism   A motive to increase another's welfare without conscious regard for one's self-interests.

social-exchange theory   The theory that human interactions are transactions that aim to maximize one's rewards and minimize one's costs.

reciprocity norm   An expectation that people will help, not hurt, those who have helped them.

social-responsibility norm   An expectation that people will help those needing help.

bystander effect   The finding that a person is less likely to provide help when there are other bystanders.

31

❖

Social Psychology and the Sustainable Future

"Have always in view not only the present but also the coming generations, even those whose faces are yet beneath the surface of the ground—the unborn of the future Nation."

—*Gayanashagowa*, the Constitution of the Iroquois Nations

(also known as "The Great Law of Peace")

Activity 31.1

Imagine yourself on a huge spaceship traveling through our galaxy. To sustain your community, a spacecraft biosphere grows plants and breeds animals. By recycling waste and managing resources, the mission has, until recently, been sustainable over time and across generations of people born onboard.

The spaceship's name is Planet Earth, and its expanding crew now numbers 7 billion. Alas, it increasingly consumes its resources at an unsustainable rate—50 percent beyond the spaceship's capacity (FootPrintNetwork .org, 2011). With the growing population and consumption have come deforestation, depletion of wild fish stocks, and climate destabilization. Some crew members are especially demanding. For all 7 billion to live the average American lifestyle would require five Planet Earths.

In 1960, the spaceship Earth carried 3 billion people and 127 million motor vehicles. Today, it has more than 7 billion people and nearly 1 billion motor vehicles (Davis & others, 2011). The greenhouse gases emitted by motor vehicles, along with the burning of coal and oil to generate electricity and heat homes and buildings, are changing the Earth's climate. To ascertain how much and how fast climate change is occurring, several thousand scientists worldwide have collaborated to create and review the

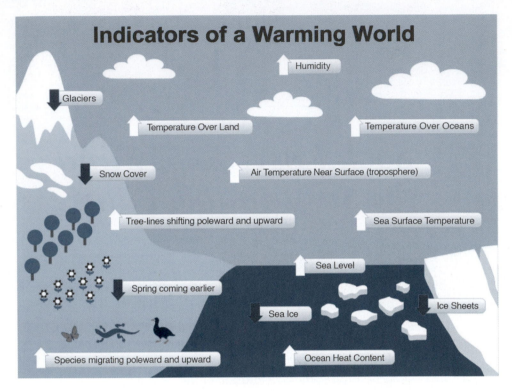

FIGURE 31-1
A synopsis of scientific indicators of global climate change.   Source: From John Cook (2010, and skepticalscience.com).

evidence via the Intergovernmental Panel on Climate Change (IPCC). The past chair of its scientific assessment committee, John Houghton (2011), reports that their conclusions—supported by the national academies of science of the world's 11 most developed countries—are undergirded by the most "thoroughly researched and reviewed" scientific effort in human history.

As the IPCC reports, and Figure 31-1 illustrates, converging evidence verifies climate change:

- *A warming greenhouse gas blanket is growing.* About half the carbon dioxide emitted by human activity since the Industrial Revolution (since 1750) remains in the atmosphere (Royal Society, 2010).
- There is now 39 percent more atmospheric carbon dioxide and 158 percent more atmospheric methane than before industrial times—and the increase has recently accelerated (World Meteorological Organization, 2011). As the permafrost thaws, methane gas release threatens to compound the problem (Gillis, 2011).

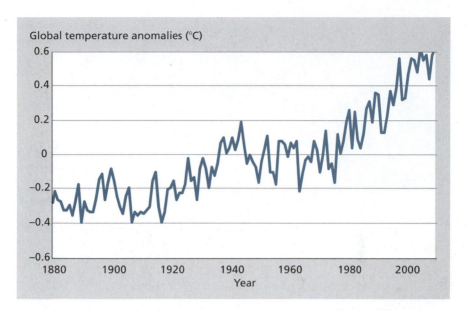

FIGURE 31-2
The warming world. Since 1980, global temperatures have trended upward, with record high temperatures greatly outnumbering record lows.   Source: NASA, 2011.

- *Sea and air temperatures are rising.* The numbers—the facts—have no political leanings. Every decade since the 1970s has been warmer than the one preceding it, with 9 of the 10 warmest years on record since 2001 (Royal Society, 2010; Figure 31-2). If the world were not warming, random weather variations should produce equal numbers of record-breaking high and low temperatures. In reality, record highs have been greatly outnumbering record lows—by about 2 to 1 in the United States, for example (Meehl & others, 2009). After amassing 1.6 billion temperature reports from more than 39,000 weather stations, one-time climate change skeptic Richard Muller (2011) became convinced: "Global warming is real."

- *Various plant and animal species are migrating.* In response to the warming world, they are creeping northward and upward, with anticipated loss of biodiversity (Harley, 2011; Houghton, 2011).

- *The Arctic sea ice is melting.* The late-summer ice cover has shrunk from nearly 3 million square miles in the late 1970s to 1.67 million square miles in 2011 (Figure 31-3). The West Antarctica and Greenland glacial ice sheets are also melting—faster than ever (Kerr, 2011).

- *The seas are rising.* Ocean water expands as it warms. Moreover, what happens in the Arctic doesn't stay in the Arctic. Projections

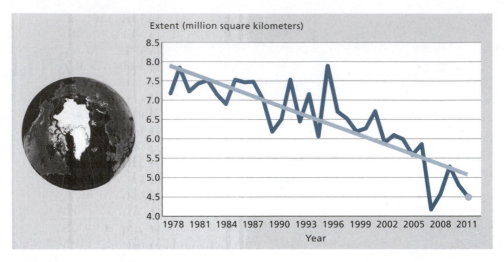

FIGURE 31-3
The shrinking ice cap. The National Snow and Ice Data Center and NASA show the September 2011, minimum Arctic ice sheet, compared with the median 1979 to 2000 minimum ice sheet. The figure depicts the shrinking September ice sheet year by year.

of rising sea levels portend large problems for coastal and low-lying areas, including Pakistan, southern China, and Indian and Pacific Ocean islands (Houghton, 2011).

- *Extreme weather is increasing.* Any single weather event—even the record European heat of 2010, or the record 2011 Mississippi floods, Missouri tornadoes, and Texas heat and drought—cannot be attributed to climate change. Weird weather happens. Nevertheless, climate scientists predict that global warming will make extreme weather events—hurricanes, heat waves, droughts, and floods—more intense (Kerr, 2011b). As precipitation in a warming and wetter world falls more as rain and less as snow, the likely result will be rainy season floods and less dry season snow and ice melt to sustain rivers.

*P*SYCHOLOGY AND CLIMATE CHANGE

Throughout its history, social psychology has responded to human events—to the civil rights era with studies of stereotyping and prejudice, to years of civil unrest and increasing crime with studies of aggression, to the women's movement with studies of gender development and gender-related attitudes. If global climate change is now "the greatest problem the world faces" (Houghton, 2011), surely we will see more and more studies of the likely effects of climate change on human behavior, of public opinion about climate change, and of ways to modify the human sources of climate change. Already, such inquiry is under way.

Psychological Effects of Climate Change

It's a national security issue, say some: Terrorist bombs and climate change are both weapons of mass destruction. "If we learned that al Qaeda was secretly developing a new terrorist technique that could disrupt water supplies around the globe, force tens of millions from their homes and potentially endanger our entire planet, we would be aroused into a frenzy and deploy every possible asset to neutralize the threat," observed essayist Nicholas Kristof (2007). "Yet that is precisely the threat that we're creating ourselves, with our greenhouse gases." Consider the human consequences.

Displacement and Trauma

In 2010, 42 million people were forced by natural disasters to leave their homes—up from 17 million in 2009. More than 90 percent of these displacements were caused by weather-related hazards, making climate-related displacement "the defining challenge of our times," said Antonio Guerres, the U.N. High Commissioner for Refugees (Amland, 2011).

If temperatures increase by the expected 2° to 4° Celsius this century, the resulting changes in water availability, agriculture, disaster risk, and sea level will necessitate massive resettlement (de Sherbinin & others, 2011). When drought or floods force people to leave their land, shelter, and work, as when sub-Saharan African farming and grazing lands become desert, the frequent result is increased poverty and hunger, earlier death, and loss of cultural identity. If an extreme weather event or climate change disrupted your ties to a place and its people, you could expect to feel grief, anxiety, and a sense of loss (Doherty & Clayton, 2011). For social and mental health, climate matters.

Climate and Conflict

Got war? Blame the climate. Such is often the case, notes Jeffrey Sachs (2006). The recent deadly carnage in Darfur, Sudan, for example, had its roots in drought and the competition for water. And so it has happened across history. Many human maladies—from economic downturns to wars—have been traced to climate fluctuations (Zhang & others, 2011). When the climate changes, agriculture often suffers, leading to increased famine, epidemics, and overall misery. Poorer countries, with fewer resources, are especially vulnerable to climate-produced misery (Fischer & Van de Vliert, 2011). And when miserable, people become more prone to anger with their governments and with one another, leading to war. For social stability, climate matters.

Public Opinion About Climate Change

Is the Earth getting warmer? Are humans responsible? Will it matter to our grandchildren? Yes, yes, and yes, say published climate scientists—97 percent of whom agree that climate change is occurring and is human caused

(Anderegg & others, 2010). As one report in *Science* explained, "Almost all climate scientists are of one mind about the threat of global warming: It's real, it's dangerous, and the world needs to take action immediately" (Kerr, 2009).

In response, the European Community, Australia, and India have all passed either a carbon tax on coal or a carbon emissions trading system, and even China now has a limited plan that will make polluters pay for excess pollution. In China, India, and South Korea, a 2010 Pew survey found more than 70 percent of people willing to address climate change by paying more for energy—compared with only 38 percent in the United States (Rosenthal, 2011).

In 2011, only 38 percent of Americans likewise agreed that there is "solid evidence" of human-caused global warming (Pew, 2011). And in 2011, their doubts supported a 240 to 184 U.S. House of Representatives vote *defeating* a resolution stating that "climate change is occurring, is caused largely by human activities, and poses significant risks for public health and welfare" (McKibben, 2011).

The enormous gulf between the scientific and U.S. public understandings of climate change intrigues social psychologists. Why the gap? Why is global warming not a hotter topic? And what might be done to align scientific and public understandings?

Personal Experience and the Availability Heuristic

By now, it's a familiar lesson: vivid and recent experiences often overwhelm abstract statistics. Despite knowing the statistical rarity of shark attacks and plane crashes, vivid images of such—being readily available in memory—often hijack our emotions and distort our judgments. We make our intuitive judgments under the influence of the availability heuristic—and thus we often fear the wrong things. If an airline misplaces our bag, we likely will overweight our immediate experience; ignoring data on the airline's overall lost-bag rate, we belittle the airline. Our ancient brains come designed to attend to the immediate situation, not out-of-sight data and beyond-the-horizon dangers (Gifford, 2011).

Likewise, people will often scorn global warming in the face of a winter freeze. One climate skeptic declared a record East Coast blizzard "a coup de grace" for global warming (Breckler, 2010). In a May 2011 survey, 47 percent of Americans agreed that "The record snowstorms this winter in the eastern United States make me question whether global warming is occurring" (Leiserowitz & others, 2011b). But then after the ensuing blistering summer, 67 percent of Americans agreed that global warming worsened the "record high summer temperatures in the U.S. in 2011" (Leiserowitz, 2011). In studies in the United States and Australia, people have expressed more belief in global warming, and more willingness to donate to a global warming charity, on warmer-than-usual days than on cooler-than-usual days (Li & others, 2011). As in so many life realms, our local experience distorts our global judgments.

Lacking Comprehension

As you may recall from Module 15, persuasive messages must first be understood. Thanks in part to the media's mixed messages—its framing of two opposing sides: those concerned about and those dismissive of climate change—only 39 percent of Americans in 2011 believed that "Most scientists think global warming is happening." More perceived "a lot of disagreement among scientists" or didn't know enough to say (Leiserowitz & others, 2011). Perceiving uncertainty, and reassured by the natural human optimism bias, people discount the threat (Gifford, 2011).

People also exhibit a "system justification" tendency—a tendency to believe in and justify the way things are in their culture, and thus, especially when comfortable, to not want to change the familiar status quo (Feygina & others, 2010). We tend to like our habitual ways of living—of traveling, of eating, and of heating and cooling our spaces.

More encouraging news comes from an experiment that showed people the global temperature trend in Figure 31-2. Regardless of their prior assumptions about global climate change, people were able to understand the trend and project it into the near future—and to adjust their beliefs. Education matters.

We also benefit from framing energy savings in attention-getting ways. An information sheet or store sign might read, "If you do not install CFL light bulbs, you will lose $____." And use long time periods. Instead of saying, "This Energy Star refrigerator will save you $120 a year on your electric bills, say it "will save you $2,400 in wasted energy bills over the next 20 years" (Hofmeister, 2010).

ENABLING SUSTAINABLE LIVING

What shall we do? Eat, drink, and be merry, for tomorrow is doom? Behave as so many participants have in prisoners' dilemma games, by pursuing self-interest to our collective detriment? ("Heck, on a global scale, my consumption is infinitesimal; it makes my life comfortable and costs the world practically nothing.") Wring our hands, dreading that fertility plus prosperity equals calamity, and vow never to bring children into a doomed world?

Those more optimistic about the future see two routes to sustainable lifestyles: (a) increasing technological efficiency and agricultural productivity, and (b) moderating consumption and population.

New Technologies

One component in a sustainable future is improved technologies. We have not only replaced incandescent bulbs with energy-saving ones, but replaced printed and delivered letters and catalogs with e-mail and e-commerce, and replaced commuter miles driven with telecommuting.

When driving, today's middle-aged adults drive cars that get twice the mileage and produce a twentieth of the pollution of the ones they drove as teenagers, and new hybrid and battery-driven cars promise greater efficiency.

Plausible future technologies include diodes that emit light for 20 years without bulbs; ultrasound washing machines that consume no water, heat, or soap; reusable and compostable plastics; cars running on fuel cells that combine hydrogen and oxygen and produce water exhaust; lightweight materials stronger than steel; roofs and roads that double as solar energy collectors; and heated and cooled chairs that provide personal comfort with less heating and cooling of rooms (N. Myers, 2000; Zhang & others, 2007).

Some energy solutions are low-tech. One Philippine nonprofit is working with the government and volunteers to install zero-energy solar light bulbs in one million low-income homes. The "bulbs" are nothing more than discarded clear plastic soda bottles that, when filled with water and wedged in a hole in the roof—with half the bottle exposed to the sun and half jutting into the room—transmit 55 watts of light. The result? Daytime light is provided without electricity bills (Orendain, 2011).

Given the speed of innovation (who could have imagined today's world a century ago?), the future will surely bring solutions that we aren't yet imagining. Surely, say the optimists, the future will bring increased material well-being for more people while requiring fewer raw materials and creating much less polluting waste.

Reducing Consumption

The second component of a sustainable future is controlling consumption. Unless we argue that today's less-developed countries are somehow less deserving of an improved standard of living, we must anticipate that their consumption will increase. As it does, the United States and other developed countries must consume less.

Thanks to family planning efforts, the world's population growth rate has decelerated, especially in developed nations. Even in less-developed countries, when food security has improved and women have become educated and empowered, birth rates have fallen. But if birth rates everywhere instantly fell to a replacement level of 2.1 children per woman, the lingering momentum of population growth, fueled by the bulge of younger humans, would continue for years to come. In 1960, after tens of thousands of years on the spaceship Earth, there were 3 billion people—which is also the number that demographers expect the human population to *grow* in just this century.

With this population size, humans have already overshot the Earth's carrying capacity, so consumption must also moderate. With our material appetites continually swelling—as more people seek personal computers, refrigeration, air-conditioning, jet travel—what can be done to moderate consumption by those who can afford to overconsume?

Incentives

One way is through public policies that harness the motivating power of incentives. As a general rule, we get less of what is taxed, and more of what is rewarded. On jammed highways, high-occupancy vehicle lanes reward carpooling and penalize driving solo. Gregg Easterbrook (2004) noted that if the United States had raised its gasoline tax by 50 cents a decade ago, as was proposed, the country would now have smaller, more fuel-efficient cars (as do the Europeans, with their higher petrol taxes) and would therefore import less oil. This, in turn, would have led to lower oil consumption, less global warming, lower gas prices, less money flowing to petro-dictators, and a smaller trade deficit weighing down the economy.

Europe leads the way in incentivizing mass transit and bicycle use over personal vehicle use. In addition to the small vehicles incentivized by high fuel taxes, cities such as Vienna, Munich, Zurich, and Copenhagen have closed many city center streets to car traffic. London and Stockholm drivers pay congestion fees when entering the heart of the city. Amsterdam is a bicycle haven. Dozens of German cities have "environmental zones" where only low CO_2 cars may enter (Rosenthal, 2011). The Netherlands has even experimented with a car meter that would tax drivers a fee for miles driven, rather like paying a phone fee for minutes talked (Rosenthal, 2011b).

Some free-market proponents object to carbon taxes because they are taxes. Others respond that carbon taxes are simply payment for external damage to today's health and tomorrow's environment. If not today's CO_2 emitters, who should pay for the cost of tomorrow's more threatening floods, tornadoes, hurricanes, droughts, and sea rise? "Markets are truly free only when everyone pays the full price for his or her actions," contends Environmental Defense Fund economist Gernot Wagner (2011). "Anything else is socialism."

Feedback

Another way to encourage greener homes and businesses is to harness the power of immediate feedback to the consumer by installing "smart meters" that provide a continuous readout of electricity use and its cost. Turn off a computer monitor or the lights in an empty room, and the meter displays the decreased wattage. Turn on the air-conditioning, and you immediately know the usage and cost. In Britain, where smart meters are being installed in businesses, Conservative Party leader David Cameron has supported a plan to have them installed in all homes. "Smart meters have the power to revolutionize people's relationship with the energy they use," he said to Parliament (Rosenthal, 2008).

Identity

In one survey, the top reason people gave for buying a Prius hybrid car was that it "makes a statement about me" (Clayton & Myers, 2009, p. 9). Indeed, argue Tom Crompton and Tim Kasser (2010), our sense of who we are—our identity—has profound implications for our climate-related behaviors. Does our social identity, the ingroup that defines our circle of concern, include only those around us now? Or does it encompass vulnerable people in places unseen, our descendants and others in the future, and even the creatures in the planet's natural environment?

Support for new energy policies will require a shift in public consciousness not unlike that occurring during the 1960s civil rights movement and the 1970s women's movement. Yale University environmental science dean James Gustave Speth (2008) is calling for an enlarged identity—a "new consciousness"—in which people

- see humanity as part of nature.
- see nature as having intrinsic value that we must steward.
- value the future and its inhabitants as well as our present.
- appreciate our human interdependence, by thinking "we" and not just "me."
- define quality of life in relational and spiritual rather than materialistic terms.
- value equity, justice, and the human community.

Is there any hope that human priorities might shift from accumulating money to finding meaning, and from aggressive consumption to nurturing connections? The British government's plan for achieving sustainable development includes an emphasis on promoting personal well-being and social health. Perhaps social psychology can help point the way to greater well-being, by suggesting *ways to reduce consumption*—and also by documenting *increased materialism,* by informing people that *economic growth does not automatically improve human morale,* and by helping people understand *why materialism and money fail to satisfy* and encouraging *alternative, intrinsic values.*

THE SOCIAL PSYCHOLOGY OF MATERIALISM AND WEALTH

Activity
31.2

Despite the recent economic recession, life for most people in Western countries is good. Today the average North American enjoys luxuries unknown even to royalty in centuries past: hot showers, flush toilets, central air-conditioning, microwave ovens, jet travel, wintertime fresh fruit, big-screen digital television, e-mail, and Post-it notes. Does money—and such associated luxuries—buy happiness? Few of us would answer yes. But ask a different question—"Would a *little* more money make you a *little* happier?"—and most of us will say yes. There is, we believe, a connection between wealth and well-being. That belief feeds what Juliet Schor (1998) has called the "cycle of work and spend"—working more to buy more.

Increased Materialism

Although the Earth asks that we live more lightly upon it, materialism has surged, most clearly in the United States. Think of it as today's American dream: life, liberty, and the purchase of happiness. The most dramatic evidence comes from the UCLA/American Council on Education annual survey of nearly a quarter million entering collegians. The proportion considering it "very important or essential" that they become "very well-off financially" rose from 39 percent in 1970 to 81 percent in 2012 (Figure 31-4). Those proportions virtually flip-flopped with those who considered it very important to "develop a meaningful philosophy of life." Materialism was up, spirituality down.

What a change in values! Among 19 listed objectives, new American collegians in most recent years have ranked becoming "very well-off financially" number 1. That outranks not only developing a life philosophy but also "becoming an authority in my own field," "helping others in difficulty," and "raising a family."

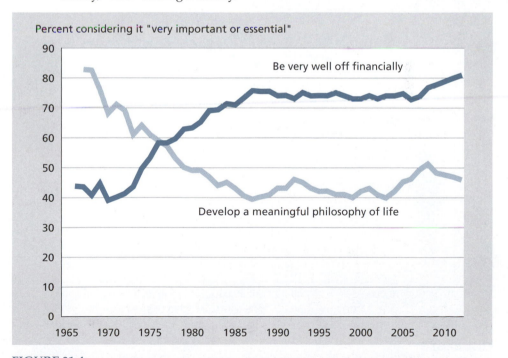

FIGURE 31-4
Changing materialism, from annual surveys of more than 200,000 entering U.S. collegians (total sample 13 million students).   Source: Data from Dey, Astin, & Korn, 1991, and subsequent annual reports.

Wealth and Well-Being

Does sustainable consumption indeed enable "the good life?" Does being well-off produce—or at least correlate with—psychological well-being? Would people be happier if they could exchange a simple lifestyle for one with palatial surroundings, ski vacations in the Alps, and executive-class travel? Would you be happier if you won a sweepstakes and could choose from its suggested indulgences: a 40-foot yacht, deluxe motor home, designer wardrobe, luxury car, or private housekeeper? Social-psychological theory and evidence offer some answers.

Are Wealthy Countries Happier?

We can observe the traffic between wealth and well-being by asking, first, if rich nations are happier places. There is, indeed, some correlation between national wealth and well-being (measured as self-reported happiness and life satisfaction). The Scandinavians have been mostly prosperous and satisfied; the Bulgarians are neither (Figure 31-5). But after nations reached

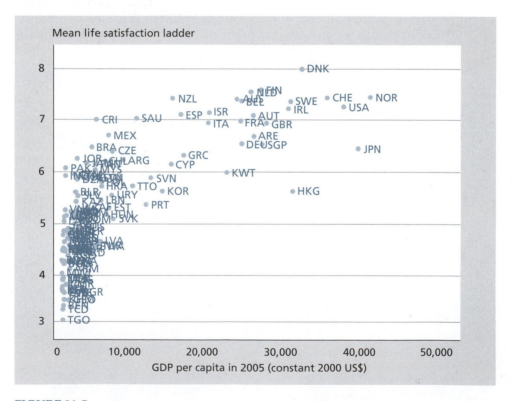

FIGURE 31-5

National wealth and well-being. Life satisfaction (on a 0 to 10 ladder) across 132 countries, as a function of national wealth (2005 gross domestic product, adjusted to the 2000 U.S. dollar value).   Source: From Di Tella & MacCullough (2008).

above $20,000 GDP per person, higher levels of national wealth are not predictive of increased life satisfaction.

Are Wealthier Individuals Happier?

We can ask, second, whether within any given nation, rich people are happier. Are people who drive their BMWs to work happier than those who take the bus? In poor countries—where low income threatens basic needs—being relatively well-off does predict greater well-being (Howell & Howell, 2008). In affluent countries, where most can afford life's necessities, affluence still matters—partly because people with more money perceive more control over their lives (Johnson & Krueger, 2006). But after a comfortable income level is reached, more and more money produces diminishing long-term returns. In Gallup surveys of more than 450,000 Americans during 2008 and 2009, daily positive feelings (the average of self-reported happiness, enjoyment, and frequent smiling and laughter) increased with income up to $75,000 (Kahneman & Deaton, 2010). The same was true for the absence of negative feelings of worry and sadness (Figure 31-6). In worldwide Gallup surveys across 123 countries, it's close relationships and

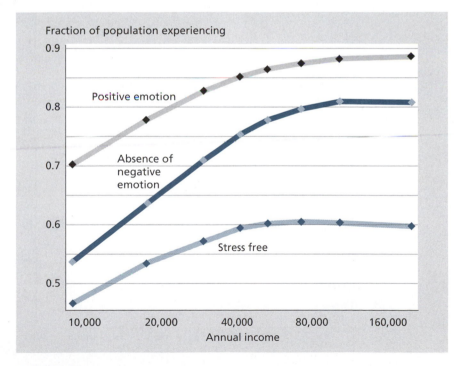

FIGURE 31-6

The diminishing effects of increasing income on positive and negative feelings. Data from Gallup surveys of more than 450,000 Americans (Kahneman & Deaton, 2010). (Note: income is reported on a log scale, which tends to accentuate the appearance of correlation between income and well-being.)

feeling empowered and competent that predict subjective well-being (Tay & Diener, 2011). When those basic needs are met, more money adds little.

Even the super-rich—the *Forbes* 100 wealthiest Americans—have reported only slightly greater happiness than average (Diener & others, 1985). And winning a state lottery seems not to enduringly elevate well-being (Brickman & others, 1978). Such jolts of joy have "a short half-life," notes Richard Ryan (1999).

Is the Wealthier Twenty-First Century Happier?

We can ask, third, whether, over time, a culture's happiness rises with its affluence. Does our collective well-being float upward with a rising economic tide?

In 1957, as economist John Kenneth Galbraith was describing the United States as *The Affluent Society*, Americans' per-person income was (in 2005 dollars) about $12,000. Today, as Figure 31-7 indicates, the United

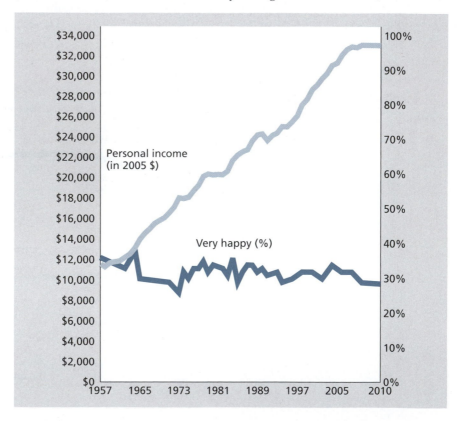

FIGURE 31-7

Has economic growth advanced human morale? While inflation-adjusted income has risen, self-reported happiness has not.   Source: Happiness data from General Social Surveys, National Opinion Research Center, University of Chicago. Income data from Bureau of the Census (1975) and *Economic Indicators.*

States is a triply affluent society. Although this rising tide has lifted the yachts faster than the dinghies, nearly all boats have risen. With double the spending power, thanks partly to the surge in married women's employment, we now own twice as many cars per person, eat out twice as often, and are supported by a whole new world of technology. Since 1960 we have also seen the proportion of households with dishwashers rise from 7 to 60 percent, with clothes dryers rise from 20 to 74 percent, and with air-conditioning rise from 15 to 86 percent (Bureau of the Census, 2009).

So, believing that it's "very important" to "be very well-off financially," and having become better off financially, are today's Americans happier? Are they happier with espresso coffee, smart phones, and suitcases on wheels than before?

They are not. Since 1957 the number of Americans who say they are "very happy" has declined slightly: from 35 to 29 percent. Twice as rich and apparently no happier. The same has been true of many other countries as well (Easterlin & others, 2010). After a decade of extraordinary economic growth in China—from few owning a phone and 40 percent owning a color television to most people now having such things—Gallup surveys revealed a *decreasing* proportion of people satisfied "with the way things are going in your life today" (Burkholder, 2005).

The findings are startling because they challenge modern materialism: *Economic growth has provided no apparent boost to human morale.* We excel at making a living but often fail at making a life. We celebrate our prosperity but yearn for purpose. We cherish our freedoms but long for connection.

Materialism Fails to Satisfy

It is striking that economic growth in affluent countries has failed to satisfy. It is further striking that individuals who strive most for wealth tend to live with lower well-being. This finding "comes through very strongly in every culture I've looked at," reported Richard Ryan (1999). Seek *extrinsic* goals—wealth, beauty, popularity, prestige, or anything else centered on external rewards or approval—and you may find anxiety, depression, and psychosomatic ills (Eckersley, 2005; Sheldon & others, 2004). Those who instead strive for *intrinsic* goals such as "intimacy, personal growth, and contribution to the community" experience a higher quality of life, concludes Tim Kasser (2000, 2002). Intrinsic values, Kasser (2011) adds, promote personal and social well-being and help immunize people against materialistic values. Those focused on close relationships, meaningful work, and concern for others enjoy inherent rewards that often prove elusive to those more focused on things or on their status and image.

Pause a moment and think: What is the most personally satisfying event that you experienced in the last month? Kennon Sheldon and his colleagues (2001) put that question (and similar questions about the last week and semester) to samples of university students. Then they asked them to rate the extent to which 10 different needs were met by the satisfying event. The students rated self-esteem, relatedness (feeling connected with others), and autonomy (feeling in control) as the emotional needs that most strongly accompanied the satisfying event. At the bottom of the list of factors predicting satisfaction were money and luxury.

People who identify themselves with expensive possessions experience fewer positive moods, report Emily Solberg, Ed Diener, and Michael Robinson (2003). Such materialists tend to report a relatively large gap between what they want and what they have, and to enjoy fewer close, fulfilling relationships. Wealthier people also tend to savor life's simpler pleasures less (Quoidbach & others, 2010). Sipping tea with a friend, savoring a chocolate, finishing a project, discovering a waterfall while hiking may pale alongside the luxuries enabled by wealth.

People focused on extrinsic and material goals also "focus less on caring for the Earth," reports Kasser (2011). "As materialistic values go up, concern for nature tends to go down. . . . When people strongly endorse money, image, and status, they are less likely to engage in ecologically beneficial activities like riding bikes, recycling, and re-using things in new ways."

But why do yesterday's luxuries, such as air-conditioning and television, so quickly become today's requirements? Two principles drive this psychology of consumption: our ability to adapt and our need to compare.

Our Human Capacity for Adaptation

The **adaptation-level phenomenon** is our tendency to judge our experience (for example, of sounds, temperatures, or income) relative to a neutral level defined by our prior experience. We adjust our neutral levels—the points at which sounds seem neither loud nor soft, temperatures neither hot nor cold, events neither pleasant nor unpleasant—on the basis of our experience. We then notice and react to up or down changes from those levels.

Thus, as our achievements rise above past levels, we feel successful and satisfied. As our social prestige, income, or in-home technology improves, we feel pleasure. Before long, however, we adapt. What once felt good comes to register as neutral, and what formerly was neutral now feels like deprivation.

Would it ever, then, be possible to create a social paradise? Donald Campbell (1975b) answered no: If you woke up tomorrow to your utopia—perhaps a world with no bills, no ills, someone who loves you unreservedly—you would feel euphoric, for a time. Yet before long, you would recalibrate your adaptation level and again sometimes feel gratified (when achievements surpass expectations), sometimes feel deprived (when they fall below), and sometimes feel neutral.

To be sure, adaptation to some events, such as the death of a spouse, may be incomplete, as the sense of loss lingers (Diener & others, 2006).

The elation from getting what we want—riches, top exam scores, the Chicago Cubs winning the World Series—evaporates more rapidly than we expect.

We also sometimes "miswant." When first-year university students predicted their satisfaction with various housing possibilities shortly before entering their school's housing lottery, they focused on physical features. "I'll be happiest in a beautiful and well-located dorm," many students seemed to think. But they were wrong. When contacted a year later, it was the social features, such as a sense of community, that predicted happiness, report Elizabeth Dunn and her colleagues (2003). The best things in life are not things.

Our Wanting to Compare

Much of life revolves around **social comparison,** a point made by the old joke about two hikers who meet a bear. One reaches into his backpack and pulls out a pair of sneakers. "Why bother putting those on?" asks the other. "You can't outrun a bear." "I don't have to outrun the bear," answers the first. "I just have to outrun you."

Similarly, happiness is relative to our comparisons with others, especially those within our own groups (Lyubomirsky, 2001; Zagefka & Brown, 2005). Whether we feel good or bad depends on whom we're comparing ourselves with. We are slow-witted or clumsy only when others are smart or agile. Let one professional athlete sign a new contract for $15 million a year and an $8-million-a-year teammate may now feel less satisfied. "Our poverty became a reality. Not because of our having less, but by our neighbors having more," recalled Will Campbell in *Brother to a Dragonfly.*

Further feeding our luxury fever is the tendency to compare upward: As we climb the ladder of success or affluence, we mostly compare ourselves with peers who are at or above our current level, not with those who have less. People living in communities where a few residents are very wealthy tend to feel envy and less satisfaction as they compare upward (Fiske, 2011).

In developed and emerging economies worldwide, inequality has grown in recent years. In the 34 Organisation for Economic Co-operation and Development (OECD, 2011) countries, the richest 10 percent now average nine times the income of the poorest 10 percent. (The gap is less in the Scandinavian countries, and is substantially greater in Israel, Turkey, the United States, Mexico, and Chile.) Countries with greater inequality not only have greater health and social problems, but also higher rates of mental illness (Pickett & Wilkinson, 2011). Likewise, U.S. states with greater inequality have higher rates of depression (Messias & others, 2011). And over time, years with more income inequality—and associated increases in perceived unfairness and lack of trust—correlate with less happiness among those with lower incomes (Oishi & others, 2011).

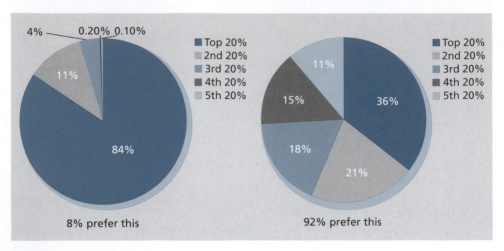

FIGURE 31-8
In an ideal society, what would be the level of income inequality? A survey of Americans provided a surprising consensus that a more equal distribution of wealth—like that shown on the right (which happened to be Sweden's distribution) would be preferable to the American status quo (shown on the left).

Although people often prefer the economic policies in place, a national survey found that Americans overwhelmingly preferred the income distribution on the right of Figure 31-8 (which, unbeknownst to the respondents, happened to be Sweden's income distribution) to the one on the left (which happened to be the United States' income distribution). Moreover, people preferred (in an ideal world) the top 20 percent income share ranging between 30 and 40 percent (rather than the actual 84 percent), with modest differences between Republicans and Democrats and between those making less than $50,000 and more than $100,000 (Norton & Ariely, 2011).

Even in China, income inequality has grown. This helps explain why rising affluence has not produced increased happiness—there or elsewhere. Rising income inequality, noted Michael Hagerty (2000), makes for more people who have rich neighbors. Television's modeling of the lifestyles of the wealthy also serves to accentuate feelings of "relative deprivation" and desires for more (Schor, 1998).

The adaptation-level and social-comparison phenomena give us pause. They imply that the quest for happiness through material achievement requires continually expanding affluence. But the good news is that adaptation to simpler lives can also happen. If we shrink our consumption by choice or by necessity, we will initially feel a pinch, but the pain likely will pass. "Weeping may tarry for the night, but joy comes with the morning," reflected the Psalmist. Indeed, thanks to our capacity to adapt and to adjust comparisons, the emotional impact of significant life events—losing a job or even a disabling accident—dissipates sooner than most people suppose (Gilbert & others, 1998).

TOWARD SUSTAINABILITY AND SURVIVAL

As individuals and as a global society, we face difficult social and political issues. How might a democratic society induce people to adopt values that emphasize psychological well-being over materialism? How might a thriving market economy mix incentives for prosperity with restraints that preserve a habitable planet? To what extent can we depend on technological innovations, such as alternative energy sources, to reduce our ecological footprints? And to what extent does the superordinate goal of preserving the Earth for our grandchildren call us each to limit our own liberties—our freedom to drive, burn, and dump whatever we wish?

A shift to postmaterialist values will gain momentum as people, governments, and corporations take these steps:

- Face the implications of population and consumption growth for climate change and environmental destruction
- Realize that extrinsic, materialist values make for *less* happy lives
- Identify and promote the things in life that can enable sustainable human flourishing

"If the world is to change for the better it must have a change in human consciousness," said Czech poet-president Vaclav Havel (1990). We must discover "a deeper sense of responsibility toward the world, which means responsibility toward something higher than self." If people were to believe that ever-bigger houses, closets full of seldom-worn clothes, and garages with luxury cars do not define the good life, then might a shift in consciousness become possible? Instead of being an indicator of social status, might conspicuous consumption become gauche?

Social psychology's contribution to a sustainable, flourishing future will come partly through its consciousness-transforming insights into adaptation and comparison. These insights also come from experiments that lower people's comparison standards and thereby cool luxury fever and renew contentment. In two such experiments, Marshall Dermer and his colleagues (1979) put university women through imaginative exercises in deprivation. After viewing depictions of the grimness of Milwaukee life in 1900, or after imagining and writing about being burned and disfigured, the women expressed greater satisfaction with their own lives.

In another experiment, Jennifer Crocker and Lisa Gallo (1985) found that people who five times completed the sentence "I'm glad I'm not a . . ." afterward felt less depressed and more satisfied with their lives than did those who completed sentences beginning "I wish I were a. . . ." Realizing that others have it worse helps us count our blessings. "I cried because I had no shoes," says a Persian proverb, "until I met a man who had no feet." *Downward* social comparison facilitates contentment.

Downward comparison to a hypothetical worse-off self also enhances contentment. In one experiment, Minkyung Koo and her colleagues (2008) invited people to write about how they might never have met their romantic partner. Compared to others who wrote about meeting their partner, those who imagined not having the relationship expressed more satisfaction with it. Can you likewise imagine how some good things in *your* life might never have happened? It's very easy for me to imagine not having chanced into an acquaintance that led to an invitation to author this book. Just thinking about that reminds me to count my blessings.

Social psychology also contributes to a sustainable and survivable future through its explorations of the good life. If materialism does not enhance life quality, what does?

- *Close, supportive relationships.* Our deep need to belong is satisfied by close, supportive relationships. People who are supported by intimate friendships or a committed marriage are much more likely to declare themselves "very happy."

- *Faith communities* and voluntary organizations are often a source of such connections, as well as of meaning and hope. That helps explain a finding from National Opinion Research Center surveys of nearly 50,000 Americans since 1972: 26 percent of those rarely or never attending religious services declared themselves very happy, as did 48 percent of those attending multiple times weekly.

- *Positive thinking habits.* Optimism, self-esteem, perceived control, and extraversion also mark happy experiences and happy lives. One analysis of 638 studies of 420,000+ people in 63 countries found that a sense of autonomy—feeling free and independent—consistently influences people's sense of well-being more than does wealth (Fischer & Boer, 2011).

- *Experiencing nature.* Carleton University students randomly assigned to a 17-minute nature walk near their campus ended up (to their and others' surprise) much happier than students who took a similar-length walk through campus walking tunnels (Nisbet & Zelenski, 2011). Japanese researchers report that "forest bathing"—walks in the woods—also help lower stress hormones and blood pressure (Phillips, 2011).

- *Flow.* Work and leisure experiences that engage one's skills mark happy lives. Between the anxiety of being overwhelmed and stressed, and the apathy of being underwhelmed and bored, notes Mihaly Csikszentmihalyi (1990, 1999), lies a zone in which people experience *flow.* Flow is an optimal state in which, absorbed in an activity, we lose consciousness of self and time. When people's experience is sampled using electronic pagers, they report greatest enjoyment not when they are mindlessly passive but when they are unselfconsciously absorbed in a mindful challenge. In fact, the less expensive (and generally more involving) a leisure activity, the *happier* people are while doing it. Most people are happier gardening than powerboating, talking to friends than watching TV. Low-consumption recreations prove most satisfying.

That is good news indeed. Those things that make for the genuinely good life—close relationships, social networks based on belief, positive thinking habits, engaging activity—are enduringly sustainable. And that is an idea close to the heart of Jigme Singye Wangchuk, former King of Bhutan. "Gross national happiness is more important than gross national product," he said. Writing from the Center of Bhutan Studies in Bhutan, Sander Tideman (2003) explained: "Gross National Happiness . . . aims to promote real progress and sustainability by measuring the quality of life, rather than the mere sum of production and consumption." Now other nations, too, are assessing national quality of life.

CONCEPTS TO REMEMBER

adaptation-level phenomenon The tendency to adapt to a given level of stimulation and thus to notice and react to changes from that level.

social comparison Evaluating one's abilities and opinions by comparing oneself with others.

References

ABELSON, R. P., KINDER, D. R., PETERS, M. D., & FISKE, S. T. (1982). Affective and semantic components in political person perception. *Journal of Personality and Social Psychology, 42,* 619–630.

ABRAMS, D., WETHERELL, M., COCHRANE, S., HOGG, M. A., & TURNER, J. C. (1990). Knowing what to think by knowing who you are: Self-categorization and the nature of norm formation, conformity and group polarization. *British Journal of Social Psychology, 29,* 97–119.

ABRAMSON, L. Y. (Ed.). (1988). *Social cognition and clinical psychology: A synthesis.* New York: Guilford.

ABRAMSON, L. Y., METALSKY, G. I., & ALLOY, L. B. (1989). Hopelessness depression: A theory-based subtype. *Psychological Review, 96,* 358–372.

ABREVAYA, J. (2009). Are there missing girls in the United States? Evidence from birth data. *American Economic Journal: Applied Economics, 1,* 1–34.

ACHA (2006). American College Health Association National College Health Assessment. Baltimore, MD: American College Health Association (acha-ncha.org).

ACKERMAN, J. M., GRISKEVICIUS, V., & LI, N. P. (2011). Let's get serious: Communicating commitment in romantic relationships. *Journal of Personality and Social Psychology, 100,* 1079–1094.

ACKERMANN, R., & DERUBEIS, R. J. (1991). Is depressive realism real? *Clinical Psychology Review, 11,* 565–584.

ADAIR, J. G., DUSHENKO, T. W., & LINDSAY, R. C. L. (1985). Ethical regulations and their impact on research practice. *American Psychologist, 40,* 59–72.

ADAMS, G., GARCIA, D. M., PURDIE-VAUGHNS, V., & STEELE, C. M. (2006). The detrimental effects of a suggestion of sexism in an instruction situation. *Journal of Experimental Social Psychology, 42,* 602–615.

ADAMS, J. M., & JONES, W. H. (1997). The conceptualization of marital commitment: An integrative analysis. *Journal of Personality and Social Psychology, 72,* 1177–1196.

ADDIS, M. E., & MAHALIK, J. R. (2003). Men, masculinity, and the contexts of help seeking. *American Psychologist, 58,* 5–14.

ADLER, N. E., BOYCE, T., CHESNEY, M. A., COHEN, S., FOLKMAN, S., KAHN, R. L., & SYME, S. L. (1993). Socioeconomic inequalities in health: No easy solution. *Journal of the American Medical Association, 269,* 3140–3145.

ADLER, N. E., BOYCE, T., CHESNEY, M. A., COHEN, S., FOLKMAN, S., KAHN, R. L., & SYME, S. L. (1994). Socioeconomic status and health: The challenge of the gradient. *American Psychologist, 49,* 15–24.

ADLER, R. P., LESSER, G. S., MERINGOFF, L. K., ROBERTSON, T. S., & WARD, S. (1980). *The effects of television advertising on children.* Lexington, MA: Lexington Books.

ADLER, S. J. (1994). *The jury.* New York: Times Books.

ADORNO, T., FRENKEL-BRUNSWIK, E., LEVINSON, D., & SANFORD, R. N. (1950). *The authoritarian personality.* New York: Harper.

AGTHE, M., SPÖRRLE, M., & FÖRSTERLING, F. (2008). Success attributions and more: Multidimensional extensions of the sexual attribution bias to failure attributions, social emotions, and the desire for social interaction. *Personality and Social Psychology Bulletin, 34,* 1627–1638.

AGTHE, M., SPÖRRLE, M., & MANER, J. K. (2011). Does being attractive always help? Positive and negative effects of attractiveness on social decision making. *Personality and Social Psychology Bulletin, 37,* 1042–1054.

AIELLO, J. R., & DOUTHITT, E. Z. (2001). Social facilitation from Triplett to electronic performance monitoring. *Group Dynamics: Theory, Research, and Practice, 5,* 163–180.

AIELLO, J. R., THOMPSON, D. E., & BRODZINSKY, D. M. (1983). How funny is crowding anyway? Effects of room size, group size, and the introduction of humor. *Basic and Applied Social Psychology, 4,* 193–207.

ALEXANDER, L., & TREDOUX, C. (2010). The spaces between us: A spatial analysis of informal segregation at a South African university. *Journal of Social Issues, 66,* 367–386.

ALLEE, W. C., & MASURE, R. M. (1936). A comparison of maze behavior in paired and isolated shell-parakeets (*Melopsittacus undulatus Shaw*) in a two-alley problem box. *Journal of Comparative Psychology, 22,* 131–155.

ALLISON, S. T., MACKIE, D. M., MULLER, M. M., & WORTH, L. T. (1993). Sequential correspondence biases and perceptions of change: The Castro studies revisited. *Personality and Social Psychology Bulletin, 19,* 151–157.

ALLISON, S. T., McQUEEN, L. R., & SCHAERFL, L. M. (1992). Social decision making processes and the equal partitionment of shared resources. *Journal of Experimental Social Psychology, 28,* 23–42.

ALLOY, L. B., & ABRAMSON, L. Y. (1979). Judgment of contingency in depressed and nondepressed students: Sadder but wiser? *Journal of Experimental Psychology: General, 108,* 441–485.

ALLOY, L. B., ABRAMSON, L. Y., GIBB, B. E., CROSSFIELD, A. G., PIERACCI, A. M., SPASOJEVIC, J., & STEINBERG, J. A. (2004). Developmental antecedents of cognitive vulnerability to depression: Review of findings from the cognitive vulnerability to depression project. *Journal of Cognitive Psychotherapy, 18,* 115–133.

ALLOY, L. B., ABRAMSON, L. Y., WHITEHOUSE, W. G., HOGAN, M. E., TASHMAN, N. A., STEINBERG, D. L., ROSE, D. T., & DONOVAN, P. (1999). Depressogenic cognitive styles: Predictive validity, information processing and personality characteristics, and developmental origins. *Behaviour Research and Therapy, 37,* 503–531.

ALLOY, L. B., ALBRIGHT, J. S., ABRAMSON, L. Y., & DYKMAN, B. M. (1990). Depressive realism and nondepressive optimistic illusions: The role of the self. In R. E. Ingram (Ed.), *Contemporary psychological approaches to depression: Theory, research and treatment.* New York: Plenum.

ALLPORT, F. H. (1920). The influence of the group upon association and thought. *Journal of Experimental Psychology, 3,* 159–182.

ALLPORT, G. W. (1958). *The nature of prejudice* (abridged). Garden City, NY: Anchor Books.

ALLPORT, G. W., & ROSS, J. M. (1967). Personal religious orientation and prejudice. *Journal of Personality and Social Psychology, 5,* 432–443.

ALTEMEYER, R. (1988). *Enemies of freedom: Understanding right-wing authoritarianism.* San Francisco: Jossey-Bass.

ALTEMEYER, R. (1992). Six studies of right-wing authoritarianism among American state legislators. Unpublished manuscript University of Manitoba.

ALTEMEYER, R., & HUNSBERGER, B. (1992). Authoritarianism, religious fundamentalism, quest, and prejudice. *International Journal for the Psychology of Religion, 2,* 113–133.

ALTMAN, I., & VINSEL, A. M. (1978). Personal space: An analysis of E. T. Hall's proxemics framework. In I. Altman & J. Wohlwill (Eds.), *Human behavior and the environment.* New York: Plenum.

AMBADY, N., BERNIERI, F. J., & RICHESON, J. A. (2000). Toward a histology of social behavior: Judgmental accuracy from thin slices of the behavioral stream. In M. P. Zanna (Ed.), *Advances in Experimental Social Psychology, 32,* 201–271.

AMBADY, N., & ROSENTHAL, R. (1993). Half a minute: Predicting teacher evaluations from thin slices of nonverbal behavior and physical attractiveness. *Journal of Personality and Social Psychology, 64,* 431–441.

AMERICAN BAR ASSOCIATION (2011). Enrollment and degrees awarded 1963–2010. (www.americanbar.org/content/dam/aba/administrative/legal_education_and_admissionsto _the_bar/stats_1.authcheckdam.pdf).

AMERICAN COLLEGE HEALTH ASSOCIATION (2009). *American College Health Association-National College Health Assessment II: Reference group executive summary Fall 2008.* Baltimore: Author.

AMERICAN ENTERPRISES (1992, January/February). Women, men, marriages and ministers, p. 106.

AMERICAN MEDICAL ASSOCIATION (2010, accessed 13 January). Women medical school applicants (Table 2 of Statistics History). (Ama-assn.org).

AMERICAN PSYCHOLOGICAL ASSOCIATION (1993). *Violence and youth: Psychology's response. Volume I: Summary report of the American Psychological Assocation Commission on Violence and Youth.* Washington DC: Public Interest Directorate, American Psychological Association.

AMERICAN PSYCHOLOGICAL ASSOCIATION (2002). *Ethical principles of psychologists and code of conduct 2002.* Washington, DC: APA (www.apa.org/ethics/code2002.html).

AMERICAN SOCIETY FOR AESTHETIC PLASTIC SURGERY (ASAPS) (2011, accessed September 16). *Highlights of the ASAPS 2010 statistics on cosmetic surgery.* ASAPS (www.asaps.com).

AMIR, Y. (1969). Contact hypothesis in ethnic relations. *Psychological Bulletin, 71,* 319–342.

AMLAND, B. H. (2011, June 6). Millions displaced by natural disasters last year. *Associated Press.*

ANASTASI, J. S., & RHODES, M. G. (2005). An own-age bias in face recognition for children and older adults. *Psychonomic Bulletin & Review, 12,* 1043–1047.

ANASTASI, J. S., & RHODES, M. G. (2006). Evidence for an own-age bias in face recognition. *North American Journal of Psychology, 8,* 237–252.

ANDERSON, C. (2011, August 2). Norway: War games and toys pulled from shelves. *New York Times* (www.nytimes.com).

ANDERSON, C. A. (2003). Video games and aggressive behavior. In D. Ravitch & J. P. Viteritti (Eds.), *Kids stuff: Marking violence and vulgarity in the popular culture.* Baltimore, MD: Johns Hopkins University Press.

ANDERSON, C. A. (2004). An update on the effects of violent video games. *Journal of Adolescence, 27,* 113–122.

ANDERSON, C. A., & ANDERSON, D. C. (1984). Ambient temperature and violent crime: Tests of the linear and curvilinear hypotheses. *Journal of Personality and Social Psychology, 46,* 91–97.

ANDERSON, C. A., BENJAMIN, A. J., JR., & BARTHOLOW, B. D. (1998). Does the gun pull the trigger? Automatic priming effects of weapon pictures and weapon names. *Psychological Science, 9,* 308–314.

ANDERSON, C. A., BERKOWITZ, L., DONNERSTEIN, E., HUESMANN, L. R., JOHNSON, J. D., LINZ, D., MALAMUTH, N. M., & WARTELLA, E. (2003). The influence of media violence on youth. *Psychological Science in the Public Interest, 4*(3), 81–110.

ANDERSON, C. A., BUCKLEY, K. E., & CARNAGEY, N. L. (2008). Creating your own hostile environment: A laboratory examination of trait aggressiveness and the violence escalation cycle. *Personality and Social Psychology Bulletin, 34,* 462–473.

ANDERSON, C. A., & BUSHMAN, B. J. (2001). Effects of violent video games on aggressive behavior, aggressive cognition, aggressive affect, physiological arousal, and prosocial behavior: A meta-analytic review of the scientific literature. *Psychological Science, 12,* 353–359.

ANDERSON, C. A., CARNAGEY, N. L., FLANAGAN, M., BENJAMIN, A. J., JR., EUBANKS, J., & VALENTINE, J. C. (2004). Violent video games: Specific effects of violent content on aggressive thoughts and behavior. *Advances in Experimental Social Psychology, 36,* 199–249.

ANDERSON, C. A., & DELISI, M. (2010). Implications of global climate change for violence in developed and developing countries. In J. Forgas, A. Kruglanski, & K. Williams (Eds.), *Social Conflict and Aggression.* New York: Psychology Press.

ANDERSON, C. A., & GENTILE, D. A. (2008). Media violence, aggression, and public policy. In E. Borgida & S. Fiske (Eds.), *Beyond common sense: Psychological science in the courtroom.* Malden, MA: Blackwell.

ANDERSON, C. A., GENTILE, D. A., & BUCKLEY, K. E. (2007). *Violent video game effects on children and adolescents: Theory, research, and public policy.* New York: Oxford University Press.

ANDERSON, C. A., & HARVEY, R. J. (1988). Discriminating between problems in living: An examination of measures of depression, loneliness, shyness, and social anxiety. *Journal of Social and Clinical Psychology, 6,* 482–491.

ANDERSON, C. A., HOROWITZ, L. M., & FRENCH, R. D. (1983). Attributional style of lonely and depressed people. *Journal of Personality and Social Psychology, 45,* 127–136.

ANDERSON, C. A., & KILDUFF, G. J. (2009). Why do dominant personalities attain influence in face-to-face groups? The competence-signaling effects of trait dominance. *Journal of Personality and Social Psychology, 96,* 491–503.

ANDERSON, C. A., LINDSAY, J. J., & BUSHMAN, B. J. (1999). Research in the psychological laboratory: Truth or triviality? *Current Directions in Psychological Science, 8,* 3–9.

ANDERSON, C. A., MILLER, R. S., RIGER, A. L., DILL, J. C., & SEDIKIDES, C. (1994). Behavioral and characterological attributional styles as predictors of depression and loneliness: Review, refinement, and test. *Journal of Personality and Social Psychology, 66,* 549–558.

ANDERSON, C. A., SAKAMOTO, A., GENTILE, D. A., IHORI, N., SHIBUYA, A., YUKAWA, S., NAITO, M., & KOBAYASHI, K. (2008). Longitudinal effects of violent video games on aggression in Japan and the United States. *Pediatrics,* **122,** e1067–e1072.

ANDERSON, S. L., ADAMS, G., & PLAUT, V. C. (2008). The cultural grounding of personal relationship: The importance of attractiveness in everyday life. *Journal of Personality and Social Psychology,* **95,** 352–368.

ANDERSON, C. A., SHIBUYA, A., IHORI, N., SWING, E. L., BUSHMAN, B. J., SAKAMOTO, A., ROTHSTEIN, C. R., & SALEEN, M. (2010). Violent video game effects on aggression, empathy, and prosocial behavior in Eastern and Western countries: A meta-analytic review. *Psychological Bulletin,* **136,** 151–173.

ANDREWS, P. W., & THOMSON, JR., J. A. (2009). The bright side of being blue: Depression as an adaptation for analyzing complex problems. *Psychological Review,* **116,** 620–654.

ANDREWS, P. W., & THOMSON, JR., J. A. (2010, January/February). Depression's evolutionary roots. *Scientific American Mind,* pp. 57–61.

ANTONAKIS, J., & DALGAS, O. (2009). Predicting elections: Child's play! *Science,* **323,** 1183.

ANTONIO, A. L., CHANG, M. J., HAKUTA, K., KENNY, D. A., LEVIN, S., & MILEM, J. F. (2004). Effects of racial diversity on complex thinking in college students. *Psychological Science,* **15,** 507–510.

AP/IPSOS (2006, May 4). Associated Press/Ipsos Poll data reported by personal correspondence with Michael Gross.

ARCHER, J. (1991). The influence of testosterone on human aggression. *British Journal of Psychology,* **82,** 1–28.

ARCHER, J. (2000). Sex differences in aggression between heterosexual partners: A meta-analytic review. *Psychological Bulletin,* **126,** 651–680.

ARCHER, J. (2004). Sex differences in aggression in real-world settings: A meta-analytic review. *Review of General Psychology,* **8,** 291–322.

ARCHER, J. (2007). A cross-cultural perspective on physical aggression between partners. *Issues in Forensic Psychology,* No. 6, 125–131.

ARCHER, J. (2009). Does sexual selection explain human sex differences? *Behavioral and Brain Sciences,* **32,** 249–311.

ARENDT, H. (1963). *Eichmann in Jerusalem: A report on the banality of evil.* New York: Viking.

ARGYLE, M., & HENDERSON, M. (1985). *The anatomy of relationships.* London: Heinemann.

ARGYLE, M., SHIMODA, K., & LITTLE, B. (1978). Variance due to persons and situations in England and Japan. *British Journal of Social and Clinical Psychology,* **17,** 335–337.

ARIZA, L. M. (2006, January). Virtual Jihad: The Internet as the ideal terrorism recruiting tool. *Scientific American,* pp. 18–21.

ARKIN, R. M., & BURGER, J. M. (1980). Effects of unit relation tendencies on interpersonal attraction. *Social Psychology Quarterly,* **43,** 380–391.

ARMOR, D. A., & SACKETT, A. M. (2006). Accuracy, error, and bias in predictions for real versus hypothetical events. *Journal of Personality and Social Psychology,* **91,** 583–600.

ARMOR, D. A., & TAYLOR, S. E. (1996). Situated optimism: Specific outcome expectancies and self-regulation. In M. P. Zanna (Ed.), *Advances in experimental social psychology* (Vol. 30). San Diego: Academic Press.

ARMS, R. L., RUSSELL, G. W., & SANDILANDS, M. L. (1979). Effects on the hostility of spectators of viewing aggressive sports. *Social Psychology Quarterly,* **42,** 275–279.

ARON, A., & ARON, E. (1989). *The heart of social psychology,* 2nd ed. Lexington, MA: Lexington Books.

ARON, A., & ARON, E. N. (1994). Love. In A. L. Weber & J. H. Harvey (Eds.), *Perspective on close relationships.* Boston: Allyn & Bacon.

ARON, A., DUTTON, D. G., ARON, E. N., & IVERSON, A. (1989). Experiences of falling in love. *Journal of Social and Personal Relationships,* **6,** 243–257.

ARON, A., FISHER, H., MASHEK, D. J., STRONG, G., LI, H., & BROWN, L. L. (2005). Reward, motivation, and emotion systems associated with early-stage intense romantic love. *Journal of Neurophysiology,* **94,** 327–337.

ARONSON, E. (2004). Reducing hostility and building compassion: Lessons from the jigsaw classroom. In A. G. Miller (Ed.), *The social psychology of good and evil.* New York: Guilford.

ARONSON, E., BREWER, M., & CARLSMITH, J. M. (1985). Experimentation in social psychology. In G. Lindzey & E. Aronson (Eds.), *Handbook of social psychology* (Vol. 1). Hillsdale, NJ: Erlbaum.

ARONSON, E., & GONZALEZ, A. (1988). Desegregation, jigsaw, and the Mexican-American experience. In P. A. Katz & D. Taylor (Eds.), *Towards the elimination of racism: Profiles in controversy.* New York: Plenum.

ARONSON, E., & MILLS, J. (1959). The effect of severity of initiation on liking for a group. *Journal of Abnormal and Social Psychology,* **59,** 177–181.

ARORA, R. (2005). China's "Gen Y" bucks tradition. Gallup Poll, (www.gallup.com/poll/15934/chinas-gen-bucks-tradition.aspx). Viewed online 1/22/09.

ARRIAGA, X. B. (2001). The ups and downs of dating: Fluctuations in satisfaction in newly formed romantic relationships. *Journal of Personality and Social Psychology, 80,* 754–765.

ARRIAGA, X. B., & AGNEW, C. R. (2001). Being committed: Affective, cognitive, and conative components of relationship commitment. *Personality and Social Psychology Bulletin, 27,* 1190–1203.

ARROW, K. J., & 21 OTHERS (2008). The promise of prediction markets. *Science, 320,* 877–878.

ASCH, S. E. (1955, November). Opinions and social pressure. *Scientific American,* pp. 31–35.

ASENDORPF, J. B. (1987). Videotape reconstruction of emotions and cognitions related to shyness. *Journal of Personality and Social Psychology, 53,* 541–549.

ASHER, J. (1987, April). Born to be shy? *Psychology Today,* pp. 56–64.

ASSOCIATED PRESS (AP) (2011, May 27). Canadian mother defends keeping baby's gender secret. *Associated Press.*

ASTIN, A. W., GREEN, K. C., KORN, W. S., & SCHALIT, M. (1987). *The American freshman: National norms for Fall 1987.* Los Angeles: Higher Education Research Institute, UCLA.

AUSTRALIAN ATTORNEY-GENERAL'S DEPARTMENT (2010, September). *Literature review on the impact of playing violent video games on aggression.* Commonwealth of Australia (www.ag.gov.au/cca).

AVERILL, J. R. (1983). Studies on anger and aggression: Implications for theories of emotion. *American Psychologist, 38,* 1145–1160.

AXSOM, D., YATES, S., & CHAIKEN, S. (1987). Audience response as a heuristic cue in persuasion. *Journal of Personality and Social Psychology, 53,* 30–40.

AZRIN, N. H. (1967, May). Pain and aggression. *Psychology Today,* pp. 27–33.

BACHMAN, J. G., & O'MALLEY, P. M. (1977). Self-esteem in young men: A longitudinal analysis of the impact of educational and occupational attainment. *Journal of Personality and Social Psychology, 35,* 365–380.

BACK, M. D., SCHMUKLE, S. C., & EGLOFF, B. (2008). Becoming friends by chance. *Psychological Science, 19,* 439–440.

BAILENSON, J. N., IYENGAR, S., YEE, N., & COLLINS, N. (2009). Facial similarity between voters and candidates causes influence. *Public Opinion Quarterly.*

BAILEY, J. M., GAULIN, S., AGYEI, Y., & GLADUE, B. A. (1994). Effects of gender and sexual orientation on evolutionary relevant aspects of human mating psychology. *Journal of Personality and Social Psychology, 66,* 1081–1093.

BAILEY, J. M., KIRK, K. M., ZHU, G., DUNNE, M. P., & MARTIN, N. G. (2000). Do individual differences in sociosexuality represent genetic or environmentally contingent strategies? Evidence from the Australian Twin Registry. *Journal of Personality and Social Psychology, 78,* 537–545.

BAIZE, H. R., JR., & SCHROEDER, J. E. (1995). Personality and mate selection in personal ads: Evolutionary preferences in a public mate selection process. *Journal of Social Behavior and Personality, 10,* 517–536.

BAKER, L., & MCNULTY, J. K. (2010). Shyness and marriage: Does shyness shape even established relationships? *Personality and Social Psychology Bulletin, 36,* 665–676.

BANAJI, M. R. (2004). The opposite of a great truth is also true: Homage of Koan #7. In J. T. Jost, M. R. Banaji, & D. A. Prentice (Eds.), *Perspectivism in social psychology: The yin and yang of scientific progress.* Washington, DC: American Psychological Association.

BANDURA, A. (1979). The social learning perspective: Mechanisms of aggression. In H. Toch (Ed.), *Psychology of crime and criminal justice.* New York: Holt, Rinehart & Winston.

BANDURA, A. (1997). *Self-efficacy: The exercise of control.* New York: Freeman.

BANDURA, A. (2004). Swimming against the mainstream: The early years from chilly tributary to transformative mainstream. *Behaviour Research and Therapy, 42,* 613–630.

BANDURA, A., PASTORELLI, C., BARBARANELLI, C., & CAPRARA, G. V. (1999). Self-efficacy pathways to childhood depression. *Journal of Personality and Social Psychology, 76,* 258–269.

BANDURA, A., ROSS, D., & ROSS, S. A. (1961). Transmission of aggression through imitation of aggressive models. *Journal of Abnormal and Social Psychology, 63,* 575–582.

BANDURA, A., & WALTERS, R. H. (1959). *Adolescent aggression.* New York: Ronald Press.

BANDURA, A., & WALTERS, R. H. (1963). *Social learning and personality development.* New York: Holt, Rinehart & Winston.

BANKS, S. M., SALOVEY, P., GREENER, S., ROTHMAN, A. J., MOYER, A., BEAUVAIS, J., & EPEL, E. (1995). The effects of message framing on mammography utilization. *Health Psychology, 14,* 178–184.

BARASH, D. P. (2003, November 7). Unreason's seductive charms. *Chronicle of Higher Education* (www.chronicle.com/free/v50/i11/11b00601.htm).

BARBER, B. M., & ODEAN, T. (2001a). Boys will be boys: Gender, overconfidence and common stock investment. *Quarterly Journal of Economics, 116,* 261–292.

BARBER, B. M., & ODEAN, T. (2001b). The Internet and the investor. *Journal of Economic Perspectives, 15,* 41–54.

BARBER, N. (2000). On the relationship between country sex ratios and teen pregnancy rates: A replication. *Cross-Cultural Research, 34,* 327–333.

BARGH, J. A., & CHARTRAND, T. L. (1999). The unbearable automaticity of being. *American Psychologist, 54,* 462–479.

BARGH, J. A., & FERGUSON, M. J. (2000). Beyond behaviorism: On the automaticity of higher mental processes. *Psychological Bulletin, 126,* 925–945.

BARGH, J. A., & McKENNA, K. Y. A. (2004). The Internet and social life. *Annual Review of Psychology, 55,* 573–590.

BARGH, J. A., McKENNA, K. Y. A., & FITZSIMONS, G. M. (2002). Can you see the real me? Activation and expression of the "true self" on the Internet. *Journal of Social Issues, 58,* 33–48.

BAR-HAIM, Y., ZIV, T., LAMY, D., & HODES, R. M. (2006). Nature and nurture in own-race face processing. *Psychological Science, 17,* 159–163.

BARLETT, C., BRANCH, O., RODEHEFFER, C., & HARRIS, R. (2009). How long do the short-term violent video game effects last? *Aggressive Behavior, 35,* 225–236.

BARLETT, C. P., HARRIS, R. J., & BRUEY, C. (2008). The effect of the amount of blood in a violence video game on aggression, hostility, and arousal. *Journal of Experimental Social Psychology, 44,* 539–546.

BARLOW, F. K., LOUIS, W. R., & HEWSTONE, M. (2009). Rejected! Cognitions of rejection and intergroup anxiety as mediators of the impact of cross-group friendships on prejudice. *British Journal of Social Psychology, 48,* 389–405.

BARNES, E. (2008, August 24). Scots heroine of Auschwitz who gave her life for young Jews. *Scotland on Sunday,* p. 3.

BARNETT, P. A., & GOTLIB, I. H. (1988). Psychosocial functioning and depression: Distinguishing among antecedents, concomitants, and consequences. *Psychological Bulletin, 104,* 97–126.

BARON, J., & HERSHEY, J. C. (1988). Outcome bias in decision evaluation. *Journal of Personality and Social Psychology, 54,* 569–579.

BARON, R. A., MARKMAN, G. D., & BOLLINGER, M. (2006). Exporting social psychology: Effects of attractiveness on perceptions of entrepreneurs, their ideas for new products, and their financial success. *Journal of Applied Social Psychology, 36,* 467–492.

BARON, R. M., MANDEL, D. R., ADAMS, C. A., & GRIFFEN, L. M. (1976). Effects of social density in university residential environments. *Journal of Personality and Social Psychology, 34,* 434–446.

BARON, R. S. (1986). Distraction-conflict theory: Progress and problems. In L. Berkowitz (Ed.), *Advances in experimental social psychology,* Orlando, FL: Academic Press.

BARON, R. S. (2000). Arousal, capacity, and intense indoctrination. *Personality and Social Psychology Review, 4,* 238–254.

BARONGAN, C., & HALL, G. C. N. (1995). The influence of misogynous rap music on sexual aggression against women. *Psychology of Women Quarterly, 19,* 195–207.

BARRY, D. (1995, January). Bored stiff. *Funny Times,* p. 5.

BARRY, D. (1998). *Dave Barry turns 50.* New York: Crown.

BAR-TAL, D. (2004). The necessity of observing real life situations: Palestinian-Israeli violence as a laboratory for learning about social behaviour. *European Journal of Social Psychology, 34,* 677–701.

BARTHOLOW, B. C., ANDERSON, C. A., CARNAGEY, N. L., & BENJAMIN, A. J., JR. (2004). Interactive effects of life experience and situational cues on aggression: The weapons priming effect in hunters and nonhunters. *Journal of Experimental Social Psychology, 41,* 48–60.

BARTHOLOW, B. C., & HEINZ, A. (2006). Alcohol and aggression without consumption: Alcohol cues, aggressive thoughts, and hostile perception bias. *Psychological Science, 17,* 30–37.

BARTHOLOW, B. C., SESTIR, M. A., & DAVIS, E. B. (2005). Correlates and consequences of exposure to video game violence: Hostile personality, empathy, and aggressive behavior. *Personality and Social Psychology Bulletin, 31,* 1573–1586.

BARTHOLOW, B. D., BUSHMAN, B. J., & SESTIR, M. A. (2006). Chronic violent video game exposure and desensitization: Behavioral and event-related brain potential data. *Journal of Experimental Social Psychology, 42*(4), 532–539.

BARTLETT, C. P., & RODEHEFFER, C. (2009). Effects of realism on extended violent and nonviolent video game play on aggressive thoughts, feelings, and physiological arousal. *Aggressive Behavior, 35,* 213–224.

BASILE, K. C., CHEN, J., LYNBERG, M. C., & SALTZMAN, L. E. (2007). Prevalence and characteristics of sexual violence victimization. *Violence and Victims, 22,* 437–448.

BASSILI, J. N. (2003). The minority slowness effect: Subtle inhibitions in the expression of views not shared by others. *Journal of Personality and Social Psychology, 84*, 261–276.

BATSON, C. D. (1991). *The altruism question: Toward a social-psychological answer.* Hillsdale, NJ: Erlbaum.

BATSON, C. D. (2006). "Not all self-interest after all": Economics of empathy-induced altruism. In D. De Cremer, M. Zeelenberg, & J. K. Murnighan (Eds.), *Social psychology and economics.* Mahwah, NJ: Erlbaum.

BATSON, C. D., & MORAN, T. (1999). Empathy-induced altruism in a prisoner's dilemma. *European Journal of Social Psychology, 29*, 909–924.

BATSON, C. D., SCHOENRADE, P., & VENTIS, W. L. (1993). *Religion and the individual: A social-psychological perspective.* New York: Oxford University Press.

BATSON, C. D., SYMPSON, S. C., HINDMAN, J. L., DECRUZ, P., TODD, R. M., JENNINGS, G., & BURRIS, C. T. (1996). "I've been there, too": Effect on empathy of prior experience with a need. *Personality and Social Psychology Bulletin, 22*, 474–482.

BATSON, C. D., & VENTIS, W. L. (1982). *The religious experience: A social psychological perspective.* New York: Oxford University Press.

BAUMAN, C. W., & SKITKA, L. J. (2010). Making attributions for behaviors: The prevalence of correspondence bias in the general population. *Basic and Applied Social Psychology, 32*, 269–277.

BAUMEISTER, R. (1996). Should schools try to boost self-esteem? Beware the dark side. *American Educator, 20*, 14–19, 43.

BAUMEISTER, R. (2005). Rejected and alone. *The Psychologist, 18*, 732–735.

BAUMEISTER, R. (2007). Is there anything good about men? Address to the American Psychological Association convention.

BAUMEISTER, R. F. (2005). *The cultural animal: Human nature, meaning, and social life.* New York: Oxford University Press.

BAUMEISTER, R. F., & BRATSLAVSKY, E. (1999). Passion, intimacy, and time: Passionate love as a function of change in intimacy. *Personality and Social Psychology Review, 3*, 49–67.

BAUMEISTER, R. F., BRATSLAVSKY, E., FINKENAUER, C., & VOHS, D. K. (2001). Bad is stronger than good. *Review of General Psychology, 5*, 323–370.

BAUMEISTER, R. F., BRATSLAVSKY, E., MURAVEN, M., & TICE, D. M. (1998). Ego depletion: Is the active self a limited resource? *Journal of Personality and Social Psychology, 74*, 1252–1265.

BAUMEISTER, R. F., CAMPBELL, J. D., KRUEGER, J. I., & VOHS, K. D. (2003). Does high self-esteem cause better performance, interpersonal success, happiness, or healthier lifestyles? *Psychological Science in the Public Interest, 4*(1), 1–44.

BAUMEISTER, R. F., DEWALL, C. N., & VOHS, K. D. (2009). Social rejection, control, numbness, and emotion: How not to be fooled by Gerber and Wheeler (2009). *Perspectives on Psychological Science, 4*, 489–493.

BAUMEISTER, R. F., & LEARY, M. R. (1995). The need to belong: Desire for interpersonal attachment as a fundamental human motivation. *Psychological Bulletin, 117*, 497–529.

BAUMEISTER, R. F., & TIERNEY, J. (2011). *Willpower: The rediscovery of humans' greatest strength.* New York: Penguin.

BAUMEISTER, R. F., & VOHS, K. (2004). Sexual economics: Sex as female resource for social exchange in heterosexual interactions. *Personality and Social Psychology Bulletin, 8*, 339–363.

BAUMEISTER, R. F., & WOTMAN, S. R. (1992). *Breaking hearts: The two sides of unrequited love.* New York: Guilford.

BAUMHART, R. (1968). *An honest profit.* New York: Holt, Rinehart & Winston.

BAXTER, T. L., & GOLDBERG, L. R. (1987). Perceived behavioral consistency underlying trait attributions to oneself and another: An extension of the actor-observer effect. *Personality and Social Psychology Bulletin, 13*, 437–447.

BAYER, E. (1929). Beitrage zur zeikomponenten theorie des hungers. *Zeitschrift fur Psychologie, 112*, 1–54.

BAZERMAN, M. H. (1986, June). Why negotiations go wrong. *Psychology Today,* pp. 54–58.

BAZZINI, D., CURTIN, L., JOSLIN, S., REGAN, S., & MARTZ, D. (2010). Do animated Disney characters portray and promote the beauty-goodness stereotype? *Journal of Applied Social Psychology, 40*, 2687–2709.

BBC (2008, November 21). Pirates "gained $150m this year" (news.bbc.co.uk).

BEALS, K. P., PEPLAU, L. A., & GABLE, S. L. (2009). Stigma management and well-being: The role of perceived social support, emotional processing, and suppression. *Personality and Social Psychology Bulletin, 35*, 867–879.

BEACH, S. R. H., HURT, T. R., FINCHAM, F. D., FRANKLIN, K. J., McNAIR, L. M., & STANLEY, S. M. (2011). Enhancing marital enrichment through spirituality: Efficacy data for prayer focused relationship enhancement. *Psychology of Religion and Spirituality, 3*, 201–216.

BEAMAN, A. L., BARNES, P. J., KLENTZ, B., & McQUIRK, B. (1978). Increasing helping rates through information dissemination: Teaching pays. *Personality and Social Psychology Bulletin, 4,* 406–411.

BEAMAN, A. L., & KLENTZ, B. (1983). The supposed physical attractiveness bias against supporters of the women's movement: A meta-analysis. *Personality and Social Psychology Bulletin, 9,* 544–550.

BEAMAN, A. L., KLENTZ, B., DIENER, E., & SVANUM, S. (1979). Self-awareness and transgression in children: Two field studies. *Journal of Personality and Social Psychology, 37,* 1835–1846.

BEARAK, B. (2010, July 9). South Africa braces for new attacks on immigrants. *New York Times* (www.nytimes.com).

BEAULIEU, C. M. J. (2004). Intercultural study of personal space: A case study. *Journal of Applied Social Psychology, 34,* 794–805.

BECK, A. T., & YOUNG, J. E. (1978, September). College blues. *Psychology Today,* pp. 80–92.

BEGUE, L., BUSHMAN, B., GIANCOLA, P., SUBRA, B., & ROSSET, E. (2010). "There is no such thing as an accident," especially when people are drunk. *Personality and Social Psychology Bulletin, 36,* 1301–1304.

BELL, P. A. (1980). Effects of heat, noise, and provocation on retaliatory evaluative behavior. *Journal of Social Psychology, 110,* 97–100.

BELLUCK, P. (2008, June 15). Gay couples find marriage is a mixed bag. *New York Times* (www.nytimes.com).

BELSON, W. A. (1978). *Television violence and the adolescent boy.* Westmead, England: Saxon House, Teakfield Ltd.

BEM, D. J. (1972). Self-perception theory. In L. Berkowitz (Ed.), *Advances in experimental social psychology* (Vol. 6). New York: Academic Press.

BEM, D. J., & McCONNELL, H. K. (1970). Testing the self-perception explanation of dissonance phenomena: On the salience of premanipulation attitudes. *Journal of Personality and Social Psychology, 14,* 23–31.

BENENSON, J. F., MARKOVITS, H., FITZGERALD, C., GEOFFROY, D., FLEMMING, J., KAHLENBERG, S. M., & WRANGHAM, R. W. (2009). Males' greater tolerance of same-sex peers. *Psychological Science, 20,* 184–190.

BENNETT, R. (1991, February). Pornography and extrafamilial child sexual abuse: Examining the relationship. Unpublished manuscript, Los Angeles Police Department Sexually Exploited Child Unit.

BENNIS, W. (1984). Transformative power and leadership. In T. J. Sergiovani & J. E. Corbally (Eds.), *Leadership and organizational culture.* Urbana: University of Illinois Press.

BERG, J. H. (1984). Development of friendship between roommates. *Journal of Personality and Social Psychology, 46,* 346–356.

BERG, J. H. (1987). Responsiveness and self-disclosure. In V. J. Derlega & J. H. Berg (Eds.), *Self-disclosure: Theory, research, and therapy.* New York: Plenum.

BERG, J. H., & McQUINN, R. D. (1986). Attraction and exchange in continuing and noncontinuing dating relationships. *Journal of Personality and Social Psychology, 50,* 942–952.

BERGER, J., & HEATH, C. (2008). Who drives divergence? Identity signaling, outgroup dissimilarity, and the abandonment of cultural tastes. *Journal of Personality and Social Psychology, 95,* 593–607.

BERKOWITZ, L. (1968, September). Impulse, aggression and the gun. *Psychology Today,* pp. 18–22.

BERKOWITZ, L. (1978). Whatever happened to the frustration-aggression hypothesis? *American Behavioral Scientist, 21,* 691–708.

BERKOWITZ, L. (1981, June). How guns control us. *Psychology Today,* pp. 11–12.

BERKOWITZ, L. (1983). Aversively stimulated aggression: Some parallels and differences in research with animals and humans. *American Psychologist, 38,* 1135–1144.

BERKOWITZ, L. (1984). Some effects of thoughts on anti- and prosocial influences of media events: A cognitive-neoassociation analysis. *Psychological Bulletin, 95,* 410–427.

BERKOWITZ, L. (1989). Frustration-aggression hypothesis: Examination and reformulation. *Psychological Bulletin, 106,* 59–73.

BERKOWITZ, L. (1995). A career on aggression. In G. G. Brannigan & M. R. Merrens (Eds.), *The social psychologists: Research adventures.* New York: McGraw-Hill.

BERKOWITZ, L. (1998). Affective aggression: The role of stress, pain, and negative affect. In R. G. Geen & E. Donnerstein (Eds.), *Human aggression: Theories, research, and implications for social policy.* San Diego: Academic Press.

BERKOWITZ, L., & GEEN, R. G. (1966). Film violence and the cue properties of available targets. *Journal of Personality and Social Psychology, 3,* 525–530.

BERKOWITZ, L., & LePAGE, A. (1967). Weapons as aggression-eliciting stimuli. *Journal of Personality and Social Psychology, 7,* 202–207.

BERNDSEN, M., SPEARS, R., VAN DER PLIGHT, J., & McGARTY, C. (2002). Illusory correlation and stereotype formation: Making sense of group differences and cognitive biases. In C. McGarty, V. Y. Yzerbyt, & R. Spears (Eds.), *Stereotypes as explanations: The formation of meaningful beliefs about social groups.* New York: Cambridge University Press.

BERNSTEIN, M. J., YOUNG, S. G., & CLAYPOOL, H. M. (2010). Is Obama's win a gain for Blacks? Changes in implicit racial prejudice following the 2008 election. *Social Psychology, 41,* 147–151.

BERNSTEIN, M. J., YOUNG, S. G., & HUGENBERG, K. (2007). The cross-category effect. Mere social categorization is sufficient to elicit an own-group bias in face recognition. *Psychological Science, 18,* 706–712.

BERSCHEID, E. (1981). An overview of the psychological effects of physical attractiveness and some comments upon the psychological effects of knowledge of the effects of physical attractiveness. In W. Lucker, K. Ribbens, & J. A. McNamera (Eds.), *Logical aspects of facial form (craniofacial growth series).* Ann Arbor: University of Michigan Press.

BERSCHEID, E. (2010). Love in the fourth dimension. *Annual Review of Psychology, 61,* 1–25.

BERSCHEID, E., BOYE, D., & WALSTER (HATFIELD), E. (1968). Retaliation as a means of restoring equity. *Journal of Personality and Social Psychology, 10,* 370–376.

BERSCHEID, E., DION, K., WALSTER (HATFIELD), E., & WALSTER, G. W. (1971). Physical attractiveness and dating choice: A test of the matching hypothesis. *Journal of Experimental Social Psychology, 7,* 173–189.

BERSCHEID, E., GRAZIANO, W., MONSON, T., & DERMER, M. (1976). Outcome dependency: Attention, attribution, and attraction. *Journal of Personality and Social Psychology, 34,* 978–989.

BERSCHEID, E., WALSTER, G. W., & HATFIELD (WAS WALSTER), E. (1969). Effects of accuracy and positivity of evaluation on liking for the evaluator. Unpublished manuscript. Summarized by E. Berscheid and E. Walster (Hatfield) (1978), *Interpersonal attraction.* Reading, MA: Addison-Wesley.

BETTENCOURT, B. A., DILL, K. E., GREATHOUSE, S. A., CHARLTON, K., & MULHOLLAND, B. (1997). Evaluations of ingroup and outgroup members: The role of category-based expectancy violation. *Journal of Experimental Social Psychology, 33,* 244–275.

BETTENCOURT, B. A., & KERNAHAN, C. (1997). A meta-analysis of aggression in the presence of violent cues: Effects of gender differences and aversive provocation. *Aggressive Behavior, 23,* 447–456.

BETTENCOURT, B. A., TALLEY, A., BENJAMIN, A. J., & VALENTINE, J. (2006). Personality and aggressive behavior under provoking and neutral conditions: A meta-analytic review. *Psychological Bulletin, 132,* 751–777.

BIANCHI, S. M., MILKIE, M. A., SAYER, L. C., & ROBINSON, J. P. (2000). Is anyone doing the housework? Trends in the gender division of household labor. *Social Forces, 79,* 191–228.

BIERNAT, M. (2003). Toward a broader view of social stereotyping. *American Psychologist, 58,* 1019–1027.

BIERNAT, M., & KOBRYNOWICZ, D. (1997). Gender- and race-based standards of competence: Lower minimum standards but higher ability standards for devalued groups. *Journal of Personality and Social Psychology, 72,* 544–557.

BIERNAT, M., VESCIO, T. K., & GREEN, M. L. (1996). Selective self-stereotyping. *Journal of Personality and Social Psychology, 71,* 1194–1209.

BILLIG, M., & TAJFEL, H. (1973). Social categorization and similarity in intergroup behaviour. *European Journal of Social Psychology, 3,* 27–52.

BINDER, J., ZAGEFKA, H., BROWN, R., FUNKE, F., KESSLER, T., MUMMENDEY, A., MAQUIL, A., DEMOULIN, S., & LEYENS, J-P. (2009). Does contact reduce prejudice or does prejudice reduce contact? A longitudinal test of the contact hypothesis among majority and minority groups in three European countries. *Journal of Personality and Social Psychology, 96,* 843–856.

BINGENHEIMER, J. B., BRENNAN, R. T., & EARLS, F. J. (2005). Firearm violence exposure and serious violent behavior. *Science, 308,* 1323–1326.

BIS (2011, February). *Women on corporate boards.* Department for Business Innovation and Skills, (www.bis.gov.uk).

BISHOP, B. (2008). *The big sort: Why the clustering of like-minded America is tearing us apart.* Boston: Houghton-Mifflin.

BJÖRKQVIST, K. (1994). Sex differences in physical, verbal, and indirect aggression: A review of recent research. *Sex Roles, 30,* 177–188.

BLACKHART, G. C., NELSON, B. C., KNOWLES, M. L., & BAUMEISTER, R. F. (2009). Rejection elicits emotional reactions but neither causes immediate distress nor lowers self-esteem: A meta-analytic review of 192 studies on social exclusion. *Personality and Social Psychology Review, 13,* 269–309.

BLACKBURN, R. T., PELLINO, G. R., BOBERG, A., & O'CONNELL, C. (1980). Are instructional improvement programs off target? *Current Issues in Higher Education, 1,* 31–48.

BLAIR, C. A., THOMPSON, L. F., & WUENSCH, K. L. (2005). Electronic helping behavior: The virtual presence of others makes a difference. *Basic and Applied Social Psychology, 27,* 171–178.

BLAKE, R. R., & MOUTON, J. S. (1962). The intergroup dynamics of win-lose conflict and problem-solving collaboration in union-management relations. In M. Sherif (Ed.), *Intergroup relations and leadership.* New York: Wiley.

BLAKE, R. R., & MOUTON, J. S. (1979). Intergroup problem solving in organizations: From theory to practice. In W. G. Austin & S. Worchel (Eds.), *The social psychology of intergroup relations*. Monterey, CA: Brooks/Cole.

BLANCHARD, F. A., & COOK, S. W. (1976). Effects of helping a less competent member of a cooperating interracial group on the development of interpersonal attraction. *Journal of Personality and Social Psychology*, **34**, 1245–1255.

BLANK, H., NESTLER, S., VON COLLANI, G., & FISCHER, V. (2008). How many hindsight biases are there? *Cognition*, **106**, 1408–1440.

BLANTON, D. (2011, April 7). *Fox News poll: 24 percent believe Obama not born in U.S.* FoxNews.com.

BLANTON, H., JACCARD, J., GONZALES, P. M., & CHRISTIE, C. (2006). Decoding the implicit association test: Implications for criterion prediction. *Journal of Experimental Social Psychology*, **42**, 192–212.

BLANTON, H., JACCARD, J., KLICK, J., MELLERS, B., MITCHELL, G., & TETLOCK P. E. (2009). Strong claims and weak evidence: reassessing the predictive validity of the IAT. *Journal of Applied Psychology*, **94**, 583–603.

BLASS, T. (1996). Stanley Milgram: A life of inventiveness and controversy. In G. A. Kimble, C. A. Boneau, & M. Wertheimer (Eds.). *Portraits of pioneers in psychology* (Vol. II). Washington, DC: American Psychological Association.

BLASS, T. (1999). The Milgram paradigm after 35 years: Some things we now know about obedience to authority. *Journal of Applied Social Psychology*, **29**, 955–978.

BLOCK, J., & FUNDER, D. C. (1986). Social roles and social perception: Individual differences in attribution and error. *Journal of Personality and Social Psychology*, **51**, 1200–1207.

BLOOM, P. (2010, May 6). The moral life of babies. *The New York Times Magazine* (www.nytimes.com).

BODEN, J. M., FERGUSSON, D. M., & HORWOOD, L. J. (2008). Does adolescent self-esteem predict later life outcomes? A test of the causal role of self-esteem. *Development and Psychopathology*, **20**, 319–339.

BODENHAUSEN, G. V. (1993). Emotions, arousal, and stereotypic judgments: A heuristic model of affect and stereotyping. In D. M. Mackie & D. L. Hamilton (Eds.), *Affect, cognition, and stereotyping: Interactive processes in group perception*. San Diego: Academic Press.

BOER, D., FISCHER, R., STRACK, M., BOND, M. H., LO, E., & LAM, J. (2011). How shared preferences in music create bonds between people: Values as the missing link. *Personality and Social Psychology Bulletin*, **37**, 1159–1171.

BONANNO, G. A., RENNICKE, C., & DEKEL, S. (2005). Self-enhancement among high-exposure survivors of the September 11th terrorist attack: Resilience or social maladjustment? *Journal of Personality and Social Psychology*, **88**, 984–998.

BOND, C. F., JR., & TITUS, L. J. (1983). Social facilitation: A meta-analysis of 241 studies. *Psychological Bulletin*, **94**, 265–292.

BOND, M. H. (2004). Culture and aggression: From context to coercion. *Personality and Social Psychology Review*, **8**, 62–78.

BONO, J. E., & JUDGE, T. A. (2004). Personality and transformational and transactional leadership: A meta-analysis. *Journal of Applied Psychology*, **89**, 901–910.

BONTA, B. D. (1997). Cooperation and competition in peaceful societies. *Psychological Bulletin*, **121**, 299–320.

BORGIDA, E., & BREKKE, N. (1985). Psycholegal research on rape trials. In A. W. Burgess (Ed.), *Rape and sexual assault: A research handbook*. New York: Garland.

BORKENAU, P., & LIEBLER, A. (1993). Convergence of stranger ratings of personality and intelligence with self-ratings, partner ratings, and measured intelligence. *Journal of Personality and Social Psychology*, **65**, 546–553.

BORNSTEIN, G., & RAPOPORT, A. (1988). Intergroup competition for the provision of step-level public goods: Effects of preplay communication. *European Journal of Social Psychology*, **18**, 125–142.

BORNSTEIN, G., RAPOPORT, A., KERPEL, L., & KATZ, T. (1989). Within- and between-group communication in intergroup competition for public goods. *Journal of Experimental Social Psychology*, **25**, 422–436.

BORNSTEIN, R. F. (1989). Exposure and affect: Overview and meta-analysis of research, 1968–1987. *Psychological Bulletin*, **106**, 265–289.

BORNSTEIN, R. F. (1999). Source amnesia, misattribution, and the power of unconscious perceptions and memories. *Psychoanalytic Psychology*, **16**, 155–178.

BORNSTEIN, R. F., GALLEY, D. J., LEONE, D. R., & KALE, A. R. (1991). The temporal stability of ratings of parents: Test-retest reliability and influence of parental contact. *Journal of Social Behavior and Personality*, **6**, 641–649.

BOSSARD, J. H. S. (1932). Residential propinquity as a factor in marriage selection. *American Journal of Sociology*, **38**, 219–224.

BOTHWELL, R. K., BRIGHAM, J. C., & MALPASS, R. S. (1989). Cross-racial identification. *Personality and Social Psychology Bulletin*, **15**, 19–25.

BOTVIN, G. J., EPSTEIN, J. A., & GRIFFIN, K. W. (2008). A social influence model of alcohol use for inner-city adolescents: Family drinking, perceived drinking norms, and perceived social benefits of drinking. *Journal of Studies on Alcohol and Drugs, 69,* 397–405.

BOTVIN, G. J., SCHINKE, S., & ORLANDI, M. A. (1995). School-based health promotion: Substance abuse and sexual behavior. *Applied & Preventive Psychology, 4,* 167–184.

BOTWIN, M. D., BUSS, D. M., & SHACKELFORD, T. K. (1997). Personality and mate preferences: Five factors in mate selection and marital satisfaction. *Journal of Personality, 65,* 107–136.

BOUAS, K. S., & KOMORITA, S. S. (1996). Group discussion and cooperation in social dilemmas. *Personality and Social Psychology Bulletin, 22,* 1144–1150.

BOURKE, M. L., & HERNANDEZ, A. E. (2009). The 'Butner study' redux: A report of the incidence of hands-on child victimization by child pornography offenders. *Journal of Family Violence, 24,* 183–191.

BOWER, G. H. (1987). Commentary on mood and memory. *Behavioral Research and Therapy, 25,* 443–455.

BOYATZIS, C. J., MATILLO, G. M., & NESBITT, K. M. (1995). Effects of the "Mighty Morphin Power Rangers" on children's aggression with peers. *Child Study Journal, 25,* 45–55.

BRAUER, M., JUDD, C. M., & JACQUELIN, V. (2001). The communication of social stereotypes: The effects of group discussion and information distribution on stereotypic appraisals. *Journal of Personality and Social Psychology, 81,* 463–464, 475.

BRAVERMAN, J. (2005). The effect of mood on detection of covariation. *Personality and Social Psychology Bulletin, 31,* 1487–1497.

BRECKLER, S. J. (2010, April). In the heat of the moment. *Monitor on Psychology,* p. 39.

BREHM, S., & BREHM, J. W. (1981). *Psychological reactance: A theory of freedom and control.* New York: Academic Press.

BRENNER, S. N., & MOLANDER, E. A. (1977, January–February). Is the ethics of business changing? *Harvard Business Review,* pp. 57–71.

BREWER, M. B. (1987). Collective decisions. *Social Science, 72,* 140–143.

BREWER, M. B., & GAERTNER, S. L. (2004). Toward reduction of prejudice: Intergroup contact and social categorization. In M. B. Brewer & M. Hewstone (Eds.), *Self and social identity.* Malden, MA: Blackwell.

BREWER, M. B., & MILLER, N. (1988). Contact and cooperation: When do they work? In P. A. Katz & D. Taylor (Eds.), *Towards the elimination of racism: Profiles in controversy.* New York: Plenum.

BREWER, M. B., & SILVER, M. (1978). In-group bias as a function of task characteristics. *European Journal of Social Psychology, 8,* 393–400.

BRICKMAN, P., COATES, D., & JANOFF-BULMAN, R. J. (1978). Lottery winners and accident victims: Is happiness relative? *Journal of Personality and Social Psychology, 36,* 917–927.

BRITISH PSYCHOLOGICAL SOCIETY (2009). *Code of ethics and conduct* (www.bps.org).

BROCKNER, J., & HULTON, A. J. B. (1978). How to reverse the vicious cycle of low self-esteem: The importance of attentional focus. *Journal of Experimental Social Psychology, 14,* 564–578.

BROCKNER, J., RUBIN, J. Z., FINE, J., HAMILTON, T. P., THOMAS, B., & TURETSKY, B. (1982). Factors affecting entrapment in escalating conflicts: The importance of timing. *Journal of Research in Personality, 16,* 247–266.

BRODT, S. E., & ZIMBARDO, P. G. (1981). Modifying shyness-related social behavior through symptom misattribution. *Journal of Personality and Social Psychology, 41,* 437–449.

BRONFENBRENNER, U. (1961). The mirror image in Soviet-American relations. *Journal of Social Issues, 17*(3), 45–56.

BROOKS, D. (2005, August 10). All cultures are not equal. *New York Times* (www.nytimes.com).

BROOKS, D. (2011, September 29). The limits of empathy. *New York Times* (www.nytimes.com).

BROWN, D. E. (1991). *Human universals.* New York: McGraw-Hill.

BROWN, D. E. (2000). Human universals and their implications. In N. Roughley (Ed.), *Being humans: Anthropological universality and particularity in transdisciplinary perspectives.* New York: Walter de Gruyter.

BROWN, H. J., JR. (1990). *P.S. I love you.* Nashville: Rutledge Hill.

BROWN, J. D., NOVICK, N. J., LORD, K. A., & RICHARDS, J. M. (1992). When Gulliver travels: Social context, psychological closeness, and self-appraisals. *Journal of Personality and Social Psychology, 62,* 717–727.

BROWN, J. D., & TAYLOR, S. E. (1986). Affect and the processing of personal information: Evidence for mood-activated self-schemata. *Journal of Experimental Social Psychology, 22,* 436–452.

BROWN, R. (1965). *Social psychology.* New York: Free Press.

BROWN, R. (1987). Theory of politeness: An exemplary case. Paper presented to the Society of Experimental Social Psychology meeting. Cited by R. O. Kroker & L. A. Wood (1992), Are the rules of address universal? IV: Comparison of Chinese, Korean, Greek, and German usage. *Journal of Cross-Cultural Psychology, 23,* 148–162.

Brown, R., Maras, P., Masser, B., Vivian, J., & Hewstone, M. (2001). Life on the ocean wave: Testing some intergroup hypotheses in a naturalistic setting. *Group Processes and Intergroup Relations, 4,* 81–97.

Brown, R., Vivian, J., & Hewstone, M. (1999). Changing attitudes through intergroup contact: The effects of group membership salience. *European Journal of Social Psychology, 29,* 741–764.

Brown, R. P., Charnsangavej, T., Keough, K. A., Newman, M. L., & Rentfrom, P. J. (2000). Putting the "affirm" into affirmative action: Preferential selection and academic performance. *Journal of Personality and Social Psychology, 79,* 736–747.

Brown, R. P., Osterman, L. L., & Barnes, C. D. (2009). School violence and the culture of honor. *Psychological Science, 20,* 1400–1405.

Brown, W. M., Price, M. E., Kang, J., Pound, N., Zhao, Y., & Yu, H. (2008). Fluctuating asymmetry and preferences for sex-typical bodily characteristics. *Proceedings of the National Academy of Sciences, 105,* 12938–12943 (pnas.org).

Buehler, R., Griffin, D., & Ross, M. (1994). Exploring the "planning fallacy": When people underestimate their task completion times. *Journal of Personality and Social Psychology, 67,* 366–381.

Buehler, R., Griffin, D., & Ross, M. (2002). Inside the planning fallacy: The causes and consequences of optimistic time predictions. In T. Gilovich, D. Griffin, & D. Kahneman (Eds.), *Heuristics and biases: The psychology of intuitive judgment.* Cambridge: Cambridge University Press.

Buehler, R., Peetz, J., & Griffin, D. (2010). Finishing on time: When do predictions influence completion times? *Organizational Behavior and Human Decision Processes, 111,* 23–32.

Bugental, D. B., & Hehman, J. A. (2007). Ageism: A review of research and policy implications. *Social Issues and Policy Review, 1,* 173–216.

Burchill, S. A. L., & Stiles, W. B. (1988). Interactions of depressed college students with their roommates: Not necessarily negative. *Journal of Personality and Social Psychology, 55,* 410–419.

Bureau of the Census (1975). *Historical abstract of the United States: Colonial times to 1970.* Washington, DC: Superintendent of Documents.

Bureau of the Census (1993, May 4). Voting survey, reported by Associated Press.

Bureau of the Census (2009). *The 2009 statistical abstract* (Table 946; www.census.gov).

Bureau of Labor Statistics (2011, June 22). American time use survey summary. Bureau of Labor Statistics (www.bls.gov).

Burger, J. M. (1987). Increased performance with increased personal control: A self-presentation interpretation. *Journal of Experimental Social Psychology, 23,* 350–360.

Burger, J. M. (2009, January). Replicating Milgram: Would people still obey today? *American Psychologist, 64,* 1–11.

Burger, J. M., & Burns, L. (1988). The illusion of unique invulnerability and the use of effective contraception. *Personality and Social Psychology Bulletin, 14,* 264–270.

Burger, J. M., & Guadagno, R. E. (2003). Self-concept clarity and the foot-in-the-door procedure. *Basic and Applied Social Psychology, 25,* 79–86.

Burger, J. M., & Palmer, M. L. (1991). Changes in and generalization of unrealistic optimism following experiences with stressful events: Reactions to the 1989 California earthquake. *Personality and Social Psychology Bulletin, 18,* 39–43.

Burger, J. M., & Pavelich, J. L. (1994). Attributions for presidential elections: The situational shift over time. *Basic and Applied Social Psychology, 15,* 359–371.

Burger, J. M., Soroka, S., Gonzago, K., Murphy, E., & Somervell, E. (2001). The effect of fleeting attraction on compliance to requests. *Personality and Social Psychology Bulletin, 27,* 1578–1586.

Burkholder, R. (2005, January 11). Chinese far wealthier than a decade ago, but are they happier? Gallup Poll (www.poll.gallup.com).

Burnham, G., Lafta, R., Doocy, S., & Roberts, L. (2006). Mortality after the 2003 invasion of Iraq: A cross-sectional cluster sample survey. *Lancet, 368,* 1421–1428.

Burns, D. D. (1980). *Feeling good: The new mood therapy.* New York: Signet.

Burns, J. F. (2003a, April 13). Pillagers strip Iraqi museum of its treasure. *New York Times* (www.nytimes.com).

Burns, J. F. (2003b, April 14). Baghdad residents begin a long climb to an ordered city. *New York Times* (www.nytimes.com).

Burnstein, E. (2009). Robert B. Zajonc (1923–2008). *American Psychologist, 64,* 558–559.

Burnstein, E., & Vinokur, A. (1977). Persuasive argumentation and social comparison as determinants of attitude polarization. *Journal of Experimental Social Psychology, 13,* 315–332.

Burnstein, E., & Worchel, P. (1962). Arbitrariness of frustration and its consequences for aggression in a social situation. *Journal of Personality, 30,* 528–540.

BURR, W. R. (1973). *Theory construction and the sociology of the family.* New York: Wiley.

BURSON, K. A., LARRICK, R. P., & KLAYMAN, J. (2006). Skilled or unskilled, but still unaware of it: How perceptions of difficulty drive miscalibration in relative comparisons. *Journal of Personality and Social Psychology,* **90,** 60–77.

BUSHMAN, B. J. (1993). Human aggression while under the influence of alcohol and other drugs: An integrative research review. *Current Directions in Psychological Science,* **2,** 148–152.

BUSHMAN, B. J. (2002). Does venting anger feed or extinguish the flame? Catharsis, rumination, distraction, anger, and aggressive responding. *Personality and Social Psychology Bulletin,* **28,** 724–731.

BUSHMAN, B. J. (2005). Violence and sex in television programs do not sell products in advertisements. *Psychological Science,* **16,** 702–708.

BUSHMAN, B. J. (2007). That was a great commercial, but what were they selling? Effects of violence and sex on memory for products in television commercials. *Journal of Applied Social Psychology,* **37,** 1784–1796.

BUSHMAN, B. J., & ANDERSON, C. A. (2001). Media violence and the American public: Scientific facts versus media misinformation. *American Psychologist,* **56,** 477–489.

BUSHMAN, B. J., & ANDERSON, C. A. (2002). Violent video games and hostile expectations: A test of the general aggression model. *Personality and Social Psychology Bulletin,* **28,** 1679–1686.

BUSHMAN, B. J., & ANDERSON, C. A. (2009). Comfortably numb: Desensitizing effects of violent media on helping others. *Psychological Science,* **20,** 273–277.

BUSHMAN, B. J., & BAUMEISTER, R. (1998). Threatened egotism, narcissism, self-esteem, and direct and displaced aggression: Does self-love or self-hate lead to violence? *Journal of Personality and Social Psychology,* **75,** 219–229.

BUSHMAN, B. J., & BAUMEISTER, R. F. (2002). Does self-love or self-hate lead to violence? *Journal of Research in Personality,* **36,** 543–545.

BUSHMAN, B. J., BAUMEISTER, R. F., & PHILLIPS, C. M. (2001). Do people aggress to improve their mood? Catharsis beliefs, affect regulation opportunity, and aggressive responding. *Journal of Personality and Social Psychology,* **81,** 17–32.

BUSHMAN, B. J., BAUMEISTER, R. F., & STACK, A. D. (1999). Catharsis, aggression, and persuasive influence: Self-fulfilling or self-defeating prophecies? *Journal of Personality and Social Psychology,* **76,** 367–376.

BUSHMAN, B. J., BAUMEISTER, R. F., THOMAES, S., RYU, E., BEGEER, S., & WEST, S. G. (2009). Looking again, and harder, for a link between low self-esteem and aggression. *Journal of Personality,* published online February **2,** 2009.

BUSHMAN, B. J., & GEEN, R. G. (1990). Role of cognitive-emotional mediators and individual differences in the effects of media violence on aggression. *Journal of Personality and Social Psychology,* **58,** 156–163.

BUSHMAN, B. J., & WHITAKER, J. L. (2010). Like a magnet: Catharsis beliefs attract angry people to violent video games. *Psychological Science,* **21,** 790–792.

BUSS, D. M. (1984). Toward a psychology of person-environment (PE) correlation: The role of spouse selection. *Journal of Personality and Social Psychology,* **47,** 361–377.

BUSS, D. M. (1985). Human mate selection. *American Scientist,* **73,** 47–51.

BUSS, D. M. (1989). Sex differences in human mate preferences: Evolutionary hypotheses tested in 37 cultures. *Behavioral and Brain Sciences,* **12,** 1–49.

BUSS, D. M. (1995). Psychological sex differences: Origins through sexual selection. *American Psychologist,* **50,** 164–168.

BUSS, D. M. (1999). Behind the scenes. In D. G. Myers, *Social psychology,* 6th edition. New York: McGraw-Hill.

BUSS, D. M. (2007). The evolution of human mating strategies: Consequences for conflict and cooperation. In S. W. Gangestad & J. A. Simpson (Eds.), *The evolution of mind: Fundamental questions and controversies.* New York: Guilford.

BUSS, D. M. (Ed.). (2005). *The handbook of evolutionary psychology.* New York: Wiley.

BUSS, D. M. (2009). The great struggles of life: Darwin and the emergence of evolutionary psychology. *American Psychologist,* **64,** 140–148.

BUTCHER, S. H. (1951). *Aristotle's theory of poetry and fine art.* New York: Dover.

BUTLER, A. C., HOKANSON, J. E., & FLYNN, H. A. (1994). A comparison of self-esteem lability and low trait self-esteem as vulnerability factors for depression. *Journal of Personality and Social Psychology,* **66,** 166–177.

BUTLER, D. M., & BROOCKMAN, D. E. (2011). Do politicians racially discriminate against constituents? A field experiment on state legislators. *American Journal of Political Science,* **55,** 463–477.

BUTLER, J. L., & BAUMEISTER, R. F. (1998). The trouble with friendly faces: Skilled performance with a supportive audience. *Journal of Personality and Social Psychology, 75,* 1213–1230.

BUUNK, B. P., & VAN DER EIJNDEN, R. J. J. M. (1997). Perceived prevalence, perceived superiority, and relationship satisfaction: Most relationships are good, but ours is the best. *Personality and Social Psychology Bulletin, 23,* 219–228.

BUUNK, B. P., & VAN YPEREN, N. W. (1991). Referential comparisons, relational comparisons, and exchange orientation: Their relation to marital satisfaction. *Personality and Social Psychology Bulletin, 17,* 709–717.

BYRNE, D. (1971). *The attraction paradigm.* New York: Academic Press.

BYRNE, D., & WONG, T. J. (1962). Racial prejudice, interpersonal attraction, and assumed dissimilarity of attitudes. *Journal of Abnormal and Social Psychology, 65,* 246–253.

BYRNES, J. P., MILLER, D. C., & SCHAFER, W. D. (1999). Gender differences in risk taking: A meta-analysis. *Psychological Bulletin, 125,* 367–383.

CACIOPPO, J. T., CLAIBORN, C. D., PETTY, R. E., & HEESACKER, M. (1991). General framework for the study of attitude change in psychotherapy. In C. R. Snyder & D. R. Forsyth (Eds.), *Handbook of social and clinical psychology.* New York: Pergamon.

CACIOPPO, J. T., FOWLER, J. H., & CHRISTAKIS, N. A. (2009). Alone in the crowd: The structure and spread of loneliness in a large social network. *Journal of Personality and Social Psychology, 97,* 977–991.

CACIOPPO, J. T., & PATRICK, W. (2008). *Loneliness: Human nature and the need for social connection.* New York: Norton.

CACIOPPO, J. T., PETTY, R. E., FEINSTEIN, J. A., & JARVIS, W. B. G. (1996). Dispositional differences in cognitive motivation: The life and times of individuals varying in need for cognition. *Psychological Bulletin, 119,* 197–253.

CACIOPPO, J. T., PETTY, R. E., & MORRIS, K. J. (1983). Effects of need for cognition on message evaluation, recall, and persuasion. *Journal of Personality and Social Psychology, 45,* 805–818.

CAI, S., KWAN, V. S. Y., & SEDIKIDES, C. (2011). The People's Republic of China: A culture of increasing narcissism. Unpublished manuscript.

CAIRNS, E., & HEWSTONE, M. (2002). The impact of peacemaking in Northern Ireland on intergroup behavior. In S. Gabi & B. Nevo (Eds.), *Peace education: The concept, principles, and practices around the world.* Mahwah, NJ: Erlbaum.

CALHOUN, J. B. (1962, February). Population density and social pathology. *Scientific American,* pp. 139–148.

CAMERON, L., & RUTLAND, A. (2006). Extended contact through story reading in school: Reducing children's prejudice toward the disabled. *Journal of Social Issues, 62,* 469–488.

CAMPBELL, D. T. (1975b). On the conflicts between biological and social evolution and between psychology and moral tradition. *American Psychologist, 30,* 1103–1126.

CAMPBELL, E. Q., & PETTIGREW, T. F. (1959). Racial and moral crisis: The role of Little Rock ministers. *American Journal of Sociology, 64,* 509–516.

CAMPBELL, W. K. (2005). *When you love a man who loves himself.* Chicago: Sourcebooks.

CAMPBELL, W. K., BOSSON, J. K., GOHEEN, T. W., LAKEY, C. E., & KERNIS, M. H. (2007). Do narcissists dislike themselves "deep down inside"? *Psychological Science, 18,* 227–229.

CAMPBELL, W. K., BUSH, C. P., BRUNELL, A. B., & SHELTON, J. (2005). Understanding the social costs of narcissism: The case of the tragedy of the commons. *Personality and Social Psychology Bulletin, 31,* 1358–1368.

CAMPBELL, W. K., & FOSTER, C. A. (2002). Narcissism and commitment in romantic relationships: An investment model analysis. *Personality and Social Psychology Bulletin, 28,* 484–495.

CAMPBELL, W. K., RUDICH, E., & SEDIKIDES, C. (2002). Narcissism, self-esteem, and the positivity of self-views: Two portraits of self-love. *Personality and Social Psychology Bulletin, 28,* 358–368.

CAMPBELL, W. K., & SEDIKIDES, C. (1999). Self-threat magnifies the self-serving bias: A meta-analytic integration. *Review of General Psychology, 3,* 23–43.

CANADIAN CENTRE ON SUBSTANCE ABUSE (1997). *Canadian profile: Alcohol, tobacco, and other drugs.* Ottawa: Canadian Centre on Substance Abuse.

CANADIAN PSYCHOLOGICAL ASSOCIATION (2000). *Canadian code of ethics for psychologists.* Ottawa: Canadian Psychological Association (www.cpa.ca/ethics2000.html).

CANTRIL, H., & BUMSTEAD, C. H. (1960). *Reflections on the human venture.* New York: New York University Press.

CAPUTO, D., & DUNNING, D. (2005). What you don't know: The role played by errors of omission in imperfect self-assessments. *Journal of Experimental Social Psychology, 41,* 488–505.

CARDUCCI, B. J., COSBY, P. C., & WARD, D. D. (1978). Sexual arousal and interpersonal evaluations. *Journal of Experimental Social Psychology, 14,* 449–457.

CARLI, L. L. (1999). Cognitive reconstruction, hindsight, and reactions to victims and perpetrators. *Personality and Social Psychology Bulletin, 25,* 966–979.

CARLI, L. L., & LEONARD, J. B. (1989). The effect of hindsight on victim derogation. *Journal of Social and Clinical Psychology, 8,* 331–343.

CARLSON, M., MARCUS-NEWHALL, A., & MILLER, N. (1990). Effects of situational aggression cues: A quantitative review. *Journal of Personality and Social Psychology, 58,* 622–633.

CARLTON-FORD, S., ENDER, M., & TABATABAI, A. (2008). Iraqi adolescents: Self-regard, self-derogation, and perceived threat in war. *Journal of Adolescence, 31,* 53–75.

CARNAGEY, N. L., ANDERSON, C. A., & BUSHMAN, B. J. (2007). The effect of video game violence on physiological desensitization to real-life violence. *Journal of Experimental Social Psychology, 43,* 489–496.

CARNEVALE, P. J., & CHOI, D-W. (2000). Culture in the mediation of international disputes. *International Journal of Psychology, 35,* 105–110.

CARPENTER, S. (2008, April/May). Buried prejudice. *Scientific American Mind,* pp. 33–39.

CARPUSOR, A. G., & LOGES, W. E. (2006). Rental discrimination and ethnicity in names. *Journal of Applied Social Psychology, 36,* 934–952.

CARRÉ, J. M., & MCCORMICK, C. M. (2008). In your face: Facial metrics predict aggressiveness behaviour in the laboratory and in varsity and professional hockey players. *Proceedings of the Royal Society B, 275,* 2651–2656.

CARRÉ, J. M., MCCORMICK, C. M., & MONDLOCH, C. J. (2009). Facial structure is a reliable cue of aggressive behavior. *Psychological Science, 20,* 1194–1198.

CARROLL, D., DAVEY SMITH, G., & BENNETT, P. (1994, March). Health and socio-economic status. *The Psychologist,* pp. 122–125.

CARROLL, J. S., PADILLA-WALKER, L. M., NELSON, L. J., OLSON, C. D., BARRY, C. M., & MADSEN, S. D. (2008). Generation XXX: Pornography acceptance and use among emerging adults. *Journal of Adolescent Research, 23,* 6–30.

CARTER, S. L. (1993). *Reflections of an affirmative action baby.* New York: Basic Books.

CARTER, S., & SNOW, C. (2004, May). Helping singles enter better marriages using predictive models of marital success. Presented to the American Psychological Society convention.

CARTWRIGHT, D. S. (1975). The nature of gangs. In D. S. Cartwright, B. Tomson, & H. Schwartz (Eds.), *Gang delinquency.* Monterey, CA: Brooks/Cole.

CARVALLO, M., & GABRIEL, S. (2006). No man is an island: The need to belong and dismissing avoidant attachment style. *Personality and Social Psychology Bulletin, 32,* 697–709.

CARVER, C. S., KUS, L. A., & SCHEIER, M. F. (1994). Effect of good versus bad mood and optimistic versus pessimistic outlook on social acceptance versus rejection. *Journal of Social and Clinical Psychology, 13,* 138–151.

CARVER, C. S., & SCHEIER, M. F. (1986). Analyzing shyness: A specific application of broader self-regulatory principles. In W. H. Jones, J. M. Cheek, & S. R. Briggs (Eds.), *Shyness: Perspectives on research and treatment.* New York: Plenum.

CASH, T. F., & JANDA, L. H. (1984, December). The eye of the beholder. *Psychology Today,* pp. 46–52.

CASPI, A., & HERBENER, E. S. (1990). Continuity and change: Assortative marriage and the consistency of personality in adulthood. *Journal of Personality and Social Psychology, 58,* 250–258.

CASPI, A., SUGDEN, K., MOFFITT, T. E., TAYLOR, A., CRAIG, I. W., HARRINGTON, H. L., MCCLAY, J., MILL, J., MARTIN, J., BRAITHWAITE, A., & POULTON, R. (2003). Influence of life stress on depression: Moderation by a polymorphism in the 5-HTT gene. *Science, 30,* 386–389.

CASTELLI, L., CARRARO, L., TOMELLERI, S., & AMARI, A. (2007). White children's alignment to the perceived racial attitudes of the parents: Closer to the mother than father. *British Journal of Developmental Psychology, 25,* 353–357.

CENTERS FOR DISEASE CONTROL (CDC) (2008, Spring). Sexual violence: Facts at a glance. Centers for Disease Control and Prevention (www.cdc.gov/injury).

CENTERS FOR DISEASE CONTROL (CDC) (2011, accessed August 5). Latest findings. Author (cdc.gov/vitalsigns/TobaccoUse/Smoking/LatestFindings.html).

CENTRAL INTELLIGENCE AGENCY (2011, May 26). *The World Factbook* (www.cia.gov).

CHAIKEN, S. (1979). Communicator physical attractiveness and persuasion. *Journal of Personality and Social Psychology, 37,* 1387–1397.

CHAIKEN, S. (1980). Heuristic versus systematic information processing and the use of source versus message cues in persuasion. *Journal of Personality and Social Psychology, 39,* 752–766.

CHAIKEN, S., & MAHESWARAN, D. (1994). Neuristic processing can bias systematic processing: Effects of source credibility, argument ambiguity, and task importance on attitude judgment. *Journal of Personality and Social Psychology, 66,* 460–473.

CHAMBERS, J. R., BARON, R. S., & INMAN, M. L. (2006). Misperceptions in intergroup conflict: Disagreeing about what we disagree about. *Psychological Science, 17,* 38–45.

CHAMBERS, J. R., & WINDSCHITL, P. D. (2004). Biases in social comparative judgments: The role of nonmotivated factors in above-average and comparative-optimism effects. *Psychological Bulletin, 130,* 813–838.

CHAMPAGNE, F., FRANCIS, D. D., MAR, A., & MEANEY, M. J. (2003). Naturally occurring variations in maternal care in the rat as a mediating influence for the effects of environment on the development of individual differences in stress reactivity. *Physiology & Behavior, 79,* 359–371.

CHAMPAGNE, F. A., & MASHOODH, R. (2009). Genes in context: Gene-environment interplay and the origins of individual differences in behavior. *Current Directions in Psychological Science, 18,* 127–131.

CHAN, M. K. H., LOUIS, W. R., & JETTEN, J. (2010). When groups are wrong and deviants are right. *European Journal of Social Psychology, 40,* 1103–1109.

CHANCE, J. E., & GOLDSTEIN, A. G. (1981). Depth of processing in response to own- and other-race faces. *Personality and Social Psychology Bulletin, 7,* 475–480.

CHANCE, J. E., GOLDSTEIN, A. G. (1996). The other-race effect and eyewitness identification. In S. L. Sporer (Ed.), *Psychological issues in eyewitness identification* (pp. 153–176). Mahwah, NJ: Erlbaum.

CHANDRA, A., MOSHER, W. D., & COPEN, C. (2011, March). Sexual behavior, sexual attraction, and sexual identity in the United States: Data from the 2006–2008 National Survey of Family Growth. *National Health Statistics Reports,* Number 36 (Centers for Disease Control and Prevention).

CHANG, L., LU, H. J., LI, H., & LI, T. (2011). The face that launched a thousand ships: The mating-warring association in men. *Personality and Social Psychology Bulletin, 37,* 976–984.

CHAPMAN, L. J., & CHAPMAN, J. P. (1969). Genesis of popular but erroneous psychodiagnostic observations. *Journal of Abnormal Psychology, 74,* 272–280.

CHAPMAN, L. J., & CHAPMAN, J. P. (1971, November). Test results are what you think they are. *Psychology Today,* pp. 18–22, 106–107.

CHATARD, A., GUIMOND, S., & SELIMBEGOVIC, L. (2007). "How good are you in math?" The effect of gender stereotypes on students' recollection of their school marks. *Journal of Experimental Social Psychology, 43,* 1017–1024.

CHECK, J., & MALAMUTH, N. (1984). Can there be positive effects of participation in pornography experiments? *Journal of Sex Research, 20,* 14–31.

CHEN, H., LUO, S., YUE, G., XU, D., & ZHAOYANG, R. (2009). Do birds of a feather flock together in China? *Personal Relationships, 16,* 167–186.

CHEN, L.-H., BAKER, S. P., BRAVER, E. R., & LI, G. (2000). Carrying passengers as a risk factor for crashes fatal to 16- and 17-year-old drivers. *Journal of the American Medical Association, 283,* 1578–1582.

CHEN, S. C. (1937). Social modification of the activity of ants in nest-building. *Physiological Zoology, 10,* 420–436.

CHEN, S., BOUCHER, H. C., & TAPIAS, M. P. (2006). The relational self revealed: Integrative conceptualization and implications for interpersonal life. *Psychological Bulletin, 132,* 151–179.

CHENEY, R. (2003, March 16). Comments on Face the Nation, CBS News.

CHIAO, J. Y., BOWMAN, N. E., & GILL, H. (2008). The political gender gap: Gender bias in facial inferences that predict voting behavior. *PLoS One* 3(10): e3666. (doi:10.1371/journal.pone.0003666).

CHODOROW, N. J. (1978). *The reproduction of mother: Psychoanalysis and the sociology of gender.* Berkeley, CA: University of California Press.

CHODOROW, N. J. (1989). *Feminism and psychoanalytic theory.* New Haven, CT: Yale University Press.

CHOI, I., & CHOI, Y. (2002). Culture and self-concept flexibility. *Personality & Social Psychology Bulletin, 28,* 1508–1517.

CHOI, I., NISBETT, R. E., & NORENZAYAN, A. (1999). Causal attribution across cultures: Variation and universality. *Psychological Bulletin, 125,* 47–63.

CHRIST, O., HEWSTONE, M., TAUSCH, N., WAGNER, U., VOCI, A., HUGHES, J., & CAIRNS, E. (2010). Direct contact as a moderator of extended contact effects: Cross-sectional and longitudinal impact on outgroup attitudes, behavioral intentions, and attitude certainty. *Personality and Social Psychology Bulletin, 36,* 1662–1674.

CHRISTENSEN, P. N., & KASHY, D. A. (1998). Perceptions of and by lonely people in initial social interaction. *Personality and Social Psychology Bulletin, 24,* 322–329.

CHRISTIAN, J. J., FLYGER, V., & DAVIS, D. E. (1960). Factors in the mass mortality of a herd of sika deer, *Cervus nippon. Chesapeake Science, 1,* 79–95.

CHUA-EOAN, H. (1997, April 7). Imprisoned by his own passions. *Time,* pp. 40–42.

CHURCH, G. J. (1986, January 6). China. *Time,* pp. 6–19.

CIALDINI, R. B. (1988). *Influence: Science and practice.* Glenview, IL: Scott, Foresman/Little, Brown.

CIALDINI, R. B., BORDEN, R. J., THORNE, A., WALKER, M. R., FREEMAN, S., & SLOAN, L. R. (1976). Basking in reflected glory: Three (football) field studies. *Journal of Personality and Social Psychology, 39,* 406–415.

CIALDINI, R. B., CACIOPPO, J. T., BASSETT, R., & MILLER, J. A. (1978). Lowball procedure for producing compliance: Commitment then cost. *Journal of Personality and Social Psychology, 36,* 463–476.

CIALDINI, R. B., DEMAINE, L. J., BARRETT, D. W., SAGARIN, B. J., & RHOADS, K. L. V. (2003). The poison parasite defense: A strategy for sapping a stronger opponent's persuasive strength. Unpublished manuscript, Arizona State University.

CICERELLO, A., & SHEEHAN, E. P. (1995). Personal advertisements: A content analysis. *Journal of Social Behavior and Personality, 10,* 751–756.

CLANCY, S. M., & DOLLINGER, S. J. (1993). Photographic depictions of the self: Gender and age differences in social connectedness. *Sex Roles, 29,* 477–495.

CLARK, K., & CLARK, M. (1947). Racial identification and preference in Negro children. In T. M. Newcomb & E. L. Hartley (Eds.), *Readings in social psychology.* New York: Holt.

CLARK, M. S. (1984). Record keeping in two types of relationships. *Journal of Personality and Social Psychology, 47,* 549–557.

CLARK, M. S. (1986). Evidence for the effectiveness of manipulations of desire for communal versus exchange relationships. *Personality and Social Psychology Bulletin, 12,* 414–425.

CLARK, M. S., LEMAY, E. P., JR., GRAHAM, S. M., PATAKI, S. P., & FINKEL, E. J. (2010). Ways of giving benefits in marriage: Norm use, relationship satisfaction, and attachment-related variability. *Psychological Science, 21,* 944–951.

CLARK, M. S., & MILLS, J. (1979). Interpersonal attraction in exchange and communal relationships. *Journal of Personality and Social Psychology, 37,* 12–24.

CLARK, M. S., & MILLS, J. (1993). The difference between communal and exchange relationships: What it is and is not. *Personality and Social Psychology Bulletin, 19,* 684–691.

CLARK, M. S., MILLS, J., & CORCORAN, D. (1989). Keeping track of needs and inputs of friends and strangers. *Personality and Social Psychology Bulletin, 15,* 533–542.

CLARK, M. S., MILLS, J., & POWELL, M. C. (1986). Keeping track of needs in communal and exchange relationships. *Journal of Personality and Social Psychology, 51,* 333–338.

CLARK, R. D., III. (1995). A few parallels between group polarization and minority influence. In S. Moscovici, H. Mucchi-Faina, & A. Maass (Eds.), *Minority influence.* Chicago: Nelson-Hall.

CLARKE, A. C. (1952). An examination of the operation of residual propinquity as a factor in mate selection. *American Sociological Review, 27,* 17–22.

CLARKE, V. (2003, March 25). Quoted in "Street fighting: A volatile enemy." *Wall Street Journal,* pp. A1, A13.

CLAYTON, S., & MYERS, G. (2009). *Conservation psychology: Understanding and promoting human care for nature.* Hoboken, NJ: Wiley-Blackwell.

CLEVSTROM, J., & PASSARIELLO, C. (2006, August 18). No kicks from "champagne." *Wall Street Journal,* p. A11.

CLIFFORD, M. M., & WALSTER, E. H. (1973). The effect of physical attractiveness on teacher expectation. *Sociology of Education, 46,* 248–258.

CLORE, G. L., BRAY, R. M., ITKIN, S. M., & MURPHY, P. (1978). Interracial attitudes and behavior at a summer camp. *Journal of Personality and Social Psychology, 36,* 107–116.

COATES, B., PUSSER, H. E., & GOODMAN, I. (1976). The influence of "Sesame Street" and "Mister Rogers' Neighborhood" on children's social behavior in the preschool. *Child Development, 47,* 138–144.

COATS, E. J., & FELDMAN, R. S. (1996). Gender differences in nonverbal correlates of social status. *Personality and Social Psychology Bulletin, 22,* 1014–1022.

CODOL, J.-P. (1976). On the so-called superior conformity of the self behavior: Twenty experimental investigations. *European Journal of Social Psychology, 5,* 457–501.

COHEN, D. (1996). Law, social policy, and violence: The impact of regional cultures. *Journal of Personality and Social Psychology, 70,* 961–978.

COHEN, D. (1998). Culture, social organization, and patterns of violence. *Journal of Personality and Social Psychology, 75,* 408–419.

COHEN, E. G. (1980). Design and redesign of the desegregated school: Problems of status, power and conflict. In W. G. Stephan & J. R. Feagin (Eds.), *School desegregation: Past, present, and future.* New York: Plenum.

COHEN, D., NISBETT, R. E., BOWDLE, B. F., & SCHWARZ, N. (1996). Insult, aggression, and the Southern culture of honor: An "experimental ethnography." *Journal of Personality and Social Psychology, 70,* 945–960.

COHEN, G. L., STEELE, C. M., & ROSS, L. D. (1999). The mentor's dilemma: Providing critical feedback across the racial divide. *Personality and Social Psychology Bulletin, 25,* 1302–1318.

COHEN, M., & DAVIS, N. (1981). *Medication errors: Causes and prevention*. Philadelphia: G. F. Stickley Co. Cited by R. B. Cialdini (1989), Agents of influence: Bunglers, smugglers, and sleuths. Paper presented at the American Psychological Association convention.

COHEN, R. (2011, January 13). Mohammed the Brit. *New York Times* (www.nytimes.com).

COHEN, S. (1980). Training to understand TV advertising: Effects and some policy implications. Paper presented at the American Psychological Association convention.

COHN, E. G. (1993). The prediction of police calls for service: The influence of weather and temporal variables on rape and domestic violence. *Environmental Psychology, 13*, 71–83.

COHRS, J. C., & IBLER, S. (2009). Authoritarianism, threat, and prejudice: An analysis of mediation and moderation. *Basic and Applied Social Psychology, 31*, 81–94.

COLARELLI, S. M., SPRANGER, J. L., HECHANOVA, M. R. (2006). Women, power, and sex composition in small groups: An evolutionary perspective. *Journal of Organizational Behavior Special Issue: Darwinian Perspectives on Behavior in Organizations, 27*, 163–184.

THE COLLEGE BOARD (2011). *Social networking sites and college-bound students*. The College Board (professionals.collegeboard.com).

COMER, D. R. (1995). A model of social loafing in a real work group. *Human Relations, 48*, 647–667.

COMSTOCK, G. (2008). A sociological perspective on television violence and aggression. *American Behavioral Scientist, 51*, 1184–1211.

CONFER, J. C., EASTON, J. A., FLEISCHMAN, D. S., GOETZ, C. D., LEWIS, D. M. G., PERILLOUX, C., & BUSS, D. M. (2010). Evolutionary psychology: Controversies, questions, prospects, and limitations. *American Psychologist, 65*, 110–126.

CONWAY, F., & SIEGELMAN, J. (1979). *Snapping: America's epidemic of sudden personality change*. New York: Delta Books.

CONWAY, M., & ROSS, M. (1986). Remembering one's own past: The construction of personal histories. In R. Sorrentino & E. T. Higgins (Eds.), *Handbook of motivation and cognition*. New York: Guilford.

COOK, T. D., & FLAY, B. R. (1978). The persistence of experimentally induced attitude change. In L. Berkowitz (Ed.), *Advances in experimental social psychology* (Vol. 11). New York: Academic Press.

COOPER, H. (1983). Teacher expectation effects. In L. Bickman (Ed.), *Applied social psychology annual* (Vol. 4). Beverly Hills, CA: Sage.

COOPER, J. (1999). Unwanted consequences and the self: In search of the motivation for dissonance reduction. In E. Harmon-Jones & J. Mills (Eds.), *Cognitive dissonance: Progress on a pivotal theory in social psychology*. Washington, DC: American Psychological Association.

CORRELL, J., PARK, B., JUDD, C. M., & WITTENBRINK, B. (2002). The police officer's dilemma: Using ethnicity to disambiguate potentially threatening individuals. *Journal of Personality and Social Psychology, 83*, 1314–1329.

CORRELL, J., PARK, B., JUDD, C. M., & WITTENBRINK, B. (2007). The influence of stereotypes on decisions to shoot. *European Journal of Social Psychology, 37*, 1102–1117.

CORRELL, J., PARK, B., JUDD, C. M., WITTENBRINK, B., SADLER, M. S., & KEESEE, T. (2007). Across the thin blue line: Police officers and racial bias in the decision to shoot. *Journal of Personality and Social Psychology, 92*, 1006–1023.

CORRELL, J., URLAND, G. R., & ITO, T. A. (2006). Event-related potentials and the decision to shoot: The role of threat perception and cognitive control. *Journal of Experimental Social Psychology, 42*, 120–128.

COSTANZO, M. (1997). *Just revenge: Costs and consequences of the death penalty*. New York: St. Martin's.

COSTANZO, M. (1998). *Just revenge*. New York: St. Martins.

COSTELLO, C., GAINES, S. D., & LYNHAM, J. (2008). Can catch shares prevent fisheries' collapse? *Science, 321*, 1678–1682.

COTA, A. A., & DION, K. L. (1986). Salience of gender and sex composition of ad hoc groups: An experimental test of distinctiveness theory. *Journal of Personality and Social Psychology, 50*, 770–776.

COTTON, J. L. (1981). Ambient temperature and violent crime. Paper presented at the Midwestern Psychological Association convention.

COTTON, J. L. (1986). Ambient temperature and violent crime. *Journal of Applied Social Psychology, 16*, 786–801.

COTTRELL, N. B., WACK, D. L., SEKERAK, G. J., & RITTLE, R. M. (1968). Social facilitation of dominant responses by the presence of an audience and the mere presence of others. *Journal of Personality and Social Psychology, 9*, 245–250.

COYNE, S. M., & ARCHER, J. (2005). The relationship between indirect and physical aggression on television and in real life. *Social Development, 14*, 324–338.

CRABTREE, S. (2002, January 22). Gender roles reflected in teen tech use. *Gallup Tuesday Briefing* (www.gallup.com).

CRAIG, W., & HAREL, Y. (2004). Bullying, physical fighting, and victimization. In C. Currie (Ed.), *Young people's health in context: International report from the HSBC 2001/2 survey. WHO Policy Series: Health policy for children and adolescents issue 4.* Copenhagen: WHO Regional Office for Europe.

CRISP, R. J., BIRTEL, M. D., & MELEADY, R. (2011). Mental simulations of social thought and action: Trivial tasks or tools for transforming social policy? *Current Directions in Psychological Science, 20,* 261–264.

CROCKER, J. (1981). Judgment of covariation by social perceivers. *Psychological Bulletin, 90,* 272–292.

CROCKER, J. (2002). The costs of seeking self-esteem. *Journal of Social Issues, 58,* 597–615.

CROCKER, J., & GALLO, L. (1985). The self-enhancing effect of downward comparison. Paper presented at the American Psychological Association convention.

CROCKER, J., HANNAH, D. B., & WEBER, R. (1983). Personal memory and causal attributions. *Journal of Personality and Social Psychology, 44,* 55–56.

CROCKER, J., & KNIGHT, K. M. (2005). Contingencies of self-worth. *Current Directions in Psychological Science, 14,* 200–203.

CROCKER, J., & LUHTANEN, R. (1990). Collective self-esteem and ingroup bias. *Journal of Personality and Social Psychology, 58,* 60–67.

CROCKER, J., & LUHTANEN, R. (2003). Level of self-esteem and contingencies of self-worth: Unique effects on academic, social, and financial problems in college students. *Personality and Social Psychology Bulletin, 29,* 701–712.

CROCKER, J., & MCGRAW, K. M. (1984). What's good for the goose is not good for the gander: Solo status as an obstacle to occupational achievement for males and females. *American Behavioral Scientist, 27,* 357–370.

CROCKER, J., & PARK, L. E. (2004). The costly pursuit of self-esteem. *Psychological Bulletin, 130,* 392–414.

CROCKER, J., THOMPSON, L. L., MCGRAW, K. M., & INGERMAN, C. (1987). Downward comparison, prejudice, and evaluations of others: Effects of self-esteem and threat. *Journal of Personality and Social Psychology, 52,* 907–916.

CROCKETT, M. J., CLARK, L., TABIBNIA, G., LIEBERMAN, M. D., & ROBBINS, T. W. (2008). Serotonin modulates behavioral reactions to unfairness. *Science, 320,* 1739.

CROMPTON, T., & KASSER, T. (2010, July/August). Human identity: A missing link in environmental campaigning. *Environment Magazine,* pp. 23–33 (www.environmentmagazine.org).

CROSBY, F., BROMLEY, S., & SAXE, L. (1980). Recent unobtrusive studies of black and white discrimination and prejudice: A literature review. *Psychological Bulletin, 87,* 546–563.

CROSBY, J. R., & MONIN, B. (2007). Failure to warn: How student race affects warnings of potential academic difficulty. *Journal of Experimental Social Psychology, 43,* 663–670.

CROSS, C. P., COPPING, L. T., & CAMPBELL, A. (2011). Sex differences in impulsivity: A meta-analysis . *Psychological Bulletin, 137,* 97–130.

CROSS, P. (1977, Spring). Not *can* but *will* college teaching be improved? *New Directions for Higher Education,* No. 17, pp. 1–15.

CROSS, S. E., LIAO, M-H., & JOSEPHS, R. (1992). A cross-cultural test of the self-evaluation maintenance model. Paper presented at the American Psychological Association convention.

CROSS-NATIONAL COLLABORATIVE GROUP (1992). The changing rate of major depression. *Journal of the American Medical Association, 268,* 3098–3105.

CSIKSZENTMIHALYI, M. (1990). *Flow: The psychology of optimal experience.* New York: Harper & Row.

CSIKSZENTMIHALYI, M. (1999). If we are so rich, why aren't we happy? *American Psychologist, 54,* 821–827.

CUDDY, A. J. C., & 23 OTHERS. (2009). Stereotype content model across cultures: Towards universal similarities and some differences. *British Journal of Social Psychology, 48,* 1–33.

CULLEN, L. T., & MASTERS, C. (2008, January 28). We just clicked. *Time,* pp. 86–89.

CUNNINGHAM, J. D. (1981). Self-disclosure intimacy: Sex, sex-of-target, cross-national, and generational differences. *Personality and Social Psychology Bulletin, 7,* 314–319.

CUNNINGHAM, W. A., JOHNSON, M. K., RAYE, C. L., GATENBY, J. C., GORE, J. C., & BANAJI, M. R. (2004). Separable neural components in the processing of black and white faces. *Psychological Science, 15,* 806–813.

D'ORLANDO, F. (2011). The demand for pornography. *Journal of Happiness Studies, 12,* 51–75.

DABBS, J. M., JR. (1992). Testosterone measurements in social and clinical psychology. *Journal of Social and Clinical Psychology, 11,* 302–321.

DABBS, J. M., JR. (2000). *Heroes, rogues, and lovers: Testosterone and behavior.* New York: McGraw-Hill.

DABBS, J. M., JR., CARR, T. S., FRADY, R. L., & RIAD, J. K. (1995). Testosterone, crime, and misbehavior among 692 male prison inmates. *Personality and Individual Differences, 18,* 627–633.

DABBS, J. M., JR., & JANIS, I. L. (1965). Why does eating while reading facilitate opinion change? An experimental inquiry. *Journal of Experimental Social Psychology, 1,* 133–144.

DABBS, J. M., JR., & MORRIS, R. (1990). Testosterone, social class, and antisocial behavior in a sample of 4,462 men. *Psychological Science, 1,* 209–211.

DABBS, J. M., JR., RIAD, J. K., & CHANCE, S. E. (2001). Testosterone and ruthless homicide. *Personality and Individual Differences, 31,* 599–603.

DABBS, J. M., JR., STRONG, R., & MILUN, R. (1997). Exploring the mind of testosterone: A beeper study. *Journal of Research in Personality, 31,* 577–588.

DAMBRUN, M., & VATINÉ, E. (2010). Reopening the study of extreme social behaviors: Obedience to authority within an immersive video environment. *European Journal of Social Psychology, 40,* 760–773.

DAMON, W. (1995). *Greater expectations: Overcoming the culture of indulgence in America's homes and schools.* New York: Free Press.

DARDENNE, B., DUMONT, M., & BOLLIER, T. (2007). Insidious dangers of benevolent sexism: Consequences for women's performance. *Journal of Personality and Social Psychology, 93,* 764–779.

DARLEY, J., & ALTER, A. (2009). Behavioral issues of punishment and deterrence. In E. Shafir (Ed.), *The behavioral foundations of policy.* Princeton, NJ: Princeton University Press.

DARLEY, J. M., & BERSCHEID, E. (1967). Increased liking as a result of the anticipation of personal contact. *Human Relations, 20,* 29–40.

DARLEY, J. M., & LATANÉ, B. (1968). Bystander intervention in emergencies: Diffusion of responsibility. *Journal of Personality and Social Psychology, 8,* 377–383.

DARLEY, S., & COOPER, J. (1972). Cognitive consequences of forced noncompliance. *Journal of Personality and Social Psychology, 24,* 321–326.

DARWIN, C. (1859/1988). *The origin of species.* Vol. 15 of *The Works of Charles Darwin,* edited by P. H. Barrett & R. B. Freeman. New York: New York University Press.

DASHIELL, J. F. (1930). An experimental analysis of some group effects. *Journal of Abnormal and Social Psychology, 25,* 190–199.

DAVIDSON, R. J., PUTNAM, K. M., & LARSON, C. L. (2000). Dysfunction in the neural circuitry of emotion regulation—A possible prelude to violence. *Science, 289,* 591–594.

DAVIES, P. G., SPENCER, S. J., QUINN, D. M., & GERHARDSTEIN, R. (2002). Consuming images: How television commercials that elicit stereotype threat can restrain women academically and professionally. *Personality and Social Psychology Bulletin, 28,* 1615–1628.

DAVIES, P. G., STEELE, C. M., & SPENCER, S. J. (2005). Clearing the air: Identity safety moderates the effects of stereotype threat on women's leadership aspirations. *Journal of Personality and Social Psychology, 88,* 276–287.

DAVIS, B. M., & GILBERT, L. A. (1989). Effect of dispositional and situational influences on women's dominance expression in mixed-sex dyads. *Journal of Personality and Social Psychology, 57,* 294–300.

DAVIS, J. A. (2004). Did growing up in the 1960s leave a permanent mark on attitudes and values? Evidence from the GSS. *Public Opinion Quarterly, 68,* 161–183.

DAVIS, K. E., & JONES, E. E. (1960). Changes in interpersonal perception as a means of reducing cognitive dissonance. *Journal of Abnormal and Social Psychology, 61,* 402–410.

DAVIS, L., & GREENLEES, C. (1992). Social loafing revisited: Factors that mitigate—and reverse—performance loss. Paper presented at the Southwestern Psychological Association convention.

DAVIS, M. H., & FRANZOI, S. L. (1986). Adolescent loneliness, self-disclosure, and private self-consciousness: A longitudinal investigation. *Journal of Personality and Social Psychology, 51,* 595–608.

DAVIS, S. C., DIEGEL, S. W., & BOUNDY, R. G. (2011, June). *Transportation Energy Data Book: Edition 30* (Tables 3.1 and 3.2). Office of Energy Efficiency and Renewable Energy, U.S. Department of Energy.

DAWES, R. (1998, October). The social usefulness of self-esteem: A skeptical view. *Harvard Mental Health Letter,* pp. 4–5.

DAWES, R. M. (1976). Shallow psychology. In J. S. Carroll & J. W. Payne (Eds.), *Cognition and social behavior.* Hillsdale, NJ: Erlbaum.

DAWES, R. M. (1990). The potential nonfalsity of the false consensus effect. In R. M. Hogarth (Ed.), *Insights in decision making: A tribute to Hillel J. Einhorn.* Chicago: University of Chicago Press.

DAWES, R. M. (1994). *House of cards: Psychology and psychotherapy built on myth.* New York: Free Press.

DAWES, R. M. (2005). The ethical implications of Paul Meehl's work on comparing clinical versus actuarial prediction methods. *Journal of Clinical Psychology, 61,* 1245–1255.

DAWKINS, R. (1993). Gaps in the mind. In P. Cavalieri & P. Singer (Eds.), *The Great Ape Project: Equality beyond Humanity.* London: Fourth Estate, pp. 80–87.

DAWSON, N. V., ARKES, H. R., SICILIANO, C., BLINKHORN, R., LAKSHMANAN, M., & PETRELLI, M. (1988). Hindsight bias: An impediment to accurate probability estimation in clinicopathologic conferences. *Medical Decision Making, 8,* 259–264.

DE HOOG, N., STROEBE, W., & DE WIT, J. B. F. (2007). The impact of vulnerability to and severity of a health risk on processing and acceptance of fear-arousing communications: A meta-analysis. *Review of General Psychology*, **11**, 258–285.

DE HOOGH, A. H. B., DEN HARTOG, D. N., KOOPMAN, P. L., THIERRY, H., VAN DEN BERG, P. T., VAN DER WEIDE, J. G., & WILDEROM, C. P. M. (2004). Charismatic leadership, environmental dynamism, and performance. *European Journal of Work and Organisational Psychology*, **13**, 447–471.

DE JONG-GIERVELD, J. (1987). Developing and testing a model of loneliness. *Journal of Personality and Social Psychology*, **53**, 119–128.

DE SHERBININ, A., & 17 OTHERS. (2011). Preparing for resettlement associated with climate change. *Science*, **334**, 456–457.

DE WIT, L., LUPPINO, F., VAN STRATEN, A., PENNINX, B., ZITMAN, F., & CUIJPERS, P. (2010). Depression and obesity: A meta-analysis of community-based studies. *Psychiatry Research*, **178**, 230–235.

DEAN, C. (2005, August 30). Scientific savvy? In U.S., not much. *New York Times* (www.nytimes.com).

DEATON, A. (2009). Religion and well-being. Unpublished manuscript, Princeton University.

DEAUX, K., & LaFRANCE, M. (1998). Gender. In D. Gilbert, S. Fiske, & G. Lindzey (Eds.), *The handbook of social psychology*, 4th edition. Hillsdale, NJ: Erlbaum.

DeBRUINE, L. M. (2002). Facial resemblance enhances trust. *Proceedings of the Royal Society of London*, **269**, 1307–1312.

DeBRUINE, L. M., JONES, B. C., WATKINS, C. D., ROBERTS, S. C., LITTLE, A. C., SMITH, F. G., & QUIST, M. C. (2011). Opposite-sex siblings decrease attraction, but not prosocial attributions, to self-resembling opposite-sex faces. *Proceedings of the National Academy of Sciences USA*, **108**, 11710–11714.

DECI, E. L., & RYAN, R. M. (1987). The support of autonomy and the control of behavior. *Journal of Personality and Social Psychology*, **53**, 1024–1037.

DECI, E. L., & RYAN, R. M. (Eds.). (2002). *Handbook of self-determination research*. Rochester, NY: University of Rochester Press.

DEMBROSKI, T. M., LASATER, T. M., & RAMIREZ, A. (1978). Communicator similarity, fear-arousing communications, and compliance with health care recommendations. *Journal of Applied Social Psychology*, **8**, 254–269.

DENISSEN, J. J. A., PENKE, L., SCHMITT, D. P., & VAN AKEN, M. A. G. (2008). Self-esteem reactions to social interactions: Evidence for sociometer mechanisms across days, people, and nations. *Journal of Personality and Social Psychology*, **95**, 181–196.

DENNETT, D. (2005, December 26). Spiegel interview with evolution philosopher Daniel Dennett: Darwinism completely refutes intelligent design. *Der Spiegel* (www.service.dspiegel.de).

DENSON, T. F., PEDERSEN, W. C., & MILLER, N. (2006). The displaced aggression questionnaire. *Journal of Personality and Social Psychology*, **90**, 1032–1051.

DePAULO, B. M., CHARLTON, K., COOPER, H., LINDSAY, J. J., & MUHLENBRUCK, L. (1997). The accuracy-confidence correlation in the detection of deception. *Personality and Social Psychology Review*, **1**, 346–357.

DERLEGA, V., METTS, S., PETRONIO, S., & MARGULIS, S. T. (1993). *Self-disclosure*. Newbury Park, CA: Sage.

DERMER, M., COHEN, S. J., JACOBSEN, E., & ANDERSON, E. A. (1979). Evaluative judgments of aspects of life as a function of vicarious exposure to hedonic extremes. *Journal of Personality and Social Psychology*, **37**, 247–260.

DERMER, M., & PYSZCZYNSKI, T. A. (1978). Effects of erotica upon men's loving and liking responses for women they love. *Journal of Personality and Social Psychology*, **36**, 1302–1309.

DESFORGES, D. M., LORD, C. G., PUGH, M. A., SIA, T. L., SCARBERRY, N. C., & RATCLIFF, C. D. (1997). Role of group representativeness in the generalization part of the contact hypothesis. *Basic and Applied Social Psychology*, **19**, 183–204.

DESFORGES, D. M., LORD, C. G., RAMSEY, S. L., MASON, J. A., VAN LEEUWEN, M. D., WEST, S. C., & LEPPER, M. R. (1991). Effects of structured cooperative contact on changing negative attitudes toward stigmatized social groups. *Journal of Personality and Social Psychology*, **60**, 531–544.

DEUTSCH, M. (1985). *Distributive justice: A social psychological perspective*. New Haven: Yale University Press.

DEUTSCH, M. (1986). Folie à deux: A psychological perspective on Soviet-American relations. In M. P. Kearns (Ed.), *Persistent patterns and emergent structures in a waning century*. New York: Praeger.

DEUTSCH, M. (1993). Educating for a peaceful world. *American Psychologist*, **48**, 510–517.

DEUTSCH, M. (1994). Constructive conflict resolution: Principles, training, and research. *Journal of Social Issues*, **50**, 13–32.

DEUTSCH, M. (1999). Behind the scenes. In D. G. Myers, *Social psychology*, 6th edition (p. 519). New York: McGraw-Hill.

DEUTSCH, M., & COLLINS, M. E. (1951). *Interracial housing: A psychological evaluation of a social experiment.* Minneapolis: University of Minnesota Press.

DEUTSCH, M., & KRAUSS, R. M. (1960). The effect of threat upon interpersonal bargaining. *Journal of Abnormal and Social Psychology, 61,* 181–189.

DEVINE, P. G., EVETT, S. R., & VASQUEZ-SUSON, K. A. (1996). Exploring the interpersonal dynamics of intergroup contact. In R. Sorrentino & E. T. Higgins (Eds.), *Handbook of motivation and cognition: The interpersonal content* (Vol. 3). New York: Guilford.

DEVINE, P. G., & MALPASS, R. S. (1985). Orienting strategies in differential face recognition. *Personality and Social Psychological Bulletin, 11,* 33–40.

DEVINE, P. G., & SHARP, L. B. (2008). Automatic and controlled processes in stereotyping and prejudice. In T. Nelson (Ed.), *Handbook of prejudice, stereotyping, and discrimination.* New York: Psychology Press.

DEVOS-COMBY, L., & SALOVEY, P. (2002). Applying persuasion strategies to alter HIV-relevant thoughts and behavior. *Review of General Psychology, 6,* 287–304.

DEWALL, C. N., BAUMEISTER, R. F., & VOHS, K. D. (2008). Satiated with belongingness? Effects of acceptance, rejection, and task framing on self-regulatory performance. *Journal of Personality and Social Psychology, 95,* 1367–1382.

DEWALL, C. N., & BUSHMAN, B. J. (2011). Social acceptance and rejection: The sweet and the bitter. *Current Directions in Psychological Science, 20,* 256–260.

DEWALL, C. N., BUSHMAN, B. J., GIANCOLA, P. R., & WEBSTER, G. D. (2010). The big, the bad, and the boozed-up: Weight moderates the effect of alcohol on aggression. *Journal of Experimental Social Psychology, 46,* 619–623.

DEWALL, C. N., POND, R. S., JR., CAMPBELL, W. K., & TWENGE, J. M. (2011). Tuning in to psychological change: Linguistic markers of psychological traits and emotions over time in popular U.S. song lyrics. *Psychology of Aesthetics, Creativity, and the Arts, 5,* 200–207.

DEY, E. L., ASTIN, A. W., & KORN, W. S. (1991). *The American freshman: Twenty-five year trends.* Los Angeles: Higher Education Research Institute, UCLA.

DICK, S. (2008). *Homophobic hate crime: The Gay British Crime Survey 2008.* Stonewall (www.stonewall.org.uk).

DICUM, J. (2003, November 11). Letter to the editor. *New York Times,* p. A20.

DIDONATO, T. E., ULLRICH, J., & KRUEGER, J. I. (2011). Social perception as induction and inference: An integrative model of intergroup differentiation, ingroup favoritism, and differential accuracy. *Journal of Personality and Social Psychology, 100,* 66–83.

DIEKMAN, A. B., BROWN, E. R., JOHNSTON, A. M., & CLARK, E. K. (2010). Seeking congruity between goals and roles: A new look at why women opt out of science, technology, engineering, and mathematics careers. *Psychological Science, 21,* 1051–1057.

DIEKMANN, K. A., SAMUELS, S. M., ROSS, L., & BAZERMAN, M. H. (1997). Self-interest and fairness in problems of resource allocation: Allocators versus recipients. *Journal of Personality and Social Psychology, 72,* 1061–1074.

DIENER, E. (1976). Effects of prior destructive behavior, anonymity, and group presence on deindividuation and aggression. *Journal of Personality and Social Psychology, 33,* 497–507.

DIENER, E. (1979). Deindividuation, self-awareness, and disinhibition. *Journal of Personality and Social Psychology, 37,* 1160–1171.

DIENER, E. (1980). Deindividuation: The absence of self-awareness and self-regulation in group members. In P. Paulus (Ed.), *The psychology of group influence.* Hillsdale, NJ: Erlbaum.

DIENER, E., HORWITZ, J., & EMMONS, R. A. (1985). Happiness of the very wealthy. *Social Indicators, 16,* 263–274.

DIENER, E., LUCAS, R. E., & SCOLLON, C. N. (2006). Beyond the hedonic treadmill: Revising the adaptation theory of well-being. *American Psychologist, 61,* 305–314.

DIENER, E., & WALLBOM, M. (1976). Effects of self-awareness on antinormative behavior. *Journal of Research in Personality, 10,* 107–111.

DIENSTBIER, R. A., ROESCH, S. C., MIZUMOTO, A., HEMENOVER, S. H., LOTT, R. C., & CARLO, G. (1998). Effects of weapons on guilt judgments and sentencing recommendations for criminals. *Basic and Applied Social Psychology, 20,* 93–102.

DIJKSTERHUIS, A., BOS, M. W., NORDGREN, L. F., & VAN BAAREN, R. B. (2006). Complex choices better made unconsciously? *Science, 313,* 760–761.

DIJKSTERHUIS, A., & NORDGREN, L. F. (2006). A theory of unconscious thought. *Perspectives on Psychological Science, 1,* 95–109.

DIJKSTERHUIS, A., SMITH, P. K., VAN BAAREN, R. B., & WIGBOLDUS, D. H. J. (2005). The unconscious consumer: Effects of environment on consumer behavior. *Journal of Consumer Psychology, 15,* 193–202.

DILL, J. C., & ANDERSON, C.A. (1999). Loneliness, shyness, and depression: The etiology and interrelationships of everyday problems in living. In T. Joiner and J. C. Coyne (Eds.) *The interactional nature of depression: Advances in interpersonal approaches.* Washington, DC: American Psychological Association.

DINDIA, K., & ALLEN, M. (1992). Sex differences in self-disclosure: A meta-analysis. *Psychological Bulletin,* **112**, 106–124.

DION, K. K. (1972). Physical attractiveness and evaluations of children's transgressions. *Journal of Personality and Social Psychology,* **24**, 207–213.

DION, K. K. (1973). Young children's stereotyping of facial attractiveness. *Developmental Psychology,* **9**, 183–188.

DION, K. K., & BERSCHEID, E. (1974). Physical attractiveness and peer perception among children. *Sociometry,* **37**, 1–12.

DION, K. K., & DION, K. L. (1985). Personality, gender, and the phenomenology of romantic love. In P. R. Shaver (Ed.), *Review of personality and social psychology* (Vol. 6). Beverly Hills, CA: Sage.

DION, K. K., & DION, K. L. (1991). Psychological individualism and romantic love. *Journal of Social Behavior and Personality,* **6**, 17–33.

DION, K. K., & DION, K. L. (1993). Individualistic and collectivistic perspectives on gender and the cultural context of love and intimacy. *Journal of Social Issues,* **49**, 53–69.

DION, K. K., & DION, K. L. (1996). Cultural perspectives on romantic love. *Personal Relationships,* **3**, 5–17.

DION, K. K., & STEIN, S. (1978). Physical attractiveness and interpersonal influence. *Journal of Experimental Social Psychology,* **14**, 97–109.

DION, K. L. (1979). Intergroup conflict and intragroup cohesiveness. In W. G. Austin & S. Worchel (Eds.), *The social psychology of intergroup relations.* Monterey, CA: Brooks/Cole.

DION, K. L., & DION, K. K. (1988). Romantic love: Individual and cultural perspectives. In R. J. Sternberg & M. L. Barnes (Eds.), *The psychology of love.* New Haven, CT: Yale University Press.

DISHION, T. J., McCORD, J., & POULIN, F. (1999). When interventions harm: Peer groups and problem behavior. *American Psychologist,* **54**, 755–764.

DIXON, J., & DURRHEIM, K. (2003). Contact and the ecology of racial division: Some varieties of informal segregation. *British Journal of Social Psychology,* **42**, 1–23.

DIXON, J., DURRHEIM, K., & TREDOUX, C. (2005). Beyond the optimal contact strategy: A reality check for the contact hypothesis. *American Psychologist,* **60**, 697–711.

DIXON, J., DURRHEIM, K., & TREDOUX, C. (2007). Intergroup contact and attitudes toward the principle and practice of racial equality. *Psychological Science,* **18**, 867–872.

DIXON, J., TREDOUX, C., & CLACK, B. (2005). On the micro-ecology of racial division: A neglected dimension of segregation. *South African Journal of Psychology,* **35**, 395–411.

DOHERTY, T. J., & CLAYTON, S. (2011). The psychological impacts of global climate change. *American Psychologist,* **66**, 265–276.

DOLLARD, J., DOOB, L., MILLER, N., MOWRER, O. H., & SEARS, R. R. (1939). *Frustration and aggression.* New Haven, CT: Yale University Press.

DOLNIK, L., CASE, T. I., & WILLIAMS, K. D. (2003). Stealing thunder as a courtroom tactic revisted: Processes and boundaries. *Law and Human Behavior,* **27**, 265–285.

DONDERS, N. C., CORRELL, J., & WITTENBRINK, B. (2008). Danger stereotypes predict racially biased attentional allocation. *Journal of Experimental Social Psychology,* **44**, 1328–1333.

DONNERSTEIN, E. (1980). Aggressive erotica and violence against women. *Journal of Personality and Social Psychology,* **39**, 269–277.

DONNERSTEIN, E. (1998). Why do we have those new ratings on television. Invited address to the National Institute on the Teaching of Psychology.

DONNERSTEIN, E. (2011). The media and aggression: From TV to the Internet. In J. Forgas, A. Kruglanski, & K. Williams (Eds.) *The psychology of social conflict and aggression* (pp. 267–284). New York: Psychology Press.

DOOB, A. N., & ROBERTS, J. (1988). Public attitudes toward sentencing in Canada. In N. Walker & M. Hough (Eds.), *Sentencing and the public.* London: Gower.

DOTAN-ELIAZ, O., SOMMER, K. L., & RUBIN, S. (2009). Multilingual groups: Effects of linguistic ostracism on felt rejection and anger, coworker attraction, perceived team potency, and creative performance. *Basic and Applied Social Psychology,* **31**, 363–375.

DOTSCH, R., & WIGBOLDUS, D. H. J. (2008). Virtual prejudice. *Journal of Experimental Social Psychology,* **44**, 1194–1198.

DOTY, R. M., PETERSON, B. E., & WINTER, D. G. (1991). Threat and authoritarianism in the United States, 1978–1987. *Journal of Personality and Social Psychology,* **61**, 629–640.

DOVIDIO, J. F., GAERTNER, S. L., ANASTASIO, P. A., & SANITIOSO, R. (1992). Cognitive and motivational bases of bias: Implications of aversive racism for attitudes toward Hispanics. In S. Knouse, P. Rosenfeld, & A. Culbertson (Eds.), *Hispanics in the workplace*. Newbury Park, CA: Sage.

DOVIDIO, J. F., GAERTNER, S. L., & SAGUY, T. (2009). Commonality and the complexity of "we": Social attitudes and social change. *Personality and Social Psychology Bulletin, 13,* 3–20.

DOVIDIO, J. F., GAERTNER, S. L., HODSON, G., HOULETTE, M., & JOHNSON, K. M. (2005). Social inclusion and exclusion: Recategorization and the perception of intergroup boundaries. In D. Abrams, M. A. Hogg, & J. M. Marques (Eds.), *The social psychology of inclusion and exclusion*. New York: Psychology Press.

DOVIDIO, J. R., BRIGHAM, J. C., JOHNSON, B. T., & GAERTNER, S. L. (1996). Stereotyping, prejudice, and discrimination: Another look. In N. Macrae, M. Hewstone, & C. Stangor (Eds.), *Stereotypes and stereotyping*. New York: Guilford.

DOYLE, J. M. (2005). *True witness: Cops, courts, science, and the battle against misidentification*. New York: Palgrave MacMillan.

DRAGUNS, J. G. (1990). Normal and abnormal behavior in cross-cultural perspective: Specifying the nature of their relationship. *Nebraska Symposium on Motivation 1989, 37,* 235–277.

DREBER, A., RAND, D. G., FUDENBERG, D., & NOWAK, M. A. (2008). Winners don't punish. *Nature, 452,* 348–351.

DROLET, A. L., & MORRIS, M. W. (2000). Rapport in conflict resolution: Accounting for how face-to-face contact fosters mutual cooperation in mixed-motive conflicts. *Journal of Experimental Social Psychology, 36,* 26–50.

DRURY, J., COCKING, C., & REICHER, S. (2009). Everyone for themselves? A comparative study of crowd solidarity among emergency survivors. *British Journal of Social Psychology, 48,* 487–506.

DRYER, D. C., & HOROWITZ, L. M. (1997). When do opposites attract? Interpersonal complementarity versus similarity. *Journal of Personality and Social Psychology, 72,* 592–603.

DUCK, J. M., HOGG, M. A., & TERRY, D. J. (1995). Me, us and them: Political identification and the third-person effect in the 1993 Australian federal election. *European Journal of Social Psychology, 25,* 195–215.

DUNN, E., & ASHTON-JAMES, C. (2008). On emotional innumeracy: Predicted and actual affective response to grand-scale tragedies. *Journal of Experimental Social Psychology, 44,* 692–698.

DUNN, E. W., WILSON, T. D., & GILBERT, D. T. (2003). Location, location, location: The misprediction of satisfaction in housing lotteries. *Personality and Social Psychology Bulletin, 29,* 1421–1432.

DUNN, J. R., & SCHWEITZER, M. E. (2005). Feeling and believing: The influence of emotion on trust. *Journal of Personality and Social Psychology, 88,* 736–748.

DUNN, M., & SEARLE, R. (2010). Effect of manipulated prestige-car ownership on both sex attractiveness ratings. *British Journal of Psychology, 101,* 69–80.

DUNNING, D. (1995). Trait importance and modifiability as factors influencing self-assessment and self-enhancement motives. *Personality and Social Psychology Bulletin, 21,* 1297–1306.

DUNNING, D. (2005). *Self-insight: Roadblocks and detours on the path to knowing thyself*. London: Psychology Press.

DUNNING, D. (2006). Strangers to ourselves? *The Psychologist, 19,* 600–603.

DUNNING, D., GRIFFIN, D. W., MILOJKOVIC, J. D., & ROSS, L. (1990). The overconfidence effect in social prediction. *Journal of Personality and Social Psychology, 58,* 568–581.

DUNNING, D., MEYEROWITZ, J. A., & HOLZBERG, A. D. (1989). Ambiguity and self-evaluation. *Journal of Personality and Social Psychology, 57,* 1082–1090.

DUNNING, D., PERIE, M., & STORY, A. L. (1991). Self-serving prototypes of social categories. *Journal of Personality and Social Psychology, 61,* 957–968.

DURANTE, K. M., LI, N. P., & HASELTON, M. G. (2008). Changes in women's dress across the ovulatory cycle: Naturalistic and laboratory task-based evidence. *Personality and Social Psychology Bulletin, 34,* 1451–1460.

DUTTON, D. G., & ARON, A. P. (1974). Some evidence for heightened sexual attraction under conditions of high anxiety. *Journal of Personality and Social Psychology, 30,* 510–517.

DUTTON, D. G., BOYANOWSKY, E. O., & BOND, M. H. (2005). Extreme mass homicide: From military massacre to genocide. *Aggression and Violent Behavior 10,* 437–473.

DYE, M. W. G., GREEN, C. S., & BAVELIER, D. (2009). Increasing speed of processing with action video games. *Current Directions in Psychological Science, 18,* 321–326.

EAGLY, A. H. (1987). Sex differences in social behavior: A social-role interpretation. Hillsdale, NJ: Erlbaum.

EAGLY, A. H. (1994). Are people prejudiced against women? Donald Campbell Award invited address, American Psychological Association convention.

EAGLY, A. H. (2009). The his and hers of prosocial behavior: An examination of the social psychology of gender. *American Psychologist, 64,* 644–658.

EAGLY, A. H., ASHMORE, R. D., MAKHIJANI, M. G., & LONGO, L. C. (1991). What is beautiful is good, but . . .: A meta-analytic review of research on the physical attractiveness stereotype. *Psychological Bulletin, 110,* 109–128.

EAGLY, A., & CARLI, L. (2007). *Through the labyrinth: The truth about how women become leaders.* Cambridge, MA: Harvard University Press.

EAGLY, A. H., & CHAIKEN, S. (1993). *The psychology of attitudes.* San Diego: Harcourt Brace Jovanovich.

EAGLY, A. H., & CROWLEY, M. (1986). Gender and helping behavior: A meta-analytic review of the social psychological literature. *Psychological Bulletin, 100,* 283–308.

EAGLY, A. H., DIEKMAN, A. B., JOHANNESEN-SCHMIDT, M. C., & KOENIG, A. M. (2004). Gender gaps in sociopolitical attitudes: A social psychological analysis. *Journal of Personality and Social Psychology, 87,* 796–816.

EAGLY, A. H., & WOOD, W. (1991). Explaining sex differences in social behavior: A meta-analytic perspective. *Personality and Social Psychology Bulletin, 17,* 306–315.

EASTERBROOK, G. (2004, May 25). The 50¢-a-gallon solution. *New York Times* (www.nytimes.com).

EASTERLIN, R. A., McVEY, L. A., SWITEK, M., SAWANGFA, O., & ZWEIG, J. S. (2010). The happiness-income paradox revisited. *PNAS, 107,* 22463–22468.

EASTWICK, P. W. (2009). Beyond the Pleistocene: Using phylogeny and constraint to inform the evolutionary psychology of human mating. *Psychological Bulletin, 135,* 794–821.

EASTWICK, P. W., FINKEL, E. J., KRISHNAMURTI, T., & LOEWENSTEIN, G. (2007). Mispredicting distress following romantic breakup: Revealing the time course of the affective forecasting error. *Journal of Experimental Social Psychology, 44,* 800–807.

EASTWICK, P. W., & FINKEL, E. J. (2008a). Speed-dating as a methodological innovation. *The Psychologist, 21,* 402–403.

EASTWICK, P. W., & FINKEL, E. J. (2008b). Sex differences in mate preferences revisited: Do people know what they initially desire in a romantic partner? *Journal of Personality and Social Psychology, 94,* 245–264.

EASTWICK, P. W., FINKEL, E. J., MOCHON, D., & ARIELY, D. (2007). Selective versus unselective romantic desire. *Psychological Science, 18,* 317–319.

EATON, A. A., VISSER, P. S., KROSNICK, J. A., & ANAND, S. (2009). Social power and attitude strength over the life course. *Personality and Social Psychology Bulletin, 35,* 1646–1660.

EBBESEN, E. B., DUNCAN, B., & KONECNI, V. J. (1975). Effects of content of verbal aggression on future verbal aggression: A field experiment. *Journal of Experimental Social Psychology, 11,* 192–204.

EBERHARDT, J. L., (2005). Imaging race. *American Psychologist, 60,* 181–190.

EBERHARDT, J. L., PURDIE, V. J., GOFF, P. A., & DAVIES, P. G. (2004). Seeing black: Race, crime, and visual processing. *Journal of Personality and Social Psychology, 87,* 876–893.

ECKERSLEY, R. (2005). Is modern Western culture a health hazard? *International Journal of Epidemiology,* published online November 22.

ECKERSLEY, R., & REEDER, L. (2008). *Violence in public places: Explanations and solutions.* Weston, ACT, Australia: Australia 21 Limited.

EDWARDS, C. P. (1991). Behavioral sex differences in children of diverse cultures: The case of nurturance to infants. In M. Pereira & L. Fairbanks (Eds.), *Juveniles: Comparative socioecology.* Oxford: Oxford University Press.

EHRLICH, P., & FELDMAN, M. (2003). Genes and cultures: What creates our behavioral phenome? *Current Anthropology, 44,* 87–95.

EIBACH, R. P., & EHRLINGER, J. (2006). "Keep your eyes on the prize": Reference points and racial differences in assessing progress toward equality. *Personality and Social Psychology Bulletin, 32,* 66–77.

EICH, E., REEVES, J. L., JAEGER, B., & GRAFF-RADFORD, S. B. (1985). Memory for pain: Relation between past and present pain intensity. *Pain, 23,* 375–380.

EISENBERG, N., & LENNON, R. (1983). Sex differences in empathy and related capacities. *Psychological Bulletin, 94,* 100–131.

EISER, J. R., SUTTON, S. R., & WOBER, M. (1979). Smoking, seat-belts, and beliefs about health. *Addictive Behaviors, 4,* 331–338.

ELDER, G. H., JR. (1969). Appearance and education in marriage mobility. *American Sociological Review, 34,* 519–533.

ELLEMERS, N., VAN RIJSWIJK, W., ROEFS, M., & SIMONS, C. (1997). Bias in intergroup perceptions: Balancing group identity with social reality. *Personality and Social Psychology Bulletin, 23,* 186–198.

ELLIS, L., HERSHBERGER, S., FIELD, E., WERSINGER, S., PELLIS, S., GEARY, D., PALMER, C., HOYENGA, K., HETRONI, A., & KARADI, K. (2008). *Sex differences: Summarizing more than a century of scientific research.* New York: Psychology Press.

ELLIS, B. J., & SYMONS, D. (1990). Sex difference in sexual fantasy: An evolutionary psychological approach. *Journal of Sex Research, 27,* 490–521.

ELLIS, H. D. (1981). Theoretical aspects of face recognition. In G. H. Davies, H. D. Ellis, & J. Shepherd (Eds.), *Perceiving and remembering faces.* London: Academic Press.

ELLISON, P. A., GOVERN, J. M., PETRI, H. L., & FIGLER, M. H. (1995). Anonymity and aggressive driving behavior: A field study. *Journal of Social Behavior and Personality, 10,* 265–272.

ELMS, A. C. (1995). Obedience in retrospect. *Journal of Social Issues, 51,* 21–31.

ENGEMANN, K. M., & OWYANG, M. T. (2003, April). So much for that merit raise: The link between wages and appearance. *The Regional Economist* (www.stlouisfed.org).

ENGS, R., & HANSON, D. J. (1989). Reactance theory: A test with collegiate drinking. *Psychological Reports, 64,* 1083–1086.

ENNIS, B. J., & VERRILLI, D. B., JR. (1989). Motion for leave to file brief amicus curiae and brief of Society for the Scientific Study of Religion, American Sociological Association, and others. U.S. Supreme Court Case No. 88–1600, Holy Spirit Association for the Unification of World Christianity, *et al.,* v. David Molko and Tracy Leal. On petition for writ of certiorari to the Supreme Court of California. Washington, DC: Jenner & Block, 21 Dupont Circle NW.

ENNIS, R., & ZANNA, M. P. (1991). Hockey assault: Constitutive versus normative violations. Paper presented at the Canadian Psychological Association convention.

EPLEY, N., AKALIS, S., WAYTZ, A., & CACIOPPO, J. T. (2008). Creating social connection through inferential reproduction: Loneliness and perceived agency in gadgets, gods, and greyhounds. *Psychological Science, 19,* 114–120.

EPLEY, N., & HUFF, C. (1998). Suspicion, affective response, and educational benefit as a result of deception in psychology research. *Personality and Social Psychology Bulletin, 24,* 759–768.

EPLEY, N., & WHITCHURCH, E. (2008). Mirror, mirror on the wall: Enhancement in self-recognition. *Personality and Social Psychology Bulletin, 34,* 1159–1170.

EPSTEIN, J. A., & BOTVIN, G. J. (2008). Media refusal skills and drug skill refusal techniques: What is their relationship with alcohol use among inner-city adolescents? *Addictive Behavior, 33,* 528–537.

EPSTEIN, R. (2007, February/March). The truth about online dating. *Scientific American Mind,* pp. 28–35.

ERICKSON, B., HOLMES, J. G., FREY, R., WALKER, L., & THIBAUT, J. (1974). Functions of a third party in the resolution of conflict: The role of a judge in pretrial conferences. *Journal of Personality and Social Psychology, 30,* 296–306.

ERON, L. D. (1987). The development of aggressive behavior from the perspective of a developing behaviorism. *American Psychologist, 42,* 425–442.

ERON, L. D., & HUESMANN, L. R. (1980). Adolescent aggression and television. *Annals of the New York Academy of Sciences, 347,* 319–331.

ERON, L. D., & HUESMANN, L. R. (1984). The control of aggressive behavior by changes in attitudes, values, and the conditions of learning. In R. J. Blanchard & C. Blanchard (Eds.), *Advances in the study of aggression* (Vol. 1). Orlando, FL: Academic Press.

ERON, L. D., & HUESMANN, L. R. (1985). The role of television in the development of prosocial and antisocial behavior. In D. Olweus, M. Radke-Yarrow, & J. Block (Eds.), *Development of antisocial and prosocial behavior.* Orlando, FL: Academic Press.

ESSES, V. M., HADDOCK, G., & ZANNA, M. P. (1993). Values, stereotypes, and emotions as determinants of intergroup attitudes. In D. Mackie & D. Hamilton (Eds.), *Affect, cognition and stereotyping: Interactive processes in intergroup perception.* San Diego, CA: Academic Press.

ETZIONI, A. (1967). The Kennedy experiment. *The Western Political Quarterly, 20,* 361–380.

EVANS, G. W. (1979). Behavioral and physiological consequences of crowding in humans. *Journal of Applied Social Psychology, 9,* 27–46.

EVANS, R. I., SMITH, C. K., & RAINES, B. E. (1984). Deterring cigarette smoking in adolescents: A psychosocial-behavioral analysis of an intervention strategy. In A. Baum, J. Singer, & S. Taylor (Eds.), *Handbook of psychology and health: Social psychological aspects of health* (Vol. 4). Hillsdale, NJ: Erlbaum.

FALK, A., KUHN, A., & ZWEIMÜLLER, J. (2011). Unemployment and right-wing extremist crime. *Scandinavian Journal of Economics, 113,* 260–285.

FARRELL, E. F. (2005, March 18). The battle for hearts and lungs. *Chronicle of Higher Education* (www.chronicle.com).

FARRELLY, M. C., DAVIS, K. C., DUKE, J., & MESSERI, P. (2008, January 17). Sustaining "truth": Changes in youth tobacco attitudes and smoking intentions after three years of a national antismoking campaign. *Health Education Research* (doi:10.1093/her/cym087).

FARRELLY, M. C., HEALTON, C. G., DAVIS, K. C., MESSERI, P., HERSEY, J. C., & HAVILAND, M. L. (2002). Getting to the truth: Evaluating national tobacco countermarketing campaigns. *American Journal of Public Health,* **92,** 901–907.

FARWELL, L., & WEINER, B. (2000). Bleeding hearts and the heartless: Popular perceptions of liberal and conservative ideologies. *Personality and Social Psychology Bulletin,* **26,** 845–852.

FAULKNER, S. L., & WILLIAMS, K. D. (1996). A study of social loafing in industry. Paper presented to the Midwestern Psychological Association convention.

FAUST, D., & ZISKIN, J. (1988). The expert witness in psychology and psychiatry. *Science,* **241,** 31–35.

FAZIO, R. H. (1990). Multiple processes by which attitudes guide behavior: The mode model as an integrative framework. *Advances in Experimental Social Psychology,* **23,** 75–109.

FAZIO. R. H. (2007). Attitudes as object-evaluation associations of varying strength. *Social Cognition,* **25,** 603–637.

FAZIO, R. H., EFFREIN, E. A., & FALENDER, V. J. (1981). Self-perceptions following social interaction. *Journal of Personality and Social Psychology,* **41,** 232–242.

FEDERAL BUREAU OF INVESTIGATION (FBI) (2008). *Uniform crime reports for the United States.* Washington, DC: Federal Bureau of Investigation.

FEDERAL BUREAU OF INVESTIGATION (FBI) (2009). Hate crime statistics, 2009. Table 1, Incidents, offenses, victims, and known offenders. Washington, DC: Federal Bureau of Investigation.

FEDERAL BUREAU OF INVESTIGATION (FBI) (2011). *Uniform Crime Reports:* Table 4. January to June 2010 offenses reported to law enforcement by state by city 100,000 and over in population. Washington, DC: Federal Bureau of Investigation. (www.fbi.gov)

FEDERAL TRADE COMMISSION (FTC) (2003, June 12). Federal Trade Commission cigarette report for 2001 (www.ftc.gov/opa/2003/06/2001cigrpt.htm).

FEENEY, J., PETERSON, C., & NOLLER, P. (1994). Equity and marital satisfaction over the family life cycle. *Personality Relationships,* **1,** 83–99.

FEIN, S., HILTON, J. L., & MILLER, D. T. (1990). Suspicion of ulterior motivation and the correspondence bias. *Journal of Personality and Social Psychology,* **58,** 753–764.

FEINBERG, J. M., & AIELLO, J. R. (2006). Social facilitation: A test of competing theories. *Journal of Applied Social Psychology,* **36,** 1–23.

FEINBERG, M., & WILLER, R. (2010). Apocalypse soon? Dire messages reduce belief in global warming by contradicting just-world beliefs. *Psychological Science,* **22,** 34–38.

FEINGOLD, A. (1988). Matching for attractiveness in romantic partners and same-sex friends: A meta-analysis and theoretical critique. *Psychological Bulletin,* **104,** 226–235.

FEINGOLD, A. (1990). Gender differences in effects of physical attractiveness on romantic attraction: A comparison across five research paradigms. *Journal of Personality and Social Psychology,* **59,** 981–993.

FEINGOLD, A. (1991). Sex differences in the effects of similarity and physical attractiveness on opposite-sex attraction. *Basic and Applied Social Psychology,* **12,** 357–367.

FEINGOLD, A. (1992a). Gender differences in mate selection preferences: A test of the parental investment model. *Psychological Bulletin,* **112,** 125–139.

FEINGOLD, A. (1992b). Good-looking people are not what we think. *Psychological Bulletin,* **111,** 304–341.

FELDMAN, R. S., & PROHASKA, T. (1979). The student as Pygmalion: Effect of student expectation on the teacher. *Journal of Educational Psychology,* **71,** 485–493.

FELDMAN, R. S., & THEISS, A. J. (1982). The teacher and student as Pygmalions: Joint effects of teacher and student expectations. *Journal of Educational Psychology,* **74,** 217–223.

FENIGSTEIN, A. (1984). Self-consciousness and the overperception of self as a target. *Journal of Personality and Social Psychology,* **47,** 860–870.

FENIGSTEIN, A., & VANABLE, P. A. (1992). Paranoia and self-consciousness. *Journal of Personality and Social Psychology,* **62,** 129–138.

FERGUSSON, D. M., HORWOOD, L. J., & SHANNON, F. T. (1984). A proportional hazards model of family breakdown. *Journal of Marriage and the Family,* **46,** 539–549.

FERGUSON, C. J., & KILBURN, J. (2010). Much ado about nothing: The misestimation and overinterpretation of violent video game effects in Eastern and Western nations: Comment on Anderson et al. (2010). *Psychological Bulletin,* **136,** 174–178.

FERRIMAN, K., LUBINSKI, D., & BENBOW, C. P. (2009). Work preferences, life values, and personal views of top math/science graduate students and the profoundly gifted: Developmental changes and gender differences during emerging adulthood and parenthood. *Journal of Personality and Social Psychology,* **97,** 517–522.

FESHBACH, S. (1980). Television advertising and children: Policy issues and alternatives. Paper presented at the American Psychological Association convention.

FESTINGER, L. (1954). A theory of social comparison processes. *Human Relations,* **7,** 117–140.

FESTINGER, L. (1957). *A theory of cognitive dissonance.* Stanford: Stanford University Press.

FESTINGER, L., & MACCOBY, N. (1964). On resistance to persuasive communications. *Journal of Abnormal and Social Psychology, 68,* 359–366.

FESTINGER, L., PEPITONE, A., & NEWCOMB, T. (1952). Some consequences of deindividuation in a group. *Journal of Abnormal and Social Psychology, 47,* 382–389.

FEYGINA, I., JOST, J. T., & GOLDSMITH, R. E. (2010). System justification, the denial of global warming, and the possibility of "system-sanctioned change." *Personality and Social Psychology Bulletin, 36,* 326–338.

FICHTER, J. (1968). *America's forgotten priests: What are they saying?* New York: Harper.

FIEDLER, F. E. (1987, September). When to lead, when to stand back. *Psychology Today,* pp. 26–27.

FIEDLER, K., SEMIN, G. R., & KOPPETSCH, C. (1991). Language use and attributional biases in close personal relationships. *Personality and Social Psychology Bulletin, 17,* 147–155.

FINCHAM, F. D., LAMBERT, N. M., & BEACH, S. R. H. (2010). Faith and unfaithfulness: Can praying for your partner reduce infidelity? *Journal of Personality and Social Psychology, 99,* 649–659.

FINDLEY, M. J., & COOPER, H. M. (1983). Locus of control and academic achievement: A literature review. *Journal of Personality and Social Psychology, 44,* 419–427.

FINKEL, E. J., EASTWICK, P. W., KARNEY, B. R., REIS, H. T., & SPRECHER, S. (2012). Online dating: A critical analysis from the perspective of psychological science. *Psychological Science in the Public Interest, 13,* 3–66.

FISCHER, K., EGERTON, M., GERSHUNY, J. I., & ROBINSON, J. P. (2007). Gender convergence in the American Heritage Time Use Study (AHTUS). *Social Indicators Research, 82,* 1–33.

FISCHER, P., & GREITEMEYER, T. (2010). A new look at selective-exposure effects: An integrative model. *Current Directions in Psychological Science, 19,* 384–389.

FISCHER, P., KRUEGER, J., GREITEMEYER, T., KASTENMÜLLER, A., VOGRINCIC, C., FREY, D., HEENE, M., WICHER, M., & KAINBACHER, M. (2011). The bystander-effect: A meta-analytic review on bystander intervention in dangerous and non-dangerous emergencies. *Psychological Bulletin, 137,* 517–537.

FISCHER, R., & BOER, D. (2011). What is more important for national well-being: Money or autonomy? A meta-analysis of well-being, burnout, and anxiety across 63 societies. *Journal of Personality and Social Psychology, 101,* 164–184.

FISCHER, R., & CHALMERS, A. (2008). Is optimism universal? A meta-analytical investigation of optimism levels across 22 nations. *Personality and Individual Differences, 45,* 378–382.

FISCHER, R., & VAN DE VLIERT, E. (2011). Does climate undermine subjective well-being? A 58-nation study. *Personality and Social Psychology Bulletin, 37,* 1031–1041.

FISHER, R. P., MILNE, R., & BULL, R. (2011). Interviewing cooperative witnesses. *Current Directions in Psychological Science, 20,* 20–23.

FISCHHOFF, B. (1982). Debiasing. In D. Kahneman, P. Slovic, & A. Tversky (Eds.), *Judgment under uncertainty: Heuristics and biases.* New York: Cambridge University Press.

FISCHTEIN, D. S., HEROLD, E. S., & DESMARAIS, S. (2007). How much does gender explain in sexual attitudes and behaviors? A survey of Canadian adults. *Archives of Sexual Behavior, 36,* 451–461.

FISHBEIN, D., & THELEN, M. H. (1981a). Husband-wife similarity and marital satisfaction: A different approach. Paper presented at the Midwestern Psychological Association convention.

FISHBEIN, D., & THELEN, M. H. (1981b). Psychological factors in mate selection and marital satisfaction: A review (Ms. 2374). *Catalog of Selected Documents in Psychology, 11,* 84.

FISHER, H. (1994, April). The nature of romantic love. *Journal of NIH Research,* pp. 59–64.

FISHER, R. J. (1994). Generic principles for resolving intergroup conflict. *Journal of Social Issues, 50,* 47–66.

FISKE, S. T. (1989). Interdependence and stereotyping: From the laboratory to the Supreme Court (and back). Invited address, American Psychological Association convention.

FISKE, S. T. (1992). Thinking is for doing: Portraits of social cognition from daguerreotype to laserphoto. *Journal of Personality and Social Psychology, 63,* 877–889.

FISKE, S. T. (2011a, January 27). *One word: Plasticity.* Presentation to the Society of Personality and Social Psychology Presidential Symposium: Visions for the next decade of personality and social psychology, San Antonio, TX.

FISKE, S. T. (2011b). *Envy up, scorn down: How status divides us.* New York: Sage Foundation.

FISKE, S. T. (2011c). *Emotions of inequality.* New York: Sage Foundation.

FISKE, S. T., HARRIS, L. T., & CUDDY, A. J. C. (2004). Why ordinary people torture enemy prisoners. *Science, 306,* 1482–1483.

FLAY, B. R., RYAN, K. B., BEST, J. A., BROWN, K. S., KERSELL, M. W., D'AVERNAS, J. R., & ZANNA, M. P. (1985). Are social-psychological smoking prevention programs effective? The Waterloo study. *Journal of Behavioral Medicine, 8,* 37–59.

FLEMING, I., BAUM, A., & WEISS, L. (1987). Social density and perceived control as mediators of crowding stress in high-density residential neighborhoods. *Journal of Personality and Social Psychology, 52,* 899–906.

FLETCHER, G. J. O., FINCHAM, F. D., CRAMER, L., & HERON, N. (1987). The role of attributions in the development of dating relationships. *Journal of Personality and Social Psychology, 53,* 481–489.

FLETCHER, G. J. O., TITHER, J. M., O'LOUGHLIN, C., FRIESEN, M., & OVERALL, N. (2004). Warm and homely or cold and beautiful? Sex differences in trading off traits in mate selection. *Personality and Social Psychology Bulletin, 30,* 659–672.

FLYNN, F. J., & WILTERMUTH, S. S. (2010). Who's with me? False consensus, brokerage, and ethical decision-making in organizations. *Academic of Management Journal, 53,* 1074–1089.

FOLEY, L. A. (1976). Personality and situational influences on changes in prejudice: A replication of Cook's railroad game in a prison setting. *Journal of Personality and Social Psychology, 34,* 846–856.

FOLLETT, M. P. (1940). Constructive conflict. In H. C. Metcalf & L. Urwick (Eds.), *Dynamic administration: The collected papers of Mary Parker Follett.* New York: Harper.

FOOTPRINTNETWORK.ORG (2011). World footprint: Do we fit on the planet? (www.footprintnetwork. org).

FORD, R. (2008). Is racial prejudice declining in Britain? *British Journal of Sociology, 59,* 609–636.

FORD, T. E., BOXER, C. F., ARMSTRONG, J., & EDEL, J. R. (2008). More than "just a joke": The prejudice-releasing function of sexist humor. *Personality and Social Psychology Bulletin, 34,* 159–170.

FORGAS, J. P. (2007). When sad is better than happy: Negative affect can improve the quality and effectiveness of persuasive messages and social influence strategies. *Journal of Experimental Social Psychology, 43,* 513–528.

FORSYTH, D. R., & LEARY, M. R. (1997). Achieving the goals of the scientist-practitioner model: The seven interfaces of social and counseling psychology. *The Counseling Psychologist, 25,* 180–200.

FOSS, R. D. (1978). The role of social influence in blood donation. Paper presented at the American Psychological Association convention.

FOSTER, C. A., WITCHER, B. S., CAMPBELL, W. K., & GREEN, J. D. (1998). Arousal and attraction: Evidence for automatic and controlled processes. *Journal of Personality and Social Psychology, 74,* 86–101.

FOURNIER, R., & TOMPSON, T. (2008, September 20). Poll: Racial views steer some white Dems away from Obama. Associated Press via news.yahoo.com (data from www.knowledgenetworks.com survey for AP-Yahoo in partnership with Stanford University).

FOWLER, J. H., & CHRISTAKIS, N. A. (2008). Dynamic spread of happiness in a large social network: Longitudinal analysis over 20 years in the Framingham Heart Study. *British Medical Journal, 337* (doi: 10.1136/bmj.a2338).

FRANK, R. (1999). *Luxury fever: Why money fails to satisfy in an era of excess.* New York: Free Press.

FRANTZ, C. M. (2006). I AM being fair: The bias blind spot as a stumbling block to seeing both sides. *Basic and Applied Social Psychology, 28,* 157–167.

FREEDMAN, J. L., BIRSKY, J., & CAVOUKIAN, A. (1980). Environmental determinants of behavioral contagion: Density and number. *Basic and Applied Social Psychology, 1,* 155–161.

FREEDMAN, J. L., & FRASER, S. C. (1966). Compliance without pressure: The foot-in-the-door technique. *Journal of Personality and Social Psychology, 4,* 195–202.

FREEDMAN, J. L., & PERLICK, D. (1979). Crowding, contagion, and laughter. *Journal of Experimental Social Psychology, 15,* 295–303.

FREEDMAN, J. L., & SEARS, D. O. (1965). Warning, distraction, and resistance to influence. *Journal of Personality and Social Psychology, 1,* 262–266.

FREEDMAN, J. S. (1965). Long-term behavioral effects of cognitive dissonance. *Journal of Experimental Social Psychology, 1,* 145–155.

FREEMAN, M. A. (1997). Demographic correlates of individualism and collectivism: A study of social values in Sri Lanka. *Journal of Cross-Cultural Psychology, 28,* 321–341.

FRENCH, J. R. P. (1968). The conceptualization and the measurement of mental health in terms of self-identity theory. In S. B. Sells (Ed.), *The definition and measurement of mental health.* Washington, DC: Department of Health, Education, and Welfare. (Cited by M. Rosenberg, 1979, *Conceiving the self.* New York: Basic Books.)

FREUND, B., COLGROVE, L. A., BURKE, B. L., & McLEOD, R. (2005). Self-rated driving performance among elderly drivers referred for driving evaluation. *Accident Analysis and Prevention, 37,* 613–618.

FRIEBEL, G., & SEABRIGHT, P. (2011). Do women have longer conversations? Telephone evidence of gendered communication strategies. *Journal of Economic Psychology, 32,* 348–356.

FRIEDMAN, T. L. (2003, April 9). Hold your applause. *New York Times* (www.nytimes.com).

FRIEDMAN, T. L. (2003, June 4). Because we could. *New York Times* (www.nytimes.com).

FRIEDRICH, J. (1996). On seeing oneself as less self-serving than others: The ultimate self-serving bias? *Teaching of Psychology, 23*, 107–109.

FRIEDRICH, L. K., & STEIN, A. H. (1973). Aggressive and prosocial television programs and the natural behavior of preschool children. *Monographs of the Society of Research in Child Development, 38* (4, Serial No. 151).

FRIEDRICH, L. K., & STEIN, A. H. (1975). Prosocial television and young children: The effects of verbal labeling and role playing on learning and behavior. *Child Development, 46*, 27–38.

FRIEZE, I. H., OLSON, J. E., & RUSSELL, J. (1991). Attractiveness and income for men and women in management. *Journal of Applied Social Psychology, 21*, 1039–1057.

FRISELL, T., LICHTENSTEIN, P., & LÅNGSTRÖM, N. (2011). Violent crime runs in families: A total population study of 12.5 million individuals. *Journal of Research in Psychiatry and the Allied Sciences, 41*, 97–105.

FURNHAM, A. (1982). Explanations for unemployment in Britain. *European Journal of Social Psychology, 12*, 335–352.

FURNHAM, A., & GUNTER, B. (1984). Just world beliefs and attitudes towards the poor. *British Journal of Social Psychology, 23*, 265–269.

GABLE, S. L., GONZAGA, G. C., & STRACHMAN, A. (2006). Will you be there for me when things go right? Supportive responses to positive event disclosures. *Journal of Personality and Social Psychology, 91*, 904–917.

GABRENYA, W. K., JR., WANG, Y.-E., & LATANÉ, B. (1985). Social loafing on an optimizing task: Cross-cultural differences among Chinese and Americans. *Journal of Cross-Cultural Psychology, 16*, 223–242.

GABRIEL, S., & GARDNER, W. L. (1999). Are there "his" and "hers" types of interdependence? The implications of gender differences in collective versus relational interdependence for affect, behavior, and cognition. *Journal of Personality and Social Psychology, 77*, 642–655.

GAERTNER, L., SEDIKIDES, C., & GRAETZ, K. (1999). In search of self-definition: Motivational primacy of the individual self, motivational primacy of the collective self, or contextual primacy? *Journal of Personality and Social Psychology, 76*, 5–18.

GAERTNER, S. L., & DOVIDIO, J. F. (2005). Understanding and addressing contemporary racism: From aversive racism to the Common Ingroup Identity Model. *Journal of Social Issues, 61*, 615–639.

GALANTER, M. (1989). *Cults: Faith, healing, and coercion.* New York: Oxford University Press.

GALANTER, M. (1990). Cults and zealous self-help movements: A psychiatric perspective. *American Journal of Psychiatry, 147*, 543–551.

GALE, C. R., BATTY, D., & DEARY, I. J. (2008). Locus of control at age 10 years and health outcomes and behaviors at age 30 years: The 1970 British cohort study. *Psychosomatic Medicine, 70*, 397–403.

GALINSKY, A. D., & MOSKOWITZ, G. B. (2000). Perspective-taking: Decreasing stereotype expression, stereotype accessibility, and in-group favoritism. *Journal of Personality and Social Psychology, 78*, 708–724.

GALINSKY, E., AUMANN, K., & BOND, J. T. (2009). *Times are changing: Gender and generation at work and at home.* New York: Families and Work Institute.

GALIZIO, M., & HENDRICK, C. (1972). Effect of musical accompaniment on attitude: The guitar as a prop for persuasion. *Journal of Applied Social Psychology, 2*, 350–359.

GALLUP, G. G., JR., & FREDERICK, D. A. (2010). The science of sex appeal: An evolutionary perspective. *Journal of General Psychology, 14*, 240–250.

GALLUP, G. G., JR., & FREDERICK, M. J., & PIPITONE, R. N. (2008). Morphology and behavior: Phrenology revisited. *Review of General Psychology, 12*, 297–304.

GALLUP, G. H. (1972). *The Gallup poll: Public opinion 1935–1971* (Vol. 3, pp. 551, 1716). New York: Random House.

GALLUP, G. H., JR., & JONES, T. (1992). *The saints among us.* Harrisburg, PA: Morehouse.

GALLUP ORGANIZATION (1990). April 19–22 survey reported in *American Enterprise,* September/October **1990**, p. 92.

GANGESTAD, S. W., SIMPSON, J. A., & COUSINS, A. J. (2004). Women's preferences for male behavioral displays change across the menstrual cycle. *Psychological Science, 15*, 203–207.

GANGESTAD, S. W., & THORNHILL, R. (1997). Human sexual selection and developmental stability. In J. A. Simpson & D. T. Kenrick (Eds.), *Evolutionary social psychology.* Mahwah, NJ: Erlbaum.

GARB, H. N. (1994). Judgment research: Implications for clinical practice and testimony in court. *Applied and Preventive Psychology, 3*, 173–183.

GARDNER, M. (1997, July/August). Heaven's Gate: The UFO cult of Bo and Peep. *Skeptical Inquirer,* pp. 15–17.

GARDNER, W. L., PICKETT, L., JEFFERIS, V., & KNOWLES, M. (2005). On the outside looking in: Loneliness and social monitoring. *Personality and Social Psychology Bulletin, 31,* 1549–1560.

GATES, G. J. (2011, April). *How many people are lesbian, gay, bisexual, and transgender?* Los Angeles: The William Institute, UCLA School of Law.

GATES, M. F., & ALLEE, W. C. (1933). Conditioned behavior of isolated and grouped cockroaches on a simple maze. *Journal of Comparative Psychology, 15,* 331–358.

GAUCHER, D., FRIESEN, J., & KAY, A. C. (2011). Evidence that gendered wording in job advertisements exists and sustains gender inequality. *Journal of Personality and Social Psychology, 101,* 109–128.

GAUNT, R. (2006). Couple similarity and marital satisfaction: Are similar spouses happier? *Journal of Personality, 74,* 1401–1420.

GAVANSKI, I., & HOFFMAN, C. (1987). Awareness of influences on one's own judgments: The roles of covariation detection and attention to the judgment process. *Journal of Personality and Social Psychology, 52,* 453–463.

GAWANDE, A. (2002). *Complications: A surgeon's notes on an imperfect science.* New York: Metropolitan Books, Holt.

GAWRONSKI, B., & BODENHAUSEN, G. V. (2006). Associative and propositional processes in evaluation: An integrative review of implicit and explicit attitude change. *Psychological Bulletin, 132,* 692–731.

GAZZANIGA, M. S. (1992). *Nature's mind: The biological roots of thinking, emotions, sexuality, language, and intelligence.* New York: Basic Books.

GAZZANIGA, M. (1998). *The mind's past.* Berkeley, CA: University of California Press.

GAZZANIGA, M. (2008). *Human: The science behind what makes us unique.* New York: Ecco.

GEEN, R. G. (1998). Aggression and antisocial behavior. In D. Gilbert, S. Fiske, & G. Lindzey (Eds.), *Handbook of social psychology,* 4th edition. New York: McGraw-Hill.

GEEN, R. G., & GANGE, J. J. (1983). Social facilitation: Drive theory and beyond. In H. H. Blumberg, A. P. Hare, V. Kent, & M. Davies (Eds.), *Small groups and social interaction* (Vol. 1). London: Wiley.

GEEN, R. G., & THOMAS, S. L. (1986). The immediate effects of media violence on behavior. *Journal of Social Issues, 42*(3), 7–28.

GELFAND, M. J., & 44 OTHERS. (2011). Differences between tight and loose cultures: A 33-nation study. *Science, 332,* 1100–1104.

GENTILE, B., TWENGE, J. M., & CAMPBELL, W. K. (2010). Birth cohort differences in self-esteem, 1988–2008: A cross-temporal meta-analysis. *Review of General Psychology, 14,* 261–268.

GENTILE, D. A. (2004, May 14). Quoted by K. Laurie in *Violent games* (ScienCentral.com).

GENTILE, D. A., & ANDERSON, C. A. (2003). Violent video games: The newest media violence hazard. In D. A. Gentile (Ed.), *Media violence and children.* Westport, CT: Ablex.

GENTILE, D. A., & ANDERSON, C. A. (2011). Don't read more into the Supreme Court's ruling on the California video game law. Iowa State University press release, June 30, 2011 (www.psychology. iastate.edu/faculty/caa/Multimedia/VGV-SC-OpEdDDAGCAA.pdf).

GENTILE, D. A., LYNCH, P. J., LINDER, J. R., & WALSH, D. A. (2004). The effects of violent video game habits on adolescent hostility, aggressive behaviors, and school performance. *Journal of Adolescence, 27,* 5–22.

GENTILE, D. A., SALEEM, M., & ANDERSON, C. A. (2007). Public policy and the effects of media violence on children. *Social Issues and Policy Review, 1,* 15–61.

GERARD, H. B., & MATHEWSON, G. C. (1966). The effects of severity of initiation on liking for a group: A replication. *Journal of Experimental Social Psychology, 2,* 278–287.

GERBER, J., & WHEELER, L. (2009a). On being rejected: A meta-analysis of experimental research on rejection. *Perspectives on Psychological Science, 4,* 468–488.

GERBER, J., & WHEELER, L. (2009b). Rejoinder to Baumeister, DeWall, and Vohs (2009). *Perspectives on Psychological Science, 4,* 494–495.

GERBNER, G. (1994). The politics of media violence: Some reflections. In C. Hamelink & O. Linne (Eds.), *Mass communication research: On problems and policies.* Norwood, NJ: Ablex.

GERRIG, R. J., & PRENTICE, D. A. (1991, September). The representation of fictional information. *Psychological Science, 2,* 336–340.

GERSHOFF, E. T. (2002). Corporal punishment by parents and associated child behaviors and experiences: A meta-analytic and theoretical review. *Psychological Bulletin, 128,* 539–579.

GERSTENFELD, P. B., GRANT, D. R., & CHIANG, C-P. (2003). Hate online: A content analysis of extremist Internet sites. *Analyses of Social Issues and Public Policy, 3,* 29–44.

GESCH, C. B., HAMMOND, S. M., HAMPSON, S. E., EVES, A., & CROWDER, M. J. (2002). Influence of supplementary vitamins, minerals and essential fatty acids on the antisocial behavior of young adult prisoners. Randomised, placebo-controlled trial. *British Journal of Psychiatry, 181,* 22–28.

GIANCOLA, P. R., & CORMAN, M. D. (2007). Alcohol and aggression: A test of the attention-allocation model. *Psychological Science, 18,* 649–655.

GIBSON, B., & SANBONMATSU, D. M. (2004). Optimism, pessimism, and gambling: The downside of optimism. *Personality and Social Psychology Bulletin, 30,* 149–160.

GIBSON, J. I., & CLAASSEN, C. (2010). Racial reconciliation in South Africa: Interracial contact. *Journal of Social Issues, 66,* 255–272.

GIFFORD, R. (2011). The dragons of inaction: Psychological barriers that limit climate change mitigation and adaptation. *American Psychologist, 66,* 290–302.

GIFFORD, R., & HINE, D. W. (1997). Toward cooperation in commons dilemmas. *Canadian Journal of Behavioural Science, 29,* 167–179.

GIFFORD, R., & PEACOCK, J. (1979). Crowding: More fearsome than crime-provoking? Comparison of an Asian city and a North American city. *Psychologia, 22,* 79–83.

GIGERENZER, G. (2004). Dread risk, September 11, and fatal traffic accidents. *Psychological Science, 15,* 286–287.

GIGERENZER, G. (2007). *Gut feelings: The intelligence of the unconscious.* New York: Viking.

GIGERENZER, G. (2010). *Rationality for mortals: How people cope with uncertainty.* New York: Oxford University Press.

GIGONE, D., & HASTIE, R. (1993). The common knowledge effect: Information sharing and group judgment. *Journal of Personality and Social Psychology, 65,* 959–974.

GILBERT, D. (2007). *Stumbling on happiness.* New York: Knopf.

GILBERT, D. (2011, June 7). Introduction (to conversation with Timothy Wilson). *The Edge* (www.edge.org).

GILBERT, D. T., & EBERT, J. E. J. (2002). Decisions and revisions: The affective forecasting of escapable outcomes. Unpublished manuscript, Harvard University.

GILBERT, D. T., LIEBERMAN, M. D., MOREWEDGE, C. K., & WILSON, T. D. (2004). The peculiar longevity of things not so bad. *Psychological Science, 15,* 14–19.

GILBERT, D. T., PINEL, E. C., WILSON, T. D., BLUMBERG, S. J., & WHEATLEY, T. P. (1998). Immune neglect: A source of durability bias in affective forecasting. *Journal of Personality and Social Psychology, 75,* 617–638.

GILBERT, D. T., & WILSON, T. D. (2000). Miswanting: Some problems in the forecasting of future affective states. In J. Forgas (Ed.), *Feeling and thinking: The role of affect in social cognition.* Cambridge, England: Cambridge University Press.

GILLHAM, J. E., SHATTE, A. J., REIVICH, K. J., & SELIGMAN, M. E. P. (2000). Optimism, pessimism, and explanatory style. In E. C. Chang (Ed.), *Optimism and pessimism.* Washington, DC: APA Books.

GILLIGAN, C. (1982). *In a different voice: Psychological theory and women's development.* Cambridge, MA: Harvard University Press.

GILLIGAN, C., LYONS, N. P., & HANMER, T. J. (Eds.) (1990). *Making connections: The relational worlds of adolescent girls at Emma Willard School.* Cambridge, MA: Harvard University Press.

GILLIS, J. (2011, December 16). As permafrost thaws, scientists study the risks. *New York Times* (www.nytimes.com).

GILLIS, J. S., & AVIS, W. E. (1980). The male-taller norm in mate selection. *Personality and Social Psychology Bulletin, 6,* 396–401.

GILOVICH, T., & DOUGLAS, C. (1986). Biased evaluations of randomly determined gambling outcomes. *Journal of Experimental Social Psychology, 22,* 228–241.

GILOVICH, T., KERR, M., & MEDVEC, V. H. (1993). Effect of temporal perspective on subjective confidence. *Journal of Personality and Social Psychology, 64,* 552–560.

GILOVICH, T., MEDVEC, V. H., & SAVITSKY, K. (2000). The spotlight effect in social judgment: An egocentric bias in estimates of the salience of one's own actions and appearance. *Journal of Personality and Social Psychology, 78,* 211–222.

GILOVICH, T., SAVITSKY, K., & MEDVEC, V. H. (1998). The illusion of transparency: Biased assessments of others' ability to read one's emotional states. *Journal of Personality and Social Psychology, 75,* 332–346.

GINSBURG, B., & ALLEE, W. C. (1942). Some effects of conditioning on social dominance and subordination in inbred strains of mice. *Physiological Zoology, 15,* 485–506.

GLADWELL, M. (2003, March 10). Connecting the dots: The paradoxes of intelligence reform. *New Yorker,* pp. 83–88.

GLASS, D. C. (1964). Changes in liking as a means of reducing cognitive discrepancies between self-esteem and aggression. *Journal of Personality, 32,* 531–549.

GLICK, P., & FISKE, S. T. (1996). The ambivalent sexism inventory: Differentiating hostile and benevolent sexism. *Journal of Personality and Social Psychology, 70,* 491–512.

GLICK, P., & FISKE, S. T. (2007). Sex discrimination: The psychological approach. In F. J. Crosby, M. S. Stockdale, & S. Ropp (Eds.), *Sex discrimination in the workplace: Multidisciplinary perspectives.* Malden, MA: Blackwell.

GLUSZEK, A., & DOVIDIO, J. F. (2010). The way *they* speak: A social psychological perspective on the stigma of nonnative accents in communication. *Personality and Social Psychology Review,* **14,** 214–237.

GOCKEL, C., KERR, N. L., SEOK, D-H., & HARRIS, D. W. (2008). Indispensability and group identification as sources of task motivation. *Journal of Experimental Social Psychology,* **44,** 1316–1321.

GOEL, S., MASON, W., & WATTS, D. J. (2010). Real and perceived attitude agreement in social networks. *Journal of Personality and Social Psychology,* **99,** 611–621.

GOETHALS, G. R., MESSICK, D. M., & ALLISON, S. T. (1991). The uniqueness bias: Studies of constructive social comparison. In J. Suls & T. A. Wills (Eds.), *Social comparison: Contemporary theory and research.* Hillsdale, NJ: Erlbaum.

GOGGIN, W. C., & RANGE, L. M. (1985). The disadvantages of hindsight in the perception of suicide. *Journal of Social and Clinical Psychology,* **3,** 232–237.

GOLDMAN, W., & LEWIS, P. (1977). Beautiful is good: Evidence that the physically attractive are more socially skillful. *Journal of Experimental Social Psychology,* **13,** 125–130.

GOLDSTEIN, A. P., GLICK, B., & GIBBS, J. C. (1998). Aggression replacement training: A comprehensive intervention for aggressive youth (rev. ed.). Champaign, IL: Research Press.

GOLDSTEIN, J. H., & ARMS, R. L. (1971). Effects of observing athletic contests on hostility. *Sociometry,* **34,** 83–90.

GOLEC DE ZAVALA, A., CICHOCKA, A., EIDELSON, R., & JAYAWICKREME, N. (2009). Collective narcissism and its social consequences. *Journal of Personality and Social Psychology,* **97,** 1074–1096.

GÓMEZ, Á., BROOKS, M. L., BUHRMEISTER, M. D., VÁQUEZ, A., JETTEN, J., & SWANN, JR., W. B. (2011). On the nature of identity fusion: Insights into the construct and a new measure. *Journal of Personality and Social Psychology,* **100,** 918–933.

GONSALKORALE, K., & WILLIAMS, K. D. (2006). The KKK would not let me play: Ostracism even by a despised outgroup hurts. *European Journal of Social Psychology,* **36,** 1–11.

GONZAGA, G. C., CAMPOS, B., & BRADBURY, T. (2007). Similarity, convergence, and relationship satisfaction in dating and married couples. *Journal of Personality and Social Psychology,* **93,** 34–48.

GONZAGA, G., KELTNER, D., LONDAHL, E. A., & SMITH, M. D. (2001). Love and the commitment problem in romantic relations and friendship. *Journal of Personality and Social Psychology,* **81,** 247–262.

GONZÁLEZ-VALLEJO, C., LASSITER, G. D., BELLEZZA, F. S., & LINDBERG, M. J. (2008). "Save angels perhaps": A critical examination of unconscious thought theory and the deliberation-without-attention effect. *Review of General Psychology,* **12,** 282–296.

GONZÁLEZ, K. V., VERKUYTEN, M., WEESIE, J., & POPPE, E. (2008). Prejudice towards Muslims in the Netherlands: Testing integrated threat theory. *British Journal of Social Psychology,* **47,** 667–685.

GOODHART, D. E. (1986). The effects of positive and negative thinking on performance in an achievement situation. *Journal of Personality and Social Psychology,* **51,** 117–124.

GORE, A. (2007, July 1). Moving beyond Kyoto. *New York Times* (www.nytimes.com).

GOTTMAN, J. (2005, April 14). The mathematics of love. *Edge,* No. 159 (www.edge.org).

GOTTMAN, J. (with N. Silver). (1994). *Why marriages succeed or fail.* New York: Simon & Schuster.

GOTTMAN, J. M. (1998). Psychology and the study of marital processes. *Annual Review of Psychology,* **49,** 169–197.

GRAY, J. D., & SILVER, R. C. (1990). Opposite sides of the same coin: Former spouses' divergent perspectives in coping with their divorce. *Journal of Personality and Social Psychology,* **59,** 1180–1191.

GREELEY, A. M. (1991). *Faithful attraction.* New York: Tor Books.

GREELEY, A. M., & SHEATSLEY, P. B. (1971). Attitudes toward racial integration. *Scientific American,* **225**(6), 13–19.

GREEN, A. R., CARNEY, D. R., PALLIN, D. J., NGO, L. H., RAYMOND, K. L., IEZZONI, L. I., & BANAJI, M. R. (2007). Implicit bias among physicians and its prediction of thrombolysis decisions for Black and White patients. *Journal of General Internal Medicine,* **22,** 1231–1238.

GREEN, D. P., GLASER, J., & RICH, A. (1998). From lynching to gay bashing: The elusive connection between economic conditions and hate crime. *Journal of Personality and Social Psychology,* **75,** 82–92.

GREEN, M. C., STRANGE, J. J., & BROCK, T. C. (Eds.). (2002). *Narrative impact: Social and cognitive foundations.* Mahwah, NJ: Erlbaum.

GREENBERG, J. (1986). Differential intolerance for inequity from organizational and individual agents. *Journal of Applied Social Psychology,* **16,** 191–196.

GREENBERG, J. (2008). Understanding the vital human quest for self-esteem. *Perspectives on Psychological Science, 3,* 48–55.

GREENBERG, J., LANDAU, M. J., KOSLOFF, S., & SOLOMON, S. (2008). How our dreams of death transcendence breed prejudice, stereotyping, and conflict. In T. Nelson (Ed.), *Handbook of prejudice, stereotyping, and discrimination.* New York: Psychology Press.

GREENBERG, J., LANDAU, M., KOSLOFF, S., & SOLOMON, S. (2009). How our dreams of death transcendence breed prejudice, stereotyping, and conflict: Terror management theory. In T. D. Nelson (Ed.), *Handbook of prejudice, stereotyping, and discrimination.* New York: Psychology Press.

GREENBERG, J., PYSZCZYNSKI, T., SOLOMON, S., ROSENBLATT, A., VEEDER, M., KIRKLAND, S., & LYON, D. (1990). Evidence for terror management theory II: The effects of mortality salience on reactions to those who threaten or bolster the cultural worldview. *Journal of Personality and Social Psychology, 58,* 308–318.

GREENBERG, J., SCHIMEL, J., MARTENS, A., SOLOMON, S., & PYSZCZYNSKI, T. (2001). Sympathy for the devil: Evidence that reminding whites of their mortality promotes more favorable reactions to white racists. *Motivation and Emotion, 25,* 113–133.

GREENBERG, J., SOLOMON, S., & PYSZCZYNSKI, T. (1997). Terror management theory of self-esteem and cultural worldviews: Empirical assessments and conceptual refinements. *Advances in Experimental Social Psychology, 29,* 61–142.

GREENWALD, A. G. (1980). The totalitarian ego: Fabrication and revision of personal history. *American Psychologist, 35,* 603–618.

GREENWALD, A. G. (1992). New look 3: Unconscious cognition reclaimed. *American Psychologist, 47,* 766–779.

GREENWALD, A. G., & BANAJI, M. R. (1995). Implicit social cognition: Attitudes, self-esteem, and stereotypes. *Psychological Review, 102,* 4–27.

GREENWALD, A. G., BANAJI, M. R., RUDMAN, L. A., FARNHAM, S. D., NOSEK, B. A., & ROSIER, M. (2000). Prologue to a unified theory of attitudes, stereotypes, and self-concept. In J. P. Forgas (Ed.), *Feeling and thinking: The role of affect in social cognition and behavior.* New York: Cambridge University Press.

GREENWALD, A. G., McGHEE, D. E., & SCHWARTZ, J. L. K. (1998). Measuring individual differences in implicit cognition: The implicit association test. *Journal of Personality and Social Psychology, 74,* 1464–1480.

GREENWALD, A. G., NOSEK, B. A., & BANAJI, M. R. (2003). Understanding and using the implicit association test: I. An improved scoring algorithm. *Journal of Personality and Social Psychology, 85,* 197–216.

GREENWALD, A. G., POEHLMAN, T. A., UHLMANN, E. L., & BANAJI, M. R. (2008). Understanding and using the Implicit Association Test: III. Meta-analysis of predictive validity. *Journal of Personality and Social Psychology, 97*(1), 17–41.

GREENWALD, A. G., & SCHUH, E. S. (1994). An ethnic bias in scientific citations. *European Journal of Social Psychology, 24,* 623-639.

GREITEMEYER, T. (2009). Stereotypes of singles: Are singles what we think? *European Journal of Social Psychology, 39,* 368–383.

GREITEMEYER, T. (2011). Exposure to music with prosocial lyrics reduces aggression: First evidence and test of the underlying mechanism. *Journal of Experimental Social Psychology, 47,* 28–36.

GREITEMEYER, T., & McLATCHIE, N. (2011). Denying humanness to others: A newly discovered mechanism by which violent video games increase aggressive behavior. *Psychological Science, 22,* 659–665.

GRIFFITT, W. (1970). Environmental effects on interpersonal affective behavior. Ambient effective temperature and attraction. *Journal of Personality and Social Psychology, 15,* 240–244.

GRIFFITT, W. (1987). Females, males, and sexual responses. In K. Kelley (Ed.), *Females, males, and sexuality: Theories and research.* Albany: State University of New York Press.

GRIFFITT, W., & VEITCH, R. (1971). Hot and crowded: Influences of population density and temperature on interpersonal affective behavior. *Journal of Personality and Social Psychology, 17,* 92–98.

GROENENBOOM, A., WILKE, H. A. M., & WIT, A. P. (2001). Will we be working together again? The impact of future interdependence on group members' task motivation. *European Journal of Social Psychology, 31,* 369–378.

GROSS, T. F. (2009). Own-ethnicity bias in the recognition of Black, East Asian, Hispanic, and White faces. *Basic and Applied Social Psychology, 31,* 128–135.

GROSSMANN, I., NA, J., VARNUM, M. E. W., PARK, D. C., KITAYAMA, S., & NISBETT, R. E. (2010). Reasoning about social conflicts improves into old age. *PNAS, 107,* 7246–7250.

GROVE, J. R., HANRAHAN, S. J., & McINMAN, A. (1991). Success/failure bias in attributions across involvement categories in sport. *Personality and Social Psychology Bulletin, 17,* 93–97.

GRUMAN, J. C., & SLOAN, R. P. (1983). Disease as justice: Perceptions of the victims of physical illness. *Basic and Applied Social Psychology, 4,* 39–46.

GRUNBERGER, R. (1971). *The 12-year Reich: A social history of Nazi Germany, 1933–1945.* New York: Holt, Rinehart & Winston.

GRUSH, J. E., & GLIDDEN, M. V. (1987). Power and satisfaction among distressed and nondistressed couples. Paper presented at the Midwestern Psychological Association convention.

GUADAGNO, R. E., RHOADS, K. V. L., & SAGARIN, B. J. (2011). Figural vividness and persuasion: Capturing the "elusive" vividness effect. *Personality and Social Psychology Bulletin, 37,* 626–638.

GUÉGUEN, N., & JACOB, C. (2001). Fund-raising on the Web: The effect of an electronic foot-in-the-door on donation. *CyberPsychology and Behavior, 4,* 705–709.

GUERIN, B. (1993). *Social facilitation.* Paris: Cambridge University Press.

GUERIN, B. (1994). What do people think about the risks of driving? Implications for traffic safety interventions. *Journal of Applied Social Psychology, 24,* 994–1021.

GUERIN, B. (1999). Social behaviors as determined by different arrangements of social consequences: Social loafing, social facilitation, deindividuation, and a modified social loafing. *The Psychological Record, 49,* 565–578.

GUINESS, O. (1993). *The American hour: A time of reckoning and the once and future role of faith.* New York: Free Press.

GUNDERSEN, E. (2001, August 1). MTV is a many splintered thing. *USA Today,* p. 1D.

GUPTA, U., & SINGH, P. (1982). Exploratory study of love and liking and type of marriages. *Indian Journal of Applied Psychology, 19,* 92–97.

HACKER, H. M. (1951). Women as a minority group. *Social Forces, 30,* 60–69.

HACKMAN, J. R. (1986). The design of work teams. In J. Lorsch (Ed.), *Handbook of organizational behavior.* Englewood Cliffs, NJ: Prentice Hall.

HADDEN, J. K. (1969). *The gathering storm in the churches.* Garden City, NY: Doubleday.

HADDOCK, G., MAIO, G. R., ARNOLD, K., & HUSKINSON, T. (2008). Should persuasion be affective or cognitive? The moderating effects of need for affect and need for cognition. *Personality and Social Psychology Bulletin, 34,* 769–778.

HADDOCK, G., & ZANNA, M. P. (1994). Preferring "housewives" to "feminists." *Psychology of Women Quarterly, 18,* 25–52.

HAEFFEL, G. J., GIBB, B. E., METALSKY, G. I., ALLOY, L. B., ABRAMSON, L. Y., HANKIN, B. L., JOINER, T. E., JR., & SWENDSEN, J. D. (2008). Measuring cognitive vulnerability to depression: Development and validation of the cognitive style questionnaire. *Clinical Psychology Review, 28,* 824–836.

HAEMMERLIE, F. M. (1987). Creating adaptive illusions in counseling and therapy using a self-perception theory perspective. Paper presented at the Midwestern Psychological Association, Chicago.

HAEMMERLIE, F. M., & MONTGOMERY, R. L. (1982). Self-perception theory and unobtrusively biased interactions: A treatment for heterosocial anxiety. *Journal of Counseling Psychology, 29,* 362–370.

HAEMMERLIE, F. M., & MONTGOMERY, R. L. (1984). Purposefully biased interventions: Reducing heterosocial anxiety through self-perception theory. *Journal of Personality and Social Psychology, 47,* 900–908.

HAEMMERLIE, F. M., & MONTGOMERY, R. L. (1986). Self-perception theory and the treatment of shyness. In W. H. Jones, J. M. Cheek, & S. R. Briggs (Eds.), *A sourcebook on shyness: Research and treatment.* New York: Plenum.

HAFER, C. L., & BÈGUE, L. (2005). Experimental research on just-world theory: Problems, developments, and future challenges. *Psychological Bulletin, 131,* 128–167.

HAGERTY, M. R. (2000). Social comparisons of income in one's community: Evidence from national surveys of income and happiness. *Journal of Personality and Social Psychology, 78,* 764–771.

HALBERSTADT, J. (2006). The generality and ultimate origins of the attractiveness of prototypes. *Personality and Social Psychology Review, 10,* 166–183.

HALEVY, N., BERSO, Y., & GALINSKY, A. D. (2011). The mainstream is not electable: When vision triumphs over representativeness in leader emergence and effectiveness. *Personality and Social Psychology Bulletin, 37,* 893–904.

HALL, D. L., MATZ, D. C., & WOOD, W. (2010). Why don't we practice what we preach? A meta-analytic review of religious racism. *Personality and Social Psychology Review, 14,* 126–139.

HALL, J. A. (1984). *Nonverbal sex differences: Communication accuracy and expressive style.* Baltimore: Johns Hopkins University Press.

HALL, J. A., COATS, E. J., & LEBEAU, L. S. (2005). Nonverbal behavior and the vertical dimension of social relations: A meta-analysis. *Psychological Bulletin, 131,* 898–924.

HALL, J. A., ROSIP, J. C., LEBEAU, L. S., HORGAN, T. G., & CARTER, J. D. (2006). Attributing the sources of accuracy in unequal-power dyadic communication: Who is better and why? *Journal of Experimental Social Psychology, 42,* 18–27.

HALL, T. (1985, June 25). The unconverted: Smoking of cigarettes seems to be becoming a lower-class habit. *Wall Street Journal*, pp. 1, 25.

HALPERN, D. F. (2010). How neuromythologies support sex role stereotypes. *Science, 330*, 1320–1321.

HAMBERGER, J., & HEWSTONE, M. (1997). Inter-ethnic contact as a predictor of blatant and subtle prejudice: Tests of a model in four West European nations. *British Journal of Social Psychology, 36*, 173–190.

HAMBLIN, R. L., BUCKHOLDT, D., BUSHELL, D., ELLIS, D., & FERITOR, D. (1969). Changing the game from get the teacher to learn. *Transaction,* January, pp. 20–25, 28–31.

HAMERMESH, D. S. (2011). *Beauty pays: Why attractive people are more successful.* Princeton, NJ: Princeton University Press.

HAMILTON, D. L., & GIFFORD, R. K. (1976). Illusory correlation in interpersonal perception: A cognitive basis of stereotypic judgments. *Journal of Experimental Social Psychology, 12*, 392–407.

HANEY, C., & ZIMBARDO, P. (1998). The past and future of U.S. prison policy: Twenty-five years after the Stanford Prison Experiment. *American Psychologist, 53*, 709–727.

HANEY, C., & ZIMBARDO, P. G. (2009). Persistent dispositionalism in interactionist clothing: Fundamental attribution error in explaining prison abuse. *Personality and Social Psychology Bulletin, 35*, 807–814.

HANSEL, T. C., NAKONEZNY, P. A., & RODGERS, J. L. (2011). Did divorces decline after the attacks on the World Trade Center? *Journal of Applied Social Psychology, 41*, 1680–1700.

HARBER, K. D. (1998). Feedback to minorities: Evidence of a positive bias. *Journal of Personality and Social Psychology, 74*, 622–628.

HARBER, K. D., STAFFORD, R., & KENNEDY, K. A. (2010). The positive feedback bias as a response to a self-image threat. *Journal of Social Psychology, 49*, 207–218.

HARDIN, G. (1968). The tragedy of the commons. *Science, 162*, 1243–1248.

HARDY, C., & LATANÉ, B. (1986). Social loafing on a cheering task. *Social Science, 71*, 165–172.

HARDY, C. L., & VAN VUGT, M. (2006). Nice guys finish first: The competitive altruism hypothesis. *Personality and Social Psychology Bulletin, 32*, 1402–1413.

HARITOS-FATOUROS, M. (1988). The official torturer: A learning model for obedience to the authority of violence. *Journal of Applied Social Psychology, 18*, 1107–1120.

HARITOS-FATOUROS, M. (2002). *Psychological origins of institutionalized torture.* New York: Routledge.

HARKINS, S. G. (1981). Effects of task difficulty and task responsibility on social loafing. Presentation to the First International Conference on Social Processes in Small Groups, Kill Devil Hills, North Carolina.

HARKINS, S. G., & JACKSON, J. M. (1985). The role of evaluation in eliminating social loafing. *Personality and Social Psychology Bulletin, 11*, 457–465.

HARKINS, S. G., & LATANÉ, B., & WILLIAMS, K. (1980), Social loafing: Allocating effort or taking it easy? *Journal of Experimental Social Psychology, 16*, 457–465.

HARKINS, S. G., & PETTY, R. E. (1982). Effects of task difficulty and task uniqueness on social loafing. *Journal of Personality and Social Psychology, 43*, 1214–1229.

HARKINS, S. G., & PETTY, R. E. (1987). Information utility and the multiple source effect. *Journal of Personality and Social Psychology, 52*, 260–268.

HARKINS, S. G., & SZYMANSKI, K. (1989). Social loafing and group evaluation. *Journal of Personality and Social Psychology, 56*, 934–941.

HARKNESS, K. L., SABBAGH, M. A., JACOBSON, J. A., CHOWDREY, N. K., & CHEN, T. (2005). Enhanced accuracy of mental state decoding in dysphoric college students. *Cognition & Emotion, 19*, 999–1025.

HARLEY, C. D. G. (2011). Climate change, keystone predation, and biodiversity loss. *Science, 334*, 1124–1127.

HARMON-JONES, E., GREENBERG, J., SOLOMON, S., & SIMON, L. (1996). The effects of mortality salience on intergroup bias between minimal groups. *European Journal of Social Psychology, 26*, 677–681.

HARRIES, K. D., & STADLER, S. J. (1988). Heat and violence: New findings from Dallas field data, 1980–1981. *Journal of Applied Social Psychology, 18*, 129–138.

HARRIS, J. R. (1998). *The nurture assumption.* New York: Free Press.

HARRIS, L. T., & FISKE, S. T. (2006). Dehumanizing the lowest of the low: Neuroimaging responses to extreme out-groups. *Psychological Science, 17*(10), 847–853.

HARRIS, M. J., & ROSENTHAL, R. (1985). Mediation of interpersonal expectancy effects: 31 meta-analyses. *Psychological Bulletin, 97*, 363–386.

HARRIS, M. J., & ROSENTHAL, R. (1986). Four factors in the mediation of teacher expectancy effects. In R. S. Feldman (Ed.), *The social psychology of education.* New York: Cambridge University Press.

HARRISON, A. A. (1977). Mere exposure. In L. Berkowitz (Ed.), *Advances in experimental social psychology* (Vol. 10, pp. 39–83). New York: Academic Press.

HART, A. J., & MORRY, M. M. (1997). Trait inferences based on racial and behavioral cues. *Basic and Applied Social Psychology, 19*, 33–48.

HART, W., ALBARRACIN, D., EAGLY, A. H., BRECHAN, I., LINDBERG, M. J., & MERRILL, L. (2009). Feeling validated versus being correct: A meta-analysis of selective exposure to information. *Psychological Bulletin, 135,* 555–588.

HASELTON, M. G., & GILDERSLEEVE, K. (2011). Can men detect ovulation? *Current Directions in Psychological Science, 20,* 87–92.

HASELTON, M. G., & NETTLE, D. (2006). The paranoid optimist: An integrative evolutionary model of cognitive biases. *Personality and Social Psychology Review, 10,* 47–66.

HASLAM, N., & KASHIMA, Y. (2010). The rise and rise of social psychology in Asia: A bibliometric analysis. *Asian Journal of Social Psychology, 13,* 202–207.

HASLAM, S. A., & REICHER, S. (2007). Beyond the banality of evil: Three dynamics of an interactionist social psychology of tyranny. *Personality and Social Psychology Bulletin, 33,* 615–622.

HASS, R. G., KATZ, I., RIZZO, N., BAILEY, J., & EISENSTADT, D. (1991). Cross-racial appraisal as related to attitude ambivalence and cognitive complexity. *Personality and Social Psychology Bulletin, 17,* 83–92.

HATFIELD (WALSTER), E., ARONSON, V., ABRAHAMS, D., & ROTTMAN, L. (1966). Importance of physical attractiveness in dating behavior. *Journal of Personality and Social Psychology, 4,* 508–516.

HATFIELD (WALSTER), E., WALSTER, G. W., & BERSCHEID, E. (1978). *Equity: Theory and research.* Boston: Allyn & Bacon.

HATFIELD, E. (1988). Passionate and compassionate love. In R. J. Sternberg & M. L. Barnes (Eds.), *The psychology of love.* New Haven, CT: Yale University Press.

HATFIELD, E., & SPRECHER, S. (1986). *Mirror, mirror: The importance of looks in everyday life.* Albany, NY: SUNY Press.

HATFIELD, E., TRAUPMANN, J., SPRECHER, S., UTNE, M., & HAY, J. (1985). Equity and intimate relations: Recent research. In W. Ickes (Ed.), *Compatible and incompatible relationships.* New York: Springer-Verlag.

HATFIELD, E., & WALSTER, G. W. (1978). *A new look at love.* Reading, MA: Addison-Wesley. (Note: originally published as Walster, E., & Walster, G. W.)

HAUSER, M. (2006). *Moral minds: How nature designed our universal sense of right and wrong.* New York: Ecco.

HAUSER, M. (2009). It seems biology (not religion) equals morality. *The Edge* (www.edge.org).

HAVEL, V. (1990). *Disturbing the peace.* New York: Knopf.

HAWKLEY, L. C., & CACIOPPO, J. T. (2010). Loneliness matters: A theoretical and empirical review of consequences and mechanisms. *Annals of Behavioral Medicine, 40,* 218–227.

HAWKLEY, L. C., WILLIAMS, K. D., & CACIOPPO, J. T. (2011). Responses to ostracism across adulthood. *Social, Cognitive, and Affective Neuroscience, 6,* 234–243.

HAZAN, C., & SHAVER, P. R. (1994). Attachment as an organizational framework for research on close relationships. *Psychological Inquiry, 5,* 1–22.

HEADEY, B., & WEARING, A. (1987). The sense of relative superiority—central to well-being. *Social Indicators Research, 20,* 497–516.

HEESACKER, M. (1989). Counseling and the elaboration likelihood model of attitude change. In J. F. Cruz, R. A. Goncalves, & P. P. Machado (Eds.), *Psychology and education: Investigations and interventions.* (Proceedings of the International Conference on Interventions in Psychology and Education, Porto, Portugal, July 1987.) Porto, Portugal: Portuguese Psychological Association.

HEGARTY, P., WATSON, N., FLETCHER, L., & McQUEEN, G. (2010). When gentlemen are first and ladies are last: Effects of gender stereotypes on the order of romantic partners' names. *British Journal of Social Psychology, 50,* 21–35.

HEINE, S. J., LEHMAN, D. R., MARKUS, H. R., & KITAYAMA, S. (1999). Is there a universal need for positive self-regard? *Psychological Review, 106,* 766–794.

HEINE, S. J., TAKEMOTO, T., MOSKALENKO, S., LASALETA, J., & HEINRICH, J. (2008). Mirrors in the head: Cultural variation in objective self-awareness. *Personality and Social Psychology Bulletin, 34,* 879–887.

HELGESON, V. S., COHEN, S., & FRITZ, H. L. (1998). Social ties and cancer. In P. M. Cinciripini & others (Eds.), *Psychological and behavioral factors in cancer risk.* New York: Oxford University Press.

HELLMAN, P. (1980). *Avenue of the righteous of nations.* New York: Atheneum.

HELWEG-LARSEN, M., CUNNINGHAM, S. J., CARRICO, A., & PERGRAM, A. M. (2004). To nod or not to nod: An observational study of nonverbal communication and status in female and male college students. *Psychology of Women Quarterly, 28,* 358–361.

HENDERSON-KING, E. I., & NISBETT, R. E. (1996). Anti-black prejudice as a function of exposure to the negative behavior of a single black person. *Journal of Personality and Social Psychology, 71,* 654–664.

HENDRICK, S. S., & HENDRICK, C. (1995). Gender differences and similarities in sex and love. *Personal Relationships, 2,* 55–65.

HENDRICK, S. S., HENDRICK, C., & ADLER, N. L. (1988). Romantic relationships: Love, satisfaction, and staying together. *Journal of Personality and Social Psychology, 54*, 980–988.

HENRICH, J., HEINE, S. J., & NORENZAYAN, A. (2010). The weirdest people in the world? *Behavioral and Brain Sciences, 33*, 61–135.

HENRY, P. J. (2008a). College sophomores in the laboratory redux: Influences of a narrow data base on social psychology's view of the nature of prejudice. *Psychological Inquiry, 19*, 49–71.

HENRY, P. J. (2008b). Student sampling as a theoretical problem. *Psychological Inquiry, 19*, 114–126.

HENRY, P. J. (2009). Low-status compensation: A theory for understanding the role of status in cultures of honor. *Journal of Personality and Social Psychology, 97*, 451–466 .

HENSLIN, M. (1967). Craps and magic. *American Journal of Sociology, 73*, 316–330.

HEPWORTH, J. T., & WEST, S. G. (1988). Lynchings and the economy: A time-series reanalysis of Hovland and Sears (1940), *Journal of Personality and Social Psychology, 55*, 239–247.

HERADSTVEIT, D. (1979). *The Arab-Israeli conflict: Psychological obstacles to peace* (Vol. 28). Oslo, Norway: Universitetsforlaget. Distributed by Columbia University Press. Reviewed by R. K. White (1980). *Contemporary Psychology, 25*, 11–12.

HERBENICK, D., REECE, M., SCHICK, V., SANDERS, S. A., DODGE, B., & FORTENBERRY, J. D. (2010). Sexual behaviors, relationships, and perceived health among adult women in the United States: Results from a national probability sample. *Journal of Sexual Medicine, 7* (suppl 5), 277–290.

HEREK, G. M. (2009). Hate crimes and stigma-related experiences among sexual minority adults in the United States: Prevalence estimates from a national probability sample. *Journal of Interpersonal Violence, 24*(1), 54–74.

HEWSTONE, M. (1994). Revision and change of stereotypic beliefs: In search of the elusive subtyping model. In S. Stroebe & M. Hewstone (Eds.), *European Review of Social Psychology* (Vol. 5). Chichester, England: Wiley.

HEWSTONE, M., HANTZI, A., & JOHNSTON, L. (1991). Social categorisation and person memory: The pervasiveness of race as an organizing principle. *European Journal of Social Psychology, 21*, 517–528.

HEWSTONE, M., HOPKINS, N., & ROUTH, D. A. (1992). Cognitive models of stereotype change: Generalization and subtyping in young people's views of the police. *European Journal of Social Psychology, 22*, 219–234.

HIGBEE, K. L., MILLARD, R. J., & FOLKMAN, J. R. (1982). Social psychology research during the 1970s: Predominance of experimentation and college students. *Personality and Social Psychology Bulletin, 8*, 180–183.

HIGGINS, E. T., & MCCANN, C. D. (1984). Social encoding and subsequent attitudes, impressions and memory: "Context-driven" and motivational aspects of processing. *Journal of Personality and Social Psychology, 47*, 26–39.

HIGGINS, E. T., & RHOLES, W. S. (1978). Saying is believing: Effects of message modification on memory and liking for the person described. *Journal of Experimental Social Psychology, 14*, 363–378.

HIMMELSTEIN, K. E. W., & BRÜCKNER, H. (2011). Criminal-justice and school sanctions against nonheterosexual youth: A national longitudinal study. *Pediatrics, 127*, 49–57.

HINE, D. W., & GIFFORD, R. (1996). Attributions about self and others in commons dilemmas. *European Journal of Social Psychology, 26*, 429–445.

HINES, M. (2004). *Brain gender*. New York: Oxford University Press.

HINKLE, S., BROWN, R., & ELY, P. G. (1992). Social identity theory processes: Some limitations and limiting conditions. *Revista de Psicologia Social*, pp. 99–111.

HINSZ, V. B., TINDALE, R. S., & VOLLRATH, D. A. (1997). The emerging conceptualization of groups as information processors. *Psychological Bulletin, 121*, 43–64.

HIRSCHMAN, R. S., & LEVENTHAL, H. (1989). Preventing smoking behavior in school children: An initial test of a cognitive-development program. *Journal of Applied Social Psychology, 19*, 559–583.

HIRT, E. R., ZILLMANN, D., ERICKSON, G. A., & KENNEDY, C. (1992). Costs and benefits of allegiance: Changes in fans' self-ascribed competencies after team victory versus defeat. *Journal of Personality and Social Psychology, 63*, 724–738.

HITSCH, G. J., HORTACSU, A., AND ARIELY, D. (2006, February). What makes you click? Mate preferences and matching outcomes in online dating. MIT Sloan Research Paper No. 4603-06 (ssrn.com/abstract (895442).

HODGES, B. H., & GEYER, A. L. (2006). A nonconformist account of the Asch experiments: Values, pragmatics, and moral dilemmas. *Personality and Social Psychology Review*, pp. 102–119.

HODSON, G. (2011). Do ideologically intolerant people benefit from intergroup contact? *Current Directions in Psychological Science, 20*, 154–159.

HOFFMAN, L. W. (1977). Changes in family roles, socialization, and sex differences. *American Psychologist, 32*, 644–657.

HOFLING, C. K., BROTZMAN, E., DAIRYMPLE, S., GRAVES, N., & PIERCE, C. M. (1966). An experimental study in nurse-physician relationships. *Journal of Nervous and Mental Disease,* **143,** 171–180.

HOFMEISTER, B. (2010). Bridging the gap: Using social psychology to design market interventions to overcome the energy efficiency gap in residential energy markets. *Southeastern Environmental Law Journal,* **19,** pp. 1ff. Available at SSRN: http://ssrn.com/abstract 5 1892906.

HOGAN, R., CURPHY, G. J., & HOGAN, J. (1994). What we know about leadership: Effectiveness and personality. *American Psychologist,* **49,** 493–504.

HOGG, M. A. (1992). *The social psychology of group cohesiveness: From attraction to social identity.* London: Harvester Wheatsheaf.

HOGG, M. A. (2008). Social identity processes and the empowerment of followers. In R. E. Riggio, I. Chaleff, & J. Lipman-Blumen (Eds.), *The art of followership: How great followers create great leaders and organizations.* San Francisco: Jossey-Bass.

HOGG, M. A. (2010). Human groups, social categories, and collective self: Social identity and the management of self-uncertainty. In R. M. Arkin, K. C. Oleson, & P. J. Carroll (Eds.), *Handbook of the uncertain self.* New York, NY, US: Psychology Press, 2010.

HOGG, M. A., HAINS, S. C., & MASON, I. (1998). Identification and leadership in small groups: Salience, frame of reference, and leader stereotypicality effects on leader evaluations. *Journal of Personality and Social Psychology,* **75,** 1248–1263.

HOGG, M. A., TURNER, J. C., & DAVIDSON, B. (1990). Polarized norms and social frames of reference: A test of the self-categorization theory of group polarization. *Basic and Applied Social Psychology,* **11,** 77–100.

HOLMBERG, D., & HOLMES, J. G. (1994). Reconstruction of relationship memories: A mental models approach. In N. Schwarz & S. Sudman (Eds.), *Autobiographical memory and the validity of retrospective reports.* New York: Springer-Verlag.

HOLMES, J. G., & REMPEL, J. K. (1989). Trust in close relationships. In C. Hendrick (Ed.), *Review of personality and social psychology* (Vol. 10). Newbury Park, CA: Sage.

HOLT-LUNSTAD, J., SMITH, T. B., & LAYTON, J. B. (2010). Social relationships and mortality risk: A meta-analytic review. *PloS Medicine,* **7**(7): e 1000316.

HOLTGRAVES, T. (1997). Styles of language use: Individual and cultural variability in conversational indirectness. *Journal of Personality and Social Psychology,* **73,** 624–637.

HOLTMAN, Z., LOUW, J., TREDOUX, C., & CARNEY, T. (2005). Prejudice and social contact in South Africa: A study of integrated schools ten years after apartheid. *South African Journal of Psychology,* **35,** 473–493.

HONIGMAN, R. J., PHILLIPS, K. A., & CASTLE, D. J. (2004). A review of psychosocial outcomes for patients seeking cosmetic surgery. *Plastic and Reconstructive Surgery,* **113,** 1229–1237.

HOORENS, V. (1993). Self-enhancement and superiority biases in social comparison. In W. Stroebe & M. Hewstone (Eds.), *European review of social psychology* (Vol. 4). Chichester: Wiley.

HOORENS, V. (1995). Self-favoring biases, self-presentation and the self-other asymmetry in social comparison. *Journal of Personality,* **63,** 793–819.

HOORENS, V., & NUTTIN, J. M. (1993). Overvaluation of own attributes: Mere ownership or subjective frequency? *Social Cognition,* **11,** 177–200.

HOORENS, V., NUTTIN, J. M., HERMAN, I. E., & PAVAKANUN, U. (1990). Mastery pleasure versus mere ownership: A quasi-experimental cross-cultural and cross-alphabetical test of the name letter effect. *European Journal of Social Psychology,* **20,** 181–205.

HOORENS, V., SMITS, T., & SHEPPERD, J. A. (2008). Comparative optimism in the spontaneous generation of future life-events. *British Journal of Social Psychology,* **47,** 441–451.

HOUGHTON, J. (2011). Global warming, climate change and sustainability: A challenge to scientists, policymakers and religious believers. Cambridge, England: The International Society for Science and Religion (www.issr.org.uk/latest-news/global-warming).

HOUSE, R. J., & SINGH, J. V. (1987). Organizational behavior: Some new directions for I/O psychology. *Annual Review of Psychology,* **38,** 669–718.

HOUSTON, V., & BULL, R. (1994). Do people avoid sitting next to someone who is facially disfigured? *European Journal of Social Psychology,* **24,** 279–284.

HOVLAND, C. I., LUMSDAINE, A. A., & SHEFFIELD, F. D. (1949). *Experiments on mass communication. Studies in social psychology in World War II* (Vol. III). Princeton, NJ: Princeton University Press.

HOVLAND, C. I., & SEARS, R. (1940). Minor studies of aggression: Correlation of lynchings with economic indices. *Journal of Psychology,* **9,** 301–310.

HOWELL, R. T., & HOWELL, C. J. (2008). The relation of economic status to subjective well-being in developing countries: A meta-analysis. *Psychological Bulletin,* **134,** 536–560.

HSEE, C. K., & HASTIE, R. (2006). Decision and experience: Why don't we choose what makes us happy? *Trends in Cognitive Sciences,* **10,** 31–37.

Huart, J., Corneille, O., & Becquart, E. (2005). Face-based categorization, context-based categorization, and distortions in the recollection of gender ambiguous faces. *Journal of Experimental Social Psychology, 41*, 598–608.

Huddy, L., & Virtanen, S. (1995). Subgroup differentiation and subgroup bias among Latinos as a function of familiarity and positive distinctiveness. *Journal of Personality and Social Psychology, 68*, 97–108.

Huesmann, L. R., Lagerspetz, K., & Eron, L. D. (1984). Intervening variables in the TV violence-aggression relation: Evidence from two countries. *Developmental Psychology, 20*, 746–775.

Huesmann, L. R., Moise-Titus, J., Podolski, C-L., & Eron, L. D. (2003). Longitudinal relations between children's exposure to TV violence and their aggressive and violent behavior in young adulthood: 1977–1992. *Developmental Psychology, 39*, 201–222.

Hugenberg, K., & Bodenhausen, G. V. (2003). Facing prejudice: Implicit prejudice and the perception of facial threat. *Psychological Science, 14*, 640–643.

Hugenberg, K., Young, S. G., Bernstein, M. J., & Sacco, D. F. (2010). The categorization-individuation model: An integrative account of the other-race recognition deficit. *Psychological Review, 117*, 1168–1187.

Hui, C. H., Triandis, H. C., & Yee, C. (1991). Cultural differences in reward allocation: Is collectivism the explanation? *British Journal of Social Psychology, 30*, 145–157.

Hull, J. G., Levenson, R. W., Young, R. D., & Sher, K. J. (1983). Self-awareness-reducing effects of alcohol consumption. *Journal of Personality and Social Psychology, 44*, 461–473.

Hull, J. G., & Young, R. D. (1983). The self-awareness-reducing effects of alcohol consumption: Evidence and implications. In J. Suls & A. G. Greenwald (Eds.), *Psychological perspectives on the self* (Vol. 2). Hillsdale, NJ: Erlbaum.

Human Security Centre (2005). *The human security report 2005: War and peace in the 21st century.* University of British Columbia.

Hunt, A. R. (2000, June 22). Major progress, inequities cross three generations. *Wall Street Journal,* pp. A9, A14.

Hunt, M. (1990). *The compassionate beast: What science is discovering about the humane side of humankind.* New York: William Morrow.

Hunt, M. (1993). *The story of psychology.* New York: Doubleday.

Hunt, P. J., & Hillery, J. M. (1973). Social facilitation in a location setting: An examination of the effects over learning trials. *Journal of Experimental Social Psychology, 9*, 563–571.

Hunt, R., & Jensen, J. (2007). *The experiences of young gay people in Britain's schools.* Stonewall (www. stonewall.org.uk).

Hunter, J. A., Stringer, M., & Watson, R. P. (1991). Intergroup violence and intergroup attributions. *British Journal of Social Psychology, 30*, 261–266.

Huo, Y. J., Smith, H. J., Tyler, T. R., & Lind, E. A. (1996). Superordinate identification, subgroup identification, and justice concerns: Is separatism the problem; is assimilation the answer? *Psychological Science, 7*, 40–45.

Huston, A. C., Donnerstein, E., Fairchild, H., Feshbach, N. D., Katz, P. A., & Murray, J. P. (1992). *Big world, small screen: The role of television in American society.* Lincoln, NE: University of Nebraska Press.

Huston, T. L. (1973). Ambiguity of acceptance, social desirability, and dating choice. *Journal of Experimental Social Psychology, 9*, 32–42.

Huston, T. L., & Chorost, A. F. (1994). Behavioral buffers on the effect of negativity on marital satisfaction: A longitudinal study. *Personal Relationships, 1*, 223–239.

Huston, T. L., Niehuis, S., & Smith, S. E. (2001). The early marital roots of conjugal distress and divorce. *Current Directions in Psychological Science, 10*, 116–119.

Hvistendahl, M. (2009). Making every baby girl count. *Science, 323*, 1164–1166.

Hvistendahl, M. (2010). Has China outgrown the one-child policy? *Science, 329*, 1458–1461.

Hvistendahl, M. (2011). *Unnatural selection: Choosing boys over girls, and the consequences of a world full of men.* New York: Public Affairs.

Hyde, J. S. (2005). The gender similarities hypothesis. *American Psychologist, 60*, 581–592.

Hyde, J. S., Mezulis, A. H., & Abramson, L. Y. (2008). The ABCs of depression: Integrating affective, biological, and cognitive models to explain the emergence of the gender difference in depression. *Psychological Review, 115*, 291–313.

Hyman, H. H., & Sheatsley, P. B. (1956 & 1964). Attitudes toward desegregation. *Scientific American, 195*(6), 35–39, and *211*(1), 16–23.

Ickes, B. (1980). On disconfirming our perceptions of others. Paper presented at the American Psychological Association convention.

ICKES, W., LAYDEN, M. A., & BARNES, R. D. (1978). Objective self-awareness and individuation: An empirical link. *Journal of Personality, 46,* 146–161.

ICKES, W., PATTERSON, M. L., RAJECKI, D. W., & TANFORD, S. (1982). Behavioral and cognitive consequences of reciprocal versus compensatory responses to preinteraction expectancies. *Social Cognition, 1,* 160–190.

ICKES, W., SNYDER, M., & GARCIA, S. (1997). Personality influences on the choice of situations. In R. Hogan, J. Johnson, & S. Briggs (Eds.), *Handbook of Personality Psychology.* San Diego: Academic Press.

IMAI, Y. (1994). Effects of influencing attempts on the perceptions of powerholders and the powerless. *Journal of Social Behavior and Personality, 9,* 455–468.

IMHOFF, R., & BANSE, R. (2009). Ongoing victim suffering increases prejudice: The case of secondary anti-Semitism. *Psychological Science, 20,* 1443–1447.

IMHOFF, R. , DOTSCH, R., BIANCHI, M., BANSE, R., & WIGBOLDUS, D. (2011). Facing Europe: Visualizing spontaneous ingroup projection. *Psychological Science, 22,* 1583–1590.

IMHOFF, R., & ERB, H-P. (2009). What motivates nonconformity? Uniqueness seeking blocks majority influence. *Personality and Social Psychology Bulletin, 35,* 309–320.

INGHAM, A. G., LEVINGER, G., GRAVES, J., & PECKHAM, V. (1974). The Ringelmann effect: Studies of group size and group performance. *Journal of Experimental Social Psychology, 10,* 371–384.

INGLEHART, M. R., MARKUS, H., & BROWN, D. R. (1989). The effects of possible selves on academic achievement—a panel study. In J. P. Forgas & J. M. Innes (Eds.), *Recent advances in social psychology: An international perspective.* North-Holland: Elsevier Science Publishers.

INGLEHART, R. (1990). *Culture shift in advanced industrial society.* Princeton, NJ: Princeton University Press.

INGLEHART, R. (2006). Cultural change and democracy in Latin America. In F. Hagopian (Ed.), *Contemporary Catholicism, religious pluralism and democracy in Latin America.* South Bend: Notre Dame University Press.

INGLEHART, R., FOA, R., PETERSON, C., & WELZEL, C. (2008). Development, freedom, and rising happiness: A global perspective (1981–2007). *Perspectives on Psychological Science, 3,* 264–285.

INGLEHART, R., & WELZEL, C. (2005). *Modernization, cultural change, and democracy: The human development sequence.* New York: Cambridge University Press.

INTERNATIONAL PARLIAMENTARY UNION (2011). *Women in national parliaments: Situation as of 30 November 2011.* Author (www.ipu.org).

INTERNATIONAL TELECOMMUNICATION UNION (ITU) (2010). *The world in 2010: ICT facts and figures.* ITU (www.itu.int/ict).

INZLICHT, M., MCKAY, L., & ARONSON, J. (2006). Stigma as ego depletion: How being the target of prejudice affects self-control. *Psychological Science, 17,* 262–269.

IRELAND, M. E., SLATCHER, R. B., EASTWICK, P. W., SCISSORS, L. E., FINKEL, E. J., & PENNEBAKER, J. W. (2011). Language style matching predicts relationship initiation and stability. *Psychological Science, 22,* 39–44.

ISOZAKI, M. (1984). The effect of discussion on polarization of judgments. *Japanese Psychological Research, 26,* 187–193.

ISR NEWSLETTER (1975). Institute for Social Research, University of Michigan, 3(4), 4–7.

ITO, T. A., MILLER, N., & POLLOCK, V. E. (1996). Alcohol and aggression: A meta-analysis on the moderating effects of inhibitory cues, triggering events, and self-focused attention. *Psychological Bulletin, 120,* 60–82.

IYENGAR, S. S., & LEPPER, M. R. (2000). When choice is demotivating: Can one desire too much of a good thing? *Journal of Personality and Social Psychology, 79,* 995–1006.

JACKMAN, M. R., & SENTER, M. S. (1981). Beliefs about race, gender, and social class different, therefore unequal: Beliefs about trait differences between groups of unequal status. In D. J. Treiman & R. V. Robinson (Eds.), *Research in stratification and mobility* (Vol. 2). Greenwich, CT: JAI Press.

JACKSON, J. M., & LATANÉ, B. (1981). All alone in front of all those people: Stage fright as a function of number and type of co-performers and audience. *Journal of Personality and Social Psychology, 40,* 73–85.

JACKSON, L. A., HUNTER, J. E., & HODGE, C. N. (1995). Physical attractiveness and intellectual competence: A meta-analytic review. *Social Psychology Quarterly, 58,* 108–123.

JACOBS, R. C., & CAMPBELL, D. T. (1961). The perpetuation of an arbitrary tradition through several generations of a laboratory microculture. *Journal of Abnormal and Social Psychology, 62,* 649–658.

JACOBY, S. (1986, December). When opposites attract. *Reader's Digest,* pp. 95–98.

JAMES, W. (1902, reprinted 1958). *The varieties of religious experience.* New York: Mentor Books.

JAMIESON, D. W., LYDON, J. E., STEWART, G., & ZANNA, M. P. (1987). Pygmalion revisited: New evidence for student expectancy effects in the classroom. *Journal of Educational Psychology, 79,* 461–466.

JANIS, I. L. (1971, November). Groupthink. *Psychology Today,* pp. 43–46.

JANIS, I. L. (1982). Counteracting the adverse effects of concurrence-seeking in policy-planning groups: Theory and research perspectives. In H. Brandstatter, J. H. Davis, & G. Stocker-Kreichgauer (Eds.), *Group decision making.* New York: Academic Press.

JANIS, I. L., KAYE, D., & KIRSCHNER, P. (1965). Facilitating effects of eating while reading on responsiveness to persuasive communications. *Journal of Personality and Social Psychology,* **1,** 181–186.

JANIS, I. L., & MANN, L. (1977). *Decision-making: A psychological analysis of conflict, choice and commitment.* New York: Free Press.

JANKOWIAK, W. R., & FISCHER, E. F. (1992). A cross-cultural perspective on romantic love. *Ethnology,* **31,** 149–155.

JAREMKA, L. M., GABRIEL, S., & CARVALLO, M. (2011). What makes us feel the best also makes us feel the worst: The emotional impact of independent and interdependent experiences. *Self and Identity,* **10,** 44–63.

JELLISON, J. M., & GREEN, J. (1981). A self-presentation approach to the fundamental attribution error: The norm of internality. *Journal of Personality and Social Psychology,* **40,** 643–649.

JENNINGS, D. L., AMABILE, T. M., & ROSS, L. (1982). Informal covariation assessment: Data-based vs theory-based judgments. In D. Kahneman, P. Slovic, & A. Tversky (Eds.), *Judgment under uncertainty: Heuristics and biases.* New York: Cambridge University Press.

JOHNSON, C. S., OLSON, M. A., & FAZIO, R. H. (2009). Getting acquainted in interracial interactions: Avoiding intimacy but approaching race. *Personality and Social Psychology Bulletin,* **35,** 557–571.

JOHNSON, D. J., & RUSBULT, C. E. (1989). Resisting temptation: Devaluation of alternative partners as a means of maintaining commitment in close relationships. *Journal of Personality and Social Psychology,* **57,** 967–980.

JOHNSON, D. W., & JOHNSON, R. T. (2000). The three Cs of reducing prejudice and discrimination. In S. Oskamp (Ed.), *Reducing prejudice and discrimination.* Mahwah, NJ: Erlbaum.

JOHNSON, D. W., & JOHNSON, R. T. (2003b). Student motivation in co-operative groups: Social interdependence theory. In R. M. Gillies & A. F. Ashman (Eds.), *Co-operative learning: The social and intellectual outcomes of learning in groups.* New York: Routledge.

JOHNSON, D. W., MARUYAMA, G., JOHNSON, R., NELSON, D., & SKON, L. (1981). Effects of cooperative, competitive, and individualistic goal structures on achievement: A meta-analysis. *Psychological Bulletin,* **89,** 47–62.

JOHNSON, J. A. (2007, June 26). Not so situational. Commentary on the SPSP listserv (spsp-discuss@stolaf.edu).

JOHNSON, J. D., BUSHMAN, B. J., & DOVIDIO, J. F. (2008). Support for harmful treatment and reduction of empathy toward blacks: "Remnants" of stereotype activation involving Hurricane Katrina and "Lil' Kim." *Journal of Experimental Social Psychology,* **44,** 1506–1513.

JOHNSON, J. D., JACKSON, L. A., & GATTO, L. (1995). Violent attitudes and deferred academic aspirations: Deleterious effects of exposure to rap music. *Basic and Applied Social Psychology,* **16,** 27–41.

JOHNSON, J. G., COHEN, P., SMAILES, E. M., KASEN, S., & BROOK, J. S. (2002). Television viewing and aggressive behavior during adolescence and adulthood. *Science,* **295,** 2468–2471.

JOHNSON, M. H., & MAGARO, P. A. (1987). Effects of mood and severity on memory processes in depression and mania. *Psychological Bulletin,* **101,** 28–40.

JOHNSON, M. K., ROWATT, W. C., BARNARD-BRAK, L. M., PATOCK-PECKHAM, J. A., LABOUFF, J. P., & CARLISLE, R. D. (2011). A mediational analysis of the role of right-wing authoritarianism and religious fundamentalism in the religiosity-prejudice link. *Personality and Individual Differences,* **50,** 851–856.

JOHNSON, R. D., & DOWNING, L. L. (1979). Deindividuation and valence of cues: Effects of prosocial and antisocial behavior. *Journal of Personality and Social Psychology,* **37,** 1532–1538.

JOHNSON, W., & KRUEGER, R. F. (2006). How money buys happiness: Genetic and environmental processes linking finances and life satisfaction. *Journal of Personality and Social Psychology,* **90,** 680–691.

JOINER, T. E., JR. (1994). Contagious depression: Existence, specificity to depressed symptoms, and the role of reassurance seeking. *Journal of Personality and Social Psychology,* **67,** 287–296.

JOINSON, A. N. (2001). Self-disclosure in computer-mediated communication: The role of self-awareness and visual anonymity. *European Journal of Social Psychology,* **31,** 177–192.

JONES, C. R., FAZIO, R. H., & OLSON, M. A. (2009). Implicit misattribution as a mechanism underlying evaluative conditioning. *Journal of Personality and Social Psychology,* **96,** 933–948.

JONES, E. E. (1976). How do people perceive the causes of behavior? *American Scientist,* **64,** 300–305.

JONES, E. E., & HARRIS, V. A. (1967). The attribution of attitudes. *Journal of Experimental Social Psychology,* **3,** 2–24.

JONES, E. E., & NISBETT, R. E. (1971). *The actor and the observer: Divergent perceptions of the causes of behavior.* Morristown, NJ: General Learning Press.

JONES, E. E., RHODEWALT, F., BERGLAS, S., & SKELTON, J. A. (1981). Effects of strategic self-presentation on subsequent self-esteem. *Journal of Personality and Social Psychology,* **41,** 407–421.

JONES, J. M. (2003). TRIOS: A psychological theory of the African legacy in American culture. *Journal of Social Issues,* **59,** 217–242.

JONES, J. M. (2011, September 12). Record-high 86% approve of Black-White marriages. Gallup (www.gallup.com).

JONES, J. T., PELHAM, B. W., CARVALLO, M., & MIRENBERG, M. C. (2004). How do I love thee? Let me count the Js: Implicit egotism and interpersonal attraction. *Journal of Personality and Social Psychology,* **87,** 665–683.

JONES, J. T., PELHAM, B. W., & MIRENBERG, M. C. (2002). Name letter preferences are not merely mere exposure: Implicit egotism as self-regulation. *Journal of Experimental Social Psychology,* **38,** 170–177.

JONES, W. H., CARPENTER, B. N., & QUINTANA, D. (1985). Personality and interpersonal predictors of loneliness in two cultures. *Journal of Personality and Social Psychology,* **48,** 1503–1511.

JOSEPHSON, W. L. (1987). Television violence and children's aggression: Testing the priming, social script, and disinhibition predictions. *Journal of Personality and Social Psychology,* **53,** 882–890.

JOST, J. T., KAY, A. C., & THORISDOTTIR, H. (Eds.) (2009). *Social and psychological bases of ideology and system justification.* New York: Oxford University Press.

JOURARD, S. M. (1964). *The transparent self.* Princeton, NJ: Van Nostrand.

JOURDEN, F. J., & HEATH, C. (1996). The evaluation gap in performance perceptions: Illusory perceptions of groups and individuals. *Journal of Applied Psychology,* **81,** 369–379.

JUDD, C. M., BLAIR, I. V., & CHAPLEAU, K. M. (2004). Automatic stereotypes vs. automatic prejudice: Sorting out the possibilities in the Payne (2001) weapon paradigm. *Journal of Experimental Social Psychology,* **40,** 75–81.

JUDGE, T. A., LEPINE, J. A., & RICH, B. L. (2006). Loving yourself abundantly: Relationship of the narcissistic personality to self and other perceptions of workplace deviance, leadership, and task and contextual performance. *Journal of Applied Psychology,* **91,** 762–776.

JUSSIM, L. (1986). Self-fulfilling prophecies: A theoretical and integrative review. *Psychological Review,* **93,** 429–445.

JUSSIM, L. (2005). Accuracy in social perception: Criticisms, controversies, criteria, components and cognitive processes. *Advances in Experimental Social Psychology,* **37,** 1–93.

JUSSIM, L. (2012). *Social perception and social reality: Why accuracy dominates bias and self-fulfilling prophecy.* New York: Oxford University Press.

JUSSIM, L., MCCAULEY, C. R., & LEE, Y-T. (1995). Introduction: Why study stereotype accuracy and innaccuracy? In Y. T. Lee, L. Jussim, & C. R. McCauley (Eds.), *Stereotypes accuracy: Toward appreciating group differences.* Washington, DC: American Psychological Association.

KAGAN, J. (1989). Temperamental contributions to social behavior. *American Psychologist,* **44,** 668–674.

KAHLOR, L., & MORRISON, D. (2007). Television viewing and rape myth acceptance among college women. *Sex Roles,* **56,** 729–739.

KAHN, M. W. (1951). The effect of severe defeat at various age levels on the aggressive behavior of mice. *Journal of Genetic Psychology,* **79,** 117–130.

KAHNEMAN, D., & DEATON, A. (2010). High income improves evaluation of life but not emotional well-being. *PNAS,* **107,** 16489–16493.

KAHNEMAN, D., & RENSHON, J. (2007, January/February). Why hawks win. *Foreign Policy* (www.foreignpolicy.com).

KAHNEMAN, D., & SNELL, J. (1992). Predicting a changing taste: Do people know what they will like? *Journal of Behavioral Decision Making,* **5,** 187–200.

KAHNEMAN, D., & TVERSKY, A. (1995). Conflict resolution: A cognitive perspective. In K. Arrow, R. Mnookin, L. Ross, A. Tversky, & R. Wilson (Eds.), *Barriers to the negotiated resolution of conflict.* New York: Norton.

KALENKOSKI, C. M., RIBAR, D. C., & STRATTON, L. S. (2009). *How do adolescents spell time use?* Institute for the Study of Labor, Bonn, Germany, Discussion Paper 4374.

KALICK, S. M. (1977). *Plastic surgery, physical appearance, and person perception.* Unpublished doctoral dissertation, Harvard University. Cited by E. Berscheid in An overview of the psychological effects of physical attractiveness and some comments upon the psychological effects of knowledge of the effects of physical attractiveness. In W. Lucker, K. Ribbens, & J. A. McNamera (Eds.), *Logical aspects of facial form* (craniofacial growth series). Ann Arbor: University of Michigan Press, 1981.

KAMEDA, T., & SUGIMORI, S. (1993). Psychological entrapment in group decision making: An assigned decision rule and a groupthink phenomenon. *Journal of Personality and Social Psychology, 65,* 282–292.

KAMMER, D. (1982). Differences in trait ascriptions to self and friend: Unconfounding intensity from variability. *Psychological Reports, 51,* 99–102.

KANAGAWA, C., CROSS, S. E., & MARKUS, H. R. (2001). "Who am I?" The cultural psychology of the conceptual self. *Personality and Social Psychology Bulletin, 27,* 90–103.

KANAZAWA, S., & KOVAR, J. L. (2004). Why beautiful people are more intelligent. *Intelligence, 32,* 227–243.

KANDEL, D. B. (1978). Similarity in real-life adolescent friendship pairs. *Journal of Personality and Social Psychology, 36,* 306–312.

KANTEN, A. B., & TEIGEN, K. H. (2008). Better than average and better with time: Relative evaluations of self and others in the past, present, and future. *European Journal of Social Psychology, 38,* 343–353.

KAPLAN, M. F. (1989). Task, situational, and personal determinants of influence processes in group decision making. In E. J. Lawler (Ed.), *Advances in group processes* (Vol. 6). Greenwich, CT: JAI Press.

KARAU, S. J., & WILLIAMS, K. D. (1993). Social loafing: A meta-analytic review and theoretical integration. *Journal of Personality and Social Psychology, 65,* 681–706.

KARAU, S. J., & WILLIAMS, K. D. (1997). The effects of group cohesiveness on social loafing and compensation. *Group Dynamics: Theory, Research, and Practice, 1,* 156–168.

KARBERG, J. C., & JAMES, D. J. (2005). Substance dependence, abuse, and treatment of jail inmates, 2002. Bureau of Justice Statistics Special Report. Washington, DC: U.S. Department of Justice.

KARNEY, B. R., & BRADBURY, T. N. (1995). The longitudinal course of marital quality and stability: A review of theory, method, and research. *Psychological Bulletin, 118,* 3–34.

KASSER, T. (2000). Two versions of the American dream: Which goals and values make for a high quality of life? In E. Diener & D. Rahtz (Eds.), *Advances in quality of life: Theory and research.* Dordrecth, Netherlands: Kluwer.

KASSER, T. (2002). *The high price of materialism.* Cambridge, MA: MIT Press.

KASSER, T. (2011). High price of materialism. Animated video. Center for the New American Dream (www.newdream.org).

KASSIN, S. M., GOLDSTEIN, C. C., & SAVITSKY, K. (2003). Behavioral confirmation in the interrogation room: On the dangers of presuming guilt. *Law and Human Behavior, 27,* 187–203.

KATZ, J., BEACH, S. R. H., & JOINER, T. E., JR. (1999). Contagious depression in dating couples. *Journal of Social and Clinical Psychology, 18,* 1–13.

KATZ-WISE, S. L., PRIESS, H. A., & HYDE, J. S. (2010). Gender-role attitudes and behavior across the transition to parenthood. *Developmental Psychology, 46,* 18–28.

KAUFMAN, J., & ZIGLER, E. (1987). Do abused children become abusive parents? *American Journal of Orthopsychiatry, 57,* 186–192.

KAWAKAMI, K., DOVIDIO, J. F., MOLL, J., HERMSEN, S., & RUSSIN, A. (2000). Just say no (to stereotyping): Effects of training in the negation of stereotypic associations on stereotype activation. *Journal of Personality and Social Psychology, 78,* 871–888.

KAWAKAMI, K., DUNN, E., KIARMALI, F., & DOVIDIO, J. F. (2009). Mispredicting affective and behavioral responses to racism. *Science, 323,* 276–278.

KAY, A. C., BAUCHER, D., PEACH, J. M., LAURIN, K., FRIESEN, J., ZANNA, M. P., & SPENCER, S. J. (2009). Inequality, discrimination, and the power of the status quo: Direct evidence for a motivation to see the way things are as the way they should be. *Journal of Personality and Social Psychology, 97,* 421–434.

KEATING, J. P., & BROCK, T. C. (1974). Acceptance of persuasion and the inhibition of counterargumentation under various distraction tasks. *Journal of Experimental Social Psychology, 10,* 301–309.

KEIZER, K., LINDENBERG, S., & STEG, L. (2008). The spreading of disorder. *Science, 322,* 1681–1685.

KELLERMAN, J., LEWIS, J., & LAIRD, J. D. (1989). Looking and loving: The effects of mutual gaze on feelings of romantic love. *Journal of Research in Personality, 23,* 145–161.

KELLEY, H. H., & STAHELSKI, A. J. (1970). The social interaction basis of cooperators' and competitors' beliefs about others. *Journal of Personality and Social Psychology, 16,* 66–91.

KELLY, D. J., LIU, S., GE, L., QUINN, P. C., SLATER, A. M., LEE, K., LIU, Q., & PASCALIS, O. (2007). Cross-race preferences for same-race faces extended beyond the African versus Caucasian contrast in 3-month-old infants. *Infancy, 11,* 87–95.

KELLY, D. J., QUINN, P. C., SLATER, A. M., LEE, K., GE, L., & PASCALIS, O. (2007). The other-race effect develops during infancy: Evidence of perceptual narrowing. *Psychological Science, 18,* 1084–1089.

KELLY, D. J., QUINN, P. C., SLATER, A. M., LEE, K., GIBSON, A., SMITH, M., GE, L., & Y PASCALIS, O. (2005). Three-month-olds, but not newborns prefer own-race faces. *Developmental Science, 8,* F31–F36.

KELMAN, H. C. (1997). Group processes in the resolution of international conflicts: Experiences from the Israeli-Palestinian case. *American Psychologist, 52,* 212–220.

KELMAN, H. C. (2007). The Israeli-Palestinian peace process and its vicissitudes: Insights from attitude theory. *American Psychologist, 62,* 287–303.

KELMAN, H. C. (2008). Evaluating the contributions of interactive problem solving to the resolution of ethnonational conflicts. *Peace and Conflict, 14,* 29–60.

KENNEDY, K. A., & PRONIN, E. (2008). When disagreement gets ugly: Perceptions of bias and the escalation of conflict. *Personality and Social Psychology Bulletin, 34,* 833–848.

KENRICK, D. T. (1987). Gender, genes, and the social environment: A biosocial interactionist perspective. In P. Shaver & C. Hendrick (Eds.), *Sex and gender: Review of personality and social psychology* (Vol. 7). Beverly Hills, CA: Sage.

KENRICK, D. T., & GUTIERRES, S. E. (1980). Contrast effects and judgments of physical attractiveness: When beauty becomes a social problem. *Journal of Personality and Social Psychology, 38,* 131–140.

KENRICK, D. T., GUTIERRES, S. E., & GOLDBERG, L. L. (1989). Influence of popular erotica on judgments of strangers and mates. *Journal of Experimental Social Psychology, 25,* 159–167.

KENRICK, D. T., & MACFARLANE, S. W. (1986). Ambient temperature and horn-honking: A field study of the heat/aggression relationship. *Environment and Behavior, 18,* 179–191.

KENRICK, D. T., & TROST, M. R. (1987). A biosocial theory of heterosexual relationships. In K. Kelly (Ed.), *Females, males, and sexuality.* Albany: State University of New York Press.

KENWORTHY, J. B., HEWSTONE, M., LEVINE, J. M., MARTIN, R., & WILLIS, H. (2008). The phenomenology of minority-majority status: Effects of innovation in argument generation. *European Journal of Social Psychology, 38,* 624–636.

KERNIS, M. H. (2003). High self-esteem: A differentiated perspective. In E. C. Chang & L. J. Sanna (Eds.), *Virtue, vice, and personality: The complexity of behavior.* Washington, DC: APA Books.

KERR, N. L. (1983). Motivation losses in small groups: A social dilemma analysis. *Journal of Personality and Social Psychology, 45,* 819–828.

KERR, N. L. (1989). Illusions of efficacy: The effects of group size on perceived efficacy in social dilemmas. *Journal of Experimental Social Psychology, 25,* 287–313.

KERR, N. L., & BRUUN, S. E. (1981). Ringelmann revisited: Alternative explanations for the social loafing effect. *Personality and Social Psychology Bulletin, 7,* 224–231.

KERR, N. L., HARMON, D. L., & GRAVES, J. K. (1982). Independence of multiple verdicts by jurors and juries. *Journal of Applied Social Psychology, 12,* 12–29.

KERR, N. L., & KAUFMAN-GILLILAND, C. M. (1994). Communication, commitment, and cooperation in social dilemmas. *Journal of Personality and Social Psychology, 66,* 513–529.

KERR, N. L. & KAUFMAN-GILLILAND, C. M. (1997). ". . . and besides, I probably couldn't have made a difference anyway": Justification of social dilemma defection via perceived self-inefficacy. *Journal of Experimental Social Psychology, 33,* 211–230.

KERR, N. L., MESSÉ, L. A., SEOK, D-H., SAMBOLEC, E. J., LOUNT, R. B., JR., & PARK, E. S. (2007). Psychological mechanisms underlying the Köhler motivation gain. *Personality and Social Psychology Bulletin, 33,* 828–841.

KERR, R. A. (2009). Amid worrisome signs of warming, "climate fatigue" sets in. *Science, 326,* 926–928.

KERR, R. A. (2011a). Antarctic ice's future still mired in its murky past. *Science, 333,* 401.

KERR, R. A. (2011b). Humans are driving extreme weather; time to prepare. *Science, 334,* 1040.

KESEBIR, S., & OISHI, S. (2010). A spontaneous self-reference effect in memory: Why some birthdays are harder to remember than others. *Psychological Science, 21,* 1525–1531.

KIESLER, C. A. (1971). *The psychology of commitment: Experiments linking behavior to belief.* New York: Academic Press.

KIHLSTROM, J. F., & CANTOR, N. (1984). Mental representations of the self. In L. Berkowitz (Ed.), *Advances in experimental social psychology* (Vol. 17). New York: Academic Press.

KIM, H., & MARKUS, H. R. (1999). Deviance of uniqueness, harmony or conformity? A cultural analysis. *Journal of Personality and Social Psychology, 77,* 785–800.

KIM, H. S., & SHERMAN, D. K. (2007). "Express yourself": Culture and the effect of self-expression on choice. *Journal of Personality and Social Psychology, 92,* 1–11.

KIMMEL, A. J. (1998). In defense of deception. *American Psychologist, 53,* 803–805.

KINDER, D. R., & SEARS, D. O. (1985). Public opinion and political action. In G. Lindzey & E. Aronson (Eds.), *The handbook of social psychology,* 3rd edition. New York: Random House.

KINGSTON, D. A., FEDOROFF, P., FIRESTONE, P., CURRY, S., & BRADFORD, J. M. (2008). Pornography use and sexual aggression: The impact of frequency and type of pornography use on recidivism among sexual offenders. *Aggressive Behavior, 34,* 341–351.

KINGSTON, D. A., MALAMUTH, N. M., FEDEROFF, P., & MARSHALL, W. L. (2009). The importance of individual differences in pornography use: Theoretical perspectives and implications for treating sexual offenders. *Journal of Sex Research, 46,* 216–232.

KINZLER, K. D., SHUTTS, K., DEJESUS, J., & SPELKE, E. S. (2009). Accent trumps race in guiding children's social preferences. *Social Cognition, 27,* 623–634.

KITAYAMA, S., & KARASAWA, M. (1997). Implicit self-esteem in Japan: Name letters and birthday numbers. *Personality and Social Psychology Bulletin, 23,* 736–742.

KITAYAMA, S., & MARKUS, H. R. (2000). The pursuit of happiness and the realization of sympathy: Cultural patterns of self, social relations, and well-being. In E. Diener & E. M. Suh (Eds.), *Subjective well-being across cultures.* Cambridge, MA: MIT Press.

KITE, M. E. (2001). Changing times, changing gender roles: Who do we want women and men to be? In R. K. Unger (Ed.), *Handbook of the psychology of women and gender.* New York: Wiley.

KLAAS, E. T. (1978). Psychological effects of immoral actions: The experimental evidence. *Psychological Bulletin, 85,* 756–771.

KLAPWIJK, A., & VAN LANGE, P. A. M. (2009). Promoting cooperation and trust in "noisy" situations: The power of generosity. *Journal of Personality and Social Psychology, 96,* 83–103.

KLAUER, K. C., & VOSS, A. (2008). Effects of race on responses and response latencies in the weapon identification task: A test of six models. *Personality and Social Psychology Bulletin, 34,* 1124–1140.

KLECK, R. E., & STRENTA, A. (1980). Perceptions of the impact of negatively valued physical characteristics on social interaction. *Journal of Personality and Social Psychology, 39,* 861–873.

KLEIN, J. G. (1991). Negative effects in impression formation: A test in the political arena. *Personality and Social Psychology Bulletin, 17,* 412–418.

KLEIN, W. M., & KUNDA, Z. (1992). Motivated person perception: Constructing justifications for desired beliefs. *Journal of Experimental Social Psychology, 28,* 145–168.

KLEINKE, C. L. (1977). Compliance to requests made by gazing and touching experimenters in field settings. *Journal of Experimental Social Psychology, 13,* 218–223.

KLENTZ, B., BEAMAN, A. L., MAPELLI, S. D., & ULLRICH, J. R. (1987). Perceived physical attractiveness of supporters and nonsupporters of the women's movement: An attitude-similarity-mediated error (AS-ME). *Personality and Social Psychology Bulletin, 13,* 513–523.

KLINESMITH, J., KASSER, T., & MCANDREW, F. T. (2006). Guns, testosterone, and aggression. *Psychological Science, 17*(7), 568–571.

KLOPFER, P. H. (1958). Influence of social interaction on learning rates in birds. *Science, 128,* 903.

KNEWTSON, H. S., & SIAS, R. W. (2010). Why Susie owns Starbucks: The name letter effect in security selection. *Journal of Business Research, 63,* 1324–1327.

KNIGHT, G. P., FABES, R. A., & HIGGINS, D. A. (1996). Concerns about drawing causal inferences from meta-analyses: An example in the study of gender differences in aggression. *Psychological Bulletin, 119,* 410–421.

KNIGHT, J. A., & VALLACHER, R. R. (1981). Interpersonal engagement in social perception: The consequences of getting into the action. *Journal of Personality and Social Psychology, 40,* 990–999.

KNOWLES, E. D., & PENG, K. (2005). White selves: Conceptualizing and measuring a dominant-group identity. *Journal of Personality and Social Psychology, 89,* 223–241.

KNOWLES, E. S. (1983). Social physics and the effects of others: Tests of the effects of audience size and distance on social judgment and behavior. *Journal of Personality and Social Psychology, 45,* 1263–1279.

KNUDSON, R. M., SOMMERS, A. A., & GOLDING, S. L. (1980). Interpersonal perception and mode of resolution in marital conflict. *Journal of Personality and Social Psychology, 38,* 751–763.

KOEHLER, D. J. (1991). Explanation, imagination, and confidence in judgment. *Psychological Bulletin, 110,* 499–519.

KOENIG, A. M., EAGLY, A. H., MITCHELL, A. A., & RISTIKARI, T. (2011). Are leader stereotypes masculine? A meta-analysis of three research paradigms. *Psychological Bulletin, 137,* 616–642.

KOENIG, L. B., MCGUE, M., & IACONO, W. G. (2008). Stability and change in religiousness during emerging adulthood. *Developmental Psychology, 44,* 531–543.

KOESTNER, R., & WHEELER, L. (1988). Self-presentation in personal advertisements: The influence of implicit notions of attraction and role expectations. *Journal of Social and Personal Relationships, 5,* 149–160.

KONRAD, A. M., RITCHIE, J. E., JR., LIEB, P., & CORRIGALL, E. (2000). Sex differences and similarities in job attribute preferences: A meta-analysis. *Psychological Bulletin, 126,* 593–641.

KONRATH, S. H., O'BRIEN, E. H., & HSING, C. (2011). Changes in dispositional empathy in American college students over time: A meta-analysis. *Personality & Social Psychology Review, 15,* 180–198.

Koo, M., Algoe, S. B., Wilson, T. D., & Gilbert, D. T. (2008). It's a wonderful life: Mentally subtracting positive events improves people's affective states, contrary to their affective forecasts. *Journal of Personality and Social Psychology,* **95,** 1217–1224.

Koole, S. L., Dijksterhuis, A., & van Knippenberg, A. (2001). What's in a name? Implicit self-esteem and the automatic self. *Journal of Personality and Social Psychology,* **80,** 669–685.

Koomen, W., & Dijker, A. J. (1997). Ingroup and outgroup stereotypes and selective processing. *European Journal of Social Psychology,* **27,** 589–601.

Koop, C. E. (1987). Report of the Surgeon General's workshop on pornography and public health. *American Psychologist,* **42,** 944–945.

Koppel, M., Argamon, S., & Shimoni, A. R. (2002). Automatically categorizing written texts by author gender. *Literary and Linguistic Computing,* **17,** 401–412.

Koriat, A., Lichtenstein, S., & Fischhoff, B. (1980). Reasons for confidence. *Journal of Experimental Social Psychology: Human Learning and Memory,* **6,** 107–118.

Korn, J. H., & Nicks, S. D. (1993). The rise and decline of deception in social psychology. Poster presented at the American Psychological Society convention.

Krackow, A., & Blass, T. (1995). When nurses obey or defy inappropriate physician orders: Attributional differences. *Journal of Social Behavior and Personality,* **10,** 585–594.

Kramer, A. E. (2008, August 32). Russia's collective farms: Hot capitalist property. *New York Times* (www.nytimes.com).

Kraus, M. W., Côté, S., & Keltner, D. (2010). Social class, contextualism, and empathic accuracy. *Psychological Science,* **21,** 1716–1723 .

Kraus, M. W., Piff, P. K., & Keltner, D. (2011). Social class as culture: the convergence of resources and rank in the social realm. *Current Directions in Psychological Science,* **20,** 246–250.

Kravitz, D. A., & Martin, B. (1986). Ringelmann rediscovered: The original article. *Journal of Personality and Social Psychology,* **50,** 936–941.

Krebs, D., & Adinolfi, A. A. (1975). Physical attractiveness, social relations, and personality style. *Journal of Personality and Social Psychology,* **31,** 245–253.

Krisberg, K. (2004). Successful "truth" anti-smoking campaign in funding jeopardy: New commission works to save campaign. *Medscape* (www.medscape.com).

Kristof, N. D. (2007, August 16). The big melt. *New York Times* (www.nytimes.com).

Kristof, N. D. (2010, September 18). Message to Muslims: I'm sorry. *New York Times* (www.nytimes.com).

Krizan, Z., & Suls, J. (2008). Losing sight of oneself in the above-average effect: When egocentrism, focalism, and group diffuseness collide. *Journal of Experimental Social Psychology,* **44,** 929–942.

Kroger, R. O., & Wood, L. A. (1992). Are the rules of address universal? IV: Comparison of Chinese, Korean, Greek, and German usage. *Journal of Cross-Cultural Psychology,* **23,** 148–162.

Krosnick, J. A., & Alwin, D. F. (1989). Aging and susceptibility to attitude change. *Journal of Personality and Social Psychology,* **57,** 416–425.

Krueger, J., & Clement, R. W. (1994a). Memory-based judgments about multiple categories: A revision and extension of Tajfel's accentuation theory. *Journal of Personality and Social Psychology,* **67,** 35–47.

Krueger, J., & Clement, R. W. (1994b). The truly false consensus effect: An ineradicable and egocentric bias in social perception. *Journal of Personality and Social Psychology,* **67,** 596–610.

Kruger, J., & Dunning, D. (1999). Unskilled and unaware of it: How difficulties in recognizing one's own incompetence lead to inflated self-assessments. *Journal of Personality and Social Psychology,* **77,** 1121–1134.

Kruger, J., & Evans, M. (2004). If you don't want to be late, enumerate: Unpacking reduces the planning fallacy. *Journal of Experimental Social Psychology,* **40,** 586–598.

Kruger, J., & Gilovich, T. (1999). "I cynicism" in everyday theories of responsibility assessment: On biased assumptions of bias. *Journal of Personality and Social Psychology,* **76,** 743–753.

Kruglanski, A. W., Chen, X., Dechesne, M., Fishman, S., & Orehek E. (2009). Fully committed: Suicide bombers' motivation and the quest for personal significance. *Political Psychology,* **30,** 331–357.

Kruglanski, A. W., & Fishman, S. (2006). The psychology of terrorism: "Syndrome" versus "tool" perspective. *Journal of Terrorism and Political Violence,* **18**(2), 193–215.

Kruglanski, A. W., & Golec de Zavala, A. (2005) Individual motivations, the group process and organizational strategies in suicide terrorism. *Psychology and Sociology (Psycologie et Sociologie).*

Kruglanski, A. W., & Webster, D. M. (1991). Group members' reactions to opinion deviates and conformists at varying degrees of proximity to decision deadline and of environmental noise. *Journal of Personality and Social Psychology,* **61,** 212–225.

KRULL, D. S., LOY, M. H-M., LIN, J., WANG, C-F., CHEN, S., & ZHAO, X. (1999). The fundamental fundamental attribution error: Correspondence bias in individualist and collectivist cultures. *Personality and Social Psychology Bulletin, 25*, 1208–1219.

KUBANY, E. S., BAUER, G. B., PANGILINAN, M. E., MUROKA, M. Y., & ENRIQUEZ, V. G. (1995). Impact of labeled anger and blame in intimate relationships. *Journal of Cross-Cultural Psychology, 26*, 65–83.

KUGIHARA, N. (1999). Gender and social loafing in Japan. *Journal of Social Psychology, 139*, 516–526.

KUIPER, N. A., & HIGGINS, E. T. (1985). Social cognition and depression: A general integrative perspective. *Social Cognition, 3*, 1–15.

KULL, S. (2003, June 4). Quoted in "Many Americans unaware WMD have not been found." Program on International Policy Attitudes (http://pipa.org/whatsnew/html/new_6_04_03.html).

KUMKALE, G. T., & ALBARRACIN, D. (2004). The sleeper effect in persuasion: A meta-analytic review. *Psychological Bulletin, 130*, 143–172.

KUNDA, Z., & OLESON, K. C. (1995). Maintaining stereotypes in the face of disconfirmation: Constructing grounds for subtyping deviants. *Journal of Personality and Social Psychology, 68*, 565–579.

KUNDA, Z., & OLESON, K. C. (1997). When exceptions prove the rule: How extremity of deviance determines the impact of deviant examples on stereotypes. *Journal of Personality and Social Psychology, 72*, 965–979.

KUTNER, L., & OLSON, C. K. (2008). *Grand theft childhood: The surprising truth about violent video games and what parents can do* (pp. 111–137). New York: Simon & Schuster.

LAGERSPETZ, K. (1979). Modification of aggressiveness in mice. In S. Feshbach & A. Fraczek (Eds.), *Aggression and behavior change.* New York: Praeger.

LAKIN, J. L., CHARTRAND, T. L., & ARKIN, R. M. (2008). I am too just like you: Nonconscious mimicry as an automatic behavioral responses to social exclusion. *Psychological Science, 19*, 816–821.

LALONDE, R. N. (1992). The dynamics of group differentiation in the face of defeat. *Personality and Social Psychology Bulletin, 18*, 336–342.

LALWANI, A. K., SHAVITT, S., & JOHNSON, T. (2006). What is the relation between cultural orientation and socially desirable responding? *Journal of Personality and Social Psychology, 90*, 165–178.

LAMAL, P. A. (1979). College student common beliefs about psychology. *Teaching of Psychology, 6*, 155–158.

LAMBERT, A. J., SCHERER, L. D., SCHOTT, J. P., OLSON, K. R., ANDREWS, R. K., O'BRIEN, T. C., & ZISSER, A. R. (2010). Rally effects, threat, and attitude change: An integrative approach to understanding the role of emotion. *Journal of Personality and Social Psychology, 98*, 886–903.

LAMBERT, N. M., DeWALL, C. N., BUSHMAN, B. J., STILLMAN, T. F., FINCHAM, F. D., & POND, R. S. (2011). Lashing out in lust: Effect of pornography on nonsexual, physical aggression against relationship partners. Unpublished manuscript, Florida State University.

LANDAU, M. J., SOLOMON, S., GREENBERG, J., COHEN, F., PYSZCZYNSKI, T., ARNDT, J., MILLER, C. H., OGILVIE, D. M., & COOK, A. (2004). Deliver us from evil: The effects of mortality salience and reminders of 9/11 on support for President George W. Bush. *Personality and Social Psychology Bulletin, 30*, 1136–1150.

LANDERS, A. (1969, April 8). Syndicated newspaper column. April 8, 1969. Cited by L. Berkowitz in, The case for bottling up rage. *Psychology Today,* September, *1973*, pp. 24–31.

LANGER, E. J. (1977). The psychology of chance. *Journal for the Theory of Social Behavior, 7*, 185–208.

LANGER, E. J., & IMBER, L. (1980). The role of mindlessness in the perception of deviance. *Journal of Personality and Social Psychology, 39*, 360–367.

LANGER, E. J., & RODIN, J. (1976). The effects of choice and enhanced personal responsibility for the aged: A field experiment in an institutional setting. *Journal of Personality and Social Psychology, 334*, 191–198.

LANGLOIS, J. H., KALAKANIS, L., RUBENSTEIN, A. J., LARSON, A., HALLAM, M., & SMOOT, M. (2000). Maxims or myths of beauty? A meta-analytic and theoretical review. *Psychological Bulletin, 126*, 390–423.

LANGLOIS, J. H., ROGGMAN, L. A., & MUSSELMAN, L. (1994). What is average and what is not average about attractive faces? *Psychological Science, 5*, 214–220.

LANGLOIS, J., KALAKANIS, L., RUBENSTEIN, A., LARSON, A., HALLAM, M., & SMOOT, M. (1996). Maxims and myths of beauty: A meta-analytic and theoretical review. Paper presented to the American Psychological Society convention.

LANKFORD, A. (2009). Promoting aggression and violence at Abu Ghraib: The U.S. military's transformation of ordinary people into torturers. *Aggression and Violent Behavior, 14*, 388–395.

LANZETTA, J. T. (1955). Group behavior under stress. *Human Relations, 8*, 29–53.

LARRICK, R. P., TIMMERMAN, T. A., CARTON, A. M., & ABREVAYA, J. (2011). Temper, temperature, and temptation: Heat-related retaliation in baseball. *Psychological Science, 22*, 423–428.

LARSEN, R. J., & DIENER, E. (1987). Affect intensity as an individual difference characteristic: A review. *Journal of Research in Personality, 21,* 1–39.

LARSON, J. R., JR., FOSTER-FISHMAN, P. G., & KEYS, C. B. (1994). Discussion of shared and unshared information in decision-making groups. *Journal of Personality and Social Psychology, 67,* 446–461.

LARSSON, K. (1956). *Conditioning and sexual behavior in the male albino rat.* Stockholm: Almqvist & Wiksell.

LARWOOD, L. (1978). Swine flu: A field study of self-serving biases. *Journal of Applied Social Psychology, 18,* 283–289.

LASSITER, G. D., DIAMOND, S. S., SCHMIDT, H. C., & ELEK, J. K. (2007). Evaluating videotaped confessions. *Psychological Science, 18,* 224–226.

LASSITER, G. D., & DUDLEY, K. A. (1991). The *a priori* value of basic research: The case of videotaped confessions. *Journal of Social Behavior and Personality, 6,* 7–16.

LASSITER, G. D., GEERS, A. L., HANDLEY, I. M., WEILAND, P. E., & MUNHALL, P. J. (2002). Videotaped interrogations and confessions: A simple change in camera perspective alters verdicts in simulated trials. *Journal of Applied Psychology, 87,* 867–874.

LASSITER, G. D., & IRVINE, A. A. (1986). Videotaped confessions: The impact of camera point of view on judgments of coercion. *Journal of Applied Social Psychology, 16,* 268–276.

LASSITER, G. D., LINDBERG, M. J., GONZÁLES-VALLEGO, C., BELLEZZA, F. S., & PHILLIPS, N. D. (2009). The deliberation-without-attention effect: Evidence for an artifactual interpretation. *Psychological Science, 20,* 671–675.

LASSITER, G. D., & MUNHALL, P. J. (2001). The genius effect: Evidence for a nonmotivational interpretation. *Journal of Experimental Social Psychology, 37,* 349–355.

LASSITER, G. D., MUNHALL, P. J., BERGER, I. P., WEILAND, P. E., HANDLEY, I. M., & GEERS, A. L. (2005). Attributional complexity and the camera perspective bias in videotaped confessions. *Basic and Applied Social Psychology, 27,* 27–35.

LATANÉ, B., & DABBS, J. M., JR. (1975). Sex, group size and helping in three cities. *Sociometry, 38,* 180–194.

LATANÉ, B., & DARLEY, J. M. (1970). *The unresponsive bystander: Why doesn't he help?* New York: Appleton-Century-Crofts.

LATANÉ, B., & NIDA, S. (1981). Ten years of research on group size and helping. *Psychological Bulletin, 89,* 308–324.

LATANÉ, B., WILLIAMS, K., & HARKINS. S. (1979). Many hands make light the work: The causes and consequences of social loafing. *Journal of Personality and Social Psychology, 37,* 822–832.

LAUMANN, E. O., GAGNON, J. H., MICHAEL, R. T., & MICHAELS, S. (1994). *The social organization of sexuality: Sexual practices in the United States.* Chicago: University of Chicago Press.

LAWLER, A. (2003a). Iraq's shattered universities. *Science, 300,* 1490–1491.

LAWLER, A. (2003b). Mayhem in Mesopotamia. *Science, 301,* 582–588.

LAWLER, A. (2003c). Ten millennia of culture pilfered amid Baghdad chaos. *Science, 300,* 402–403.

LAWSON, T. J. (2010). The social spotlight increases blindness to change blindness. *Basic and Applied Social Psychology, 32,* 360–368.

LAYDEN, M. A. (1982). Attributional therapy. In C. Antaki & C. Brewin (Eds.), *Attributions and psychological change: Applications of attributional theories to clinical and educational practice.* London: Academic Press.

LAZARSFELD, P. F. (1949). The American soldier—an expository review. *Public Opinion Quarterly, 13,* 377–404.

LAZER, D., & OTHERS. (2009). Computational social science. *Science, 323,* 721–723.

LEAPER, C., & ROBNETT, R. D. (2011). Women are more likely than men to use tentative language, aren't they? A meta-analysis testing for gender differences and moderators. *Psychology of Women Quarterly, 35,* 129–142.

LEARY, M. (1994). *Self-presentation: Impression management and interpersonal behavior.* Pacific Grove, CA: Brooks/Cole.

LEARY, M. R. (1998). The social and psychological importance of self-esteem. In R. M. Kowalski & M. R. Leary (Eds.), *The social psychology of emotional and behavioral problems.* Washington, DC: American Psychological Association.

LEARY, M. R. (1999). The social and psychological importance of -self-esteem. In R. M. Kowalski & M. R. Leary (Eds.), *The social psychology of emotional and behavioral problems.* Washington, DC: APA Books.

LEARY, M. R. (2004b). The self we know and the self we show: Self-esteem, self-presentation, and the maintenance of interpersonal relationships. In M. Brewer & M. Hewstone (Eds.), *Emotion and motivation.* Malden, MA: Usishers.

LEARY, M. R. (2007). Motivational and emotional aspects of the self. *Annual Review of Psychology, 58,* 317–344.

LEARY, M. R. (2010). Affiliation, acceptance, and belonging: The pursuit of interpersonal connection. In S. T. Fiske, D. T. Gilbert, & G. Lindzey (Eds.), *Handbook of social psychology,* 5th edition. Hoboken, NJ: Wiley.

LEARY, M. R., & KOWALSKI, R. M. (1995). *Social anxiety.* New York: Guilford.

LEARY, M. R., TWENGE, J. M., & QUINLIVAN, E. (2006). Interpersonal rejection as a determinant of anger and aggression. *Personality and Social Psychology Review,* **10,** 111–132.

LEDOUX, J. (2002). *Synaptic self: How our brains become who we are.* New York: Viking.

LEE, F., HALLAHAN, M., & HERZOG, T. (1996). Explaining real-life events: How culture and domain shape attributions. *Personality and Social Psychology Bulletin,* **22,** 732–741.

LEE, I.-C., PRATTO, F., & JOHNSON, B. T. (2011). Intergroup consensus/disagreement in support of group-based hierarchy: An examination of socio-structural and psycho-cultural factors. *Psychological Bulletin,* **137,** 1029–1064.

LEISEROWITZ, A. (2011, November 17). Do Americans connect climate change and extreme weather events? E-mail of Yale/GMU survey, from Yale Project on Climate Change Communication.

LEISEROWITZ, A., MAIBACH, E., ROSER-RENOUF, C., & SMITH, N. (2011a). *Global warming's six Americas, May 2011.* Yale University and George Mason University. New Haven, CT: Yale Project on Climate Change Communication.

LEISEROWITZ, A., MAIBACH, E., ROSER-RENOUF, C., & SMITH, N. (2011b). *Climate change in the American mind: Americans' global warming beliefs and attitudes in May 2011.* Yale University and George Mason University. New Haven, CT: Yale Project on Climate Change Communication.

LEMAY, E. P., JR., CLARK, M. S., & GREENBERG, A. (2010). What is beautiful is good because what is beautiful is desired: Physical attractiveness stereotyping as projection of interpersonal goals. *Personality and Social Psychology Bulletin,* **36,** 339–353.

LENCH, H. C., QUAS, J. A., & EDELSTEIN, R. S. (2006). My child is better than average: The extension and restriction of unrealistic optimism. *Journal of Applied Social Psychology,* **36,** 2963–2979.

LENHART, A. (2010, April 20). *Teens, cell phones and texting.* Pew Internet and American Life Project. Pew Research Center (www.pewresearch.org).

LENTON, A. P., & FRANCESCONI, M. (2010). How humans cognitively manage an abundance of mate options. *Psychological Science,* **21,** 528–533.

LERNER, M. J. (1980). *The belief in a just world: A fundamental delusion.* New York: Plenum.

LERNER, M. J., & MILLER, D. T. (1978). Just world research and the attribution process: Looking back and ahead. *Psychological Bulletin,* **85,** 1030–1051.

LERNER, M. J., & SIMMONS, C. H. (1966). Observer's reaction to the "innocent victim": Compassion or rejection? *Journal of Personality and Social Psychology,* **4,** 203–210.

LERNER, M. J., SOMERS, D. G., REID, D., CHIRIBOGA, D., & TIERNEY, M. (1991). Adult children as caregivers: Egocentric biases in judgments of sibling contributions. *The Gerontologist,* **31,** 746–755.

LESHNER, A. I. (2005, October). Science and religion should not be adversaries. *APS Observer* (www.psychologicalscience.org).

LEVENTHAL, H. (1970). Findings and theory in the study of fear communications. In L. Berkowitz (Ed.), *Advances in experimental social psychology* (Vol. 5). New York: Academic Press.

LEVINE, J. M. (1989). Reaction to opinion deviance in small groups. In P. Paulus (Ed.), *Psychology of group influence: New perspectives.* Hillsdale, NJ: Erlbaum.

LEVINE, R. (2003). *The power of persuasion: How we're bought and sold.* New York: Wiley.

LEVINSON, H. (1950). *The science of chance: From probability to statistics.* New York: Rinehart.

LEVITAN, L. C., & VISSER, P. S. (2008). The impact of the social context on resistance to persuasion: Effortful versus effortless responses to counter-attitudinal information. *Journal of Experimental Social Psychology,* **44,** 640–649.

LEVY, K. N., & KELLY, K. M. (2010). Sex differences in jealousy: A contribution from attachment theory. *Psychological Science,* **21,** 168–173.

LEVY, S. R., STROESSNER, S. J., & DWECK, C. S. (1998). Stereotype formation and endorsement: The role of implicit theories. *Journal of Personality and Social Psychology,* **74,** 1421–1436.

LEVY-LEBOYER, C. (1988). Success and failure in applying psychology. *American Psychologist,* **43,** 779–785.

LEWANDOWSKI, G. W., & BIZZOCO, N. M. (2007). Addition through subtraction: Growth following the dissolution of a low-quality relationship. *Journal of Positive Psychology,* **2,** 40–54.

LEWANDOWSKI, G. W., JR., ARON, A., & GEE, J. (2007). Personality goes a long way: The malleability of opposite-sex physical attractiveness. *Personal Relationships,* **14,** 571–585.

LEWIN, K. (1936). *A dynamic theory of personality.* New York: McGraw-Hill.

LEWINSOHN, P. M., HOBERMAN, H., TERI, L., & HAUTZINER, M. (1985). An integrative theory of depression. In S. Reiss & R. Bootzin (Eds.), *Theoretical issues in behavior therapy.* New York: Academic Press.

LEWINSOHN, P. M., & ROSENBAUM, M. (1987). Recall of parental behavior by acute depressives, remitted depressives, and nondepressives. *Journal of Personality and Social Psychology, 52,* 611–619.

LEWIS, C. S. (1952). *Mere Christianity.* New York: Macmillan.

LEWIS, D. O. (1998). *Guilty by reason of insanity.* London: Arrow.

LEYENS, J.-P., CAMINO, L., PARKE, R. D., & BERKOWITZ, L. (1975). Effects of movie violence on aggression in a field setting as a function of group dominance and cohesion. *Journal of Personality and Social Psychology, 32,* 346–360.

LI, N. P., BAILEY, J. M., KENRICK, D. T., & LINSENMEIER, J. A. W. (2002). The necessities and luxuries of mate preferences: Testing the tradeoffs. *Journal of Personality and Social Psychology, 82,* 947–955.

LI, Y., JOHNSON, E. J., & ZAVAL, L. (2011). Local warming: Daily temperature change influences belief in global warming. *Psychological Science, 22,* 454–459.

LICHTBLAU, E. (2003, March 18). U.S. seeks $289 billion in cigarette makers' profits. *New York Times* (www.nytimes.com).

LICHTENSTEIN, S., & FISCHHOFF, B. (1980). Training for calibration. *Organizational Behavior and Human Performance, 26,* 149–171.

LIEHR, P., MEHL, M. R., SUMMERS, L. C., & PENNEBAKER, J. W. (2004). Connecting with others in the midst of stressful upheaval on September 11, 2001. *Applied Nursing Research, 17,* 2–9.

LILIENFELD, S. O., FOWLER, K. A., LOHR, J. M., & LYNN, S. J. (2005). Pseudoscience, nonscience, and non-sense in clinical psychology: Dangers and remedies. In R. H. Wright & N. A. Cummings (Eds.), *Destructive trends in mental health: The well-intentioned path to harm.* New York: Routledge.

LILIENFELD, S. O., WOOD, J. M., & GARB, H. N. (2000). The scientific status of projective techniques. *Psychological Science in the Public Interest, 1,* 27–66.

LINDSKOLD, S. (1978). Trust development, the GRIT proposal, and the effects of conciliatory acts on conflict and cooperation. *Psychological Bulletin, 85,* 772–793.

LINDSKOLD, S. (1979a). Conciliation with simultaneous or sequential interaction: Variations in trustworthiness and vulnerability in the prisoner's dilemma. *Journal of Conflict Resolution, 27,* 704–714.

LINDSKOLD, S. (1979b). Managing conflict through announced conciliatory initiatives backed with retaliatory capability. In W. G. Austin & S. Worchel (Eds.), *The social psychology of intergroup relations.* Monterey, CA: Brooks/Cole.

LINDSKOLD, S. (1981). The laboratory evaluation of GRIT: Trust, cooperation, aversion to using conciliation. Paper presented at the American Association for the Advancement of Science convention.

LINDSKOLD, S. (1983). Cooperators, competitors, and response to GRIT. *Journal of Conflict Resolution, 27,* 521–532.

LINDSKOLD, S., & ARONOFF, J. R. (1980). Conciliatory strategies and relative power. *Journal of Experimental Social Psychology, 16,* 187–198.

LINDSKOLD, S., BENNETT, R., & WAYNER, M. (1976). Retaliation level as a foundation for subsequent conciliation. *Behavioral Science, 21,* 13–18.

LINDSKOLD, S., & COLLINS, M. G. (1978). Inducing cooperation by groups and individuals. *Journal of Conflict Resolution, 22,* 679–690.

LINDSKOLD, S., & FINCH, M. L. (1981). Styles of announcing conciliation. *Journal of Conflict Resolution, 25,* 145–155.

LINDSKOLD, S., & HAN, G. (1988). GRIT as a foundation for integrative bargaining. *Personality and Social Psychology Bulletin, 14,* 335–345.

LINDSKOLD, S., HAN, G., & BETZ, B. (1986a). Repeated persuasion in interpersonal conflict. *Journal of Personality and Social Psychology, 51,* 1183–1188.

LINDSKOLD, S., HAN, G., & BETZ, B. (1986b). The essential elements of communication in the GRIT strategy. *Personality and Social Psychology Bulletin, 12,* 179–186.

LINDSKOLD, S., WALTERS, P. S., KOUTSOURAIS, H., & SHAYO, R. (1981). Cooperators, competitors, and response to GRIT. Unpublished manuscript, Ohio University.

LIPPA, R. A. (2007). The preferred traits of mates in a cross-national study of heterosexual and homosexual men and women: An examination of biological and cultural influences. *Archives of Sexual Behavior, 36,* 193–208.

LIPPA, R. A. (2008a). Sex differences and sexual orientation differences in personality: Findings from the BBC Internet survey. *Archives of Sexual Behavior, 37,* 173–187.

LIPPA, R. A. (2008b). Sex differences in sex drive, sociosexuality, and height across 53 nations: Testing evolutionary and social structural theories. *Archives of Sexual Behavior* (www.springerlink.com/content/x754q0433g18hg81/).

LIPSITZ, A., KALLMEYER, K., FERGUSON, M., & ABAS, A. (1989). Counting on blood donors: Increasing the impact of reminder calls. *Journal of Applied Social Psychology, 19,* 1057–1067.

LITTLE, A. C., JONES, B. C., & DeBRUINE, L. M. (2008). Preferences for variation in masculinity in real male faces change across the menstrual cycle: Women prefer more masculine faces when they are more fertile. *Personality and Individual Differences, 45,* 478–482.

LIVINGSTON, R. W. (2001). What you see is what you get: Systematic variability in perceptual-based social judgment. *Personality and Social Psychology Bulletin, 27,* 1086–1096.

LIVINGSTON, R. W., & DRWECKI, B. B. (2007). Why are some individuals not racially biased? Susceptibility to affective conditioning predicts nonprejudice toward Blacks. *Psychological Science, 18,* 816–823.

LIVINGSTONE, S., & HADDON, L. (2009). *EU Kids Online; Final report.* LSE, London: EU Kids Online.

LOCKE, E. A., & LATHAM, G. P. (1990). Work motivation and satisfaction: Light at the end of the tunnel. *Psychological Science, 1,* 240–246.

LOCKE, E. A., & LATHAM, G. P. (2002). Building a practically useful theory of goal setting and task performance. *American Psychologist, 57,* 705–717.

LOCKE, E. A., & LATHAM, G. P. (2009). Has goal setting gone wild, or have its attackers abandoned good scholarship? *Academy of Management Perspectives, 23,* 17–23.

LOCKSLEY, A., BORGIDA, E., BREKKE, N., & HEPBURN, C. (1980). Sex stereotypes and social judgment. *Journal of Personality and Social Psychology, 39,* 821–831.

LOFLAND, J., & STARK, R. (1965). Becoming a worldsaver: A theory of conversion to a deviant perspective. *American Sociological Review, 30,* 862–864.

LOFTIN, C., McDOWALL, D., WIERSEMA, B., & COTTEY, T. J. (1991). Effects of restrictive licensing of handguns on homicide and suicide in the District of Columbia. *New England Journal of Medicine, 325,* 1615–1620.

LOFTUS, E. F., & KLINGER, M. R. (1992). Is the unconscious smart or dumb? *American Psychologist, 47,* 761–765.

LOGEL, C., WALTON, G. M., SPENCER, S. J., ISERMAN, E. C., VON HIPPEL, W., & BELL, A. E. (2009). Interacting with sexist men triggers social identity threat among female engineers. *Journal of Personality and Social Psychology, 96,* 1089–1103.

LOMBARDO, J. P., WEISS, R. F., & BUCHANAN, W. (1972). Reinforcing and attracting functions of yielding. *Journal of Personality and Social Psychology, 21,* 359–368.

LONNER, W. J. (1980). The search for psychological universals. In H. C. Triandis & W. W. Lambert (Eds.), *Handbook of cross-cultural psychology* (Vol. 1). Boston: Allyn & Bacon.

LORD, C. G., ROSS, L., & LEPPER, M. (1979). Biased assimilation and attitude polarization: The effects of prior theories on subsequently considered evidence. *Journal of Personality and Social Psychology, 37,* 2098–2109.

LOVETT, F. (1997). Thinking about values (report of December 13, 1996 *Wall Street Journal* national survey). *The Responsive Community, 7*(2), 87.

LOWENSTEIN, D. (2000, May 20). Interview. *The World* (www.cnn.com/TRANSCRIPTS/0005/20/stc.00.html).

LOEWENSTEIN, G., & SCHKADE, D. (1999). Wouldn't it be nice? Predicting future feelings. In D. Kahneman, E. Diener, & N. Schwarz (Eds.), *Understanding well-being: Scientific perspectives on enjoyment and suffering.* New York: Russell Sage Foundation, pp. 85–105.

LÜCKEN, M., & SIMON, B. (2005). Cognitive and affective experiences of minority and majority members: The role of group size, status, and power. *Journal of Experimental Social Psychology, 41,* 396–413.

LUEPTOW, L. B., GAROVICH, L., & LUEPTOW, M. B. (1995). The persistence of gender stereotypes in the face of changing sex roles: Evidence contrary to the sociocultural model. *Ethology and Sociobiology, 16,* 509–530.

LUMENG, J. C., FORREST, P., APPUGLIESE, D. P., KACIROTI, N., CORWYN, R. F., BRADLEY, R. H. (2010). Weight status as a predictor of being bullied in third through sixth grades. *Pediatrics, 125,* e1301–e1307.

LUMSDEN, A., ZANNA, M. P., & DARLEY, J. M. (1980). *When a newscaster presents counter-additional information: Education or propaganda?* Paper presented at the Canadian Psychological Association annual convention.

LUN, J., MESQUITA, B., & SMITH, B. (2011). Self- and other-presentation styles in the Southern and Northern United States: An analysis of personal ads. *European Journal of Social Psychology, 41,* 435–445.

LUNTZ, F. (2003, June 10). Quoted by T. Raum, "Bush insists banned weapons will be found." Associated Press (story.news.yahoo.com).

LUPPINO, F. S., DE WIT, L. M., BOUVY, P. F., STIJNEN, T., CUIJPERS, P., PENNINX, W. J. H., & ZITMAN, F. G. (2010). Overweight, obesity, and depression. *Archives of General Psychiatry, 67,* 220–229.

LUTSKY, L. A., RISUCCI, D. A., & TORTOLANI, A. J. (1993). Reliability and accuracy of surgical resident peer ratings. *Evaluation Review, 17,* 444–456.

LYDON, J., & DUNKEL-SCHETTER, C. (1994). Seeing is committing: A longitudinal study of bolstering commitment in amniocentesis patients. *Personality and Social Psychology Bulletin, 20,* 218–227.

LYKKEN, D. T. (1997). The American crime factory. *Psychological Inquiry, 8,* 261–270.

LYNN, M., & OLDENQUIST, A. (1986). Egoistic and nonegoistic motives in social dilemmas. *American Psychologist, 41,* 529–534.

LYONS, P. A., KENWORTHY, J. B., & POPAN, J. R. (2010). Ingroup identification and group-level narcissism as predictors of U.S. citizens' attitudes and behavior toward Arab immigrants. *Personality and Social Psychology Bulletin, 36,* 1267–1280.

LYUBOMIRSKY, S. (2001). Why are some people happier than others? The role of cognitive and motivational processes in well-being. *American Psychologist, 56,* 239–249.

MA, V., & SCHOENEMAN, T. J. (1997). Individualism versus collectivism: A comparison of Kenyan and American self-concepts. *Basic and Applied Social Psychology, 19,* 261–273.

MAASS, A. (1998). Personal communication from Universita degli Studi di Padova.

MAASS, A., VOLPARO, C., & MUCCHI-FAINA, A. (1996). Social influence and the verifiability of the issue under discussion: Attitudinal versus objective items. *British Journal of Social Psychology, 35,* 15–26.

MACCOBY, E. E. (2002). Gender and group process: A developmental perspective. *Current Directions in Psychological Science, 11,* 54–58.

MACDONALD, G., ZANNA, M. P., & HOLMES, J. G. (2000). An experimental test of the role of alcohol in relationship conflict. *Journal of Experimental Social Psychology, 36,* 182–193.

MACDONALD, T. K., & ROSS, M. (1997). Assessing the accuracy of predictions about dating relationships: How and why do lovers' predictions differ from those made by observers? Unpublished manuscript, University of Lethbridge.

MACK, D., & RAINEY, D. (1990). Female applicants' grooming and personnel selection. *Journal of Social Behavior and Personality, 5,* 399–407.

MACKINNON, S. P., JORDAN, C. H., & WILSON, A. E. (2011). Birds of a feather sit together: Physical similarity predicts seating choice. *Personality and Social Psychology Bulletin, 37,* 879–892.

MACRAE, C. N., ALNWICK, M. A., MILNE, A. B., & SCHLOERSCHEIDT, A. M. (2002). Person perception across the menstrual cycle: Hormonal influences on social-cognitive functioning. *Psychological Science, 13,* 532–536.

MACRAE, C. N., & BODENHAUSEN, G. V. (2000). Social cognition: Thinking categorically about others. *Annual Review of Psychology, 51,* 93–120.

MACRAE, C. N., & BODENHAUSEN, G. V. (2001). Social cognition: Categorical person perception. *British Journal of Psychology, 92,* 239–255.

MACRAE, C. N., BODENHAUSEN, G. V., MILNE, A. B., & JETTEN, J. (1994). Out of mind but back in sight: Stereotypes on the rebound. *Journal of Personality and Social Psychology, 67,* 808–817.

MACRAE, C. N., & JOHNSTON, L. (1998). Help, I need somebody: Automatic action and inaction. *Social Cognition, 16,* 400–417.

MADDUX, J. E. (1993). The mythology of psychopathology: A social cognitive view of deviance, difference, and disorder. *The General Psychologist, 29*(2), 34–45.

MADDUX, J. E., & GOSSELIN, J. T. (2003). Self-efficacy. In M. R. Leary & J. P. Tangney (Eds.), *Handbook of self and identity.* New York: Guilford.

MADDUX, J. E., & ROGERS, R. W. (1983). Protection motivation and self-efficacy: A revised theory of fear appeals and attitude change. *Journal of Experimental Social Psychology, 19,* 469–479.

MADDUX, W. W., GALINSKY, A. D., CUDDY, A. J. C., & POLIFRONI, M. (2008). When being a model minority is good . . . and bad: Realistic threat explains negativity towards Asian Americans. *Personality and Social Psychology Bulletin, 34,* 74–89.

MADDUX, W. W., MULLEN, E., & GALINSKY, A. D. (2008). Chameleons bake bigger pies and take bigger pieces: Strategic behavioral mimicry facilitates negotiation outcomes. *Journal of Experimental Social Psychology, 44,* 461–468.

MADERA, J. M., HEBL, M. R., & MARTIN, R. C. (2009). Gender and letters of recommendation for academia: Agentic and communal differences. *Journal of Applied Psychology, 94,* 1591–1599.

MADON, S., JUSSIM, L., & ECCLES, J. (1997). In search of the powerful self-fulfilling prophecy. *Journal of Personality and Social Psychology, 72,* 791–809.

MAJOR, B., KAISER, C. R., & MCCOY, S. K. (2003). It's not my fault: When and why attributions to prejudice protect self-esteem. *Personality and Social Psychology Bulletin, 29,* 772–781.

MALAMUTH, N. M., & CHECK, J. V. P. (1981). The effects of media exposure on acceptance of violence against women: A field experiment. *Journal of Research in Personality, 15,* 436–446.

MALKIEL, B. (2011). *A random walk down Wall Street: The time-tested strategy for successful investing.* New York: Norton.

MALLE, B. F. (2006). The actor-observer asymmetry in attribution: A (surprising) meta-analysis. *Psychological Bulletin, 132,* 895–919.

MANER, J. K., GAILLIOT, M. T., & MILLER, S. L. (2009). The implicit cognition of relationship maintenance: Inattention to attractive alternatives. *Journal of Experimental Social Psychology, 45,* 174–179.

MANIS, M., CORNELL, S. D., & MOORE, J. C. (1974). Transmission of attitude-relevant information through a communication chain. *Journal of Personality and Social Psychology, 30,* 81–94.

MANN, L. (1981). The baiting crowd in episodes of threatened suicide. *Journal of Personality and Social Psychology, 41,* 703–709.

MANNING, R., LEVINE, M., & COLLINS, A. (2007). The Kitty Genovese murder and the social psychology of helping: The parable of the 38 witnesses. *American Psychologist, 62,* 555–562.

MAR, R. A., & OATLEY, K. (2008). The function of fiction is the abstraction and simulation of social experience. *Perspectives on Psychological Science, 3,* 173–192.

MARCUS, S. (1974). Review of *Obedience to authority.* New York Times Book Review, January 13, pp. 1–2.

MARCUS-NEWHALL, A., PEDERSEN, W. C., CARLSON, M., & MILLER, N. (2000). Displaced aggression is alive and well: A meta-analytic review. *Journal of Personality and Social Psychology, 78,* 670–689.

MARKEY, P. M., WELLS, S. M., & MARKEY, C. N. (2002). In S. P. Shohov (Ed.), *Advances in psychology research, 9,* 94–113. Huntington, NY: Nova Science.

MARKEY, P. M., & KURTZ, J. E. (2006). Increasing acquaintanceship and complementarity of behavioral styles and personality traits among college roommates. *Personality and Social Psychology Bulletin, 32,* 907–916.

MARKMAN, H. J., FLOYD, F. J., STANLEY, S. M., & STORAASLI, R. D. (1988). Prevention of marital distress: A longitudinal investigation. *Journal of Consulting and Clinical Psychology, 56,* 210–217.

MARKS, G., & MILLER, N. (1987). Ten years of research on the false-consensus effect: An empirical and theoretical review. *Psychological Bulletin, 102,* 72–90.

MARKUS, H. (2001, October 7). Culture and the good life. Address to the Positive Psychology Summit conference, Washington, DC.

MARKUS, H. R., & CONNER, A. (2011). The culture cycle. *The Edge* (www.edge.org).

MARKUS, H., & KITAYAMA, S. (1991). Culture and the self: Implications for cognition, emotion, and motivation. *Psychological Review, 98,* 224–253.

MARKUS, H. R., & KITAYAMA, S. (2010). Cultures and selves: A cycle of mutual constitution. *Perspectives on Psychological Science, 5,* 420–430.

MARKUS, H., & NURIUS, P. (1986). Possible selves. *American Psychologist, 41,* 954–969.

MARKUS, H., & WURF, E. (1987). The dynamic self-concept: A social psychological perspective. *Annual Review of Psychology, 38,* 299–337.

MARSDEN, P., & ATTIA, S. (2005). A deadly contagion? *The Psychologist, 18,* 152–155.

MARSHALL, R. (1997). Variances in levels of individualism across two cultures and three social classes. *Journal of Cross-Cultural Psychology, 28,* 490–495.

MARSHALL, W. L. (1989). Pornography and sex offenders. In D. Zillmann & J. Bryant (Eds.), *Pornography: Research advances and policy considerations.* Hillsdale, NJ: Erlbaum.

MARTENS, A., KOSLOFF, S., GREENBERG, J., LANDAU, M. J., & SCHMADER, R. (2007). Killing begets killing: Evidence from a bug-killing paradigm that initial killing fuels subsequent killing. *Personality and Social Psychology Bulletin, 33,* 1251–1264.

MARTIN, R., HEWSTONE, M., & MARTIN, P. Y. (2008). Majority versus minority influence: The role of message processing in determining resistance to counter-persuasion. *European Journal of Social Psychology, 38,* 16–34.

MARTIN, R., MARTIN, P. Y., SMITH, J. R., & HEWSTONE, M. (2007). Majority versus minority influence and prediction of behavioural intentions and behaviour. *Journal of Experimental Social Psychology, 43,* 763–771.

MARUYAMA, G., RUBIN, R. A., & KINGBURY, G. (1981). Self-esteem and educational achievement: Independent constructs with a common cause? *Journal of Personality and Social Psychology, 40,* 962–975.

MARVELLE, K., & GREEN, S. (1980). Physical attractiveness and sex bias in hiring decisions for two types of jobs. *Journal of the National Association of Women Deans, Administrators, and Counselors, 44*(1), 3–6.

MASI, C. M., CHEN, H-Y., HAWKLEY, L. C., & CACIOPPO, J. T. (2011). A meta-analysis of interventions to reduce loneliness. *Personality and Social Psychology Review, 15,* 219–266.

MASSEY, C., SIMMONS, J. P., & ARMOR, D. A. (2011). Hope over experience: Desirability and the persistence of optimism. *Psychological Science, 22,* 274–281.

Mast, M. S., & Hall, J. A. (2006). Women's advantage at remembering others' appearance: A systematic look at the why and when of a gender difference. *Personality and Social Psychology Bulletin, 32,* 353–364.

Mastroianni, G. R., & Reed, G. (2006). Apples, barrels, and Abu Ghraib. *Sociological Focus, 39,* 239–250.

Masuda, T., & Kitayama, S. (2004). Perceiver-induced constraint and attitude attribution in Japan and the U.S.: A case for the cultural dependence of the correspondence bias. *Journal of Experimental Social Psychology, 40,* 409–416.

Mayer, J. D., & Salovey, P. (1987). Personality moderates the interaction of mood and cognition. In K. Fiedler & J. Forgas (Eds.), *Affect, cognition, and social behavior.* Toronto: Hogrefe.

McAlister, A., Perry, C., Killen, J., Slinkard, L. A., & Maccoby, N. (1980). Pilot study of smoking, alcohol and drug abuse prevention. *American Journal of Public Health, 70,* 719–721.

McCarthy, J. F., & Kelly, B. R. (1978a). Aggression, performance variables, and anger self-report in ice hockey players. *Journal of Psychology, 99,* 97–101.

McCarthy, J. F., & Kelly, B. R. (1978b). Aggressive behavior and its effect on performance over time in ice hockey athletes: An archival study. *International Journal of Sport Psychology, 9,* 90–96.

McCauley, C. (1989). The nature of social influence in groupthink: Compliance and internalization. *Journal of Personality and Social Psychology, 57,* 250–260.

McCauley, C. R. (2002). Psychological issues in understanding terrorism and the response to terrorism. In C. E. Stout (Ed.), *The psychology of terrorism* (Vol. 3). Westport, CT: Praeger/Greenwood.

McCauley, C. R., & Segal, M. E. (1987). Social psychology of terrorist groups. In C. Hendrick (Ed.), *Group processes and intergroup relations: Review of personality and social psychology* (Vol. 9). Newbury Park, CA: Sage.

McConahay, J. B. (1981). Reducing racial prejudice in desegregated schools. In W. D. Hawley (Ed.), *Effective school desegregation.* Beverly Hills, CA: Sage.

McCullough, J. L., & Ostrom, T. M. (1974). Repetition of highly similar messages and attitude change. *Journal of Applied Psychology, 59,* 395–397.

McDermott, T. (2005). *Perfect soldiers: The hijackers: Who they were, why they did it.* New York: HarperCollins.

McDonald, M. M., Asher, B. D., Kerr, N. L., & Navarrete, C. D. (2011). Fertility and intergroup bias in racial and minimal-group contexts: Evidence for shared architecture. *Psychological Science, 22,* 860–865.

McFarland, C., & Ross, M. (1985). The relation between current impressions and memories of self and dating partners. Unpublished manuscript, University of Waterloo.

McFarland, S., & Carnahan, T. (2009). A situation's first powers are attracting volunteers and selecting participants: A reply to Haney and Zimbardo (2009). *Personality and Social Psychology Bulletin, 35,* 815–818.

McGillicuddy, N. B., Welton, G. L., & Pruitt, D. G. (1987). Third-party intervention: A field experiment comparing three different models. *Journal of Personality and Social Psychology, 53,* 104–112.

McGowan, P. O., Sasaki, A., D'Alessio, A. C., Dymov, S., Labonté, B., Szyl, M., Turecki, G., & Meaney, M. J. (2010). Epigenetic regulation of the glucocorticoid receptor in human brain associates with childhood abuse. *Nature Neuroscience, 12,* 342–348.

McGregor, I., Zanna, M. P., Holmes, J. G., & Spencer, S. J. (2001). Conviction in the face of uncertainty: Going to extremes and being oneself. *Journal of Personality and Social Psychology, 80,* 472–478.

McGuire, A. (2002, August 19). Charity calls for debate on adverts aimed at children. *The Herald* (Scotland), p. 4.

McGuire, W. J. (1964). Inducing resistance to persuasion: Some contemporary approaches. In L. Berkowitz (Ed.), *Advances in experimental social psychology* (Vol. 1). New York: Academic Press.

McGuire W. J., & McGuire, C. V. (1986). Differences in conceptualizing self versus conceptualizing other people as manifested in contrasting verb types used in natural speech. *Journal of Personality and Social Psychology, 51,* 1135–1143.

McGuire, W. J., McGuire, C. V., Child, P., & Fujioka, T. (1978). Salience of ethnicity in the spontaneous self-concept as a function of one's ethnic distinctiveness in the social environment. *Journal of Personality and Social Psychology, 36,* 511–520.

McGuire, W. J., McGuire, C. V., & Winton, W. (1979). Effects of household sex composition on the salience of one's gender in the spontaneous self-concept. *Journal of Experimental Social Psychology, 15,* 77–90.

McGuire, W. J., & Padawer-Singer, A. (1978). Trait salience in the spontaneous self-concept. *Journal of Personality and Social Psychology, 33,* 743–754.

McKelvie, S. J. (1995). Bias in the estimated frequency of names. *Perceptual and Motor Skills, 81,* 1331–1338.

McKelvie, S. J. (1997). The availability heuristic: Effects of fame and gender on the estimated frequency of male and female names. *Journal of Social Psychology, 137,* 63–78.

McKenna, F. P., & Myers, L. B. (1997). Illusory self-assessments—Can they be reduced? *British Journal of Psychology, 88,* 39–51.

McKenna, K. Y. A., & Bargh, J. A. (1998). Coming out in the age of the Internet: Identity demarginalization through virtual group participation. *Journal of Personality and Social Psychology, 75,* 681–694.

McKenna, K. Y. A., & Bargh, J. A. (2000). Plan 9 from cyberspace: The implications of the Internet for personality and social psychology. *Personality and Social Psychology Review, 4,* 57–75.

McKenna, K. Y. A., Green, A. S., & Gleason, M. E. J. (2002). What's the big attraction? Relationship formation on the Internet. *Journal of Social Issues, 58,* 9–31.

McKibben, B. (2011, May 23). A link between climate change and Joplin tornadoes? Never! *Washington Post* (www.washingtonpost.com).

McNeel, S. P. (1980). *Tripling up: Perceptions and effect of dormitory crowding.* Paper presented at the American Psychological Association convention.

McNeill, B. W., & Stoltenberg, C. D. (1988). A test of the elaboration likelihood model for therapy. *Cognitive Therapy and Research, 12,* 69–79.

McNulty, J. K. (2010). When positive processes hurt relationships. *Current Directions in Psychological Science, 19,* 167–171.

McPherson, M., Smith-Lovin, L., & Cook, J. M. (2001). Birds of a feather: Homophily in social networks. *Annual Review of Sociology, 27,* 415–444.

Meehl, G. A., Tebaldi, C., Walton, G., Easterling, D., & McDaniel, L. (2009). Relative increase of record high maximum temperatures compared to record low minimum temperatures in the U.S. *Geophysical Research Letters, 36,* L23701.

Meehl, P. E. (1954). *Clinical vs. statistical prediction: A theoretical analysis and a review of evidence.* Minneapolis: University of Minnesota Press.

Meehl, P. E. (1986). Causes and effects of my disturbing little book. *Journal of Personality Assessment, 50,* 370–375.

Mehl, M. R., & Pennebaker, J. W. (2003). The sounds of social life: A psychometric analysis of students' daily social environments and natural conversations. *Journal of Personality and Social Psychology, 84,* 857–870.

Mehl, M. R., Vazire, S., Holleran, S. E., & Clark, C. S. (2010). Eavesdropping on happiness: Well-being is related to having less small talk and more substantive conversations. *Psychological Science, 21,* 539–541.

Meissner, C. A., & Brigham, J. C. (2001). Thirty years of investigating the own-race bias in memory for faces: A meta-analytic review. *Psychology, Public Policy, & Law, 7,* 3–35.

Mendes, E. (2010, February 9). Six in 10 overweight or obese in U.S., more in '09 than in '08. (www.gallup.com)

Merari, A. (2002). Explaining suicidal terrorism: Theories versus empirical evidence. Invited address to the American Psychological Association.

Mesoudi, A. (2009). How cultural evolutionary theory can inform social psychology and vice versa. *Psychological Review, 116,* 929–952.

Messé, L. A., & Sivacek, J. M. (1979). Predictions of others' responses in a mixed-motive game: Self-justification or false consensus? *Journal of Personality and Social Psychology, 37,* 602–607.

Messias, E., Eaton, W. W., & Grooms, A. N. (2011). Income inequality and depression prevalence across the United States: An ecological study. *Psychiatric Services, 62,* 710–712.

Messick, D. M., & Sentis, K. P. (1979). Fairness and preference. *Journal of Experimental Social Psychology, 15,* 418–434.

Michaels, J. W., Blommel, J. M., Brocato, R. M., Linkous, R. A., & Rowe, J. S. (1982). Social facilitation and inhibition in a natural setting. *Replications in Social Psychology, 2,* 21–24.

Mikula, G. (1984). Justice and fairness in interpersonal relations: Thoughts and suggestions. In H. Taijfel (Ed.), *The social dimension: European developments in social psychology* (Vol. 1). Cambridge: Cambridge University Press.

Mikulincer, M., Florian, V., & Hirschberger, G. (2003). The existential function of close relationships: Introducing death into the science of love. *Personality and Social Psychology Review, 7,* 20–40.

MILGRAM, A. (2000). My personal view of Stanley Milgram. In T. Blass (Ed.), *Obedience to authority: Current perspectives on the Milgram paradigm*. Mahwah, NJ: Erlbaum.

MILGRAM, S. (1961, December). Nationality and conformity. *Scientific American*, pp. 45–51.

MILGRAM, S. (1965). Some conditions of obedience and disobedience to authority. *Human Relations*, **18**, 57–76.

MILGRAM, S. (1974). *Obedience to authority*. New York: Harper and Row.

MILLER, A. G. (1986). *The obedience experiments: A case study of controversy in social science*. New York: Praeger.

MILLER, A. G. (2004). What can the Milgram obedience experiments tell us about the Holocaust? Generalizing from the social psychological laboratory. In A. G. Miller (Ed.), *The social psychology of good and evil*. New York: Guilford.

MILLER, A. G., ASHTON, W., & MISHAL, M. (1990). Beliefs concerning the features of constrained behavior: A basis for the fundamental attribution error. *Journal of Personality and Social Psychology*, **59**, 635–650.

MILLER, D. T., DOWNS, J. S., & PRENTICE, D. A. (1998). Minimal conditions for the creation of a unit relationship: The social bond between birthdaymates. *European Journal of Social Psychology*, **28**, 475.

MILLER, G. (2011, April 29). Using the psychology of evil to do good. *Science*, **332**, 530–532.

MILLER, G., TYBUR, J. M., & JORDAN, B. D. (2007). Ovulatory cycle effects on tip earnings by lap dancers: Economic evidence for human estrus? *Evolution and Human Behavior*, **28**, 375–381.

MILLER, J. B. (1986). *Toward a new psychology of women*, 2nd ed. Boston, MA: Beacon Press.

MILLER, J. G. (1984). Culture and the development of everyday social explanation. *Journal of Personality and Social Psychology*, **46**, 961–978.

MILLER, K. I., & MONGE, P. R. (1986). Participation, satisfaction, and productivity: A meta-analytic review. *Academy of Management Journal*, **29**, 727–753.

MILLER, L. C. (1990). Intimacy and liking: Mutual influence and the role of unique relationships. *Journal of Personality and Social Psychology*, **59**, 50–60.

MILLER, L. C., BERG, J. H., & ARCHER, R. L. (1983). Openers: Individuals who elicit intimate self-disclosure. *Journal of Personality and Social Psychology*, **44**, 1234–1244.

MILLER, N., & MARKS, G. (1982). Assumed similarity between self and other: Effect of expectation of future interaction with that other. *Social Psychology Quarterly*, **45**, 100–105.

MILLER, N., PEDERSEN, W. C., EARLEYWINE, M., & POLLOCK, V. E. (2003). A theoretical model of triggered displaced aggression. *Personality and Social Psychology Review*, **7**, 75–97.

MILLER, N. E. (1941). The frustration-aggression hypothesis. *Psychological Review*, **48**, 337–342.

MILLER, P. A., & EISENBERG, N. (1988). The relation of empathy to aggressive and externalizing/antisocial behavior. *Psychological Bulletin*, **103**, 324–344.

MILLER, R. L., BRICKMAN, P., & BOLEN, D. (1975). Attribution versus persuasion as a means for modifying behavior. *Journal of Personality and Social Psychology*, **31**, 430–441.

MILLER, R. S. (1997). Inattentive and contented: Relationship commitment and attention to alternatives. *Journal of Personality and Social Psychology*, **73**, 758–766.

MILLER, R. S., & SCHLENKER, B. R. (1985). Egotism in group members: Public and private attributions of responsibility for group performance. *Social Psychology Quarterly*, **48**, 85–89.

MILLETT, K. (1975, January). The shame is over. *Ms.*, pp. 26–29.

MILYAVSKAYA, M., GINGRAS, I., MAGEAU, G. A., KOESTNER, R., GAGNON, H., FANG, J., & BOICHÉ, J. (2009). Balance across contexts: Importance of balanced need satisfaction across various life domains. *Personality and Social Psychology Bulletin*, **35**, 1031–1045.

MIRELS, H. L., & MCPEEK, R. W. (1977). Self-advocacy and self-esteem. *Journal of Consulting and Clinical Psychology*, **45**, 1132–1138.

MISHNA, F., COOK, C., GADALLO, T., DACIUK, J., & SOLOMON, S. (2010). Cyberbullying behaviors among middle and high school students. *American Journal of Orthopsychiatry*, **80**, 362–374.

MITA, T. H., DERMER, M., & KNIGHT, J. (1977). Reversed facial images and the mere-exposure hypothesis. *Journal of Personality and Social Psychology*, **35**, 597–601.

MITCHELL, T. R., & THOMPSON, L. (1994). A theory of temporal adjustments of the evaluation of events: Rosy prospection and rosy retrospection. In C. Stubbart, J. Porac, & J. Meindl (Eds.), *Advances in managerial cognition and organizational information processing*. Greenwich, CT: JAI Press.

MITCHELL, T. R., THOMPSON, L., PETERSON, E., & CRONK, R. (1997). Temporal adjustments in the evaluation of events: The "rosy view." *Journal of Experimental Social Psychology*, **33**, 421–448.

MOFFITT, T., & 12 OTHERS. (2011). A gradient of childhood self-control predicts health, wealth, and public safety. *PNAS*, **108**(7): 2693–2698.

MOGHADDAM, F. M. (2005). The staircase to terrorism: A psychological exploration. *American Psychologist, 60,* 161–169.

MOJZISCH, A., & SCHULZ-HARDT, S. (2010). Knowing others' preferences degrades the quality of group decisions. *Journal of Personality and Social Psychology, 98,* 784–808.

MOLLER, I., & KRAHE, B. (2008). Exposure to violent video games and aggression in German adolescents: A longitudinal analysis. *Aggressive Behavior, 34,* 1–14.

MONTOYA, R. M. (2008). I'm hot, so I'd say you're not: The influence of objective physical attractiveness on mate selection. *Personality and Social Psychology Bulletin, 34,* 1315–1331.

MOODY, K. (1980). *Growing up on television: The TV effect.* New York: Times Books.

MOONS, W. G., & MACKIE, D. M. (2007). Thinking straight while seeing red: The influence of anger on information processing. *Personality and Social Psychology Bulletin, 33,* 706–720.

MOOR, B. G., CRONE, E. A., & VAN DER MOLEN, M. W. (2010). The heartbrake of social rejection: Heart rate deceleration in response to unexpected peer rejection. *Psychological Science, 21,* 1326–1333.

MOORE, D. L., & BARON, R. S. (1983). Social facilitation: A physiological analysis. In J. T. Cacioppo & R. Petty (Eds.), *Social psychophysiology.* New York: Guilford.

MOR, N., & WINQUIST, J. (2002). Self-focused attention and negative affect: A meta-analysis. *Psychological Bulletin, 128,* 638–662.

MORALES, L. (2011, May 27). *U.S. adults estimate that 25% of Americans are gay or lesbian.* (www.gallup.com).

MORLING, B., & LAMOREAUX, M. (2008). Measuring culture outside the head: A meta-analysis of individualism-collectivism in cultural products. *Personality and Social Psychology Bulletin, 12,* 199–221.

MORRISON, D. M. (1989). Predicting contraceptive efficacy: A discriminant analysis of three groups of adolescent women. *Journal of Applied Social Psychology, 19,* 1431–1452.

MOSCOVICI, S. (1985). Social influence and conformity. In G. Lindzey & E. Aronson (Eds.), *The handbook of social psychology,* 3rd edition. Hillsdale, NJ: Erlbaum.

MOSCOVICI, S., & ZAVALLONI, M. (1969). The group as a polarizer of attitudes. *Journal of Personality and Social Psychology, 12,* 124–135.

MOTHERHOOD PROJECT (2001, May 2). Watch out for children: A mothers' statement to advertisers. Institute for American Values (www.watchoutforchildren.org).

MOYER, K. E. (1976). *The psychobiology of aggression.* New York: Harper & Row.

MOYER, K. E. (1983). The physiology of motivation: Aggression as a model. In C. J. Scheier & A. M. Rogers (Eds.), *G. Stanley Hall lecture series* (Vol. 3). Washington, DC: American Psychological Association.

MSNBC (2010, October 6). *Man who saved abducted child says he was "beyond fear."* (www.msnbc.msn.com).

MUELLER, C. W., DONNERSTEIN, E., & HALLAM, J. (1983). Violent films and prosocial behavior. *Personality and Social Psychology Bulletin, 9,* 83–89.

MULLEN, B. (1986a). Atrocity as a function of lynch mob composition: A self-attention perspective. *Personality and Social Psychology Bulletin, 12,* 187–197.

MULLEN, B. (1986b). Stuttering, audience size, and the other-total ratio: A self-attention perspective. *Journal of Applied Social Psychology, 16,* 139–149.

MULLEN, B., & BAUMEISTER, R. F. (1987). Group effects on self-attention and performance: Social loafing, social facilitation, and social impairment. In C. Hendrick (Ed.), *Group processes and intergroup relations: Review of personality and social psychology* (Vol. 9). Newbury Park, CA: Sage.

MULLEN, B., BROWN, R., & SMITH, C. (1992). Ingroup bias as a function of salience, relevance, and status: An integration. *European Journal of Social Psychology, 22,* 103–122.

MULLEN, B., BRYANT, B., & DRISKELL, J. E. (1997). Presence of others and arousal: An integration. *Group Dynamics: Theory, Research, and Practice, 1,* 52–64.

MULLEN, B., & COPPER, C. (1994). The relation between group cohesiveness and performance: An integration. *Psychological Bulletin, 115,* 210–227.

MULLEN, B., COPPER, C., & DRISKELL, J. E. (1990). Jaywalking as a function of model behavior. *Personality and Social Psychology Bulletin, 16,* 320–330.

MULLEN, B., & GOETHALS, G. R. (1990). Social projection, actual consensus and valence. *British Journal of Social Psychology, 29,* 279–282.

MULLEN, B., & RIORDAN, C. A. (1988). Self-serving attributions for performance in naturalistic settings: A meta-analytic review. *Journal of Applied Social Psychology, 18,* 3–22.

MULLER, R. A. (2011, October 21). The case against global-warming skepticism. *Wall Street Journal* (online.wsj.com).

MULLER, S., & JOHNSON, B. T. (1990). Fear and persuasion: A linear relationship? Paper presented to the Eastern Psychological Association convention.

MULLIN, C. R., & LINZ, D. (1995). Desensitization and resensitization to violence against women: Effects of exposure to sexually violent films on judgments of domestic violence victims. *Journal of Personality and Social Psychology, 69,* 449–459.

MUNRO, G. D., DITTO, P. H., LOCKHART, L. K., FAGERLIN, A., GREADY, M., & PETERSON, E. (1997). *Biased assimilation of sociopolitical arguments: Evaluating the 1996 U.S. presidential debate.* Unpublished manuscript, Hope College.

MURPHY, C. (1990, June). New findings: Hold on to your hat. *The Atlantic,* pp. 22–23.

MURRAY, S. L., GELLAVIA, G. M., ROSE, P., & GRIFFIN, D. W. (2003). Once hurt, twice hurtful: How perceived regard regulates daily marital interactions. *Journal of Personality and Social Psychology, 84,* 126–147.

MURRAY, S. L., HOLMES, J. G., GELLAVIA, G., GRIFFIN, D. W., & DOLDERMAN, D. (2002). Kindred spirits? The benefits of egocentrism in close relationships. *Journal of Personality and Social Psychology, 82,* 563–581.

MURRAY, S. L., HOLMES, J. G., & GRIFFIN, D. W. (1996a). The benefits of positive illusions: Idealization and the construction of satisfaction in close relationships. *Journal of Personality and Social Psychology, 70,* 79–98.

MURRAY, S. L., HOLMES, J. G., & GRIFFIN, D. W. (1996b). The self-fulfilling nature of positive illusions in romantic relationships: Love is not blind, but prescient. *Journal of Personality and Social Psychology, 71,* 1155–1180.

MURRAY, S. L., HOLMES, J. G., & GRIFFIN, D. W. (2000). Self-esteem and the quest for felt security: How perceived regard regulates attachment processes. *Journal of Personality and Social Psychology, 78,* 478–498.

MURRAY, S. L., HOLMES, J. G., MACDONALD, G., & ELLSWORTH, P. C. (1998). Through the looking glass darkly? When self-doubts turn into relationship insecurities. *Journal of Personality and Social Psychology, 75,* 1459–1480.

MURSTEIN, B. L. (1986). *Paths to marriage.* Newbury Park, CA: Sage.

MUSON, G. (1978, March). Teenage violence and the telly. *Psychology Today,* pp. 50–54.

MYERS, D. G. (1978). Polarizing effects of social comparison. *Journal of Experimental Social Psychology, 14,* 554–563.

MYERS, D. G. (2000). *The American paradox: Spiritual hunger in an age of plenty.* New Haven, CT: Yale University Press.

MYERS, D. G. (2001, December). Do we fear the right things? *American Psychological Society Observer,* p. 3.

MYERS, D. G., & BISHOP, G. D. (1970). Discussion effects on racial attitudes. *Science, 169,* 778–789.

MYERS, J. E., MADATHIL, J., & TINGLE, L. R. (2005). Marriage satisfaction and wellness in India and the United States: A preliminary comparison of arranged marriages and marriages of choice. *Journal of Counseling and Development, 83,* 183–190.

MYERS, N. (2000). Sustainable consumption: The meta-problem. In B. Heap & J. Kent (Eds.), *Towards sustainable consumption: A European perspective.* London: The Royal Society.

NADLER, A., GOLDBERG, M., & JAFFE, Y. (1982). Effect of self-differentiation and anonymity in group on deindividuation. *Journal of Personality and Social Psychology, 42,* 1127–1136.

NADLER, J. T., & CLARK, M. H. (2011). Stereotype threat: A meta-analysis comparing African Americans to Hispanic Americans. *Journal of Applied Social Psychology, 41,* 872–890.

NAGAR, D., & PANDEY, J. (1987). Affect and performance on cognitive task as a function of crowding and noise. *Journal of Applied Social Psychology, 17,* 147–157.

NAIL, P. R., MACDONALD, G., & LEVY, D. A. (2000). Proposal of a four-dimensional model of social response. *Psychological Bulletin, 126,* 454–470.

NARIO-REDMOND, M. R. (2010). Cultural stereotypes of disabled and non-disabled men and women: Consensus for global category representations and diagnostic domains. *British Journal of Social Psychology, 49,* 471–488.

NATIONAL CENTER FOR HEALTH STATISTICS (1991). Family structure and children's health: United States, 1988 (by Deborah A. Dawson). *Vital and Health Statistics,* Series **10,** No. **178,** CHHS Publication No. PHS 91–1506.

NATIONAL RESEARCH COUNCIL (2010). *Advancing the science of climate change.* Washington, DC: National Academies Press.

NATIONAL SAFETY COUNCIL (2008). Transportation mode comparisons, from *Injury Facts* (via correspondence with Kevin T. Fearn, Research & Statistical Services Department).

NATIONAL TELEVISION VIOLENCE STUDY (1997). Thousand Oaks, CA: Sage.

NAVARRETE, C. D., FESSLER, D. M. T., FLEISCHMAN, D. S., & GEYER, J. (2009). Race bias tracks conception risk across the menstrual cycle. *Psychological Science, 20,* 661–665.

NAVARRETE, C. D., McDONALD, M. M., MOLINA, L. E., & SIDANIUS, J. (2010). Prejudice at the nexus of race and gender: An outgroup male target hypothesis. *Journal of Personality and Social Psychology,* **98,** 933–945.

NEFF, K. D. (2011). Self-compassion, self-esteem, and well-being. *Social and Personality Psychology Compass,* **5,** 1–12.

NEFF, L. A., & KARNEY, B. R. (2005). To know you is to love you: The implications of global adoration and specific accuracy for marital relationships. *Journal of Personality and Social Psychology,* **88,** 480–497.

NEIMEYER, G. J., MacNAIR, R., METZLER, A. E., & COURCHAINE, K. (1991). Changing personal beliefs: Effects of forewarning, argument quality, prior bias, and personal exploration. *Journal of Social and Clinical Psychology,* **10,** 1–20.

NELSON, L. D., & MORRISON, E. L. (2005). The symptoms of resource scarcity: Judgments of food and finances influence preferences for potential partners. *Psychological Science,* **16,** 167–173.

NELSON, L. J., & MILLER, D. T. (1995). The distinctiveness effect in social categorization: You are what makes you unusual. *Psychological Science,* **6,** 246.

NEMETH, C. (1979). The role of an active minority in intergroup relations. In W. G. Austin & S. Worchel (Eds.), *The social psychology of intergroup relations.* Monterey, CA: Brooks/Cole.

NEMETH, C. J. (2011). Minority influence theory. In P. Van Lange, A. Kruglanski, & E. T. Higgins (Eds.), *Handbook of theories in social psychology.* New York: Sage.

NEMETH, C., & CHILES, C. (1988). Modelling courage: The role of dissent in fostering independence. *European Journal of Social Psychology,* **18,** 275–280.

NEMETH, C., & WACHTLER, J. (1974). Creating the perceptions of consistency and confidence: A necessary condition for minority influence. *Sociometry,* **37,** 529–540.

NEMETH, C. J. (1997). Managing innovation: When less is more. *California Management Review,* **40,** 59–74.

NEMETH, C. J. (1999). Behind the scenes. In D. G. Myers, *Social psychology,* 6th edition. New York: McGraw-Hill.

NEMETH, C. J., BROWN, K., & ROGERS, J. (2001). Devil's advocate versus authentic dissent: Stimulating quantity and quality. *European Journal of Social Psychology,* **31,** 1–13.

NEMETH, C. J., CONNELL, J. B., ROGERS, J. D., & BROWN, K. S. (2001). Improving decision making by means of dissent. *Journal of Applied Social Psychology,* **31,** 48–58.

NESTLER, S., BLANK, H., & EGLOFF, B. (2010). Hindsight ≠ hindsight: Experimentally induced dissociations between hindsight components.

NEW YORK TIMES (2010, April 25). Questions surround a delay in help for a dying man. (www.nytimes.com).

NEWCOMB, T. M. (1961). *The acquaintance process.* New York: Holt, Rinehart & Winston.

NEWELL, B., & LAGNADO, D. (2003). Think-tanks, or think *tanks. The Psychologist,* **16,** 176.

NEWELL, B. R., WONG, K. Y., CHEUNG, J. C. H., & RAKOW, T. (2008, August 23). Think, blink, or sleep on it? The impact of modes of thought on complex decision making. *Quarterly Journal of Experimental Psychology* (DOI: 10.1080/17470210802215202).

NEWMAN, H. M., & LANGER, E. J. (1981). Post-divorce adaptation and the attribution of responsibility. *Sex Roles,* **7,** 223–231.

NEWMAN, L. S. (1993). How individualists interpret behavior: Idiocentrism and spontaneous trait inference. *Social Cognition,* **11,** 243–269.

NEWPORT, F. (2011). Americans prefer boys to girls, just as they did in 1941. (www.gallup.com).

NEWPORT, F. (2012, December 5). Religion big factor for Americans against same-sex marriage. Gallup Poll (www.gallup.com).

NIAS, D. K. B. (1979). Marital choice: Matching or complementation? In M. Cook & G. Wilson (Eds.), *Love and attraction.* Oxford: Pergamon.

NICHOLSON, C. (2007, January). Framing science: Advances in theory and technology are fueling a new era in the science of persuasion. *APS Observer* (www.psychologicalscience.org).

NIE, N. H., & ERBRING, L. (2000, February 17). Internet and society: A preliminary report. Stanford, CA: Stanford Institute for the Quantitative Study of Society.

NIEDERMEIER, K. E., KERR, N. L., & MESSE, L. A. (1999). Jurors' use of naked statistical evidence: Exploring bases and implications of the Wells effect. *Journal of Personality and Social Psychology,* **76,** 533–542.

NIELSEN (2008a, May). *Nielsen's three screen report.* The Nielsen Company (www.nielsen.com).

NIELSEN (2008b, February 14). Nielsen reports DVR playback is adding to TV viewing levels. The Nielsen Company (www.nielsen.com).

NIEMI, R. G., MUELLER, J., & SMITH, T. W. (1989). *Trends in public opinion: A compendium of survey data.* New York: Greenwood Press.

NISBET, E. K., & ZELENSKI, J. M. (2011). Underestimating nearby nature: Affective forecasting errors obscure the happy path to sustainability. *Psychological Science, 22,* 1101–1106.

NISBETT, R. E. (1990). Evolutionary psychology, biology, and cultural evolution. *Motivation and Emotion, 14,* 255–263.

NISBETT, R. E. (1993). Violence and U.S. regional culture. *American Psychologist, 48,* 441–449.

NIX, G., WATSON, C., PYSZCZYNSKI, T., & GREENBERG, J. (1995). Reducing depressive affect through external focus of attention. *Journal of Social and Clinical Psychology, 14,* 36–52.

NOLAN, S. A., FLYNN, C., & GARBER, J. (2003). Prospective relations between rejection and depression in young adolescents. *Journal of Personality and Social Psychology, 85,* 745–755.

NOLEN-HOEKSEMA, S. (2003). *Women who think too much: How to break free of overthinking and reclaim your life.* New York: Holt.

NOLLER, P., & FITZPATRICK, M. A. (1990). Marital communication in the eighties. *Journal of Marriage and Family, 52,* 832–843.

NOOR, M., BROWN, R., GONZALEZ, R., MANZI, J., & LEWIS, C. A. (2008). On positive psychological outcomes: What helps groups with a history of conflict to forgive and reconcile with each other? *Personality and Social Psychology Bulletin, 34,* 819–832.

NORC (National Opinion Research Center) (1996). General social survey. National Opinion Research Center, University of Chicago (courtesy Tom W. Smith).

NORDGREN, L. F., BANAS, K., & MACDONALD, G. (2011). Empathy gaps for social pain: Why people underestimate the pain of social suffering. *Journal of Personality and Social Psychology, 100,* 120–128.

NOREM, J. K. (2000). Defensive pessimism, optimism, and pessimism. In E. C. Chang (Ed.), *Optimism and pessimism.* Washington, DC: APA Books.

NOREM, J. K., & CANTOR, N. (1986). Defensive pessimism: Harnessing anxiety as motivation. *Journal of Personality and Social Psychology, 51,* 1208–1217.

NORENZAYAN, A., & HEINE, S. J. (2005). Psychological universals: What are they and how can we know? *Psychological Bulletin, 131,* 763–784.

NORTH, A. C., HARGREAVES, D. J., & MCKENDRICK, J. (1997). In-store music affects product choice. *Nature, 390,* 132.

NORTON, M. I., & ARIELY, D. (2011). Building a better America—One wealth quintile at a time. *Perspectives on Psychological Science, 6,* 9–12.

NOSEK, B. A. (2007). Implicit-explicit relations. *Current Directions in Psychological Science, 16,* 65–69.

NOSEK, B. A., SMYTH, F. L., HANSEN, J. J., DEVOS, T., LINDNER, N. M., RANGANATH, K. A., SMITH, C. T., OLSON, K. R., CHUGH, D., GREENWALD, A. G., & BANAJI, M. R. (2007). Pervasiveness and correlates of implicit attitudes and stereotypes. *European Review of Social Psychology, 18,* 36–88.

NOTARIUS, C., & MARKMAN, H. J. (1993). *We can work it out.* New York: Putnam.

NOVELLI, D., DRURY, J., & REICHER, S. (2010). Come together: Two studies concerning the impact of group relations on "personal space." *British Journal of Social Psychology, 49,* 223–236.

NURMI, J-E., & SALMELA-ARO, K. (1997). Social strategies and loneliness: A prospective study. *Personality and Individual Differences, 23,* 205–215.

NURMI, J-E., TOIVONEN, S., SALMELA-ARO, K., & ERONEN, S. (1996). Optimistic, approach-oriented, and avoidance strategies in social situations: Three studies on loneliness and peer relationships. *European Journal of Personality, 10,* 201–219.

NUTTIN, J. M., JR. (1987). Affective consequences of mere ownership: The name letter effect in twelve European languages. *European Journal of Social Psychology, 17,* 318–402.

O'DEA, T. F. (1968). Sects and cults. In D. L. Sills (Ed.), *International encyclopedia of the social sciences* (Vol. 14). New York: Macmillan.

O'HEGARTY, M., PEDERSON, L. L., YENOKYAN, G., NELSON, D., & WORTLEY, P. (2007). Young adults' perceptions of cigarette warning labels in the United States and Canada. *Preventing Chronic Disease: Public Health Research, Practice, and Policy, 30,* 467–473.

O'KEEFE, D. J., & JENSEN, J. D. (2011). The relative effectiveness of gain-framed and loss-framed persuasive appeals concerning obesity-related behaviors: Meta-analytic evidence and implications. In R. Batra, P. A. Keller, & V. J. Strecher (Eds.), *Leveraging consumer psychology for effective health communications: The obesity challenge* (pp. 171–185). Armonk, NY: Sharpe.

O'LEARY, K. D., CHRISTIAN, J. L., & MENDELL, N. R. (1994). A closer look at the link between marital discord and depressive symptomatology. *Journal of Social and Clinical Psychology, 13,* 33–41.

OATEN, M., & CHENG, K. (2006b). Longitudinal gains in self-regulation from regular physical exercise. *British Journal of Health Psychology, 11,* 717–733.

ODDONE-PAOLUCCI, E., GENUIS, M., & VIOLATO, C. (2000). A meta-analysis of the published research on the effects of pornography. In C. Violata (Ed.), *The changing family and child development.* Aldershot, England: Ashgate Publishing.

OHBUCHI, K., & KAMBARA, T. (1985). Attacker's intent and awareness of outcome, impression management, and retaliation. *Journal of Experimental Social Psychology, 21,* 321–330.

OISHI, S., KESEBIR, S., & DIENER, E. (2011). Income inequality and happiness. *Psychological Science, 22,* 1095–1100.

OISHI, S., ROTHMAN, A. J., SNYDER, M., SU, J., ZEHM, K., HERTEL, A. W., GONZALES, M. H., & SHERMAN, G. D. (2007). The socioecological model of procommunity action: The benefits of residential stability. *Journal of Personality and Social Psychology, 93,* 831–844.

OKIMOTO, T. G., & BRESCOLL, V. L. (2010). The price of power: Power seeking and backlash against female politicians. *Personality and Social Psychology Bulletin, 36,* 923–936.

OLSON, I. R., & MARSHUETZ, C. (2005). Facial attractiveness is appraised in a glance. *Emotion, 5,* 498–502.

OLSON, J. M., ROESE, N. J., & ZANNA, M. P. (1996). Expectancies. In E. T. Higgins & A. W. Kruglanski (Eds.), *Social psychology: Handbook of basic principles* (pp. 211–238). New York: Guilford.

OLSON, J. M., & ZANNA, M. P. (1981, November). Promoting physical activity: A social psychological perspective. Report prepared for the Ministry of Culture and Recreation, Sports and Fitness Branch, 77 Bloor St. West, 8th Floor, Toronto, Ontario M7A 2R9.

OLSON, K. R., DUNHAM, Y., DWECK, C. S., SPELKE, E. S., & BANAJI, M. R. (2008). Judgments of the lucky across development and culture. *Journal of Personality and Social Psychology, 94,* 757–776.

OLWEUS, D. (1979). Stability of aggressive reaction patterns in males: A review. *Psychological Bulletin, 86,* 852–875.

OLWEUS, D., MATTSSON, A., SCHALLING, D., & LOW, H. (1988). Circulating testosterone levels and aggression in adolescent males: A causal analysis. *Psychosomatic Medicine, 50,* 261–272.

ORBELL, J. M., VAN DE KRAGT, A. J. C., & DAWES, R. M. (1988). Explaining discussion-induced cooperation. *Journal of Personality and Social Psychology, 54,* 811–819.

ORENDAIN, S. (2011, December 29). In Philippine slums, capturing light in a bottle. National Public Radio (www.npr.org).

ORENSTEIN, P. (2003, July 6). Where have all the Lisas gone? *New York Times* (www.nytimes.com).

ORGANISATION FOR ECONOMIC CO-OPERATION AND DEVELOPMENT (2011). An overview of growing income inequalities in OECD countries: Main findings. Paris: Author (www.oecd.org/dataoecd/40/12/49170449.pdf).

ORIVE, R. (1984). Group similarity, public self-awareness, and opinion extremity: A social projection explanation of deindividuation effects. *Journal of Personality and Social Psychology, 47,* 727–737.

ORNSTEIN, R. (1991). *The evolution of consciousness: Of Darwin, Freud, and cranial fire: The origins of the way we think.* New York: Prentice Hall.

OSBORNE, J. W. (1995). Academics, self-esteem, and race: A look at the underlying assumptions of the disidentification hypothesis. *Personality and Social Psychology Bulletin, 21,* 449–455.

OSGOOD, C. E. (1962). *An alternative to war or surrender.* Urbana, IL: University of Illinois Press.

OSGOOD, C. E. (1980). GRIT: A strategy for survival in mankind's nuclear age? Paper presented at the Pugwash Conference on New Directions in Disarmament, Racine, WI.

OSKAMP, S. (1991). Curbside recycling: Knowledge, attitudes, and behavior. Paper presented at the Society for Experimental Social Psychology meeting, Columbus, OH.

OSOFSKY, M. J., BANDURA, A., & ZIMBARDO, P. G. (2005). The role of moral disengagement in the execution process. *Law and Human Behavior, 29,* 371–393.

OSTERHOUSE, R. A., & BROCK, T. C. (1970). Distraction increases yielding to propaganda by inhibiting counterarguing. *Journal of Personality and Social Psychology, 15,* 344–358.

OSTROM, T. M., & SEDIKIDES, C. (1992). Out-group homogeneity effects in natural and minimal groups. *Psychological Bulletin, 112,* 536–552.

OYSERMAN, D., COON, H. M., & KEMMELMEIER, M. (2002). Rethinking individualism and collectivism: Evaluation of theoretical assumptions and meta-analyses. *Psychological Bulletin, 128,* 3–72.

OYSERMAN, D., KEMMELMEIER, M., & COON, H. M. (2002). Cultural psychology, a new look: Reply to Bond (2002), Fiske (2002), Kitayama (2002), and Miller (2002). *Psychological Bulletin, 128,* 110–117.

PACKER, D. J. (2008). Identifying systematic disobedience in Milgram's obedience experiments: A meta-analytic review. *Perspectives on Psychological Science, 3*(4), 301–304.

PADGETT, V. R. (1989). Predicting organizational violence: An application of 11 powerful principles of obedience. Paper presented at the American Psychological Association convention.

PAGE, S. E. (2007). *The difference: How the power of diversity creates better groups, firms, schools, and societies.* Princeton, NJ: Princeton University Press.

PAGE-GOULD, E., MENDOZA-DENTON, R., ALEGRE, J. M., & SIY, J. O. (2010). Understanding the impact of cross-group friendship on interactions with novel outgroup members. *Journal of Personality and Social Psychology, 98,* 775–793.

PAGE-GOULD, E., MENDOZA-DENTON, R., & TROPP, L. R. (2008). With a little help from my cross-group friend: Reducing anxiety in intergroup contexts through cross-group friendship. *Journal of Personality and Social Psychology, 95,* 1080–1094.

PALLAK, S. R., MURRONI, E., & KOCH, J. (1983). Communicator attractiveness and expertise, emotional versus rational appeals, and persuasion: A heuristic versus systematic processing interpretation. *Social Cognition, 2,* 122–141.

PALMER, D. L. (1996). Determinants of Canadian attitudes toward immigration: More than just racism? *Canadian Journal of Behavioural Science, 28,* 180–192.

PALMER, E. L., & DORR, A. (Eds.) (1980). *Children and the faces of television: Teaching, violence, selling.* New York: Academic Press.

PALUCK, E. L. (2009). Reducing intergroup prejudice and conflict using the media: A field experiment in Rwanda. *Journal of Personality and Social Psychology, 96,* 574–587.

PANDEY, J., SINHA, Y., PRAKASH, A., & TRIPATHI, R. C. (1982). Right-left political ideologies and attribution of the causes of poverty. *European Journal of Social Psychology, 12,* 327–331.

PAOLINI, S., HEWSTONE, M., CAIRNS, E., & VOCI, A. (2004). Effects of direct and indirect cross-group friendships on judgments of Catholics and Protestants in Northern Ireland: The mediating role of an anxiety-reduction mechanism. *Personality and Social Psychology Bulletin, 30,* 770–786.

PAPASTAMOU, S., & MUGNY, G. (1990). Synchronic consistency and psychologization in minority influence. *European Journal of Social Psychology, 20,* 85–98.

PAPE, R. A. (2003, September 22). Dying to kill us. *New York Times* (www.nytimes.com).

PARASHAR, U. D., GIBSON, C. J., BRESSE, J. S., & GLASS, R. I. (2006). Rotavirus and severe childhood diarrhea. *Emerging Infectious Diseases, 12,* 304–306.

PARK, B., & ROTHBART, M. (1982). Perception of out-group homogeneity and levels of social categorization: Memory for the subordinate attributes of in-group and out-group members. *Journal of Personality and Social Psychology, 42,* 1051–1068.

PARK, J., MALACHI, E., STERNIN, O., & TEVET, R. (2009). Subtle bias against Muslim job applicants in personnel decisions. *Journal of Applied Social Psychology, 39,* 2174–2190.

PARKE, R. D., BERKOWITZ, L., LEYENS, J. P., WEST, S. G., & SEBASTIAN, J. (1977). Some effects of violent and nonviolent movies on the behavior of juvenile delinquents. In L. Berkowitz (Ed.), *Advances in experimental social psychology* (Vol. 10). New York: Academic Press.

PASCARELLA, E. T., & TERENZINI, P. T. (1991). *How college affects students: Findings and insights from twenty years of research.* San Francisco: Jossey-Bass.

PATTERSON, D. (1996). *When learned men murder.* Bloomington, IN: Phi Delta Kappa.

PATTERSON, G. R., CHAMBERLAIN, P., & REID, J. B. (1982). A comparative evaluation of parent training procedures. *Behavior Therapy, 13,* 638–650.

PATTERSON, G. R., LITTMAN, R. A., & BRICKER, W. (1967). Assertive behavior in children: A step toward a theory of aggression. *Monographs of the Society of Research in Child Development* (Serial No. 113), *32,* 5.

PATTERSON, T. E. (1980). The role of the mass media in presidential campaigns: The lessons of the 1976 election. *Items, 34,* 25–30. Social Science Research Council, 605 Third Avenue, New York, NY 10016.

PAYNE, B. K. (2001). Prejudice and perception: The role of automatic and controlled processes in misperceiving a weapon. *Journal of Personality and Social Psychology, 81,* 181–192.

PAYNE, B. K. (2006). Weapon bias: Split-second decisions and unintended stereotyping. *Current Directions in Psychological Science, 15,* 287–291.

PAYNE, B. K., KROSNICK, J. A., PASEK, J., LELKES, Y., AKHTAR, O., & TOMPSON, T. (2010). Implicit and explicit prejudice in the 2008 American presidential election. *Journal of Experimental Social Psychology, 46,* 367–374.

PEDERSEN, A., & WALKER, I. (1997). Prejudice against Australian Aborigines: Old-fashioned and modern forms. *European Journal of Social Psychology, 27,* 561–587.

PEDERSEN, W. C., BUSHMAN, B. J., VASQUEZ, E. A., & MILLER, N. (2008). Kicking the (barking) dog effect: The moderating role of target attributes on triggered displaced aggression. *Personality and Social Psychology Bulletin, 34,* 1382–1395.

PEDERSEN, W. C., GONZALES, C., & MILLER, N. (2000). The moderating effect of trivial triggering provocation on displaced aggression. *Journal of Personality and Social Psychology, 78,* 913–927.

PEGALIS, L. J., SHAFFER, D. R., BAZZINI, D. G., & GREENIER, K. (1994). On the ability to elicit self-disclosure: Are there gender-based and contextual limitations on the opener effect? *Personality and Social Psychology Bulletin, 20,* 412–420.

PELHAM, B., & CARVALLO, M. (2011). The surprising potency of implicit egotism: A reply to Simonsohn. *Journal of Personality and Social Psychology, 101,* 25–30.

PELHAM, B. W. (2009, October 22). About one in six Americans report history of depression. (www.gallup.com).

PELHAM, B. W., MIRENBERG, M. C., & JONES, J. T. (2002). Why Susie sells seashells by the seashore. Implicit egotism and major life decisions. *Journal of Personality and Social Psychology, 82,* 469–487.

PENNEBAKER, J. W., & LAY, T. C. (2002). Language use and personality during crises: Analyses of Mayor Rudolph Giuliani's press conferences. *Journal of Research in Personality, 36,* 271–282.

PENTON-VOAK, I. S., JONES, B. C., LITTLE, A. C., BAKER, S., TIDDEMAN, B., BURT, D. M., & PERRETT, D. I. (2001). Symmetry, sexual dimorphism in facial proportions and male facial attractiveness. *Proceedings of the Royal Society of London, 268,* 1–7.

PEPLAU, L. A., & FINGERHUT, A. W. (2007). The close relationships of lesbians and gay men. *Annual Review of Psychology, 58,* 405–424.

PEREIRA, C., VALA, J., & COSTA-LOPES, R. (2010). From prejudice to discrimination: The legitimizing role of perceived threat in discrimination against immigrants. *European Journal of Social Psychology, 40,* 1231–1250.

PEREIRA, J. (2003, January 10). Just how far does First Amendment protection go? *Wall Street Journal,* pp. B1, B3.

PERLS, F. S. (1973, July). *Ego, hunger and aggression: The beginning of Gestalt therapy.* Random House, 1969. Cited by Berkowitz in The case for bottling up rage. *Psychology Today,* pp. 24–30.

PERRETT, D. (2010). *In your face: The new science of human attraction.* New York: Palgrave Macmillan.

PERSICO, N., POSTLEWAITE, A., & SILVERMAN, D. (2004). The effect of adolescent experience on labor market outcomes: The case of height. *Journal of Political Economy, 112,* 1019–1053.

PESSIN, J. (1933). The comparative effects of social and mechanical stimulation on memorizing. *American Journal of Psychology, 45,* 263–270.

PESSIN, J., & HUSBAND, R. W. (1933). Effects of social stimulation on human maze learning. *Journal of Abnormal and Social Psychology, 28,* 148–154.

PETERS, E., ROMER, D., SLOVIC, P., JAMIESON, K. H., WHASFIELD, L., MERTZ, C. K., & CARPENTER, S. M. (2007). The impact and acceptability of Canadian-style cigarette warning labels among U.S. smokers and nonsmokers. *Nicotine and Tobacco Research, 9,* 473–481.

PETERSEN, J. L., & HYDE, J. S. (2010) A meta-analytic review of research on gender differences in sexuality, 1993–2007. *Psychological Bulletin, 136,* 21–38.

PETERSEN, J. L., & HYDE, J. S. (2011). Gender differences in sexual attitudes and behaviors: A review of meta-analytic results and large datasets. *Journal of Sex Research, 48,* 149–165.

PETERSON, C., SCHWARTZ, S. M., & SELIGMAN, M. E. P. (1981). Self-blame and depression symptoms. *Journal of Personality and Social Psychology, 41,* 253–259.

PETERSON, C., & STEEN, T. A. (2002). Optimistic explanatory style. In C. R. Snyder & S. J. Lopez (Eds.), *Handbook of positive psychology.* London: Oxford University Press.

PETTIGREW, T. F. (1958). Personality and socio-cultural factors in intergroup attitudes: A cross-national comparison. *Journal of Conflict Resolution, 2,* 29–42.

PETTIGREW, T. F. (1969). Racially separate or together? *Journal of Social Issues, 2,* 43–69.

PETTIGREW, T. F. (1986). The intergroup contact hypothesis reconsidered. In M. Hewstone & R. Brown (Eds.), *Contact and conflict in intergroup encounters.* Oxford: Blackwell.

PETTIGREW, T. F. (1988). Advancing racial justice: Past lessons for future use. Paper for the University of Alabama conference "Opening Doors: An appraisal of Race Relations in America."

PETTIGREW, T. F. (1997). Generalized intergroup contact effects on prejudice. *Personality and Social Psychology Bulletin, 23,* 173–185.

PETTIGREW, T. F. (2004). Intergroup contact: Theory, research, and new perspectives. In J. A. Banks & C. A. McGee Banks (Eds.), *Handbook of research on multicultural education.* San Francisco: Jossey-Bass.

PETTIGREW, T. F. (2006). A two-level approach to anti-immigrant prejudice and discrimination. In R. Mahalingam (Ed.), *Cultural psychology of immigrants.* Mahwah, NJ: Erlbaum.

PETTIGREW, T. F., JACKSON, J. S., BRIKA, J. B., LEMAINE, G., MEERTENS, R. W., WAGNER, U., & ZICK, A. (1998). Outgroup prejudice in western Europe. *European Review of Social Psychology, 8,* 241–273.

PETTIGREW, T. F., & TROPP, L. R. (2000). Does intergroup contact reduce prejudice? Recent meta-analytic findings. In S. Oskamp (Ed.), *Reducing prejudice and discrimination* (pp. 93–114). Mahwah, NJ: Erlbaum.

PETTIGREW, T. F., & TROPP, L. R. (2008). How does intergroup contact reduce prejudice? Meta-analytic tests of three mediators. *European Journal of Social Psychology, 38,* 922–934.

PETTIGREW, T. F., & TROPP, L. R. (2011). *When groups meet: The dynamics of intergroup contact.* New York: Psychology Press.

PETTIGREW, T. F., WAGNER, U., & CHRIST, O. (2008). Who opposes immigration? Comparing German with North American findings. *DuBois Review, 4,* 19–40.

PETTIGREW, T. F., WAGNER, U., & CHRIST, O. (2010). Population ratios and prejudice: Modeling both contact and threat effects. *Journal of Ethnic and Migration Studies, 36,* 635–650.

PETTY, R. E., & BRINOL, P. (2008). Persuasion: From single to multiple to metacognitive processes. *Perspectives on Psychological Science, 3,* 137–147.

PETTY, R. E., & CACIOPPO, J. T. (1986). *Communication and persuasion: Central and peripheral routes to attitude change.* New York: Springer-Verlag.

PETTY, R. E., CACIOPPO, J. T., & GOLDMAN, R. (1981). Personal involvement as a determinant of argument-based persuasion. *Journal of Personality and Social Psychology, 41,* 847–855.

PETTY, R. E., CACIOPPO, J. T., STRATHMAN, A. J., PRIESTER, J. R., BROCK, T. C., & GREEN, M. C. (2005). To think or not to think. In T. C. Brock & M. C. Greene (Eds.), *Persuasion: Psychological insights and perspectives,* 2nd ed. Thousand Oaks, Calif.: Sage.

PETTY, R. E., SCHUMANN, D. W., RICHMAN, S. A., & STRATHMAN, A. J. (1993). Positive mood and persuasion: Different roles for affect under high and low elaboration conditions. *Journal of Personality and Social Psychology, 64,* 5–20.

PEW RESEARCH CENTER (2000, May 10). Tracking online life: How women use the Internet to cultivate relationships with family and friends. Washington, DC: Pew Internet and American Life Project.

PEW RESEARCH CENTER (2006, February 13). Not looking for love: Romance in America. Pew Internet and American Life Project (pewresearch.org).

PEW RESEARCH CENTER (2006, March 30). America's immigration quandary. Pew Research Center (www.people-press.org).

PEW RESEARCH CENTER (2006, July 12). Little consensus on global warming: Partisanship drives opinion. Pew Research Center (people-press.org).

PEW RESEARCH CENTER (2007a, May 22). *Muslim Americans: Middle class and mostly mainstream* (www.pewresearch.org).

PEW RESEARCH CENTER (2007b, July 18). Modern marriage: "I like hugs. I like kisses. But what I really love is help with the dishes." Pew Research Center (pewresearch.org).

PEW RESEARCH CENTER (2008). *Video Gamers Galore.* Retrieved from pewresearch.org/databank/dailynumber/?NumberID=787, June 5, 2009.

PEW RESEARCH CENTER (2010a, July 10). *Gender equality universally embraced, but inequalities acknowledged.* Pew Research Center (www.pewresearch.org).

PEW RESEARCH CENTER (2010b, August 19). *Growing number of Americans say Obama is a Muslim.* Pew Research Center (www.pewresearch.org).

PEW RESEARCH CENTER (2011a, January 27). *The future of the global Muslim population: Projections for 2010–2030* (www.pewforum.org).

PEW RESEARCH CENTER (2011b, July 21). *Muslim-Western tensions persist: Common concerns about Islamic extremism.* Pew Global Attitudes Project (www.pewresearch.org).

PEW RESEARCH CENTER (2011c, December 1). *Modest rise in number saying there is "solid evidence" of global warming* (www.pewresearch.org).

PEW RESEARCH CENTER (2012, October 15). More say there is solid evidence of global warming. Pew Research Center for the People & the Press (www.people-press.org).

PHELAN, J. E., & RUDMAN, L. A. (2010). Reactions to ethnic deviance: The role of backlash in racial stereotype maintenance. *Journal of Personality and Social Psychology, 99,* 265–281.

PHILLIPS, A. L. (2011). A walk in the woods. *American Scientist, 69,* 301–302.

PHILLIPS, D. L. (2003, September 20). Listening to the wrong Iraqi. *New York Times* (www.nytimes.com).

PICKETT, K., & WILKINSON, R. (2011). *The spirit level: Why greater equality makes societies stronger.* New York: Bloomsbury.

PINCUS, J. H. (2001). *Base instincts: What makes killers kill?* New York: Norton.

PINKER, S. (1997). *How the mind works.* New York: Norton.

PINKER, S. (2002). *The blank slate.* New York: Viking.

PINKER, S. (2008). *The sexual paradox: Men, women, and the real gender gap.* New York: Scribner.

PINKER, S. (2011, September 27). A history of violence. *The Edge* (www.edge.org).

PIPHER, M. (2002). *The middle of everywhere: The world's refugees come to our town.* Harcourt.

PLACE, S. S., TODD, P. M., PENKE, L., & ASENDORPF, J. B. (2009). The ability to judge the romantic interest of others. *Psychological Science, 20,* 22–26.

PLAKS, J. E., & HIGGINS, E. T. (2000). Pragmatic use of stereotyping in teamwork: Social loafing and compensation as a function of inferred partner-situation fit. *Journal of Personality and Social Psychology, 79,* 962–974.

PLANT, E. A., GOPLEN, J., & KUNSTMAN, J. W. (2011). Selective responses to threat: The roles of race and gender in decisions to shoot. *Personality and Social Psychology, 37,* 1274–1281.

PLAUT, V. C., ADAMS, G., & ANDERSON, S. L. (2009). Does attractiveness buy happiness? "It depends on where you're from." *Personal Relationships, 16,* 619–630.

PLAUT, V. C., MARKUS, H. R., & LACHMAN, M. E. (2002). Place matters: Consensual features and regional variation in American wellbeing and self. *Journal of Personality and Social Psychology,* **83,** 160–184.

POLK, M., & SCHUSTER, A. M. H. (2005). *The looting of the Iraq museum, Baghdad: The lost legacy of ancient Mesopotamia.* New York: Harry N. Abrams.

PONIEWOZIK, J. (2003, November 24). All the news that fits your reality. *Time,* p. 90.

POPENOE, D. (2002). The top ten myths of divorce. Unpublished manuscript, National Marriage Project, Rutgers University.

POST, J. M. (2005). The new face of terrorism: Socio-cultural foundations of contemporary terrorism. *Behavioral Sciences and the Law,* **23,** 451–465.

POSTMES, T., & SPEARS, R. (1998). Deindividuation and antinormative behavior: A meta-analysis. *Psychological Bulletin,* **123,** 238–259.

PRATKANIS, A. R., GREENWALD, A. G., LEIPPE, M. R., & BAUMGARDNER, M. H. (1988). In search of reliable persuasion effects: III. The sleeper effect is dead. Long live the sleeper effect. *Journal of Personality and Social Psychology,* **54,** 203–218.

PRATTO, F. (1996). Sexual politics: The gender gap in the bedroom, the cupboard, and the cabinet. In D. M. Buss & N. M. Malamuth (Eds.), *Sex, power, conflict: Evolutionary and feminist perspectives.* New York: Oxford University Press.

PRATTO, F., STALLWORTH, L. M., & SIDANIUS, J. (1997). The gender gap: Differences in political attitudes and social dominance orientation. *British Journal of Social Psychology,* **36,** 49–68.

PRENTICE, D. A., & CARRANZA, E. (2002). What women and men should be, shouldn't be, are allowed to be, and don't have to be: The contents of prescriptive gender stereotypes. *Psychology of Women Quarterly,* **26,** 269–281.

PRENTICE-DUNN, S., & ROGERS, R. W. (1980). Effects of deindividuating situational cues and aggressive models on subjective deindividuation and aggression. *Journal of Personality and Social Psychology,* **39,** 104–113.

PRENTICE-DUNN, S., & ROGERS, R. W. (1989). Deindividuation and the self-regulation of behavior. In P. B. Paulus (Ed.), *Psychology of group influence,* 2nd edition. Hillsdale, NJ: Erlbaum.

PRESSON, P. K., & BENASSI, V. A. (1996). Illusion of control: A meta-analytic review. *Journal of Social Behavior and Personality,* **11,** 493–510.

PRICE, G. H., DABBS, J. M., JR., CLOWER, B. J., & RESIN, R. P. (1974). At first glance—Or, is physical attractiveness more than skin deep? Paper presented at the Eastern Psychological Association convention. Cited by K. L. Dion & K. K. Dion (1979). Personality and behavioral correlates of romantic love. In M. Cook & G. Wilson (Eds.), *Love and attraction.* Oxford: Pergamon.

PRITCHARD, I. L. (1998). The effects of rap music on aggressive attitudes toward women. Master's thesis, Humboldt State University.

PROHASKA, V. (1994). "I know I'll get an A": Confident overestimation of final course grades. *Teaching of Psychology,* **21,** 141–143.

PRONIN, E., LIN, D. Y., & ROSS, L. (2002). The bias blind spot: Perceptions of bias in self versus others. *Personality and Social Psychology Bulletin,* **28,** 369–381.

PRONIN, E., & ROSS, L. (2006). Temporal differences in trait self-ascription: When the self is seen as an other. *Journal of Personality and Social Psychology,* **90,** 197–209.

PRUITT, D. G. (1986). Achieving integrative agreements in negotiation. In R. K. White (Ed.), *Psychology and the prevention of nuclear war.* New York: New York University Press.

PRUITT, D. G. (1998). Social conflict. In D. Gilbert, S. T. Fiske, & G. Lindzey (Eds.), *Handbook of social psychology,* 4th edition. New York: McGraw-Hill.

PRUITT, D. G., & KIMMEL, M. J. (1977). Twenty years of experimental gaming: Critique, synthesis, and suggestions for the future. *Annual Review of Psychology,* **28,** 363–392.

PRUITT, D. G., & LEWIS, S. A. (1975). Development of integrative solutions in bilateral negotiation. *Journal of Personality and Social Psychology,* **31,** 621–633.

PRUITT, D. G., & LEWIS, S. A. (1977). The psychology of integrative bargaining. In D. Druckman (Ed.), *Negotiations: A social-psychological analysis.* New York: Halsted.

PRYOR, J. H., EAGAN, K., BLAKE, L. P., BURTADO, S., BERDAN, J., & CASE, M. H. (2012). *The American freshman: National norms fall 2012.* Los Angeles: Higher Education Institute, UCLA.

PRYOR, J. H., HURTADO, S., DEANGELO, L., BLAKE, L. P., & TRAN, S. (2010). *The American freshman: National norms fall 2010.* Los Angeles: Higher Education Research Institute, UCLA.

PRYOR, J. H., HURTADO, S., SAENZ, V. B., LINDHOLM, J. A., KORN, W. S., & MAHONEY, K. M. (2005). *The American freshman: National norms for Fall 2005.* Los Angeles: Higher Education Research Institute, UCLA.

PRYOR, J. H., HURTADO, S., SHARKNESS, J., & KORN, W. S. (2007). *The American freshman: National norms for Fall 2007.* Los Angeles: Higher Education Research Institute, UCLA.

PRZYBYLSKI, A. K., RIGBY, C. S., & RYAN, R. M. (2010). A motivational model of video game engagement. *Review of General Psychology,* **14,** 154–166.

PTC (2007, January 10). *Dying to entertain: Violence on prime time broadcast TV, 1998 to 2006.* Parents Television Council (www.parentstv.org).

PUBLIC OPINION (1984, August/September). *Vanity Fair,* p. 22.

PUHL, R. M., & HEUER, C. A. (2009). The stigma of obesity: A review and update. *Obesity,* **17,** 941–964.

PUHL, R. M., & HEUER, C. A. (2010). Obesity stigma: Important considerations for public health. *American Journal of Public Health,* **100,** 1019–1028.

PURVIS, J. A., DABBS, J. M., JR., & HOPPER, C. H. (1984). The "opener": Skilled user of facial expression and speech pattern. *Personality and Social Psychology Bulletin,* **10,** 61–66.

PUTNAM, R. (2000). *Bowling alone.* New York: Simon & Schuster.

PUTNAM, R. (2006, July 3). You gotta have friends: A study finds that Americans are getting lonelier. *Time,* p. 36.

PYSZCZYNSKI, T., ABDOLLAHI, A., SOLOMON, S., GREENBERG, J., COHEN, F., & WEISE, D. (2006). Mortality salience, martyrdom, and military might: The great Satan versus the axis of evil. *Personality and Social Psychology Bulletin,* **32,** 525–537.

PYSZCZYNSKI, T., HAMILTON, J. C., GREENBERG, J., & BECKER, S. E. (1991). Self-awareness and psychological dysfunction. In C. R. Snyder & D. O. Forsyth (Eds.), *Handbook of social and clinical psychology: The health perspective.* New York: Pergamon.

QIRKO, H. N. (2004). "Fictive kin" and suicide terrorism. *Science,* **304,** 49–50.

QUARTZ, S. R., & SEJNOWSKI, T. J. (2002). *Liars, lovers, and heroes: What the new brain science reveals about how we become who we are.* New York: Morrow.

QUOIDBACH, J., DUNN, E., PETRIDES, K., & MIKOLAJCZAK, M. (2010). Money giveth, money taketh away: The dual effect of wealth on happiness. *Psychological Science,* **21,** 759–763.

RAINE, A. (2005). The interaction of biological and social measures in the explanation of antisocial and violent behavior. In D. M. Stoff & E. J. Susman (Eds.), *Developmental psychobiology of aggression.* New York: Cambridge University Press.

RAINE, A. (2008). From genes to brain to antisocial behavior. *Current Directions in Psychological Science,* **17,** 323–328.

RAINE, A., LENCZ, T., BIHRLE, S., LACASSE, L., & COLLETTI, P. (2000). Reduced prefrontal gray matter volume and reduced autonomic activity in antisocial personality disorder. *Archives of General Psychiatry,* **57,** 119–127.

RAINE, A., STODDARD, J., BIHRLE, S., & BUCHSBAUM, M. (1998). Prefrontal glucose deficits in murderers lacking psychosocial deprivation. *Neuropsychiatry, Neuropsychology, & Behavioral Neurology,* **11,** 1–7.

RAJECKI, D. W., BLEDSOE, S. B., & RASMUSSEN, J. L. (1991). Successful personal ads: Gender differences and similarities in offers, stipulations, and outcomes. *Basic and Applied Social Psychology,* **12,** 457–469.

RAMIREZ, J. M., BONNIOT-CABANAC, M-C., & CABANAC, M. (2005). Can aggression provide pleasure? *European Psychologist,* **10,** 136–145.

RANDLER, C., & KRETZ, S. (2011). Assortative mating in morningness-eveningness. *International Journal of Psychology,* **46,** 91–96.

RANK, S. G., & JACOBSON, C. K. (1977). Hospital nurses' compliance with medication overdose orders: A failure to replicate. *Journal of Health and Social Behavior,* **18,** 188–193.

RAPOPORT, A. (1960). *Fights, games, and debates.* Ann Arbor: University of Michigan Press.

RAY, D. G., MACKIE, D. M., RYDELL, R. J., & SMITH, E. R. (2008). Changing categorization of self can change emotions about outgroups. *Journal of Experimental Social Psychology,* **44,** 1210–1213.

REARDON, S. (2011). Antismoking drive tries cigarettes ads, in reverse. *Science,* **333,** 33–34.

REED, D. (1989, November 25). Video collection documents Christian resistance to Hitler. Associated Press release in *Grand Rapids Press,* pp. B4, B5.

REGAN, D. T., & CHENG, J. B. (1973). Distraction and attitude change: A resolution. *Journal of Experimental Social Psychology,* **9,** 138–147.

REICHER, S., SPEARS, R., & POSTMES, T. (1995). A social identity model of deindividuation phenomena. In W. Storebe & M. Hewstone (Eds.), *European review of social psychology* (Vol. 6). Chichester, England: Wiley.

REIJNTJES, A., THOMAES, S., KAMPHUIS, J. H., BUSHMAN, B. J., DE CASTRO, B. O., & TELCH, M. J. (2011). Explaining the paradoxical rejection–aggression link: The mediating effects of hostile intent attributions, anger, and decreases in state self-esteem on peer rejection-induced aggression on youth. *Personality and Social Psychology Bulletin,* **37,** 955–963.

REINER, W. G., & GEARHART, J. P. (2004). Discordant sexual identity in some genetic males with cloacal exstrophy assigned to female sex at birth. *New England Journal of Medicine, 350,* 333–341.

REIS, H. T., & ARON, A. (2008). Love: Why is it, why does it matter, and how does it operate? *Perspectives on Psychological Science, 3,* 80–86.

REIS, H. T., MANIACI, M. R., CAPRARIELLO, P. A., EASTWICK, P. W., & FINKEL, E. J. (2011). Familiarity does indeed promote attraction in live interaction. *Journal of Personality and Social Psychology, 101,* 557–570.

REIS, H. T., NEZLEK, J., & WHEELER, L. (1980). Physical attractiveness in social interaction. *Journal of Personality and Social Psychology, 38,* 604–617.

REIS, H. T., & SHAVER, P. (1988). Intimacy as an interpersonal process. In S. Duck (Ed.), *Handbook of personal relationships: Theory, relationships and interventions.* Chichester, England: Wiley.

REIS, H. T., SMITH, S. M., CARMICHAEL, C. L., CAPRARIELLO, P. A., TSA, F.-F., RODRIGUES, A., & MANIACI, M. R. (2010). Are you happy for me? How sharing positive events with others provides personal and interpersonal benefits. *Journal of Personality and Social Psychology, 99,* 311–329.

REIS, H. T., WHEELER, L., SPIEGEL, N., KERNIS, M. H., NEZLEK, J., & PERRI, M. (1982). Physical attractiveness in social interaction: II. Why does appearance affect social experience? *Journal of Personality and Social Psychology, 43,* 979–996.

RENAUD, H., & ESTESS, F. (1961). Life history interviews with one hundred normal American males: "Pathogenecity" of childhood. *American Journal of Orthopsychiatry, 31,* 786–802.

RENNER, M. (1999). *Ending violent conflict.* Worldwatch Paper **146,** Worldwatch Institute.

RESSLER, R. K., BURGESS, A. W., & DOUGLAS, J. E. (1988). *Sexual homicide patterns.* Boston: Lexington Books.

REYNOLDS, J., STEWART, M., MACDONALD, R., & SISCHO, L. (2006). Have adolescents become too ambitious? High school seniors' educational and occupational plans, 1976 to 2000. *Social Problems, 53,* 186–206.

RHODES, G. (2006). The evolutionary psychology of facial beauty. *Annual Review of Psychology, 57,* 199–226.

RHODES, G., SUMICH, A., & BYATT, G. (1999). Are average facial configurations attractive only because of their symmetry? *Psychological Science, 10,* 52–58.

RHODEWALT, F., & AGUSTSDOTTIR, S. (1986). Effects of self-presentation on the phenomenal self. *Journal of Personality and Social Psychology, 50,* 47–55.

RHOLES, W. S., NEWMAN, L. S., & RUBLE, D. N. (1990). Understanding self and other: Developmental and motivational aspects of perceiving persons in terms of invariant dispositions. In E. T. Higgins & R. M. Sorrentino (Eds.), *Handbook of motivation and cognition: Foundations of social behavior* (Vol. 2). New York: Guilford.

RICE, B. (1985, September). Performance review: The job nobody likes. *Psychology Today,* pp. 30–36.

RICHARD, F. D., BOND, C. F., JR., & STOKES-ZOOTA, J. J. (2003). One hundred years of social psychology quantitatively described. *Review of General Psychology, 7,* 331–363.

RICHARDS, Z., & HEWSTONE, M. (2001). Subtyping and subgrouping: Processes for the prevention and promotion of stereotype change. *Personality and Social Psychology Review, 5,* 52–73.

RICHARDSON, B. B. (2005, Spring–Summer). A conversation with Judith Lichtman, a.k.a. "the 101st Senator." ABA/YLD Women in the Profession Committee newsletter.

RICHARDSON, D. S. (2005). The myth of female passivity: Thirty years of revelations about female aggression. *Psychology of Women Quarterly, 29,* 238–247.

RICHARDSON, J. D., HUDDY, W. P., & MORGAN, S. M. (2008). The hostile media effect, biased assimilation, and perceptions of a presidential debate. *Journal of Applied Social Psychology, 38,* 1255–1270.

RICHARDSON, L. F. (1960). Generalized foreign policy. *British Journal of Psychology Monographs Supplements, 23.* Cited by A. Rapoport in *Fights, games, and debates* (p. 15). Ann Arbor: University of Michigan Press.

RICHTEL, M. (2007, June 2). For pornographers, Internet's virtues turn to vices. *New York Times* (www.nytimes.com).

RIORDAN, C. A. (1980). Effects of admission of influence on attributions and attraction. Paper presented at the American Psychological Association convention.

RISEN, J. L., & CRITCHER, C. R. (2011). Visceral fit: While in a visceral state, associated states of the world seem more likely. *Journal of Personality and Social Psychology, 100,* 777–793.

RISEN, J. L., GILOVICH, T., & DUNNING, D. (2007). One-shot illusory correlations and stereotype formation. *Personality and Social Psychology Bulletin, 33,* 1492–1502.

RIVA, P., WIRTH, J. H., & WILLIAMS, K. D. (2011). The consequences of pain: The social and physical overlap on psychological responses. *European Journal of Social Psychology, 41,* 681–687.

ROBBERSON, M. R., & ROGERS, R. W. (1988). Beyond fear appeals: Negative and positive persuasive appeals to health and self-esteem. *Journal of Applied Social Psychology, 18,* 277–287.

ROBERTSON, I. (1987). *Sociology*. New York: Worth Publishers.

ROBINS, R. W., & BEER, J. S. (2001). Positive illusions about the self: Short-term benefits and long-term costs. *Journal of Personality and Social Psychology, 80*, 340–352.

ROBINSON, J. (2002, October 8). What percentage of the population is gay? *Gallup Tuesday Briefing* (www.gallup.com).

ROBINSON, J. P., & MARTIN, S. (2009). Changes in American daily life: 1965–2005. *Social Indicators Research, 93*, 47–56.

ROBINSON, M. D., & RYFF, C. D. (1999). The role of self-deception in perceptions of past, present, and future happiness. *Personality and Social Psychology Bulletin, 25*, 595–606.

ROBINSON, M. S., & ALLOY, L. B. (2003). Negative cognitive styles and stress-reactive rumination interact to predict depression: A prospective study. *Cognitive Therapy and Research, 27*, 275–291.

ROBINSON, T. N., WILDE, M. L., NAVRACRUZ, L. C., HAYDEL, F., & VARADY, A. (2001). Effects of reducing children's television and video game use on aggressive behavior. *Archives of Pediatric and Adolescent Medicine, 155*, 17–23.

ROCHAT, F. (1993). How did they resist authority? Protecting refugees in Le Chambon during World War II. Paper presented at the American Psychological Association convention.

ROCHAT, F., & MODIGLIANI, A. (1995). The ordinary quality of resistance: From Milgram's laboratory to the village of Le Chambon. *Journal of Social Issues, 51*, 195–210.

ROEHLING, M. V., ROEHLING, P. V., & ODLAND, I. M. (2008). Investigating the validity of stereotypes about overweight employees. *Group and Organization Management, 23*, 392–424.

ROEHLING, P. V., ROEHLING, M. V., JOHNSTON, A., BRENNAN, A., & DREW, A. (2010). Weighty decisions: The effect of weight bias on the selection and election of U.S. political candidates. Unpublished manuscript, Hope College.

ROEHLING, P. V., ROEHLING, M. V., VANDLEN, J. D., BLAZEK, J., & GUY, W. C. (2009). Weight discrimination and the glass ceiling effect among top U.S. male and female CEOs. *Equal Opportunities International, 28*, 179–196.

ROGERS, C. R. (1980). *A way of being*. Boston: Houghton Mifflin.

ROGERS, R. W., & PRENTICE-DUNN, S. (1981). Deindividuation and anger-mediated interracial aggression: Unmasking regressive racism. *Journal of Personality and Social Psychology, 41*, 63–73.

ROKEACH, M., & MEZEI, L. (1966). Race and shared beliefs as factors in social choice. *Science, 151*, 167–172.

RONEY, J. R. (2003). Effects of visual exposure to the opposite sex: Cognitive aspects of mate attraction in human males. *Personality and Social Psychology Bulletin, 29*, 393–404.

ROOK, K. S. (1984). Promoting social bonding: Strategies for helping the lonely and socially isolated. *American Psychologist, 39*, 1389–1407.

ROOTH, D-O. (2007). Implicit discrimination in hiring: Real-world evidence. IZA Discussion Paper No. 2764, University of Kalmar, Institute for the Study of Labor (IZA).

ROSE, A. J., & RUDOLPH, K. D. (2006). A review of sex differences in peer relationship processes: Potential trade-offs for the emotional and behavioral development of girls and boys. *Psychological Bulletin, 132*, 98–131.

ROSENHAN, D. L. (1973). On being sane in insane places. *Science, 179*, 250–258.

ROSENTHAL, E. (2008, July 15). Britons shine a light on energy use at home. *New York Times* (www.nytimes.com).

ROSENTHAL, E. (2010, May 24). Climate fears turn to doubts among Britons. *New York Times* (www.nytimes.com).

ROSENTHAL, E. (2011a, June 26). Europe stifles drivers in favor of alternatives. *New York Times* (www.nytimes.com).

ROSENTHAL, E. (2011b, August 10). In auto test in Europe, meter ticks off miles, and fee to driver. *New York Times* (www.nytimes.com).

ROSENTHAL, E. (2011c, October 15). Where did global warming go? *New York Times* (www.nytimes.com).

ROSENTHAL, R. (1985). From unconscious experimenter bias to teacher expectancy effects. In J. B. Dusek, V. C. Hall, & W. J. Meyer (Eds.), *Teacher expectancies*. Hillsdale, NJ: Erlbaum.

ROSENTHAL, R. (1991). Teacher expectancy effects: A brief update 25 years after the Pygmalion experiment. *Journal of Research in Education, 1*, 3–12.

ROSENTHAL, R. (2002). Covert communication in classrooms, clinics, courtrooms, and cubicles. *American Psychologist, 57*, 839–849.

ROSENTHAL, R. (2003). Covert communication in laboratories, classrooms, and the truly real world. *Current Directions in Psychological Science, 12*, 151–154.

ROSENTHAL, R. (2006). Applying psychological research on interpersonal expectations and covert communication in classrooms, clinics, corporations, and courtrooms. In S. I. Donaldson, D. E. Berger, & K. Pezdek (Eds.), *Applied psychology: New frontiers and rewarding careers*. Mahwah, NJ: Erlbaum.

Rosenthal, R. (2008). Introduction, methods, results, discussion: The story of a career. In R. Levin, A. Rodriques, & L. Zelezny (Eds.), *Journeys in social psychology: Looking back to inspire the future*. New York: Psychology Press.

Rosenzweig, M. R. (1972). Cognitive dissonance. *American Psychologist, 27,* 769.

Ross, L. (1977). The intuitive psychologist and his shortcomings: Distortions in the attribution process. In L. Berkowitz (Ed.), *Advances in experimental social psychology* (Vol. 10). New York: Academic Press.

Ross, L. (1981). The "intuitive scientist" formulation and its developmental implications. In J. H. Havell & L. Ross (Eds.), *Social cognitive development: Frontiers and possible futures*. Cambridge, England: Cambridge University Press.

Ross, L. (1988). Situationist perspectives on the obedience experiments. Review of A. G. Miller's *The obedience experiments. Contemporary Psychology, 33,* 101–104.

Ross, L., Amabile, T. M., & Steinmetz, J. L. (1977). Social roles, social control, and biases in social-perception processes. *Journal of Personality and Social Psychology, 35,* 485–494.

Ross, L., & Ward, A. (1995). Psychological barriers to dispute resolution. In M. P. Zanna (Ed.), *Advances in experimental social psychology* (Vol. 27). San Diego: Academic Press.

Ross, M., McFarland, C., & Fletcher, G. J. O. (1981). The effect of attitude on the recall of personal histories. *Journal of Personality and Social Psychology, 40,* 627–634.

Ross, M., & Sicoly, F. (1979). Egocentric biases in availability and attribution. *Journal of Personality and Social Psychology, 37,* 322–336.

Rossi, A. S., & Rossi, P. H. (1990). *Of human bonding: Parent-child relations across the life course*. Hawthorne, NY: Aldine de Gruyter.

Roszell, P., Kennedy, D., & Grabb, E. (1990). Physical attractiveness and income attainment among Canadians. *Journal of Psychology, 123,* 547–559.

Rothbart, M., & Birrell, P. (1977). Attitude and perception of faces. *Journal of Research Personality, 11,* 209–215.

Rothbart, M., & Taylor, M. (1992). Social categories and social reality. In G. R. Semin & K. Fielder (Eds.), *Language, interaction and social cognition*. London: Sage.

Rothblum, E. D. (2007). Same-sex couples in legalized relationships: I do, or do I? Unpublished manuscript, Women's Studies Department, San Diego State University.

Rotter, J. (1973). Internal-external locus of control scale. In J. P. Robinson & R. P. Shaver (Eds.), *Measures of social psychological attitudes*. Ann Arbor: Institute for Social Research.

Rotton, J., & Cohn, E. G. (2004). Outdoor temperature, climate control, and criminal assault: The spatial and temporal ecology of violence. *Environment and Behavior, 36,* 276–306.

Roy, M. M., Christenfeld, N. J. S., & McKenzie, C. R. M. (2005). Underestimating the duration of future events: Memory incorrectly used or memory bias? *Psychological Bulletin, 131,* 738–756.

Royal Society (2010, September). *Climate change: A summary of the science*. London: The Royal Society.

Ruback, R. B., Carr, T. S., & Hoper, C. H. (1986). Perceived control in prison: Its relation to reported crowding, stress, and symptoms. *Journal of Applied Social Psychology, 16,* 375–386.

Rubin, J. Z. (1986). Can we negotiate with terrorists: Some answers from psychology. Paper presented at the American Psychological Association convention.

Rubin, L. B. (1985). *Just friends: The role of friendship in our lives*. New York: Harper & Row.

Rubin, Z. (1973). *Liking and loving: An invitation to social psychology*. New York: Holt, Rinehart & Winston.

Ruiter, R. A. C., Abraham, C., & Kok, G. (2001). Scary warnings and rational precautions: A review of the psychology of fear appeals. *Psychology and Health, 16,* 613–630.

Ruiter, S., & De Graaf, N. D. (2006). National context, religiosity, and volunteering: Results from 53 countries. *American Sociological Review, 71,* 191–210.

Rule, B. G., Taylor, B. R., & Dobbs, A. R. (1987). Priming effects of heat on aggressive thoughts. *Social Cognition, 5,* 131–143.

Rule, N. O., Rosen, K. S., Slepian, M. L., & Ambady, N. (2011). Mating interest improves women's accuracy in judging male sexual orientation. *Psychological Science, 22,* 881–886.

Rupp, H. A., & Wallen, K. (2008). Sex differences in response to visual sexual stimuli: A review. *Archives of Sexual Behavior, 37,* 206–218.

Rusbult, C. E., Johnson, D. J., & Morrow, G. D. (1986). Impact of couple patterns of problem solving on distress and nondistress in dating relationships. *Journal of Personality and Social Psychology, 50,* 744–753.

Rusbult, C. E., Martz, J. M., & Agnew, C. R. (1998). The investment model scale: Measuring commitment level, satisfaction level, quality of alternatives, and investment size. *Personal Relationships, 5,* 357–391.

RUSBULT, C. E., MORROW, G. D., & JOHNSON, D. J. (1987). Self-esteem and problem-solving behaviour in close relationships. *British Journal of Social Psychology, 26*, 293–303.

RUSSELL, B. (1930/1980). *The conquest of happiness.* London: Unwin Paperbacks.

RUSSELL, G. W. (1983). Psychological issues in sports aggression. In J. H. Goldstein (Ed.), *Sports violence.* New York: Springer-Verlag.

RUSSELL, N. J. C. (2011). Milgram's obedience to authority experiments: Origins and early evolution. *British Journal of Social Psychology, 50*, 140–162.

RYAN, R. (1999, February 2). Quoted by A. Kohn, In pursuit of affluence, at a high price. *New York Times* (www.nytimes.com).

RYDELL, R. J., RYDELL, M. T., & BOUCHER, K. L. (2010). The effect of negative performance stereotypes on learning. *Journal of Personality and Social Psychology, 99*, 883–896.

SAAD, L. (2002, November 21). Most smokers wish they could quit. Gallup News Service (www.gallup.com/poll/releases/pr021121.asp).

SABINI, J., & SILVER, M. (1982). *Moralities of everyday life.* New York: Oxford University Press.

SACERDOTE, B., & MARMAROS, D. (2005). How do friendships form? NBER Working Paper No. 11530 (www.nber.org/papers/W11530).

SACHS, J. D. (2006, July). Ecology and political upheaval. *Scientific American, 291*, 37.

SACK, K., & ELDER, J. (2000, July 11). Poll finds optimistic outlook but enduring racial division. *New York Times* (www.nytimes.com).

SACKS, C. H., & BUGENTAL, D. P. (1987). Attributions as moderators of affective and behavioral responses to social failure. *Journal of Personality and Social Psychology, 53*, 939–947.

SAFER, M. A., BONANNO, G. A., & FIELD, N. P. (2001). It was never that bad: Biased recall of grief and long-term adjustment to the death of a spouse. *Memory, 9*, 195–204.

SAGARIN, B. J., RHOADS, K. V. L., & CIALDINI, R. B. (1998). Deceiver's distrust: Denigration as a consequence of undiscovered deception. *Personality and Social Psychology Bulletin, 24*, 1167–1176.

SAID, C. P., & TODOROV, A. (2011). A statistical model of facial attractiveness. *Psychological Science, 22*, 1183–1190.

SAKS, M. J. (1974). Ignorance of science is no excuse. *Trial, 10*(6), 18–20.

SALES, S. M. (1972). Economic threat as a determinant of conversion rates in authoritarian and nonauthoritarian churches. *Journal of Personality and Social Psychology, 23*, 420–428.

SALES, S. M. (1973). Threat as a factor in authoritarianism: An analysis of archival data. *Journal of Personality & Social Psychology, 28*, 44–57.

SALGANIK, M. J., DODDS, P. S., & WATTS, D. J. (2006). Experimental study of inequality and unpredictability in an artificial cultural market. *Science, 311*, 854–856.

SALMELA-ARO, K., & NURMI, J-E. (2007). Self-esteem during university studies predicts career characteristics 10 years later. *Journal of Vocational Behavior, 70*, 463–477.

SALMIVALLI, C. (2009). Bullying and the peer group: A review. *Aggression and Violent Behavior, 15*, 112–120.

SANDE, G. N., GOETHALS, G. R., & RADLOFF, C. E. (1988). Perceiving one's own traits and others': The multifaceted self. *Journal of Personality and Social Psychology, 54*, 13–20.

SANDERS, G. S. (1981a). Driven by distraction: An integrative review of social facilitation and theory and research. *Journal of Experimental Social Psychology, 17*, 227–251.

SANDERS, G. S. (1981b). Toward a comprehensive account of social facilitation: Distraction/conflict does not mean theoretical conflict. *Journal of Experimental Social Psychology, 17*, 262–265.

SANDERS, G. S., BARON, R. S., & MOORE, D. L. (1978). Distraction and social comparison as mediators of social facilitation effects. *Journal of Experimental Social Psychology, 14*, 291–303.

SANI, F., HERRERA, M., & BOWE, M. (2009). Perceived collective continuity and ingroup identification as defence against death awareness. *Journal of Experimental Social Psychology, 45*, 242–245.

SANISLOW, C. A., III, PERKINS, D. V., & BALOGH, D. W. (1989). Mood induction, interpersonal perceptions, and rejection in the roommates of depressed, nondepressed-disturbed, and normal college students. *Journal of Social and Clinical Psychology, 8*, 345–358.

SANITIOSO, R., KUNDA, Z., & FONG, G. T. (1990). Motivated recruitment of autobiographical memories. *Journal of Personality and Social Psychology, 59*, 229–241.

SANTOS, A., MEYER-LINDENBERG, A., & DERUELLE, C. (2010). Absence of racial, but not gender, stereotyping in Williams syndrome children. *Current Biology, 20*, R307–R308.

SAPADIN, L. A. (1988). Friendship and gender: Perspectives of professional men and women. *Journal of Social and Personal Relationships, 5*, 387–403.

SARNOFF, I., & SARNOFF, S. (1989). *Love-centered marriage in a self-centered world.* New York: Schocken Books.

SASAKI, J. Y., & KIM, H. S. (2011). At the intersection of culture and religion: A cultural analysis of religion's implications for secondary control and social affiliation. *Journal of Personality and Social Psychology, 101,* 401–414.

SASSENBERG, K., MOSKOWITZ, G. B., JACOBY, J., & HANSEN, N. (2007). The carry-over effect of competition: The impact of competition on prejudice towards uninvolved outgroups. *Journal of Experimental Social Psychology, 43,* 529–538.

SATO, K. (1987). Distribution of the cost of maintaining common resources. *Journal of Experimental Social Psychology, 23,* 19–31.

SAUCIER, D. A., & MILLER, C. T. (2003). The persuasiveness of racial arguments as a subtle measure of racism. *Personality and Social Psychology Bulletin, 29,* 1303–1315.

SAUCIER, G., AKERS, L. G., SHEN-MILLER, S., KNEŽEVIĆ, G., & STANKOV, L. (2009). Patterns of thinking in militant extremism. *Perspectives on Psychological Science, 4,* 256–271.

SAVITSKY, K., EPLEY, N., & GILOVICH, T. (2001). Do others judge us as harshly as we think? Overestimating the impact of our failures, shortcomings, and mishaps. *Journal of Personality and Social Psychology, 81,* 44–56.

SAVITSKY, K., VAN VOVEN, L., EPLEY, N., & WRIGHT, W. M. (2005). The unpacking effect in allocations of responsibility for group tasks. *Journal of Experimental Social Psychology, 41,* 447–457.

SAX, L. J., LINDHOLM, J. A., ASTIN, A. W., KORN, W. S., & MAHONEY, K. M. (2002). *The American freshman: National norms for Fall, 2002.* Los Angeles: Cooperative Institutional Research Program, UCLA.

SCALIA, A. (2011). *Opinion of the Supreme Court of the United States, Brown v. Entertainment Merchants Association.* June 27, 2011.

SCHACHTER, S., & SINGER, J. E. (1962). Cognitive, social and physiological determinants of emotional state. *Psychological Review, 69,* 379–399.

SCHAFER, R. B., & KEITH, P. M. (1980). Equity and depression among married couples. *Social Psychology Quarterly, 43,* 430–435.

SCHAFFNER, P. E., WANDERSMAN, A., & STANG, D. (1981). Candidate name exposure and voting: Two field studies. *Basic and Applied Social Psychology, 2,* 195–203.

SCHEIN, E. H. (1956). The Chinese indoctrination program for prisoners of war: A study of attempted brainwashing. *Psychiatry, 19,* 149–172.

SCHIFFENBAUER, A., & SCHIAVO, R. S. (1976). Physical distance and attraction: An intensification effect. *Journal of Experimental Social Psychology, 12,* 274–282.

SCHIMEL, J., ARNDT, J., PYSZCZYNSKI, T., & GREENBERG, J. (2001). Being accepted for who we are: Evidence that social validation of the intrinsic self reduces general defensiveness. *Journal of Personality and Social Psychology, 80,* 35–52.

SCHIMEL, J., SIMON, L., GREENBERG, J., PYSZCZYNSKI, T., SOLOMON, S., & WAXMONSKY, J. (1999). Stereotypes and terror management: Evidence that mortality salience enhances stereotypic thinking and preferences. *Journal of Personality and Social Psychology, 77,* 905–926.

SCHIMMACK, U., OISHI, S., & DIENER, E. (2005). Individualism: A valid and important dimension of cultural differences between nations. *Personality and Social Psychology Review, 9,* 17–31.

SCHKADE, D. A., & KAHNEMAN, D. (1998). Does living in California make people happy? A focusing illusion in judgments of life satisfaction. *Psychological Science, 9,* 340–346.

SCHKADE, D. A., & SUNSTEIN, C. R. (2003, June 11). Judging by where you sit. *New York Times* (www.nytimes.com).

SCHKADE, D., SUNSTEIN, C. R., & HASTIE, R. (2007). What happened on deliberation day? *California Law Review, 95,* 915–940.

SCHLENKER, B. R. (1976). Egocentric perceptions in cooperative groups: A conceptualization and research review. Final Report, Office of Naval Research Grant NR 170–797.

SCHLENKER, B. R., & LEARY, M. R. (1982). Social anxiety and self-presentation: A conceptualization and model. *Psychological Bulletin, 92,* 641–669.

SCHLENKER, B. R., & LEARY, M. R. (1985). Social anxiety and communication about the self. *Journal of Language and Social Psychology, 4,* 171–192.

SCHLENKER, B. R., & MILLER, R. S. (1977a). Group cohesiveness as a determinant of egocentric perceptions in cooperative groups. *Human Relations, 30,* 1039–1055.

SCHLENKER, B. R., & MILLER, R. S. (1977b). Egocentrism in groups: Self-serving biases or logical information processing? *Journal of Personality and Social Psychology, 35,* 755–764.

SCHLESINGER, A. M., JR. (1965). *A thousand days.* Boston: Houghton Mifflin. Cited by I. L. Janis (1972) in *Victims of groupthink.* Boston: Houghton Mifflin.

SCHLESINGER, A., JR. (1949). The statistical soldier. *Partisan Review, 16,* 852–856.

SCHLESINGER, A., JR. (1991, July 8). The cult of ethnicity, good and bad. *Time,* p. 21.

SCHMID, R. E. (2008, July 8). Pet owners prefer McCain over Obama. Associated Press (news.yahoo. com).

SCHMITT, D. P. (2003). Universal sex differences in the desire for sexual variety; tests from 52 nations, 6 continents, and 13 islands. *Journal of Personality and Social Psychology, 85,* 85–104.

SCHMITT, D. P. (2005). Sociosexuality from Argentina to Zimbabwe: A 48-nation study of sex, culture, and strategies of human mating. *Behavioral and Brain Sciences, 28,* 247–311.

SCHMITT, D. P. (2007). Sexual strategies across sexual orientations: How personality traits and culture relate to sociosexuality among gays, lesbians, bisexuals, and heterosexuals. *Journal of Psychology and Human Sexuality, 18,* 183–214.

SCHMITT, D. P., & ALLIK, J. (2005). Simultaneous administration of the Rosenberg Self-Esteem Scale in 53 nations: Exploring the universal and culture-specific features of global self-esteem. *Journal of Personality and Social Psychology, 89,* 623–642.

SCHOFIELD, J. (1982). *Black and white in school: Trust, tension, or tolerance?* New York: Praeger.

SCHOFIELD, J. W. (1986). Causes and consequences of the colorblind perspective. In J. F. Dovidio & S. L. Gaertner (Eds.), *Prejudice, discrimination, and racism.* Orlando, FL: Academic Press.

SCHOR, J. B. (1998). *The overworked American.* New York: Basic Books.

SCHULZ, J. W., & PRUITT, D. G. (1978). The effects of mutual concern on joint welfare. *Journal of Experimental Social Psychology, 14,* 480–492.

SCHUMAN, H., & SCOTT, J. (1989). Generations and collective memories. *American Sociological Review, 54,* 359–381.

SCHWARTZ, B. (2000). Self-determination: The tyranny of freedom. *American Psychologist, 55,* 79–88.

SCHWARTZ, B. (2004). *The tyranny of choice.* New York: Ecco/HarperCollins.

SCHWARTZ, S. H., & GOTTLIEB, A. (1981). Participants' post-experimental reactions and the ethics of bystander research. *Journal of Experimental Social Psychology, 17,* 396–407.

SCHWARTZ, S. H., & RUBEL, T. (2005). Sex differences in value priorities: Cross-cultural and multimethod studies. *Journal of Personality and Social Psychology, 89,* 1010–1028.

SCHWARZ, N., & CLORE, G. L. (1983). Mood, misattribution, and judgments of well-being: Informative and directive functions of affective states. *Journal of Personality and Social Psychology, 45,* 513–523.

SCHWEINLE, W., ICKES, W. AND BERNSTEIN, I. (2002). Empathic inaccuracy in husband to wife aggression: The overattribution bias. *Personal Relationships, 9,* 141–158.

SCOTT, J. P., & MARSTON, M. V. (1953). Nonadaptive behavior resulting from a series of defeats in fighting mice. *Journal of Abnormal and Social Psychology, 48,* 417–428.

SEARS, D. O. (1979). Life stage effects upon attitude change, especially among the elderly. Manuscript prepared for Workshop on the Elderly of the Future, Committee on Aging, National Research Council, Annapolis, MD, May 3–5.

SEARS, D. O. (1986). College sophomores in the laboratory: Influences of a narrow data base on social psychology's view of human nature. *Journal of Personality and Social Psychology, 51,* 515–530.

SEDIKIDES, C. (1993). Assessment, enhancement, and verification determinants of the self-evaluation process. *Journal of Personality and Social Psychology, 65,* 317–338.

SEGAL, H. A. (1954). Initial psychiatric findings of recently repatriated prisoners of war. *American Journal of Psychiatry, 61,* 358–363.

SEGALL, M. H., DASEN, P. R., BERRY, J. W., & POORTINGA, Y. H. (1990). *Human behavior in global perspective: An introduction to cross-cultural psychology.* New York: Pergamon.

SEGERSTROM, S. C. (2001). Optimism and attentional bias for negative and positive stimuli. *Personality and Social Psychology Bulletin, 27,* 1334–1343.

SELIGMAN, M. (1994). *What you can change and what you can't.* New York: Knopf.

SELIGMAN, M. E. P. (1975). *Helplessness: On depression, development, and death.* San Francisco: W. H. Freeman.

SELIGMAN, M. E. P. (1991). *Learned optimism.* New York: Knopf.

SELIGMAN, M. E. P. (1998). The prediction and prevention of depression. In D. K. Routh & R. J. DeRubeis (Eds.), *The science of clinical psychology: Accomplishments and future directions.* Washington, DC: American Psychological Association.

SELIGMAN, M. E. P. (2002). *Authentic happiness: Using the new positive psychology to realize your potential for lasting fulfillment.* New York: Free Press.

SENGUPTA, S. (2001, October 10). Sept. 11 attack narrows the racial divide. *New York Times* (www.nytimes.com).

SENTYRZ, S. M., & BUSHMAN, B. J. (1998). Mirror, mirror, on the wall, who's the thinnest one of all? Effects of self-awareness on consumption of fatty, reduced-fat, and fat-free products. *Journal of Applied Psychology, 83,* 944–949.

SHAFFER, D. R., PEGALIS, L. J., & BAZZINI, D. G. (1996). When boy meets girls (revisited): Gender, gender-role orientation, and prospect of future interaction as determinants of self-disclosure among same- and opposite-sex acquaintances. *Personality and Social Psychology Bulletin, 22,* 495–506.

SHANKAR, A., McMUNN, A., BANKS, J., & STEPTOE, A. (2011). Loneliness, social isolation, and behavioral and biological health indicators in older adults. *Health Psychology, 30,* 377–385.

SHAPIRO, D. L. (2010). Relational identity theory: A systematic approach for transforming the emotional dimension of conflict. *American Psychologist, 65,* 634–645.

SHARPE, D., & FAYE, C. (2009). A second look at debriefing practices: Madness in our method? *Ethics and Behavior, 19,* 432–447.

SHEESE, B. E., & GRAZIANO, W. G. (2005). Deciding to defect: The effects of video-game violence on cooperative behavior. *Psychological Science, 16,* 354–357.

SHELDON, K. M., ELLIOT, A. J., YOUNGMEE, K., & KASSER, T. (2001). What is satisfying about satisfying events? Testing 10 candidate psychological needs. *Journal of Personality and Social Psychology, 80,* 325–339.

SHELDON, K. M., RYAN, R. M., DECI, E. L., & KASSER, T. (2004). The independent effects of goal contents and motives on well-being: It's both what you pursue and why you pursue it. *Personality and Social Psychology Bulletin, 30,* 475–486.

SHELDON, K. M., & NIEMIEC, C. P. (2006). It's not just the amount that counts: Balanced need satisfaction also affects well-being. *Journal of Personality and Social Psychology, 91,* 331–341.

SHELTON, J. N., & RICHESON, J. A. (2005). Intergroup contact and pluralistic ignorance. *Journal of Personality and Social Psychology, 88,* 91–107.

SHEPPERD, J. A. (2003). Interpreting comparative risk judgments: Are people personally optimistic or interpersonally pessimistic? Unpublished manuscript, University of Florida.

SHEPPERD, J. A., GRACE, J., COLE, L. J., & KLEIN, C. (2005). Anxiety and outcome predictions. *Personality and Social Psychology Bulletin, 31,* 267–275.

SHEPPERD, J. A., & WRIGHT, R. A. (1989). Individual contributions to a collective effort: An incentive analysis. *Personality and Social Psychology Bulletin, 15,* 141–149.

SHERGILL, S. S., BAYS, P. M., FRITH, C. D., & WOLPERT, D. M. (2003). Two eyes for an eye: The neuroscience of force escalation. *Science, 301,* 187.

SHERIF, M. (1966). *In common predicament: Social psychology of intergroup conflict and cooperation.* Boston: Houghton Mifflin.

SHERMAN, D. K., NELSON, L. D., & ROSS, L. D. (2003). Naive realism and affirmative action: Adversaries are more similar than they think. *Basic and Applied Social Psychology, 25,* 275–289.

SHERMAN, J. W. (1996). Development and mental representation of stereotypes. *Journal of Personality and Social Psychology, 70,* 1126–1141.

SHERMAN, J. W., KRUSCHKE, J. K., SHERMAN, S. J., PERCY, E. J., PETROCELLI, J. V., & CONREY, F. R. (2009). Attentional processes in stereotype formation: A common model for category accentuation and illusory correlation. *Journal of Personality and Social Psychology, 96,* 305–323.

SHERMAN, J. W., LEE, A. Y., BESSENOFF, G. R., & FROST, L. A. (1998). Stereotype efficiency reconsidered: Encoding flexibility under cognitive load. *Journal of Personality and Social Psychology, 75,* 589–606.

SHERMAN, S. J., CIALDINI, R. B., SCHWARTZMAN, D. F., & REYNOLDS, K. D. (1985). Imagining can heighten or lower the perceived likelihood of contracting a disease: The mediating effect of ease of imagery. *Personality and Social Psychology Bulletin, 11,* 118–127.

SHIPMAN, P. (2003). We are all Africans. *American Scientist, 91,* 496–499.

SHOOK, N. J., & FAZIO, R. H. (2008). Interracial roommate relationships: An experimental field test of the contact hypothesis. *Psychological Science, 19,* 717–723.

SHORT, J. F., JR. (Ed.) (1969). *Gang delinquency and delinquent subcultures.* New York: Harper & Row.

SHOSTAK, M. (1981). *Nisa: The life and words of a !Kung woman.* Cambridge, MA: Harvard University Press.

SHOWERS, C., & RUBEN, C. (1987). Distinguishing pessimism from depression: Negative expectations and positive coping mechanisms. Paper presented at the American Psychological Association convention.

SHRIVER, E. R., YOUNG, S. G., HUGENBERG, K., BERNSTEIN, M. J., & LANTER, J. R. (2008, February). Class, race, and the face: Social context modulates the cross-race effect in face recognition. *Personality and Social Psychology Bulletin, 34,* 260–274.

SIDANIUS, J., & PRATTO, F. (1999). *Social dominance: An intergroup theory of social hierarchy and oppression.* New York: Cambridge University Press.

SIDANIUS, J., PRATTO, F., & BOBO, L. (1994). Social dominance orientation and the political psychology of gender: A case of invariance? *Journal of Personality and Social Psychology, 67,* 998–1011.

SIDANIUS, J., VAN LAAR, C., LEVIN, S., & SINCLAIR, S. (2004). Ethnic enclaves and the dynamics of social identity on the college campus: The good, the bad, and the ugly. *Journal of Personality and Social Psychology, 87,* 96–110.

SIGALL, H. (1970). Effects of competence and consensual validation on a communicator's liking for the audience. *Journal of Personality and Social Psychology, 16,* 252–258.

SILKE, A. (2003). Deindividuation, anonymity, and violence: Findings from Northern Ireland. *Journal of Social Psychology, 143,* 493–499.

SILVER, M., & GELLER, D. (1978). On the irrelevance of evil: The organization and individual action. *Journal of Social Issues, 34,* 125–136.

SILVER, N. (2009, May 9). Bush may haunt Republicans for generations (www.fivethirtyeight.com).

SIMON, R. (2011). SCOTUS: Violence OK. Sex? Maybe. Politico.com column, June 28, 2011.

SIMONSOHN, U. (2011a). Spurious? Name similarity effects (implicit egotism) in marriage, job, and moving decisions. *Journal of Personality and Social Psychology, 101,* 1–24.

SIMONSOHN, U. (2011b). Spurious also? Name-similarity effects (implicit egotism) in employment decisions. *Psychological Science, 22,* 1087–1089.

SIMONTON, D. K. (1994). *Greatness: Who makes history and why.* New York: Guilford.

SIMPSON, J. A. (1987). The dissolution of romantic relationships: Factors involved in relationship stability and emotional distress. *Journal of Personality and Social Psychology, 53,* 683–692.

SIMPSON, J. A., GANGESTAD, S. W., & LERMA, M. (1990). Perception of physical attractiveness: Mechanisms involved in the maintenance of romantic relationships. *Journal of Personality and Social Psychology, 59,* 1192–1201.

SINCLAIR, S., DUNN, E., & LOWERY, B. S. (2004). The relationship between parental racial attitudes and children's implicit prejudice. *Journal of Experimental Social Psychology, 41,* 283–289.

SINGER, M. (1979). Cults and cult members. Address to the American Psychological Association convention.

SINGER, T., SEYMOUR, B., O'DOHERTY, J. P., STEPHAN, K. E., DOLAN, R. J., & FRITH, C. D. (2006). Empathic neural responses are modulated by the perceived fairness of others. *Nature, 439,* 466–469.

SIO, U. N., & ORMEROD, T. C. (2009). Does incubation enhance problem solving? A meta-analytic review. *Psychological Bulletin, 135,* 94–120.

SIPRI (2011). Appendix 4A. Military expenditure data, 2001–10. Stockholm International Peace Research Institute (www.sipri.org/yearbook/2011/04/04A).

SKAALVIK, E. M., & HAGTVET, K. A. (1990). Academic achievement and self-concept: An analysis of causal predominance in a developmental perpsective. *Journal of Personality and Social Psychology, 58,* 292–307.

SKITKA, L. J. (1999). Ideological and attributional boundaries on public compassion: Reactions to individuals and communities affected by a natural disaster. *Personality and Social Psychology Bulletin, 25,* 793–808.

SKITKA, L. J., BAUMAN, C. W., & MULLEN, E. (2004). Political tolerance and coming to psychological closure following the September 11, 2001, terrorist attacks: An integrative approach. *Personality and Social Psychology Bulletin, 30,* 743–756.

SLATCHER, R. B., & PENNEBAKER, J. W. (2006). How do I love thee? Let me count the words: The social effects of expressive writing. *Psychological Science, 17,* 660–664.

SLAVIN, R. E. (1990, December/January). Research on cooperative learning: Consensus and controversy. *Educational Leadership,* pp. 52–54.

SLOTTER, E. B., & GARDNER, W. L. (2009). Where do you end and I begin? Evidence for anticipatory, motivated self-other integration between relationship partners. *Journal of Personality and Social Psychology, 96,* 1137–1151.

SLOTTER, E. B., GARDNER, W. L., & FINKEL, E. (2010). Who am I without you? The influence of romantic breakup on the self-concept. *Personality and Social Psychology Bulletin, 36,* 147–160.

SLOVIC, P. (1972). From Shakespeare to Simon: Speculations—and some evidence—about man's ability to process information. *Oregon Research Institute Research Bulletin, 12*(2).

SLOVIC, P., & FISCHHOFF, B. (1977). On the psychology of experimental surprises. *Journal of Experimental Psychology: Human Perception and Performance, 3,* 455–551.

SMEDLEY, J. W., & BAYTON, J. A. (1978). Evaluative race-class stereotypes by race and perceived class of subjects. *Journal of Personality and Social Psychology, 3,* 530–535.

SMELSER, N. J., & MITCHELL, F. (Eds.) (2002). *Terrorism: Perspectives from the behavioral and social sciences.* Washington, DC: National Research Council, National Academies Press.

SMITH, A. (1976). *The wealth of nations.* Book 1. Chicago: University of Chicago Press. (Originally published, 1776.)

SMITH, D. E., GIER, J. A., & WILLIS, F. N. (1982). Interpersonal touch and compliance with a marketing request. *Basic and Applied Social Psychology, 3,* 35–38.

SMITH, H. (1976) *The Russians.* New York: Balantine Books. Cited by B. Latané, K. Williams, and S. Harkins in "Many hands make light the work." *Journal of Personality and Social Psychology, 1979, 37,* 822–832.

SMITH, H. J., & TYLER, T. R. (1997). Choosing the right pond: The impact of group membership on self-esteem and group-oriented behavior. *Journal of Experimental Social Psychology, 33,* 146–170.

SMITH, H. W. (1981). Territorial spacing on a beach revisited: A cross-national exploration. *Social Psychology Quarterly, 44,* 132–137.

SMITH, J. (2011, August 14). Lack of empathy made it easier to wreck and rob. *The Independent* (www.independent.co.uk).

SMITH, L. G. E., & POSTMES, T. (2011). The power of talk: Developing discriminatory group norms through discussion. *British Journal of Social Psychology, 50,* 193–215.

SMITH, P. B., & TAYEB, M. (1989). Organizational structure and processes. In M. Bond (Ed.), *The cross-cultural challenge to social psychology.* Newbury Park, CA: Sage.

SMITH, R. H., TURNER, T. J., GARONZIK, R., LEACH, C. W., URCH-DRUSKAT, V., & WESTON, C. M. (1996). Envy and Schadenfreude. *Personality and Social Psychology Bulletin, 22,* 158–168.

SMITH, S. J., AXELTON, A. M., & SAUCIER, D. A. (2009). The effects of contact on sexual prejudice: A meta-analysis. *Sex Roles, 61,* 178–191.

SMITH, T. W. (1998, December). *American sexual behavior: Trends, socio-demographic differences, and risk behavior.* National Opinion Research Center GSS Topical Report No. 25.

SMOREDA, Z., & LICOPPE, C. (2000). Gender-specific use of the domestic telephone. *Social Psychology Quarterly, 63,* 238–252.

SNODGRASS, M. A. (1987). The relationships of differential loneliness, intimacy, and characterological attributional style to duration of loneliness. *Journal of Social Behavior and Personality, 2,* 173–186.

SNYDER, C. R. (1978). The "illusion" of uniqueness. *Journal of Humanistic Psychology, 18,* 33–41.

SNYDER, C. R. (1980), March. The uniqueness mystique. *Psychology Today,* pp. 86–90.

SNYDER, C. R., & FROMKIN, H. L. (1980). *Uniqueness: The human pursuit of difference.* New York: Plenum.

SNYDER, C. R., & HIGGINS, R. L. (1988). Excuses: Their effective role in the negotiation of reality. *Psychological Bulletin, 104,* 23–35.

SNYDER, C. R., & SMITH, T. W. (1986). On being "shy like a fox": A self-handicapping analysis. In W. H. Jones et al. (Eds.), *Shyness: Perspectives on research and treatment.* New York: Plenum.

SNYDER, M. (1981). Seek, and ye shall find: Testing hypotheses about other people. In E. T. Higgins, C. P. Herman, & M. P. Zanna (Eds.), *Social cognition: The Ontario symposium on personality and social psychology.* Hillsdale, NJ: Erlbaum.

SNYDER, M. (1983). The influence of individuals on situations: Implications for understanding the links between personality and social behavior. *Journal of Personality, 51,* 497–516.

SNYDER, M. (1984). When belief creates reality. In L. Berkowitz (Ed.), *Advances in experimental social psychology* (Vol. 18). New York: Academic Press.

SNYDER, M., & ICKES, W. (1985). Personality and social behavior. In G. Lindzey & E. Aronson (Eds.), *Handbook of social psychology,* 3rd edition. New York: Random House.

SNYDER, M., TANKE, E. D., & BERSCHEID, E. (1977). Social perception and interpersonal behavior: On the self-fulfilling nature of social stereotypes. *Journal of Personality and Social Psychology, 35,* 656–666.

SOLBERG, E. C., DIENER, E., & ROBINSON, M. D. (2003). Why are materialists less satisfied? In T. Kasser & A. D. Kanner (Eds.), *Psychology and consumer culture: The struggle for a good life in a materialistic world.* Washington, DC: APA Books.

SOMAIYA, R. (2011, August 13). After British riots, conflicting answers as to "why." *New York Times* (www.nytimes.com).

SOROKOWSKI, P., & OTHERS. (2011). Attractiveness of leg length: Report from 27 nations. *Journal of Cross-Cultural Psychology, 42,* 131–139.

SOMMER, R. (1969). *Personal space.* Englewood Cliffs, NJ: Prentice Hall.

SPARRELL, J. A., & SHRAUGER, J. S. (1984). Self-confidence and optimism in self-prediction. Paper presented at the American Psychological Association convention.

SPEARS, R., ELLEMERS, N., & DOOSJE, B. (2009). Strength in numbers or less is more? A matter of opinion and a question of taste. *Personality and Social Psychology Bulletin, 35,* 1099–1111.

SPECTOR, P. E. (1986). Perceived control by employees: A meta-analysis of studies concerning autonomy and participation at work. *Human Relations, 39,* 1005–1016.

SPEER, A. (1971). *Inside the Third Reich: Memoirs.* (P. Winston & C. Winston, trans.). New York: Avon Books.

SPENCER, S. J., STEELE, C. M., & QUINN, D. M. (1999). Stereotype threat and women's math performance. *Journal of Experimental Social Psychology, 3,* 4–28.

SPETH, J. G. (2008). Foreword. In A. A. Leiserowitz & L. O. Fernandez, *Toward a new consciousness: Values to sustain human and natural communities*. New Haven: Yale School of Forestry & Environmental Studies.

SPIEGEL, H. W. (1971). *The growth of economic thought*. Durham, NC: Duke University Press.

SPIELMANN, S. S., MacDONALD, G., & WILSON, A. E. (2009). On the rebound: Focusing on someone new helps anxiously attached individuals let go of ex-partners. *Personality and Social Psychology Bulletin, 35,* 1382–1394.

SPITZBERG, B. H., & HURT, H. T. (1987). The relationship of interpersonal competence and skills to reported loneliness across time. *Journal of Social Behavior and Personality, 2,* 157–172.

SPIVAK, J. (1979, June 6). *Wall Street Journal*.

SPORER, S. L., & HORRY, R. (2011). Recognizing faces from ethnic of outer face features and effects of retention interval. *Applied Cognitive Psychology, 25,* 424–431.

SPORER, S. L., TRINKL, B., & GUBEROVA, E. (2007). Matching faces. Differences in processing speed of out-group faces by different ethnic groups. *Journal of Cross-Cultural Psychology, 38,* 398–412.

SPRECHER, S. (1987). The effects of self-disclosure given and received on affection for an intimate partner and stability of the relationship. *Journal of Personality and Social Psychology, 4,* 115–127.

SPRECHER, S., ARON, A., HATFIELD, E., CORTESE, A., POTAPOVA, E., & LEVITSKAYA, A. (1994). Love: American style, Russian style, and Japanese style. *Personal Relationships, 1,* 349–369.

SPRECHER, S., SULLIVAN, Q., & HATFIELD, E. (1994). Mate selection preferences: Gender differences examined in a national sample. *Journal of Personality and Social Psychology, 66,* 1074–1080.

SPRECHER, S., & TORO-MORN, M. (2002). A study of men and women from different sides of Earth to determine if men are from Mars and women are from Venus in their beliefs about love and romantic relationships. *Sex Roles, 46,* 131–147.

SRIVASTAVA, S., McGONIGAL, K. M., RICHARDS, J. M., BUTLER, E. A., & GROSS, J. J. (2006). Optimism in close relationships: How seeing things in a positive light makes them so. *Journal of Personality and Social Psychology, 91,* 143–153.

STALDER, D. R. (2008). Revisiting the issue of safety in numbers: The likelihood of receiving help from a group. *Social Influence, 3,* 24–33.

STANGOR, C., JONAS, K., STROEBE, W., & HEWSTONE, M. (1996). Influence of student exchange on national stereotypes, attitudes and perceived group variability. *European Journal of Social Psychology, 26,* 663–675.

STANGOR, C., LYNCH, L., DUAN, C., & GLASS, B. (1992). Categorization of individuals on the basis of multiple social features. *Journal of Personality and Social Psychology, 62,* 207–218.

STANOVICH, K. E., & WEST, R. F. (2008). On the relative independence of thinking biases and cognitive ability. *Journal of Personality and Social Psychology, 94,* 672–695.

STARK, E., KIM, A., MILLER, C., & BORGIDA, E. (2008). Effects of including a graphic warning label in advertisements for reduced-exposure products: Implications for persuasion and policy. *Journal of Applied Social Psychology, 38,* 281–293.

STARK, R., & BAINBRIDGE, W. S. (1980). Networks of faith: Interpersonal bonds and recruitment of cults and sects. *American Journal of Sociology, 85,* 1376–1395.

STASSER, G. (1991). Pooling of unshared information during group discussion. In S. Worchel, W. Wood, & J. Simpson (Eds.), *Group process and productivity*. Beverly Hills, CA: Sage.

STATISTICS CANADA (2010). *Victims and persons accused of homicide, by age and sex*. Table 253-0003.

STAUB, E. (1989). *The roots of evil: The origins of genocide and other group violence*. Cambridge: Cambridge University Press.

STAUB, E. (1997a). Blind versus constructive patriotism: Moving from embeddedness in the group to critical loyalty and action. In D. Bar-Tal & E. Staub (Eds.), *Patriotism in the lives of individuals and nations*. Chicago: Nelson-Hall.

STAUB, E. (1997b). *Halting and preventing collective violence: The role of bystanders*. Background paper for symposium organized by the Friends of Raoul Wallenberg, Stockholm, June 13–16.

STAUB, E. (1999). The origins and prevention of genocide, mass killing, and other collective violence. *Peace and Conflict, 5,* 303–336.

STAUB, E. (2003). *The psychology of good and evil: Why children, adults, and groups help and harm others*. New York: Cambridge University Press.

STAUB, E. (2005a). The origins and evolution of hate, with notes on prevention. In R. J. Sternberg (Ed.), *The psychology of hate*. Washington, DC: American Psychological Association.

STAUB, E. (2005b). The roots of goodness: The fulfillment of basic human needs and the development of caring, helping and nonaggression, inclusive caring, moral courage, active bystandership, and altruism born of suffering. In G. Carlo & C. P. Edwards (Eds.), *Moral motivation through the life span: Theory, research, applications. Nebraska Symposium on Motivation* (Vol. 51). Lincoln, NE: University of Nebraska Press.

STEELE, C. M. (2010). *Whistling Vivaldi: And other clues to how stereotypes affect us.* New York: Norton.

STEELE, C. M., & ARONSON, J. (1995). Stereotype threat and the intellectual test performance of African Americans. *Journal of Personality and Social Psychology, 69,* 797–811.

STEELE, C. M., SPENCER, S. J., & ARONSON, J. (2002). Contending with group image: The psychology of stereotype and social identity threat. In M. P. Zanna (Ed.), *Advances in experimental social psychology,* 34, 379–440. San Diego: Academic Press.

STEIN, A. H., & FRIEDRICH, L. K. (1972). Television content and young children's behavior. In J. P. Murray, E. A. Rubinstein, & G. A. Comstock (Eds.), *Television and social learning.* Washington, DC: Government Printing Office.

STEIN, D. D., HARDYCK, J. A., & SMITH, M. B. (1965). Race and belief: An open and shut case. *Journal of Personality and Social Psychology, 1,* 281–289.

STELTER, B. (2008, November 25). Web suicide viewed live and reaction spur a debate. *New York Times* (www.nytimes.com).

STEPHAN, W. G. (1987). The contact hypothesis in intergroup relations. In C. Hendrick (Ed.), *Group processes and intergroup relations.* Newbury Park, CA: Sage.

STEPHAN, W. G. (1988). School desegregation: Short-term and long-term effects. Paper presented at the national conference "Opening Doors: An Appraisal of Race Relations in America," University of Alabama.

STEPHAN, W. G., BERSCHEID, E., & WALSTER, E. (1971). Sexual arousal and heterosexual perception. *Journal of Personality and Social Psychology, 20,* 93–101.

STERNBERG, R. J. (1988). Triangulating love. In R. J. Sternberg & M. L. Barnes (Eds.), *The psychology of love.* New Haven, CT: Yale University Press.

STERNBERG, R. J. (1998). *Cupid's arrow: The course of love through time.* New York: Cambridge University Press.

STERNBERG, R. J. (2003). A duplex theory of hate and its development and its application to terrorism, massacres, and genocide. *Review of General Psychology, 7,* 299–328.

STEWART, K. D., & BERNHARDT, P. C. (2010). Comparing Millennials to pre-1987 students and with one another. *North American Journal of Psychology, 12,* 579–602.

STILLINGER, C., EPELBAUM, M., KELTNER, D., & ROSS, L. (1991). The "reactive devaluation" barrier to conflict resolution. Unpublished manuscript, Stanford University.

STIRRAT, M., & PERRETT, D. I. (2010). Valid facial cues to cooperation and trust: Male facial width and trustworthiness. *Psychological Science, 21,* 349–354.

ST. LAWRENCE, J. S., & JOYNER, D. J. (1991). The effects of sexually violent rock music on males' acceptance of violence against women. *Psychology of Women Quarterly, 15,* 49–63.

STOCKDALE, J. E. (1978). Crowding: Determinants and effects. In L. Berkowitz (Ed.), *Advances in experimental social psychology* (Vol. 11). New York: Academic Press.

STONE, A. A., HEDGES, S. M., NEALE, J. M., & SATIN, M. S. (1985). Prospective and cross-sectional mood reports offer no evidence of a "blue Monday" phenomenon. *Journal of Personality and Social Psychology, 49,* 129–134.

STONE, J. (2000, November 6). Quoted by Sharon Begley, The stereotype trap. *Newsweek.*

STONE, J., LYNCH, C. I., SJOMELING, M., & DARLEY, J. M. (1999). Stereotype threat effects on Black and White athletic performance. *Journal of Personality and Social Psychology, 77,* 1213–1227.

STONER, J. A. F. (1961). A comparison of individual and group decisions involving risk. Unpublished master's thesis, Massachusetts Institute of Technology, 1961. Cited by D. G. Marquis in Individual responsibility and group decisions involving risk, *Industrial Management Review, 3,* 8–23.

STORMS, M. D., & THOMAS, G. C. (1977). Reactions to physical closeness. *Journal of Personality and Social Psychology, 35,* 412–418.

STOUFFER, S. A., SUCHMAN, E. A., DeVINNEY, L. C., STAR, S. A., & WILLIAMS, R. M., JR. (1949). *The American soldier: Adjustment during army life* (Vol. 1.). Princeton, NJ: Princeton University Press.

STOUT, J. G., DASGUPTA, N., HUNSINGER, M., & McMANUS, M. A. (2011). STEMing the tide: Using ingroup experts to inoculate women's self-concept in science, technology, engineering, and mathematics (STEM). *Journal of Personality and Social Psychology, 100,* 255–270.

STRACK, F., & DEUTSCH, R. (2004). Reflective and impulsive determinants of social behavior. *Personality and Social Psychology Review,* 8(3), 220–247.

STRACK, S., & COYNE, J. C. (1983). Social confirmation of dysphoria: Shared and private reactions to depression. *Journal of Personality and Social Psychology, 44,* 798–806.

STRASBURGER, V. C., JORDAN, A. B., & DONNERSTEIN, E. (2010). Health effects of media on children and adolescents. *Pediatrics, 125,* 756–767.

STRAUS, M. A., & GELLES, R. J. (1980). *Behind closed doors: Violence in the American family.* New York: Anchor/Doubleday.

STRICK, M., DIJKSTERHUIS, A., & VAN BAAREN, R. B. (2010). Unconscious-thought effects take place off-line, not on-line. *Psychological Science, 21,* 484–488.

STRICK, M., VAN BAAREN, R. B., HOLLAND, R. W., & VAN KNIPPENBERG, A. (2009). Humor in advertisements enhances product liking by mere association. *Journal of Experimental Psychology: Applied, 15,* 35–45.

STROEBE, W. (2012). The truth about Triplett (1898), but nobody seems to care. *Perspectives on Psychological Science, 7,* 54–57.

STROESSNER, S. J., HAMILTON, D. L., & LEPORE, L. (1990). Intergroup categorization and intragroup differentiation: Ingroup-outgroup differences. Paper presented at the American Psychological Association convention.

STRONG, S. R. (1968). Counseling: An interpersonal influence process. *Journal of Counseling Psychology, 17,* 81–87.

STRONG, S. R. (1978). Social psychological approach to psychotherapy research. In S. L. Garfield & A. E. Bergin (Eds.), *Handbook of psychotherapy and behavior change,* 2nd edition. New York: Wiley.

STRONG, S. R., WELSH, J. A., CORCORAN, J. L., & HOYT, W. T. (1992). Social psychology and counseling psychology: The history, products, and promise of an interface. *Journal of Personality and Social Psychology, 39,* 139–157.

STRUBE, M. J. (2005). What did Triplett really find? A contemporary analysis of the first experiment in social psychology. *American Journal of Psychology, 118,* 271–286.

SUNDIE, J. M., KENRICK, D. T., GRISKEVICIUS, V., TYBUR, J. M., VOHS, K. D., & BEAL, D. J. (2011). Peacocks, porches, and Thorstein Veblen: Conspicuous consumption as a sexual signaling system . *Journal of Personality and Social Psychology, 100,* 664–680.

SULLIVAN, A. (1999, September 26). What's so bad about hate? *New York Times Magazine* (www.nytimes.com).

SULS, J., & TESCH, F. (1978). Students' preferences for information about their test performance: A social comparison study, *Journal of Applied Social Psychology, 8,* 189–197.

SUMMERS, G., & FELDMAN, N. S. (1984). Blaming the victim versus blaming the perpetrator: An attributional analysis of spouse abuse. *Journal of Social and Clinical Psychology, 2,* 339–347.

SUN, C., BRIDGES, A., WOSNITZER, R., SCHARRER, E., & LIBERMAN, R. (2008). A comparison of male and female directors in popular pornography: What happens when women are at the helm? *Psychology of Women Quarterly, 32,* 312–325.

SUNSTEIN, C. R. (2001). *Republic.com.* Princeton: Princeton University Press.

SUNSTEIN, C. R. (2007a). Group polarization and 12 angry men. *Negotiation Journal, 23,* 443–447.

SUNSTEIN, C. R. (2007b). On the divergent American reactions to terrorism and climate change. *Columbia Law Review, 107,* 503–557.

SUNSTEIN, C. R. (2009). *Going to extremes: How like minds unite and divide.* New York: Oxford University Press.

SVENSON, O. (1981). Are we all less risky and more skillful than our fellow drivers? *Acta Psychologica, 47,* 143–148.

SWAMI, V., CHAN, F., WONG, V., FURNHAM, A., & TOVÉE, M. J. (2008). Weight-based discrimination in occupational hiring and helping behavior. *Journal of Applied Social Psychology, 38,* 968–981.

SWANN, W. B., JR. (1996). *Self-traps: The elusive quest for higher self-esteem.* New York: Freeman.

SWANN, W. B., JR. (1997). The trouble with change: Self-verification and allegiance to the self. *Psychological Science, 8,* 177–180.

SWANN, W. B., JR., & GILL, M. J. (1997). Confidence and accuracy in person perception: Do we know what we think we know about our relationship partners? *Journal of Personality and Social Psychology, 73,* 747–757.

SWANN, W. B., JR., GÓMEZ, Á., SEYLE, D. C., MORALES, J. F., & HUICI, C. (2009). Identity fusion: The interplay of personal and social identities in extreme group behavior. *Journal of Personality and Social Psychology, 96,* 995–1011.

SWANN, W. B., JR., & PREDMORE, S. C. (1985). Intimates as agents of social support: Sources of consolation or despair? *Journal of Personality and Social Psychology, 49,* 1609–1617.

SWANN, W. B., JR., RENTFROW, P. J., & GOSLING, S. D. (2003). The precarious couple effect: Verbally inhibited men + critical, disinhibited women = bad chemistry. *Journal of Personality and Social Psychology, 85,* 1095–1106.

SWANN, W. B., JR., SELLERS, J. G., & MCCLARTY, K. L. (2006). Tempting today, troubling tomorrow: The roots of the precarious couple effect. *Personality and Social Psychology Bulletin, 32,* 93–103.

SWEENEY, J. (1973). An experimental investigation of the free rider problem. *Social Science Research, 2,* 277–292.

SWEENY, K., MELNYK, D., MILLER, W., & SHEPPERD, J. A. (2010). Information avoidance: Who, what, when, and why. *Review of General Psychology, 14,* 340–353.

Sweeney, P. D., Anderson, K., & Bailey, S. (1986). Attributional style in depression: A meta-analytic review. *Journal of Personality and Social Psychology, 50,* 947–991.

Swets, J. A., Dawes, R. M., & Monahan, J. (2000). Psychological science can improve diagnostic decisions. *Psychological Science in the Public Interest, 1,* 1–26.

Swim, J. K. (1994). Perceived versus meta-analytic effect sizes: An assessment of the accuracy of gender stereotypes. *Journal of Personality and Social Psychology, 66,* 21–36.

Swim, J. K., Cohen, L. L., & Hyers, L. L. (1998). Experiencing everyday prejudice and discrimination. In J. K. Swim & C. Stangor (Eds.), *Prejudice: The target's perspective.* San Diego: Academic Press.

Swim, J. K., & Hyers, L. L. (1999). Excuse me—What did you just say?!: Women's public and private reactions to sexist remarks. *Journal of Experimental Social Psychology, 35,* 68–88.

Swindle, R., Jr., Heller, K., Bescosolido, B., & Kikuzawa, S. (2000). Responses to nervous breakdowns in America over a 40-year period: Mental health policy implications. *American Psychologist, 55,* 740–749.

Symons, D. (1979). *The evolution of human sexuality.* New York: Oxford University Press.

Tafarodi, R. W., Lo, C., Yamaguchi, S., Lee, W. W-S., & Katsura, H. (2004). The inner self in three countries. *Journal of Cross-Cultural Psychology, 35,* 97–117.

Tajfel, H. (1970, November). Experiments in intergroup discrimination. *Scientific American,* pp. 96–102.

Tajfel, H. (1981). *Human groups and social categories: Studies in social psychology.* London: Cambridge University Press.

Tajfel, H. (1982). Social psychology of intergroup relations. *Annual Review of Psychology, 33,* 1–39.

Tajfel, H., & Billig, M. (1974). Familiarity and categorization in intergroup behavior. *Journal of Experimental Social Psychology, 10,* 159–170.

Tamres, L. K., Janicki, D., & Helgeson, V. S. (2002). Sex differences in coping behavior: A meta-analytic review and an examination of relative coping. *Personality and Social Psychology Review, 6,* 2–30.

Tan, H. H., & Tan, M. L. (2008). Organizational citizenship behavior and social loafing: The role of personality, motives, and contextual factors. *Journal of Psychology, 142,* 89–108.

Tannen, D. (1990). *You just don't understand: Women and men in conversation.* New York: Morrow.

Tarmann, A. (2002, May/June). Out of the closet and onto the Census long form. *Population Today, 30,* 1, 6.

Tausch, N., Hewstone, M., Kenworthy, J. B., Psaltis, C., Schmid, K., Popan, J. R., Cairns, E., & Hughes, J. (2010). Secondary transfer effects of intergroup contact: Alternative accounts and underlying processes. *Journal of Personality and Social Psychology, 99,* 282–302.

Tavris, C., & Aronson, E. (2007). *Mistakes were made (but not by me): Why we justify foolish beliefs, bad decisions, and hurtful acts.* New York: Harcourt.

Tay, L., & Diener, E. (2011). Needs and subjective well-being around the world. *Journal of Personality and Social Psychology, 101,* 354–365.

Taylor, D. M., & Doria, J. R. (1981). Self-serving and group-serving bias in attribution. *Journal of Social Psychology, 113,* 201–211.

Taylor, L. S., Fiore, A. T., Mendelsohn, G. A., & Cheshire, C. (2011). "Out of my league": A real-world test of the matching hypothesis. *Personality and Social Psychology Bulletin, 37,* 942–954.

Taylor, S. E. (1981). A categorization approach to stereotyping. In D. L. Hamilton (Ed.), *Cognitive processes in stereotyping and intergroup behavior.* Hillsdale, NJ: Erlbaum.

Taylor, S. E. (1989). *Positive illusions: Creative self-deception and the healthy mind.* New York: Basic Books.

Taylor, S. E. (2002). *The tending instinct: How nurturing is essential to who we are and how we live.* New York: Times Books.

Taylor, S. E., Crocker, J., Fiske, S. T., Sprinzen, M., & Winkler, J. D. (1979). The generalizability of salience effects. *Journal of Personality and Social Psychology, 37,* 357–368.

Taylor, S. E., & Fiske, S. T. (1978). Salience, attention, and attribution: Top of the head phenomena. In L. Berkowitz (Ed.), *Advances in experimental social psychology* (Vol. 11). New York: Academic Press.

Taylor, S. E., Fiske, S. T., Etcoff, N. L., & Ruderman, A. J. (1978). Categorical and contextual bases of person memory and stereotyping. *Journal of Personality and Social Psychology, 36,* 778–793.

Taylor, S. E., Lerner, J. S., Sherman, D. K., Sage, R. M., & McDowell, N. K. (2003a). Are self-enhancing cognitions associated with healthy or unhealthy biological profiles? *Journal of Personality and Social Psychology 85,* 605–615.

Taylor, S. E., Saphire-Bernstein, S., & Seeman, T. E. (2010). Are plasma oxytocin in women and plasma vasopressin in men biomarkers of distressed pair-bond relationships? *Psychological Science, 21,* 3–7.

TAYLOR, S. E., LERNER, J. S., SHERMAN, D. K., SAGE, R. M., & McDOWELL, N. K. (2003b). Portrait of the self-enhancer: Well adjusted and well liked or maladjusted and friendless? *Journal of Personality and Social Psychology*, **84**, 165–176.

TAYLOR, S. P., & CHERMACK, S. T. (1993). Alcohol, drugs and human physical aggression. *Journal of Studies on Alcohol*, Supplement No. 11, 78–88.

TEGER, A. I. (1980). *Too much invested to quit*. New York: Pergamon.

TEIGEN, K. H. (1986). Old truths or fresh insights? A study of students' evaluations of proverbs. *British Journal of Social Psychology*, **25**, 43–50.

TELCH, M. J., KILLEN, J. D., McALISTER, A. L., PERRY, C. L., & MACCOBY, N. (1981). Long-term follow-up of a pilot project on smoking prevention with adolescents. Paper presented at the American Psychological Association convention.

TESSER, A. (1988). Toward a self-evaluation maintenance model of social behavior. In L. Berkowitz (Ed.), *Advances in experimental social psychology* (Vol. 21). San Diego, CA: Academic Press.

TESSER, A., MILLAR, M., & MOORE, J. (1988). Some affective consequences of social comparison and reflection processes: The pain and pleasure of being close. *Journal of Personality and Social Psychology*, **54**, 49–61.

TESSER, A., ROSEN, S., & CONLEE, M. C. (1972). News valence and available recipient as determinants of news transmission. *Sociometry*, **35**, 619–628.

TESTA, M. (2002). The impact of men's alcohol consumption on perpetration of sexual aggression. *Clinical Psychology Review*, **22**, 1239–1263.

TETLOCK, P. E. (1983). Accountability and complexity of thought. *Journal of Personality and Social Psychology*, **45**, 74–83.

TETLOCK, P. E. (1985). Integrative complexity of American and Soviet foreign policy rhetoric: A time-series analysis. *Journal of Personality and Social Psychology*, **49**, 1565–1585.

TETLOCK, P. E. (1998). Close-call counterfactuals and belief-system defenses: I was not almost wrong but I was almost right. *Journal of Personality and Social Psychology*, **75**, 639–652.

TETLOCK, P. E. (1999). Theory-driven reasoning about plausible pasts and probable futures in world politics: Are we prisoners of our preconceptions? *American Journal of Political Science*, **43**, 335–366.

TETLOCK, P. E. (2005). *Expert political judgment: How good is it? How can we know?* Princeton, NJ: Princeton University Press.

THAKAR, M., & EPSTEIN, M. (2011, November 16). *How love emerges in arranged marriages: A follow-up cross-cultural study*. Paper presented to the National Council on Family Relations.

THELWALL, M. (2008). Social networks, gender and friending: An analysis of MySpace member profiles. *Journal of the American Society for Information Science and Technology*, **59**, 1321–1330.

THOMAS, E. F., & McGARTY, C. A. (2009). The role of efficacy and moral outrage norms in creating the potential for international development activism through group-based interaction. *British Journal of Psychology*, **48**, 115–134.

THOMAS, K. W., & PONDY, L. R. (1977). Toward an "intent" model of conflict management among principal parties. *Human Relations*, **30**, 1089–1102.

THOMPSON, L. (1990a). An examination of naive and experienced negotiators. *Journal of Personality and Social Psychology*, **59**, 82–90.

THOMPSON, L. (1990b). The influence of experience on negotiation performance. *Journal of Experimental Social Psychology*, **26**, 528–544.

THOMPSON, L., VALLEY, K. L., & KRAMER, R. M. (1995). The bittersweet feeling of success: An examination of social perception in negotiation. *Journal of Experimental Social Psychology*, **31**, 467–492.

THOMPSON, L. L., & CROCKER, J. (1985). Prejudice following threat to the self-concept. Effects of performance expectations and attributions. Unpublished manuscript, Northwestern University.

THOMPSON, S. C., ARMSTRONG, W., & THOMAS, C. (1998). Illusions of control, underestimations, and accuracy: A control heuristic explanation. *Psychological Bulletin*, **123**, 143–161.

THOMSON, R., & MURACHVER, T. (2001). Predicting gender from electronic discourse. *British Journal of Social Psychology*, **40**, 193–208 (and personal correspondence from T. Murachver, May 23, 2002).

THORNTON, B., & MAURICE, J. (1997). Physique contrast effect: Adverse impact of idealized body images for women. *Sex Roles*, **37**, 433–439.

TIDEMAN, S. (2003, undated). Announcement of Operationalizing Gross National Happiness conference, February 18–20, 2004. Distributed via the Internet.

TIERNEY, J. (2008, January 29). Hitting it off, thanks to algorithms of love. *New York Times* (www.nytimes.com).

TIME (1992, March 30). The not so merry wife of Windsor, pp. 38–39.

TIMMERMAN, T. A. (2007). "It was a thought pitch": Personal, situational, and target influences on hit-by-pitch events across time. *Journal of Applied Psychology, 92*, 876–884.

TODD, A. R., BODENHAUSEN, G. V., RICHESON, J. A., & GALINSKY, A. D. (2011). Perspective taking combats automatic expressions of racial bias. *Journal of Personality and Social Psychology, 100*, 1027–1042.

TODOROV, A. (2011). Evaluating faces on social dimensions. In A. Todorov, S. T. Fiske, & D. A. Prentice (Eds.), *Social neuroscience: Toward understanding the underpinnings of the social mind.* New York: Oxford University Press.

TODOROV, A., MANDISODZA, A. N., GOREN, A., & HALL, C. C. (2005). Inferences of competence from faces predict election outcomes. *Science, 308*, 1623–1626.

TORMALA, Z. L., BRINOL, P., & PETTY, R. E. (2006). When credibility attacks: The reverse impact of source credibility on persuasion. *Journal of Experimental Social Psychology, 42*, 684–691.

TRAIL, T. E., SHELTON, J. N., & WEST, T. V. (2009). Interracial roommate relationships: Negotiating daily interactions. *Personality and Social Psychology Bulletin, 35*, 671–684.

TRAUTWEIN, Ul, & LÜDTKE, O. (2006). Self-esteem, academic self-concept, and achievement: How the learning environment moderates the dynamics of self-concept. *Journal of Personality and Social Psychology, 90*, 334–349.

TRAVIS, L. E. (1925). The effect of a small audience upon eye-hand coordination. *Journal of Abnormal and Social Psychology, 20*, 142–146.

TRAWALTER, S., TODD, A. R., BAIRD, A. A., & RICHESON, J. A. (2008). Attending to threat: Race-based patterns of selective attention. *Journal of Experimental Social Psychology, 44*, 1322–1327.

TREDOUX, C., & FINCHILESCU, G. (2010). Mediators of the contact-prejudice relation amongst South African students on four university campuses. *Journal of Social Issues, 66*, 289–308.

TREWIN, D. (2001). *Australian social trends 2001.* Canberra: Australian Bureau of Statistics.

TRIANDIS, H. C. (1981). Some dimensions of intercultural variation and their implications for interpersonal behavior. Paper presented at the American Psychological Association convention.

TRIANDIS, H. C. (1982). Incongruence between intentions and behavior: A review. Paper presented at the American Psychological Association convention.

TRIANDIS, H. C. (1994). *Culture and social behavior.* New York: McGraw-Hill.

TRIANDIS, H. C. (2000). Culture and conflict. *International Journal of Psychology, 55*, 145–152.

TRIANDIS, H. C., BONTEMPO, R., VILLAREAL, M. J., ASAI, M., & LUCCA, N. (1988). Individualism and collectivism: Cross-cultural perspectives on self-ingroup relationships. *Journal of Personality and Social Psychology, 54*, 323–338.

TRIPLETT, N. (1898). The dynamogenic factors in pacemaking and competition. *American Journal of Psychology, 9*, 507–533.

TROLIER, T. K., & HAMILTON, D. L. (1986). Variables influencing judgments of correlational relations. *Journal of Personality and Social Psychology, 50*, 879–888.

TROPP, L. R., & PETTIGREW, T. F. (2005a). Differential relationships between intergroup contact and affective and cognitive dimensions of prejudice. *Personality and Social Psychology Bulletin, 31*, 1145–1158.

TROPP, L. R., & PETTIGREW, T. F. (2005b). Relationships between intergroup contact and prejudice among minority and majority status groups. *Psychological Science, 16*, 951–957.

TROST, M. R., MAASS, A., & KENRICK, D. T. (1992). Minority influence: Personal relevance biases cognitive processes and reverses private acceptance. *Journal of Experimental Social Psychology, 28*, 234–254.

TRZESNIEWSKI, K. H., & DONNELLAN, M. B. (2010). Rethinking "Generation Me": A study of cohort effects from 1976–2006. *Perspectives in Psychological Science, 5*, 58–75.

TRZESNIEWSKI, K. H., DONNELLAN, M. B., MOFFITT, T. E., ROBINS, R. W., POULTON, R., & CASPI, A. (2006). Low self-esteem during adolescence predicts poor health, criminal behavior, and limited economic prospects during adulthood. *Developmental Psychology, 42*, 381–390.

TSANG, J-A. (2002). Moral rationalization and the integration of situational factors and psychological processes in immoral behavior. *Review of General Psychology, 6*, 25–50.

TURNER, C. W., HESSE, B. W., & PETERSON-LEWIS, S. (1986). Naturalistic studies of the long-term effects of television violence. *Journal of Social Issues, 42*(3), 51–74.

TURNER, J. C. (1981). The experimental social psychology of intergroup behaviour. In J. Turner & H. Giles (Eds.), *Intergroup behavior.* Oxford, England: Blackwell.

TURNER, J. C., & HASLAM, S. A. (2001). Social identity, organizations, and leadership. In M. E. Turner (Ed.), *Groups at work: Theory and research.* Mahwah, NJ: Erlbaum.

TURNER, J. C., & REYNOLDS, K. J. (2004). The social identity perspective in intergroup relations: Theories, themes, and controversies. In M. B. Brewer & M. Hewstone (Eds.), *Self and social identity.* Malden, MA: Blackwell.

TURNER, M. E., & PRATKANIS, A. R. (1994). Social identity maintenance prescriptions for preventing groupthink: Reducing identity protection and enhancing intellectual conflict. *International Journal of Conflict Management*, **5**, 254–270.

TURNER, M. E., PRATKANIS, A. R., PROBASCO, P., & LEVE, C. (1992). Threat cohesion and group effectiveness: Testing a social identity maintenance perspective on groupthink. *Journal of Personality and Social Psychology*, **63**, 781–796.

TURNER, N., BARLING, J., & ZACHARATOS, A. (2002). Positive psychology at work. In C. R. Snyder & S. J. Lopez (Eds.), *The handbook of positive psychology*. New York: Oxford University Press.

TURNER, R. N., & CRISP, R. J. (2010). Imagining intergroup contact reduces implicit prejudice. *British Journal of Social Psychology*, **49**, 129–142.

TURNER, R. N., HEWSTONE, M., & VOCI, A. (2007). Reducing explicit and implicit outgroup prejudice via direct and extended contact: The mediating role of self-disclosure and intergroup anxiety. *Journal of Personality and Social Psychology*, **93**, 369–388.

TURNER, R. N., HEWSTONE, M., VOCI, A., PAOLINI, S., & CHRIST, O. (2007). Reducing prejudice via direct and extended cross-group friendship. *European Review of Social Psychology*, **18**, 212–255.

TURNER, R. N., HEWSTONE, M., VOCI, A., & VONOFAKOU, C. (2008). A test of the extended intergroup contact hypothesis: The mediating role of intergroup anxiety, perceived ingroup and outgroup norms, and inclusion of the outgroup in the self. *Journal of Personality and Social Psychology*, **95**, 843–860.

TV GUIDE (1977, January 26), pp. 5–10.

TVERSKY, A., & KAHNEMAN, D. (1973). Availability: A heuristic for judging frequency and probability. *Cognitive Psychology*, **5**, 207–232.

TVERKSY, A., & KAHNEMAN, D. (1974). Judgment under uncertainty: Heuristics and biases. *Science*, **185**, 1123–1131.

TWENGE, J. M. (2006). *Generation me: Why today's young Americans are more confident, assertive, entitled—and more miserable than ever before.* New York: Free Press.

TWENGE, J. M., ABEBE, E. M., & CAMPBELL, W. K. (2010). Fitting in or standing out: Trends in American parents' choices for children's names, 1880–2007. *Social Psychological and Personality Science*, **1**, 19–25.

TWENGE, J. M., BAUMEISTER, R. F., TICE, D. M., & STUCKE, T. S. (2001). If you can't join them, beat them: Effects of social exclusion on aggressive behavior. *Journal of Personality and Social Psychology*, **81**, 1058–1069.

TWENGE, J. M., & CAMPBELL, W. K. (2008). Increases in positive self-views among high school students: Birth cohort changes in anticipated performance, self-satisfaction, self-liking, and self-competence. *Psychological Science*, **19**, 1082–1086.

TWENGE, J. M., & CAMPBELL, W. K. (2009). *The narcissism epidemic: Living in the age of entitlement.* New York: Atria Paperback.

TWENGE, J. M., CAMPBELL, W. K., & GENTILE, B. (2011). Generational increases in agentic self-evaluations among American college students, 1966–2009. *Self and Identity*, **11**, 409–427.

TWENGE, J. M., CATANESE, K. R., & BAUMEISTER, R. F. (2002). Social exclusion causes self-defeating behavior. *Journal of Personality and Social Psychology*, **83**, 606–615.

TWENGE, J. M., CATANESE, K. R., & BAUMEISTER, R. F. (2003). Social exclusion and the deconstructed state: Time perception, meaninglessness, lethargy, lack of emotion, and self-awareness. *Journal of Personality and Social Psychology*, **85**, 409–423.

TWENGE, J. M., & FOSTER, J. D. (2008). Mapping the scale of the narcissism epidemic: Increases in narcissism 2002–2007 within ethnic groups. *Journal of Research in Personality*, **42**, 1619–1622.

TWENGE, J. M., & FOSTER, J. D. (2010). Birth cohort increases in narcissistic personality traits among American college students, 1982–2009. *Social Psychological and Personality Science*, **1**, 99–106.

TWENGE, J. M., KONRATH, S., FOSTER, J. D., CAMPBELL, W. K., & BUSHMAN, B. J. (2008). Egos inflating over time: A cross-temporal meta-analysis of the Narcissistic Personality Inventory. *Journal of Personality*, **76**, 875–901.

TWENGE, J. M., ZHANG, L., CATANESE, K. R., DOLAN-PASCOE, B., LYCHE, L. F., & BAUMEISTER, R. F. (2007). Replenishing connectedness: Reminders of social activity reduce aggression after social exclusion. *British Journal of Social Psychology*, **46**, 205–224.

TYKOCINSKI, O. E., & BAREKET-BOJMEL, L. (2009). The lost e-mail technique: Use of an implicit measure to assess discriminatory attitudes toward two minority groups in Israel. *Journal of Applied Social Psychology*, **39**, 62–81.

TZENG, M. (1992). The effects of socioeconomic heterogamy and changes on marital dissolution for first marriages. *Journal of Marriage and the Family*, **54**, 609–619.

U.S. SENATE (2004, July 9). *Report on the U.S. Intelligence community's prewar intelligence assessments on Iraq.* Washington, DC: United States Select Senate Committee on Intelligence. Retrieved from (www.intelligence.senate.gov).

UNITED NATIONS (UN) (1991). *The world's women, 1970–1990: Trends and statistics.* New York: United Nations.

UNITED NATIONS (UN) (2006). *Ending violence against women: From words to action.* Study of the Secretary-General. New York: United Nations (www.un.org).

UNITED NATIONS (UN) (2010). *The world's women 2010 trends and statistics.* United Nations Department of Economic and Social Affairs. (www.unstats.un.org).

UNKELBACH, C., FORGAS, J. P., & DENSON, T. F. (2008). The turban effect: The influence of Muslim headgear and induced affect on aggressive responses in the shooter bias paradigm. *Journal of Experimental Social Psychology, 44,* 1409–1413.

UNKELBACH, C., & MEMMERT, D. (2010). Crowd noise as a cue in referee decisions contributes to the home advantage. *Journal of Sport & Exercise Psychology, 32,* 483–498.

VAILLANT, G. E. (1977). *Adaptation to life.* Boston: Little, Brown.

VALCOUR, M. (2007). Work-based resources as moderators of the relationship between work hours and satisfaction with work-family balance. *Journal of Applied Psychology, 92,* 1512–1523.

VALLONE, R. P., GRIFFIN, D. W., LIN, S., & ROSS, L. (1990). Overconfident prediction of future actions and outcomes by self and others. *Journal of Personality and Social Psychology, 58,* 582–592.

VALLONE, R. P., ROSS, L., & LEPPER, M. R. (1985). The hostile media phenomenon: Biased perception and perceptions of media bias in coverage of the "Beirut Massacre." *Journal of Personality and Social Psychology, 49,* 577–585.

VAN DIJK, W. W., FINKENAUER, C., & POLLMANN, M. (2008). The misprediction of emotions in track athletics: Is experience the teacher of all things? *Basic and Applied Social Psychology, 30,* 369–376.

VAN KNIPPENBERG, D., & WILKE, H. (1992). Prototypicality of arguments and conformity to ingroup norms. *European Journal of Social Psychology, 22,* 141–155.

VAN LAAR, C., LEVIN, S., SINCLAIR, S., & SIDANIUS, J. (2005). The effect of university roommate contact on ethnic attitudes and behavior. *Journal of Experimental Social Psychology, 41,* 329–345.

VAN STRAATEN, I., ENGELS, R. C. M. E., FINKENAUER, C., & HOLLAND, R. W. (2009). Meeting your match: How attractiveness similarity affects approach behavior in mixed-sex dyads. *Personality and Social Psychology Bulletin, 35,* 685–697.

VAN VUGT, M., & SPISAK, B. R. (2008). Sex differences in the emergence of leadership during competitions within and between groups. *Psychological Science, 19,* 854–858.

VAN YPEREN, N. W., & BUUNK, B. P. (1990). A longitudinal study of equity and satisfaction in intimate relationships. *European Journal of Social Psychology, 20,* 287–309.

VANDELLO, J. A., & COHEN, D. (1999). Patterns of individualism and collectivism across the United States. *Journal of Personality and Social Psychology, 77,* 279–292.

VANDELLO, J. A., COHEN, D., & RANSOM, S. (2008). U.S. southern and northern differences in perceptions of norms about aggression: Mechanisms for the perpetuation of a culture of honor. *Journal of Cross-Cultural Psychology, 39,* 162–177.

VANDERSLICE, V. J., RICE, R. W., & JULIAN, J. W. (1987). The effects of participation in decision-making on worker satisfaction and productivity: An organizational simulation. *Journal of Applied Social Psychology, 17,* 158–170.

VANDERWEELE, T. J., HAWKLEY, L. C., THISTED, R. A., & CACIOPPO, J. C. (2011). A marginal structural model analysis for loneliness: Implications for intervention trials and clinical practice. *Journal of Consulting and Clinical Psychology, 79,* 225–235.

VARNUM, M. E. W., & KITAYAMA, S. (2011). What's in a name? Popular names are less common on frontiers. *Psychological Science, 22,* 176–183.

VASQUEZ, E. A., DENSON, T. F., PEDERSEN, W. C., STENSTROM, D. M., & MILLER, N. (2005). The moderating effect of trigger intensity on triggered displaced aggression. *Journal of Experimental Social Psychology, 41,* 61–67.

VAZIRE, S., & MEHL, M. R. (2008). Knowing me, knowing you: The accuracy and unique predictive validity of self-ratings and other-ratings of daily behavior. *Journal of Personality and Social Psychology, 95,* 1202–1216.

VEGA, V., & MALAMUTH, N. M. (2007). Predicting sexual aggression: The role of pornography in the context of general and specific risk factors. *Aggressive Behavior, 33,* 104–117.

VERKUYTEN, M., & YILDIZ, A. A. (2007). National (dis)identification and ethnic and religious identity: A study among Turkish-Dutch Muslims. *Personality and Social Psychology, 33,* 1448–1462.

VERWOERD, H. (1958, November). "Good neighborliness" speech. The Johannesburg Museum of Apartheid.

VESCIO, T. K., GERVAIS, S. J., SNYDER, M., & HOOVER, A. (2005). Power and the creation of patronizing environments: The stereotype-based behaviors of the powerful and their effects on female performance in masculine domains. *Journal of Personality and Social Psychology, 88,* 658–672.

VEYSEY, B. M., & MESSNER, S. F. (1999). Further testing of social disorganization theory: An elaboration of Sampson and Groves's "Community structure and crime." *Journal of Research in Crime and Delinquency, 36,* 156–174.

VIKEN, R. J., TREAT, T. A., BLOOM, S. L., & McFALL, R. M. (2005). Illusory correlation for body type and happiness: Covariation bias and its relationship to eating disorder symptoms. *International Journal of Eating Disorders, 38,* 65–72.

VISSER, P. S., & KROSNICK, J. A. (1998). Development of attitude strength over the life cycle: Surge and decline. *Journal of Personality and Social Psychology, 75,* 1389–1410.

VISSER, P. S., & MIRABILE, R. R. (2004). Attitudes in the social context: The impact of social network composition on individual-level attitude strength. *Journal of Personality and Social Psychology, 87,* 779–795.

VITELLI, R. (1988). The crisis issue assessed: An empirical analysis. *Basic and Applied Social Psychology, 9,* 301–309.

VOHS, K. D., BAUMEISTER, R. F., SCHMEICHEL, B. J., TWENGE, J. M., NELSON, N. M., & TICE, D. M. (2008). Making choices impairs subsequent self-control: A limited-resource account of decision making, self-regulation, and active initiative. *Journal of Personality and Social Psychology, 94,* 883–898.

VOLLHARDT, J. R. (2010). Enhanced external and culturally sensitive attributions after extended intercultural contact. *British Journal of Social Psychology, 49,* 363–383.

VON HIPPEL, F. N. (2011, March 22). It could happen here. *New York Times* (www.nytimes.com).

VON HIPPEL, W., BRENER, L., & VON HIPPEL, C. (2008). Implicit prejudice toward injecting drug users predicts intentions to change jobs among drug and alcohol nurses. *Psychological Science, 19,* 7–12.

VORAUER, J. D. (2001). The other side of the story: Transparency estimation in social interaction. In G. Moskowitz (Ed.), *Cognitive social psychology: The Princeton symposium on the legacy and future of social cognition.* Mahwah, NJ: Erlbaum.

VORAUER, J. D. (2005). Miscommunications surrounding efforts to reach out across group boundaries. *Personality and Social Psychology Bulletin, 31,* 1653–1664.

VORAUER, J. D., & RATNER, R. K. (1996). Who's going to make the first move? Pluralistic ignorance as an impediment to relationship formation. *Journal of Social and Personal Relationships, 13,* 483–506.

VORAUER, J. D., & ROSS, M. (1999). Self-awareness and feeling transparent: Failing to suppress one's self. *Journal of Experimental Social Psychology, 35,* 415–440.

VUKOVIC, J., JONES, B. C., DeBRUINE, L. M., LITTLE, A. C., FEINBERG, D. R., & WELLING, L. L. M. (2008). Circum-menopausal changes in women's face preferences. *Biology Letters* (DOI: 10.1098/rsbl.2008.0478).

WAGNER, G. (2011, September 7). Going green but getting nowhere. *New York Times* (www.nytimes.com).

WAGNER, U., CHRIST, O., & PETTIGREW, T. F. (2008). Prejudice and group-related behavior in Germany. *Journal of Social Issues, 64,* 403–416.

WAGSTAFF, G. F. (1983). Attitudes to poverty, the Protestant ethic, and political affiliation: A preliminary investigation. *Social Behavior and Personality, 11,* 45–47.

WALD, M. L. (2008, July 27). Flight's first fatal trip. *New York Times* (www.nytimes.com).

WALKER, P. M., & HEWSTONE, M. (2008). The influence of social factors and implicit racial bias on a generalized own-race effect. *Applied Cognitive Psychology, 22,* 441–453.

WALLACE, D. S., PAULSON, R. M., LORD, C. G., & BOND, C. F., JR. (2005). Which behaviors do attitudes predict? Meta-analyzing the effects of social pressure and perceived difficulty. *Review of General Psychology, 9,* 214–227.

WALLACE, M. *New York Times,* November 25, 1969.

WALLER, J. (2002). *Becoming evil: How ordinary people commit genocide and mass killing.* New York: Oxford University press.

WALSTER (HATFIELD), E. (1965). The effect of self-esteem on romantic liking. *Journal of Experimental Social Psychology, 1,* 184–197.

WALSTER (HATFIELD), E., ARONSON, V., ABRAHAMS, D., & ROTTMAN, L. (1966). Importance of physical attractiveness in dating behavior. *Journal of Personality and Social Psychology, 4,* 508–516.

WALSTER (HATFIELD), E., WALSTER, G. W., & BERSCHEID, E. (1978). *Equity: Theory and research.* Boston: Allyn & Bacon.

WALTHER, E., WEIL, R., & DÜSING, J. (2011). The role of evaluative conditioning in attitude formation. *Current Directions in Psychological Science, 20,* 190–196.

WANG, Q., BOWLING, N. A., & ESCHLEMAN, K. J. (2010). A meta-analytic examination of work and general locus of control. *Journal of Applied Psychology, 95,* 761–768.

WARD, W. C., & JENKINS, H. M. (1965). The display of information and the judgment of contingency. *Canadian Journal of Psychology, 19*, 231–241.

WARREN, N. C. (2005, March 4). Personal correspondence from founder of eHarmony.com.

WASON, P. C. (1960). On the failure to eliminate hypotheses in a conceptual task. *Quarterly Journal of Experimental Psychology, 12*, 129–140.

WATERS, E. A., KLEIN, W. M. P., MOSER, R. P., YU, M., WALDRON, W. R., McNEEL, T. S., & FREEDMAN, A. N. (2011). Correlates of unrealistic risk beliefs in a nationally representative sample. *Journal of Behavioral Medicine, 34*, 225–235.

WATKINS, D., AKANDE, A., & FLEMING, J. (1998). Cultural dimensions, gender, and the nature of self-concept: A fourteen-country study. *International Journal of Psychology, 33*, 17–31.

WATKINS, D., CHENG, C., MPOFU, E., OLOWU, S., SINGH-SENGUPTA, S., & REGMI, M. (2003). Gender differences in self-construal: How generalizable are Western findings? *Journal of Social Psychology, 143*, 501–519.

WATKINS, E. R. (2008). Constructive and unconstructive repetitive thought. *Psychological Bulletin, 134*, 163–206.

WATSON, D. (1982, November). The actor and the observer: How are their perceptions of causality divergent? *Psychological Bulletin, 92*, 682–700.

WATSON, R. I., JR. (1973). Investigation into deindividuation using a cross-cultural survey technique. *Journal of Personality and Social Psychology, 25*, 342–345.

WATT, S. E., & BADGER, A. J. (2009). Effects of social belonging on homesickness: An application of the belongingness hypothesis. *Personality and Social Psychology Bulletin, 35*, 516–530.

WATT, S. E., & LARKIN, C. (2010). Prejudiced people perceive more community support for their views: The role of own, media, and peer attitudes in perceived consensus. *Journal of Applied Social Psychology, 40*, 710–731.

WEBER, B., & HERTEL, G. (2007). Motivation gains of inferior group members: A meta-analytical review. *Journal of Personality and Social Psychology, 93*, 973–993.

WEBLEY, K. (2009, June 15). Behind the drop in Chinese adoptions. *Time*, p. 55.

WEGNER, D. M., & ERBER, R. (1992). The hyperaccessibility of suppressed thoughts. *Journal of Personality and Social Psychology, 63*, 903–912.

WEHR, P. (1979). *Conflict regulation.* Boulder, CO: Westview.

WEINER, B. (1981). The emotional consequences of causal ascriptions. Unpublished manuscript, UCLA.

WEINER, B., OSBORNE, D., & RUDOPH, U. (2011). An attributional analysis of reactions to poverty: The political ideology of the giver and the perceived morality of the receiver. *Personality and Social Psychology Review, 15*, 199–213.

WEINSTEIN, N. D. (1980). Unrealistic optimism about future life events. *Journal of Personality and Social Psychology, 39*, 806–820.

WEINSTEIN, N. D. (1982). Unrealistic optimism about susceptibility to health problems. *Journal of Behavioral Medicine, 5*, 441–460.

WEIS, R., & CERANKOSKY, B. C. (2010). Effects of video-game ownership on young boys' academic and behavioral functioning: A randomized, controlled study. *Psychological Science, 21*, 463–470.

WEISS, J., & BROWN, P. (1976). Self-insight error in the explanation of mood. Unpublished manuscript, Harvard University.

WENER, R., FRAZIER, W., & FARBSTEIN, J. (1987, June). Building better jails. *Psychology Today*, pp. 40–49.

WHITE, G. L. (1980). Physical attractiveness and courtship progress. *Journal of Personality and Social Psychology, 39*, 660–668.

WHITE, G. L., & KIGHT, T. D. (1984). Misattribution of arousal and attraction: Effects of salience of explanations for arousal. *Journal of Experimental Social Psychology, 20*, 55–64.

WHITE, J. W., & KOWALSKI, R. M. (1994). Deconstructing the myth of the nonaggressive woman. *Psychology of Women Quarterly, 18*, 487–508.

WHITE, L., & EDWARDS, J. (1990). Emptying the nest and parental well-being: An analysis of national panel data. *American Sociological Review, 55*, 235–242.

WHITE, M. (2000). *Historical atlas of the twentieth century* (users.erols.com/mwhite28/warstat8.htm).

WHITE, P. A., & YOUNGER, D. P. (1988). Differences in the ascription of transient internal states to self and other. *Journal of Experimental Social Psychology, 24*, 292–309.

WHITE, R. K. (1996). Why the Serbs fought: Motives and misperceptions. *Peace and Conflict: Journal of Peace Psychology, 2*, 109–128.

WHITE, R. K. (1998). American acts of force: Results and misperceptions. *Peace and Conflict, 4*, 93–128.

WHITECHURCH, E. R., WILSON, T. D., & GILBERT, D. T. (2011). "He loves me, he loves me not . . ."; Uncertainty can increase romantic attraction. *Psychological Science, 22*, 172–175.

WHITMAN, D. (1996, December 16). I'm OK, you're not. *U.S. News and World Report,* p. 24.

WHITMAN, D. (1998). *The optimism gap: The I'm OK—They're not syndrome and the myth of American decline.* New York: Walker.

WHITMAN, R. M., KRAMER, M., & BALDRIDGE, B. (1963). Which dream does the patient tell? *Archives of General Psychology,* **8,** 277–282.

WHITSON, J. A., & GALINSKY, A. D. (2008). Lacking control increases illusory pattern perception. *Science,* **322,** 115–117.

WICKER, A. W. (1971). An examination of the "other variables" explanation of attitude-behavior inconsistency. *Journal of Personality and Social Psychology,* **19,** 18–30.

WIDOM, C. S. (1989). Does violence beget violence? A critical examination of the literature. *Psychological Bulletin,* **106,** 3–28.

WIEGMAN, O. (1985). Two politicians in a realistic experiment: Attraction, discrepancy, intensity of delivery, and attitude change. *Journal of Applied Social Psychology,* **15,** 673–686.

WIESELQUIST, J., RUSBULT, C. E., FOSTER, C. A., & AGNEW, C. R. (1999). Commitment, pro-relationship behavior, and trust in close relationships. *Journal of Personality and Social Psychology,* **77,** 942–966.

WIKE, R., & GRIM, B. J. (2007, October 30). Widespread negativity: Muslims distrust Westerners more than vice versa. Pew Research Center (pewresearch.org).

WILDER, D. A. (1978). Perceiving persons as a group: Effect on attributions of causality and beliefs. *Social Psychology,* **41,** 13–23.

WILDER, D. A. (1981). Perceiving persons as a group: Categorization and intergroup relations. In D. L. Hamilton (Ed.). *Cognitive processes in stereotyping and intergroup behavior.* Hillsdale, NJ: Erlbaum.

WILDER, D. A. (1990). Some determinants of the persuasive power of in-groups and out-groups: Organization of information and attribution of independence. *Journal of Personality and Social Psychology,* **59,** 1202–1213.

WILDER, D. A., & SHAPIRO, P. N. (1984). Role of out-group cues in determining social identity. *Journal of Personality and Social Psychology,* **47,** 342–348.

WILDER, D. A., & SHAPIRO, P. N. (1989). Role of competition-induced anxiety in limiting the beneficial impact of positive behavior by out-group members. *Journal of Personality and Social Psychology,* **56,** 60–69.

WILDSCHUT, T., INSKO, C. A., & PINTER, B. (2007). Interindividual-intergroup discontinuity as a joint function of acting as a group and interacting with a group. *European Journal of Social Psychology,* **37,** 390–399.

WILDSCHUT, T., PINTER, B., VEVEA, J. L., INSKO, C. A., & SCHOPLER, J. (2003). Beyond the group mind: A quantitative review of the interindividual-intergroup discontinuity effect. *Psychological Bulletin,* **129,** 698–722.

WILKOWSKI, B. M., & ROBINSON, M. D. (2008). The cognitive basis of trait anger and reactive aggression: An integrative analysis. *Personality and Social Psychology Bulletin,* **12,** 3–21.

WILLIAMS, E. F., & GILOVICH, T. (2008). Do people really believe they are above average? *Journal of Experimental Social Psychology,* **44,** 1121–1128.

WILLIAMS, J. E., & BEST, D. L. (1990). *Measuring sex stereotypes: A multination study.* Newbury Park, CA: Sage.

WILLIAMS, J. E., SATTERWHITE, R. C., & BEST, D. L. (1999). Pancultural gender stereotypes revisited: The Five Factor model. *Sex Roles,* **40,** 513–525.

WILLIAMS, J. E., SATTERWHITE, R. C., & BEST, D. L. (2000). Five-factor gender stereotypes in 27 countries. Paper presented at the XV Congress of the International Association for Cross-Cultural Psychology, Pultusk, Poland.

WILLIAMS, K. D. (2002). *Ostracism: The power of silence.* New York: Guilford.

WILLIAMS, K. D. (2007). Ostracism. *Annual Review of Psychology,* **58,** 425–452.

WILLIAMS, K. D. (2009). Ostracism: A temporal need-threat model. *Advances in Experimental Social Psychology,* **41,** 275–313.

WILLIAMS, K. D. (2011, January/February). The pain of exclusion. *Scientific American Mind,* pp. 30–37.

WILLIAMS, K. D., CHEUNG, C. K. T., & CHOI, W. (2000). Cyberostracism: Effects of being ignored over the Internet. *Journal of Personality and Social Psychology,* **79,** 748–762.

WILLIAMS, K. D., & KARAU, S. J. (1991). Social loafing and social compensation: The effects of expectations of coworker performance. *Journal of Personality and Social Psychology,* **61,** 570–581.

WILLIAMS, K. D., & NIDA, S. A. (2011). Ostracism: Consequences and coping. *Current Directions in Psychological Science,* **20,** 71–75.

WILLIAMS, K. D., NIDA, S. A., BACA, L. D., & LATANÉ, B. (1989). Social loafing and swimming: Effects of identifiability on individual and relay performance of intercollegiate swimmers. *Basic and Applied Social Psychology,* **10,** 73–81.

WILLIAMS, M. J., & EBERHARDT, J. L. (2008). Biological conceptions of race and the motivation to cross racial boundaries. *Journal of Personality and Social Psychology, 94,* 1033–1047.

WILLIS, F. N., & HAMM, H. K. (1980). The use of interpersonal touch in securing compliance. *Journal of Nonverbal Behavior, 5,* 49–55.

WILSON, A. E., & ROSS, M. (2001). From chump to champ: People's appraisals of their earlier and present selves. *Journal of Personality and Social Psychology, 80,* 572–584.

WILSON, D. (2011, June 21). U.S. releases graphic images to deter smokers. *New York Times* (www. nytimes.com).

WILSON, R. S., & MATHENY, A. P., JR. (1986). Behavior-genetics research in infant temperament: The Louisville twin study. In R. Plomin & J. Dunn (Eds.), *The study of temperament: Changes, continuities, and challenges.* Hillsdale, NJ: Erlbaum.

WILSON, S. J., & LIPSEY, M. W. (2005). The effectiveness of school-based violence prevention programs for reducing disruptive and aggressive behavior. Revised Report for the National Institute of Justice School Violence Prevention Research Planning Meeting, May 2005.

WILSON, T. D. (1985). Strangers to ourselves: The origins and accuracy of beliefs about one's own mental states. In J. H. Harvey & G. Weary (Eds.), *Attribution in contemporary psychology.* New York: Academic Press.

WILSON, T. D. (2002). *Strangers to ourselves: Discovering the adaptive unconscious.* Cambridge: Harvard University Press.

WILSON, T. D., & BAR-ANAN, Y. (2008). The unseen mind. *Science, 321,* 1046–1047.

WILSON, T. D., DUNN, D. S., KRAFT, D., & LISLE, D. J. (1989). Introspection, attitude change, and attitude-behavior consistency: The disruptive effects of explaining why we feel the way we do. In L. Berkowitz (Ed.), *Advances in experimental social psychology* (Vol. 22). San Diego: Academic Press.

WILSON, T. D., & GILBERT, D. T. (2003). Affective forecasting. *Advances in Experimental Social Psychology, 35,* 346–413.

WILSON, T. D., & GILBERT, D. T. (2005). Affective forecasting: Knowing what to want. *Current Directions in Psychological Science, 14,* 131–134.

WILSON, T. D., LASER, P. S., & STONE, J. I. (1982). Judging the predictors of one's mood: Accuracy and the use of shared theories. *Journal of Experimental Social Psychology, 18,* 537–556.

WILSON, T. D., LINDSEY, S., & SCHOOLER, T. Y. (2000). A model of dual attitudes. *Psychological Review, 107,* 101–126.

WINCH, R. F. (1958). *Mate selection: A study of complementary needs.* New York: Harper & Row.

WINES, M. (2005, September 23). Crime in South Africa grows more vicious. *New York Times* (www. nytimes.com).

WINQUIST, J. R., & LARSON, J. R., JR. (2004). Sources of the discontinuity effect: Playing against a group versus being in a group. *Journal of Experimental Social Psychology, 40,* 675–682.

WINTER, F. W. (1973). A laboratory experiment of individual attitude response to advertising exposure. *Journal of Marketing Research, 10,* 130–140.

WIRTH, J. H., SACCO, D. F., HUGENBERG, K., & WILLIAMS, K. D. (2010). Eye gaze as relational evaluation: Averted eye gaze leads to feelings of ostracism and relational devaluation. *Personality and Social Psychology Bulletin, 36,* 869–882.

WISMAN, A., & KOOLE, S. L. (2003). Hiding in the crowd: Can mortality salience promote affiliation with others who oppose one's worldviews? *Journal of Personality and Social Psychology, 84,* 511–526.

WITTENBERG, M. T., & REIS, H. T. (1986). Loneliness, social skills, and social perception. *Personality and Social Psychology Bulletin, 12,* 121–130.

WITTENBRINK, B. (2007). Measuring attitudes through priming. In B. Wittenbrink & N. Schwarz (Eds.), *Implicit measures of attitudes.* New York: Guilford.

WITTENBRINK, B., JUDD, C. M., & PARK, B. (1997). Evidence for racial prejudice at the implicit level and its relationship with questionnaire measures. *Journal of Personality and Social Psychology, 72,* 262–274.

WIXON, D. R., & LAIRD, J. D. (1976). Awareness and attitude change in the forced-compliance paradigm: The importance of when. *Journal of Personality and Social Psychology, 34,* 376–384.

WOHL, M. J. A., & ENZLE, M. E. (2002). The deployment of personal luck: Sympathetic magic and illusory control in games of pure chance. *Personality and Social Psychology Bulletin, 28,* 1388–1397.

WOLF, S. (1987). Majority and minority influence: A social impact analysis. In M. P. Zanna, J. M. Olson, & C. P. Herman (Eds.), *Social influence: The Ontario symposium on personality and social psychology,* Vol. 5. Hillsdale, NJ: Erlbaum.

WOLF, S., & LATANÉ, B. (1985). Conformity, innovation and the psycho-social law. In S. Moscovici, G. Mugny, & E. Van Avermaet (Eds.), *Perspectives on minority influence.* Cambridge: Cambridge University Press.

WOOD, J. V., HEIMPEL, S. A., & MICHELA, J. L. (2003). Savoring versus dampening: Self-esteem differences in regulating positive affect. *Journal of Personality and Social Psychology, 85,* 566–580.

WOOD, W., & EAGLY, A. H. (2007). Social structural origins of sex differences in human mating. In S. W. Gangestad & J. A. Simpson (Eds.), *The evolution of mind: Fundamental questions and controversies.* New York: Guilford.

WOODBERRY, R. D., & SMITH, C. S. (1998). Fundamentalism et al: Conservative Protestants in America. *Annual Review of Sociology, 24,* 25–56.

WOODZICKA, J. A., & LaFRANCE, M. (2001). Real versus imagined gender harassment. *Journal of Social Issues, 57*(1), 15–30.

WORCHEL, S., & BROWN, E. H. (1984). The role of plausibility in influencing environmental attributions. *Journal of Experimental Social Psychology, 20,* 86–96.

WORCHEL, S., ROTHGERBER, H., DAY, E. A., HART, D., & BUTEMEYER, J. (1998). Social identity and individual productivity within groups. *British Journal of Social Psychology, 37,* 389–413.

WORD, C. O., ZANNA, M. P., & COOPER, J. (1974). The nonverbal mediation of self-fulfilling prophecies in interracial interaction. *Journal of Experimental Social Psychology, 10,* 109–120.

WORLD METEOROLOGICAL ORGANIZATION (2011, November). *WMO greenhouse gas bulletin: The state of greenhouse gases in the atmosphere based on global observations through 2010.* Geneva: World Meteorological Organization.

WORRINGHAM, C. J., & MESSICK, D. M. (1983). Social facilitation of running: An unobtrusive study. *Journal of Social Psychology, 121,* 23–29.

WRIGHT, D. B., BOYD, C. E., & TREDOUX, C. G. (2001). A field study of own-race bias in South Africa and England. *Psychology, Public Policy, & Law, 7,* 119–133.

WRIGHT, R. (1998, February 2). Politics made me do it. *Time,* p. 34.

WRIGHT, R. (2003, June 29). Quoted by Thomas L. Friedman, "Is Google God?" *New York Times* (www.nytimes.com).

WRIGHT, R. (2003, September 11). Two years later, a thousand years ago. *New York Times* (www.nytimes.com).

WRIGHT, S. C., ARON, A., McLAUGHLIN-VOLPE, T., & ROPP, S. A. (1997). The extended contact effect: Knowledge of cross-group friendships and prejudice. *Journal of Personality and Social Psychology, 73,* 73–90.

WROSCH, C., & MILLER, G. E. (2009). Depressive symptoms can be useful: Self-regulatory and emotional benefits of dysphoric mood in adolescence. Unpublished manuscript.

WYLIE, R. C. (1979). *The self-concept (Vol. 2): Theory and research on selected topics.* Lincoln, NE: University of Nebraska Press.

YBARRA, M. L., MITCHELL, K. J., HAMBURGER, M., DIENER-WEST, M., & LEAF, P. J. (2011). X-rated material and perpetration of sexually aggressive behavior among children and adolescents: Is there a link? *Aggressive Behavior, 37,* 1–18.

YBARRA, M. L., WEST, M. D., MARKOW, D., LEAF, P. J., HAMBURGER, M. & BOXER, P. (2008). Linkages between Internet and other media violence with seriously violent behavior by youth. *Pediatrics, 122,* 929–937.

YBARRA, O. (1999). Misanthropic person memory when the need to self-enhance is absent. *Personality and Social Psychology Bulletin, 25,* 261–269.

YELSMA, P., & ATHAPPILLY, K. (1988). Marriage satisfaction and communication practices: Comparisons among Indian and American couples. *Journal of Comparative Family Studies, 19,* 37–54.

YOUNG, S. G., BERNSTEIN, M. J., & HUGENBERG, K. (2010). When do own-group biases in face recognition occur? Encoding versus post-encoding. *Social Cognition, 28,* 240–250.

YOUNG, W. R. (1977, February). There's a girl on the tracks! *Reader's Digest,* pp. 91–95.

YOUNGER, J., ARON, A., PARKE, S., CHATTERJEE, N., & MACKEY, S. (2010). Viewing pictures of a romantic partner reduces experimental pain: Involvement of neural reward systems. *PLoS One, 5*(10), e13309.

YOVETICH, N. A., & RUSBULT, C. E. (1994). Accommodative behavior in close relationships: Exploring transformation of motivation. *Journal of Experimental Social Psychology, 30,* 138–164.

YUKL, G. (1974). Effects of the opponent's initial offer, concession magnitude, and concession frequency on bargaining behavior. *Journal of Personality and Social Psychology, 30,* 323–335.

YZERBYT, V. Y., & LEYENS, J-P. (1991). Requesting information to form an impression: The influence of valence and confirmatory status. *Journal of Experimental Social Psychology, 27,* 337–356.

ZADRO, L., BOLAND, C., & RICHARDSON, R. (2006). How long does it last? The persistence of the effects of ostracism in the socially anxious. *Journal of Experimental Social Psychology, 42,* 692–697.

ZAGEFKA, H., & BROWN, R. (2005). Comparisons and perceived deprivation in ethnic minority settings. *Personality and Social Psychology Bulletin, 31,* 467–482.

Zajonc, R. B. (1965). Social facilitation. *Science,* **149,** 269–274.

Zajonc, R. B. (1968). Attitudinal effects of mere exposure. *Journal of Personality and Social Psychology,* **9,** Monograph Suppl. No. **2,** part 2.

Zajonc, R. B. (1970, February). Brainwash: Familiarity breeds comfort. *Psychology Today,* pp. 32–35, 60–62.

Zajonc, R. B. (1998). Emotions. In D. Gilbert, S. T. Fiske, & G. Lindzey (Eds.), *Handbook of social psychology,* 4th edition. New York: McGraw-Hill.

Zajonc, R. B. (2000). Massacres: Mass murders in the name of moral imperatives. Unpublished manuscript, Stanford University.

Zakaria, F. (2008). We need a wartime president. *Newsweek* (www.newsweek.com).

Zauberman, G., & Lynch, J. G., Jr. (2005). Resource slack and propensity to discount delayed investments of time versus money. *Journal of Experimental Psychology: General,* **134,** 23–37.

Zebrowitz, L. A., White, B., & Wieneke, K. (2008). Mere exposure and racial prejudice: Exposure to other-race faces increases liking for strangers of that race. *Social Cognition,* **26,** 259–275.

Zebrowitz-McArthur, L. (1988). Person perception in cross-cultural perspective. In M. H. Bond (Ed.), *The cross-cultural challenge to social psychology.* Newbury Park, CA: Sage.

Zhang, D. D., Lee, H. F., Wong, C., Li, B., Pei, Q., Zhang, J., & An, Y. (2011). The causality analysis of climate change and large-scale human crisis. *PNAS,* **108,** 17296–17301.

Zhang, Y. F., Wyon, D. P., Fang, L., & Melikov, A. K. (2007). The influence of heated or cooled seats on the acceptable ambient temperature range. *Ergonomics,* **50,** 586–600.

Zhong, C.-B., Bohns, V. K., & Gino, F. (2010). Good lamps are the best police: Darkness increases dishonesty and self-interested behavior. *Psychological Science,* **21,** 311–314.

Zhong, C-B, & Leonardelli, G. F. (2008). Cold and lonely: Does social exclusion literally feel cold? *Psychological Science,* **19,** 838–842.

Zhou, X., Sedikides, C., Wildschut, T., & Gao, D-G. (2008). Counteracting loneliness: On the restorative function of nostalgia. *Psychological Science,* **19,** 1023–1029.

Zhu, W. X., Lu, L., & Hesketh, T. (2009). China's excess males, sex selective abortion, and one child policy: Analysis of data from 2005 national intercensus survey. *British Medical Journal (BMJ),* **338,** b1211.

Zhu, Y., Zhang, L., Fan, L., & Han, S. (2007). Neural basis of cultural influence on self-representation. *NeuroImage,* **34,** 1310–1316.

Zick, A., Pettigrew, T. F., & Wagner, U. (2008). Ethnic prejudice and discrimination in Europe. *Journal of Social Issues,* **64,** 233–251.

Zick, A., Wolf, C., Küpper, B., Davidov, E., Schmidt, P., & Heitmeyer, W. (2008). The syndrome of group-focused enmity: The interrelation of prejudices tested with multiple cross-sectional and panel data. *Journal of Social Issues,* **64,** 363–383.

Zillmann, D. (1989a). Aggression and sex: Independent and joint operations. In H. L. Wagner & A. S. R. Manstead (Eds.), *Handbook of psychophysiology: Emotion and social behavior.* Chichester: Wiley.

Zillmann, D. (1989b). Effects of prolonged consumption of pornography. In D. Zillmann & J. Bryant (Eds.), *Pornography: Research advances and policy considerations.* Hillsdale, NJ: Erlbaum.

Zillmann, D., & Paulus, P. B. (1993). Spectators: Reactions to sports events and effects on athletic performance. In R. N. Singer, N. Murphey, & L. K. Tennant (Eds.), *Handbook of research on sport psychology.* New York: Macmillan.

Zillmann, D., & Weaver, J. B., III. (1999). Effects of prolonged exposure to gratuitous media violence on provoked and unprovoked hostile behavior. *Journal of Applied Social Psychology,* **29,** 145–165.

Zillmann, D., & Weaver, J. B. (2007). Aggressive personality traits in the effects of violence imagery on unprovoked impulsive aggression. *Journal of Research in Personality,* **41,** 753–771.

Zillmer, E. A., Harrower, M., Ritzler, B. A., & Archer, R. P. (1995). *The quest for the Nazi personality: A psychological investigation of Nazi war criminals.* Hillsdale, NJ: Erlbaum.

Zimbardo, P. G. (1970). The human choice: Individuation, reason, and order versus deindividuation, impulse, and chaos. In W. J. Arnold & D. Levine (Eds.), *Nebraska symposium on motivation, 1969.* Lincoln: University of Nebraska Press.

Zimbardo, P. G. (1971). *The psychological power and pathology of imprisonment.* A statement prepared for the U.S. House of Representatives Committee on the Judiciary, Subcommittee No. 3: Hearings on Prison Reform, San Francisco, October 25.

Zimbardo, P. G. (1972). The Stanford prison experiment. A slide/tape presentation produced by Philip G. Zimbardo, Inc., P. O. Box 4395, Stanford, CA 94305.

Zimbardo, P. G. (2002, April). Nurturing psychological synergies. *APA Monitor,* pp. 5, 38.

Zimbardo, P. G. (2004a). A situationist perspective on the psychology of evil: Understanding how good people are transformed into perpetrators. In A. G. Miller (Ed.), *The social psychology of good and evil.* New York: Guilford.

Zimbardo, P. G. (2004b, May 3). Awful parallels: Abuse of Iraqi inmates and SPE. Comments to Social Psychology of Personality and Social Psychology listserv.

Zimbardo, P. G. (2007, September). Person x situation x system dynamics. *The Observer* (Association for Psychological Science), p. 43.

Zitek, E. M., & Hebl, M. R. (2007). The role of social norm clarity in the influenced expression of prejudice over time. *Journal of Experimental Social Psychology, 43,* 867–876.

Zuckerman, E. W., & Jost, J. T. (2001). What makes you think you're so popular? Self-evaluation maintenance and the subjective side of the "friendship paradox." *Social Psychology Quarterly, 64,* 207–223.

Credits

❖

Name Index

Subject Index

❖

Note: Page numbers followed by a "f" indicate figures.